Orlando Reade

View here the Authors high Designe,
His Book displaid, his Tapers shine,
Y⁼ Athenian Bird, the Dog, and Cat,
Which watchfull Study intimate.
THEOPHILA doth before Him stand
Amused with erected Hand;
And, like an Eagle, upward flies,
Rapt by bright ANGELS to the SKIES.

FRONTISPIECE TO THEOPHILA (CANTO V, P. 66, OF ORIGINAL
REDUCED FROM 10½ INCHES BY 5½)

Minor Poets of the Caroline Period

VOLUME I

CONTAINING

CHAMBERLAYNE'S *PHARONNIDA*
AND *ENGLAND'S JUBILEE*

BENLOWES' *THEOPHILA*

AND THE POEMS OF
KATHERINE PHILIPS AND
PATRICK HANNAY

EDITED BY

GEORGE SAINTSBURY

OXFORD
AT THE CLARENDON PRESS

Oxford University Press, Ely House, London W. 1

GLASGOW NEW YORK TORONTO MELBOURNE WELLINGTON
CAPE TOWN SALISBURY IBADAN NAIROBI LUSAKA ADDIS ABABA
BOMBAY CALCUTTA MADRAS KARACHI LAHORE DACCA
KUALA LUMPUR HONG KONG TOKYO

FIRST PUBLISHED 1905
REPRINTED LITHOGRAPHICALLY IN GREAT BRITAIN
AT THE UNIVERSITY PRESS, OXFORD
BY VIVIAN RIDLER
PRINTER TO THE UNIVERSITY
1968

GENERAL INTRODUCTION

A GREAT English critic, Mr. Matthew Arnold, and a great French man of letters, Mérimée, though they might not agree in all points agreed in one—in disparaging and discountenancing the study of minor literature. Mr. Arnold's utterances on the subject (or some of them, for they are numerous and sometimes inconsistent) are probably well known to most readers of this book ; of Mérimée's, his qualification of the praise which it was impossible for him to refuse to Ticknor's *History of Spanish Literature*, with blame for the inclusion of the *numerus*, may serve as a sufficient example. Both are formidable antagonists : and Goethe, from whom it is not improbable that both derived at least support for their opinion, and who notoriously, in his later days at any rate, held it himself, will seem to most people, no doubt, an antagonist more formidable still. But one of the cardinal principles of literary as of other knight-errantry is that the adventurer is not to be too careful—if he is to be careful at all—of the number, or of the individual prowess and reputation, of his adversaries. The greater and the more they are, the greater his success if he triumphs, the less his discredit if he succumbs— when his case is the right and theirs is the wrong. I have no doubt that in this respect Goethe and Mérimée and Mr. Arnold were wrong. It is not difficult to trace various causes of their error, the chief of which are that all three were in a certain sense disenchanted lovers of Romanticism ; that Romanticism, as it was bound to do by mere filial piety, enjoined the study of *all* literature ; and (further) that none of them had any special bent towards literary history. Mr. Arnold regarded all history with an impartial dislike ; Goethe probably did not find this kind scientific enough : and Mérimée, though no mean historical student in his own way, was a student of manners, of politics, of archaeology rather than of literature.

Yet there can be no doubt that from the point of view of literary history, and not from that point only, the neglect of minorities is a serious, and may be a fatal mistake. It is a mistake which used to prevail in the elder offspring of Clio herself ; but in most of her family it has been long outgrown. There is even at the present day, perhaps, a danger of too much attention being paid to small things—the complaint is all but unanimous that the document is killing the historian. Literary history, however, is a very youthful member of the historical household : it is not, in any fully developed condition, much more than two hundred years old, and its classics are few and disputed. Most of those which could pretend to the

General Introduction

position have been constructed on the very principle here attacked; such a book as Taine's, for instance, deliberately ignores whole schools, whole periods, whole departments, and is even extremely eclectic and anomalous in its treatment of principals. Yet it surely should not require much argument to show that this proceeding is not only absolutely unscientific, but inartistic in the last degree from one point of view, and perilous to the last degree from another. Even in the sphere of inorganic or inanimate or irrational things no reasonable physicist would care to generalize from a single example, or a few, leaving many unexamined. And the expressions of the human mind and sense in art are infinitely more individual and individually differentiated than chunks of the same rock, or blooms of the same flower, or specimens of the same animal race. Every fresh example *may*—it may almost be asserted that every fresh example *does*—give the rule with a difference; and by far the larger number of these differences are at least illustrative. From the confinement of the attention to a few examples, however brilliant and famous, come hasty generalizations, insufficient exposition, not seldom downright errors. Nor is it enough that the historian, as he too seldom does, should have made an examination, more or less exhaustive, for himself; it is desirable that the opportunity of controlling, checking, illustrating that examination should be in the hands of the student.

This opportunity, in regard to the poets now collected, few students who have not easy access to the very largest libraries can possibly have enjoyed. The invaluable collection of Chalmers—which ought long ago to have been supplemented by a similar *corpus* for the late eighteenth and early nineteenth centuries—contains a very fair number of mid-seventeenth century poets, but not one of those here presented. Nor has any one of them enjoyed the good fortune—I do not for a moment insinuate that any one has deserved it—of Herrick, who was himself omitted by Chalmers. The best and largest thing here given, Chamberlayne's *Pharonnida*, was indeed reprinted by Singer eighty years ago: but his edition is now scarce and dear. Very few of the others have been reprinted at all, and in every case the familiar adjectives just used apply to the reprints where they exist. As for the originals, though the extreme collector's mania point has not been yet reached in their case, as in that of the books of the period immediately preceding and some (especially first editions of plays) of a later time, yet most of them are excessively costly—twenty or thirty shillings, or two or three pounds having to be given for small duodecimos of large print. And what is more, copies are not to be obtained on the asking even at these fancy prices. To collect the texts which we here propose to give would cost anything from twenty to fifty pounds in money, and I really do not think it would be an exaggeration to say that it might cost from twenty to fifty weeks, if not months, in

time. And while it is certainly not extravagant to say that most
students have neither too much time nor too much money at
command, it is not, I think, illiberal to say that at least some
collectors who have plenty of both do not exactly collect for the
purposes of study.

So far, little answer is likely to be attempted ; but there remains
a different set of objections to face. 'Are these things *worth* collecting
and reprinting?' it may be asked—'Is either the *prodesse* or the
delectare likely to be got from them?' Nor do I propose to answer
this in the lofty manner of some, by saying that knowledge is
knowledge, and to be striven for, and imparted, putting all questions
of profit or of delectation aside. This (to split the old commendation)
may be 'the most orgilous' fashion of defence ; but it is not 'the
best,' perhaps, and it is certainly not the most prudent, especially
as there are divers others. The importance of the matter here
given for the proper comprehension of English literary history is
really great. It may be best classed and indicated under three
heads, those of Versification, Diction, and Subject.

In Versification, the poems here set before the reader, being mostly
in rhyme, do not illustrate one of the main features of their period,
that disintegration or disvertebration of blank verse which the
contemporary plays display so remarkably. But their exposition of
the rhymed couplet of the period comes very close to this : and
indeed, as contrast-pendant, practically forms part of the same
subject. We give here, in the forefront of the book, the greatest
poem, in bulk and merit alike, which was ever written in this
particular form of heroic : and the special *Introduction* to *Pharon-
nida* will be found to contain some further remarks on the matter.
It is sufficient here to say that what this poem shows on the great
scale many others show more or less :—the conflict of the two
principles of 'stop' and *enjambement* which goes on everlastingly
in this province of English Prosody. When the couplet[1] first
'emerges from the heap' (to use Guest's excellent but for himself
rather damaging phrase on a more general point) its examples
are almost necessarily ' stopped '—as in the *Orison of Our Lady*,
in Hampole and elsewhere—because the fact of the writer having
no more to say in the space almost of itself determined his limita-
tion to ten feet. But when Chaucer first took it up as a poetic
medium and vehicle on the great scale, his genius could not fail,
whether consciously or not, to discover the double capacity of the
metre. He has sometimes been claimed as a great exemplar of
enjambement ; but as a matter of fact he is quite as great a one
of the stopped couplet when he chooses : and neither Dryden nor

---

[1] These remarks, necessarily made here *obiter*, the writer hopes to develop in
a *History of English Prosody*, on which he has been for some time engaged. The
observation is made simply to guard them against the supposition of being idle or
random *dicta*.

Leigh Hunt could have been under the slightest difficulty in learning from him and quoting from him examples of the form which each preferred. The remarkable instances of 'clench' and 'stop' which are found in *Mother Hubberd's Tale* could escape no careful reader of Spenser: and those who like to discover literary anticipations and 'false dawns' have had no difficulty in finding many others in Elizabethan poetry. In particular, those final couplets of Fairfax's stanzas which had such a great influence on Waller and his followers, necessarily take the stopped form as a rule, and sometimes equal in emphasis anything in Pope himself.

But the dramatic model of the rhymed couplet, very frequently used and never quite expelled by blank verse in its palmiest days, as necessarily inclined to overlapping : and both the pregnancy of thought and the rather undisciplined exuberance of Jacobean and Caroline times favoured the same tendency. This, undoubtedly, caught or lent contagion from or to the other tendency to licence in blank verse itself. The sliding, slipping flow of Wither and Browne was consequently most alluring, in decasyllables and octosyllables alike : and for some time very few writers even tried to resist the allurement. Chamberlayne himself, and Shakerley Marmion earlier, are the chief of not a few who have displayed the sin and its solace. There is indeed no doubt of either. Hardly any metrical device so well deserves the hackneyed praise of 'linked sweetness long drawn out' as these verse-paragraphs, punctuated by rhyme as well as pause, when they are successful. Nothing so well enables us to understand Milton's otherwise almost unintelligible wrath with the rhyme he had managed so exquisitely as the same paragraphs, or rather paragraph-heaps, when they are not successful. And the odds are undoubtedly rather against their succeeding. Even Keats, a greater poet by far than any one here presented, and endowed with a miraculous finger for poetic music, cannot always— cannot very often—keep them straight or curl them satisfactorily. They encourage themselves by their own transgression : the poet who drinks of them will almost certainly drink to excess. And there is nothing for it, as Keats himself found, but one or other of the astringent antidotes which Milton and Dryden respectively applied. Yet, as we have seen in the nineteenth century, from Keats himself to Mr. William Morris, poetry will turn to them, and will not be denied the indulgence. Nay, there is the curious fact that, after Keats had discarded the decasyllabic *enjambement* of *Endymion*, he fell back upon the octosyllabic *enjambement* of the *Eve of St. Mark*, and would obviously have done great things in it had he had time.

It is, therefore, by no means an unimportant thing, in the interests of the history of English Prosody and of English Literature, that the documents of this period of unbridled overlapping should be put completely within the reach of the student and reader :—first, that he may understand and appreciate them in themselves; secondly, that he may understand and appreciate the reaction against them; thirdly, that he may understand and appreciate the new reaction to something like them more than a century later. They have a great deal to teach us; they are a 'source' or a main part of one; they cannot be dismissed, except by the most short-sighted impatience, as things dead and obsolete. The newer tendency to extend the view of literature laterally, and take in what other nations and other languages are doing, is valuable and to be encouraged, but not at the expense of retrospection and of the maintenance of continuity in the study of particular literatures. Nowhere is it truer that the thing that hath been shall be than in this field: nowhere are the ancestral heirlooms—less as well as more precious—to be more carefully treasured and looked up from time to time.

The other points chiefly noticeable in regard to Versification are two—the practice of irregular 'Pindaric' metres, and the peculiar tone and colour of the 'common measure' and the quatrain of eights. The popularity of Cowley was sure to encourage the practice of the first, but Cowley's own addiction to it was, of course, only an instance, not a cause, of the general fondness for it. This fondness was also itself, no doubt, but a sort of evidence of discontent or want of skill with previously popular metrical arrangements, like the restless liberties taken with the Spenserian stanza by poets from the Fletchers to Prior. We have nothing of the very first excellence to promise in this form—nothing like the best of Crashaw or of Vaughan—certainly nothing equal to that splendid anonymous piece [1] which Mr. Bullen discovered in the Christ Church Library. But it must be remembered that Cowley himself is by no means invariably or even very often successful with it, and that its apparent promise of *numeros lege solutos* is the most treacherous and dangerous of deceits. The poet (or perhaps hardly the poet but the verse-writer) thinks he has got rid of an incumbrance, when he has in reality thrown away the staff that supports his steps and the girdle that strengthens his loins. Only masters of euphony and harmony can really triumph with these irregular arrangements which require such a transcendental regularity. Nay more, we know from the remarkable example of Tennyson's early verse, and its effect on Coleridge, that the very masters themselves cannot always appreciate others' mastery in it. So that, in our range of sixty years and more from Patrick Hannay to Ayres, we shall not see many successes here: yet the lesson of their absence will not be idle or superfluous.

But the third and last general metrical 'colour' of this verse is the most satisfactory; it is indeed one of the principal evidences in English poetry of the almost incomprehensible blowing of the wind of the spirit in a particular direction for a certain space of time. Whether it was the special accomplishment of Ben Jonson, the

---

[1] 'Yet if His Majesty, Our Sovereign Lord,' &c.

greatest single tutor and teacher of the verse of the mid-seventeenth
century, or whether this accomplishment itself was but the first and
greatest instance of a prevalent phenomenon, it would be uncritical
rashness to attempt to decide. But what is certain is that the
new, the wonderful, the delightful cadences which we find in such
mere anonymities as—

> Thou sent'st to me a heart was crowned,
> I took it to be thine :
> But when I saw it had a wound
> I knew that heart was mine.
> A bounty of a strange conceit !
> To send mine own to me—
> And send it in a worse estate
> Than when it came to thee !

or in Marvell's magnificent—

> My love is of a birth as rare
> As 'tis, for object, strange and high—
> It was begotten by Despair
> Upon Impossibility.

meet us often here, even in the warblings of the mild if matchless
muse of 'Orinda.' Some of course will say, according to their usual
saying, that it is the thought which is charming in both these
—that it is the Caroline conceit, not the Caroline cadence, which is
so bewitching. Let us distinguish. The thought, the conceit, is
caressing : but it would be perfectly possible so to put it that it
should not have this rushing soar, this dying fall ; and it would not
be very hard to get the soar and fall with much less fantastically
gracious fancies. In fact, we should have to go to these very Carolines
to borrow them. Nobody, except by imitation, has got it since ;
nobody had it before. It is only when one appreciates it that it
becomes evident how some of those thus gifted managed also to
strike out (quite casually it would seem) the matchless *In Memo-
riam* variation of eights, which also dates from this time, and which
carries its own music so indissolubly bound up in it that only
violence, or dulness unspeakable, can effect a divorce between them.
If these notes—not exactly wood-notes but notes of a slightly
sophisticated yet exquisitely tempered society—came first into
existence a little before the accession of the first Charles, they
hardly survived the death of the second, under whom very worth-
less and unpoetical persons still, in some strange fashion, were able
to produce them, while later, very respectable and even poetical
persons were unable to produce them at all. We shall not, indeed,
find any of the very best examples of them here ; those very best
examples are so irresistibly and so universally charming that they
have, in almost all cases, long ago served as passports to at least
the modified general knowledge given by anthologies. I can promise

General Introduction

my readers no Herrick, nor even any Sedley or Aphra Behn. But
the purpose of the collection will be fully attained by showing that
in lesser degree, the gift prevailed:—that even the minor poet had
it, that it was an appanage and a privilege not of the individual but
of the time. Not until such points as these have been mastered—
with the result and reward of being able to distinguish what is of
the time and what of the individual—is a real grasp of the history
of literature and especially of poetry possible. The process corrects
at once the extreme determinism of the Taine school, and the
extreme individualism which will not look at filiations and groups
and *milieux* at all; it turns the student, if he will be turned, into a
scholar who can appreciate, and a lover who can understand.

In point of Diction the authors here given add a good deal to the
word- and phrase-book of the period; and I have thought it worth
while to draw attention to some of these additions in the several
Introductions, and to all the more remarkable ones in the glossarial
notes. The general tendency is double: and the evidences of this
duplicity are perhaps more striking than those in most of the better
known poetry of the time, though not more so than those in its
slightly more accessible, but not really much more generally read,
drama. One set is in the direction of a sort of new 'aureate'
diction—of 'inkhorn terms' corresponding to those of which the
mighty chief of contemporary prose-writers, Sir Thomas Browne, is
so prodigal. Chamberlayne, though not quite so lavish of them,
is a thorough contemporary of Browne's in his 'enthean' and his
'astracisms.' But, as is well known, all Jacobean and Caroline
writers, from Bacon and Greville to Thomas Burnet, succumb to
this temptation, the indulgence in which was no doubt a main cause
of the imminent reaction to 'a naked natural way of speaking,'
though some of the greatest men on that side, notably Dryden,
never quite relinquished their fondness for 'traduction' and the
like. This indulgence is certainly more pardonable in poetry than
in prose, where also it is not unpardonable to some tastes; it only
becomes so when (as, it must be confessed, often happens) it is either
pushed to the verge of the burlesque in itself or associated with
grotesque and vernacular locutions. Benlowes is a particular offender
in this way; but it can hardly be said that any one of the Caroline
minors is entirely to be trusted to escape the danger and the offence.
Yet the better of these *inusitata* may be regarded with a little
affectionate regret by those who hold that in language, as elsewhere,
the old motto 'keep a thing, its use will come' has its value; and that
it is hardly possible for any tongue to be too rich or too hospitable
provided only its treasures or its guests do not underlie the reproach
of barbarism. There is a charm in such a phrase as 'the epact of the
heart[1]' which none but word-lovers and thought-lovers know.

The other tendency connects itself forwards rather than backwards

[1] In the anonymous song, 'Why should I wrong my judgement so?'

in respect of development, though one of its sources is to be sought in an earlier age. It is the indulgence in familiar and slovenly forms of speech which grew upon writers during the later years of the seventeenth century, and against which Swift, at the beginning of the next, delivered his famous onslaught in the *Tatler*. This, as has been said, is particularly painful when it is found in close proximity to the 'aureate' phrases just discussed; but its worst instances possess an offensiveness which is independent and intrinsic, and which is perhaps the great drawback to the enjoyment of this poetry. These take the most slipshod conversational contractions —not merely such as 'they're' for 'they are,' and 'she's' for 'she is,' but such as the horrors, now luckily obsolete even in conversation, of 'do's,' not for 'does' but for 'do his,' 'th' castle' for 'the castle,' 'b' the' for 'by the,' and the like. In some cases, of course, a mere slur of the voice will get over the difficulty: but in many it will not. And the result is then one of the most jarring grains of sand between the teeth, one of the most loathsome flies in the ointment. Some of the passages where it occurs are utterly ruined by it; there are none, I think, where it is not a more or less serious drawback to the poetic pleasure. It is noticeable more or less in all the poets of the time except Milton, whose ear saved him, almost if not quite invariably, from anything that cannot be resolved into a tolerable trisyllabic foot: and it continued for a long time after our strict period. Even Dryden is not proof against it, in the verse of his plays, though he too was kept by his genius from often (not from sometimes) committing it in his strictly poetic verse. Of the others, persons not represented here as different as Crashaw and Marvell, persons represented here as different as Chamberlayne and Benlowes, are almost indiscriminately guilty of it [1].

This always uncomely and sometimes hideous and horrible fault was at least partly due to a wrong theory, not of Diction itself but once more of Versification—to the strange delusion (first put into words by Gascoigne, who laments what he thought thirty or forty years before the beginning of our time, and finally formulated by Bysshe twelve or fifteen beyond the end of it) that, either universally or in all but a very few trivial song metres, English prosody admitted of nothing but disyllabic feet. It was to get back the ten syllables into the heroic line, the eight into the 'short' line (as Butler calls it) and no more, that these abominable Procrustean tortures were committed. It is possible—the contrary may seem indeed *im*possible —that the fantastic combinations of consonants sometimes produced, were not intended to be pronounced as they are printed—that, as was observed above, a saving slur was allowed. But in some cases at least no sleight of tongue with the actual syllables is itself possible: the verse simply cannot be made euphonious by any acrobatism of

---

[1] It is to the credit of 'J. D.,' the introducer of Joshua Poole's *English Parnassus*, that he protests against mere 'apostrophation,' as he calls it.

pronunciation. And it is not surprising that, in order to get rid of it, Dryden tended more and more to the rigid decasyllable, with an occasional indulgence in the complete Alexandrine when he could not suit himself with less room. Never till Shenstone, and then only by a kind of timid suggestion, was the 'dactyl' (of course it was not as a rule a dactyl at all) allowed back into English heroic or blank verse ; and during this period of proscription there was practically no alternative between inconvenience and cacophony for those poets who were not consummate masters. Hardly one of ours deserves that grudgingly-to-be-allotted description, and accordingly they nearly all succumb.

Yet again, there is special interest of Subject about not a few of the poets and poems here given ; and this has not, like the others, been in any great part anticipated by previous collections and editions. Of the 'Heroic Poem' on which the mind of the late sixteenth and the whole of the seventeenth century was so much set, only Davenant's *Gondibert*, the most popular example doubtless of the kind at its own time, has been hitherto accessible with any ease ; and *Gondibert*, though the most considerable English piece save one in bulk, has the disadvantage of having been written by a man who is not single-minded in his ideas of poetry, who with much of the actual has more of the coming taste and fashion. Here we give, not only *Pharonnida* the queen of the whole bevy, but some others, of much less merit and importance no doubt, but still constituting a body of evidence and not a mere isolated example. Of the kind itself something is said in the *Introduction* to Chamberlayne's romance: but something more may fitly, and almost necessarily must, be said here. It is, for the reasons just now hinted at and others, not at all a well-known kind ; and with all the abundance of monographs—German, American, and English— on English Literature which the last few decades have seen, no one has yet summoned up courage to take it with its analogues, the 'Heroic Prose Romance,' and the 'Heroic Play,' for thorough and ✳ synoptic treatment. Except in cases which break through and above its limitations, such as Milton's *Paradise Lost*, which, be it remembered, takes to itself the actual style and title[1], or as Cowley's *Davideis*, it is a kind which incurs the familiar dangers of sitting (or attempting to sit) on two stools. Starting from the theory and practice of Tasso, who wished to effect a *modus vivendi* between the Virgilians and the partisans of Ariosto, and from the doctrine of Scaliger that the *Aethiopica* of Heliodorus was a perfect prose epic, writers, first in Italy and Spain, then in France, and almost contemporaneously in England, endeavoured to secure the variety, the freedom to some extent, and the sentimental and story-telling attractions of the Romance, with something of the majesty, unity, and prestige of the Epic. They very seldom achieved these

---

[1] At the close of the prefatory note on ' The Verse.'

(xi)

latter; and if like Milton they did, it was almost necessarily at the cost and to the neglect of the former. The smaller ' Heroic' poems are often mere narrative love-pieces, scarcely more than lyric in appeal, though unwisely divesting themselves of the lyric charm in form. But *Pharonnida* is much more than this, and though, no doubt, the versification and the diction subject it to risks which need not necessarily have been run, yet, to some extent, the Heroic Poem might not do unwisely to choose Chamberlayne as its champion.

At any rate, the greater and smaller examples here presented will supply materials for information and judgement on two points of literary history and criticism, neither of which is without very considerable interest and importance. In the first place, we have here a definite species (or chapter) of the general class (or history) of Verse-Narrative. This, even in ancient times, had some difficulty in subjecting itself to the rigid theory of Epic Unity. The *Iliad* obeys this pretty fairly—which is the less wonderful inasmuch as the theory was certainly deduced from the *Iliad*, if not from the *Iliad* alone. But the *Odyssey* and even the *Aeneid* have to take the benefit of all sorts of subterfuges in order to comply with it: and disastrous as is the shipwreck of ancient epic generally, we can see from writers like Nonnus on the one hand and Statius on the other, that orthodoxy was by no means universal if it was even general. Mediaeval verse knew nothing of it, and the mighty genius of Ariosto flouted it unceremoniously not to say wantonly. An intending verse tale-teller, in the middle of the seventeenth century, might well ' not know what to think of it' even in face of Tasso and Spenser, much more of Marini and Chiabrera and the French ' long poem' writers from Ronsard to Chapelain. Either because of such bewilderment, or for other reasons, he generally fortified himself with certain things; a punctilious extravagance of sentimental interest, often suggesting the tone of the *Amadis* cycle; a curious nomenclature of a rococo-Romance kind which has perhaps some indebtedness to the same source; intricately and almost violently entangled adventures, revolutions, discoveries, and the like. In many cases it seems to have been more or less a chance whether he wrote in prose or in verse.

In fact (and this brings us to the second point), the kind supplies another important link or chapter in the history of Fiction generally. Very much of it, one might almost be sure, would not have been written in this form if the prose-novel had taken forms more definite and variously available. And yet it is necessary to repeat the ' almost.' For the verse-novel itself, we must remember, has made its appearance as late as the nineteenth century in some very notable examples in English. It may almost claim *Sordello* and *The Princess*; it may quite claim *Festus*, and *Aurora Leigh*, and *Lucile* and *Glenaveril*. If Mr. William Morris led verse-narrative

General Introduction

back to more natural ways, it does not follow that it will always abide in them. At any rate, here are examples—little known, not so little worth knowing,—of one of the forms which it has taken in the past of English poetry and English literature. That this form has been much neglected hitherto is certainly not a reason for continuing the neglect. It certainly *is* a reason for repairing it in the most important point, the provision of the actual materials for study.

To these considerations of direct interest and importance, from the point of view of the history of literature, there remain to be added some of an indirect kind.

Most, though not all, of the writers here reprinted were forgotten during the eighteenth century; but some at least of them were of note in the seventeenth, and more than one has been a power of this or that moment during the last hundred years. The influence which they—or rather the spirit which they exhibit—exerted upon Dryden has sometimes been exaggerated, but more generally overlooked: and it is a matter of real and great importance. It is not merely that he mentions ' Orinda ' with admiration [1] and Cleveland with contempt [2]; nor that he confesses, in somewhat other but closely allied matter, how conceit and bombast and ' alembicated ' metaphysicalities for a long time were the Delilahs of his imagination [3]. It is not merely that the Lines on Lord Hastings are in existence to show that he could as a boy out-Benlowes Benlowes and out-catachresis Cleveland himself. From these first puerilities to those almost last and almost noblest lines where he addresses—

> [The] daughter of the rose, whose cheeks unite
> The differing titles of the Red and White,

he is the servant of misguiding or rightly guiding fantasy—a fantasy at the worst the by-blow and bastard of older *Furor Poeticus*, at the best its legitimate offspring. It is this quality which differentiates him from the mere prose-and-sense versifiers, and which is so unfortunately missed by those who cannot appreciate him because they appreciate Milton, just as others cannot appreciate Keats because they appreciate Byron. And our poets are almost the last, except a few well-known exceptions, for a hundred years, to show the constant presence of this will-o'-the-wisp which does not always lead astray, and which is at any rate better than darkness, and perhaps than common daylight. So, too, how appreciate the justice (in this case one may be frank enough to say the injustice) of *Mac Flecknoe*, when the songs that Flecknoe actually sang are more unknown than those to which Browne (forgetful of δεῦρ' ἄγε νῦν and its music) made the famous reference? How apportion the

---

[1] In the ' Anne Killigrew' *Ode*, viii. 162.
[2] In the *Essay of Dramatic Poesy*.
[3] Dedication of *The Spanish Friar*.

(xiii)

office of the true critic and that of the mere satirist in Butler
without having *Theophila* before us? How fully comprehend the
to us rather incomprehensible wrath and ridicule with which
Addison and others pursue the childish, but not wholly unamiable,
practice of making verses in the shape of altars, and candle-
sticks, and frying-pans, without a full collection of the original
offences?

The other source of interest referred to is less equivocal. There
is no doubt that some of these seventeenth-century writers were
extremely influential in the Romantic Revolt of the nineteenth.
They could not but be so, inasmuch as they were precisely the
persons against whom the neoclassic poets—the 'school of prose
and sense'—had themselves revolted. The poetic blood of these
old martyrs was the necessary seed of the new Church, and not
only the seed but the fostering soil and the kindly fertilizer. That
Keats must have had direct obligations to *Pharonnida* has never
been matter of doubt since people began to study Keats seriously;
but there is fair reason to believe that he knew others of our
collection. One ceases to think his famous and very ugly rhyme
of 'favour' and 'behaviour' a mere cockneyism, when one finds
it in Shakerley Marmion. Not, of course, that it may not be found
elsewhere, but that both in subject and execution *Cupid and Psyche*
is exactly one of the poems which Keats is most likely to have read,
enjoyed, and followed. Southey's relish of *Pharonnida* is cited in
the proper place, as is Campbell's, which caused, more surprisingly
to those who know Jeffrey only at second hand, Jeffrey's. Sir
Egerton Brydges, whose influence was much greater than is perhaps
now generally appreciated, paid much attention to the writers of
this time and class in the *Censura Literaria*: and the invaluable
Retrospective Review did what it could to reintroduce them, whilst
Singer, if he had met with more encouragement, would probably have
reprinted more of them than he actually did. No one can mistake
—as a result no doubt not of any 'plagiarism' nor even of following
in the sense too commonly understood by the collectors of parallel
passages, but of kindred in spirit, and perhaps of actual familiarity—the
resemblances to the poetry of these, as of other seventeenth-century
men, which are found in early nineteenth-century poets like Beddoes
and Darley, not to mention the 'Spasmodics' and other outlying
groups or individuals. It is impossible to imagine a better antidote
or alterative to Blackmore and Glover than Chamberlayne; to the
average minor poet of the eighteenth century than Benlowes or
Katherine Philips or even Philip Ayres. Even the extremest
minority is worn with a difference: and with a difference which
is still agreeable and refreshing. 'Agreeable and refreshing.'
Dulce refrigerium! It sounds better in Latin, though the sense is
pretty exactly the same: and the Latin phrase at least expresses
the charm of these writers perhaps as well as any that could be

invented. There is no need to relinquish a jot of the pedagogic or, if the shibboleth of the day be preferred, the ' scientific ' arguments and claims just advanced ; but in a matter of art, and especially of poetical art, they can never be quite victoriously decisive. ' Is the delight here ? ' is a question which anybody has the right to ask at any moment, and it moves the case into another court.

But there is no difficulty in giving the affirmative answer though, of course, that answer must itself be subject, like all such, to the yet further, and in this case final tribunal of individual taste. Some people will not like even Chamberlayne, much less Benlowes and the rest ; it has even been admitted that they can find reasons for not liking, if they choose to seek them. But it must be remembered that in Art, and especially in Poetry, the potency of the negative and the potency of the affirmative in replies to this question are utterly different in weight and scope. The negative is final as regards the individual ; *he* has a right to dislike if he does dislike, though there may be subsequent questions as to his competence. But it is not in the least final as to the work in question. It is (let it be granted) not good for *him* ; it does not follow that it is not good in itself. Now the affirmative carries with it results of a very different character. *This* is final in regard to the work as well as to the reader. That which should be delectable has delighted in one proven and existing case : and nothing—not the crash of the world— can alter the fact. It has achieved—though the value of the achievement in different cases may be different.

From this point of view, few of the poets now presented need fall back on the mere scholastic-historic estimate : though one or two may have to do so. Puzzling as it may be to extract and define the essence of the charm which is found in almost every page of Chamberlayne and which is not so rare elsewhere, the examples already referred to will show that that charm itself has been felt by persons whose competence is too certain, and whose idiosyn-crasies are too various, to permit the poohpoohing of it as an effect of crotchet, or *engouement*, or simple bad taste. The fact is that it is as genuine as it is elusive, and almost as all-pervading as it is sometimes faint and felt from far. If it can be explained in any way it is by the constant presence of the worship of Imagination, and of the reward which Imagination bestows upon even her most mistaken worshippers. Sometimes they are mistaken enough; they confuse their Goddess with a Fancy which is not even ' Fancy made of golden air ' but an earthy Fancy bedizened with tinsel. But the better Fancy is only Imagination a little human-ized, and even the worst has something not quite alien from the divine. As we come closer to the confines of the period, it is most curious to see the last flutters and flashes of the wings of this Fancy as she takes her leave in such things as Ayres's *Fair Beggar,* and his *Lydia Distracted.* Earlier, she is always with us,

General Introduction

and Imagination herself not seldom. There are who like not these for companions, no doubt ; for those who do, let us cut short this ushership at once and allow the music to begin [1].

GEORGE SAINTSBURY.

[1] NOTE TO INTRODUCTION. The principles of editing which have been adopted can be very shortly set forth. In all cases, whether the texts have been set up from reprints, as in a few cases, or from the originals, as in most, they have been carefully collated with these originals themselves and all important variations noted, and where necessary explained. The spelling has been subjected to the very small amount of modernization necessary to make it uniform with the only uniformity which is at all possible. At this time no texts were printed with very antique spelling, and some present for whole pages nothing that is not modern, except an occasional capital Initial. A very few readers might prefer the reproduction of anomalous and contradictory archaisms ; but these would certainly repel a much larger number, and interfere with the acquaintance which it is desired to bring about. With regard to punctuation, the fantastic and irregular clause- and sentence-architecture of the time hardly admits of a strict application of any system. This is partly remedied, or at least recognized, in the originals by an extremely liberal use of the semicolon, which has been generally retained, except where means of improvement are obvious. Glossarial notes have been added where they seemed necessary or very desirable, but with a sparing hand ; and notes, explanatory of matter, with a hand more sparing still. The object constantly kept in view by the editor has been the provision, not of biographical, bibliographical, or commentatorial minutiae, but of a sufficient and trustworthy text for the student and the lover of literature. (*Unforeseen and unavoidable circumstances have hitherto prevented the accomplishment of the collation of Hannay. I trust to complete it shortly and to give the results, if any, in Vol. II.*—G. S.)

CONTENTS

(xvii)

Contents

Pharonnida:

A

HEROICK
POEM.

BY

WILLIAM CHAMBERLAYNE
Of *Shaftsbury* in the County of *Dorcet.*

Ἴσκε Ψύδεα πολλὰ λέγων ἐτύμοισιν ὁμοῖα.
Hom. Odyſſ. Lib. XIX.

LONDON,
Printed for *Robert Clavell,* at the Sign of the
Stags-head neer St. *Gregories* Church in
St. *Pauls* Church-yard, 1 6 8 9.

[Two vols. in one of 258 and 215 pp. respectively. The print and leading of these is quite different, the first having small type and thirty-four lines to the page, the second a larger letter and twenty-six or twenty-eight lines.]

INTRODUCTION TO
WILLIAM CHAMBERLAYNE

THE extreme scantiness of our biographical knowledge [1] of the author of *Pharonnida* has not, even in recent or comparatively recent years, been compensated by any fullness of critical or general acquaintance with his works. He was even more unfortunate than Herrick as regards the time at which he came and his chances of popularity : and his kind of work was a great deal less likely to recommend itself to future generations. That the original edition is very rare indeed, and that Singer's reprint eighty years ago was published in no very great numbers, and is now far from common or cheap, are facts which no doubt have had a good deal to do with the general neglect : but criticism is not quite blameless in the matter. That Langbaine should have seen nothing in *Pharonnida* is indeed itself nothing ; if there ever has been anything which may possibly have ruffled the smoothness of Shakespeare's brow since his death, it must have been Langbaine's admiration. That the eighteenth century should have left our poet not contemptuously but utterly alone is not wonderful : for his system of versification is simply anathema to the orthodoxy of which Bysshe was the lawgiver and which Johnson did not disdain to profess.

Southey, who read *Pharonnida* early and might have been expected to like it, has indeed left a pleasant tribute [2]. But the author of an elaborate and useful argument, with extracts, in the *Retrospective Review* [3], which no doubt served as shoehorn to draw on Singer's reprint, gives very little criticism, and that little by turns extravagant and grudging. I have myself a very great admiration for Chamberlayne, but I fear I could not, except

---

[1] It is practically limited to what can be found in the prefatory matter of his poem, with a very few external contributions—as that he was born in 1619 ; practised as a physician at Shaftesbury ; died there on Jan. 11, 1679, and was buried ; his son, Valentine, putting up a monument to him. *Pharonnida* appeared (London : R. Clavell), with a portrait (? generally absent), in 1659. The tragi-comedy of *Love's Victory*, which accompanies it in Singer's reprint, but (as a play) is not given here, had been published the year before, and was reprinted in 1678, with alterations, as *Wits Led by the Nose*, a title not obviously applicable. At the Restoration, Chamberlayne published a short poem of some interest, *England's Jubile[e]*, which has never, I think, been reprinted, but which is given at the end of *Pharonnida*.

[2] In a note to *The Vision of the Maid of Orleans* (*Poems*, one vol. edition, p. 79), he gives a considerable extract from Pharonnida's remarkable dream in Book I, Canto v, and speaks of the author as 'a poet to whom I am indebted for many hours of delight.' But even he, while acknowledging 'an interesting story, sublimity of thought, and beauty of expression,' excepts against 'the uncouth rhymes, the quaintest conceits, and the most awkward inversions.'

[3] I. pp. 21–48, with a further article on *Love's Victory*, pp. 258-71.

(3)

as regards the inequality, say that 'his main story is carried on with deep and varied interest and developed with great but unequal power,' or grant 'individuality' to 'the character of Almanzor.' On the other hand, to speak of the 'involved and inharmonious' diction, and still more of 'the poverty and insignificance of the rhyme,' is as excessive in the other direction, though it may not be utterly untrue : and the remark about the rhyme in particular shows that the critic had not grasped Chamberlayne's system. We can come together again on 'richness of imagery,' 'impassioned and delightful poetry,' &c.

The first person to do some real justice to *Pharonnida* was Campbell in his *Specimens*, which again give not much criticism and chiefly praise the story—the weakest part—but provide admirable selections, the perusal of which stirred Jeffrey himself to admiration and desire for more. Of late years things have been better [1], but even yet the poem is far too little known, and the hope of extending the knowledge of it was one of my main motives in suggesting and planning this edition.

The points of interest from which *Pharonnida* can be regarded are neither few nor unimportant. In the first place it is, with Davenant's much better known but far inferior *Gondibert*, the chief English example of that curious kind the 'Heroic poem'—the romanticized epic which, after the deliberations of the Italian critics and the example of Tasso, spread itself over Europe in the late sixteenth century and held the field for the greater part of the seventeenth. With something of the late romance of the *Amadis* type in it, this poem had a good deal of intended reference to the *Aeneid*; but perhaps linked itself most of all to the prose *Aethiopica* of Heliodorus, which attracted great attention from the Renaissance and had been pronounced by Scaliger himself the model of a prose epic. The resemblance, indeed, between *Pharonnida* and the type of the Greek romance generally is very strong—in the prominence and persistent persecutions of the heroine, in the constant voyages and travels, alarums and excursions, ambushes and abductions, and, it may be added, in the very subordinate position of Character. Indeed Chariclea and some of her sisters are much less open to Pope's libel than the good Pharonnida and the bad Amphibia of our poem.

An even greater attraction to some readers is its position at the very end (indeed, in a sort of appendix to the great volume) of Elizabethan verse, in conception, in versification, and in phrase. Like the whole body of this verse, from Spenser downwards, it is of imagination (or at worst of fancy) all compact: the restraints of prose and common sense are utterly alien to it. Its author has passed from the merely 'conceited'

---

[1] Mr. Gosse in *From Shakespeare to Pope* did, perhaps, most to draw attention once more to Chamberlayne.

to the 'metaphysical' stage; and if his excursions into the *au delà* do not reach the sublimity or the subtlety of Donne, the flaming fantasy and passion of Crashaw, they leave very little to desire in their fidelity to the Gracianic motto *En Nada Vulgar.* The immense length of his verse paragraphs (to be referred to further) is closely connected with this intricacy and excursiveness of thought, and so no doubt, at least according to the present writer's idea, is the 'impassioned and delightful' poetry. But so also is the extreme incoherence not merely of the story as a whole, but, and still more, of its component incidents and episodes. It is, of course, impossible not to think of *Sordello* in reading it : and I should say myself that the poem which has rather absurdly become a proverb for incomprehensibility in the. proper sense of the word, is much the more easily comprehensible of the two. Mr. Browning's thought pursues the most astonishing zigzags and whirligigs and shifts, but it is solid : and you can, if you are nimble enough, keep your clutch on it. Chamberlayne's constantly sublimes itself off into a kind of mist before making a fresh start as a solid, at quite a different point from that at which it was last perceived in that condition.

So, too, with the versification. Although it is, of course, quite possible to trace the stopped and stable couplet, not merely in drama but in narrative and miscellaneous poetry, from Spenser and Drayton and Daniel downwards, the general tendency of the Elizabethan distich had been towards an undulating *enjambement,* and this had grown much stronger, both in octosyllable and decasyllable, with strictly Jacobean poets like Wither and Browne. But Chamberlayne serpentines it to a still greater extent. Indeed, it is impossible not to discern in him something akin to that extraordinary *unscrewing* of blank verse itself which is noticeable in his dramatic contemporaries, and which might have disvertebrated English verse altogether if it had not been for the tonic, in different forms, of Milton and Dryden. The 'poverty and insignificance' of rhyme, on which our *Retrospective* friend is so severe, are of course deliberate. The rhymes are intended, not as a stop-signal at the end of the couplet, but as an accompanying music to the run of the paragraph. Unfortunately the possession of this accompaniment is too likely to dispense a poet from that attention to varied pause, and to careful selection of value in individual words, with which the blank verse paragrapher cannot dispense if he is to do anything distinguished. It would be interesting if one could know whether Milton ever heard of *Pharonnida,* but I think I do know what he would have said of it. It is not insignificant that his nephew Phillips, while mentioning the unimportant *Robert* Chamberlain, says nothing about William in a tale of Caroline poets which descends to 'Pagan' Fisher and Robert Gomersal. But, for all its dangers and all its actual lapses, it makes a medium frequently delightful even if we had not *Endymion*, and more, not less, seeing that we have that.

It is in his diction, using that word widely to include composition and grammar, that Chamberlayne's state is least gracious. His ugliest fault he shares with most of his contemporaries, even with Dryden occasionally, and it is so ugly that it constitutes perhaps the most serious drawback to the enjoyment of him by modern readers. Partly owing to that gradual vulgarization of the language which Dryden arrested to some extent, but which it is a redeeming merit of the eighteenth century in prose and verse to have cauterized—but partly also to the prevailing critical error as to the strictly· syllabic character of English verse, *Pharonnida* swarms with things like ' in 's hand,' ' t' the coach,' ' Perform 't.' These uglinesses cannot always (as, by the way, they generally can in Dryden) be smoothed away by printing in full and allowing trisyllabic feet; they are too often ' in grain.' Very much more tolerable, but occasionally unsatisfactory, is his indulgence, generally a repeated indulgence, in such words as *remora, enthean, catagraph, astracism*. And disapproval must begin again, not so much in regard to the licentiousness of his syntax—for English grammar, after all, is made by good English writers, and not vice versa—as to the extraordinary haphazardness of syntax, phrase, and composition alike. I do not wish to burden this introduction with extracts of any length, but those who turn to the passage about the governor of the fort in Book II, Canto ii, lines 123–132, will find a capital example of our poet at his very worst. It is perhaps well that this worst should be got over beforehand, so that things like it may not possess the additional disgust of surprise. But it must be admitted that the greatest danger in reading him is lest the reader, by too frequent occurrence of these choke-passages, may be tempted to skip, and that in the lack of *ordonnance* which has been noted, he may find himself hopelessly befogged at the point where he alights from his skipping-pole.

As if all this were not enough, Chamberlayne has multiplied his obstacles of commission by an omission which nearly all of his few critics have noticed, but which none of them has fully followed out. We know from his own words at the end of the Second Book that the poem was thus far written, but broken off, at the second battle of Newbury in October, 1644. And whether its author resumed it at once after the complete disaster of the Royal arms next year, or earlier, or later[1], it was certainly not published for fifteen years afterwards. This would, in itself, render inconsistencies and gaps likely enough: but it would not account for the

---

[1] It has been thought, from bibliographical peculiarities in the original, that the *last* part was printed later than the rest. The last *volume* (see note on reverse of half-title) is certainly quite different in typography and arrangement from the first.

extraordinary *incuria* which Chamberlayne constantly displays. One would imagine not merely that he had never read his MS. through, but that he had never taken the trouble to read his proofs: a process which could hardly have failed to reveal to the most careless author some, if not all, of the discrepancies of nomenclature, &c. In the first few pages he calls one of his characters indifferently 'Ariamnes' and 'Aminander,' but here this slip of the pen is so glaring that it hardly misleads. A little later he puts the careful (the careless will not mind) hopelessly out, by transferring the name 'Aphron' to one 'Andremon,' both persons having already appeared and being entirely distinct. He never seems to know whether his main scene of action is in the Morea (where it certainly opens) or in Sicily; and there may, perhaps, be corroborative evidence of some passing intention to change the whole *venue* from Greece to Italy in his calling the same person at one time an 'Epirot' and at another a 'Calabrian.' Although the exits and the entrances of his characters are very complicated, and sometimes correspond at long intervals, he will (there is an example at I. iv. 109) omit to name them, and describe them in such a round-about fashion that anybody but a very wary and attentive reader must be, at least for a time, at sea. Finally, as indeed Thackeray and others have done, he will kill and bring alive again with the completest nonchalance. At least, though his phrase is constantly enigmatic, it is hard to understand the lines at IV. i. 192, where, in reference to the wicked Amphibia and her paramour Brumorchus, it is said that the prince

'refers
Their punishment to death's dire messengers,'

in any other sense than that both were executed. Yet at V. iii. 360 Amphibia is still alive, still a lady in waiting to Pharonnida, and in case to execute the crowning treason of the story which kills the princess's father and very nearly brings herself to the scaffold as his murderess.

This being the case and the 'arguments' prefixed by the author being almost useless[1], it may be well to present a brief analysis, canto by canto, of a poem which one tolerably practised reader had to read three times before its general subject was at all clearly imprinted on his mind.

Book I, Canto i[2]. Aminander [Ariamnes], a Spartan lord, hunting on the shore of the Gulf of Lepanto, sees a naval combat between Turks and Christians; and when the combatants, wrecked by a squall, are still fighting on the beach, rescues the Christian heroes Argalia and Aphron.

Canto ii. Another lord, Almanzor, the villain of the piece, finds two damsels, Carina and Florenza, in a wood. He offers violence to Florenza,

---

[1] The abstract in the *Retrospective Review* is a little scrappy and capricious.
[2] Observe the *five* books, and the *five* cantos in each. This was one of the curious 'heroic' punctilios, to bring the construction nearer to the *five* acts of Drama.

and her lover, Andremon, though coming in time to save her, falls before his sword. But Argalia, who has been sleeping near, is waked by the scuffle, takes her part, and severely wounds Almanzor, despite the succour of his friends. Forces come up, and, appearances being against Argalia, take him into custody.

Canto iii. He is conveyed to the capital, where, according to the custom of the country, it is the duty of the king's daughter, Pharonnida, whose mother is dead, to preside over the tribunal. She falls in love with Argalia at first sight, but he is condemned, receiving three days' respite as an Epirot, a citizen of an allied state, which is confirmed by ambassadors from Epirus then present.

Canto iv. This is however not sufficient to obtain his pardon: and he is about to suffer when Aminander reappears with Florenza herself, who tells the whole story. Argalia is set at liberty and is about to depart with the ambassadors (who have become 'Calabrians' and who have told what they know of his origin) when a fresh adventure happens. Molarchus the Morean (now Sicilian) admiral, who has been charged to convoy the envoys, invites the king, princess and court on board his flag-ship and makes sail, having formed a design to carry off Pharonnida. This he does, though there is a fierce fight on board, by throwing her into a prepared boat and making off, while the crew do the same, having previously scuttled the ship. Argalia, however, with the help of his friend Aphron, though at the cost of the latter's life, secures one of the boats, rescues the king, and lands on a desolate island, where they find that Molarchus has conveyed Pharonnida to a fortress. Argalia, always fertile in resource, makes a ladder of the tackling of some stranded boats, scales the walls, slays Molarchus, and rescues the princess.

Canto v tells of a halcyon time at Corinth, where Pharonnida and Argalia, who is captain of her bodyguard, fall more and more deeply in love with one another, till the usual romance-mischance of a proposed betrothal to a foreign prince interrupts it: and the book finishes with this agony further agonized by Argalia's appointment on the very embassy destined to reply favourably to the Epirot suitor.

In Book II, Canto i we return to Almanzor, who forms a plot to abduct the princess, succeeds at first by turning a masque into a massacre, but is defeated by the rising of the country people, who half ignorantly rescue her. But her ravisher, in

Canto ii, thinking he has gone too far to retreat, sets up a rebellion and garrisons the castle of a city named Alcithius, which the king at first retakes, but which only serves him as a place of refuge when Almanzor has beaten him in the field. He has just time to send to Epirus for help before the place is invested.

Introduction

Canto iii. It is almost reduced by famine, and the besieged are meditating the forlorn hope of a sally when Zoranza the Epirot prince arrives with a large army, the vanguard of which, commanded by Argalia and supported from the castle, disperses the rebel forces, though not at first completely. After a glowing interview between the lovers the hero has to expel the remnant of the foe from a strange cavern-fastness where he finds a secret treasury with mysterious inscription.

Canto iv. Another interval of war. The unwelcome suitor is called off by troubles at home: and the lovers (Argalia still commanding the princess's guard) enjoy discreet but delightful hours in an island paradise.

Canto v. Episode of two Platonic-Fantastic lovers, Acretius and Philanta, on whom a practical joke is played. Intrigues of Amphibia, who excites the king's jealousy, and induces him to send Argalia at the head of a contingent to Epirus. After pathetic parting scenes, Argalia leaves Pharonnida, and the poet 'leaves the Muses to converse with men,' that is to say to fight the Roundheads at Newbury.

Book III, Canto i opens with a semi-episode of the rival loves of Euriolus and Mazara for Florenza, and Mazara's consolation with Carina, Florenza's companion at her original appearance. In

Canto ii the princess, unwarily reading aloud a letter from Argalia with her door open, is overheard by her father, who is furiously angry and sends letters of Bellerophon to the Prince of Syracuse [Epirus] as to Argalia. Zoranza, nothing loth, makes Argalia captain of the fortress Ardenna, with a secret commission to the actual governor to make away with him. He is saved from death for the moment by a convenient local superstition, and carried off (still prisoner) by an invading fleet, which fails to capture Ardenna. But Pharonnida is strictly imprisoned in the castle of Gerenza. In

Canto ii Argalia, after a rapid series of adventures at sea and in Rhodes, is captured by the Turkish chief Ammurat and sent to his wife Janusa in Sardinia to be tortured and executed. But Janusa falls in love with him, and this and the next Canto contain the best known and perhaps the most sustained chapter of the poem, Argalia being not merely

'Like Paris handsome and like Hector brave,'

but also like Joseph chaste. The passage having ended happily for him, tragically for Janusa and her husband, he seizes ships, mans them with Christian slaves, rescues the Prince of Cyprus from a new Turkish fleet, returns to the Morea, and after a time resolves, aided by his Cyprian friend, to release Pharonnida. In this, at first, they succeed.

Book IV, Canto i. Episode of Orlinda and the Prince of Cyprus. Pharonnida and Argalia enjoy a new respite in a retired spot, but are attacked by outlaws, who wound Argalia and carry off the princess. Their chief is Almanzor, who in

Canto ii tries to force Pharonnida to accept him by threats, and immures her in a living tomb from which she is rescued by Euriolus (mentioned before) and Ismander, on whom and Aminda there is fresh episode continued into

Canto iii by entrances of certain persons named Vanlore [1], Amarus, and Silvandra, but not concluded. The rest of Canto iii, Canto iv, and

Canto v contain an account of Argalia's recovery, and long conversations, in which he reveals what he knows of his youth to a friendly hermit.

Book V, Canto i. Meanwhile Pharonnida has retired to a monastery and is about to take the veil (has actually done so after a fashion) when Almanzor attacks the convent and once more carries her off, but surrenders her to her father that he may obtain his own pardon and plot further.

Canto ii. Argalia goes to Aetolia, of which he is the rightful heir, and fights his way to his own.

Canto iii. He is however rejected as suitor and attacked by his rival Zoranza. But Almanzor procures both this prince's murder and that of King Cleander (who is never named till very late in the story). Then Pharonnida in Canto iv undergoes her last danger, and in Canto v is finally freed by Argalia as her champion from Almanzor, whom he at last slays, and from all her other ills by marriage with her deliverer.

Now for my part I am entirely unable to pronounce this 'one of the most interesting stories ever told in verse.' As a whole it is romance 'common-form,' of by no means a specially good kind, only heightened by the telling in a few passages—the dream, the story of Janusa, the entombment of the heroine, and two or three others. I would, as Blair's typical person of bad taste said of Homer, 'as soon read any old romance of knight-errantry,' and would a great deal sooner read most of them *for the story*. If anybody agrees with Pope that 'the fable is the soul or immortal part of poetry,' Chamberlayne is not the poet for him. But he is, if not *the* poet, a poet and little less than a great one, for those who enjoy the 'poetic moment,' the ' single-instant pleasure' of image and phrase and musical accompaniment of sound. The extraordinary abundance of these things is the solace of those sins of his in *ordonnance* and versification and diction which have been so frankly and amply acknowledged above. It is hit or miss with him, no doubt: and equally without doubt, he misses too often—far oftener than a poet of the School of Good Sense would do. But he hits not only much oftener than the poet of good sense would do,

---

[1] It will be observed that Chamberlayne's nomenclature, mainly of the odd rococo-romantic type popular in seventeenth-century literature, is still more oddly mixed. This particular name must have been a favourite, for it recurs in *Love's Victory*.

but also as the poet of good sense rarely does at all. He is far too careless
of what he says, and of its exact meaning, and of the concatenation thereof
with other meanings. But he always tries, in the great adverb of the Italian
Platonist-critic Patrizzi, to say it *poeticamente*, or as Hazlitt (who certainly
did not know Patrizzi) unconsciously translates it, 'in a poetical way.'
Chamberlayne's sky and landscape are occasionally very dark—it is difficult
to find one's way about under the one and across the other : but both are
constantly lighted up by splendid shooting-stars. The road through his
story is as badly laid, made, and kept, as road can be : but fountains and
wildflower banks are never long wanting by its sides, and it occasionally
opens prospects of enchanting beauty.

There is at least not disgrace of incongruity in this eulogy, for
Chamberlayne's own style is nothing if not starry and flowery. His
metaphors and similes and imagery generally for atmospheric phenomena,
and especially for Night and Day, are inexhaustible :

> 'Day's sepulchre, the ebon-archèd night
> Was raised above the battlements of light,'

he writes here ; there

> 'And now the spangled squadrons of the night
> Encountering beams had lost the field to light.'

And again :

> 'The day was on the glittering wings of light
> Fled to the western wild, and swarthy night
> In her black empire thronèd.'

And again :

> 'Now at the great'st antipathy to-day
> The silent earth oppressed with midnight lay,
> Vested in clouds black as they had been sent
> To be the whole world's mourning monument';—

passages which could be added to almost indefinitely. Nor is his
imagination limited, according to Addison's rule, to 'ideas furnished by
sight': there is more than this in the phrase 'Desire, the shady porch of
Love,' analogues of which will be found in almost every page. In fact
Pharonnida is simply a Sinbad's Valley of poetic jewels, though here as
there it may be a little difficult to get at them. The practice of filling
Introductions with extracts instead of leaving the reader to find them for
himself is, I have said, an objectionable one. But I may take the
middle course and instance as more than purple patches :—the picture of
Argalia at the bar (I. iii. 165 sq.); Pharonnida's dream, already mentioned (I.
v. 153 sq.), one of the longest and finest of the bursts ; the mystic chamber
in the outlaw's cavern (II. iii. 480 sq.) ; Pharonnida's island (II. iv. 129 sq.) ;
the close of Book III, Canto i and the beginning of the next Canto where

she reads the letter; the valley of Florenza's home, and the lovers' sojourn there. These are but a few, and the reader will find plenty more for himself.

One point, uninteresting to some, will be of the very highest interest to others; and that is what may be called the Battle of the Couplets in *Pharonnida*. It is, as has been said, the last, and in more senses than one the greatest, of poems written in that 'enjambed' and paragraphed variety of the heroic, which was driven out and replaced by its rival a very few years afterwards, when that rival had secured the assistance of Dryden. But as everybody ought to know, the stopped dissyllabic couplet itself is of an ancient house, though its supremacy was modern. It made perhaps the very first appearance in the scattered couplets of Hampole and others before Chaucer. It is very much less absent from Chaucer himself than those who call the metre of *Endymion* Chaucerian appear to imagine; Spenser shows himself a master of it in *Mother Hubberd's Tale*, and it is abundant not merely in the dramatists but in the non-dramatic Elizabethans. Ben Jonson seems to have thought it the best of all metres; but, above all, the tails of Fairfax's stanzas, from which so many of the later seventeenth-century poets learnt, are full of it. Chamberlayne, who was not much more than ten years older than Dryden, could not miss it unless he had set himself the sternest rules of self-criticism : and, as we have seen, he never criticized himself at all. Even the few examples given in this Introduction will show its presence : but much more remarkable ones, both of the completed couplet and of the Drydenian single line which helps to constitute and clench it, will be easily found by the inquirer. Just at the beginning such a formation as

> 'From all the warm society of flesh'

is unmistakable in its tendency, though it actually forms part of a couplet very much 'enjambed.' There is no need to draw the moral of

> 'Dropt as their foes' victorious fate flew by
> To shew his fortune and their royalty.'

or

> 'Rebellion's subtle engineer might sit
> To wreck the weakness of a female wit.'

or

> 'The vexed Epirots who for comfort saw
> Revenge appearing in the form of law.'

These are the single spies which forerun the battalions.

I have no desire to expatiate in these Introductions, or to take up room better occupied by the too long neglected texts; and there remains little that it is desirable and less that it is necessary to say. Chamberlayne's other work of substance, his play of *Love's Victory*, contains many fine passages in the serious blank verse, most of which will be found extracted in the article upon it in the same volume of the *Retrospective Review*;

nor is even the comic part, though it shares the ribaldry and the crudity common in such productions, devoid of some of Chamberlayne's audacious felicities of expression. If that supplementary Dodsley, which has long been wanted, should ever appear, the piece should certainly find a place there : but it is out of our way. His poem to the King at the Restoration may be worth subjoining to *Pharonnida*.

On the whole he is not quite so much of an ' awful example ' as even his panegyrists, Campbell and others, used to make him. At his date, and with the idiosyncrasy shown by the fact that he spent at least fifteen years over his poem as it was, it was practically impossible that he should in any case have devoted to it the critical Medea-sorcery which made perfect things of such very imperfect ones as the original *Palace of Art* and the original *Lady of Shalott.* He might, of course, not have written it at all, and he might possibly have written it in the other vein of stopped couplet, epigrammatic clench and emphasis, and more suppressed conceit. In either case it would not be what it is. We should have lost (in words of its own) ' acquaintance with *Pharonnida.*' And by some that acquaintance would not willingly be relinquished for the possession not merely of one but of a dozen long poems, written in the strictest and most savourless orthodoxy of Le Bossu and La Harpe[1].

---

[1] Most of the few accounts of Chamberlayne mention a prose version of *Pharonnida*, entitled *Eromena, or The Noble Stranger,* which appeared, four years after his death, in 1683 (London : Norris). One naturally imagines—the present editor certainly did so till he read it—a book of length *à la Scudéry.* The actual work is a tiny pamphlet containing some seventy small pages of large print, but adorned with a fresh Pindaric motto (τίνα θεόν, τίν' ἥρωα, τίν' ἄνδρα κελαδήσομεν ;) and a dedication to Madam Sarah Monday. The earlier cantos are paraphrased with some fullness ; the bulk of the story is altogether omitted. As Pharonnida becomes Eromena, so does Argalia take the alias of Horatio. The thing, which acknowledges no indebtedness, is worthless enough ; and only curious because of the admixture of Chamberlayne's own original and highly poetic phrases with the flattest prose.

To the Right Worshipful
Sir William Portman, Baronet[1]

HONOURED SIR,

Though, by that splendour[2] with which the bountiful hand of fortune, illustrated by the more excellent gifts of nature, hath adorned you, to the illuminating the hopes of all your expecting friends, I might justly fear these glow-worms of fancy may be outshone, to the obscurity of a contemptible neglect; you being like, ere long, to prove that glorious luminary, to whose ascending brightness the happiest wits that grace the British hemisphere, like Persian priests prostrated to the rising sun, will devote the morning sacrifices of their muses: yet, animated by your late candid reception of my more youthful labours, whose humble flights, having your name to beautify their front, passed the public view unsullied by the cloudy aspect of the most critic spectator, I have once more assumed the boldness to let the infirmities of my fancy take sanctuary under the name of so honoured a patron. Though my abilities could not clothe her in such robes as would render her a fit companion for your serious studies, yet I hope her dress is not so sordid, but she may prove an acceptable attendant on your more vacant hours. For my subject (it being heroic poesy) it is such as the wiser part of the world hath always held in a venerable esteem; the extracts of fancy being that noble elixir, which heaven ordained to immortalize

their memories, whose worthy actions, being the products of that nobler part of man—the soul, are by this made almost commensurate with her eternity; which otherwise, (to the sorrow of succeeding ages, who are in debt for much of their virtue to a noble emulation of their glorious ancestors), had either terminated in a circle of no larger a diameter than life; or, like short-breathed ephemeras, only survived a while in the airy region of discourse.

This, sir, having been the past fortune of our predecessors; and, as the pregnant hopes of your blooming spring promises[3] the world, like to be yours in the future; yours, when both the splendid beauties of your most glorious palace, and the lasting structure of your marble dormitory, time shall have so levigated, that the wanton winds dally with their dust; I doubt not but to find you so much a Mæcenas, as to affect the eternizing of your name, more from the lasting lineaments of learning than those vain phainomena of pleasures, which are the low delights of more vulgar spirits.

Though I confess these papers beneath the serious view, which a wit, acuated with the best adjuncts of art, will, ere long, render the ordinary recreations of your progressive studies, yet, as in relation to the latitude for which they were calculated, I hope they may not appear unworthy a

---

[1] This was the sixth Baronet (1641?-90), who succeeded to the title in 1648, and matriculated at All Souls in the very year of the appearance of *Pharonnida*. He was a great Tory, and captured Monmouth; but joined William of Orange.

[2] Orig. 'splen*dor*,' on the strength of which, I suppose, Singer has altered 'hono*u*red' before, and 'labo*u*rs' just below, to the same form, though they were correct in text. I shall, therefore, print -*our* throughout, following the original in almost every case.

[3] Singer altered 'promises' to 'promise' and 'serenities' to 'serenity.' But these false concords are too constant in Chamberlayne, and too often made certain by the rhyme to be mere slips of pen or press. I have therefore restored the original forms: as also in al cases (oversights excepted) where the reprint of 1820 unnecessarily changes 'in' to 'on,' &c.

Dedication

present supervisal ; it being intended (like the weak productions of the early spring) but for the April of your age ; where, though my hopes tell me it may subsist, whilst irrigated by those balmy dews of passion which are the usual concomitants of youth ; I am not guilty of so unbecoming a boldness, as to think it fit to stand the heat of your more vigorous maturity, when the meridian altitude of your comprehensive judgement shall have attained so near an universality of knowledge, as the sun, when in its apogæum, doth of light ; that being only hindered by a comparatively punctillo of earth, as the powerful energies of noble souls are, by the upper garments of their mortality, from being at once ubiquitary blessings.

Shaftesbury, May 12, 1659.

Fortified by these considerations with the hope of your acceptance, and assured that prefixing your name is an amulet of sufficient power to preserve me from the contagion of censure, I have, with an unruffled confidence, given these papers a capacity of being publicly viewed. If their being liked attain but near the dimensions of your being beloved, it will co-equate the knowledge the world shall have of them, that being so universal; as the serenities [1] of your bliss is the happiness of your nearest relations, so is it much of the hopes of those that only know you at a remoter distance: And shall be still the prayer of,

Sir,
Your devoted Servant,
WILLIAM CHAMBERLAYNE.

The Epistle to the Reader

SINCE custom obliges me to give a welcome at the gate, I shall not be so irregular as not to meet that common civility with a fair compliance. And though, like the passive elements, I lie open to all the incongruity of aspects, (of which I have some reason to doubt, the most powerful may be found in a disdainful opposition), yet, like the noblest of active creatures—light, I shall not think myself sullied by every vapour ; nor solicit his acquaintance that cannot so long spare his eyes from beholding more active vanities.

I have always held it a solecism for entertainers to be beggars ; and, although by exposing these papers to the public view I must consequently expect variety of censures, should be loath to descend so low to court the applause of every reader ; from whose various genii I am necessitated to take such welcome, as affection in most, though judgement in some, shall incline them to give. For the first of which, as their censures are doubtful, so their calumnies are small—not of weight

sufficient to balance the indifferent temper of my thoughts : but for the latter (since looked upon as competent judges) though their sentence may be formidable, I shall beg no further favour than what their ability thinks fit to bestow ; only, for what they may justly except against, could rather wish that, whilst these papers were private, I had had their advice to reform, than now they are published, their censure to condemn. Fortune hath placed me in too low a sphere. to be happy in the acquaintance of the age's more celebrated wits : wherefore, wonder not that I appear unushered in with a train of encomiums, which though, I confess, if from knowing and judicious friends, add a lustre to the author's ensuing labours ; yet the custom of these times often . makes them appear as ridiculous as a splendid and beautiful front to an empty and contemptible cottage.

I have made bold with the title of heroic, but have a late example [2] that deters me from disputing upon what grounds I assumed it : if it suits not

---

[1] See previous note.   [2] No doubt the Preface to *Gondibert*.

with the abilities of my pen, yet it is no unbecoming epithet for the eminence of those personated in my poem. For the place of my scene, manner of composure, and the like, (though in prefaces they often find an immature discovery, and, perhaps, but acuate an appetite to what, on further progress, may prove but a distasteful banquet), I hold them so impertinent, that, if will and leisure serve you to read, you may suddenly, with more advantage, satisfy yourself; if not, omit them as strangers to your other affairs, and not to be understood but in their own dialect.

I have done with all that in probability may prove my readers, and now a word to such, whom I presume will be none ; for they are desired to do no more than the epistle, it being fit to serve them. Like vagabonds, let them enter no farther than the gate ; —I mean, all squint-eyed sectaries, from the spawn of Geneva to the black brood of Amsterdam ; together with some rascals of a lower rank, such as usurp the abused title of Sons of Art, and, with an empty impudence, endeavour to pollute those immaculate virgins ; whilst the other, with an exalted villany, sully the celestial beauties of divine truth. For the first of which, the preposterous genius of the times hath so far favoured them, that now nothing is more vendible than the surreptitious offsprings of their imagined wit : every stationer's shop affording pregnant examples of it, in big bulked volumes of physic, astrology, and the like, by these indigent vermin ; either to satisfy their clamorous wants, or enhance their esteem in the vulgar opinion, basely prostituted to every illiterate spectator ; whilst truth, and a guilty conscience, tells them nought is their own but the hyperbolical titles ; which, to discerning eyes, appear but the glorious outsides to tainted sepulchres, in which their detected villany shall be abominated by more knowing posterity. These cry down all things of this nature for subjects of inutility, not tending to the improvement of science, which, in the most genuine construction of it, hath no enemy from which her ruin is more formidable than from them.

But for my more dangerous sceptic, (who yet is so much like the foal of an ass, that he appears to the world with his spleen in his mouth), I mean my pretended zealous censurer, from whom in me it were an overweening boldness to expect civility ; since, (though not for the nature, which he understands not, yet for the name, which he hath only heard of), he is so much an enemy to the muses, that should the seraphic strains of majestic David, or the flaming raptures of elegiac Jeremiah, appear to the world in their pristine and unpolluted purity, his ignorance would extend to so vast an error, to censure them of levity.

But as no man will esteem the sun less glorious, for that the hated owl avoids its sight ; so I presume none, except their own deluded followers, will betray so palpable a dearth of judgement, as to bear the less esteem to majestic poetry, for the illiterate scandal of flattering ignorance. Poesy, (if justly meriting to be invested in that glorious title) being so attractive a beauty that it doth rather, like an Orphean harmony, draw that emblem of a beast, the unpolished clown, to a listening civility, than, like Circe's enchantments, change the more happily educated to a swinish and sordid lethargy. But her defence being a burthen which already stands firm on so many noble supporters, whose monuments will remain till time itself shall be lost in eternity, I need not add my weak endeavours to illustrate a Beauty which the wiser world already admires. Now, though she want the applause of some, attribute it not to the defect, either of her excellency, or their judgement ; but to that various dress of humours, wherewith nature hath chequered the universe. Concluding with that honour of ancient Thebes—

Τερπνὸν δ᾽ ἐν ἀνθρώποις ἴσον ἔσσεται οὐδέν.
Pindarus in Olympiorum octavo.

W. C.

PHARONNIDA

BOOK I. Canto I[1]

THE ARGUMENT

From sea's wild fury, and the wilder rage
  Of faithless Turks, two noble strangers freed,
Let courtesy their grateful souls engage
  To such a debt as doth obstruct their speed:

Where they, to fill those scenes inactive rest
  Would tedious make, in fair description saw,
How Sparta's Prince, for his queen's loss opprest,
  Found all those ills cured in Pharonnida[2].

THE earth, which lately lay, like nature's tomb,
Marbled in frosts, had from her pregnant womb
Displayed the fragrant spring; when, courted by
A calm fresh morning, ere heaven's brightest eye
Adorned the east, a Spartan lord, (whom fame,
Taught from desert, made glorious by the name
Of Aminander), with a noble train,
Whose active youth did sloth, like sin, disdain,
Attended, had worn out the morning in
Chase of a stately stag; which, having been   10
Forced from the forest's safe protection to
Discovering plain, his clamorous foes had drew
Up to a steep cliff's lofty top; where he,
As if grown proud so sacrificed to be
To man's delight, 'mongst the pursuing cry,
Who make the valleys echo victory,
Sinks weeping; whilst exalted shouts did tell
The distant herds—their ancient leader fell.
    The half-tired hunters, their swift game stopt here
By death, like noble conquerors appear   20
To give that foe, which now resistless lies,
With their shrill horns his funeral obsequies;
Which whilst performing, their diverted sight
Turns to behold a far more fatal fight—

---

[1] These headings were in orig. 'The First Book. Canto the First,' &c., in two lines. So, too, each verse paragraph begins with an indented couplet.
[2] This initial passage may deserve a note which I shall not repeat, though it describes a process frequently necessary. Singer read 'Were they' for 'Where they,' but kept the comma of the orig. at 'rest' and inserted none at 'they' or 'make,' while he did insert an apostrophe at 'scenes.' His text thus becomes unintelligible, which mine, I hope, is not.
    8 sloth, like] Orig. 'sloth-like.'

(17)

That since-famed gulf, (where the brave Austrian made
The Turkish crescents an eternal shade
Beneath dishonour seek) Lepanto, lay
So near, that from their lofty station they,
A ship upon whose streamers there were fixt
The Christian badge, saw in fierce battle mixt   30
With a prevailing Turkish squadron, that
With shouts assault what now lay only at
That feeble guard, which, under the pretence
Of injuring others, seeks its own defence.
   Clear was the day, and calm the sea so long,
Till now the Turks, whose numbers grew too strong
For all that could no other help afford
But human strength, within their view did board
The wretched Christians; to whose sufferings they
Can lend no comfort, but what prayers convey   40
To helpful heaven; by whose attentive ear,
Both heard and pitied, mercy did appear
In this swift change:—A hollow wind proclaims
Approaching storms, the black clouds burst in flames,
Imprisoned thunder roars, and in a shower,
Dark as the night, dull sweaty vapours pour
Themselves on the earth, to enrich whom nature vents
·The ethereal fabric's useless excrements,
Whose flatuous pride, as if it did disdain
Such base descents, rolling the liquid plain   50
Into transparent mountains, hurls them at
The brow of heaven, whose lamps, by vapours that
Their influence raised, are crampt; whilst the sick day
Was languishing to such a night, as lay
O'er the first matter, when confusion dwelt
In the vast chaos, ere the rude mass felt
Heaven's segregating breath—but long this fierce
Conflict endures not, ere the sun-beams pierce
The scattered clouds, which, whilst wild winds pursue,
Through sullied air in reeking vapours flew.   60
   In this encounter of the storm, before
Its sable veil let them discover more
Than contained horror, a loud dreadful shriek,
Piercing the thick air, at their ears did seek
For trembling entrance: being transported by
Uncertain drifts, rent sails and tackling fly
Amongst the towering cliffs,—a sure presage
That adverse winds did in that storm engage
Some vessel, which did from her cordage part,
With such sad pangs—as from the dying heart   70
Convulsions tear the fibres. But the day,
Recovering her lost reign, made clearer way

27 seek] Orig. 'seeks.'

(18)

For a more sad discovery. They behold
The brackish main in funeral pomp unfold
The trophies of her cruelty. Her brow,
Uncurled with waves, was only spotted now
With scattered ruins ; here, engaged within
The ruffled sails, some sad souls that had been,
For life long struggling, tired, at length are forced
To sink and die ; yonder, a pair, divorced   80
From all the warm society of flesh,
With cold stiff arms embrace their fate ;—the fresh
And tender virgin in her lover's sight,
The sea-gods ravish, and the enthean light
Of those bright orbs, her eyes, which could by nought
But seas be quenched, t' eternal darkness brought.
    Whilst pitying these, a sudden noise, whose strange
Confusion did their passion's object change,
Assaults their wonder ; which, by this surprise
Amazed, persuades them to inform their eyes   90
With its obscure original : when, led
By sounds that might in baser souls have bred
A swift aversion, clashing weapons they
Might soon behold—upon the sands that lay
Beneath the rock a troop of desperate men,
Unstartled with those dangers (which e'en then
Their ruined ship and dropping garments showed
Heaven freed them from—what mercy had bestowed)
Let their own anger loose ; which, flaming in
A fatal combat, had already been   100
In blood disfigured : but when now so near
Them drawn, that every object did appear
In true distinction, they, with wonder raised
To such a height as poets would have praised
Their heroes in, a noble Christian saw,
Whose sword (as if, by the eternal law
Of Providence, to punish infidels,
Directed) with each falling stroke expels
A Turk's black soul : yet valour, being opprest
By multitudes, must have at length sought rest   110
From death, had not brave Ariamnes, by
His hunters followed, brought him victory ;
Whilst the approaching danger did exclude
E'en hope, the last support of fortitude.
    The desperate Turks, that chose the sea to be
Their sad redeemer of captivity,
Though from that fear they fled to death, had now
Upon the shore left none life could allow

---

84 enthean] This, a rather favourite word with Chamberlayne and his contem-
poraries, ought not to have become obsolete ; for we have no single equivalent to
' *divinely* inspired ' or ' furnished.'

But motion to; though, stopped by death such store,
All the escaped appeared, but such as bore　　120
The fatal story of destruction to
Their distant friends.　When now a serious view,
By Ariamnes and that noble youth,
(Whose actions, honoured as authentic truth,
Made all admire him), of their pitied dead
With sorrow took, one worthy soul unfled
From life they found, which, by Argalia seen,
With joy recals those spirits that had been
In busy action lost; but danger, that
Toward the throne of life seemed entering at　　130
Too many wounds, denies him to enlarge
The stream of love, as noble Virtue's charge
To him, her follower.　Ariamnes, by
His goodness and their sad necessity
Prompted to pity, fearing slow delays
As danger's fatal harbinger, conveys
The wounded strangers to the place where he
His palace made the throne of charity.
　'Twas the short journey 'twixt the day and night,
The calm fresh evening, time's hermaphrodite,　　140
The sun, on light's dilated wings, being fled,
To call the western villagers from bed,
Ere at his castle they arrive, which stood
Upon a hill, whose basis, fringed with wood,
Shadowed the fragrant meadows; thorough which
A spacious river, striving to enrich
The flowery valleys with whatever might
At home be profit, or abroad delight,
With parted streams that pleasant islands made,
Its gentle current to the sea conveyed.　　150
　In the composure of this happy place
Wherein he lived, as if framed to embrace
So brave a soul as now did animate
It with his presence, strength and beauty sate
Combined in one: 'twas not so vastly large,
But fair convenience countervailed the charge
Of reparations, all that modest art
Affords to sober pleasure's every part,
More for its ornament; but none were drest
In robes so rich, but what alone exprest　　160
Their master's providence and care to be,
A prop to falling hospitality.
For he, not comet-like, did blaze out in
This country sphere what had extracted been
From the court's lazy vapours, but had stood
There like a star of the first magnitude,
With a fixed constancy so long, that now,
Grown old in virtue, he began to bow

Beneath the weight of time ; and, since the calm
Of age had left him nothing to embalm   170
His name but virtue, strives in that to be
The glorious wonder of posterity :
Each of his actions being so truly good,
That, like the ground where hallowed temples stood,
Although by age the ruins ruined seem,
The people bear a reverend esteem
Unto the place ; so they preserve his name—
A yet unwasted pyramid of fame.
   Rich were his public virtues, but the price
Of those was but the world to Paradise,   180
Compared with that rare harmony that dwells
Within his walls ; each servant there excels
All but his fellows in desert ; each knew—
First, when,—then, how his lord's commands to do ;
None more enjoyed than was enough, none less,
All did of plenty taste, none of excess ;
Riot was here a stranger, but far more,
Repining penury ; ne'er from that door
The poor man went denied, nor did the rich
E'er surfeit there ; 'twas the blest medium which,   190
Extracted from all compound virtues, we
Make, and then Christian Mediocrity.
Within the compass of his spacious hall,
Stood no vain pictures to obscure the wall,
Which useful arms adorned ; and such as when
His prince required assistance, his own men,
Valiant and numerous, managed to defend
That righteous cause, but never to attend
A popular faction, whose corrupted seed
Hell did engender, and ambition feed.   200
   His judgement, that, like life's attendant—sense,
To try each object's various difference,
Fit mediums chose, (which he made virtue), here
Beholding (though these wandering stars appear
Now in their greatest detriment) the rays
Of perfect worth, he to that virtue pays
Those attributes of honour, which unto
Their births, though now in coarse disguise, was due.
To Aphron's wounds successful art applies
Prevailing medicines, whilst invention flies   210
To the aphelion of her orb to seek
Such modest pleasures as might smooth the cheek
Of ruffled passion ; which, being found, are spent
To cure the sad Argalia's discontent :
Which, long being lost to all delight, at length
Revives again his friend's recovered strength.

192 Christian] This must be in the sense of 'christen' ; so Singer.

They, having now no remora to stay
Them here but what their gratitude did pay
To his desires, (whose courtesy had made
Those bonds of love with as much zeal obeyed   220
As those which duty locks), preparing are
To take their leave; even in whose civil war
Whilst they contend with courtesies, as sent
To rescue, when his eloquence was spent,
Brave Aminander, with such haste as shewed
His speed to some supreme injunction owed
Such diligence, a messenger brings in
A packet, which that noble lord had been
Too frequently acquainted with to fear
The unseen contents, which opened did appear—   230
A mandate from his royal master to
Attend him ere the next day's beauties grew
Deformed with age; which honoured message read,
To banish what suspicion might have bred
In's doubtful friends, he, the enclosed contents,
With cheerful haste, unto their view presents.
    Their fear thus cured by information, he,
That his appearance in the court might be
More glorious made by such attendants, to
Incite in them a strong desire to view   240
Those royal pastimes, thus relates that story,
Whose fatal truth transferred the Morea's glory
So often thither. ''Twas, my honoured friends,
My fate ('mongst some that yet his court attends)
Then to be near my prince, when what now draws
Him to these parts did prove at once the cause
Of joy and grief. Not far from hence removed
The vale of Ceres lies, where his beloved
Pharonnida remains; a lady that
Nature ordained for man to wonder at,   250
She not being more the comfort of his age
Than glory of her sex: but I engage
Myself to a more large discovery, which
Thus take in brief—When youth did first enrich
Beauty with manly strength, his happy bed
Was with her royal mother blest; who fed
A flame of virtue in her soul, that lent
Light to a beauty, which, being excellent,
In its own sphere by that reflection shone
So heavenly bright—perfection's height of noon   260
Dwelt only there. Some years had circled in
Time's revolutions, since they first had been
Acquainted with those private pleasures that
Attend a nuptial bed, ere she did at
Lucina's temple offer; whose barred gate,
Once open flow, both their good angels sate

In council for her safety. Hopes of a boy,
To be Morea's heir, fill high with joy
The ravished parents ; subjects did no less,
In the loud voice of triumph, theirs express.   270
'But when the active pleasures of their love,
Which filled her womb, had taught the babe to move
Within the morys mount, preceding pains
Tell the fair queen, that the dissolving chains,
Nature enclosed it in, were grown so weak
That the imprisoned infant soon would break
Those slender guards. The gravest ladies were
Called to assist her, whose industrious care
Lend nature all the helps of art, but in
Despair of safety send their prayers to win   280
Relief from heaven, which swift assistance lent
To unload the burthen ; but those cordials sent
By harbingers, with whom the fair queen fled
To deck the silent dwellings of the dead,
And lodge in sheets of lead ; o'er which were cast
A coverlet of the spring's infants past
From life like her—e'en whilst Earth's teeming womb,
Promised the world, and not a silent tomb,
That beauteous issue. But those nymphs, which spun
Her thread of life, the slender twine begun   290
Too fine to last long, undenied by
The ponderous burthen of mortality;
Beneath whose weight, she sinking now to death,
The unhappy babe was by the mother's breath
No sooner welcomed into life before
She bids farewell; of power to do no more
But, whilst her spirits with each word expires,
Thus to her lord express her last desires.—
"Receive this infant from thy dying queen,
Name her Pharonnida."—At which word between   300
His trembling arms she sunk ; and had e'en then
Breathed forth her soul, if not recalled again
By their loud mournings from the icy sleep,
Which, like a chilling frost, did softly creep
Through the cold channels of her blood to bar
The springs of life ; in which defensive war,
The hasty summons, sent by death, allow
Her giddy eyes, whose heavy lids did bow
Toward everlasting slumber, no more light
Than what affords a dim imperfect sight,—   310
Such as the troubled optics, being by
Dying convulsions wrested, could let fly

273 morys] Orig. 'mory,' qu. 'ivory'? The orig. looks like a misprint, and 'ivory
mount' is a favourite Elizabethanism.
278 care] Again, a note on Chamberlayne's singular habit of putting a plural noun
to a singular verb may serve once for all.

Thorough their sullied crystals, to behold
Her woeful lord, whilst she did thus unfold
Her dying thoughts:—"O hear, O hear, (quoth she) I do
By all our mutual vows conjure thee to
Let this sweet babe—all thou hast left of me,
Within thy thoughts preserve my memory.
And since, poor infant, she must lose her mother,
To beg an entrance here, oh let no other   320
Have more command o'er her than what may bear
An equal poise with thy paternal care.
This, this is all that I shall leave behind;
An earnest of our loves here thou may'st find,
Perhaps, my image may'st behold, whilst I,
Resolving into dust, embraced do lie
By crawling worms—followers that nature gave
To attend mortality, whilst the tainted grave
Is ripening us for judgement. O my lord,
Death were the smile of fate, would it afford   330
Me time to see this infant's growth, but oh!
I feel life's cordage crackt, and hence must go
From time and flesh,—like a lost feather, fall
From th' wings of vanity, forsaking all
The various business of the world, to see
What wondrous change dwells in eternity."
    'This said, she faintly bids farewell, then darts
An eager look on all; but, ere she parts,
E'en whilst the breath, with which in thin air slips
Departing spirits, on her then cold lips   340
In clammy dews did hang, she of them takes
Her last farewell, whilst her pure soul forsakes
Its brittle cabinet, and those orbs of light,
That swam in death, sunk in eternal night.
    'Thus died the queen, Pharonnida thus lost,
Ere knew, her mother, when her birth had cost
A price so great, that brought her infancy
In debt to grief, until maturity
Ripened her age to pay it. After long
And vehement lamentation, such whose strong   350
Assaults had almost shook his soul into
A flight from the earth, her father doth renew
His long lost mirth, at the delight he took
In his soul's darling; whose each cheerful look
Crimsoned those sables, which e'en whilst he wore,
A flood of woes his head had silvered o'er,
Had not this comfort stopt them, which beguiles
Sorrow of some few hours; those pretty smiles
That drest her fair cheeks, like a gentle thief,
Stealing his heart through all the guards of grief.   360

315 The first Alexandrine. But the duplication of 'O hear' may be a slip.

'But when that time's expunging hand had more
Defaced those sable characters he wore
For sorrow's livery o'er his soul, and she,
Having out-grown her tender infancy,
Did now (her thoughts composed of heavenly seed)
To guide her life no other guardian need,
But native virtue ; for her calm retreat,
When burthened Corinth was with throngs replete,
He chose this seat, whose venerable shade,
(Waving what blind antiquity had made)   370
For sacred held, is not so slighted, but
A custom, ancient as our law, hath shut
Hence (as the hateful marks of servitude)
All that unbounded power did e'er obtrude
On suffering subjects ; which this happy place
Fits so serene a blessing to embrace
As is this lady : whose illustrious court,
Though now augmented by the full resort
Of her great father's train, doth still appear
This happy kingdom's brightest hemisphere.   380
'A hundred noble youths in Sparta bred,
Of valour high as e'er for beauty bled,
All loyal lovers, and that love confined
Within the court, are for her guard assigned.
But what (if aught in such an orb of all
That's great or good may low as censure fall)
The court hath questioned, is—the cause that moved
The prince to give a party so beloved
Into his hands that leads them ; being one,
Whose birth excepted, (that being near a throne),   390
Those virtues wants, on whose foundation, wise
Considerate princes let their favours rise.
Like the abortive births of vapours, by
Their male-progenitors enforced to fly
Above the earth their proper sphere, and there
Lurk in imperfect forms, his breast doth bear
Some seeds of goodness, which the soil, too hot
With rank ambition, doth in ripening rot.
Yet, though from those that praise humility
He merits not, a dreaded power, (which he   400
Far more applauds) raised on the wings of's own
Experienced valour, hath so long been known
His foes' pale terror, that 'tis feared he bends
That engine to the ruin of his friends,
Whose equal merits claim as much of fame
As e'er was due to proud Almanzor's name.
'Yet what may raise more strong desires to see
Her court than valour's wished society,
Is one unusual custom, which the love
Of her kind father hath so far above   410

All past example raised—that, for the time
He here resides, no cause, although a crime
Which death attends, but is by her alone
Both heard and judged, he seeming to unthrone
His active power, whilst justice doth invest
His beauteous daughter; which, to the opprest,
Whose hopes e'en shrunk into despair, hath in
That harsh extreme their safe asylum been:
So that e'en those that feared the event could now
Mix their desires,—the custom would allow   420
Her reign a longer date.   But that I may
Illustrate this by a more full survey
Of her excelling virtues, no pretence
Of harsh employment shall command you hence,
Till you have been spectators of that court,
Whose glories are too spacious for report.'
    The noble youths, beholding such a flame
Of virtue shewn them through the glass of Fame,
First gaze with wonder on it, which ascends
Into desire, a rivulet which ends   430
Not till its swelling streams had drawn them through
All weak excuses, and engaged them to
Attend on Ariamnes: when, to show
How much man's vain intentions fall below
Mysterious fate, e'en in the height of all
Their full resolves, her countermands thus call
Back their intentions, by a summons that
The uncertain world hath often trembled at.—
The late recovered Aphron, whether by
Too swift a cure, life's springs, being raised too high,   440
Flowed to a dangerous plethora, or whe'er
Some cause occult the humours did prepare
For that malignant ill, did, whilst he lay
In tedious expectation of the day
Shook with a shivering numbness, first complain
Through all his limbs of a diffusive pain:
Which, searching each to find the fittest part
For its contagion, on the labouring heart
Fixes at length; which, being with grief opprest,
By the extended arteries to the rest   450
O' the body sends its flames.   The poisoned blood
Through every vein streams in a burning flood;
His liver broils, and his scorched stomach turns
The chyle to cinders; in each cold cell burns
The humid brains.   A violent earthquake shakes
The crackling nerves, sleep's balmy dew forsakes
The shrivelled optics; in which trembling fits,
'Mongst tortured senses, troubled Reason sits
So long opprest with passion, till at length,
Her feeble mansion, battered by the strength   460

(26)

Of a disease, she leaves to entertain
The wild chimeras of a sickly brain.
And, what must yet to 's friend's affliction add
More weights of grief, their courteous host, which had
Stayed to the latest step of time, must now
Comply with those commands, which could allow
No more delays, and leave Argalia to
Be the sole mourner for his friend, which drew
(As far as human art could guess) so near
His end, that life did only now appear   470
In thick, short sobs,—those frequent summons that
Souls oft forsake their ruined mansions at.

THE END OF THE FIRST CANTO.

Canto II

THE ARGUMENT

Whilst here Argalia in a calm retreat
Allays the sorrow felt for 's sickly friend,
Two blooming virgins near him take their seat,
Whose harmless mirth soon finds a hapless end.

The fairest seized on, and near ruined by
Impetuous lust, had not Andremon's speed
Protected her, till from his fall drawn nigh
The same sad fate the brave Argalia freed.

THAT sad slow hour, which Art e'en thought his last,
With the sharp fever's paroxysm past,
Sick Aphron's spirits to a cool retreat,
Beneath a slumber, life's remotest seat,
Was gently stol'n, which did so long endure,
Till, in that opiate quenched, the calenture
Decayed forsakes him, leaving nought behind,
But such faint symptoms as from time might find
An easy cure; which, though no perfect end
Is lent to th' care of his indulgent friend,   10
Yet gives him so much liberty, that now
Fear dares, without his friendship's breach, allow
Sometime to leave him slumbering, whilst that he
Contemplates nature's fresh variety.
     The full-blown beauties of the spring were not
By summer sun-burnt yet, though Phœbus shot
His rays from Cancer, when, prepared to expand
Imprisoned thoughts from objects near at hand
To eye-shot rovers, freed Argalia takes
A noon-tide walk through a fair glade, that makes   20
Her aged ornaments their stubborn head
Fold into verdant curtains, which she spread

In cooling shadows o'er the bottoms; where
A crystal stream, unfettered by the care
Of nicer art, in her own channel played
With the embracing banks, until betrayed
Into a neighbouring lake; whose spacious womb
Looked at that distance like a crystal tomb
Frâmed to inter the Naiades. Not far
From hence an oak, (whose limbs defensive war   30
'Gainst all the winds a hundred winters knew,
Stoutly maintained), on a small rising grew,
Under whose shadow whilst Argalia lies,
This object tempts his soul into his eyes—
A pair of virgins, fairer than the spring;
Fresher than dews, that, ere the glad birds sing
The morning's carols, drop; with such a pace
As in each act showed an unstudied grace,
Crossing the neighbouring plain, were now so near
Argalia drew, that what did first appear   40
But the neglected object of his eye,
More strictly viewed, calls fancy to comply
With so much love, that, though no wilder fire
Ere scorched his breast, he here learnt to admire
Love's first of symptoms. To a shady seat,
Near that which he had made his cool retreat,
Being come, beneath a spreading hawthorn they,
Seating themselves, the sliding hours betray
From their short lives, by such discourse as might
Have made e'en Time, if young, lament his flight.   50
  Retired Argalia, at the sight of these,
Though no obscener vanity did please
His eyes, than anch'rites are possest with, when
Numb'ring their beads, or from a sacred pen
Distilling Heaven's blest oracles, yet he,
Wondering to find such sweet civility
Mixt with thàt place's rudeness, long beholds
That lovely pair, whose every act unfolds
Such linked affections as wise nature weaves
In dearest sisters; but their form bereaves   60
That thought ere feathered with belief: although,
To admiration, Beauty did bestow
Her gifts on both, she had those darlings drest
In various colours;—what could be exprest
By objects, fair as new created light;
By roseal mixtures, with immaculate white;

40 drew, 122 withdrew] Another not-to-be-repeated note may call attention here to
Chamberlayne's singular liberties with preterite and past participle. In the first of
these two instances one is actually tempted to read ' where ' which, as it happens, makes
ordinary grammar. But it is evidently not the sense, and ' drew '=' drawn ' as ' with-
drew '=' withdrawn.'
  66 roseal] Singer *putidé* ' rosea*te*,' thereby effacing a delightful word and substituting
a very inferior one.

By eyes that emblemed heaven's pure azure, in
The youngest nymph, Florenza, there was seen ;
To which she adds behaviour far more free,
Although restrained to strictest modesty,   70
Than the more sad Carina, who, if there
Were different years in that else equal pair,
Something the elder seemed ; her beauty—such
As Jove-loved Leda's was, not praised so much
For rose' or lily's residence, though they
 Did both dwell there, as to behold the day
Lose its antipathy to night ; such clear
And conquering beams, so full of light, to appear
Thorough her eyes, showed like a diamond set,
To mend its lustre, in a foil of jet.   80
Nor doth their dress of nature differ more
In colour than the habits which they wore,
Though fashioned both alike ; Florenza's, green
As the fresh Spring, when her first buds are seen
To clothe the naked boughs ; Carina's, white
As Innocence, before she takes a flight
In thought from cold virginity. Their hair,
Wreathed in contracting curls beneath a fair
But often parting veil, attempts to hide
The naked ivory of their necks—that pride   90
Of beauty's frontispiece. On their heads sate
Lovely, as if unto a throne of state
From their first earth advanced, two flowery wreaths,
(From whose choice mixture in close concord breathes
The fragrant odour of the fields), placed by
Them in such order, as antiquity
Mysterious held. Being set, to pass away
The inactive heat of the exalted day,
They either tell old harmless tales, or read
Some story where forsaken lovers plead   100
Unpitied causes, then betwixt a smile
And tear bewail passion should ere beguile
Poor reason so ; at length, as if they meant
To charm him who, far from each ill intent,
So near them lay, melting the various throng
Of their discourse into a well-tuned song ;
Whose swift division moulds the air into
Such notes, as did the spheres' first tunes out-do.
   Argalia, in his labyrinth of delight
To action lost, had drawn the veil of night,   110
In quiet slumbers, o'er his heavy eyes :
Locked in whose arms whilst he securely lies,
Lest the mistakes of vain mortality
The brittle glass of earth should take to be
Perfection's lasting adamant, this sad
Chance did unravel all their mirth.—There had

(29)   D   811846·1

Some of the prince's noblest followers, in
That morning's nonage, led by pleasure been
Far from their sphere—the court; and now, to shun
The unhealthy beams of the reflected sun,　　　　120
Whilst it its shortest shadows made, were to
The cool protection of the woods withdrew:
In which retreat, as if conducted by
Their evil genius, (all his company
An awful distance keeping) none but proud
Almanzor, in those guilty groves which shroud
The hapless virgins, enters; who so near
Him sitting, that soon his informing ear
Thither directs his eye. Unto his view
Ere scarce thought obvious, swiftly they withdrew,　　　130
But with untimely haste. His soul, that nurst
Continual flames within it, at the first
Sight kindles them, ere he discovers more
Than difference in the sex; such untried ore,
Hot heedless lust, when made by practice bold,
I' th' flame of passion ventures on for gold.
But when drawn nearer to the place he saw
Such beauties, whose magnetic force might draw
Souls steeled with virtue, custom having made
His impious rhetoric ready to invade,　　　　140
He towards them hastes, with such a pace as might
Excuse their judgements, though in open flight
They strove to shun him, but in vain; so near
Them now he's drawn, that the effects of fear
Obscuring reason, as if safety lay
In separation, each a several way
From danger flies; but since both could not be
By that secure, whilst her blest stars do free
The glad Carina from his reach, the other
He swiftly seizes on: hot kisses smother　　　　150
Her out-cries in the embryo, and to death
Near crushed virginity, ere, from lost breath,
She could a stock of strength enough recover
To spend in prayers. The tempting of a lover,
Mixt with the force of an adulterer, did
At once assail, and with joined powers forbid
All hopes of safety; only, whilst Despair
Looked big in apprehension, whilst the air
Breathed nought but threatenings; promising him to pay
For't in her answers, she doth lust betray　　　　160
Of some few minutes, which, with all the power
Of prayer, she seeks to lengthen; sheds a shower
Of tears to quench those flames. But sooner might

122 withdrew] See note on p. 28.
138 force] So Singer for 'form,' which I think quite possible.

Hell's sooty lamp extinguished be ; the sight
Of such a fair, but pitiful aspect,
When lust assails, wants power to protect.
By this hot parley, whilst she strove to shun
His loathed embraces, the thronged spirits run
To fortify her heart, but vainly seek
For entrance there, being back into her cheek   170
Sent in disdainful blushes : now she did
Entreat civility, then sharply chid
His blushless impudence ; but he, whose skill
In rhetoric was pregnant to all ill,
Though barren else, summons up all the choice
Of eloquence, that might produce a voice
To win fair virtue's fortress, though her chaste
Soul, armed against those battering engines, past
That conflict without danger ; when, enraged
By being denied, with passion that presaged   180
A dangerous consequence, his fierce eyes fixt
On hers, that, melting with pale terror, mixt
Floods with their former flames, her soul's sad doubt
He thus resolves—'Unworthy whore, that, out
Of hate to virtue, dost deny me what
Thou freely grant'st to every rude swain that
But courts thee in a dance—think not these tears
Shall make me waive a pleasure, that appears
Worth the receiving. Can your sordid earth
Be honoured more than in the noble birth   190
Of such a son, as, wouldst thou yield to love,
Might call thee mother, and hereafter prove
The glory of your family? From Jove,
The noblest mortals, heretofore that strove
To fetch their pedigree, thought it no stain
So to be illegitimate ; as vain
Is this in thee, there being as great an odds
'Twixt you and us, as betwixt us and gods.'
Trembling Florenza, on her bended knees,
Thus answers him :—'That dreadful power that sees   200
All our disveloped thoughts, my witness be
You wrong my innocence ; I yet am free
From every thought of lust. I do confess
The unfathomed distance 'twixt our births, but less
That will not make my sin ; it may my shame
The more, when my contaminated name
Shall in those ugly characters be shown
To the world's public view, that now is known
B' the blush of honesty ; whose style, though poor,
Exceeds the titles of a glorious whore—   210
Attended, whilst youth doth unwithered last,
With envied greatness ; but, frail beauty past
Into a swift decay, assaulted by

Rottenness within, and black-mouthed calumny
Without, cast off, blushing for guilt, the scorn
Of all my sex. My mother would unborn
Wish her degenerate issue, my father curse
The hour he got me. As infection worse
Than mortal plagues, each virgin, that hath nought
To glory in but what she with her brought   220
Into the world—an unstained soul, would fly
The air I breathe ; cast whores being company
For none but devils, when corrupted vice
A wilderness makes Beauty's paradise.
To this much ill, dim-eyed mortality
A prospect lends ; but what, oh ! what should be
When we must sum up all our time in one
Eternal day, since to our thoughts unknown,
Is only feared ; but if our hallowed laws
Are more than fables, the everlasting cause,   230
'Twill of our torment be. If all this breath,
Formed into prayers, no entrance finds, my death
Shall buy my virgin-freedom, ere I will
Consent to that, which, being performed, will kill
My honour to preserve my life, and turn
The unworthy beauty, which now makes you burn
In these unhallowed flames, into a cell
Which none but th' black inhabitants of hell
Will e'er possess. Those private thoughts, which give,
If we continue virtuous whilst we live   240
On earth, our souls commerce with angels, shall
Be turned to furies, if we yield to fall
Beneath our vices thus. O ! then take heed—
Do not defile a temple ; such a deed
Will, when in labour with your latest breath,
With horror curtain the black bed of death.'
    Though prayers in vain strove to divert that crime
He prosecutes, yet, to protract the time,
She more had said, had not all language been
Lost in a storm of 's lust ; which, raging in   250
His fury, gives a fresh assault unto
Weak innocence : for mercy now to sue—
To hope—seems vain ; robustious strength did bar
The use of language, which defensive war
Continuing, till the breathless maid was wrought
Almost beneath resistance, just heaven brought
This unexpected aid. A lowly swain,
Whose large possessions in the neighbouring plain
Had styled him rich, and powerful which to improve,
To that fair stock, his virtue added love ;   260

257 lowly] Orig. 'lovely,' which again is quite possible, though the words are often
confounded in the very bad printing of the original.

Which, ⟨un⟩to flattery since it lost its eyes,
The world but seldom sees without disguise.
This sprightly youth, led by the parallels
Of birth and fortune—whate'er else excels
Those fading blessings—to Florenza, in
His youth's fresh April, had devoted been,
With so much zeal, that what that heedless age
But dallied with, (like customs which engage
Themselves to habits), ere its growth he knew,
Love, equal with his active manhood, grew;   270
Which noble plant, though, in the torrid zone
Of her disdain, 't had ne'er distemper known,
Yet oft those sad vicissitudes doth find,
For which none truly loved that ne'er had pined.
Which pleasing passion, though his judgement knew
How to divert, ere reason it out-grew,
It often from important action brought
Him to those shades, where contemplation sought
Calm solitude; in whose soft raptures, Love,
Refining fancy, lifts his thoughts above   280
Those joys, which, when by trial brought t' the test,
Prove Thought's bright heaven dull earth, when once possest.
    Whilst seated here, his eyes did celebrate,
As to those shades Florenza oft had sat
Beneath kind looks; to ravish that delight,
The tired Carina, in her breathless flight
Come near the place, assaults his wonder in
That dreadful sound, which tells him what had been
Her cause of fear; which doleful story's end,
Arrived t' the danger of his dearest friend,   290
Leaves him no time for language, ere, winged by
Anger and love, his haste strives to outfly
His eager thoughts. Being now arrived so near
Unto the place, that his informing ear
Thither directs his steps, with such a haste,
As nimble souls, when they are first uncased,
From bodies fly, he thither speeds; and now
Being come, where he beheld with horror how
His better angel injured was, disputes
Neither with fear nor policy—they're mutes   300
When anger's thunder roars—but swiftly draws
His falchion, and the justice of his cause
Argues with eager strokes, but spent in vain
'Gainst that unequal strength, which did maintain
The more unlawful; all his power could do,
Is but to show the effects of love unto
Her he adored, few strokes being spent before
His feeble arm, of power to do no more,

261 ⟨un⟩to] Altered from 'to' by Singer. I am not sure that Chamberlayne would
not have risked the double trochee 'Whĭch, tŏ | flāttĕ | ry.'

Faints with the loss of blood ; and, letting fall
The ill-managed weapon, for his death doth call,   310
By the contempt of mercy, so to prove
A sacrifice, slain to Florenza's love.
The cursed steel, by the robustious hand
Of fierce Almanzor guided, now did stand
Fixed in his breast, whilst, with a purple flood,
His life sails forth i' the channel of his blood.
This remora removed, the impious deed
No sooner was performed, but, ere the speed
Florenza made (though to her eager flight
Fear added wings) conveyed her from his sight,   320
His rude hand on her seizes. Now in vain
She lavished prayers, the groans in which her slain
Friend breathes his soul forth, with her shrieks, did fill
The ambient air, struck lately with the still
Voice of harmonious music. But the ear
Of penetrated heaven not long could hear
Prayers breathed from so much innocence, yet send
Them back denied ; white Mercy did attend
Her swift delivery, when obstructing fear
Through reason let no ray of hope appear.   330
   Startled Argalia, who was courted by
Her pleasing voice's milder harmony
Into restrictive slumbers, wakened at
Their altered tone, hastes to discover what
Had caused that change ; and soon the place attains,
Where, in the exhausted treasure of his veins,
Andremon wallows, and Florenza lies,
Bathed in her tears, ready to sacrifice
Her life with her virginity ; which sight
Provoked a haste, such as his presence might   340
Protect the trembling virgin ; which perceived
By cursed Almanzor, mad to be bereaved
O' the spoils of such a wicked victory
As lust had then near conquered, fiercely he
Assails the noble stranger ; who, detesting
An act so full of villany, and resting
On the firm justice of his cause, had made
His guiltless sword as ready to invade
As was the other's, that had surfeited
In blood before. Here equal valour bred   350
In both a doubtful hope ; Almanzor's lust
Had fired his courage, which Argalia's just
Attempts did strive to quench. The thirsty steel
Had drunk some blood from both, ere fortune's wheel
Turned to the righteous cause. That vigour which
Through rivulets of veins spread the salt itch
Of feverish lust before, was turned into
A flame of anger ; whilst his hands did do

What rage doth dictate, fury doth assist
With flaming paroxysms, and each nerve twist   360
Into a double strength : yet not that flood,
Which in this ebullition of his blood
Did through the channels boil till they run o'er
With flaming spirits, could depress that store
Of manly worth, which in Argalia's breast
Did with a quiet even valour rest ;
Moving as in its natural orb, unstrained
By any violent motion ; nor yet chained
By lazy damps of faint mistrust, but in
Danger's extreme, still confident to win   370
A noble victory; or, i' the loss of breath,
If his fate frowned, to find an honoured death.
   Filled with these brave resolves, until the heat
Of their warm fury had alarums beat
T' the neighbouring fields, they fought ; which tumult, by
Such of Almanzor's followers as were nigh
The grove reposed, with an astonishment
That roused them, heard, they hasten to prevent
The sad effects that might this cause ensue,
Ere more of danger than their fear they knew.   380
Arrived e'en with that fatal minute, he
Who against justice strove for victory,
With such faint strokes that their descent did give
Nought but assurance that his foe must live
A happy conqueror, they usurp the power
Of Heaven—revenge ; and, in a dreadful shower
Of danger, with their fury's torrent strive
To o'erwhelm the victor : but the foremost drive
Their own destruction on, and fall beneath
His conquering sword, ere he takes time to breathe   390
Those spirits, which, when near with action tired,
Valour breathed fresh, fast as the spent expired.
   Here rash Araspes and bold Leovine,
Two whose descent i' the nearest collateral line
Unto Almanzor's stood, beholding how
His strength decayed must unto conquest bow
In spite of valour, to revenge his fate
With so much haste, attempt, as if too late
They'd come to rescue, and would now, to shun
His just reproof, by rashness strive to run   400
To death before him, finding from that sword
Their life's discharge ; which did to him afford
Only those wounds, whose scars must live to be
The badges of eternal infamy.
   But here, o'erwhelmed by an unequal strength,
The noble victor soon to the utmost length
Had life's small thread extended, if not in
The dawn of hope, some troops, (whose charge had been,

(35)

Whilst the active gentry did attend the court,
To free the country from the feared resort 410
Of wild bandits), these, being directed by
Such frighted rurals as employment nigh
The grove had led, arriving at that time
When his slain foes made the mistaken crime
Appear Argalia's, soon by power allay
That fatal storm; which done, (a full survey
Of them that death freed from distress being took),
Them, through whose wounds Life had not yet forsook
Her throne, they view; 'mongst whom, through the disguise
Of 's blood, Almanzor, whose high power they prize 420
More than discovered innocence, being found,
As Justice had by close decree been bound
To espouse his quarrels; whilst his friends convey
Him safely thence, those ponderous crimes they lay
Unto Argalia's charge, whose just defence
Pleads but in vain for injured innocence.
　　Now, near departing, whilst his helpful friends
Bore off Almanzor, where he long attends
The cure of 's wounds, though they less torment bred
Than to behold how his lost honour bled; 430
The sad Florenza comes to take her last
Leave of her lost Andremon, ere she past
That sad stage o'er. To his cold clammy lips
Joining her balmy twins, she from them sips
So much of death's oppressing dews, that, by
That touch revived, his soul, though winged to fly
Her ruined seat, takes time enough to breathe
These sad notes forth :—' Farewell, my dear, beneath
The ponderous burthen of mortality
My fainting spirits sink. Oh ! mayest thou be 440
Blest in a happier love ; all that I crave
Is, that my now departing soul may have
Thy virgin prayers for her companions, through
Those gloomy vaults, which she must pass, unto
Eternal shades. Had fate assigned my stay,
Till we'd together gone, the horrid way
Had then been made delightful; but I must
Depart without thee, and convert to dust,
Whilst thou art flesh and blood : I in a cold
Dark urn must lie, whilst a warm groom doth hold 450
Thee in thy nuptial bed; yet there I shall—
If fled souls know what doth on earth befal,—
Mourn for thy loss, and to eternity
Wander alone. The various world shall be
Refined in flames ; Time shall afford no place
For vanity, ere I again embrace
Society with flesh ; which, ere that, must
Change to a thousand forms her varied dust.

What we shall be, or whither we shall go,
When gone from hence—whe'er unto flames below,   460
Or joys above—or whe'er in death we may
Know our departed friends, or tell which way
They went before us—these, oh ! these are things
That pause our divinity. Sceptred kings,
And subjects die alike, nor can we tell,
Which doth in joy, or which in torments dwell.
Oh, sad, sad ignorance ! Heaven guide me right,
Or I shall wander in eternal night,
To whose dark shades my dim eyes sink apace.
Farewell, Florenza ! when both time and place   470
My separated soul hath left, to be
A stranger masked in immortality,
Think on thy murthered friend ; we now must part
Eternally ! the cordage of my heart
That last sigh broke.' With that the breath, that long
Had hovered in his breast, flew with a strong
Groan from that mortal mansion ; which beheld
By such of 's friends whom courtesy compelled
To that sad charge, the bloodless body they
With sad slow steps to 's father's home convey.   480

THE END OF THE SECOND CANTO.

Canto III

THE ARGUMENT

The brave Argalia, who designed to raise
   Through all approaching ills his weighty fate,
In smooth compliance that harsh guard obeys,
   Who towards his death did prosecute their hate :

To death, which here unluckily had stained
   Maugre his friends, the ill-directed sword
Of justice, had not secret love obtained
   More mercy than the strict laws dare afford.

Low in a fruitful pasture, where his flocks
Cloud with their breath those plains, whose leafy locks
Could hardly shadow them—those meadows need
No shearing—where in untold droves did feed
His bellowing herds, of which enough did come
Each day to 's yoke to serve a hecatomb,
Lay old Andremon's country farm : in which,
Happy till now, being made by fortune rich,
And goodness honest ; from domestic strife
Still calm and free ; the upper robes of life,   10

466 in joy] Altered by Singer from 'enjoy,' plausibly, but perhaps idly.

Till withered, he had worn; to ease whose sad
And sullen cares less bounteous nature had
Lent him no numerous issue—all he'd won
By prayer, confined unto his murthered son,
The blasted blossom of whose tender age,
When blooming first, taught hope how to presage
Those future virtues, which, interpreted
By action, had such fruitful branches spread,
That all indulgent parents wished to be
Immortalized in blest posterity,   20
Had seen in him; who, innocently good,
Still let his heart by's tongue be understood,
In such a sacred dialect, that all
Which verged within deliberate thought did fall,
Towards heaven was graced, and in descent did prove
To's parents duty, and to's neighbours love.
   This hopeful youth, their age's chief support,
Whose absence, though by's own desires made short,
Their love thought tedious, having now expired
His usual hours, the aged couple tired   30
With expectation, to anticipate
His slow appearance, to their mansion's gate
Were softly walked, where coolly shadowed by
An elm, which, planted at his birth, did vie
Age with his lord; whilst their desires pursue
Its first design, they with some pleasure view
Their busy servants, whose industrious pain
Sweats out diseases in pursuit of gain.
All which, although the chiefest pleasure that
Their thoughts contain—whose best are busied at   40
The mart o' the world, such small diversion lent
The aged pair, that his. kind mother, spent
With a too long protracted hope, had let
E'en that expire, had not his father set
Props to that weakness, 'and, that mutual fear
Which filled their breasts, let his sound judgement clear,
By the proposing accidents that might,
Untouched, detain their darling from their sight.
   But many minutes had not left their seals
On the records of time, ere truth reveals   50
Her horrid secrets.—A confusèd noise
First strikes their ears, which suddenly destroys
Its own imperfect embryocs, to transfer
Its object to that nearer messenger
O' the soul—the eyes, whose beamy scouts convey
A trembling fear into their souls, whilst they,
That bore their murthered son, arrived to tell
Their doleful message; which so fierce storm fell

33 Were] Singer, officiously, ' Had.'

Not long in those remoter drops, before,
Swelled to a deluge, the swift torrent bore　　　　60
The bays of reason down, and in one flood
Drowned all their hopes. When purpled in his blood,
Yet pale with death—untimely death, she saw
Her hopeful son, grief violates the law
Of slower nature, and his mother's tears
In death congeals to marble : her swoln fears,
Grown for her sex a burthen far too great,
Had only left death for her dark retreat.
　　Although from grief's so violent effects,
Reason, conjoined with manly strength, protects　　　70
His wretched father, at that stroke his limbs
Slack their unwieldly nerves, faint sorrow dims
His eyes more than his age, his hands bereft
His hoary head of all that time had left
Unplucked before ; nor had the expecting grave
Gaped longer for him, if they then had gave
His passion freedom—his own guilty hand
Had broke the glass, and shook that little sand
That yet remained into thin air, that so,
Unclogged with earth, his tortured ghost might go　　　80
Beyond that orb of atoms that attend
Mortality ; and at that journey's end
Meet theirs, soon as swift Destiny enrols
Those new-come guests within the sphere of souls.
By these sad symptoms of infectious grief,
Those best of friends that came for the relief
Of sorrow's captives, being by that surprised
They hoped to conquer, sadly sympathized
With him in woe, till the epidemic ill,
Stifling each voice, drest sorrow in a still　　　90
And dismal silence : in which sad aspect,
None needing robes or cypress to detect
A funeral march, each dolefully attends,
To death's dark mansion, their lamented friends.
Where, having now the earthy curtain drawn
O'er their cold bed, till doomsday's fatal dawn
Rally their dust, they leave them ; and retire
To sorrow, which can ne'er hope to expire
In just revenge, since kept by fear in awe—
Where power offends, the poor scarce hope for law.　　100
　　By sad example to confirm this truth—
From innocent and early hopes of youth
Led toward destruction, let's return to see
That noble stranger, whose captivity,
Like an unlucky accident, depends
On this sad subject. By the angry friends
Of those accused, which in that fatal strife
To death resigned the charter of their life,

(39)

He's brought unto the princess' palace; where
That age, (whose customs knew not how to bear   110
Such sails as these have filled with pride), was placed
The seat of justice; whose stern sword defaced
Not Pleasure's smoothest front, since now 'twas by
Her fair hand guided, whose commanding eye,
If armed with anger, seemed more dreadful then
The harshest law e'er made by wrathful men.
  Here, strictly guarded, till the important crime,
Which urged her to anticipate the time
By custom known, had called her forth to that
Unwilling office, still unstartled at   120
The frowns of danger, did Argalia lie
An injured captive; till, commanded by
The stern reformers of offended law,
He hastes t' the bar; where come, though death ne'er saw
A brow more calm, or breast more confident,
To meet his darts, yet since the innocent
Are stained with guilt, when, in contempt of fate,
They silent fall, he means to meet their hate
With all that each beholder could expect
From dying valour, when it had to protect   130
An envied stranger, left no more defence
But what their hate obscures—his innocence.
  The clamorous friends of Aphron, backed by those
Which knew his death the only mean to close
Almanzor's bleeding honour, to the fair   ,
And pitiful Pharonnida repair,
With cries of vengeance; whose unwelcome sound
She by her father's strict command was bound
To hear, since that those rivulets of law,
Which from the sea of regal power did draw   140
Their several streams, all flowed to her, and in
That crystal fountain, pure as they had been
From heaven dispensed ere just Astræa fled
The earth, remained; yet such aversion bred
In her soft soul, that to these causes, where
The law sought blood, slowly as those that bear
The weight of guilt, she came; whose dark text she
Still comments on with noble charity.
High mounted on an ebon throne, in which
The embellished silver shewed so sadly rich,   150
As if its varied form strove to delight
Those solemn souls which death's pale fear did fright,
In Tyrian purple clad, the princess sate,
Between two sterner ministers of fate,
Impartial judges, whose distinguished tasks
Their varied habit to the view unmasks.

133 Aphron] Mistake for 'Andremon.'   149 in] Singer alters to on.'

One, in whose looks, as pity strove to draw
Compassion in the tablets of the law,
Some softness dwelt, in a majestic vest
Of state-like red was clothed ; the other, dressed   160
In dismal black, whose terrible aspect
Declared his office, served but to detect
Her slow consent, if, when the first forsook
The cause, the law so far as death did look.
  Silence proclaimed, a harsh command calls forth
The undaunted prisoner, whose excelling worth,
In this low ebb of fortune, did appear
Such as we fancy virtues that come near
The excellence of angels—fear had not
Rifled one drop of blood, nor rage begot   170
More colour in his cheeks—his soul in state
Throned in the medium, constant virtue, sat,
Not slighting, with the impious atheists, that
Loud storm of danger, but, safe anchored at
Religious hope, being firmly confident
Heaven would relieve whom earth knew innocent.
  All thus prepared, he hears his wrongful charge
(Envy disguising injured truth) at large,
Before the people, in such language read,
As checked their hopes in whom his worth had bred   180
Some seeds of pity ; and to those, whose hate
Pursued him to this precipice of fate,
Dead Aphron's friends, such an advantage gave,
That Providence appeared too weak to save
One so assaulted : yet, though now depressed
E'en in opinion, which oft proves the best
Support to those whose public virtues we
Adore before their private guilt we see,
His noble soul still wings itself above
Passion's dark fogs ; and like that prosperous dove,   190
The world's first pilot for discovery sent,
When all the floods that bound the firmament
O'erwhelmed the earth, Conscience' calm joys to increase,
Returns, fraught with the olive branch of peace.
  Thus fortified from all that tyrant fear
E'er awed the guilty with, he doth appear
The court's just wonder in the brave defence
Of what, (though power, armed with the strong pretence
Of right, opposed), so prevalent had been,
T' have cleared him ; if, when near triumphing in   200
Victorious truth, to cloud that glorious sun,
Some faithless swains, by large rewards being won

---

162 detect] For the sake of rhyme, no doubt.   It can just be interpreted as = ' remove
the concealment from,' ' extract.'
183 Aphron] Mistake as before.

To spot their souls, had not, corrupted by
His foes, been brought, falsely to justify
Their accusations. Which beheld by him,
Whose knowledge now did hope's clear optics dim,
He ceased to plead ; justly despairing then,
That innocence 'mongst mortals rested, when
Banished her own abode; so thinks it vain
To let truth's naked arms strive to maintain   210
The field 'gainst his more powerful foes. Not all
His virtues now protect him, he must fall
A guiltless sacrifice, to expiate
No other crime but their envenomed hate.
An ominous silence—such as oft precedes
The fatal sentence—whilst the accuser reads
His charge, possessed the pitying court, in which
Presaging calm Pharonnida, too rich
In mercy, Heaven's supreme prerogative,
To stifle tears, did with her passion strive   220
So long, till what at first assaulted in
Sorrow's black armour, had so often been
For pity cherished, that at length her eyes
Found there those spirits that did sympathize
With those that warmed her blood, and, unseen, move
That engine of the world, mysterious love,
The way that fate predestinated, when
'Twas first infused i' the embryo; it being then
That which espoused the active form unto
Matter, and from that passive being drew   230
Divine ideas; which, subsisting in
Harmonious Nature's highest sphere, do win,
In the perfection of our age, a more
Expansive power; and, nature's common store
Still to preserve, unites affections by
The mingled atoms of the serious eye.
    Whilst Nature's priest, the cause of each effect,
Miscalled disease, endeavours to detect
Its unacquainted operations in
The beauteous princess, whose free soul had been   240
Yet guarded in her virgin ice, and now
A stranger is to what she doth allow
Such easy entrance—by those rays that fall
From either's eyes, to make reciprocal
Their yielding passions, brave Argalia felt,
E'en in the grasp of death, his functions melt
To flames, which on his heart an onset make
For sadness, such as weaker mortals take
Eternal farewells in. Yet in this high
Tide of his blood, in a soft calm to die,   250
His yielding spirits now prepare to meet
Death, clothed in thoughts white as his winding-sheet.

(42)

That fatal doom, which unto heaven affords
The sole appeal, one of the assisting lords
Had now pronounced, whose horrid thunder could
Not strike his laurelled brow ; that voice, which would
Have petrified a timorous soul, he hears
With calm attention. No disordered fears
Ruffled his fancy, nor domestic war
Raged in his breast ; his every look, so far   260
From vulgar passions, that unless amazed
At Beauty's majesty, he sometimes gazed
Wildly on that as emblems of more great
Glories than earth afforded, from the seat
Of resolution his fixed soul had not
Been stirred to passion, which had now begot
Wonder, not fear, within him. No harsh frown
Contracts his brow, nor did his thoughts pull down
One fainting spirit, wrapt in smothered groans,
To clog his heart. From her most eminent thrones   270
Of sense, the eyes, the lightning of his soul
Flew with such vigour forth, it did control
All weaker passions, and at once include
With Roman valour Christian fortitude.

Pharonnida, from whom the rigid law
Extorts his fate, being now enforced to draw
The longest line she e'er could hope to move
Over his face, that beauteous sphere of love,
Unto its great'st obliquity, she leaves
Him, in his winter solstice, and bereaves   280
Love's hemisphere of light, not heat ; yet, oft
Retreating, wished those stars, fate placed aloft
In the first magnitude of honour, might
Prove retrograde ; so their contracted light
Might unto him part of their influence
In life bestow, passion would fain dispense
So far with reason, to recal again
The sentence she had past : but hope in vain
Those false suggestions moves. His jailors are
The undaunted prisoner hurrying from the bar,   290
His fair judge rising, the corrupted court
Upon removing, all the ruder sort
Of hearers rushing out, when, through the throng,
Kind Ariamnes (being detained so long
By strict employment) comes ; at whose request
The court their seats resuming, he addrest
Himself t' the princess in a language that,
(Whilst all Argalia's foes were storming at),
E'en on her justice so prevails, that he
Reprieved till all hope could produce, to free   300

257 petrified] Orig. 'putrefied,' which I shall not say that Chamberlayne *could* not
have meant.   291 corrupted] Apparently in the derivative sense of 'broken up.'

Her love's new care, might be examined by
His active friend ; who now, being seated nigh
Pharonnida, whilst all attentive sate,
The stranger's story doth at large relate.
　Pleased at this full relation, near as much
As grieved to see those jewels placed in such
A coarse cheap metal, which could never hold
The least proportion with her regal gold,
Pharonnida had now removed, if not
Thus once more stayed :—The rumour, first begot　　310
From this sad truth, had, with the common haste
Of ill, arrived where his disease had placed
Aphron, whose ears, assaulted now with words
Of more infection than that plague, affords
Room for the stronger passion : though offended,
To leave a hold it had at first intended
To keep till ruined, the imprisoned blood,
And spirits are unfettered, by that flood
To wash usurping grief from off that part
Where most she reigned; but they, drawn near the heart, 320
And finding enemies too strong to be
Encountered, mix in their society ;
Which, thus supplied with auxiliaries, in
Contempt of weakness, (when he 'long had been
Languishing, underneath a tedious load
Of sickness), sends him from his safe abode,
'Mongst dangers which in death's black shape attend
His bold design, to seek his honoured friend.
　Come on the spur of passion to the court,
A flux of spirits from all parts resort　　　　330
To prompt his anger, which abruptly broke
Forth in this language :—' Do not, sirs, provoke
A foreign power thus·far—I speak to you
That have condemned this stranger—as to do
An act so opposite to all the law
Of nations,—here within your realm to draw
Blood that 's near and allied unto the best
Of an adjacent state. If this request
Of mine too full of insolence appear,
We are spirits nobly born, and we are near　　340
Enough to have 't, whatever crime 's the cause
Of this harsh sentence, tried by our own laws.'—
　This bold opposer of stern justice (here
Pausing to see what clouds there did appear

---

313 Aphron] The real Aphron.
　315 offended] Another *exemplary* note may call attention to this characteristic instance
of Chamberlayne's syntax. 'Offended' and 'it' can only refer to 'disease,' or 'plague,'
though they have not the least grammatical connexion therewith or with anything else.
For though grammar permits junction with 'the imprisoned blood,' sense forbids.
　337 near] Singer alters to 'so near,' without any need.

In that fair heaven, whose influence only now
Could light to's friend's declining stars allow),
To free the troubled court, which struggled in
A strange dilemma, had commanded been
To a more large discovery, if not by
His pitying friend discharged in a reply,   350
Doubting how far irregular boldness had
Provoked just wrath. Argalia thus unclad
Amazement's dark disguise :—'To you that awe
This court' (with that kneels to Pharonnida)
'I now for mercy flee, that scorn to run
From my own doom, so I might have begun
The doubtful task alone ; but here to leave
My friend, from whom your justice did receive
This bold affront, in danger, is a crime
That not approaching death, which all my time   360
Too little for repentance calls, can be
A just excuse for; let me then set free
His person with your doubts, and joined to those
What both their varied stories may compose.—
'For what this noble lord, whose goodness we
First found in needful hospitality,
From him hath differed in, impute it not
To either's error ; both reports begot
From such mistakes, as nature made to be
The careful issues of necessity :   370
That fatal difference, whose vestigia stood,
When we Epirus left, fresh filled with blood,
By league so lately with Calabria made,
Being composed, that fame did not invade
Our ears with the report, till we had been
By a disguise secured ; which, shaded in,
Whilst fearing danger, we ne'er thought to leave
Till safe at home. Thus, what did first deceive
Kind Aminander, you have heard ; and now,
Without the stain of boasting, must allow   380
Me leave to tell you, that we there have friends,
On whom the burthen of a state depends.'
When, to the court's just wonder, thus far he,
With such unshaken confidence as we
Pray on the expanded wings of faith, displayed
His soul's integrity, the royal maid,
Whom a repented destiny had made
His pitying judge, endeavouring to evade
That doom's harsh rigour, grants him a reprieve,
Till thrice the sun, returning to relieve   390

---

352 wrath] I have tried various punctuations for this passage, but it defies all. The
sense is clear enough, however.   379 Aminander] i. e. Ariamnes.   383 court's]
Orig. 'court,' not quite impossibly.

Night's drooping sentinels, had circled in
So many days.   In which short time, to win
The fair advantage of discovering truth,
Old Aminander, active as fresh youth
In all attempts of charity, to know
From what black spring those troubled streams did flow,
Hastes toward Andremon's; whilst Pharonnida,
Active as he toward all whence she might draw
A consequence of hope, lays speedy hold
On this design:—Commissioned to unfold   400
Their master's love toward her, there long had been
Ambassadors from the Epirot in
Her father's court; whose message, though it might
Wear love's pure robes, yet, in her reason's light,
Seems so much stained with policy, that all
Those blessings, which the wise foresaw to fall
As influence from that conjunction, she
Opposes as her stars' malignity.
    Proud of this new command, with such a haste
As those that fear more slow delays may waste   410
Their precious time, the ambassadors attain
The princess' court; where come, though hoped in vain,
Only expect a speedy audience; they,
That frustrated, are soon taught to betray
More powerful passions:—the first glance o' the eye
They on the prisoners cast, kind sympathy
Proclaimed,—love gave no leave for time to rust
Their memories—both the old lords durst trust
Eyes dimmed with tears, whilst their embraces give
A sad assurance there did only live   420
Their last and best of comforts.   Which beheld
By those from whom kind pity had expelled
All thoughts of the vindictive law, they strive
By all the power of rhetoric to drive
Those sad storms over; which good office done,
They each inform the prince, which was the son
Of nature, which adoption; withal tell how,
By their persuasions moved, they did allow
Them time to travel, which disasters had
So long protracted; for some years, with sad   430
And doubtful hopes, they had in vain expected
Their wished return, but that their stars directed
Their course so ill, as now near home to be
O'ertaken with so sad a destiny.—
Since such a sorrow could be cured by none,
They sadly crave the time to mourn alone.

THE END OF THE THIRD CANTO.

398 draw] In this rhyme, which is common, it is more likely that 'draw' was
pronounced 'dra'' than that 'Pharonnida' became 'Pharonnida*w*.'
412 hoped] Orig. 'hope.'

Canto IV

THE ARGUMENT

At length the veil from the deluded law,
  With active care by Aminander took,
The startled court in their own error saw
  How lovely truth did in Argalia look.

The story of our youth discovered, he,
  His merits yet in higher pitch to raise,
Morea's prince doth from a danger free,
  Which unto death his noblest lords betrays.

THAT last sad night, the rigid law did give
The late reprieved Argalia leave to live,
Was now, wrapt in her own obscurity,
Stolen from the stage of time, when light, got free
From his nocturnal prison, summons all
Almanzor's friends to see the longed-for fall
Of the envied stranger; whose last hour was now
So near arrived, faint hope could not allow
So much of comfort to his powerful'st friend
As told her fears—she longer might suspend   10
His fatal doom. Mournful attendants on
That serene sufferer, all his friends are gone
Unto the sable scaffold that's ordained,
By the decree of justice, to be stained
With guiltless blood; all sunk in grief—but she,
Who by inevitable destiny
Doomed him to death, most deep. Dull sorrow reigns
In her triumphant; sad and alone remains
She in a room, whose window's prospect led
Her eye to the scaffold, whither, from the bed   20
Where sorrow first had cast her, she did oft
Repair to see him; but her passion's soft
Temper, soon melting into tears, denies
Her soul a passage through o'erflowing eyes.
Often she would in vain expostulate
With those two subtle sophisters that sate
Clothed in the robes of fancy, but they still
O'erthrow her weaker arguments, and fill
Her breast with love and wonder; passion gave
Such fierce assaults, no virgin vow could save   30
Her heart's surrender—she must love and lose
In one sad hour; thus grief doth oft infuse
Those bitter pills, where hidden poisons dwell,
In the smooth pleasures of sweet oxymel.
  Argalia's friends, that did this minute use
As if the last of mortal interviews,

28 o'erthrow] Orig. 'o'erthrew.'

(47)

Had now reversed their eyes, expecting nought
But that stroke's fall, whose fatal speed had brought
Him to eternal rest; when by a loud
And busy tumult, as if death, grown proud,   40
Expected triumphs, to divert their sight,
They from the scaffold's lofty station might,
Within the reach of an exalted voice,
Behold a troop, who (as the leader's choice,
Confined to strait necessity, had there
Enrolled all comers, if of strength to bear
Offensive arms) did first appear to be
Some tumult drest in the variety
Of sudden rage: for here come headlong in
A herd of clowns, armed as they then had been   50
From labour called; near them, well ordered ride
(As greatness strove no longer to divide
Societies) some youths, brave as they had
Been in the spoils of conquered nations clad.
    This sudden object, first obstructing all
Their court's proceedings, prompts their doubts to call
Their absent prince; who, being too wise for fear's
Uncertain fictions, with such speed appears
As checks the tumult; when, to tell them who
Had from their homes the frighted people drew,   60
I' the van of a well-ordered troop rides forth
Loved Aminander, whose unquestioned worth,
That strong attractive of the people's love,
Expunged suspicion: whilst his troops did move
With a commanded slowness to inform
The expecting prince, from whence this sudden storm
Contracted clouds, he to his view presents
Andremon's friends; whose looks—the sad contents
Of sorrow, with a silent oratory
Beg pity, whilst he thus relates their story.—   70
    'That we, great prince, we, whom a loyal fear
To strict obedience prompts, dare thus appear
Before your sacred person, were a sin
Mercy would blush to own, had we not been
Forced to offensive arms, by such a cause
As tore the sceptre-regulated laws
Forth of your royal hand, to vindicate
This suffering stranger, whom a subtle hate,
Not solemn law, pursued. I here have brought
Such witnesses as have their knowledge bought   80
At the expense of all their joy, whom I
Found so confined, as if their misery
Were in their houses sepulchred; a sad
And general sorrow in one dress had clad
So many, that their only sight did prove—
Lost virtue caused such universal love.

To free this noble youth, whose valour lent
A late protection to this innocent
But injured maid, they, unconstrained, had here
Implored your aid, had not too just a fear,   90
Caused from some troops, raised by a wronged pretence
Of your commands, checked their intelligence,
With such illegal violence that I
Had shared their sufferings, if not rescued by
These following friends, whose rude conjunction shows
It was no studied plot did first compose
So loose a body. But, lest it appear
In me like envy, should I strive to clear
This doubtful story, here are those, (with that
Calls forth Andremon's friends), instructed at   100
The dearest price, which, by discovering truth,
Will not alone rescue this noble youth
From falling ruin—but, lest he retreat
Into rebellion, force before this seat
A man, whose power the people thought had been
To punish vice, not propagate a sin.'
      Having thus far past toward discovery, here
The grave lord ceased : and, that truth might appear
From its first fair original, to her
Whose virtue, Heaven's affected messenger,   110
Commands attention, the more horrid part
Of his relation leaves. And here, vain Art,
Look on and envy, to behold how far
Thy strict rules (which our youth's afflictions are)
Nature transcends, in a discourse which she,
With all the flowers of virgin modesty,
Not weeds of rhetoric, strewed; to hear her miss,
Or put a blush for a parenthesis,
In the relating that uncivil strife,
Which her sad subject was—so near the life   120
Limns lovely virtue, that, that copy whence
Art took those graces, she doth since dispense
T' the best of women. Fair Pharonnida,
Taught by that sympathy, which first did draw
Those lovely transcripts of herself, although
Varied as much as humble flowers, that grow
Dispersed in shady deserts, are from those
That nice art in enamelled gardens shows ;
Yet, like bright planets which communicate
To earth their influence, from exalted state   130
She now descends to cherish virtue in
Those lovely nymphs, whose beauties, though they'd been
Yet in the country clouded from report,
Soon grow the praise or envy of the court.
      Emboldened by that gracious favour shown
To these fair nymphs, to prosecute their own

Most just complaints, Andremon's wretched friends,
With prayers perceive that mercy which descends,
O'er all their sufferings, on the expanded wings
Of noble pity; whose fair hand first brings   140
Argalia from the sable scaffold, to
Meet those rewards to his high merits due,
Not only in what death's dark progress stays,
But life's best joy—an universal praise
Acquired from just desert. Next she applies
Herself to those poor burthened souls, whose eyes
Look e'en on comforts through their tears, the dead
Andremon's mourners ; whose lost joy, though fled
For ever from those wintring regions, yet
As much received as sorrow would permit   150
Souls so opprest ; the splendid court they leave
With thankful prayers. And now called to receive
His sin's reward Almanzor is, whose shame,
Its black attendant, when b' his hated name
He'd oft been summoned, prompts him to deny
That legal call; which being an act too high
For a depending power to patronise,
To shun feared justice' public doom, he flies
His prince's mandates, an affront that sent
Him to 's desert—perpetual banishment.   160
  This comet lost in clouds of infamy,
The court, which had too long been burthened by
His injured power, with praises entertain
Impartial justice ; whilst to call again
Those pleasures which had in this interval
Of law been lost, the prince, convening all
That shared those sufferings, as the centre whence
Joy spread itself t' the court's circumference,
Crowns all their wishes, which, by that bright star
In honour's sphere—the auspicious princess, are   170
Exalted to their highest orbs. Her love
Unto Argalia, though it yet must move
As an unnoted constellation, here
Begins its era, which, that 't might appear
Without suspicion, she disguises in
The public joy. Which, 'mongst those that had been
His serious mourners, to participate,
That kind Epirot, who first taught his fate
The way to glory, comes; to whom he now
Was on those knees merit had taught to bow,   180
With as much humble reverence as if all
The weights of nature made those burthens fall
A sacrifice to love, fixed to implore
Its constant progress, but he needs no more

178 Epirot] Observe the jumble with ‘Calabrian,’ l. 189.

For confirmation, since his friend could move
But the like joy, where nature taught to love.
  Passion's encounter, which too high to last,
Into a calm of thankful prayers being past,
The prince from the Calabrian seeks to know
By what collateral streams he came to owe   190
Such love unto a stranger—one that stood
Removed from him i' the magnetism of blood ;
Whom thus the lord resolves :—'When blooming in
The pride of youth, whose varied scenes did win
Time on the morning of my days, a while,
To taste the pleasures of a summer's smile,
I left the court's tumultuous noise and spent
Some happy time blest with retired content,
In the calm country, where Art's curious hand,
As centre to a spacious round of land,   200
Had placed a palace, in whose lovely dress,
The city might admire the wilderness ;
Yet, though that ill civility was in
Her marble circle, Nature's hand had been
As liberal to the neighbouring fields, and deckt
Each rural nymph as gaudy, till neglect
Or slovenly necessity had drawn
Her canvass furrows o'er their vales of lawn.
  'Near this fair seat, fringed with an ancient wood,
A fertile valley lay, where scattered stood   210
Some homely cottages, the happy seats
Of labouring swains, whose careful toil completes
Their wishes in obtaining so much wealth
To conquer dire necessity ; firm health,
Calm thoughts, sound sleeps, unstarted innocence,
Softened their beds, and, when roused up from thence,
Suppled their limbs for labour. Amongst these,
My loved Argalia, (for till fate shall please
His dim stars to uncertain, and salute
His better fortune with each attribute   220
Due to a nobler birth, his name must be
Contracted into that stenography)
Life's scenes began, amongst his fellows that
There first drew breath, being true heirs to what,
Whilst all his stars were retrograde and dim,
Unlucky fortune but adopted him.
  'Whilst there residing, I had oft beheld
The active boy, whose childhood's bud excelled
More full-blown youths, gleaning the scattered locks
Of new-shorn fields amongst the half-clad flocks   230
Of their unripe but healthful issue ; by
Which labour tired, sometimes I see them try
The strength of their scarce twisted limbs, and run
A short breathed course ; whose swift contention done,

(51)

And he (as in each other active sport)
With victory crowned, they make their next resort
T' the spring's cheap bounties ; but what did of all
His first attempts give the most powerful call
Both to my love and wonder was, what chanced
From one rare act :—The morning had advanced   240
Her tempting beauties to assure success
To these young huntsmen, who, with labour less
Made by the pleasure of their journey, had
The forest reached, where, with their limbs unclad
For the pursuit, they follow beasts that might
Abroad be recreation, and, when night
Summoned them home, the welcomest supply
Both to their own and parents' quality.
An angry boar, chafed with a morning's chase,
And now near spent, was come so near the place,   250
Where, though secured, on the stupendous height
Of a vast rock they stood, that now no flight
Could promise safety ; that wild rage, which sent
Him from the dogs, his following foes, is spent
In the pursuit of them ; which, to my grief,
Had suffered ere we could have lent relief,
Had not Argalia, e'en when danger drew
So near as death, turned on the beast, and threw
His happy javelin ; whose well-guided aim,
Although success it knew not how to claim   260
From strength, yet is so much assisted by
Fortune, that, what before had scorned to die
By all our power when contending in
Nice art, the honour of that day to win
To him alone, falls by that feeble stroke
From all his speed ; which seen, he, to provoke
His hastier death, seconds those wounds which in
Their safety are by those with terror seen,
That had escaped the danger, and e'en by
Us that pursued with such amaze, that I,   270
Who had before observed those rays of worth
Obscured in clouds, here let my love break forth
In useful action, such as from that low
Condition brought him where I might bestow
On him what art required, to perfect that
Rare piece of nature which we wondered at.
From those whom I, 'mongst others, thought to be
Such whose affection the proximity
Of nature claimed, with a regret that showed
Their poverty unwillingly bestowed   280

238 give the most powerful call] This is Singer's mending of the orig. repetition
did give the powerful call.'
  280 bestowed] This bewildering Chamberlaynean construction seems = ' *Of* those *from*
whom I, *thinking them* to be, &c., had procured.' But in this as in hundreds of future

So loved a jewel, had procured the youth—
His foster father, loath to waive a truth
That in the progress of his fate might be
Of high account, discovers unto me
The world's mistake concerning him, and thus
Relates his story:—" He was brought to us,
(Quoth the good man) some ten years since, by two
Who (could men be discovered to the view
Of knowledge by their habits) seemed but such
As Fortune's narrow hand had gave not much   290
More than necessity requires to be
Enjoyed of every man, whom life makes free
Of Nature's city; though their bounty showed
To our dim judgements, that they only owed
Mischance for those coarse habits, which disguised
What once the world at higher rates had prized.
I' the worst extreme of time, about the birth
O' the sluggish morning, when the crusted earth
Was tinselled o'er with frost, and each sprig clad
With winter's wool, I, whom cross Fortune had   300
Destined to early labours, being abroad,
Met two benighted men, far from the road,
Wandering alone; no skilful guide their way
Directing in that infancy of day,
But the faint beams of glimmering candles, that
Shone from our lowly cottage windows, at
Which marks they steered their course: one of them bore
This boy, an infant then, which knew no more
Than Nature's untrod paths. These, having spied
Me through the morning's mists, glad of a guide,   310
Though to a place whose superficial view
Lent small hopes of relief, went with me to
Mine own poor home; where, with such coarse cheap fare
As must content us that but eat to bear
The burthens of a life, refreshed, they take
A short repose; then, being to forsake
Their new-found host, desire with us to leave
The child, till time should some few days bereave
Of the habiliments of light. We stood
Not long to parl, but, willing to do good   320
To strangers so distressed, were never by
Our poverty once tempted to deny.
My wife, being then a nurse, upon her takes
The pretty charge, and with our own son makes
Him fellow-commoner at the full breast,
And partner of the cradle's quiet rest.
Now to depart, one that did seem to have
The near'st relation to the infant gave

instances the reader must take his own choice of several doubtfully possible inter-
pretations.

Him first this jewel, (at which word they showed
One which upon Argalia was bestowed   330
By those that left him), then, that we might be
Not straitened by our former poverty,
Leaves us some gold, by which we since have been
Enabled to maintain him, though not in
That equipage, which we presume unto
His birth (although to us unknown) is due.
This done, with eyes that lost their light in tears,
They take their leaves ; since when, those days to years
Are grown, in which we did again expect
They should return ; but whether 't be neglect   340
Or else impossibility detain
Them from his sight, our care hath sought in vain."
  'Having thus plainly heard as much as Fate
Had yet of him discovered, I, that late
Desired him for his own, now for the sake
Of 's friends, (whate'er they were), resolved to take
Him from that barren rudeness, and transplant
So choice a slip where he might know no want
Of education ; with some labour, I
Having obtained him, till virility   350
Rendered him fit for nobler action, stayed
Him always with me, when my love obeyed
His reason ; and then, in the quest of what
Confined domestics do but stumble at—
Exotic knowledge, with this noble youth,
To whom his love grew linked, like spotless truth
To perfect virtue,—sent him to pursue
His wished design, from whence this interview
First took its fatal rise : '—And here the lord,
That a more full discovery might afford   360
Them yet more wonder, shows the jewel to
Sparta's pleased prince ; at whose most serious view
The skilfullest lapidaries, judging it,
Both for its worth and beauty, only fit
To sparkle in the glorious cabinet
Of some great queen, such value on it set,
That all conclude the owner of 't must be
Some falling star, i' the night of royalty,
From honour's sphere, the glories of a crown
To vaunt, the centre of our fears, dropt down.   370
  And now the court, whose brightest splendour in
These fatal changes long eclipsed had been,
Resumes its lustre ; which to elevate,
With all the pleasures of a prosperous state,
For that contracted span of time designed
For th' prince's stay, fancies are racked to find

367 owner] Orig. 'honour,' a strange mistake elsewhere repeated.

New forms of mirth, such whose invention might
Inform the ear, whilst they the eye delight.
All which, whilst to the less concerned they lent
A flux of joy, yet lost their first intent—   380
To please the princess; who from mirth did move
Eccentrical, since first inflamed with love,
Which did soon from her fancy's embryon grow
A large-limbed tyrant; when, prepared to go,
She sees Argalia, who, engaged to attend
The ambassadors, here soon put an end
To what, e'en from those unto love unkind,
Must now force tears ere it a period find.
  That time expired—ordained to terminate
Her father's stay, and so that splendid state   390
That yet adorned the princess' court, to show
How much he did for 's frontiers' safety owe
Unto those moving citadels—a fleet,
His mandates call each squadron for to meet
Within Lepanto, in whose harbours lay
Those ships that were ordained for a convey
To the Calabrian's messengers; who now,
With all that love or honour could allow
To noble strangers, being attended by
The brightest glories of two courts, draw nigh   400
A royal fleet, whose glittering streamers lent
Dull waves the beauties of a firmament:
Amongst which numbers, one, too stately far
For rough encounters of defacing war,
Whose gilded masts their crimson sails had spread
In silken flakes, advanced her stately head,
High as where clouds condense, where a light stands,
Took for a comet by far distant lands;
For cabins—where the imprisoned passenger
Wants air to breathe,—she 's stored with rooms that were 410
So fair without, and yet so large within,
A Persian sophi might have revelled in
Their spacious hulks. To this, Molarchus, he
Whom greatness, joined to know ability,
Had made Sicilia's admiral, invites
The royal train; where, with whate'er delights
(Although invention all her stock had spent)
Could be upon that liquid element
Prepared their welcome; whilst, at every bowl
A health inters, the full-mouthed cannons troul   420
A peal of thunder, which in white waves drowned,
The softer trumpets do their dirges sound.
  Now in the full career of mirth, whilst all
Their thoughts in perpendiculars did fall

414 know] One conjectures 'known,' but the other is more like our author.

From honour's zenith, none incurvated
With common cares—parents that might have bred
A sly suspicion; whilst neglective mirth
Keeps all within, from their deep bed of earth
Molarchus hoist his anchors, whilst that all
The rest lay still, expecting when his call   430
Commands their service: but when they beheld
His spread sails with a nimble gale were swelled;
An oppressed slave, which lay at rest before,
Was, with stretched limbs, tugging his finny oar;
Conceiving it but done to show the prince
That galley's swiftness, let that thought convince
Fear's weak suggestions, and, invited by
Their tempting mirth, still safe at anchor lie.
  But now, when they not only saw the night
Draw sadly on, but what did more affright   440
Their loyal souls—the distant vessel, by
Doubling a cape, lost to the sharpest eye,
For hateful treason taxing their mistake,
With anchors cut and sails spread wide they make
The lashed waves roar. Whilst those enclosed within
The galley, by her unknown speed had been
Far more deceived—being so far conveyed,
Ere care arrives to tell them they're betrayed
Through mirth's neglective guards. Who now, in haste
With anger raised, in vain those flames did waste   450
In wild attempts to force a passage to
The open decks, whither before withdrew
Molarchus was; who now prepared to give
That treason birth, whose hated name must live
In bloody lines of infamy. Before
They could expect it, opening wide the door
That led them forth, the noble captives fly
To seek revenge; but, being encountered by
An armèd crew, so fierce a fight begin,
That night's black mantle ne'er was lined within   460
With aught more horrid; in which bloody fray,
The subtle traitor, valiant to betray—
Though abject else, unnoted, seizing on
The unguarded princess, from their rage is gone,
Through night's black mask, with that rich prize into
A boat, that, placed for that design, was drew
Near to the galley; whose best wealth being now
Thus made their own, no more they study how
To save the rest—all which for death designed.
The conquered rebels soon their safety find   470

429 hoist] Singer 'hoists,' but it is no doubt preterite.
  434 oar] Orig. and Singer 'ore,' which must be wrong. In anybody but Chamber-
layne we should expect '*And* oppressed slaves' with no 'was.'

From other boats, but first, that all but she
O' the royal train secured by death might be,
So large a leak in the brave vessel make,
That thence her womb soon too much weight did take
For her vast bulk to wield, which, sinking now,
No safety to her royal guests allow.
    The ship thus lost, and now no throne but waves
Left the Sicilian prince, just Heaven thus saves
His sacred person :—Amongst those that fought
For timely safety, nimble strength had brought   480
Argalia and his following friend so near
One of the boats, in which, secured from fear,
The rebels sailed, that now they both had took
A hold so sure, that, though their foes forsook
Their oars to hinder 't, spite of all their force,
Argalia enters ; which, a sad divorce
From life, as he by strength attempts to rise
From falling wounds, unhappily denies
The valiant Aphron ; who, by death betrayed
From time and strength, had now left none to aid   490
His friend, but those attending virtues, that,
Ne'er more than now, for th' world to wonder at,
Brave trophies built. With such a sudden rage,
As all his foes did to defence engage,
Those bolder souls that durst resist, he had
From their disordered robes of flesh unclad ;
Which horrid sight forced the more fearful to
Such swift submission, that, ere fear outgrew
His hope, assisted by that strength which bought
Their lives' reprieve, their oars reversed had brought   500
Him back t' the place, in which the guilty flood
Was stained with fair Sicilia's noblest blood.
    Assisted by those silver streams of light
The full-faced moon shot through the swarthy night
On the smooth sea, he first his course directs
Toward one, whose robes, studded with gems, reflects
Those feeble rays, like new-fallen stars ; he there
Finds Sparta's prince, then sinking from the sphere
Of mortal greatness in the boundless deep,
To calm life's cares in an eternal sleep.   510
From unexpected death, the grave's most grim
And ghastly tyrant, having rescued him—
With as much speed, as grief's distractions, joined
To night's confusion, could give leave, to find
More friends, before that all were swallowed by
The sea, he hastes ; when, being by chance brought nigh
Dead Aphron's father, to be partner in
Their cares, who, as they only saved had been

---

475 bulk] Singer, as elsewhere, arbitrarily prints ' *h*ulk,' which is possible but by no
means necessary.

To mourn the rest, he from the rude sea saves
Him, to be drowned in sorrow's sable waves.   520
Now in the quest of that deserving lord,
Whose goodness did to 's infancy afford
Life's best of comforts—education, he,
To balk that needless diligence, might see
At one large draught the wide waves swallow all
Who vainly did till that sad minute call
To Heaven for help; which dismal sight, beheld
By those that saved by accident, expelled
Their own just fears—for them to entertain
As just a grief. Their needful time in vain   530
They spend no longer in their search, but, though
Unwieldy grief yet made their motion slow,
Haste from that horrid place, where each must leave
Such valued friends. Numbers that did receive
Their blood, descended to nobility,
From th' royal spring, here the grieved prince might see
Interred in the ocean; the Epirot lord,
His late found son, whom love could scarce afford
A minute's absence; nor 's Argalia less
Engaged to grief—to leave whom the distress   540
Of 's youth relieved; but what from each of these
Borrowed some streams of sorrow, to appease
A grief which since so many floods hath cost—
The noble Aminander here was lost.
Rowed with such speed as their desire, joined to
That fear which from the conquered rebels drew
A swift obedience, being conducted by
A friendly light, their boat is now drawn nigh
A rocky island; in whose harbour they
Found where the boat that had outsailed them lay,   550
Drawn near the shore: but all the passengers
Being gone, the sight of that alone confers
No other comfort than to inform them that
The ravished princess had been landed at
That port; which by their sailors they are told
Belongs unto a castle, kept to hold
That island, though but one unnoted town,
T' the scarce known laws of the Sicilian crown.
This heard b' the prince, who formerly had known
That castle's strength, being vexed (although his own)   560
That now 'twas such; leaving the vessel, they,
Protected by night's heaviest shades, convey
Themselves into a neighbouring cottage, where
The prince, who now externally did bear
No forms of greatness, left to his repose.
Argalia, whilst night's shadows yet did close

558 Sicilian] i. e. Morean.

Discovering eyes, hastes back t' the harbour ; whence,
To give the royal fleet intelligence
O' the king's distress, he sends forth all but one,
Whose stoutness had best made his valour known,   570
Of those which, conquered by his sword, are now
By bounty made too much his own, to allow
E'en slight suspicion room. This being done,
That valour, though with love 'twere winged, might run
On no rash precipice, assisted by
That skilful seaman, from some ships that lie
Neglected, 'cause by time decayed, he takes
So much o' the tackling, as of that he makes
Ladders of length sufficient to ascend
The castle walls ; which, having to defend   580
Them nought but slave security, is done
With so much ease, that what 's so well begun
They boldly second, and first entering in
A tower, (which had b' the prudent founder been
Built to command the haven's mouth, which lay
Too low for th' castle), where, when come, all they
Found to resist, is one poor sentry, bound
In sleep, which soon by death is made more sound.
    To lodge the prince in that safe place, before
His active valour yet attempted more,   590
The gate 's secured that led t' the castle. He,
Protected by that night's obscurity,
By a concealed small sally-port is to
Its strength soon brought ; when now prepared to view
More dreadful dangers, in such habit clad,
As by the out-guard's easy error had,
Soon as a soldier, gave him entrance, come
T' the hall he is : there being informed by some
O' the drowsy guards, where his pretended speed
Might find Molarchus, to perform a deed,   600
That future ages (if that honour's fire
Lose not its light), shall worthily admire,
His valour hastes :—Within a room,—whose pride
Of art, though great, was far more glorified
By that bright lustre the spectators saw,
Through sorrow's clouds, in fair Pharonnida,—
He finds the impious villain, heightened in
His late success to such rude acts of sin,
That servile baseness, the low distance whence
He used to look, grew 'saucy impudence.   610
    Inflamed Argalia, who at once beholds
Objects to which the soul enlarged unfolds
Its passions in the various characters
Of love and anger, now no more defers
The execution of his rage, but in
So swift a death, as if his hand had been

(59)

Guided by lightning, to Molarchus sent
His life's discharge; which, with astonishment,
Great as if by their evil angels all
Their sins had been displayed, did wildly fall   620
Upon his followers; whom, ere haste could save,
Or strength resist, Argalia's sword had gave
Such sudden deaths, that, whilst amazements reigned
O'er all, he from the heedless tumult gained
That glorious prize—the royal lady; who,
In all assaults of fears, not lost unto
Her own clear judgement, as a blessing sent
From Heaven, (whilst her base foes confusion lent
That action safety), follows that brave friend,
Whose sword redeemed her, till her journey's end,   630
Through threatening dangers, brought her to that place
Where, with such passion as kind wives embrace
Husbands returned from bondage, she is by
Her father welcomed into liberty.
    Thus rescued, whilst exalted rumours swelled
To such confusion as from sense expelled
Reason's safe conduct, whilst each soldier leaves
His former charge, fear's pale disease receives
This paroxysm:—The fleet, which yet had in
A doubtful quest of their surprised prince been,   640
Directed hither with the new-born day,
Their streamers round the citadel display;
Which seen by them that, being deluded by
The dead Molarchus, to his treachery
Had joined their strength, guilt, the original
Of shame, did to defend the platform call
Their bold endeavour; but, when finding it
Too strongly manned for undermining wit
Or open strength to force, despairing to
Be long secure, prompted by fear, they threw   650
Themselves on mercy; which calm grace, among
Heaven's other blessings, whilst it leads along
The prince toward victory, made his conquest seem—
Such as came not to punish, but redeem.

THE END OF THE FOURTH CANTO.

Canto V

THE ARGUMENT

The grateful prince, to show how much he loved
This noble youth, whose merit's just reward
Too great for less abilities had proved,
Makes him commander of his daughter's guard.

Where seated in the most benign aspect
Kind love could grant to fair Pharonnida,
A sacred vision doth her hopes detect,
Whose waking joys his absence doth withdraw.

FREED from those dangers which this bold attempt
Made justly feared, whilst joy did yet exempt
Those cares, which, when by time concocted, shall
His kingdom to a general mourning call,
Sparta's pleased prince, with all the attributes
E'er gratitude learned from desert, salutes
That noble youth, which, even when hope was spent,
Kind Heaven had made his safety's instrument,
By acts of such heroic virtue, that,
Whilst all the less concerned are wondering at,   10
The grateful prince in all the noble ways
Of honour, lasting as his life, repays.
By whose example the fair princess taught,
To shadow love (her soul's most perfect draught)
In friendship's veil, so free a welcome gave
The worthy stranger, that all prayer durst crave,
Though sacrificed in zeal's most perfect fire,
Seemed now from Heaven dropt on his pleased desire.
    Some days spent here, whilst justice vainly sought
That treason's root, whose base production, brought   20
Unto an unexpected period in
Molarchus' death, with him had buried been
To future knowledge—all confessions, though
In torments they extracted were, bestow
Upon their knowledge, being the imperfect shade
Of supposition, which too weak to invade
E'en those whose doubtful loyalty looked dim,
The prudent prince, burying mistrust with him,
Leaving the island with 's triumphant fleet,
On the Sicilian shore prepares to meet   30
That joy in triumph which, a blessing brought,
His loyal subjects with their prayers had sought.
    To cure those hot distemperatures, which in
His absence had the court's quotidian been,
The princess' guard (as being an honour due
To noble valour) having left unto

That worthy stranger, whose victorious hand
Declared a soul created for command,
The prince departs from his loved daughter's court
To joyful Corinth; where, though the resort   40
Of such as by their service strove to express
An uncorrupted loyalty made less
That mourning, which the kingdom's general loss
Claimed from all hearts, yet, like a sable cross,
Which amongst trophies noble conquerors bear,
All did some signs o' the public sorrow wear.
　But leaving these to rectify that state
This fever shook, return to whom we late
Left gently calmed—that happy pair, which in
Desire, the shady porch of love, begin   50
That lasting progress, which ere ended shall
So oft their fate to strong assistance call.
Some months in happy free delights—before
Passion got strength enough to dictate more
Than Reason could write fair—they'd spent; in which
Slumber of fancy, popular love grown rich,
Soon becomes factious, and engages all
The powers of Nature to procure the fall
Of the soul's lawful sovereign. Either, in
Each action of the other's, did begin   60
To place an adoration—she doth see
Whate'er he doth, as shining majesty
Beneath a cloud, or books, where Heaven transfers
Their oracles in unknown characters;
Like gold yet unrefined, or the adamant
Wrapt up in earth, he only seemed to want
Knowledge of worth. Her actions in his sight
Appear like fire's feigned element, with light,
But not destruction, armed; like the fair sun,
When through a crystal aqueduct he'th run   70
His piercing beams, until grown temperate by
That cooling medium, through humility,
Shuns her majestic worth. In either's eyes,
The other seemed to wear such a disguise
As poets clothed their wandering gods in, when
In forms disguised they here conversed with men.
　But long this conflict of their passions, ere
Resisted, lasts not; when, disdained to bear
Those leaden fetters, the great princess tries
To quench that fire i' the embryo, ere it rise   80
To unresisted blazes—but in vain;
What her tears smother are by sighs again
Blown into flames, such as, since not to be
By aught extinguished, her sweet modesty
Strives to conceal, nor did them more betray
Than by such fugitives as stole away

Through her fair eyes, those sally-ports of love,
From her besiegèd heart, now like to prove
(Had not her honour called the act unjust)
So feeble to betray her soul's best trust;   90
Her flames being not as each vulgar breast
Feels in the fires of fancy, when oppressed
With gloomy discontents; her bright stars sate
Enthroned so high, that, like the bays of Fate,
It stopped the current of the stream, and, to
The sea of honour, love's fresh rivers drew.

Thus whilst the royal eaglet doth, i' the high
Sublimer region of bright majesty,
Upon affection's wings still hover, yet,
Loath to descend, on th' humble earth doth sit;   100
Her worthy lover, like that amorous vine,
When crawling o'er the weeds, it strives to twine
Embraces with the elm, he stands; whilst she
Desires to bend, but, like that love-sick tree,
By greatness is denied.   He that ne'er knew
A swelling tumour of conceit, nor flew,
Upon the waxen wings of vain ambition,
A thought above his own obscure condition,
Thinks that the princess, by her large respect
Conferred on him, but kindly doth reflect   110
His father's beams ; and, with a reverent zeal
Sees those descending rays, that did reveal
Love's embassies, transported on the quick
Wings of that heart-o'ercoming rhetoric,
Instructing that the weakness of his eye,
Dazzled with beams of shining majesty,
Might, for too boldly gazing on a sight
So full of glory, be deprived of light—
Stifling his fancy, till it turned the air
That fanned his heart to flames, which pale despair   120
Chilled into ice soon as he went about
With them to breathe a storm of passion out.

But vain are all these fears—his eagle sight
Is born to gaze upon no lesser light
Than that from whence all other beauties in
The same sphere borrow theirs; he else had been
Degenerate from that royal eyrie whence
He first did spring, although he fell from thence
Unfledged, the growing pinions of his fame
Wanting the purple tincture of his name   130
And titles—both unknown ; yet shall he fly,
On his own merit's strength, a pitch as high,
Though not so boldly claimed, and such as shall
Enhance the blessing, when the dull mists fall

95 It] Singer, again arbitrarily, 'They.'   For 'bays' in this sense see inf. II. v. 174.

(63)

From truth's benighted eyes, whispering in
His soul's pleased ear—her passion did begin
Whilst all the constellations of her fate,
Fixed in the zenith of bright honour, sate ;
Whilst his, depressed by adverse fortune, in
Their nadir lay—even to his hopes unseen.   140
  Whilst thus enthean fire did lie concealed
With different curtains, lest, by being revealed,
Cross fate, which could not quench it, should to death
Scorch all their hopes, burned in the angry breath
Of her incensèd father—whilst the fair
Pharonnida was striving to repair
The wakeful ruins of the day, within
Her bed, whose down of late by love had been
Converted into thorns, she having paid
The restless tribute of her sorrow, staid   150
To breathe awhile in broken slumbers, such
As with short blasts cool feverish brains ; but much
More was in hers—A strong pathetic dream,
Diverting by enigmas Nature's stream,
Long hovering through the portals of her mind
On vain phantastic wings, at length did find
The glimmerings of obstructed reason, by
A brighter beam of pure divinity
Led into supernatural light, whose rays
As much transcended reason's, as the day's   160
Dull mortal fires, faith apprehends to be
Beneath the glimmerings of divinity.
Her unimprisoned soul, disrobed of all
Terrestrial thoughts, like its original
In heaven, pure and immaculate, a fit
Companion did for those bright angels sit,
Which the gods made their messengers to bear
This sacred truth, seeming transported where,
Fixed in the flaming centre of the world,
The heart o' the microcosm, 'bout which is hurled   170
The spangled curtains of the sky, within
Whose boundless orbs, the circling planets spin
Those threads of time, upon whose strength rely
The ponderous burthens of mortality.
An adamantine world she sees, more pure,
More glorious far than this,—framed to endure
The shock of dooms-day's darts, in which remains
The better angels of what earth contains,
Placed there to govern all our acts, and be
A medium 'twixt us and eternity.   180
Hence Nature, from a labyrinth half above,
Half underneath, that sympathetic love,

Which warms the world to generation, sends
On unseen atoms; each small star attends
Here for his message, which received, is by
Their influence to the astral faculty
That lurks on earth communicated; hence
Informing Forma sends intelligence
To the material principles of earth—
Her upper garments, Nature's second birth.   190
Upon each side of this large frame, a gate
Of different use was placed—At one there sate
A sprightly youth, whose angel's form delights
Eyes dimmed with age, whose blandishments invites
Infants i' the womb to court their woe, and be
By his false shape tempted to misery.
Millions of thousands swarm about him, though
Diseases do each minute strive to throw
Them from his presence; since, being tempted by
His flattering form, all court it, though they lie   200
On beds of thorns to look on 't, saving some
More wretched malcontents, that hither come
With souls so sullen, that, whilst Time invites
Them to his joys, they shun those smooth delights.
This, the world's favourite, had a younger brother
Of different hue, each more unlike the other
Than opposite aspects; antipathy
Within their breast, though they were forced to be
Almost inseparable, dwelt. This fiend
A passage guarded, which at the other end   210
O' the spacious structure stood; betwixt each gate
Was placed a labyrinth, in whose angles sate
The Vanities of life, attempting to
Stay death's pale harbingers, but that black clew,
Time's dusky girdle, Fate's arithmetic,
Grief's slow-paced snail, Joys more than eagle-quick,—
That chain whose links composed of hours and days,—
Thither at length spite of delay conveys
The slow-paced steps of Time. There always stood
Near him one of the triple sisterhood,   220
Who, with deformity in love, did send
Him troops of servants, hourly to attend
Upon his harsh commands, which he, from all ·
Society of flesh, without the wall,
Down a dark hill conveyed; at whose foot stood
An ugly lake, black as that horrid flood,
Gods made by men did fear. Myriads of boats
On the dark surface of the water floats,

---

216 Grief's slow-paced snail] Singer has altered this to 'Griefs, slow, snail-paced,'
which, from what follows, an ordinary writer might more probably have written. But
it by no means follows that Chamberlayne did not deliberately write the other.

Containing passengers, whose different hue ·
Tell them that from the walls do trembling view   230
Their course—that there's no age of man to be
Exempted from that powerful tyranny.
A tide, which ne'er shall know reflux, beyond
The baleful stream, unto a gloomy strond,
Circled with black obscurity, conveys
Each passenger, where their torn chain of days
Is in eternity peeked-up.   Between
These different gates, the princess having seen
Life's various scenes wrought to a method by
Disposing angels, on a rock more high   240
Than Nature's common surface, she beholds
The mansion house of Fate, which thus unfolds
Its sacred mysteries :—A trine without
A quadrate placed, both those encompassed in
A perfect circle, was its form ; but what
Its matter was—for us to wonder at—
Is undiscovered left ; a tower there stands
At every angle, where Time's fatal hands,
The impartial Parcae, dwell.—I' the first she sees
Clothe, the kindest of the Destinies,   250
From immaterial essences to cull
The seeds of life, and of them frame the wool
For Lachesis to spin ; about her fly
Myriads of souls that yet want flesh to lie
Warmed with their functions in, whose strength bestows
That power by which man ripe for misery grows.
Her next of objects was that glorious tower,
Where that swift-fingered nymph that spares no hour
From mortal's service, draws the various threads
Of life in several lengths—to weary beds   260
Of age extending some, whilst others in
Their infancy are broke ; some blacked in sin,
Others the favourites of heaven, from whence
Their origin, candid with innocence ;
Some purpled in afflictions, others dyed
In sanguine pleasures ; some in glittering pride,
Spun to adorn the earth, whilst others wear
Rags of deformity ; but knots of care
No thread was wholly freed from.   Next to this
Fair glorious tower was placed that black abyss   270
Of dreadful Atropos, the baleful seat
Of death and horror ; in each room replete
With lazy damps, loud groans, and the sad sight
Of pale grim ghosts—those terrors of the night.

237 peeked] This odd word ('peeckt' in orig.) suggests (1) 'peak' in the Shake-
spearean sense of 'peak and pine,' (2) the same in that of 'brought to a point,'
'finished off,' (3) 'picked.'   It seems to recur below (II. v. 383) in 'night-peect,' which
Singer has altered to 'specked.'   250 Clothe] *Sic in orig.*

To this, the last stage that the winding clew
Of life can lead mortality unto,
Fear was the dreadful porter, which let in
All guests sent thither by destructive Sin.
As its firm basis, on all these depends
A lofty pyramid, to which each sends   280
Some gift from Nature's treasury to Fame's
Uncertain hand. The hollow room with names
And empty sounds was only filled, of those
For whom the Destinies 'dained to compose
Their fairest threads ; as if but born to die—
Here all Ephemeras of report did fly
On feeble wings, till, being like to fall,
Some faintly stick upon thé slimy wall,
Till the observant antiquary rents
Them thence to live in paper monuments ;   290
In whose records they are preserved to be
The various censures of posterity.
I' the upper room, as favourites to Fate,
There only Poets, rich in fancy sate ;
In that beneath—Historians, whose records
Do themes unto those pregnant wits afford ;
Yet both preparing everlasting bays
To crown their glorious dust, whose happy days
Were here spent well. Beneath these, covered o'er
With dim oblivion's shadows, myriads more,   300
Till dooms-day shall the gaudy world undress,
Lay huddled up in dark forgetfulness.
All which, as objects not of worth to cast
A fixed eye on, the princess' genius past
In heedless haste, until obstructed by
Visions, that thus fixed her soul's wandering eye.
A light, as great as if that dooms-day's flame
Were for a lamp hung in the court of Fame,
Directs her—where on a bright throne there sate
Sicilia's better Genius : her proud state   310
(Courted by all earth's greatest monarchs) by
Three valiant knights supported was, whose high
Merits, disdaining a reward less great,
With equal hopes aimed at the royal seat ;
Which since all could not gain, betwixt her three
Fair daughters both her crown and dignity
Is equally bestowed, by giving one
To each of them. When the divided throne
Had on each angle fixed a diadem,
Her vision thus proceeds .—The royal stem   320

284 'dained] Orig. ' dained,' which looks like ' deigned.' But the sense shows that
Chamberlayne must have further shortened the more usual contraction ' 'sdained.'
289 rents] Of course ' rends,' for the sake of rhyme. Chamberlayne interchanges
d and *t* endings freely, as ' reveren*d* ' for ' reveren*t*.'

That bore her father's crown, to view first brings
Its golden fruit—a glorious race of kings,
Led by the founder of their fame, their rear
Brought by her father up; next, those that bear
Epirus' honoured arms, the royal train
Concluding in Zoranza; this linked chain
Drawn to an end, the princes that had swayed
Argalia's sceptre, fill the scene, till, stayed
By the Epirot's sword, their conquered crown
From agèd Gelon's hoary head dropt down   330
At fierce Zoranza's feet. This she beholds
With admiration, whilst hid truth unfolds
Itself in plainer objects :—The distressed
Ætolian prince again appears, but dressed
In a poor pilgrim's weed; in 's hand he leads
A lovely boy, in whose sweet look she reads
Soft Pity's lectures; but whilst gazing on
This act, till lost in admiration,
By sudden fate he seemed transformed to what
She last beheld him, only offering at   340
Love's shrine his heart to her Idea. There
Joy had bereaved her slumbers, had not fear
Clouded the glorious dream—A dreadful mist,
Black as the steams of hell, seeming to twist
Its ugly vapours into shades more thick
Than night-engendering damps, had with a quick
But horrid darkness veiled the room; to augment
Whose terror, a cloud's sulphury bosom, rent
With dreadful thunder-claps, darting a bright
But fearful blaze through the artificial night,   350
Lent her so much use of her eyes—to see
Argalia grovelling in his blood, which she
Had scarce beheld ere the malignant flame
Vanished again. She shrieks, and on his name
Doth passionately call; but here no sound
Startles her ear but hollow groans, which drowned
Her soul in a cold sweat of fears. Which ended,
A second blaze lends her its light, attended
With objects, whose wild horror did present
Her father's ghost, then seeming to lament   360
Her injured honour. In his company
The slain Laconian's spirit, which, let free
From the dark prison of the cold grave, where
In rusty chains he lay, was come to bear
Her to that sad abode; but, as she now
Appeared to sink, a golden cloud did bow
From heaven's fair arch, in which Argalia seemed,
Clad in bright armour, sitting, who redeemed
Her from approaching danger; which being done,
The darkness vanished, and a glorious sun   370

Of welcome light displayed its beams ; by which,
A throne the first resembling, but more rich
In its united glory, to the eye
Presents its lustre, where in majesty,
The angels that attend their better fate
Placed her and brave Argalia.—In which state,
The unbarred portals of her soul let fly
The golden slumber, whose dear memory
Shall live within her noble thoughts, until,
Treading o'er all obstructions, fate fulfil   380
These dark predictions, whose obscurity
Must often first her soul's affliction be.

　　When now the morning's dews—that cool allay
Which cures the fever of the intemperate day,—
Were rarified to air, the princess, to
Improve her joy in private thoughts, withdrew
From burthensome society within
A silent grove's cool shadows—what had been
Her midnight's joy to recollect. In which
Delightful task, whilst memory did enrich   390
The robes of fancy, to divert the stream
Of thoughts, intentive only on her dream,
Argalia enters, with a speed that showed
He unto some supreme commander owed
That diligence ; but, when arrived so near
As to behold, stopped with a reverent fear,
Lest this intrusion on her privacies
Might ruffle passion, which now floating lies
In a calm stream of thought. He stays till she
By her commands gave fresh activity   400
To his desires, then with a lowly grace,
Yet such to which Pride's haughty sons gave place
For native sweetness, he on 's knee presents
A packet from her father, whose contents,
If love can groan beneath a greater curse
Than desperation, made her sufferings worse
Than fear could represent them—'twas expressed
In language that not wholly did request,
Nor yet command consent ; only declare
His royal will, and the paternal care   410
He bore his kingdom's safety, which could be
By nought confirmed more than affinity
With the Laconian prince, whose big fame stood
Exalted in a spacious sea of blood,
On honour's highest pyramid. His hand
Had made the triple-headed spot of land
One of her stately promontories bow
Beneath his sword, and with his sceptre now

412 Laconian] This should be 'Epirot,' but Chamberlayne, as the reader has been
warned, uses these appellations almost at random.

He at the other reaches; which, if love
But gently smile on's new-born hopes, and prove   420
Propitious as the god of war, his fate
Climbs equal with his wishes. But too late
That slow-paced soldier bent his forces to
Storm that fair virgin citadel, which knew,
Ere his pretences could a parley call,
Beneath what force that royal fort must fall.

Enclosed within this rough lord's letter, she
Received his picture, which informed her he
Wanted dissimulation (that worst part
Of courtship) to put complements of art   430
On his effigies; his stern brow far more
Glorying i' the scars, than in the crown he wore,
His active youth made him retainer to
The court of Mars, something too long to sué
For entrance into Love's; like mornings clad
In grizzled frosts ere plump-cheeked Autumn had
Shorn the glebe's golden locks, some silver hairs
Mixed with his black appeared; his age despairs
Not of a hopeful heir, nor could his youth
Promise much more; the venerable truth   440
Of glorious victories, that stuck his name
For ornament i' the frontispiece of fame,
Together with his native greatness, were
His orators to plead for love: but where
Youth, beauty, valour, and a soul as brave,
Though not known great as his, before had gave
Love's pleasing wounds, Fortune's neglected gain
In fresh assaults but spends her strength in vain.

With as much ease as souls, when ripened by
A well-spent life, haste to eternity,   450
She had sustained this harsh encounter, though
Backed with her father's threats, did it not show
More dreadful yet—in a command which must
Call her Argalia from his glorious trust;
Her guardian to a separation in
An embassy to him, whose hopes had been
Her new-created fears. Which sentence read
By the wise lady, though her passions bred
A sudden tumult, yet her reason stays
The torrent, till Argalia, who obeys   460
The strictest limits of observance to
Her he adored, being reverently withdrew,
Enlarged her sorrows in so loud a tone,
That ere he's through the winding labyrinth gone
So far, but that he could distinctly hear
Her sad complaints, they thus assault his ear:—
'Unhappy soul! born only to infuse
Pearls of delight with vinegar, and lose

Content for honour; is 't a sin to be
Born high, that robs me of my liberty?   470
Or is 't the curse of greatness to behold
Virtue through such false optics as unfold
No splendour, 'less from equal orbs they shine?
What heaven made free, ambitious men confine
In regular degrees. Poor Love must dwell
Within no climate but what 's parallel
Unto our honoured births; the envied fate
Of princes oft these burthens finds from state,
When lowly swains, knowing no parent's voice
A negative, make a free happy choice.'—   480
And here she sighed ; then with some drops, distilled
From Love's most sovereign elixir, filled
The crystal fountains of her eyes, which e'er
Dropped down, she thus recalls again—'But ne'er,
Ne'er, my Argalia, shall these fears destroy
My hopes of thee : Heaven! let me but enjoy
So much of all those blessings, which their birth
Can take from frail mortality ; and earth,
Contracting all her curses, cannot make
A storm of danger loud enough to shake   490
Me to a trembling penitence ; a curse,
To make the horror of my suffering worse,
Sent in a father's name, like vengeance fell
From angry Heaven, upon my head may dwell
In an eternal stain ; my honoured name
With pale disgrace may languish; busy fame
My reputation spot; affection be
Termed uncommanded lust ; sharp poverty,
That weed which kills the gentle flower of love,
As the result of all these ills, may prove   500
My greatest misery,—unless to find
Myself unpitied. Yet not so unkind
Would I esteem this mercenary band,
As those far more malignant powers that stand,
Armed with dissuasions, to obstruct the way
Fancy directs ; but let those souls obey
Their harsh commands, that stand in fear to shed
Repentant tears : I am resolved to tread
These doubtful paths, through all the shades of fear
That now benight them. Love! with pity hear   510
Thy suppliant's prayers, and when my clouded eyes
Shall cease to weep, in smiles I'll sacrifice
To thee such offerings, that the utmost date
Of Death's rough hands shall never violate.'
  Whilst our fair virgin sufferer was in
This agony, Argalia, that had been
Attentive as an envied tyrant to
Suspected counsels, from her language drew

So much, that that pure essence, which informs
His knowledge, shall in all the future storms   520
Of fate protect him, from a fear that did
Far more than death afflict, whilst love lay hid
In honour's upper region. Now, whilst she
Calmly withdraws, to let her comforts be
Hopes of 's return, his latest view forsook
His soul's best comfort, who hath now betook
Herself to private thoughts ; where, with what rest
Love can admit, I leave her, and him blest
In a most prosperous voyage, but happier far
In being directed by so bright a star.   530

THE END OF THE FIRST BOOK

BOOK II. Canto I

THE ARGUMENT

Still wakeful guilt, Almanzor's rebel sin,
Taking advantage of unguarded mirth,
Which now without mistrust did revel in
The princess' court, gives thence new treason birth.

By treachery seized, and through night's shades conveyed,
She had for ever in this storm been lost,
Had not its rage by such rude hands been staid,
That safety near as much as danger cost.

THESE hell-engendered embryos, which had long
Lay hid within Almanzor's breast, grown strong,
Now for delivery strive; clandestine plots,
Ripened with age and lust, dissolve the knots
Wherein his fear had fettered them, and fly
Beyond the circle of his loyalty.
Since his deserts made him a stranger to
His princess' court, he'd lived like those that do
Fly that pursuing vengeance which attends
A rebel's acts, seen only to such friends,   10
Whose blemished honour suffering in his fall,
Assist his rising, though they venture all
By that unlawful act, on paths that may
Precipitate to ruin. The dark way
Had long been sought for, consultations did
Whisper rebellion in soft airs, forbid
To live in louder language, until, like
Inevitable thunder, it could strike
As swift, as secret, and as sure as those,
Heaven's anger hurls through all that durst oppose. 20
  In all the progress of that dark design,
Whose unseen engines strove to undermine
That power, which since Heaven doth in kings infuse,
None but unhallowed rebels durst abuse,
Time, treason's secret midwife, did produce
No birth like this.—Such friends, as often use
Had taught him their soul's characters, he makes
Sharers of 's guilt; but, whilst he troubled takes
A care to fit each smaller wheel unto
This fatal engine, those black powers, that do   30
Assist such dark designs, a moving spirit
Supply it with. Although Almanzor's merit
Purchased few friends, yet had his tempting gold
Corrupted some, 'mongst which it surest hold

Upon Amphibia took; a lady who,
Before Florenza's sweeter virtues drew
Her favour to a better object, swayed
The princess' choice affections; she, betrayed
By glittering charms, persuades her thoughts—no deed
For guilt is branded, whose attempts may feed   40
Ambition's malice, and at one blow give
Envy and avarice a hope to live,
Pleased with their ruin, whose fair merits dwell
High in those thoughts from whence she justly fell.
　To rack revenge unto as large extent
As hate could wish, what hell could ne'er invent
Without assistance of a female wit—
Man's first betrayer—all that seemed but fit
From treason's close embrace to propagate
Revenge, she lights him.　What, though close as Fate   50
When parling with the Destinies, is by
Her counsel acted, swift as stories fly
From vulgar tongues, her treachery makes known
To the bold rebel; whose intentions grown
Hence ripe for action, when his secret guilt
A strong retreat had for rebellion built,
By laying the foundation on 't in those
Who, since by want or envy made the foes
T' the public peace, are soon persuaded by
Their princess' fall to cure that malady.   60
　This platform laid—some, whose wise valour he
By practice knew adorned with secrecy,
Amongst the number of his guilty friends,
Selected in its first attempt, attends
Treason's dark walks, which, now more secret by
Night's dismal shadows made, had brought them nigh
The princess' palace.　Through the hemisphere's
Dark curtain now the big-bulked roof appears,
And dappled windows showed their several light,
Like rich enamel in the jet of night.   70
All rocked in sweet security they found
By Fate's false smiles, triumphant mirth had crowned
The glorious train, whose height of joy could taste
No poison of suspicion, each embraced
His free delights, yet feared no snake should lie
Lurking within those flowers.　Amidst which high
Divine flames of enthean joy, to her
That levelled had their way, a messenger
Makes known their near approach; for which before
She had prepared, and veiled the pavement o'er   80
In thin, but candid innocence.　Accurst
By all that e'er knew virtue! oh, how durst

45 rack] Singer 'wreak,' which seems unnecessary.
57 on 't] Singer 'of 't,' which loses an idiom.

Thy envy turn these comic scenes into
So red a tragedy as must ensue
Thy guilt's stenography, which thus writes fate
In characters of blood! But now too late
'Tis to repent; when punishment wrought fair
Shows thy foul crimes, thou only may'st despair.
  Leaving this fiend to hatch her vipers here,
Let's breathe awhile, although in full career,   90
Stay on the brow o' the precipice to view
The court's full joys; which, being arrived unto
Their zenith, seemed, to fate-discerning eyes,
Like garlands wore before a sacrifice.
The cornucopiae, from the tables now
Removed by full-fed rurals, did allow
Time for discourse, as much as modest mirth
Durst stretch her wings; crowned cups gave lusty birth
To active sports; the hearth's warm bounties flame
From lofty piles, and in their pride became   100
The lustre of the roof. To glorify
Which yet imperfect festival, the eye
That lent to this large body light divine,
Pharonnida, at whose adorèd shrine
These sacrifices offered were, appears
Within the hall, and with her presence clears
Each supercilious brow,—if hopes to see
What's now enjoyed suffered such there to be.
The princess on her honoured throne reposed,
A fancy-tempting music first unclosed   110
The winding portals of the soul; which done,
Four swains, whose time-directed knowledge won
Attention with credulity, by turn
Sicilia's annals sung, and from the urn
Of now almost forgotten truth did raise
Their fame—those branches of eternal bays:
Which sober mirth, preparatives unto
More active sports, continuing, whilst the new
Model of treason was disguising in
A mask ordained to candy o'er their sin,   120
To gild those pills of poison with delight,
And strew with roses deadly aconite,
Was now drawn near an end, when from without
A murmuring noise of several sounds about
The palace gates was heard; which suddenly,
Dissolving to an antic harmony,
Proclaims their entrance, whose first solemn sight,
In dreadful shapes, mixed terror with delight.
  In the black front of that slow march appears
A train, whose difference both in sex and years   130

---

94 wore] Orig. 'were.'   99 hearth's] Orig. 'hearts.'

Had spoke confusion, if agreement in
Their acclamation had no prologue been.
A dance, where method in disorder lay,
Where each seemed out, though all their rules obey,
Was first in different measures trod ; which done,
Twelve armed viragoes, whose strange habit won
More 'admiration than their beauty, led
As many captive satyrs ; in the head
O' the Amazonian troop, a matron, by
Two younger nymphs supported till come nigh   140
Pharonnida's bright throne, presents the rest—
Her issue ; who externally exprest
So many fair-souled virtues, born to be
Protectors of their mother—Chastity,
Who wants their help, although supported by
Her weaker daughters—Fear and Modesty.
   Those obscene vices, whose rude hands betray
Nature's deformities forced to obey
Their brave opposing virtues, did appear
I' the captive satyrs ; who being now brought near,   150
A dreadful music 's heard without, whose sound
Did gentler airs in their first births confound.
Which being a signal to that act of blood
That soon ensues, whilst all expecting stood
Some happier change, the false viragoes drew
Their swords, and with a speedy fury slew
The struggling knights, who thus disguised had been,
With the more horror to be murthered in
Their royal mistress' sight, whose shrieks did tell
What trembling guests within her breast did dwell.   160
   Sudden and cruel was the act ; yet stands
Not treason here ; but whilst their purpled hands
Yet reeked in blood, their guilty souls to stain
With blacker sins, her weak defenders slain,
Rush toward the trembling princess, who now lies
Betrayed by the soul's janitors—her eyes,
To passions insupportable, which grown
A burthen to her spirits, all were flown
T' the porch of death for rest. If souls new fled
From tainted bodies, that have surfeited   170
On studied sins, could be discerned when they,
Unarmed with penitence, are hurled away
By long-armed fiends—less pale, less horrid would
Their guilty looks appear. Confusion could
Not live in livelier emblem ; each appears
To fly the danger, but about him bears
Its pale effects—so passengers forsake
A sinking ship ; such strong convulsions shake

172 hurled] Another would probably have written ' whirled' or ' haled.'

Suiprisèd forts; so dooms-day's trumpet shall
Startle the unpreparèd world, when all   180
Her atoms in their then worn robes shall be
Ravished in flames to meet eternity.
The unguarded princess, being by all forsook
But poor Florenza, both from thence are took,
Whilst neither in that horrid agony
Beheld their danger, and transported by
Almanzor to his coach, which near attended
On his assured success; who now, befriended
With the protecting darkness, hastes away,
Swift as desire, with the fair trembling prey.   190
Those few opposing friends, whose will was more
Than power to relieve her, overbore
By the victorious rebels, did in vain
Attempt her rescue; which, since fruitless slain,
Her martyrs fall leaving their lives to be
An evidence of dying loyalty,
Success attends thus far; but Fortune now
Left off to smile on villany, her brow
Contracted into frowns, she swiftly sent
This countermand:—Her followers, having spent   200
Their own endeavours to no purpose, raise
In haste the neighbouring villages; nor stays
The swift alarum, till it had outfled
The speed Almanzor made. Roused from his bed,
And warm embraces of his wife, by those
Which had outrun the danger of their foes,
The drowsy villager in trembling haste
Snatches such arms as former fear had placed
Fit to defend; with which, whilst horn-pipes call
In tones more frantic than a bacchinal,   210
They stumble to their rendezvous, which none
But only by the louder cries had known.
This giddy multitude, which no command
Knew, but what rage did dictate, hovering stand,
Like big swoln clouds drove by a doubtful wind,
Uncertain where to fall: one cries 'Behind
The greatest danger lies'; some like his choice,
And speedily retreat, until a voice
More powerful, though from the like judgement sprung,
Persuades them on again; some madly rung   220
The jarring bells—as far from harmony
As their opinions; all which disagree
About the place whence the alarums come:
One cries—the princess' court; until struck dumb
By a more terrifying fool that swears
The next port is surprised, toward which he stares,

209 horn-pipes] Orig. 'horn-*pies*.'

To see the beacon's blaze, but is from far
Deceived b' the light of an ascending star.
So many shapes bear their weak fancies, that
All would do something, but there's none knows what.   230
In this strange medley of confusion, they
That could command, want such as would obey,
To exercise their power; each thinks his own
Opinion best, so must perform't alone,
Or else remain, as hitherto they had,
Busy in doing nothing. In which mad
Fit of distracted fury, like to fight,
For want of foes, amongst themselves, the night,
Grown grey with age, foreshowed her death; when each,
Thinking that now he'd done enough to teach   240
An active soldier vigilance in spending
A night abroad, which they will call defending
Their prince and country from a danger, but
What't was they know not, swearing't shall be put
In the next chronicle, they disunite
Their ne'er well-jointed forces, and a flight,
Rather than march t' the several hamlets take,
From whence at first, being scarce half awake,
Not so much clothed, their heedless haste had sent
Them only noise and number to augment.   250
    One troop of this disbanded company,
Which, though but few, more than could well agree
To march together, by mistake being cast
Into a narrow strait, met, as they past,
The coach that bore the princess, being by those
That stole her guarded : the mad rout oppose
Their further passage, not because they thought
Them to be those their ignorance had sought
In their late meeting—the antipathy
'Twixt them and th' gentry is enough to be   260
That quarrel's parent, whose event shall make
Their prince and country blessed in their mistake.
    Startled from all his temperate joys with this
Unlooked-for remora i' the road of bliss,
Enraged Almanzor vows to ford the flood
O' the present danger, or with his own blood
Augment the stream. With that he flies among
Those that are nearest of the numerous throng,
Who, when they found what difference was between
Their clubs (blunt as their valours) and the keen   270
Edge of his sword, would have fell back, but are
Forced on by those behind, who, being far

---

256 oppose] Orig. 't' oppose.'
262 mistake] One suspects, in this and other passages, satire on the very ineffectual
'Clubmen' of the Western counties in the Rebellion.
265 vows] Orig. 'rows.'

From danger, fear it not.　Thus some are forced
To fight, till their unwilling souls, divorced
From their cold lodgings, made their peace.　But here,
Whilst he a conqueror reigns, ingenious fear
Taught them that durst no nearer come, to do
Most mischief at a distance ; climbed unto
The rock's inequitable clifts, 'from thence
They shower down stones that equally dispense　　　　280
Danger 'mongst friends and foes.　Had she not been
Defended by her coach, their princess in
This storm had perished ; or, had fear of death
Unfixed her thoughts, she'd spent that precious breath
Now sacrificing in her prayers to be
From their wild rage delivered safe ; but she,
Oppressed with lethargies of sorrow, lends
No ear to this rude fight, on which depend
So much of fate,—danger appears to lie
Not more in the disease than remedy.　　　　290
　Whilst the opposed Almanzor now had near
Hewed forth his way through all of them, appear
More company by their loud clamours drew
Unto their timely aid.　Now danger grew
Horrid and threatening, till the impetuous shower,
Wetting the wings of the fierce rebel's power,
Clog all his hopes of flight, unless he leave
His trembling prey behind him.　To bereave
Him of his last of hopes, he sees his train
Begin to droop.　With those that yet remain　　　　300
He thinks it time, whilst undiscovered, to
Secure himself ; which difficult to do,
At length (though not unwounded) he alone
Breaks through their forces, blest in being unknown ;
Else had their battered weapons spared to shed
The blood of others, and had surfeited
On his, which, adding knowledge to the fire
Of rage, they had most reason to desire.
　The unsuccessful rebel thus secured
By speedy flight, his train not long endured　　　　310
The circling danger, which from each side sends
Symptoms so deadly, all their strength defends
Not the rude torrent, nor their prayers could calm
Their foes' stern rage.　Sweet mercy's healing balm
Is the extraction of brave spirits, which,
By innate valour rarified, enrich
With that fair gem the triumphs of success,
Whilst cowards make the victors' glory less—
Their highest flame of rage being but dull earth
Fired into tyranny, the spurious birth　　　　320

　279 clifts] This word does double duty for ‘ cliff’ and ‘ cleft.’

Of a precedent fear, whose baseness knows
No calm, but what from others' danger grows.
　And now the field, scoured by the beastly rage
O' the savage clowns, had left no foe to engage
A life, nor could their policy persuade
Them to let one survive, till he had made
The plot discovered. With rude haste they crush
Their trembling souls out, and all weapons blush
In part o' the blood; so many hands had gave
Them hurtless wounds, that the expecting grave　　330
Needs only take their bones, for madly they
Had minced their flesh for the vulture's easier prey.
　This victory gained, they haste t' the coach, and thence
The unknown princess take, no large expense
Of prayers, poured from Florenza's fears, could be
So powerful to obtain civility.
She tells them whom their rage profanes, and by
Their princess' name conjures them; but the high
Exalted outcries drown her voice, till one,
Who had the rape of the sad lady known,　　340
When first performed, did with a louder voice
Proclaim her there; and, having first made choice
Of a more civil company to oppose
The uncivil clowns, rescues her; and then shows
How near their heedless rage had cast away
The glorious prize of that victorious day.
　From fainting slumbers raised, the princess, now
Secure in their discovery, taught them how
To turn their fury into zeal, and show,
By serving her, the allegiance that they owe　　350
Her royal father. To the palace come,
Rewarding all, she there commands that some
Stay for her guard; but soon that order grew
A troublesome obedience, none would to
His cottage whilst that any staid within
The palace gates. But long they had not been
Thus burthensomely diligent, ere, on
A new design, each struggles to be gone
From 's former charge; a messenger is sought,
Who to the court must post, but each one thought　　360
Himself of most ability, so all
Or none must go; yet, ere the difference fall
Into a near approaching quarrel, he
Who rescued her, the princess chose to be
Her messenger. Euriolus, (for so
The youth was called), disdaining to be slow
Where such commands gave wings, with speed unto
The court was come; but busy fame outflew

335 their] Orig. 'her.'

His eager haste, and ere 's arrival spread
Some scattered fragments of the news, which bred   370
Suspicion of that doubtful truth, from whence
His message leads to doleful confidence.

THE END OF THE FIRST CANTO.

Canto II

THE ARGUMENT

Freed from suspicion by a cause that tells
  His injured prince, Almanzor's guilt exceeds
His great'st mistrust—from thence just anger swells,
  Till for that fever the whole nation bleeds.

Armies united in a dreadful haste
  From distant places sad spectators bring,
To see by fortune justice so defaced,
  The subjects here pursue a conquered king.

MOREA'S prudent prince, whose fears had been
Before this message but like truths wrapped in
Dark oracles, now, with a sense enlarged
Beyond imperfect doubts, no longer charged
His judgement with dilemmas, but, in all
The haste indulgent love, when by the call
Of danger frighted, could procure, without
Staying to let slow counsel urge a doubt
Which might but seem a remora unto
His fixed desires, having together drew   10
His guard, was marching ; when, in such a haste
As breathless speed foreshowed they had been chased
By some approaching danger, such as were
Too full of truth and loyalty to bear
Rebellion longer than their thoughts could be
Eased of the burthen by discovery,
Arrive at th' court with this sad news—that by
Almanzor, who, forgetting loyalty,
Had seized Alcithius' castle, they were drove
To fly their country, since that there he strove   20
To raise an army, by whose strength he might
To the sword's power subject the sceptre's right.
  By this sad news startled out of his late
Fixed resolutions, the vexed prince, whose fate
Had not through all the progress of his reign
Darted so many plagues, to entertain
Them now with strength unballast, calls in haste
His late neglected council, and embraced

1 Morea's] 'Morea' again : it was Sicilia at II. i. 114.

This sudden, but mature advice—that he
Should with such forces as could soonest be   30
Prepared for service, having only seen
Pharonnida, possess that strait between
The castle and the mountains; from whose rude
Inhabitants, which Nature did include
Within those rocks, rebellion soonest might
Grow to a dangerous tumour: the dim light
Of scarce discernèd majesty, so far
Being from them removed, that, lest a war
Enforced him to command their aid, they ne'er
Heard of his mandates; being more fit to bear   40
The weight of armour on their bodies, than
Of taxes on estates—so small that, when
With all the art of industry improved,
For want were kept, but not for ease beloved.
  Through paths that no vestigia showed, to these,
As being retained or lost with greatest ease,
Since naturally unconstant, comes the king.
Not much too late, majestic rays did bring
Props to their wavering faith that yet remained
Unclad in lawless arms; some being gained   50
Unto Almanzor, whose revolt had brought
That freedom, those, whose subtle plots long sought
For innovations, wished. The sickly state,
In sad irruptions—such as future fate,
From sacred truths, speaks deadly symptoms in—
Relaxes all that order which had been
Till now her cement; the soft harmony
Of peaceful contracts, sadly silenced by
That discord in whose flames the kingdom burned,
Had all their measures into marches turned.   60
  Through't his dominions speedy orders flew
For raising troops; whilst, with such haste as new-
Shorn meadows, when approaching storms are nigh,
Tired labourers huddle up, both parties try
To levy armies. The sad scholar throws
His books aside, and now in practice shows
His studied theorics; the stiff labourer leaves
I' the half-shorn fields the uncollected sheaves
To female taskers, and exchanged his hook
Into a sword; each busy trade, that took   70
Pains in the nicer ornaments of peace,
Sit idle till want forced them to increase
The new-raised troops; that ornament o' the hall,
Old armours, which had nothing but a wall
Of long time saved from the invading dust,
From cobwebs swept, though its enamel rust
Stick close, and on the unpractised soldier put,
Forth of their breasts, nor fear, nor danger shut.

Yet, with an army of this temper in
Haste huddled up, the wandering prince had been   80
Enforced to fight, had not his just cause brought
Some loyal gentry, such whose virtue sought
Truth for reward, unto his side; with which
He now advances, more completely rich
In noble valour, than 's rebellious foes
In numerous troops. No enemies oppose
His speedy march, till being now come near
Alcithius' fort, Almanzor's timely fear
Hurries him thence. His better fate depends
On larger hopes : unto such constant friends   90
As equal guilt by sympathy secured,
To them he leaves the castle; and assured
Them of relief, with what convenient speed
Those of his faction (which did only need
His presence to confirm rebellion by
An injured power) could draw their armies nigh.

As hence he marches, each successful hour
Augments his strength, till the unlawful power
Trebled his injured prince's. But as they
Who carry Guilt about them, do betray   100
Her by her sister, Fear, so these, whose crimes
Detected, durst not, in more peaceful times,
Look justice in the face, and therefore now
Stood veiled in arms against her, fearing how
She might prevail 'gainst power, march not till
A greater strength their empty bosoms fill
With hope—a tumour which doth oft dilate
The narrow souls of cowards, till their fate
Flatter them into ruin, then forsakes
Them in an earthquake, whose pale terror shakes   110
Base souls to flight, whilst noble valour dies
Adorned with wounds, fame's bleeding sacrifice.

Almanzor's doubtful army, since that here
The threatening storm at distance did appear
Locked in a calm, possessed with confidence,
Slowly their squadrons moves ; but had from thence
Not a day's journey marched, before the sad
News of Alcithius' desperate danger had
Paled o'er their camp ; which whilst the leaders strove
To animate, Almanzor faster drove   120
On those designs, which, prospering, might prevent
It from surrender; but the time was spent
Too far before. The governor that kept
It now against his prince, too long had slept
In the preceding down of peace, to be
Awakened into valour. Only he
Had seen 't kept clean from cobwebs, and perhaps
The guns shot off, when those loud thunderclaps

Proclaimed a storm of healths; yet, till he saw
The threatening danger circularly draw   130
An armèd line about him, in as high
A voice as valour could a foe defy,
He clothes his fears, which shook the false disguise
Off with the first assault, and swiftly flies
To 's prince's mercy; whose pleased soul he found
Heightened to have his first attempt thus crowned
With victory, which nor made his army less,
Nor steeped in blood, though travailed to success.
   To this new conquest, as a place whose strength
He best might trust, if, to a tedious length,   140
Or black misfortune, the ensuing war
His fate should spin, his choicest treasures are,
Together with her in whose safety he
Placed life itself, brought for security.
This done, that now no slow delays might look
Like fear, he with his loyal army took
The field; in which he'd scarce a level chose
To rally 's army, ere his numerous foes
Appear o' the tops of the adjacent hill,
Like clouds, which, when presaging storms, do fill   150
Dark southern regions. In a plain that lay
So near that both the armies' full survey
Might from the clifts on which Alcithius stands
Be safely viewed, were the rebellious bands
Of 's enemies descending, on each side
Flanked by a river which did yet divide
Him from the prince; who, having time to choose
What ground to fight on, did that blessing use
To 's best advantage. On a bridge, which by
Boards closely linked had forced an unity   160
Betwixt the banks, his army passed. He now
Within a plain, whose spacious bounds allow,
Together with a large extension, all
An ancient leader could convenient call.
Removed no tedious distance from his rear
Stood a small town, which, as the place took care
How to advance so just an interest, might
Be useful—when, tired in the heat of fight,
Strength lost in wounds should force some thither by
Wants which a camp's unfurnished to supply.   170
More near his front, betwixt him and the plain
Through which Almanzor led his spacious train,
On a small hill, which gently rose as though

137 nor] Orig. 'nere,' which for 'never,' is not impossible. In the next line one
suspects '*ex*cess': but with Chamberlayne, more than with others, the least probable
is the most likely.
   149 tops] Singer 'top,' which seems unnecessary.

Its eminence but only strove to show
The fragrant vale, how much nice art outwent
Her beauties in her brow's fair ornament,
A splendid palace stood; which, having been
Built but for wanton peace to revel in,
Was as unfit for the rough hand of war
As boisterous arms for tender virgins are.   180
    To this, since now of consequence unto
The first possessor, had both armies drew.
Commanded parties, which ere night shut in
Light's latest rays, did furiously begin
The first hot skirmish; which, continuing till
Dark shadows all the hemisphere did fill,
To such as fear or novelty had sent
T' the hills' safe tops, such dreadful prospect lent.
By the swift rising of those sudden fires,
In whose short close that fatal sound expires,   190
Which tells each timorous auditor—its breath,
To distant breasts, bears unexpected death,
That, whilst their eyes direct their thoughts unto
Their danger whom reward or honour drew
To the encounter, all the uncouth sight
Affords—to horror turns that strange delight.
    These circling fires drawn near their centre, in
Such tumult as armies engaged begin
Death's fatal task, a dreadful sound surprised
The distant ear. Danger, that lay disguised   200
In darkness yet, now, as if wakened by
The conquerors' shouts, so general and so high,
That it e'en drowned the clamorous instruments
Of fatal war, her veil of sables rents
From round the palace, by that horrid light
Which her own turrets through the steams of night
In dreadful blazes sent, discovering both
The shadowed armies; who, like mourners loath
To draw too near their sorrow's centre, while
Their friends consume, surround the blazing pile,   210
In such a sad and terrible aspect,
That those engaged in action could neglect
Approaching danger, to behold how they
Like woods grown near the foot of Ætna lay,
Whilst the proud palace from her sinking walls
In this sharp fever's fiery crisis falls.
    But now the night, as wearied with a reign
So full of trouble, had resigned again
The earth's divided empire, and the day,
Grown strong in light, both armies did display   220

203 it] Singer 'they,' as he usually reads in such cases. But 'it' is idiomatic and
probable.

To their full view, who to the mountain (in
Sad expectation of the event) had been
Early spectators called. Here, seated nigh
Their female friends, old men, exempted by
Weakness from war's too rough encounters, show
Those colours which their active youth did know
Adorn the field, when those that now engage,
Like tender plants kept for the future age,
In blooming childhood were ; 'mongst this they tell
What heroes in preceding battles fell,   230
Where victory stooped to valour, and where rent
From brave desert by fatal accident ;
Then, ere their story can a period have,
Show wounds they took, and tell of some they gave.
   This sad preludium to an action far
More dismal past, the unveiled face of War
Looks big with horror : now both armies draw
So near, that their divided brothers saw
Each other's guilt—that too too common sin
Of civil war. Rebellious sons stood in   240
Arms 'gainst their fathers clad ; friends, that no cross
Could disunite, here found the fatal loss
Of amity, and as presaging blood
I' the worst aspect, sad opposition, stood :
One was their fashion, form, and discipline ;
Strict heralds in one scutcheon did combine
The arms of both armies—yet all this must be
By war's wild rage robbed of its unity.
   Whilst like sad Saturn, ominous and slow,
Each army moved, some youths, set here to grow,   250
By forward actions, stately cedars to
Adorn Fame's court, like shooting stars were flew,
So bright, so glittering, from the unwieldy throng
Of either army ; which, being mixed among
Each other, in a swift Numidian fight,
Like air's small atoms when discovering light
Betrays their motions, show ; some hours had past
In this light skirmish—till now, near war's last
Sad scene arrived, as the distressed heart calls,
Before the body death's pale victim falls,   260
Those spirits that dispersed by actions were,
Back to their centre, their commander's care
Summons these in ; that so united strength
Might swiftly end—or else sustain the length
Of that black storm, where yet that danger stood,
Which must ere long fall in a shower of blood.
   A dismal silence, such as oft attends
Those that surround the death-beds of their friends .

240 Rebellious] Orig. ' Rebellion's,' *nescio an recte.*

(86)

In the departing minute, reigns throughout
Both armies' troops; who, gathered now about   270
Their several standards, and distinguished by
Their several colours, such variety
Presents the eye with, that, whilst the sad thought
Beholds them but as fallen branches brought
To the decay of time, their view did bring
In all the pleasures of the checkered spring;
Like a large field, where being confined unto
Their several squares—here blushing roses grew,
There purpled hyacinths, and, near to them,
The yellow cowslip bends its tender stem,   280
T' the mountain's tops, the army, marching low
Within the vale, their several squadrons show.
    This silent time, which by command was set
Aside to pay confession's needful debt
To oft-offended Heaven, whose aid, though gave
Ere asked, yet, since our duty is to crave,
Expects our prayers. The armies, from their still
Devotion raised, declare what spirits fill
Their breast, by such an universal joy,
As, to get young, and not the old destroy,   290
Each had by beauteous paranymphs been led,
Not to rough war, but a soft nuptial bed.
    That fatal hour, by time, which, though it last
Till fixed stars have a perfect circle past,
We still think short, to action brought; which now
So near approached, it could no more allow
The generals to consult, although there need
Nought to augment, when valour's flame doth feed
High on the hopes of victory, the rage
Of eager armies. Ere their troops engage,   300
Their several leaders all that art did use,
By which loud war's rough rhetoric doth infuse
Into those bodies, on whose strength consists
Their safety, souls whose brave resolves might twist
Them into chains of valour, which no force,
Than death less powerful, ever should divorce.
    The prince, as more depending on the just
Cause that had drawn his sword, which to distrust
Looks like a crime, soonest commits the day
To Fate's arbitrement. No more delay   310
Comforts the fainting coward,—a sad sound
Of cannon gave the signal, and had drowned
The murmuring drum in silence; Earth did groan
In trembling echoes; on her sanguine throne,
High mounted, Horror sits; wild Rage doth fill
Each breast with fury, whose fierce flames distil

273 presents] Singer, as always where he notices, ' present.' I think it well to draw
occasional but not constant attention to this.

Life through the alembics of their veins : that cloud
Of dust, which, when they first did move, a shroud
Of darkness veiled them in, allayed with blood,
Fell to the earth; whose clefts a crimson flood   320
Filled to the brim, and, when it could contain
No more, let forth those purple streams to stain
The blushing fields, which being made slippery by
The unnatural shower, there lets them sink and die ;
Whose empty veins rent in this fatal strife,
Here dropped the treasure of exhausted life.
In sad exchange of wounds, whilst the last breath,
E'en flying forth to give another death,
Supports the fainting spirits, all were now
Sadly employed; armed Danger could allow   330
In this loud storm of action, none to stand
Idle spectators ; but each busy hand
Labours, in death's great work, his life to sell
At rates so dear—that foe by which he fell,
To boast his gain, survives not. But now, in
This mart of death, blind Fortune doth begin
To show herself antagonist unto
Less powerful Justice. In the common view
Of Reason, which by the external shape
Of actions only judges, no escape   340
From their desert—captivity, was left
The rebels' army, but the unmanly theft
Of secret flight to some, protected by
Their fellows' loss ; when, in a rage as high
As if it had attempted to outroar
The battle's thunder, a rude tempest, bore
From southern climates on the exalted wings
Of new-raised winds, a change so fatal brings
T' the royal army, that from victory's near
Successful pride, unto extremes which fear   350
Did ne'er suggest, it brought them back to view
Their glorious hopes thus sadly overthrew.—
    A strong reserve, raised by his friends to be
Almanzor's rescue, if that victory
Seemed to assist the juster part, was now
Brought near the river ; which endeavouring how
To ford, they there unwillingly had been
Detained, till strength had proved but useless in
The prince's conquest, if the swelling flood,
Whose added streams, too strong to be withstood,   360
Had not in that impetuous torrent tore
That bridge which passed the royal army o'er ;
Whose severed boats born down the river made
So sad a change, that, whilst their foes invade

317 veins] Orig. 'reins' which, again, is quite possibly not wrong.

Their rear on them, the late lamented loss
Forbid the others when dispersed to cross
The waves by dangers, which in each breast bred
Terrors as great as those from whence they fled.
  The valiant army, like life's citadel—
The heart, when nought but poisonous vapours swell   370
Every adjacent part, long struggling in
Death's sharp convulsions, out of hopes to win
Aught there but what buys the uncertain breath
Of future fame at the high price of death;
At length, not conquered, but o'erburthened by
A flood of power, in night's obscurity,
When dreadful shadows had the field o'erspread,
As darkness were a herse-cloth for the dead,
That this day's losses might not grow too great
For reparation, by a hard retreat,   380
Attempt to save such of their strengths, as, since
Enforced to fly, might safely guard the prince
From dangers; which could but his foes have viewed,
Their motions all had unto death pursued.
  In this distress, from that vast sea of blood—
The field where late his army marshalled stood—
The wretched prince retires; but with a train
So small, they seemed like those that did remain
After a deluge. Where the river's course,
Stopped with dead bodies, ran with smallest force,   390
He ventures o'er the flood, whose guilty waves
Blushes in blood. Some few, whom Fortune saves
To attend on him, alike successful by
That bold adventure, whilst the prince doth fly
To guard Alcithius, by his mandates are,
Since the disasters of this fatal war
Forced him to seek for more assistance, sent
To the Epirot. Striving to prevent
Those wild reports, that, on the quick belief
Of female fear, might be imposed by grief,   400
He hastes to bear the sad report to her,
Whose sorrow's lost to see the messenger.

368 whence] Singer, in an arbitrary mood of book-grammar, 'which.'

THE END OF THE SECOND CANTO.

Canto III

THE ARGUMENT

Through the dark terrors of a dreadful night,
  The prince to 's daughter comes with flying speed;
From dangers, great as those he feared in flight,
  Is by Argalia's forward valour freed.

Who having with successful fortune gave
  His master freedom, their joint strength pursue
Their flying foes unto an uncouth cave,
  In whose vast womb Fate's dark decrees they view.

THIS last retreat, which seemed but to defer
Danger by being Honour's sepulchre,
Attained in haste; there, calming all the strife
Of various passion, since her father's life
Paid all the tears she owed his losses, he
His virtuous daughter found, prepared to be
No sad addition to his sorrow by
The faults of female imbecility—
Untimely tears; but with a confidence
High as e'er taught brave valour to dispense   10
With sad disasters, armed to entertain
The worst of ills: to ease the wounded's pain,
Or stop their blood, those hands which once she thought
Should have to victors Triumph's garlands brought,
Are now employed; yet, that her acts may be
The best examples to posterity,
Her present ill, she with such strength withstood—
Its power was lost in hopes of future good.
    Precipitated from a throne to be
Subjected by a subject's tyranny;   20
To want their pity—who of late did know
No peace, but what his influence did bestow;
With sad presaging fears, to think his fair,
His virtuous daughter, his rich kingdom's heir,
Like to be ravished from his baffled power—
A trophy to a rebel conqueror;
With such afflicting griefs as did exclude
The comforts of his passive fortitude,
Oppressed the prince: when now an army, led
By their pursuing enemies, o'erspread   30
The circling fields, and brings their fear within
The reach o' the eye. Heightened with hope to win
That now by parl, which, ere the sad success
Of battle made their conquered numbers less,
He feared in fight; the confidently bold
Almanzor, in a scroll that did unfold

A language, whose irreverent style affords
Far more of anger than his soldiers' swords
Had ere stirred fear within his prince's breast,
His fixed intentions thus in brief exprest :—   40

———GREAT SIR,
No airy tumour of untamed desire,
Nursed my ambition, prompts me to aspire
To any action that may soar above
My birth or loyalty ;—it was the love
I bore your virtuous daughter that first clad
Me in defensive arms, which never had
Been else unsheathed, though't had been to defend
Me from injustice—should your sword extend
Its power to tyranny; but, failing in   50
That first attempt, ere streams of blood had been
Shed in addition to those drops, my hand
Had broke my sword as guilty, had this land
To whom I owe for the first air I breathed,
Not washed the stain in tears, and since unsheathed
It in the name of Justice. To their good,
Which trembling on uncertain hopes hath stood,
Whilst fearing foreign governors; I have
Added my love, and satisfaction crave
For both, before a greater ill may fall,   60
To make our sufferings epidemical—
By being slaves to some proud tyrant, that
In politic ambition reaches at
A kingdom by professed affection, and
Marries your daughter, to command your land.

This scroll, spotted with impudence, received
By the vexed prince, whom passion had bereaved
Of politic evasions, he returns
A swift defiance ; but his high rage burns
Nought but his own scorched breast—the fainting fire,   70
Quenched by constraint, wants fuel to blaze higher
Than flashy threatenings, which, since proved a folly,
Sink in the ashes of melancholy ;
For which his ablest council could prepare
No cordial of advice—they rather share
With him in sorrow, whose harsh burthen grows
Not lighter by the company of those
That now lend hearts to bear it. Only in
This sullen cloud's obscurity, this sin
Of their nativity, the noble soul   80
Of the undaunted princess did control

---

37 irreverent] Orig. ' irreveren*d*.'   43 my] ' by ' ?
73 Singer inserts ' his ' before melancholy, but Chamberlayne may have accented
the antepenultimate, without scruple as to the rhyme.

The harshest lectures of her stars, and sate
Unshaken in this hurricane of fate;
Calming her father's hot adversity
With dews of comfort, taught him how to be
Prince of his passions—a command more great
Than his that trembles in a regal seat.
   The enemy, that vainly had till now
Toiled forth their strength, no more endeavours how
By force to conquer; some small time, they knew,   90
Would, with the bloodless sword of famine, do
More than their cannon could.—The meagre fen
Already grew tyrannical, his men,
Like walking ghosts, wait on their prince, and stand
For shadows on their platforms; not a hand,
But was unnerved with want; yet, whilst each párt
Languished toward death, each bosom held a heart,
Which, though most large, could never empty be,
Being doubly filled with grief and loyalty;
Amongst both which, hope for a part puts in—   100
As the supporter of what else had been
A burthen insupportable, and spoke
This pleasing language—That the royal oak,
Beneath whose winter fortune now they stood,
Pining for want—the withered underwood
That all his miseries dropped on—yet they shall,
Whene'er his brighter stars again do call
His fortune into light, be comforted
By his kind shadow; which shall those, that fled
Him in this sad extreme, then leave to be   110
Scorched in the rays of angry majesty.
   Reduced unto this pitied exigence,
Yet, by his honour, which could not dispense
With aught that like suspicion looked, detained
From what by parl might have their freedom gained,
The loyal sufferers, to declare how far
They fear declined; those mourning weeds of war,
Whose sight a desperate valour doth betray,
Black ensigns, on their guarded walls display.
When to augment their high resolves, with what   120
Their valour was to pity softened at,
After, with all those coarse, though scarce cates, they
By sparing, first attempted to betray
Time till relief with, they'd been fed till now
There nought remained, that longer could allow
Life further hopes of sustenance, to do
An act so great, all ages to ensue,
Shall more admire than imitate; within
The hall appears their sovereign, leading in
His .hand the princess; whose first view, though drest   130
In robes as sad as sorrows e'er exprest,

Was but the frontiers of their grief to what,
When nearer seen, whilst sorrow silenced at
So sad an object, might for death be took,
Made solemn grief like grave religion look.
   Whilst all thus in sad expectation stand
Of future fate, disdaining to command
Those whom an equal sorrow seemed to make
His fellow sufferers, the sad prince thus spake
His fixed resolves :—' Brave souls, whose loyal love,   140
Oppressed by my unhappy woes, must prove
Part of my grief, since by my wretched fate
Forced with my own life to precipitate
Your's into danger; from whose reach, (since by
No crime—until the love of loyalty
Become a sin—you are called guilty), yet
Seek some evasion : 'tis not you that sit
Upon the throne he aims at, nor doth here
A rival in Pharonnida appear.
No, 'tis our lives, our lives, brave subjects, that   150
His bold ambition only reaches at ;
By this pretence—what to my daughter, love,
To 's country, 's pity called,—could he remove
Those now but small obstructions soon would grow,
To 's pride united, till it overflow
All limits of a subject's duty by
Rebellious reach, usurpèd tyranny.
   ' Go then, and let not my unhappiness
Afflict you more i' the shadow of distress :
'Twill like warm comfort swell my soul, to know   160
That to his favour you for safety owe.
Did not those sacred canons, that include
All virtue in a Christian's fortitude,
Obstruct our passion's progress, we, ere this,
In death had made the haughty rebel miss
The glory of his conquest; which since now
Denied, although unwieldly age allow
Not strength to sell my life at such a rate
Honour aims at, yet shall the slow debate,
E'en in my fall, let the world know I died,   170
Scorning his pity, as they hate his pride.'
   Here stopped the prince ; when, as if every breast
One universal sorrow had possest,
Grief (grown into more noble passion) broke
The attentive silence, and thus swiftly spoke
Their resolutions :—' On, on, and lead
Us unto death, no critic eye shall read
Fear through the optics of our souls ; but give
Command to act—here 's not a heart durst live
Without obedience.' Comforted with this   180
Rich cordial, from his sorrow's dark abyss

(93)   H

Raised to resolves, whose greatness equalled all
His former glory, by their fatal fall
To darken the ensuing day, the prince
Gives a command to all his train—that since
Their own free votes elected death, they now
With souls that no terrestrial thought allow
A residence, 'gainst the next morn prepare
That wished-for freedom with himself to share.
   All sadly sat, expecting but that light   190
Whose near approach must to eternal night
Their last conductor be. A sudden, still,
And doleful silence, such as oft doth fill
The room where sick men slumber, when their friends
Stand weeping by, to contemplation bends
Their busy thoughts; within each troubled breast,
Being to leave the mansion she'd possessed
So long, yet with so short a warning, all
Her faculties the frighted soul did call
Forth of the bosom of those causes, in   200
Whose form they'd fettered to their crasis been,
To join those powers (yet strong in living breath)
For her assistance in the grasp of death.
   The whispering trumpet having called them by
Such sharp notes, as, when powerful foes are nigh
Retreating, parties use, all swiftly rise
From bended knees, and the last sacrifice
They e'er expect to pay to Heaven, until
Their soul's last gasp the vocal organs fill.
Concluded was the last sad interview,   210
The prince was marched, Pharonnida withdrew.
And now, all from the opened ports were in
A swift march sallying, had their speed not been
Thus swiftlier stopped:—Those scattered horse that fled
The battle to the Epirot's court had sped
So well in their embassage, that the prince,
Whom the least negligence might now convince
Of want of love, proud of so fair a chance
To show 's affection, swiftly doth advance
With a vast army toward them. Lest the fear   220
Prevailing danger, ere their strength come near
To their necessitated friends, might force
Them to unworthy articles, some horse
Selected are, whose swifter speed might, by
A desperate charge broke through their foes, supply
Their fainting friends. The much desired command
Of these few men, committed to the hand
Of brave Argalia, (ne'er more blest than now
In serving the fair princess), did allow
His sword so fair a field to write the story   230
Of honour in, that his unblasted glory

Beyond this day shall live—outlive the reach
Of long-armed envy, and those weak souls teach,
That fear the frowns of Fate, in spite of all,
Heroic Virtue sits too high to fall.
  With the day's close they take their march, and, ere
The silver morning on her brow did bear
The burnished guilt o' the sun's warm rays, arrive
In view o' the place. When Fortune, that did strive
To crown their hopes, had wrapped the earth in thick   240
And heavy mists, the sluggish morning, sick
Of midnight surfeits, from her dewy bed
Pale and discoloured rose. This curtain spread
To veil their plot in, they assault their foes ;
Which when surprised could not themselves dispose
Fit for resistance, but whilst some did fly
From the distracting danger, others die
To their neglect a sacrifice. The swift
Alarum, like a rude wind's circling drift,
Hurries confusion through the field, and shook   250
The trembling soldier ; some unclad forsook
Their half-fired cabins ; death's large gripe did take
Whole troops that destiny ordained to wake
No more till dooms-day, and in 's march prevents
The unition of unrallied regiments.
  This frighted language of confusion heard
By those o' the castle, which were now prepared
For their last desperate sally, swiftly draws
Them to assist their friends ; and though the cause,
Being yet unknown, was only thought to be   260
Some private jar grown to a mutiny ;
Or else the noise the enemy had made,
When all their force was drawing to invade
Them in their works : howe'er they stand not to
Consult with reason, but, as striving who
Shall first encounter death, each several hand
Sought for his own from those that did withstand
His rage-directed strength. Their cannon in
A funeral peal went off, whose steam had been
Their covert to the camp ; where finding such   270
A wild confusion, they assisted much
The fortune of the day, which now was grown
Indubitable—they might call their own
A glorious conquest. The thick sulphury cloud,
Whose dismal shade did that destruction shroud,
Rent with those thunder claps, dissolved into
A shower of blood ; what she vouchsafed to do,
Fortune lends light to show them. Having left
Their camp, whilst darkness did protect a theft

255 unition] Singer ' union,' which seems to me rather a bad emendation.

That only stole dishonour, which they were 280
Now in an open flight enforced to bear,
They see Almanzor's broken troops o'erspread
The neighbouring fields: those clouds of men that fled,
Being pursued by companies so small,
That they appeared but like those drops that fall
After a storm. Yet, as the labouring heart
Long struggles for that life, which doth depart
From the less noble members to lend aid
To her in death's pale conflict, having staid
Some of his best commanders, hoping by 290
Their valour to recall the rest, with high
Undaunted force, Almanzor doth oppose
His enemy's pursuit, till like to enclose
Him in, disdaining the reproachful end
He must expect, no longer stands to attend
The glimmering light of hope: the field he leaves
To conquering Argalia, but deceives
Him of himself—the prize most sought for; which
When lost beyond recovery, he grown rich
In shining honour, that, like sun-beams placed 300
Within a field of gules, by being defaced,
Had beautified his armour. That dark mist,
Which did at first such contradictions twist,
That he both curst, and blest it—one, 'cause 't did
Aid his design, the other, 'cause it hid.
His heaven of beauty in their dewy bed
Had left the blushing roses, and was fled
Upon the wings o' the wind. With wonder now
Discovered colours taught each party how
To know their friends. The royal standard in 310
The prince's party had developed been,
By that fair signal to discover who
Was present there. But ere Argalia to
That place arrived, Pharonnida, who had,
Whilst desperation all her beauties clad
In the pale robes of fear, heard all the loud
Shock of the conflict; but, until the cloud
Removed his fatal curtain, never knew
How near the hour of her delivery drew;
That being dissolved, through those which grief had raised 320
In her fair eyes, did see, and seeing praised
Just Heaven which sent it. Each of those that
Fought for her she commends; but wonders at,
Although unknown, the lightning valour she
Saw in Argalia, whilst with just rage he
Unravels nature's workmanship—a rent
Which were a sin, if not a punishment,

304 did] The text, which is probable and characteristic enough, is Singer's. Orig.
one cause did ' and in next line ' cause' without apostrophe.

And from the slender web of life did send
Forth rebels' souls, fast as each busy fiend
That wait their fall transport them. Fain she would,	330
Ere known, conceit 'twere he, but how he should
Come there, and so attended, did exceed
Imagination. Thus whilst her hopes feed
On strange desires, being come near unto
The coach wherein she sat, prepared to do
His love's oblations, he that face disarms;
Which, when beheld, by those attractive charms,
Within the centre of her best desires,
Contracted all her hopes, whose life expires
Soon as they're crowned with wished success. Too great	340
A distance parts them yet—she leaves her seat,
And flies to his embraces, but concealed
Her passion in his merit, being revealed
To him alone, whose better judgement knew,
That, in those spirit-breathing beams that flew
Through the fair casements of her eyes, did move
The secret language of an ardent love.
　　This conflict of her passions, which had been
Fought betwixt fear and hope, was settled in
A silent joy, that from her noble breast	350
Struggled for passage; whilst Argalia, blest
Above his hopes, in burning kisses seals
His service on her virgin hand, that steals
From thence new flames into her heart; which ere
Fed with desire, e'en whilst she did prepare
To entertain those welcome guests, appears
The prince, who now, thawed from the icy fears
Of desperation, was come there to give
Thanks to his unknown friends; but words did live
Within a place too barren to bestow	360
That fruitful zeal, whose plenty did o'erflow
His eyes, those clouded orators, which till
Disburthened did capacious passion fill.
　　This moist gale o'er, when now they had awhile
Melted in joy, clothing it with a smile,
He thus unfolds his comfort: ' Blessed Fates,
You have out-tried my charity, he hates
All real virtue, that confesses not
My care of thee was but an unknown spot
To this large world of satisfaction.'—Here	370
Kind sorrow stopped his voice again. When fear
Their enemies might rally, and i' the bud
Blast all their blooming joys, even whilst the blood
Reeked on his sword, leaving their eyes to pay
Pursuing prayers, Argalia posts away,

<hr>

330 wait, transport] Singer, with his usual well-intentioned officiousness, 'waite'
and 'transports.'

But finds his foes dispersed, excepting one
Stout regiment, whose desperation, grown
To valour, spite of all pursuers, made
Good their retreat; till forced at length to shade
Themselves from the pursuing danger in 380
A deep dark cave, whose spacious womb had been
Their receptacle, when unlawful theft
Was their profession. In this place they'd left
Their dearest pledges, as most confident
Those dark meanders would their loss prevent.
 These stout opposers being protected here,
Before Argalia brought his army near,
Had fortified the narrow pass, and now
Presume of safety, since none else knew how
Without their leave to enter. Hemmed about 390
With all the castle foot, his horse sent out
To clear the field, the careful general sees;
Then every quarter made secure, he frees
His own from all suspected danger. While
This busy siege did better things beguile
Of some few steps of time, the prince arrives,
To see the leaguer, where each captain strives
With entrance to be honoured: but in vain
The subtle engineer here racks his brain;
The mountains yield not to their cannon shock, 400
Nor mine could pierce the marble-breasted rock.
 Thus whilst they lay despairing e'er to force
A place so difficult, with some few horse
Only attended, the vexed prince surrounds
The spacious hill, whose uncouth sight confounds
His ablest guides; making a stand to view
A promontory, on whose brow there grew
A grove of stately cedars, from a dark
And hidden cleft, proud of so rich a mark,
Some muskets are discharged; which missing, by 410
A desperate sally's seconded. To fly
The danger thorough such a dreadful way
As now they were to pass, was not to stay—
But hasten ruin; though too weak, in fight
More safety lay, than an unworthy flight.
 But valour, like the royal eagle by
A cloud of crows o'ermastered, less to die
With honour, had no refuge left; and that
Here each plebeian gains. When, frighted at
The unusual clamour, with such troops as were 420
Most fit for speed, Argalia was come there—
Arrived even with that minute which first saw
His prince a captive. Now the rebels draw
Back to their private sally-port, but are
      415 an] Singer ' in ' perhaps unnecessarily.

Too speedily pursued to enter far
Within their dark meanders, ere o'ertook
By their enraged foes, who had forsook
Their other stations, and to this alone
Drew all their forces, entering the unknown
And horrid cave, whose troubled womb till then   430
Ne'er such a colic felt. Argalia's men,
Following so brave a leader, boldly tread
Through the rock's rugged entrails ; those that fled,
Though better skilled in their obscure retreat,
No safety find. The cave's remotest seat
Was now the stage of death ; together thronged,
After their swords had life's last step prolonged,
There all the villains in despair had died,
Had not the fear their prince in such a tide
Of blood might have been shipwrecked ; whom to save,   440
A general pardon to the rest is gave.
   And now the dreadful earthquake, which had turned
The rock to Ætna, could its top have burned
With subterranean fires, being ceased ; the prince,
Desirous by his knowledge to convince
Those word-deep wonders, which report had spread
Of that strange cave, commands some to be led
By an old outlaw, whose experience knew
The uncouth vault's remotest corners, to
Those seats of horror. Which performed, and word   450
Returned again, the danger did afford
Subject for nobler spirits ; forthwith he,
Attended by Argalia, goes to see
What had affrighted them. The dreadful way
Through which he passed, being steep and rugged, lay
Between two black and troubled streams, that through
The cleft rock rolled with horrid noise, till to
An ugly lake, whose heavy streams did lie
Unstirred with air, they come, and there are by
That black asphaltos swallowed. A strange sound   460
Of yelling dragons, hissing snakes, confound
Each trembling auditor ; till comforted
By bold Argalia venturing first to tread
On stones, which did like ruined arches lie
Above the surface of the lake, he 's by
Their aid brought to an ancient tower, that stood
Fixed in the centre of the lazy flood :—
Its basis founded on a rock, whose brow,
With age disfigured into clefts, did now
With loud and speedy ruin threaten to   470
Crush all beneath it ; round about it flew
On sooty wings such ominous birds as hate
The cheerful day ; vipers and scorpions sate
Circled in darkness, till the cold damp breath

(99)

Of near concreted vapours, singed to death
B' the numerous light of torches, which did shine
Through the whole mountain's convex, and refine
Air with restraint corrupted, forcing way
By conquering flames recalls the banished day.
  Come now to a black tower, which seemed to be   480
The throne of some infernal deity,
That his extended laws reaches unto
The brazen gate, whose folded leaves withdrew
Assaults their eyes with such a flux of light,
That, as the dim attendants of the night
In bashful duty shun the prince of day,
So their lost tapers unto this give way;
Whilst it, with wonder that belief outgrew,
Transports their sights to the amazing view
Of so much beauty, that the use of sense   490
Was lost in more than human excellence.
  A glorious room, so elegantly fair
In 'ts various structure, that the riotous heir
O' the eastern crescent that might choose to be
The theatre of shining majesty,
They now behold; yet than its mighty strength,
Which had preserved such beauty from the length
Of Age's iron talons, there appear
More rare perfections—the large floor, of clear
Transparent emeralds, lent a lustre to   500
The oval roof; whose scarce seen ground was blue,
Studded with sparkling gems, whose brightness lent
The beauties of the vaulted firmament
To all beneath their beams; the figured walls,
Embossed with rare and antic sculptury, calls
For th' next observance: though the serious eye,
The way to truth in secret mystery
Here having lost, lets the dark text alone,
To view the beauties of a glorious throne,
Which, placed within the splendid room, did stand   510
Beneath an ivory arch, o'er which the hand
Of art, in golden hieroglyphics, had
The story of ensuing fate unclad,
But vainly, since the art-defective times
Struck nought but discords on those well-tuned chimes.
  Upon the throne, in such a glorious state
As earth's adorèd favourites, there sate
The image of a monarch, vested in
The spoils of nature's robes, whose price had been
A diadem's redemption; his large size,   520
Beyond this pigmy age, did equalize
The admired proportion of those mighty men,
Whose cast-up bones, grown modern wonders, when
Found out, are carefully preserved to tell

(100)

Posterity—how much these times are fell
From Nature's youthful strength; if ['t] be not worse,
Our sin's stenography, the dwarfish curse
Ordained for large-sized luxury. Before
The throne, a lamp, whose fragrant oils had more
Perfumed the room than all the balmy wealth   530
Of rich Arabia, stood; light, life, and health,
Dwelt in its odours, but what more contents
The pleased spectators, that fair hand presents
The rest t' the view :—the image to declare
Of whom the effigies was, on 's front did bear
A regal crown, and in his hand sustained
A threatening sceptre; but what more explained
Antiquity's mysterious dress was seen
In a small tablet; which, as if 't had been
Worth more observance than what Fate exprest   540
In unknown figures, he did gently rest
His left hand on, as if endeavouring by
That index to direct posterity,
How in their wonder's altitude to praise
The deeper knowledge of those wiser days,
By reading in such characters as Time
Learned in her nonage—this—in antic rhyme,

    When striving to remove this light,
    It princes leaves involved to night,
    The time draws near, that shall pull down   550
    My old Morea's triple crown;
    Uniting, on one royal head,
    What to disjoin such discord bred:
    But let the more remote take heed,
    For there's a third ordained to bleed;
    For when I'm read, not understood,
    Then shall Epirus' royal blood,
    By ways no mortal yet must know,
    Within the Aetolian channel flow.

This strange inscription read, not only by   560
The prince, but those whom wonder had drawn nigh
The sacred room, their fancies' civil war
Grows full of trouble; 'tis a text so far
Beyond a comment, that their judgements, in
Enigmas mazed, had long let motion been
In epileptic wonder lost, until
(As that alone contained their dreaded ill)
The greater part with joined consents advise
To have the lamp removed, since in it lies,
If those lines prove prophetic, the linked fate   570
Of all Ietian princes. Which debate

549 to] Singer 'in.'   571 Ietian] In the extraordinary confusion of proper names,
which has been already noticed, it would probably be quite vain to guess at this.

Being carried in the affirmative, the rest
Drew back, whilst bold Argalia forward prest;
But's thus soon staid;—the stone, on which he stept
Next, was by art so framed, that it had kept
Concealed an engine's chiefest spring, which, by
The least weight touched, in furious haste let fly
Unpractised wheels, and with such vigour strook
The sceptre on the long-lived lamp—it shook
Its crystal walls to dust;—not thunder's strong   580
Exagitations, when it roars among
Heaps of congested elements, a sound
More dreadful makes. But what did most confound
Weak trembling souls, was the thick darkness that
Succeeds the dying flame; which wondering at,
Whilst all remain, art's feeble aids supply
The lamp's lost virtue with new lights, but by
Cold damps so darkened, that contracted night
Scorned their weak flames, showing that hallowed light
Contained more sacred virtues. Now, as Fate   590
Had only to that hour prolonged the date
Of all within, a sudden change, to dust
The mighty body turns; consuming rust
Had ate the brazen imagery, and left
No sign of what till then safe from the theft
Of time remained; darkness had repossessed
The sullen cave to an eternal rest;
In the rude chaos of their ashes, all
Art's lively figures in an instant fall.
     Pleased with the sight of these strange objects more   600
Than with war's dangers he was vexed before,
The prince with all his train of conquerors now
Is gone to teach the expecting army how
To share their wonder; but not far from thence
Removes, before confirmed intelligence
Acquaints him with the Epirot's march; who in
His swift advance so fortunate had been,
That falling on such as the morning's flight
Flattered with hope, they there met endless night
At unawares: but of these added numbers   610
Was cursed Almanzor none; yet Justice slumbers
I' the prosecution of his unripe fate,
Which must more horrid sins accumulate:
Before cut off, his clamorous guilt must call
For vengeance louder, and grow hectical
With custom, till the tables of his shame
Into oblivion rot his loathèd name.

THE END OF THE THIRD CANTO.

Canto IV

THE ARGUMENT

From war's wide breaches, whence his brave friends had
  With victory brought him, the old prince arrived
In safety, whilst fear punishes the bad,
  Rewards that virtue which his cause revived.

In which brave act, Argalia's merits met
  With a reward that e'en desert outgrew,
Whilst him it the fair princess' guardian set,
  The root on which love's fruit to ripeness grew.

THAT too inferior branch, which strove to rise
With the basilic to anastomize,
Thus drained, the state's plethoric humours are
Reduced to harmony ; that blazing star,
Which had been lifted by rebellious breath
To 's exaltation, in the House of Death
Now lay oppressed. Which victory complete,
Leaving his army where before the seat
O' the rebels was, his entertainment by
The welcome harbinger of victory   10
Before prepared, the pleased Epirot goes
With an exalted joy to visit those
His goodness, whilst unknown, relieved ; where he
Such noble welcome finds, as not to be
Imagined but by grateful souls that know
The strength of courtesy, when 'twould o'erflow
Those merits, which, whilst love incites to praise
Our friend's deserts, to pyramids we raise.
    The narrow confines of Alcithius' wall,
Which kept them safe from dangers past, too small   20
Grows for that present triumph, that blots out
All thoughts of grief, but what are spent about
Thanksgiving for delivery ; which they do
Perform in sports, whose choice delights might woo
Cold anchorites from their sullen cells. The earth,
The air, the sea, all, in a plenteous birth,
Exhausted their rich treasuries to pay
Tribute to their desires ; which, could Time stay
Her chariot wheels from hurrying down the hill
Of feeble nature, man's vain thoughts would fill   30
With subaltern delights, most highly prized,
Till the conclusion, Death, hath annalized
The doubtful text with what lets mortals know
Their blooming joys must drop to shades below.

29 Her] Singer alters, on general principles, to ' His.' But Chamberlayne is
so eccentric that he might have imagined Time as feminine, which is not at all
unthinkable.

That great eclipse of glory's rays, within
Whose shades sad Corinth had benighted been,
Since, like a widowed turtle, first she sate
A mourner for her wandering prince's fate ;
Now, like the day's recovered reign, breaks forth
In fuller lustre. All excelling worth,   40
That honoured virtue, or loved beauty, placed,
Her ornaments, with their appearance graced
Those public triumphs she prepares to meet
The princes in ; in every splendid street
The various pride of Persia strove to outvie
Rich English wool dipped in the Tyrian dye :
Each shop shines bright, and every merchant shows
How little to domestic toil he owes,
By the displaying beauteous wardrobes, where-
The world's each part may justly claim a share :   50
Though what in all art's stiff contention lent
Most lustre, was the windows' ornament—
Fair constellations of bright virgins, that,
Like full-blown flowers, first to be wondered at,
Display their beauties, but that past withal,
Tempt some kind hand to pluck them ere they fall.
    Their entrance in this triumph made, whilst now
Each busy artist is endeavouring how
To court their fancies, Time's small stock to improve,
The grave Epirot, whose designs toward love   60
Yet only by ambition led, had made
His first approach so seeming retrograde
By state's nice cautions, and what did presage
More ill—the inequality of age,
That when converse his private captive led,
His largest hopes on the thin diet fed
Of a paternal power ; assisted by
Whose useful aid, with all the industry
Of eager love, he still augments that fire
Which must consume, not satisfy desire.   70
But, as occasion warned him to prevent
Unequal flames, he but few days had spent
In love's polemics, ere unpractised art,
From this calm field to war's more serious part
Is sadly summoned. Those large conquests he
Had triumphed in, whilst glorious victory
Waited on 's sword, too spacious to be kept
Obedient whilst that glittering terror slept
In an inactive peace, disclaiming all
The harsh injunctions of proud victors, fall   80
Off from 's obedience ; and to justify
Their bold revolt, to the unsafe refuge fly
Of a defensive power. To crush whose pride,
With such a force as an impetuous tide

Assaults the shore's defence, he's forced to take
A march so sad, as souls when they forsake
The well-known mansions of their bodies to
Tread death's uncertain paths, and there renew
Acquaintance with eternity; perplexed
To hear those new combustions, but more vexed   90
With love's proud flames burning. In which we'll leave
Him on his hasty voyage, and receive
A smile from the fair princess' fate ; which, till
Enjoyment stifles strong desire, will fill
The tragic scene no more, but, with as sad
A progress to her hopes, as ever had
Poor virgin to the throne of Love, will frame
Those harsh phylacteries, which in Cupid's name
She must obey, unless she will dispense
With sacred vows, and martyr innocence.   100
    These storms blown o'er, and the Epirot gone,
Her father, that till now had waited on
His entertainment, with a serious eye
Looks o'er his kingdom's wounds, and doth supply
Each part, which in this late unnatural war
Was grown defective. Unto some that are
Not lethargized in ill he gently lays
Refreshing mercies ; sometimes, danger stays
From an approaching gangrene, by applying
Corroding threats ; but unto those that, flying   110
All remedies prescribed, had mortified
Their loyalty, stern justice soon applied
The sword of amputation : which care past,
As 'twas his greatest, so becomes his last—
Pharonnida he places, where she might
At once enjoy both safety and delight.
    Her thoughts' clear calm, too smooth for th' turbulent
And busy city, wants that sweet content
The private pleasures of the country did
Afford her youth ; but late attempts forbid   120
All places far remote : which to supply,
He unto one directs his choice, that by
Its situation did participate
Of all those rural privacies, yet sate
Clothed in that flowery mantle, in the view
O' the castle walls, which, as placed near it to
Delight not trouble, in full bulk presents
Her public buildings' various ornaments.
    This beauteous fabric, where the industrious hand
Of Art had Nature's midwife proved, did stand   130
Divided from the continent b' the wide
Arms of a spacious stream, whose wanton pride
In cataracts from the mountains broke, as glad
Of liberty to court the valley, had

Curled his proud waves, and stretched them to enclose
That type of paradise, whose crown-top rose
From that clear mirror, as the first light saw
Fair Eden 'midst the springs of Havilah ;
So fresh as if its verdant garments had
Been in the first creation's beauties clad,   140
Ere, by mistaking of the fatal tree,
That blooming type of blest eternity,
Subjected was, by man's too easy crime,
Unto the sick vicissitudes of time.
    Nor was she in domestic beauty more
Than prospect rich—the wandering eye passed o'er
A flowery vale, smooth, as it had been spread
By nature for the river's fragrant bed.
At the opening of that lovely angle met
The city's pride, as costlier art had set   150
That masterpiece of wit and wealth to show—
Unpolished nature's pleasures were below
Her splendid beauties, and unfit to be
Looked on, 'less in the spring's variety :
Though from the palace where in prospect stood
All that nice art or plainer nature would,
If in contention, show to magnify
Their power, did stand, yet now appeared to vie
That prospect which the city lent ; unless,
Diverted from that civil wilderness,   160
The pathless woods, and ravenous beasts within,
Whose bulk were but the metaphors for sin,
We turn to view the stately hills, that fence
The other side o' the happy isle, from whence
All that delight or profit could invent
For rural pleasures, was for prospect sent.
    As Nature strove fór something uncouth in
So fair a dress, the struggling streams are seen,
With a loud murmur rolling 'mongst the high
And rugged clifts ; one place presents the eye   170
With barren rudeness, whilst a neighbouring field
Sits clothed in all the bounteous spring could yield
Here lovely landscapes, where thou might'st behold,
When first the infant morning did unfold
The day's bright curtains, in a spacious green,
Which Nature's curious art had spread between
Two bushy thickets, that on either hand
Did like the fringe of the fair mantle stand,
A timorous herd of grazing deer ; and by
Them in a shady grove, through which the eye   180
Could hardly pierce, a well-built lodge, from whence
The watchful keeper's careful diligence

162 bulk] Singer ' bulks ' obviously but perhaps unnecessarily.
170 clifts] Orig. ' clefts ' as often.

Secures their private walks; from hence to look
On a deep valley, where a silver brook
Doth in a soft and busy murmur slide
Betwixt two hills, whose shadows strove to hide
The liquid wealth they were made fruitful by,
From full discoveries of the distant eye.

Here, from fair country farms that had been
Built 'mongst those woods as places happy in   190
Their privacy, the first salutes of light
Fair country virgins meet, cleanly and white
As were their milky loads: so free from pride,
Though truly fair, that justly they deride
Court's nice contentions, and by freedom prove
More blest their lives—more innocent their love.
Early as these, appears within the field
The painful husbandman, whose labour steeled
With fruitful hopes, in a deep study how
To improve the earth, follows his slow-paced plough.   200

Near unto these, a shepherd, having took
On a green bank placed near a purling brook
Protection from the sun's warm beams, within
A cool fresh shade, truly contented in
That solitude, is there endeavouring how
On 's well-tuned pipe to smooth the furrowed brow
Of careful Want, seeing not far from hence
His flock, the emblems of his innocence.
Where the more lofty rock admits not these
Domestic pleasures, Nature there did please   210
Herself with wilder pastimes ;—on those clifts,
Whose rugged heads the spacious mountain lifts
To an unfruitful height, amongst a wild
Indomitable herd of goats, the mild
And fearful cony, with her busy feet,
Makes warmth and safety in one angle meet.

From this wild range, the eye, contracted in
The island's narrow bounds, would think 't had been
I' the world before, but now were come to view
An angel-guarded paradise; till to   220
A picture's first rude catagraph the art
Of an ingenious pencil doth impart
Each complement of skill: or as the court
To the rude country; as each princely sport
That brisks the blood of kings, to those which are
The gross-souled peasant's rude delight—so far
These objects differ: here well-figured Nature
Had put on form, and to a goodly stature,
On whose large bulk more lasting arts were spent,
Added the dress of choicest ornament.   230

---

189 **farms**] Chamberlayne, who always spells 'alarum' 'alarm,' apparently gave
'farm' the sound of 'farum.'

The stately mount, whose artificial crown
The palace was, to meet the vale stole down
In soft descents, by labour forced into
A sliding serpentine, whose winding clew
An easy but a slow descent did give
Unto a purling stream ; whose spring did live,
When from the hill's cool womb broke forth, within
A grotto ; whence before it did begin
To take its weeping farewell, into all
The various forms restrictive Art could call   240
Her elemental instruments unto
Obedience by, it courts the admiring view
Of pleased spectators—here, exalted by
Clear aqueducts, in showers it from those high
Supporters falls ; now turned into a thin
Vapour, in that heaven's painted bow is seen ;
Now it supplies the place of air, and to
A choir of birds gives breath, which all seemed flew
From thence for fear, when the same element,
With such a noise as seas imprisoned rent   250
Including rocks, doth roar : which rude sound done,
As noble conquerors who, the battle won,
From the loud thunders of impetuous war
To the calm fields of peaceful mercies, are
By manly pity led ; so, Proteus-like,
Returned from what did fear or wonder strike,
The liquid nymph, resuming her own shape
Within a marble square, a clear escape,
Till from her winding stream the river takes
Still fresh supplies, from that fair fountain makes.   260
    Upon those banks which guarded her descent,
Both for her odour and her ornament,
Lilies and fragrant roses there were set ;
To heighten whose perfume, the violet
And maiden primrose, in their various dress,
Steal through that moss, whose humble lowliness
Preserves their beauties ; whilst Aurora's rose,
And that ambitious flower that will disclose
The full-blown beauties of herself to none
Until the sun mounts his meridian throne,   270
(Like envied Worth, together with the view
Of the beholders), being exposed unto
Each storm's rough breath, in that vicissitude
Find that their pride their danger doth include,
When scorched with heat or burthened with a shower,
From blooming beauty sinks the fading flower ;
Though here defended by a grove that twined
Mutual embraces, and with boughs combined,
Protects the falling stream, which it ne'er leaves,
Till thence the vale its flowery wealth receives.   280

Placed as the nobler faculty to this
Of vegetation, like an emphasis
Amongst the flowers of rhetoric, did stand
The gorgeous palace; where Art's curious hand
Had, to exceed example, centred in
One exact model what had scattered been—
But as those fragments which she now selects,
The glory of all former architects.
Here did the beauties of those temples shine,
Which Ephesus or sacred Palestine   290
Once boasted in; the Persian might from this
Take patterns for his famed Persepolis;
This, which had that fair Carian widow known,
Mausolus' tomb had ne'er a proverb grown,
But been esteemed, after her cost, by her
That did erect, a homely sepulchre.
    Though to describe this fabric be as far
Above my art as imitations are
Beneath its worth, yet if thy Fancy's eye
Would at its outside glance, receive it by   300
This cloudy medium.—On a stately square,
Which powerful art forced to a level where
The mountain highest rose, compassed about
With a thick grove, whose leafy veil let out
Its beauties so, 'tis at a distance seen,
A silver mount enamelled o'er with green,
The shining palace stood; whose outward form
Though such as if built for perpetual storm,
Yet in that strength appeared but armed to be
Beauty's protector: whose variety,   310
Though all met in an artful gracefulness,
In every square put on a several dress.
The sides, whose large balcones conveyed the eye
T' the fields' wild prospects, were supported by
A thousand pillars; where in mixture shone
The Parian white and red Corinthian stone,
Supporting frames, where in the like art stood
Smooth ivory mixed with India's swarthy wood:
All which, with gold, and purer azure brought
From Persian artists, in mosaics wrought,   320
The curious eye into meanders led,
Until diverted by a sight that bred
More real wonder.—The rich front wherein
By antic sculpture, all that ere had been
The various acts of their preceding kings,
So figured was; no weighty metal brings

296 erect] Singer supplies ' 't'—' erect—'t.' But though Chamberlayne certainly
does not go out of his way to avoid these uglinesses, one need not go out of one's way
to insert them.
324 antic] ' antic' of course = ' antique.'

Aught to enhance its worth, Art did compose
Each emblem of such various gems—all chose
Their several colours—Under a sapphire sky
Here cheerful emeralds, chaste smaragdi lie—   330
A fresh green field, in which the armèd knights
Were all clad in heart-cheering chrysolites,
With rubies set, which to adorn them twist
Embraces with the temperate amethyst ;
For parts unarmed—here the fresh onyx stood,
And Sardia's stone appeared like new-drawn blood ;
The Proteus-like achates here was made
For swords' fair hilts, but for the glittering blade,
Since all of rich and precious gems was thus
Composed, was showed of flaming pyropus :   340
And lest aught here that's excellent should want,
The ladies' eyes were shining adamant.
These glorious figures, large as if that in
Each common quar these glittering gems had been
By sweaty labourers digged, united by
Successful art, unto the distant eye
Their mixed beams with such splendid lustre sent,
That comets, with whose fall the firmament
Seems all on fire, amazes not the sight
With such a full and sudden flux of light.   350
    As lines extended from their centre, hence
Unto the island's clear circumference,
Four flowery glades, whose odoriferous dress
Tempted the weary to forgetfulness,
Cutting the mountain into quadrants, led
Into the valley—Pleasure's humbler bed.
Where come, if Nature's stock can satisfy
The fancy at the fountains of the eye,
'Twas here performed, in all that did include
What active mirth or sacred solitude   360
Could happy call—Groves never seen b' the eye
O' the universe, whose pleasing privacy
Was more retired from treacherous light than those,
To hide from Heaven, Earth's first Offender chose.
    When Contemplation, the kind mother to
All thoughts that e'er in sacred rapture flew
Toward celestial bowers, had here refined
The yet imperfect embryos of the mind ;
To recreate contracted spirits by
The soul's best medicine—fresh variety,   370
An easy walk conducts them unto all
That active sports did e'er convenient call.
All which, like a fair theatre b' the bank
O' the river verged, was guarded by a rank
Of ancient elms ; whose lofty trunks, embraced
By clasping vines, with various colours graced

Their spreading branches—Whose proud brows, being crowned
With stately walks, did from that ample round
The well-pleased eye to every place convey,
That in the island's humble level lay.   380
   To guard her court, a hundred gentlemen,
Such as had glorified their valour, when
Tried in her father's wars, attended; which,
Commanded by Argalia, did enrich
His merit with such fair reward, that all
His better stars, should they a synod call,
Those fires convened ne'er with more glorious light
Could clothe his hopes; his fortune's dim-eyed night
Enflamed to noon, and the fair princess blest
By the same power; for though his fate invest   390
His noble soul within the obscure mask
Of an unknown descent, his fame shall ask,
In time to come, a chronicle, and be
The glory of that royal family
From whence he sprung. But ere he must attain
The top of Fortune's wheel, that iron chain,
By whose linked strength it turns, too oft will grate
Him with most hot afflictions; his wise fate
Digs deep with miseries, before it lays
The ground-work of his fame, which then shall raise,   400
On the firm basis of authentic story,
To him eternal pyramids of glory.
   Thou that art skilled in Love's polemics here
Wish they may rest awhile; and though drawn near
A sadder fate, if Pity says—too rath
'Tis to let Sorrow sad the scene, we'll bathe
Our pen awhile in nectar, though we then
Steep it in gall again. The Spring did, when
The princess first did with her presence grace
This house of pleasure, with soft arms embrace   410
The Earth—his lovely mistress—clad in all
The painted robes the morning's dew let fall
Upon her virgin bosom; the soft breath
Of Zephyrus sung calm anthems at the death
Of palsy-shaken Winter, whose large grave—
The earth, whilst they in fruitful tears did lave,
Their pious grief turned into smiles, they throw
Over the hearse a veil of flowers; the low
And pregnant valleys swelled with fruit, whilst Heaven
Smiled on each blessing its fair hand had given.   420
   Becalmed on this pacific sea of pleasure,
No boisterous wave appearing, the rich treasure
Of Love, being ballast with content, did fear
No threatening storm, so safe a harbour near,

400 ground-work] Orig. ' ground-*fork*' not perhaps possibly.
416 lave] Orig. 'leave' which is obviously worth noting.

As the object whence it sprung. Such royal sports,
As take their birth from the triumphant courts
Of happy princes, did contract the day
To pitied beauty; Time steals away
On downy feet, whose loss since it bereaves
Them of no more than what new birth receives   430
From the next teeming day, by none is thought
Worth the lamenting. Sometimes, rocked i' the soft
Arms of the calmest pleasures, they behold
A sprightly comedy the sins unfold
Of more corrupted times; then, in its high
Cothurnal scenes, a lofty tragedy
Erects their thoughts, and doth at once invite,
To various passions, sorrow and delight.
    Time, motion's aged measurer, includes
Not more, in all the hours' vicissitudes,   440
Than their oft changing recreations; that,
When the sun's lofty pride sat smiling at
The earth's embroidered robes, or Winter's cold
And palsied hand did those fresh beauties fold
Up in her hoary plush, each season lends
Delights of 'ts own—such a beguiled time spends
Its stock of hours unwasted on, in chaste
Though private sports. Here happy lovers past
Fancy's fresh youth, whose first attempts did prove
Too innocent for th' sophistry of love;   450
There scornful beauty, or the envious eye
Of jealous rivals, ne'er afflicts—all by
An equal and a noble height so blest,
Pride none had raised, nor poverty depressed.

THE END OF THE FOURTH CANTO.

Canto V

THE ARGUMENT

Whilst serene joy sat smiling in her court,
    As shadows to illustrate virtue by.
Fantastic Love becomes the princess' sport,
    Whose harsher dictates she ere long must try.

For now suspicion, Virtue's secret foe,
    Fired with Argalia's just-deserved fame,
Makes her great father think each minute slow,
    Till separation had allayed the flame.

LEST that her court, which seems composed of all
That's great or good, the o'erweening world should call
Perfection's height—a word which, whilst on earth,
Vain as Delight, only from name takes birth—

In this the largest and most glorious sphere
E'er greatness moved in, some few stars appear
To virtue retrograde. The informing spirit—
Love, by whose motion on the pole of merit
This bright orb turned, e'en 'mongst these heroes finds
A pair of followers, whose imperfect minds   10
Transgressed his dictates; and, though no offence
So full of guilt as foul incontinence
Durst here approach, by ways less known unto
What love intends, those various figures drew,
Whose aspects ne'er more near conjunction move,
Than eyes—the slight astronomy of love.
   That new Platonic malady, the way
By which imperfect eunuchs do betray
Nature's diseases to contempt, whilst by
Such slight repast they strive to satisfy   20
Love's full desires, which pines or else must crave
More than thin souls in separation have,
Being lately by some sick fantastics brought
But near the Court, within it long had sought
For residence, till entertained by two
Whose meeting souls no more distinction knew
Than sex, a difference which, whilst here it grows
Toward Heaven, it to corporeal organs owes.
But since that these so uncouth actors here
But as intruders on the scene appear,   30
Ere in their story we engulph too far,
Let's first behold them in their character.
   If e'er thy sober reason did submit
To suppling Mirth, that wanton child of Wit,
Beholding a Fantastic, drest in all
His vain delights, what's analogical
To our Acretius then conceive thou'st seen;
Though if compared, those short to him had been
As transcripts are to copies: to complete
A humorist, here Folly had chose a seat   40
'Mongst more than vulgar knowledge, and might pass
The same account an academic ass
Makes of his father's four-year charge, when he
Frights villagers with shreds of sophistry.
'Mongst foreign parts, of which, like Coriate,
He'd run through some, he had acquired to prate
By privilege; and, as if every nation
Contributed, is in each several fashion;
Which, like their tongues, all so imperfect find,
That both disguised his body and his mind.   50
Though self-conceit, vain youth's fantastic crime,
Made him steal singly from the front of time,
I' the medium, which but seldom proves the seat
For lust's wild fire or zeal's reflected heat,

(113)

He amorous grows; and doubting to prevail,
For all his wings caught Pegasus b' the tail,
And being before with Cupid's engines fired,
From his posteriors doubly was inspired.
  She that at first this sympathetic flame
Inspired him with, the court knew by the name   60
Of Philanta; to whom, all would impair
Their skill, that gave the epithet of fair,
Except Acretius,—since her beauty fit
For praises was, where paralleled by wit.
Yet now, although time's sad discovery tells—
Her Autumn's furrows were no parallels
In Beauty's sphere, those youthful forms being grown
So obsolete, scarce the vestigia 's shown:
A native pride and strange fantastic dress,
More admiration than e'er comeliness   70
Could do, acquires. She formerly had been
A great admirer of romances, in
Whose garb she now goes drest; a medley piece
Made up of India, Turkey, Persia, Greece,
With other nations, all enforced to be
Comprised within five foot's stenography.
Her wit, that had been critical, and ranged
'Mongst ladies' more than the ushers' legs, was changed
To gratify; and every word she said,
An apophthegm unto the chamber-maid,   80
From whom, her long experienced knowledge in
Some of the female mysteries of sin,
Had gained the applause of being skilled in all
That could prevent decaying beauty's fall.
  Acretius and she, being such a pair
As Nature when tired with more serious care
For recreation made, instructed by
Their meeting natures' secret sympathy,
Soon learn to love; but, as if now too wise
For youth's first dictates, Love's loose rules comprise   90
In such strict bounds, that each the object saw
Of their desires, like sacred things, some law,
Fear made obeyed, forbids the world to use,
Lest the adored enjoyment should abuse
Into contempt; nor are their meetings in
Those plainer paths—which their nice art calls sin—
At all performed;—that, the dull road unto
The bridal bed; this, the fantastic clew
To a delight, which doth in labyrinths sit,
None e'er beheld while they preserved their wit.   100
  Like wanton Jove committing secret rapes
On mortal beauties, they transmute their shapes
At every interview; now, in a dress
Resembling an Arcadian shepherdess,

(114)

She in the woods encounters him, whilst he,
Armed like a furious knight, resolved to be
Her ravisher, approaches, but, being by
Her prayers charmed into pity, there doth lie
Fettered in soft embraces; now he must
Turn hermit, and be tempted unto lust   110
By her, a lady errant; like distressed
Lovers, whose hopes by rigid friends oppressed
Pine to despair, they now are wandering in
Unhaunted groves, whose pensive shades had been
So oft their shady veil, that every tree,
In wreaths where love lay wrapped in mystery,
Held their included names—a subtile way
To the observant courtiers to betray
Their serious folly, which, from being their own
Delight, was now the sport o' the pages grown;   120
The pleasant offsprings of whose wanton wit
Disturb their peace, that, though secured they sit
In shady deserts, with as much of fear,
As wandering ladies, when the giant 's near,
They're still possessed; less terrible were all
The dreadful objects, Amadis de Gaul
Or wittier Quixote from their enemies
E'er met, than was the fear of a surprise
By those which did such strict observance take.
They thus their folly the court's laughter make.—   130
    Near to the island's utmost verge did lie
Retired e'en from Heaven's universal eye,
A deep dark vale; whose night-concealing shade
By a fresh river's silver stream was made
So sweetly cool, it often did invite
Pharonnida to meet the smooth delight
Of calm retirement there. Where, to impart
With Nature's bounty all that liberal Art
Thought fit for so remote a pleasure, stood
A grotto, where the macrocosm's cold blood   140
Ran more dispersed in various labyrinths then
It circulates within the veins of men.
    Hither the inventive lovers, who long sought
Some way which Fancy ne'er her followers taught
To express their serious folly in, repair,
Oft as the sun made the insalubrious air
Unfit for publick walks. To entertain
Them here with what exceeded all their vain
Delights before,—newly erected by
Successful art, each various deity   150
Old Fancy placed the sea's commanders, here
They with delight behold; but when drawn near
They saw, i' the midst o' the blue-eyed Tritons, placed
Neptune's and Thetis' chariot—yet not graced

With their unfinished figures, this they took
For so much favour, as they had forsook
Their thrones to give them place. But what adds yet
More to the future mirth, they swiftly fit
Themselves with habits, such as art had drew
Its fancies in—both of their robes being blue   160
Enchased with silver streams ; their heads, with fair
Dishevelled periwigs of sea-green hair,
Were both adorned ; circling whose crowns they wore
Wreathed coronets of flags ; his right hand bore
A golden trident ; hers, yet hardly red,
As if new plucked from the sea's frothy bed,
A branch of coral.—But whilst here they sit
Proudly adorned, both void of fear as wit,
The gates o' the grotto swiftly shutting in,
A torrent, such as if they'd seated been   170
At Nile's loud cataracts, by ways (before
Unseen) breaks forth ; by which the engine bore
From its firm station, floats aloft, and, by
A swift withdrawing of those bays which tie
Floods from commerce, is wafted forth into
A spacious pool ; where the bold artist drew
The unfathomed sea's epitome within
A circling wall, but such as might have been
A pattern to Rome's big-bulked pride, when they
Showed sea's loud battles for the land's soft play.   180
   Our amorous humorists, that must now appear,
This narrow sea's commanders, shook with fear,
Sit trembling—whilst the shrill-voiced Tritons sound
Their crooked shells, whose watery notes were drowned
B' the lofty laughter of that troop, they saw
Their pleased spectators ; for Pharonnida,
Being now with all her beauteous train come to
Behold this pageant, taught them how to view
A shame as dreadful as their fear, which yet
Was full of horror ; for though safe they sit   190
I' the floating chariot, yet the mounting waves
So boisterous grew, that e'en great Neptune craves
Himself relief, till frighted from all sense
By second dangers :—From that port from whence
They sallied forth, two well-rigged ships are now
Seen under sail, whose actions taught them how
Sea fights are managed, in a method that
They being too near engaged to tremble at,
By fear's slow conduct to confusion led,
Fall from their thrones ; and through the waves had fled 200
From shame to death, had they not rescued been
By swift relief—a courtesy that, in
Its first approach, though welcomed—when they come
To stand the shock o' the court's loud mirth, as dumb

As were the fishes they so late forsook,
Makes Mercy court them in a dreadful look.
   But, leaving these to pay with future hate
Each courtier's present mirth, a sadder fate
Commands my pen no longer to attend
On smooth delights, before it gives an end   210
To that ephemera of pleasure; which,
Whilst a free conversation did enrich
Their thoughts, too fast did ripen in the breasts
Of both our royal lovers, whose fate rests
Not long in downy slumbers, ere it starts
In vain phantasmas—Hope herself departs
In a distracted trembling. Their bright sphere
Of milder stars had now continued clear
So long, till what their smiling influence drew
From the unthankful earth contracted to   220
A veil of clouds; whose coolness, whilst some praised,
Obscured those beams by which they first were raised.
   Hell's subtle embryos—the ingratitudes
Of cursed Amphibia, whose disguise includes
Mischief's epitome, had often strook
In secret at their envied joys, which took
Ne'er its effects till now. So heavenly free
The virtuous princess was from what could be
Of human vice, she knew not to mistrust
It in another, but thinks all as just   230
As her own even thoughts; wherefore, without
Oppressing of her soul with the least doubt
Raised from suspicion, she dares let her see
She loved Argalia, though it could not be
Yet counted more than what his merits might
Claim as desert. But this small beam of light,
Through the prospective of suspicion to
Envy's malignant eye conveyed, to do
An act, informs the cursed Amphibia, that
Makes love lament for what she triumphed at.   240
Since virtue, Heaven's unspotted character,
On the beloved Argalia did transfer
Merits of too sublime a height to be
Shadowed with vice—from that flower's fragrancy
She sucks her venom ; and, from what had built
His glory, now intends to raise his guilt.
For though the prince no engines need to move
His passion's frame, but just desert—his love—
Her close endeavours are to heighten 't by
Praises that make affection jealousy;   250
Whose venom, having once possessed his soul,
It swiftly doth, like fatal charms, control

237 prospective] Singer 'perspective,' unnecessarily.

Reason's fair dictates; and although no fear
From such well-ordered actions could appear
To strengthen it, Argalia's merits caused
Some sad and sullen doubts, such as, when paused
Awhile upon, resolve their cure must be—
Their cause removed—though in that action he
From his breast's royal mansion doth exclude
The noblest virtue—generous gratitude.   260

  To cure this new-felt wound, and yet not give
Strong arguments—great virtues cannot live
Safe in corrupted courts—the poison's sent
In gilded pills.—A specious compliment,
To call him from his calm and quiet charge,
Pretends by new additions to enlarge
His full-blown fame, to an extent as far
As valour climbs in slippery heights of war :
Which now, though calmed in 's own dominions, by
A friendly league invites him to supply   270
The stout Epirot with an army that,
Though rich in valour, more was trembled at
For being commanded by Argalia, than
Composed of Sparta's most selected men.

  As if no grief could be commensurate
Unto their joys, but what did blast their fate
In its most blooming spring: our lovers were,
When first assaulted by the messenger
Of this sad news, sate, in the quiet shade—
A meeting grove of amorous myrtles, made   280
To veil the brow of a fair mount, whose sides
A beauteous robe of full-blown roses hides ;
In such discourse, the flying minutes spending,
As passion dictates, when firm vows are ending
Those parles by which love toward perfection went
In the obliging bliss of full consent.

  The fatal scroll received, and read until
She finds their parting doom ; the spring-tides fill
Her eyes, those crystal seas of grief—she stops—
Fans with a sigh her heart, then sheds some drops   290
Upon the guilty paper. Trembling fear
Plucks roses from her cheeks, which soon appear
Full-blown again with anger—red and white
Did in this conflict of her passions fight
For the pre-eminence. Which agony
Argalia noting, doubtful what might be
The cause of so much ill, he in his arms
Circles his saint ; with all the powerful charms
Of love's soft rhetoric, her lost pleasure strives
To call again ;—but no such choice flower thrives,   300

279 sate] Singer ' set ' : but I am not sure that the other is not right.

Though springs of tears thither invite this rest,
In the cold region of her grief-swollen breast.
   Long had she strove with grief's oppressive load
Ere sighs make way for this :—'Is thy abode
Become the parent of suspicion ? Look
On this, Argalia, there hath poison took
Its lodging underneath these flowers, whose force
Will blast our hopes—there, there, a sad divorce
'Twixt our poor loves is set, ere we more near
Than in desires have met.' As much of fear,   310
As could possess his mighty soul, did shake
His strenuous hand, whilst 'twas stretched forth to take
The letter from Pharonnida. Which he
Having looked o'er, and finding it to be
An honourable policy to part
Them without noise, he curtains o'er his heart,
Pale as was hers with fear, in a disguise
Which, though rage drew his soul into his eyes,
So polished o'er his passion—to her grief,
His own concealed, he thus applies relief :—   320
   'Dear virtuous princess, give your reason leave
But to look through this cloud, which doth receive
Its birth from nought but fear.—This honour, which
Your royal father pleases to enrich
My worthless fortunes with, will but prepare
Our future happiness.—The time we spare
From feeding on ambrosia, will increase
Our wealthy store, when the white wings of peace
Shall bear us back with victory ; there may,
Through the dark chaos of my fate, display   330
Some beam of honour ; though compared with thine
(That element of living flame) it shine
Dim as the pale-faced moon, when she lets fall
Through a dark grove her beams :—thy virtues shall
Give an alarum to my sluggish soul,
Whene'er it droops ; thy memory control
The weakness of my passions. When we strive
I' the heat of glorious battle, I'll revive
My drooping spirits with that harmony
Thy name includes—thy name, whose memory   340
(Dear as those relics a protecting saint
Sends humble votaries) mentioned, will acquaint
My thoughts with all that's good. Then calm again
This conflict of thy fears, I shall remain
Safe in the hail of death, if guarded by
Thy pious prayers—Fate's messengers that fly
On wings invisible, will lose the way,
Aimed at my breast, if thou vouchsafe to pray

345 hail] Singer 'vale'—a possibly right but rather large change.

(119)

To Heaven for my protection.—But if we
Ne'er meet again—yet, oh! yet let me be   350
Sometimes with pity thought on.'   At which word
His o'ercharged eyes no longer could afford
A room to entertain their tears; both wept,
As if they strove to quench that fire which kept
Light in the lamps of life, whose fortunes are
I' the House of Death, whilst Mars the regal star.
    Some time in silent sorrow spent, at length
The fair Pharonnida recovers strength,
Though sighs each accent interrupted, to
Return this answer:—'Wilt, oh! wilt thou do   360
Our infant love such injury—to leave
It ere full grown?   When shall my soul receive
A comfortable smile to cherish it,
When thou art gone?   They're but dull joys that sit
Enthroned in fruitless wishes; yet I could
Part, with a less expense of sorrow, would
Our rigid fortune only be content
With absence; but a greater punishment
Conspires against us—Danger must attend
Each step thou tread'st from hence; and shall I spend   370
Those hours in mirth, each of whose minutes lay
Wait for thy life?   When Fame proclaims the day
Wherein your battles join, how will my fear
With doubtful pulses beat, until I hear
Whom victory adorns!   Or shall I rest
Here without trembling, when, lodged in thy breast,
My heart's exposed to every danger that
Assails thy valour, and is wounded at
Each stroke that lights on thee—which absent I,
Prompted by fear, to myriads multiply.   380
—But these are Fancy's wild-fires, we in vain
Do spend unheard orisons, and complain
To unrelenting rocks—this night-peekt scroll,
This bill of our divorcement, doth enrol
Our names in sable characters nought will
Expunge, till death obliterate our ill.'—
    'Oh! do not, dear commandress of my heart,
(Argalia answers), let our moist eyes part
In such a cloud as will for ever hide
Hope's brightest beams;—those deities that guide   390
The secret motions of our fate will be
More merciful, than to twist destiny
In such black threads.   Should Death unravel all
The feeble cordage of our lives, we shall,

356 Mars] i. e. Mars *is* in the ascendant.   Chamberlayne dares these clashes of *s* imperturbably.
    383 night-peekt] Singer 'night-speckt.'   But we have had this odd word 'peekt,' 'peect,' &c. before.

Spite of that Prince of Terrors, in the high
And glorious palace of Eternity,
Being met again, renew that love, which we
On earth were forced, before maturity
Had ripened it, to leave. I' the numerous throng
Of long departed souls, that stray among   400
The myrtles in Elysium, I will find
Thy virgin ghost; and whilst the rout, inclined
To sensual pleasures here, refining are
In purging flames, laugh at each envious star
Whose aspect, if ill sited at our birth,
With poisonous influence blasts the joys of earth.'
   'Oh! waste not (cries the princess) dear time in
These shadows of conceit—the hours begin
To be 'mongst those inserted that have tried
The actions of the world, which must divide   410
Us from our joy. The sea through which we sail
Works high with woe, nor can our prayers prevail
To calm its angry brow—the glorious freight
Of my unwelcome honours hangs a weight
Too ponderous on me for to steer the way
Thy humbler fortunes do; else, ere I'd stay
To mourn without thee, I would rob my eyes
Of peaceful slumbers, and in coarse disguise,
Whilst love my sex's weakness did control,
Command my body to attend my soul—   420
My soul, my dear, which hovering near thee, not
Midnight alarums, that appear begot
By truth, should startle: 'twixt the clamorous camp,
Lightened with cannons, and the peaceful lamp
That undisturbed here wastes its oil, I know
No difference, but what doth from passion flow,
Whose close assaults do more afflict us far,
Than all the loud impetuous storms of war.'
   'We must, we must (replies Argalia) stand
This thunderbolt, unmoved,—since his command—   430
Whose will confirms our law. Happy had we,
Great princess, been, if in that low degree,
From whence my infancy was raised, I yet
Had lived a toiling rural; then, when fit
For Hymen's pleasures, uncontrolled I'd took
Some homely village girl, whose friends could look
After no jointure for to equalize
Her portion but my love; no jealous eyes
Had waited on our meetings, we had made
All our addresses free; the friendly shade   440
Cast from a spreading oak, as soon as she
Had milked her cows, had proved our canopy;
Where our unpolished courtship had a love
As chaste concluded, as, from the amorous dove

Perched near us, we had learned it. When arrived
Unto love's zenith, we had, undeprived
By disagreeing parents, soon been led
To church b' the sprucest swains ; our marriage-bed,
Though poor and thin, would have been neatly drest
By rural paranymphs, clad in the best   450
Wool their own flocks afforded. In a low
And humble shed, on which we did bestow
Nought but our labour to erect, we might
Have spent our lusty youth with more delight
Than glorious courts are guilty of; and, when
Age had decayed our strength, grown up to men,
Beheld our large coarse issue. Our days ended,
Unto the church been solemnly attended
By those of our own rank, and buried been
Near to the font that we were christened in.   460
Whilst I in russet weeds of poverty
Had spun these coarse threads, shining majesty
Would have exhausted all her stock to frame
A match for thy desert—some prince, whose name
The neighbouring regions trembled at, from whom
The generous issue of thy fruitful womb
Might have derived a stock of fame to build
A future greatness on, such as should yield
Subjects of wonder to the world.' About
To interrupt him, ere he had drawn out   470
This sad theme, she began to speak, but by
Night's swift approach was hindered. Now drew nigh
The time of his departure. Whilst he bleeds
At thought o' the first, a second summons speeds
His preparations to the city, where
That big-bulked body, unto which his care
Must add a soul, was now drawn up, and staid
Only to have his wished commands obeyed.
    His powerful passion, love's strict rules respecting
More than bright honour's dictates, yet, neglecting   480
All summons, staid him till he'd sacrificed
His vows to her, whose every smile he prized
Above those trivial glories. Ere from hence
He dares depart, each, with a new expense
Of tears, pays interest to exacting Fate
For every minute she had lent of late
Unto poor Love, whose stock since not his own,
Although no spendthrift, is a bankrupt grown.
    Look how a bright and glorious morning, which
The youthful brow of April doth enrich,   490
Smiles, till the rude winds blow the troubled clouds
Into her eyes, then in a black veil shrouds
Herself, and weeps for sorrow—so wept both
Our royal lovers—each would, and yet was loath

To bid farewell, till stubborn time enforced
Them to that task. First his warm lips divorced
From the soft balmy touch of hers ; next parts
Their hands, those frequent witnesses o' the heart's
Indissoluble contracts ; last and worst,
Their eyes—their weeping eyes—(O fate accurst,   500
That lays so hard a task upon my pen—
To write the parting of poor lovers) when
They had e'en lost their light in tears, were in
That shade—that dismal shade, forced to begin
The progress of their sorrow.—He is gone.
Sweet sad Pharonnida is left alone
To entertain grief in soft sighs ; whilst he
'Mongst noise and tumult, oft finds time to be
Alone with sorrow, though encompassed by
A numerous army, whose brave souls swelled high   510
With hopes of honour ;—lest Fame's trump lost breath,
Haste to supply 't by victory or death.
  But, ere calmed thoughts to prosecute our story,
Salute thy ears with the deserved glory
Our martial lover purchased here, I must
Let my pen rest awhile, and see the rust
Scoured from my own sword ; for a fatal day
Draws on those gloomy hours, whose short steps may
In Britain's blushing chronicle write more
Of sanguine guilt than a whole age before—   520
To tell our too neglected troops that we
In a just cause are slow. We ready see
Our rallied foes, nor will 't our slothful crime
Expunge, to say—Guilt wakened them betime.
From every quarter the affrighted scout
Brings swift alarums in ; hovering about
The clouded tops of the adjacent hills,
Like ominous vapours, lie their troops ; noise fills
Our yet unrallied army ; and we now
Grown legible, in the contracted brow   530
Discern whose heart looks pale with fear. If in
This rising storm of blood, which doth begin
To drop already, I 'm not washed into
The grave, my next safe quarter shall renew
Acquaintance with Pharonnida.—Till then,
I leave the Muses to converse with men.

THE END OF THE SECOND BOOK.

BOOK III. Canto I

THE ARGUMENT

Beneath the powerful tyranny of love,
    Whilst the fair princess weeps out every star
In pleasure's sphere, those dark clouds to remove,
    All royal pastimes in it practised are.

Amongst whose triumphs, that her train might lend
    Her their attendance in the shades of grief,
Passion brings some so near a fatal end,
    That timely pity scarce affords relief.

SOME months now spent, since, in the clouded court
Of sad Pharonnida, each princely sport
Was with Argalia's absence masked within
Sables of discontent, robes that had been
Of late her chiefest dress : no cheerful smile
E'er cheered her brow ; those walks which were erewhile
The schools where they disputed love, were now
Only made use of, when her grief sought how
To hide its treacherous tear : the unfilled bed
O' the widow, whose conjugal joy is fled,   10
I' the hot and vigorous youth of fancy, to
Eternal absence, sooner may renew
(Though she for tears repeated praises seeks)
The blooming spring of beauty on her cheeks.
    When bright-plumed Day on the expanded wings
Of air approaches, Light's fair herald brings
No overtures of peace to her ; each prayer
In pious zeal she makes, a pale despair
In their celestial journey clogs.   But long
Her feeble sex could not endure these strong   20
Assaults of passion, ere the red and white,
Vanquished, from beauty's throne had took their flight,
And nought but melancholy paleness left
To attend the light of her dim eyes—bereft
Of all their brightness ; pining agues in
The earthquake of each joint, leaving within
The veins more blood than dwelt in hers which beat
The heart's slow motions with a hectic heat.
    Long passion's tyrant reigns not, ere this change
Of mirth and beauty, letting sorrow range   30
Beyond the circle of discretion, in
Her father that suspicion which had been
Kindled before, renewing, he removes
His court to hers ; but the kind visit proves

A paroxysm unto that strong disease
Which combats in her blood. No mirth could please
Her troubled soul, since barred society
With all its better angels—gone to be
Attendant on Argalia ; she beholds
Those studied pleasures which the prince unfolds   40
His love and greatness in, with no delight
More smooth than that a sullen anchorite,
Which a harsh vow hath there enforced to dwell,
Sees the cold wants of his unhaunted cell.
　　Amongst these sports, whose time-betraying view
Ravished each pleased spectator, the fair clew
Contracts some sable knots, of which my pen
Is only one bound to unravel. When
War had unclasped that dreadful book of hers,
Where honoured names in sanguine characters   50
Brave valour had transcribed, fair virtue fixed
Euriolus in honour's orb, and mixed
Him with the court's bright stars : but he who had,
Whilst unregarded poverty had clad
His virtues in obscurity, learned how
To sail in fortune's boisterous storms, is now
By her false smiles becalmed and sunk, before
Desert (bound thither) touched love's treacherous shore.
　　I' the playful freedom of their youth, when she
Was only a fair shepherdess, and he   60
A humble swain, he truly did adore
The fair Florenza ; but aspired no more,
Since poverty clogged love's ambitious wing,
Than by his private muse alone to sing
Her praise—with such a flame of wit, that they
Which have compared, say, envied Laura may
Look pale with spleen, to hear those lines expressed,
Though in her great Platonic raptures dressed.
　　But now his worth, by virtue raised, did dwell
High as his hopes, and that a parallel   70
To hers appearing ; either's merits had
A climax to preferment, and thus clad
Virtue in honour's robes ; which equal fate
Gave his affection language to relate
What their disparity kept dumb : nor did
Those motions find acceptance, such as chid
Them for presumption, rather 'twas a frost
Of virgin ice, than fire of pride that crost
His masculine desires ; her eyes unfold
So much of passion, as by them she told   80
Who had most interest in her heart, which she
From all brave rivals his resolves shall be.

76 chid] Orig. 'hid.'

'Mongst thóse, Mazara, one whose noble blood
Enriched the gems of virtue, though they stood
In honour's altitude, was chief; nor could
A nobler choice, were her affections ruled
By worth, commend her judgement,—his fresh youth
Being crowned with virtues which might raise a truth
Above hyperboles; his nature mild,
As was the gall-less dove, yet not the wild   90
And furious lion, when provoked, could have
More daring valour; an untimely grave,
Whilst it i' the embryo was, to every vice,
But unto virtue a fair paradise;
Whose weedless banks no pining winter knew
Till death the influence of warm life withdrew.
   That sympathy of meeting virtues, which
Did both their souls with equal worth enrich,
'Twixt him and brave Euriolus had tied
A league not to be broke,—could Love divide   100
His blessings amongst friends; but that of all
Our passions brooks no rival: Fear may call
Friends to partake of palsies, Anger strives
To fire each neighbouring bosom, Envy thrives
By being transplanted, but a lover's pure
Flames, though converted to a calenture,
Unwillingly with the least flame will part—
Although to thaw another's frozen heart.
   Few 'mongst the observant wits o' the court yet knew
(Though it with twisted eye-beams strengthened grew   110
At every interview, and often dropped
Some tears to water it) whose love 'twas stopped
Mazara's suit. Euriolus, to her
Whose melting pity only could confer
A cure, unlocks the secret; whilst the other,
More confident to win, ne'er strives to smother
A passion so legitimate, but, by
All actual compliments, declares how high
He prized her virtues: but this worthy's fate
Fixed him in love's intemperate zone; too late   120
The pining fruit was sown, the spring so far
Being spent, its days were grown canicular,
Scorching all hopes, but what made able were
By fruitful tears—love's April showers,—to bear
Neglect's untimely frosts; which oft have lost,
In bloomy springs, the unhappy lover's cost.
   When this accomplished youth, whose tongue and pen,
With negatives more firm and frequent then
Cursed usurers give impoverished clients, oft
Had been repulsed, truth for discovery brought   130

        128 then] 'then' for 'than' as often.

This accident—Within the royal court
Of bright Pharonnida, a full resort
Of valiant knights were met, convened to try
Whose valour fortune meant to glorify.
Of which selected number there was one,
Who, though a stranger, virtue soon made known
To all, 'cause feared of most; his valour had,
Before the first triumphant day unclad
The silver-vested hemisphere, been oft
Clothed in the ornaments of honour—brought   140
On fame's fair wings from the opposing part,
Uncresting them to crown his high desert.
But now, when this new constellation near
Its zenith drew in honour's hemisphere,
Called thither by deciding lots, the brave
Euriolus appears, whom victory gave
In the first shock success, and placed his name
In the meridian altitude of fame;
Where, though the valiant stranger prove no foe
So fortunately valiant to o'erthrow   150
The structure of his fate, yet his close stars
Now sink a mine, to which those open wars
But easy dangers were. Mazara, in
His crest, a scarf that formerly had been
Known for Florenza's, seeing, jealous love
Converted into rage, his passions move
Above the sphere of reason, and, what late
Was but a gentle blaze, by altered fate,
Fires to a comet, whose malignant beams
Foretold sad ills, attending love's extremes.   160
   Loath to betray his passions in so great
A breach of friendship, to a close retreat
Mazara summons forward rage; yet in
The stranger's name, whose fortune might have been
The parent of a private quarrel, sends
To call Euriolus, (who now attends
Nought but triumphant mirth), unguarded by
Applauding friends, in secret fight to try
What power did him from threatening danger guard,
When public fame was victory's reward.   170
   This fatal scroll received by him that thought
It real truth, since passion might have sought
In him the same delay, a swift consent
Returns his answer. But the message went
So far from its directed road, that, ere
It reached Mazara's, loose neglect did bear
It to Carina's ear;—a lady that
In silent tears her heart had offered at
His virtue's shrine, yet with such secret zeal,
Her eyes forbid their Cupids to reveal   180

(127)

That language of her heart. She knew that in
Florenza's sea of merits, hers had been
Shipwrecked and lost; yet, with a soul as far
From envying her, as hating him, this war
Of factious passions she maintains, and since
Reason now wanted language to convince
Those headstrong rebels, she resolves to be,
Though ruined, ruled by their democracy.

    The information her officious maid
Had from Mazara's careless page betrayed,   190
Assures Carina—the preceding night,
Such horse and armour as the stranger knight
Euriolus had conquered in, had been
By his most cautious diligence within
A not far distant wood, in whose black shade
He meant his fury should his foe invade,
Lodged by his master. Which discovered truth,
Frightening her tears from the swift chase of youth
And beauty into froward age, to meet
Sorrow in private shades, withdraws the sweet   200
But sad Carina, who resolves to spend
Her sighs unnoted by her dearest friend.

    This in Florenza, who foresaw that nought
But passions more than common could have wrought
So swift a change, works high; who, that she might
Displume these ravens ere the babes of light
Smile in their weeping mother's face, prepares
To see Carina: who, with wakeful cares,
(Her sad companions) by her friend surprised,
No longer in their ebon veil disguised   210
Her thoughts' pure candour; but with looks that did
Seem to implore assistance, whilst they chid
Her own indulgent nature, shows her how
Preposterous love made her to passions bow,
Whose fruit, since none of her first planters came
From forward man, could be but female shame.

    This, with its fatal author, known, to free
Her friend from shame, herself from cruelty,
Unto Mazara, whose firm love attends
Her least commands, incensed Florenza sends.   220
Whose zeal-transported soul no sooner hears
That welcome sound, but, though presaging fears
Prompt him to stay, lest haughty honour fall,
Ruined by fame, he lets her standards fall
Before commanding love, and goes to wait
On 's honoured mistress. But this sly deceit
Of hope no cordial proves unto the sad
Carina's grief; the long experience had
Of his affection to Florenza, tells
Her doubtful soul, those even parallels   230

Could not by all her friend's persuasions be
Wrested into the least obliquity.
Which sad mistrust did love precipitate
On paths whose danger frights protecting fate.
   Assured the combat's hour drew on, and that
Mazara's love-sick soul was offering at
Florenza's shrine, and by that willing stay
Might be enforced some minutes to delay
The time, in which his readier opposite
Expected him, she, being resolved to write   240
Affection in her blood, with love's wild haste
Makes toward the lists ; there finds his armour placed
Within the dark shade of an ancient wood,
In whose black breast that place of horror stood
Where they appoint to meet, like those of fate
Obscure and dark, by beasts and birds that hate
The light alone frequented ; but love had
Displumed fear's haggars : being resolved, she clad
Beauty's fair pearl, where smooth delights did dwell,
I' the rough-cast mould of that Cyclopian shell.   250
   But that no arms nor bounding steeds affright,
Where love's fair hand hath valour's passport writ,
Here we should pause, and pity her that now
Fancy beholds, whilst she is learning how
To manage stubborn steel within her sleek
And polished hand, through devious paths to seek
For doubtful dangers, such whose horrid shape
On man's best judgement might commit a rape.
   Her swift conductor, love, ere this had brought
Her to the place, where passion had not sought   260
Long for the object of her hate, ere she
Her valiant brother, that was come to be
His fame's protector, sees, but so disguised
In 's arms, that both, with envy unadvised
By knowledge, an unthought-of guilt prepare
In blood to meet. Their foaming horses were
Now freed from the commanding rein, and in
Their full career ; but love in vain to win
The field from valour strives, her eager haste
But argues such an envy as did waste   270
Itself in weak attempts ; which, to the length
Of power extended, falls beneath the strength
Of her victorious foe, whose fortune had
In robes of joy, what he must weep for, clad.
   Conquered Carina, now dismounted, lay

---

248 haggars] It is a pity that 'haggars' has been allowed to become obsolete : for
we want something answering to the French *affres*. At the same time, the word may
be used in a sense closer to the usual one of 'haggard,' in relation to the person,—' those
who are made wild and haggard by fear.' In either case, of course, the poet has the
' untamed hawk ' in mind : and, *perhaps*, nothing else.

Struggling for life; whose fortress to betray
Toward nature's tyrant, death, her blood transports
False spirits through their purple sallyports.
Her brother, with an anger that was grown
Into disdain, his fury should be shown   280
On such resistless subjects, ere he knows
How much of grief his soul to sorrow owes
For this unhappy act, from 's finished course
Was now returning, not by strength to force
The harsh commands of tyrant victors, but
By calm advice a bloodless end to put
To that ill-managed quarrel: but before
He there arrives, to make his sorrows more
When truth unveils their dark design, a knight,
With haste as speedy as the secret flight   290
Of wrath when winged from angry Heaven, he saw,
Bolted into the lists; who soon did draw
Too near, in sober language to dispute
Their fatal quarrel. Both with rage grown mute,
Disdaining conference, found no place for words
Amidst the mortal language of their swords;
Which, the first shock passed o'er and lances broke,
In haste took place, and at each furious stroke
Unbayed the fountains of their blood, to stain
With purple guilt the flower-enamelled plain.   300
  Whilst each did thus with silent rage employ
An art-directed fury to destroy
The other's strength, the bordering shadows weep
In trickling dews, and with sad murmurs keep
Time with the hollow and ill-boding note
Sent from a fatal raven's stretched-out throat,
Which from an old oak's withered top did sing
A baleful dirge. But these sad omens bring
No terror to their busy thoughts, which were
Too much employed in action, to take care   310
For any danger more remote than what
With the next stroke might fall. Perceiving that
Their horses faint, they both dismount, and do
On equal terms the fight on foot renew,
Till a cessation, from the want of breath
Not valour, was enforced. The veil, which death
Contracted from those steams his reeking blood
Breathed forth its spirits in, already stood
Over Mazara's eyes, which clouded sees
Not that approach of night; his trembling knees   320
Stagger beneath their fainting load, which in-
T' the grave had dropped, had not their fury been,
When its last heat was with life's flame near spent,
From further rage restrained by accident.
  Some of the lost Carina's frighted friends,

Fearing those ills which desperate love attends,
Spending that morning in the fruitless quest
Of her had been, and now (their hopes distrest
With vain inquiries) to communicate
Their grief returning were; which secret fate   330
To interpose through dark meanders brought
Neglect, to find what care in vain had sought.
    Whilst yet no more than brave humanity
Prompts them to part a quarrel that might be
Defiled with blood, which, if not shed in wars,
With murder stains what it doth gild with scars,
They toward them haste, even in that critical
And dangerous minute when Mazara's fall,
With victory's laurels to adorn his crest,
His valiant friend had robbed of future rest,   340
Had not this blest relief of innocence,
The one from death, the other from expense
Of tears, restrained, before revenge had found
So much of guilt as might his conscience wound.
    His high-wrought rage stopped by too many hands
To vent its heat, Euriolus now stands,
Shook with the fever of his anger, till
Those friends, which saw Mazara grown so ill
With wounds to gasp for breath, by giving way
For air, they to the victor's view betray   350
His best of friends. At which afflicting sight,
Cursing the cause of that unhappy fight,
His sword as guilty thrown aside, he hastes
To his relief; in which kind act none wastes
Their friendly help: life, as but stolen from pain
Behind the veil of death, appears again
On Nature's frontiers; whose returning flame,
Though scarce of strength to warm, looked red with shame,
When he so many well-known friends beheld,
Sad witnesses, how much his passion swelled   360
Above the banks, where reason should have staid,
When to that meeting it his friend betrayed.
    Their veils of steel removed, each now beholds
What shame and wonder in firm contracts folds.
Amazed stands brave Euriolus to see,
None but his friend—his honoured friend—should be
The parent of that quarrel; shame confounds
Mazara more, and from internal wounds,
Though like the Red Sea's springs his other bled,
Perhaps less danger, but more torment bred.   370
Both now by his unforced confession knew
Whose equal-honoured beauty 'twas that drew
Them to this fatal combat, whose event
Him near the grave on love's vain errand sent.

    372 equal-honoured] Orig. 'equalled-honoured.'

Friendship renewed in strict embraces, they
Are now arrived where weak Carina lay,
So faint with love's phlebotomy that she,
Masked in forgetful slumbers, could not see
Approaching shame ; which, when discovered, sticks
Life's fair carnations on her death-like cheeks.   380
    Hasting to see what over-forward rage
That unknown stranger's weakness did engage
In that unhappy quarrel, they beheld,
At the first glance, an object that expelled
Into the shades of sorrow's wilderness
All temperate thoughts :—his sister's sad distress,
Wrought by his arm whose strength betrayed her near
The grave, did to Euriolus appear,
Dreadful as if some treacherous friend had shown
Those flames in which his scorched companions groan.   390
Nor did Mazara, though but prompted by
Pity, that tender child of sympathy,
With less relenting sorrow live to see
Love's bloody trophies, though unknown to be
By his victorious beauty reared. To save
From the cold grasp of an untimely grave
So ripe a virgin, whilst her brother stands
Unnerved with grief, amongst the helpful hands
Of other friends are his employed, till, by
Their useful aid, fled life returns to try   400
Once more the actions of the world, before
It shot the gulf of death ; but on the shore
Of active Nature was no sooner set,
But that, together with the light, she met
Her far more welcome lover. Whom whilst she
Beholds with trembling, Heaven, resolved to free
A suffering captive, turns his pity to
So much of passion, as ere long love grew
On the same stem ; whose flowers to propagate,
She in these words uncurtains mystic fate :—   410
' Forbear your aid, brave sir, and let me die,
Ere live the author of a prodigy
That future times shall curse ! Yet pardon me,
Dear brother, Heaven will ne'er impute to thee
The guilt of blood—'twas my unhappy love
Which raised this storm ; which, if my prayers may prove
In death successful, let me crave of you,
Dear sir, to whom I long have borne a true
But indiscreet affection, that from hence,
For poor Carina's sake, for this expense   420
Of tears and blood, you would preserve those dear
Respects of friendship, that did once appear
Confirmed betwixt you ; and, although my fate
Unto the worst of ills precipitate

(132)

My fame and life, oh! let my name not be
Offensive to your ear. This, this for me,
Is all you shall perform.'—Which spoke, she'd let
Her hovering soul forth, to have paid the debt
Of nature to the grave, had not she been
By some assisting friends, whilst dropping in,   430
Staid at the last step, and brought back to meet
The bridal pair, no single winding sheet.
This doubtful combat ended, they are to
The court conveyed; where Fame, upon this new
Text commenting, in various characters
Transcribes her sense :—some this bold act of hers
Term unbecoming passion, others brave,
Heroic love. But what most comfort gave
To cured Carina, was, that this lost blood
Had proved love's balm, and in a purple flood   440
Washed from her heart grief's sable stains ; for now
Merit had taught her dear Mazara how
To prize her virtuous love, and for its sake
Its cabinet her heart's best temple make.
   Thus passion's troubled sea had settled in
A smooth and gentle calm, had there not been
Unhappily, to blast their sweet content,
Not long before an act, for th' banishment
Of all such courtiers, made, as should, without
A licence from the council, fight about   450
Whatever private quarrel. But not this
Mazara or his new choice frights—their bliss
Stood on more firm foundations than the court's
Uncertain favours were : whose glorious sports
Although he left, it was not to retire
To sullen cares ; what honour could require,
A state, which called him her unquestioned lord,
Without depending favours did afford.
   But whilst we leave this noble lover, by
This mandate freed from what before did tie   460
Unto a troublesome attendance, we
From brave Euriolus are forced to be
With sorrow parted, since the general love
His virtue had obtained, wants strength to move
The ponderous doom. Ere his impoverished heart,
Grown poor in streams, could from life's springs impart
Warm blood enough for his pale cheeks to drink
A health to beauty, he's enforced to think
Of that sad theme of parting; on whose sense
His grieved soul dictates sighs, yet could dispense   470
Even with its harshest rigour, were there but
Any exception in it, that might put

472 exception] Orig. ' acception.'

Out parting with Florenza, that though he
Were shrunk into his former poverty,
Calling the rugged frowns of Fate, would bear
A brow unclouded with Ambition's care.
But he must go :—not all the rhetoric
Of tempting love could plead against the quick
Approach of time ; whose speedy motion now
Only some·slippery minutes did allow   480
Their parting tears : in whose exalted flood,
Had reason not with future hopes withstood
The rising stream, Love's summer fruits had been,
O'erwhelmed with grief, for ever buried in
A deluge of despair ; but that, whilst she,
With such sad looks as wintering Scythians see
The sun haste toward the arctic pole, beholds
His slow departure, glimmering hope unfolds
Twilight, which now foretells their frozen fear—
Day may return to Love's cold hemisphere.   490

THE END OF THE FIRST CANTO.

Canto II

THE ARGUMENT

The princess, by unlucky accident,
   Having Love's secret embassies betrayed
To her great father, by that action spent
   That stock of hope which promised future aid.

His rage being to such rash extremes inflamed,
   That he, whose mandates none durst disobey,
As if his power were of such acts ashamed,
   Shrinks from 't himself, and poorly doth betray.

If angry Age, the enemy to love,
Tells thy grave pride—thy judgement is above
What with contempt, although it injure truth,
Thy spleen miscalls the vanity of youth ;
If harsh employment, gross society,
That feast of brutes, make thee an enemy
To love, the soul's commercive language, then
Remove thy eye, whilst my unenvied pen,
That long to passion hath a servant been,
Confines the fair Pharonnida's within   10
These paper limits.   Frozen still she lies
Beneath opposing passions ; her bright eyes,

Arg. **8,** 't himself] Orig. ' itself.'
  1 Age] Orig. 'Aid,' which is of course pure nonsense and betrays, only more
distinctly than many other misprints, the fact that the copy was set up from dictation,
and never ' read.'

Those stars whose best of influence scarce had power
To thaw what grief congealed into a shower
Of heart-disburthening tears, their influence spend
In sorrow's polar circles, and could lend
No light to beauty's world. I' the vigorous reign
Of this pale tyrant, whilst she did remain
Unlightened with a beam of comfort, in
A bower being set, that formerly had been   20
Her seat when she heard the unhappy news
Of parting with Argalia ; whilst she views
She blames the guiltless shadows, who, to ask
Pardon, in trembling murmurs did unmask
Their naked limbs, and scattered at her feet
The fragrant veil ; in's death-bed sat the sweet
But pining rose, each grass its heavy head,
Laden with tears, did hang, whilst her eyes shed
A pattern to instruct them. Hence, whilst she
Looks thorough on a way conceived to be   30
The same her lord marched with his army when
He left Gerenza, with a haste more then
A common traveller, she sees one post
Towards her court, whose visage had not lost
Its room within her memory—he's known
Argalia's page. And now, each minute grown
A burthen to her thoughts that did defer
A nearer interview, the messenger
Arrives, and to her eager view presents
His master's letters : whose enclosed contents   40
Are now the object her expecting soul
Courts with desire, nor doth she long control
Their forward haste—a diamond being by
The messenger returned, whose worth might vie
Price with an Indian fleet when it sails slow
With 'ts glittering burthen. Though each word o'erflow
With joy, whilst her inquisitive discourse
Was on this pleasing theme, time did enforce
The page's swift departure ; who, with all
Affected epithets that love can call   50
To gild invention, when it would express
Things more sublime than mortal happiness,
Is gone to carry his expecting lord
What pleasure could, when rarified, afford.
Whilst this sweet joy was only clothed in fresh
Blossoms of hope, like souls ere mixt with flesh,
She only by desire subsisted ; but
Now to her chamber come, and having shut
The treacherous door, from the conjugal seal
The white-lipped paper freed, doth soon reveal   60

32 Gerenza] I follow Singer in adopting this form. The orig. wanders between
'Ghirenza,' 'Ghieranza,' &c.

Love's welcome embassies.—She reads, and, by
Each line transported to an ecstasy,
In fancy's wild meanders lost the way
She rashly entered ; faint desire would stay
At every word in amorous sighs to breathe
A love-sick groan, but she is yet beneath
The mount of joy, and must not rest until
Her swift-paced eye had climbed the flowery hill ;
Which now passed lightly o'er, with an intent
Of a review to its best ornament,   70
His name, she comes ; which whilst bathed in the balm
Of fragrant kisses, from joy's gentle calm
She thus is startled—A redoubled groan,
That sign of neighbouring sorrow, though unknown
From whence, affrights her soul ; but she too soon,
Too sadly knows the cause. The height of noon
Raged in reflected heat, when, walking in
Those outer rooms, her father long had been
In expectation of her sight ; but not
Finding her there, a golden slumber got   80
The start of 's meditations : to comply
With whose calm council, he did softly lie
Down on a stately couch, whose glittering pride
A curtain from the public view did hide.
Where, having plucked from off the wing of Time
Some of her softest down, the dews, that climb
In sleep to stop each ventricle, begin
To steal a soft retreat : hovering within
His stretched-out limbs sleep's vapours lie ; his hand
Rubs from his eyes those leaden bolts that stand   90
Over their heavy lids ; which scarce was done,
When first surprised Pharonnida begun
To read her letter, and by that sad chance
Betray her love. Passion strove to advance
Her father from his lodging when he first
Heard the discovery, but though anger thirst
For swift revenge, yet policy persuades
Him to hear further, ere his sight invades
Her troop of pleasures. Whose thin squadrons broke
By what she'd heard, before she could revoke   100
Her vanquished spirits, that were fled to seek
Protection in her heart, robbing her cheek
Of all the blood to waft in ; whilst she stands
A burthen to her trembling legs, her hands
Wringing each other's ivory joints, her bright
Eyes scattering their distracted beams, the flight
O' the curtain from her father's angry touch,
Discovers whence that groan, which caused so much
Her wonder, came. Grief and amazement strives
Awhile with love, which soon victorious drives   110

(136)

Those pale guests from her cheeks; unto whose aid
Her noble heart, secure from being betrayed
By its own strength, did send a quick supply
Of its warm blood; her conscience knows not why
To fear, 'cause knows no guilt, nor could have been
By love so virtuous e'er drawn near a sin.
But as the evening blushes for the rude
Winds of the ensuing day, so fortitude,
Upon the lovely roses that did grow
Within her face, a deeper dye bestow   120
Than fear could e'er have done, and did presage
The ensuing storm's exagitated rage.
  Silent with passion, which his eyes inflamed,
The prince awhile beholds her, ere he blamed
The frailty of affection; but at length,
Through the thick throng of thoughts, armed with a strength
Which crushed the soft smiles of paternal love,
He thus begins: 'And must, oh, must that prove
My greatest curse, on which my hopes ordained
To raise my happiness? Have I refrained   130
The pleasures of a nuptial bed, to joy
Alone in thee, not trembled to destroy
My name, so that, advancing thine, I might
Live to behold my sceptre take its flight
To a more spacious empire? Have I spent
My youth till, grown in debt to age, she hath sent
Diseases to arrest me, that impair
My strength and hopes e'er to enjoy an heir
Which might preserve my name, that only now
Must in our dusty annals live; whilst thou   140
Transfer'st the glory of our house on one,
Which, had not I warmed into life, had gone,
A wretch forgotten of the world, to the earth
From whence he sprung? But tear this monstrous birth
Of fancy from thy soul, quick as thou'dst fly
Descending wrath, if visible,—or I
Shall blast thee with my anger, till thy name
Rot in my memory; not as the same
That once thou wert behold thee, but as some
Dire prodigy, which to foreshow should come   150
All ills, which through the progress of my life
Did chance, were sent. I lost a queen and wife,
Thy virtuous mother, who for her goodness might
Have here supplied, before she took her flight
To heaven, my better angel's place; have since
Stood storms of strong affliction; still a prince
Over my passions until now—but this
Hath proved me coward. Oh! thou dost amiss

132 not] Singer 'nor' perhaps unnecessarily.

To grieve me thus, fond girl.   With that he shook
His reverend head; beholds her with a look   160
Composed of grief and anger, which she sees
With melting sorrow: but resolved love frees
Her from more yielding pity.   To begin
The prologue to obedience, which within
Her breast still dwelt, though swayed by love, she falls
Prostrate at 's feet; to his remembrance calls
Her dying mother's will, by whose pale dust,
She now conjures him not to be unjust
Unto that promise, with which her pure soul
Fled satisfied from earth, as to control   170
Her freedom of affection.   Rather she
Desires her interest in his crown might be
Denied her, than the choice of one to sway
It in her right.   She urges how it may
Be by his virtue far more glorified
Whom she had chose, than if by marriage tied
To any neighbouring prince, who only there
Would rule by proxy, whilst his greater care
Secured his own inheritance.   She then
Calls to remembrance who relieved him when   180
Distressed within Alcithius' walls; the love
His subjects bore Argalia, which might prove
Her choice their happiness; with all, how great
A likelihood it was—but the retreat
Of royalty to a more safe disguise,
Had showed him to their state's deluded eyes
So mean a thing.   Love's boundless rhetoric
About to dictate more, he with a quick
And furious haste forsakes the room, his rage
Thus boiling o'er:—'And must my wretched age   190
Be thus by thee tormented?   But take heed,
Correct thy passions, or their cause must bleed
Until he quench the flame.'   At which harsh word
He leaves the room, nor could her strength afford
Her power to rise; which whilst she strives to do,
Her memory adding more weights unto
The burthen of her thoughts, her soul opprest
Sinks in a pale swoon, catching at the rest
It must not yet enjoy; swift help lends light,
Though faint and glimmering, to behold what night   200
Of grief o'ershadowed her.   You that have been,
Upon the rack of passion, tortured in
The engines of forbidden love, that have
Shed fruitless tears, spent hopeless sighs to crave
A rigid parent's fair aspect, conceive
What wild distraction seized her.   I must leave

201 distraction] Orig. 'destruction.'

Her passion's volume only to be read,
Within the breasts of such whose hearts have bled
At the like dangerous wounds. Whilst she sits here
Amazed with grief, know that no smiles appear   210
To smooth her father's angry brow : yet to
None he unfolds his thoughts, but, bent to do
Whate'er his rage should dictate, to appease
This high-wrought storm, which turned into disease
Each motion of the brain, he only takes
Scorn and revenge, to whose ill counsel shakes
The quiet of the soul, to be his guides
Thorough those night-specked walks, whose shadow hides
The languished beams of love. Awhile their strong
Ingredients boil in 's blood, before they throng   220
The scattered thoughts into a quintessence
Of poisonous resolutions. First from thence
There sprung this black disaster to attend
Argalia's fortune—He doth forthwith send
A secret messenger t' the warlike prince
Of Syracuse, to let him know that since
He sent those forces to assist him in
His war, their general, that till late had been
The darling of his love, by arguments
Too strong was proved a traitor, whose intents   230
Aimed at his crown and life. To aggravate
His spleen the more, he writes him word—their fate
On the same ominous pinions flew, if that
He proved successful. Having warmed him at
This flame of passion, he concludes with—' Sir,
You guess my meaning, I would have no stir
About dispatching of him, for he 's grown
Strong in affection, and may call his own
The hearts of half my kingdom. Let this give
Your justice power ; he 's too much loved to live.'   240
    The startled Syracusan having read
These bloody lines, which had not only bred
A new, but nourished growing envy in
His mighty soul—a stranger to all sin—
So full of guilt, as to dissemble till
The new made general's just deserts did fill
Fame's still augmented volume, and was grown
More legible than what he called his own.
What in a rival prince had been a high
And noble emulation, kindled by   250
A smaller star, blasts virtue. He beholds
His lightning valour, which each hour unfolds
Examples for posterity, destroy
What, though he trembled at, creates no joy
Within his sullen soul ; a secret hate
By envy fed, strives to unhinge his fate

From off its lofty pyramids, and throw
What merit raised unto a place more low
Than their first step to glory : yet, whilst nought
But honour was engaged, disdain ne'er sought   260
For life-excluding corrosives; but love
Bearing a part, two suns might sooner move
In the same sphere, than that hot guest endure
A rival flame. Desert could not secure
Worth thus besieged; yet this accurst intent
Dares not unveil itself. The army sent
By him from fair Gerenza, ere the sun
Performed his summer's progress, had begun
To garrison their weary force within
Such towns as their own valour first did win   270
From the retired Aetolians. Ere this task
Was fully ended, curtained in the mask
Of merit's lawful claim, reward, there came
A large commission, which Zoranza's name
Had made authentic—That the government
Of Ardenna, a town whose strength had spent
The baffled foe whole fields of blood, should be
Conferred on him. By the vicinity
O' the place freed from a tedious journey, in
The city he arrives; and, what had been   280
Sent from his prince, presents those mandates that
Informed the governor : who, frighted at
The strange commands, lets a pale guilt o'ertake
His swift resolves, till glorious hopes did shake
Those mourning robes of conscience off; and, in
The purple garments of a thriving sin,
Shadows his trembling soul, lest she appear
Shook with a cold fit of religious fear.
   The discomposure of his look, which did
Appear the birth of discontent, forbid   290
Suspicion of a blacker sin. That night,
As being the last of 's charge, he did invite
Argalia to remain his guest, the next
Promising to be his ; yet seeming vext
To leave the place, though only to conceal
His dark design, that did itself reveal
To none but some selected soldiers, by
Whose help he meant to murther him. To vie
Its benefits with the day's, night had bestowed
Refreshing slumbers upon all that owed   300
It to the last day's labour; when, without
Fear of approaching danger, hemmed about
With guards of honest valour, all his train,
Save such as mere necessity detain,

Lodged in the city, fearless Argalia in
The castle lies : where having tempted been
By midnight revels, full crowned cups, to be
Betrayed from reason to ebriety,
But nought prevailing, he at length is led,
Like an intended sacrifice, t' the bed   310
Ordained to be his last, until the earth
Within her womb afford him one. The birth
O' the morn grew near her slow approach, ere all
Those engines, by whose strength they meant his fall,
Could be prepared. The governor, that held
The helm of this black mischief, had expelled
The poisonous guilt of staining his own sword
With blood, providing villains that abhorred
No sin's contagion, though revenge did wait
On every guilty step. That evening's bait   320
Their liquid mirth had laid, although it took
No use of reason from his soul, had shook
Its labouring faculties into a far
More sudden slumber ; which composed the war
Of wandering fancy in a harmony
Of the concordant humours, until, by
The sudden noise of those ordained to be
His murderers, he wakes. Amazed to see
His chamber so possessed, he catches hold
On one of them, but finds his strength controlled   330
By the assistance of the other : in
The embryo of this treachery, ere their sin
Was past to execution, he conjures
Them to forbear so black a deed, assures
Them of rewards, greater than hope could call
A debt from him that basely sought his fall.
But deadly silence had barred up the gates
Of every voice ; those cursed assassinates
Prepared for action were ; but Heaven prevents
That aged sin of murdering innocents   340
With miracles of mercy. There was found
Not long before an ancient story, crowned
With a prophetic honour, that contained
This sacred truth :—'When Ardenna is stained
With treachery, in friendship's veil disguised,
Her sable tower shall be by foes surprised.'
    This known, but misconceived, to cozen Fate,
They did unwounded bear without the gate
The now resistless lion, that did lie,
Like that brave prince o' the forest, fettered by   350
A crew of trembling hunters. To the brow
Of a high promontory, that did bow
Its black clifts o'er the clamorous waves, they had
Conveyed the noble youth. The place a sad

And dismal horror wore ; the grim aspects
Of lowering rocks the grey-eyed sea reflects
In ugly glaring beams ; the night-raven beats
His rusty wings, and from their squalid seats
The baleful screech-owls fly, to bear their parts
In the sad murmur of the night. Those hearts   360
Custom had steeled with crimes, perhaps had been
Here frighted to repentance, had not sin,
Assisted by the hands of avarice, drawn
The bridge of reason, and obscured the dawn
Of infant goodness. To redeem the time
Astonishment had lost, towards their crime
They now themselves precipitate ; the hand
Ordained to ruin that fair structure, and
Unravel his life's even thread, prepares
To strike the fatal blow ; but He that dares   370
Obstruct commanded villany forbid
The further progress of their guilt, and chid
That pale sin in rough language of a strange
Confused sound, striking their ears—did change
The ominous dirges of the night into
A various noise of human voices. Who
Durst in that secret place approach, 'twas now
Too late to think on ; the rock's spacious brow
Was clouded o'er with men, whose glittering arms
Threatened destruction, ere their swift alarms   380
Could summon sleep's enfeebled aid. Whilst they
Forsake their prisoner, who becomes a prey
To the invaders, seeking safety in
Their flight, they fall before him that had been
Ordained to speedier ruin ; entering at
The open sallyport, they give by that
Rash act directions to the foe that mixed
Promiscuously with them, and now had fixed
Their standards on the gates. The castle, in
Feverish alarums sweating, did begin   390
To ease her fiery stomach, by the breath
O' the full-mouthed cannon : ministers of death
In this hot labour busily distils
Extracted spirits ; noise and tumult fills
The frighted city, whose fired turrets lent
A dismal light. But the assailants spent
Their blood in vain, the soldiers that had been
At the first trembling fit distracted in
Confusion's giddy maze, had rallied now
Their scattered spirits, and were seeking how   400
To purge dishonour's stains in the bright fire
Of rage-contracted valour. To retire

393, 4 distils, fills] Singer corrects both false concords—things which, it may be
well to repeat just once, Chamberlayne certainly commits knowingly in some places.

Unto their ships in safety, now is all
The invaders hope for ; but so many fall
In that attempt, it leaves no triumph due
To Fortune's temple. By this winding clew
Of various fate, Argalia only finds
That stroke of death deceived ; no hand unbinds
His corded arms, but that which meant to lay
Bondage as hard ; so corrosives do stay   410
A gangrene, fed by springs of poisonous blood,
When reaching at the heart, as these withstood
The cataracts of death. With tyrants more
Indomitable than the sea that bore
Their black fleet, leave our hero to untie
This knotty riddle of his fate, whilst, by
The ignis fatuus of a fancy led,
With slow-paced feet through other paths we tread.
   The tumults of the city silenced in
A peaceful calm ; what the effects had been   420
Of those loud clamours, whilst all seek to know,
Argalia's loss makes giddy wonder grow
Into suspicion—that this act might be
Some stratagem o' the governor, to free
Himself from a successor. But those sly
Darts of mistrust were rendered hurtless by
His prince's mandates, whose envenomed hate
That spurious birth had made legitimate.
Yet swift revenge affronts his treason in
Its full career ; his master, having been   430
By him informed of a surprisal where
All sounds but death affrighted, could not bear
The burthen of his fears, and yet not sink
Deeper in sin. Ere the poor wretch could think
On aught but undeserved rewards, he, by
A brace of mutes being strangled, from the high
But empty clouds of expectation drops,
To let the world know what vain shadow props
Those blood-erected pyramids that stand
On secret murder's black and rotten sand.   440
   When thus the Syracusan had secured
His future fame, passion, that still endured
A strong distemperature, slept not until
The story of their crossed design did fill
Palermo's prince's ear. Argalia's loss
Was now the ball that babbling Fame did toss
Thorough the court ; upon whose airy wing,
Reaching the island, it too soon did bring
The heavy news, disguised in robes more sad
Than truth, to her, whose stock of virtues had   450

444 crossed] Orig. 'cross*e*' : and 'cross' is not at all impossible.
445 Palermo's] 'Palermo' introduces a fresh confusion of scene.

Been ventured on that sea of merit.   In
Such forms of grief, as princes that have been
Hurled from the splendent glories of a throne
Into a dungeon, her great soul did groan
Beneath the weights of grief: the doleful tale
Had thunder-struck all joy; her spirits exhale
Their vigour forth in sighs, and faintly let
That glorious fabric, unto which they're set
Supporters, fall to the earth.   Yet sorrow stays
Not in this frigid zone, rude grief betrays   460
Her passions to her father's jealous ear,
Who, fearing least Argalia's stars might clear
Their smoky orbs, and once more take a flight
From death's cold house, by a translated light,
To separate from sorrow, and again,
In fortune's house, lord of the ascendant reign;
He doubts that island's safety, and from thence
Removes her with what speedy diligence
Fear could provoke suspicion to.   Her train,
Shook with that sudden change, desire in vain   470
The island's pleasure, ere they know how much
Their fates must differ.   As it oft in such
Unlooked for changes happens, each man vents
His own opinion;—some said, discontents
Of the young princess; others, that the season
O' the year was cause: but though none know his reason,
All must obey his will.   The pleasant isle,
Whose walks, fair gardens, prospects, did beguile
Time of so many happy hours, must now,
A solitary wilderness whose brow   480
Winter had bound in folds of ice, be left
To wail their absence; whilst each tree, bereft
Of leaves, did like to virgin mourners stand,
Clothed in white veils of glittering icelets, and
Shook with the breath of those sharp winds that brought
The hoary frost.   The pensive birds had sought
Out springs that were unbarred with ice, and there
Grew hoarse with cold; the crusted earth did wear
A rugged armour; every bank, unclad
With flowers, concealed the juicy roots that had   490
Adorned their summer's dress; the meadows' green
And fragrant mantle, withering, lay between
The grizly mountain's naked arms;—all grows
Into a swift decay, as if it owes
That tribute unto her departure, by
Whose presence 'twas adorned.   Seated did lie,
Within the circuit of Gerenza's wall,
Though stretched to embrace, a castle, which they call

474 said] Orig. ' did.'   486 frost] 'Frost' is Singer's correction for 'fish'
which cannot be right, and was probably suggested by 'birds.'

The prince's tower—a place whose strength had stood
Unshook with danger.—When that violent flood   500
Of war raged in the land hither were brought
Such, if of noble blood, whose greatness sought
From treacherous plots extension; yet, although
To those a prison, here he did bestow
His best of treasure: briefly, it had been
Unto the Spartan kings a magazine
Since first they ruled that kingdom, and, whene'er
A war drew near them, their industrious care
Made it their place of residence. The hill
'Twas built upon, with's rocky feet did fill   510
A spacious isthmus; at its depth a lake,
Supplied b' the neighbouring sea let in to make
The fort the more impregnable, with slow
But a deep current running, did bestow
A dreadful prospect on the bended brow
O' the hill; which, covered with no earth, did bow
Its torn clifts o'er the heavy stream. The way
That led to it was o'er a bridge, which they
That guard it did each night draw up; from whence
A steep ascent, whose natural defence   520
Assisted by all helps of art, had made
The fatal place so dangerous to invade—
Each step a death presented. Here when he
Had placed his daughter, whose security
Rocks, walls, nor rivers warranted, without
A trusty guard of soldiers hemmed about
The walls less hard than they. Those gentlemen
That on her happier court attended, when
Argalia did command them, as too mild
Were now discharged; their office on a wild   530
Band of those mountain soldiers, who had in
His last great war most famed for valour been,
Being conferred; and these, lest they should be
Forced by commands into civility,
Bestowed upon the fierce Brumorchus; one
Whose knotty disposition nature spun
With all her coarsest threads, composing it
For strength, not beauty, yet a lodging fit
For such a rough unpolished guest as that
Black soul; whose dictates it oft trembled at   540
In feverish glooms, whose subterranean fire
Inflamed that ill-formed chaos with desire
Its vigour to employ in nought of kin
To goodness, till 'twas better tempered in
The prince's court; where, though he could not cast
His former rudeness off, yet having past

540 oft] Orig. ' ought,' another, no doubt, of the slips of *ear.*

The filing of the courtiers' tongues, at length
It thus far wrought him—he converts that strength
To 's prince's service, which till then had lay
In passion's fetters, learning to obey   550
The gentle strokes of government. Though bred
In savage wildness, nurst with blood, and fed
With hourly rapine, since he had forsook
Those desert haunts a firm obedience took
Hold on 's robustious nature, not to be
By that effeminate wanton, Flattery,
Stroked to a yielding mildness. Which being known
To the mistrustful prince, whose passions, grown
So far above the reach of reason that
Her strength could not support them, bending at   560
Their own unwieldy temper, sunk into
Acts that his milder thoughts would blush to do,
Make him from all his nobler captains choose
Forth this indomitable beast. To use
So harsh a discipline unto the sole
Heir to his crown, a lady that did roll
More virtues on the spindle of her life,
Than Fate days' length of thread, had raised a strife
So high in his vexed subjects' blood, that all
Murmur in secret; but there 's none durst call   570
His prince's acts in question : to behold
Her prison through their tears, and then unfold
Their friends a veil of sorrow, is the most
Their charity durst do. But that which crost
Distressed Pharonnida above the grief
Of her restraint, or aught but the belief
Of her Argalia's death, is—now to be
Barred, when she wants it most, society
With sorrowful Florenza, whilst she staid,
The partner of her secrets, now betrayed   580
By false Amphibia to her father, and
Banished the court, retiring, to withstand
The storms of greatness, to her father's own
Poor quiet home ; which, as if ne'er she'd known
The beauties of a palace, did content
Her even thoughts, at leisure to lament
In pensive tears her wretched mistress' fate,
Whose joys eclipsed, converts her robes of state
To mourning sables. What delights the place
Was capable of having, to deface   590
The characters of grief, her father strives
To make them hers; but no such choice flower thrives
In the cold region of her breast,—she makes
Her prison such as theirs, whose guilt forsakes
All hopes of mercy. The slow-footed day,
Hardly from night distinguished, steals away

Few beams from her tear-clouded eyes, and those
A melancholy pensiveness bestows
On saddest objects. The o'ershadowed room,
Wherein she sat, seemed but a large-sized tomb,   600
Where beauty buried lay ; its furniture
Of doleful black hung in it, to inure
Her eyes to objects like her thoughts. In which
Night-dress of sorrow, till a smile enrich
Impoverished beauty, I must leave her to
Her sighs, those sad companions ! and renew
His fatal story, for whose love alone
She dares exchange the glories of a throne.

THE END OF THE SECOND CANTO.

Canto III

THE ARGUMENT

From treachery, which two princes' annals stained,
  The brave Argalia by protecting fate
Delivered, land on Rhodes' fair isle attained,
  Being there elected champion for their state.

In which design, although with victory blest,
  The common fate him soon a prisoner makes
To a proud Turk, beneath whose power distressed,
  His virtue proffered liberty forsakes.

THROUGH the dark paths of dusty annals, we,
Led by his valour's light, return to see
Argalia's story ; who hath, since that night
Wherein he took that strange distracted flight
From treacherous Ardenna, performed a course
So full of threatening dangers, that the force
Of his protecting angel trembled to
Support his fate, which cracked the slender clew
Of destiny almost to death. His stars,
Doubting their influence when such horrid wars   10
The gods proclaimed, withdrew their languished beams
Beneath heaven's spangled arch. In pitchy streams
The heavy clouds unlade their wombs, until
The angry winds, fearing the flood should fill
The air, their region where they ruled, did break
Their marble lodgings ; nature's self grew weak

Arg. 3, on] Orig. ' or,' and I would not undertake that Chamberlayne's restless and unconventional thought did not understand by ' land ' ' continent ' or ' main,' and suggest a sort of parenthesis of correction.
  15 their] Singer ' the region,' to some positive loss.

(147)

With these distemperatures, and seemed to draw
Toward dissolution; her neglected law
Each element forgot—the imprisoned flame,
When the clouds' stock of moisture could not tame   20
Its violence, in sulphury flashes break
Thorough the glaring air; the swoln clouds speak
In the loud voice of thunder; the sea raves
And foams with anger, hurls his troubled waves
High as the moon's dull orb, whose waning light
Withdrew to add more terror to the night.
　　When the black curtain of this storm that took
The use of art away, had made them look
For nought but swift destruction, being so vain
For th' mariners to row that the proud main   30
Scorned to be lashed with oars, to ease distress,
The night forsook them: but a day no less
Dreadful succeeds it; by whose doubtful light
The wretched captives soon discover right
Near them a Turkish navy; to whose aid
The renegadoes (having first displayed
Their silver crescents) join. Nor did they meet
That help untimely; a brave Rhodian fleet
Set forth from those, the Christian bulwarks, to
Obstruct the Turks' invasions, was in view.   40
　　To meet the threatening danger, which 'twas then
Too late to waive, that miracle of men,
The brave Argalia, chained unto an oar,
Is with a thousand noble captives more
Forced to assist damned infidels. And now
The well-armed fleets draw near, their swift keels plough
The ocean's angry front. First, they salute
Each other with their cannon; those grown mute,
Come to more desperate fight; unfriendly bands
Unite their vessels; the fierce soldier stands   50
Firm on his hatches, whilst another boards
His active enemies, whose ship affords
No room for such unwelcome guests, but sends
Their scattered limbs into thin air; each bends
His strength to 's foe's destruction. Plunging in
Which bloody sweat, the Rhodians' hopes had been
Lost with their fleet, had not kind fortune smiled
Thus on their fear.—Whilst action had beguiled
Each soul of passive cares, Argalia sees
A way to unlock his rusty chain, and frees   60
Himself and fellows from their bank; which done,
Those that continued at their oars did run
The vessel from the rest, and, ere unto
Their sight betrayed, the trembling pirates slew.

34 right] Orig. ' night.'

Then, closing with their unsuspicious foes,
I' the vigour of the fight, they discompose
Their well-ranged fleet, and such confusion strook
Into the van, to see their rear thus shook
With an unlooked for hurricane, that in
A fearful haste the numerous Turks begin   70
To stretch their fins and flee.   But all their speed
Was spent in vain, Argalia's hand had freed
So many captives, that their galleys must
Unto the winds' uncertain favour trust,
Or else, becalmed, but feebly crawl before
Their eager foes, who both with sail and oar
Chased them to ruin.   Glorious victory
Thus to the Christian party being by
A stranger purchased, with such high applause
As those that rescue a declining cause   80
From the approach of ruin, welcomed, he
Is now received into th' society
Of the brave Christian order.   But they not
Long joyed in victory, ere the Turk, to blot
The stains of being conquered out, had made
A mighty army ready to invade
The valiant Rhodians ; where Argalia shows
So brave a spirit, their whole army owes
His valour for example.   The Turks had oft
Made desperate onslaughts on the isle, but brought   90
Nought back but wounds and infamy ; but now,
Wearied with toil, they are resolved to bow
Their stubborn resolutions with the strength
Of not-to-be-resisted want.   The length
O' the chronical disease extended had
To some few months, since, to oppress the sad
But constant islanders, the army lay
Circling their confines.   Whilst this tedious stay
From battle rusts the soldier's valour in
His tainted cabin, there had often been,   100
With all variety of fortune, fought
Brave single combats, whose success had brought
Honour's unwithered laurels on the brow
Of either party ; but the balance now,
Forced by the hand of a brave Turk, inclined
Wholly to them.   Thrice had his valour shined
In victory's refulgent rays, thrice heard
The shouts of conquest, thrice on 's lance appeared
The heads of noble Rhodians, which had strook
A general sorrow 'mongst the knights.   All look   110

89 oft] Orig. 'ought.' There can be no doubt about the right word in meaning,
but it is an interesting point in the History of Rhyme, whether 'brought' was pro-
nounced 'broft,' with the sound of 'cough,' or whether 'oft' was forced, in a
plusquam-Spenserian fashion, to suit the eye.

Who next the lists should enter; each desires
The task were his, but honour now requires
A spirit more than vulgar, or she dies
The next attempt, their valour's sacrifice;
To prop whose ruins, chosen by the free
Consent of all, Argalia comes to be
Their happy champion. Truce proclaimed until
The combat end, the expecting people fill
The spacious battlements, the Turks forsake
Their tents, of whom the city ladies take   120
A dreadful view, till a more noble sight
Diverts their looks. Each part behold their knight
With various wishes, whilst in blood and sweat
They toil for victory. The conflict's heat
Raged in their veins, which honour more inflamed
Than burning calentures could do; both blamed
The feeble influence of their stars that gave
No speedier conquest; each neglects to save
Himself—to seek advantage to offend
His eager foe. The dreadful combat's end   130
Nought but their loss of blood proclaims; their spirits
In that reflux of heat and life inherits
Valour's unconquered throne. But now so long
The Turks' proud champion had endured the strong
Assaults of the stout Christian, till his strength
Cooled on the ground, with 's blood, he fell at length
Beneath his conquering sword. The barbarous crew
O' the villains, that did at a distance view
Their champion's fall, all bands of truce forgot,
Running to succour him, begin a hot   140
And desperate combat with those knights that stand
To aid Argalia, by whose conquering hand
Whole squadrons of them fall: but here he spent
His mighty spirit in vain, their cannons rent
His scattered troops, who for protection fly
T' the city gates; but, closely followed by
Their foes, did there for sad oblations fall
To dying liberty. Their battered wall
Groaned with the wondrous weight of lead, and in
Its ruins hides her battlements; within   150
The bloody streets the Turkish crescents are
Displayed, whilst all the miseries of war
Raged in their palaces. The common sort
Of people make the barbarous soldier sport
In dying, whilst those that survive them crave
Their fate in vain; here cruelty did save
And mercy only kill, since death set free
Those happier souls from dire captivity,
At length the unrestrained soldier tires,
Although not satisfies his foul desires,   160

With rapes and murder. When, amongst those poor
Distressed captives that from thence they bore,
Argalia lies in chains, ordained to die
A sacrifice unto the cruelty
Of the fierce bashaw, whose loved favourite in
The combat late he slew; yet had not been
In that so much unhappy, had not he,
That honoured then his sword with victory,
Half-brother to Janusa been,—a bright
But cruel lady, whose refined delight,   170
Her slave, though husband, Ammurat, durst not
Ruffle with discontent. Wherefore to cool that hot
Contention of her blood, which he foresaw
That heavy news would from her anger draw,
To quench with the brave Christian's death, he sent
Him living to her, that her anger, spent
In flaming torments, might not settle in
The dregs of discontent. Staying to win
Some Rhodian castles, all the prisoners were
Sent with a guard into Sardinia, there   180
To meet their wretched thraldom. From the rest
Argalia severed, soon hopes to be blest
With speedy death, though waited on by all
The hell-instructed torments that could fall
Within invention's reach. But he's not yet
Arrived to's period, his unmoved stars sit
Thus in their orbs secured.—It was the use
O' the Turkish pride, which triumphs in the abuse
Of suffering Christians, once, before they take
The ornaments of nature off, to make   190
Their prisoners public to the view, that all
Might mock their miseries. This sight did call
Janusa to her palace window, where,
Whilst she beholds them, love resolved to bear
Her ruin on her treacherous eye-beams, till
Her heart infected grew; their orbs did fill,
As the most pleasing object, with the sight
Of him whose sword opened a way for th' flight
Of her loved brother's soul. At the first view
Passion had struck her dumb, but when it grew   200
Into desire, she speedily did send
To have his name; which known, hate did defend
Her heart, besieged with love; she sighs, and straight
Commands him to a dungeon; but Love's bait
Cannot be so cast up, though to deface
His image in her soul she strives. The place
For's execution she commands to be
'Gainst the next day prepared; but rest and she
Grow enemies about it: if she steal
A slumber from her thoughts, that doth reveal   210

Her passions in a dream ; sometimes she thought
She saw her brother's pale grim ghost, that brought
His grisly wounds to show her, smeared in blood,
Standing before her sight, and, by that flood
Those red streams wept, imploring vengeance ; then,
Enraged, she cries—Oh, let him die. But when
Her sleep-imprisoned fancy, wandering in
The shades of darkened reason, did begin
To draw Argalia's image on her soul,
Love's sovereign power did suddenly control   220
The strength of those abortive embryoes, sprung
From smothered anger. The glad birds had sung
A lullaby to night, the lark was fled,
On drooping wings, up from his dewy bed,
To fan them in the rising sun-beams ; ere
Whose early reign, Janusa, that could bear
No longer locked within her breast so great
An army of rebellious passions, beat
From Reason's conquered fortress, did unfold
Her thoughts to Manto, a stout wench, whose bold   230
Wit, joined with zeal to serve her, had endeared
Her to her best affections. Having cleared
All doubts with hopeful promises, her maid,
By whose close wiles this plot must be conveyed
To secret action, of her council makes
Two eunuch-panders ; by whose help she takes
Argalia from his keeper's charge, as to
Suffer more torments than the rest should do,
And lodged him in that castle, to affright
And soften his great soul with fear. The light,   240
Which lent its beams unto the dismal place
In which he lay, without presents the face
Of horror smeared in blood—A scaffold, built
To be the stage of murder, blushed with guilt
Of Christian blood, by several torments let
From the imprisoning veins. This object set
To startle his resolves if good, and make
His future joys more welcome, could not shake
The heaven-built pillars of his soul, that stood
Steady, though in the slippery paths of blood.   250
The gloomy night now sat enthroned in dead
And silent shadows, midnight curtains spread
The earth in black for what the falling day
Had blushed in fire, whilst the brave prisoner lay
Circled in darkness ; yet in those shades spends
The hours with angels, whose assistance lends
Strength to the wings of Faith, which, mounted on
The rock of hope, was hovering to be gone
Towards her eternal fountain, from whose source
Celestial love enjoined her lower course.   260

(152)

Whilst in this holy ecstasy, his knees'
Descent did mount his heart to Him that sees
His thoughts developed ; whilst dull shades opprest
The drowsy hemisphere ; whilst all did rest,
Save those whose actions blushed at day-light, or
Such wretched souls whose sullen cares abhor
Truce with refreshing slumbers ; he beholds
A glimmering light, whose near approach unfolds
The leaves of darkness. Whilst his wonder grows
Big with amazement, the dim taper shows   270
What hand conveyed it thither ; he might see
False Manto entered, who, prepared to be
A bawd unto her lustful mistress, came,
Not with persuasive rhetoric to inflame
A heart congealed with death's approach, but thaw
Him from the frozen rocks of rigid law
With brighter constellations, that did move
In spheres, where every star was fired with love.
    The siren, yet to show that she had left
Some modesty, unrifled by the theft   280
Of mercenary baseness, sadly wept—
Her errand's prologue ; but guilt was not kept
Within the curtain long, she only sate
A mourner for the sickness of his fate
Until esteemed for pitiful, and then
Prescribes this remedy :—' Most blest of men
Compose thy wonder, and let only joy
Dwell in thy soul; my coming 's to destroy,
Not nurse thy trembling fears. Be but so wise
To follow thy swift fate, and thou may'st rise   290
Above the reach of danger. In thy arms
Circle that power, whose radiant brightness charms
Fierce Ammurat's anger, when his crescents shine
In a full orb of forces. What was thine
Ere made a prisoner, though the doubtful state
Of the best Christian monarch, will abate
Its splendour, when that daughter of the night,
Thy feeble star, shines in a heaven of light.
If life or liberty, then, bear a shape
Worthy thy courting, swear not to escape   300
By the attempts of strength, and I will free
The iron bonds of thy captivity.'
    A solemn oath, by that Great Power he served,
Took and believed, his hopes no longer starved
In expectation. From that swarthy seat
Of sad despair, his narrow jail, replete
With lazy damps, she leads him to a room,
In whose delights Joy's summer seemed to bloom ;
There left him to the brisk society
Of costly baths and Corsic wines, whose high   310

(153)

And sprightly temper from cool sherbets found
A calm allay.   Here his harsh thoughts unwound
Themselves in pleasure, as not fearing fate
So much, but that he dáres to recreate
His spirits, by unwieldy action tired,
With all that lust into no crime had fired.
    By mutes, those silent ministers of sin,
His sullied garments were removed, and in
Their place such various habits laid, as Pride
Would clothe her favourites with, she means to hide   320
From those deformities, which, accident,
On Nature's issue, striving to prevent
Form's even progress, casts, when she would twine
That active male with matter feminine.
    Unruffled here by the rash wearer, rests
Fair Persian mantles, rich Sclavonian vests.
The gaudy Tuscan, or transmuted shape
Of the fantastic French—the British ape,
The grave and constant Spaniard, all might here
Find garments, such as princes would appear   330
To grace their honoured nuptials in, or tell
Strangers how much their treasure doth excel.
Though on this swift variety of fate
He looks with wonder, yet his brave soul sate
Too safe within her guards of reason, to
Be shook with passion : that there's something new
And strange approaching after such a storm,
This gentle calm assures him ; but the form
Of pleasure softens not that which the other
And worse extreme not with fear's damps could smother.   340
He flies not with the rugged separatist
Pleasure's smooth walks, nor doth, enjoying twist
Those threads of gold to fetters ; he dares taste
All mirth, but what religion's stock would waste.
His limbs, from wounds but late recovered, now
Refreshed with liquid odours, did allow
Their suppled nerves no softer rest, but in
Such robes as wore their ornament within,
Veiled o'er their beauty.   Linen, smooth and soft
As Phœnix' down, and whiter than what's brought   350
From furthest China, he puts on ; and then,
What habit custom made familiar, when
Clothed in his own, makes choice of for to be
Most honoured of that rich variety.
    In an Italian garb t' the doublet clad,
Manto, lust's swift and watchful spy, that had
With an officious care attended on
That motion, entering, hastes him to be gone

312 allay] Orig. ' ally.'

Toward more sublime delights. Which though a just
And holy doubt proclaim the road of lust,   360
Knowing his better angel did attend
Upon each step, he ventures to descend
The dreadful precipice so far, until
The burning vale was seen, then mounts the hill
Of heaven-bred fortitude, from whence disdain
Floods of contempt on those dark fires did rain.
His guilty conduct now had brought him near
Janusa's room ; the glaring lights appear
Thorough the window's crystal walls ; the strong
Perfumes of balmy incense, mixed among   370
The wandering atoms of the air, did fly ;
Sight's nimble scouts yet were made captive by
A slower sense, as if but to reveal
What breathed within, those fugitives did steal
Thorough their unseen sallyports, which now
Were useless grown ; The open doors allow
A free access into the room, where come,
Such real forms he saw as would strike dumb
Their Alcoran's tales of paradise ; the fair
And sparkling gems i' the gilded roof impair   380
Their tapers' fires, yet both themselves confess
Weak to those flames Janusa's eyes possess.
   With such a joy as bodies that do long
For souls, shall meet them in the doomsday's throng,
She that ruled princes, though not passions, sate
Waiting her lover, on a throne whose state
Epitomized the empire's wealth ; her robe,
With costly pride, had robbed the chequered globe
Of its most fair and orient jewels, to
Enhance its value ; captive princes, who   390
Had lost their crowns, might here those gems have seen
That did adorn them : yet she trusts not in
These auxiliary strengths, her confidence
In her own beauty rests, which no defence
Of chastity ere yet withstood ; and now
She scorns to fear it, when her power did bow
Unto a slave condemned, that ne'er could look
To see the light, but whilst some torment took
The use of eyes away. Whilst he draws near
By her command, no less it did appear   400
Her wonder, to behold his dauntless spirit,
Than his, what virtue to applaud as merit.
   Placed in a seat near her bright throne, to stir
His settled thoughts, she thus begins :—' From her
Your sword hath so much injured, as to shed
Blood so near kin to mine, that it was fed

367 conduct] 'Conduct' for 'conductress' may just deserve a note because of the
odd reversal of meaning involved.   383, 4 Blake !   398 light] Orig. 'sight.'

(155)

By the same milky fountains, and within
One womb warmed into life, is such a sin
I could not pardon, did not love commit
A rape upon my mercy : all the wit   410
Of man in vain inventions had been lost,
Ere thou redeemed ; which now, although it cost
The price of all my honours, I will do :—
Be but so full of gratitude as to
Repay my care with love. Why dost thou thus
Sit dumb to my discourse ? It lies in us
To raise or ruin thee, and make my way
Thorough their bloods that our embraces stay.'
   This on the spur of passion spoke, she strains
His hand in hers ; where feeling the big veins   420
Beat with intemperate heat, conceiving it
The strokes of lust, to aggravate the fit
Into a paroxysm of guilt, she shows
More than with modesty, how much she owes
To Nature's treasure, for that ill-spent stock
Of beauty she enjoyed :—Her eyes unlock
Two cabinets of sparkling diamonds, which
The even foils of ebon brows enrich
With a more orient brightness ; on her cheek
The roses, conquering the pale lily, seek   430
To counterfeit a blush, but vanquished shame
Submits to love, in whose insulting flame
The modest virgin a sad martyr dies,
And at Fame's wounds bleeds—Passion's sacrifice ;
Nature's embossed work, her soft swelling breasts,
Those balls of living ivory, unprest
Even with the weight of tiffany, displays
Whiteness that shamed the swan's : the blood, that strays
In azure channels over them, did show
By their swelled streams, how high the tide did flow   440
Wherein her passions sailed ; the milky way,
Love's fragrant valley that betwixt them lay,
Was moist with balmy dew, extracted by
The busy spirits that did hovering fly
Thorough her boiling blood, whose raging flame
Had scorched to death the April flowers of shame.
   To charm those sullen spirits that within
The dark cells of his conscience might have been
Yet by religion hid—that gift divine,
The soul's composure, music, did refine   450
The lazy air ; whose polished harmony,
Whilst dancing in redoubled echoes, by
A wanton song was answered, whose each part
Invites the hearing to betray the heart.

434 bleeds] Orig. 'bled.'

Having with all these choice flowers strewed the way
That leads to lust, to shun the slow delay
Of his approach, her sickly passions haste
To die in action. 'Come (she cries) we waste
The precious minutes. Now thou know'st for what
Thou'rt sent, for hither, which if active at,   460
Thou only liv'st in my esteem.' And then,
Oh, impudence! which from the worst of men
Might force a blush, she swiftly hastes to tread
Within lust's tropics, her polluted bed.
And here, black sinner, thou, whose blood's disease,
Of kin to hell's, wants numbers to appease
Its flaming calenture, blush to behold
A virgin virtue spotless leaves unfold
In youthful volume, whilst thy ripe years, spent
In lust, hath lost thy age's ornament.   470
   In this, as hot and fierce a charge of vice,
As, since he lost the field in Paradise,
Man ever felt, the brave Argalia sits,
With virtue cooled in passion's feverish fits:
Yet at life's garrisons his pulses beat
In hot alarums, till, to a soft retreat
Called by that fair commandress, spite of all
Beauty's prevailing rhetoric, though he fall
Ruined beneath her anger, he by this
Unwelcome language her expected bliss   480
Converts to rage:—'And must my freedom then
At such a rate be purchased? Rather, when
My life expires in torments, let my name
Forgotten die, than live in black-mouthed fame,
A servant to thy lust. Go, tempt thy own
Damned infidels to sin, that ne'er had known
The way to virtue : not this cobweb veil
Of beauty, which thou wear'st but as a jail
To a soul pale with guilt, can cover o'er
Thy mind's deformities ; a tainted whore   490
Conscience proclaim thee will, when thou shalt sit,
Shook with this spotted fever's trembling fit.
Rent from these gilded pleasures, send me to
A dungeon dark as hell, where shadows do
Reign in eternal silence ; let these rich
And costly robes, the gaudy trappings which
Thou mean'st to clothe my sin in, be exchanged
For sordid rags. When thy fierce spleen hath ranged
Through all invented torments, choose the worst
To punish my denial ; less accursed   500
I so shall perish, than if by consent
I'd taught thy guilty thoughts how to augment

470 hath] Singer, as usual, changes to 'have.'

Their sins in action, and, by giving ease
To thy blood's fever, took its loathed disease.'
  To have the spring-tide of her pleasures, swelled
By lust's salt waters, thus by force expelled
Back to confusion's troubled sea, had made
Such troops of passion ready to ' invade
An ill-defended conscience, that her look,
Like a cast felon's out of hopes o' the book,   510
Was sad with silent guilt. The room she leaves
To her contemner, who not long receives
The benefit of rest; she that had been
The prologue unto this obstructed sin,
With six armed slaves was entered, thence to force
Him to his dismal jail: but the divorce
Of life from those which first approached, joined to
The others' flight, had put her to renew
That scattered strength, had not that sacred tie,
His solemn oath, from laurelled victory   520
Snatched the fair wreath, and, though brave valour strives
To reach at freedom through a thousand lives,
At her command more tamely made him yield,
Than conquered virgins in the bridal field.

THE END OF THE THIRD CANTO.

Canto IV

THE ARGUMENT

Anger, improved by lust's enormous flame,
  Fires vexed Janusa with such sad extremes
Of rage, that her sweet sex's native shame
  Is scorched to death in those prodigious beams.

Which whilst they to her angry lord betray
  Her honour's loss, such tumults in him breed,
That both their deaths must serve for an allay;
  Whose sudden fall our Christian champion freed.

OUR noble captive, to fair Virtue's throne
In safety passed, though through Lust's burning zone,
Finds in his dungeon's lazy damps a rest
More sweet, though with the heavy weights opprest
Of iron bondage, than if they had been
Love's amorous wreaths, Janusa's arms, within
Whose ivory circles he had slept. But she,
Her grief composed of all malignity,
Lust's flames unquenched converts to, whilst they burn,
Black thoughts within her breast—the beauteous urn   10

      510 hopes o' the book] i. e. ' benefit of clergy.'

Of lust's corruption. Sometimes anger flies
Above the sphere of reason, and there dies
With tears extinguished ; she breathes curses in
Her soul's pale agony, such as had been
More deadly than infectious damps if not
Strangled in the embryo,—dead before their hot
Poison could work upon her fancy more
Than spleenful thoughts, which were recalled before
Ripened for execution. Now she steeps
Her down in tears, a flood of sorrow weeps,   20
Of power, if penitent, to expiate
Youth's vigorous sins ; but all her mourning sate
Beneath a darker veil than that which shades
Repentant grief, since sin but wished invades
The soul with that which leads to horror, when
Grief for sins past brings into light again :
One through a sea of trouble leads the way
To a safe harbour, the other casts away
Poor shipwrecked mortals, when by death's swift stroke
Life's feeble hold is from Hope's anchor broke.   30
    So far the fair Janusa in this sad
Region of grief had gone, till sorrow had
That fever turned, upon whose flaming wings
At first lust only sat, to one which brings
Death's symptoms near her heart ; which had so long
Beneath the burden groaned, until the strong
Disease had wrought up all the blood within
Her cheeks into consuming flames ; the skin
Had lost its soft repose of flesh, and lay
On nought but bones, whose sharpness did betray   40
Their macerated nerves ; the rose had lost
His ensigns in her cheeks, and though it cost
Pains near to death, the lily had alone
Set his pale banners up ; no brightness shone
Within her eyes' dim orbs, whose fading light,
Being quenched in death, had set in endless night,
Had not the wise endeavours of her maid,
The careful Manto, grief's pale scouts betrayed
By sly deceit : knowing if she should want
Health, until cured by that exotic plant,   50
The captive's love, what lust at first did burn
With inflammations might a gangrene turn.
Although she cures not, yet gives present ease
By laying opiates to the harsh disease.
    A letter, which did for uncivil blame
His first denial, in the stranger's name
Disguised, she gives her ; which, with eyes that did
O'erflow with joy, read o'er, had soon forbid
Grief's sullen progress, whose next stage had been
O'er life's short road, the grave—death's quiet inn.   60

(159)

From whose dark terror, by this gleam of light,
Like trembling children by a lamp's weak light
Freed from night's dreadful shadows, she'd embraced
Sleep, Nature's darkness, had not joy defaced
Those sooty characters, and on the wings
Of airy hope—that wanton bird which sings
As soon as fledged—advanced her to survey
The dawning beauties of a longed-for day.
  But ere this pyramid of pleasure to
Its height arrives, with 's presence to undo 70
The golden structure, dreadful Ammurat
From 's floating mansion safely landed at
The city's port, impatient love had brought
In an untimely visit : ere swift thought,
Fettered with guilt, could from his eager eye
By an excuse to sanctuary fly,
He enters, and she faints! In which pale trance
His pity finds her, but to no such chance
Imputes the cause ; rather conceives it joy,
Whose rushing torrent made her heart employ 80
Its nimble servants, all her spirits, to
Prevent a deluge, which might else undo
Love's new-made commonwealth. But whilst his care
Hastens to help, her fortune did declare
Her sorrow's dark enigma : from her bed
The letter drops—which, when life's army fled
Their frontier garrisons, neglected had
Been left within 't ;—this seen, declares a sad
Truth to the amazed bassa, though 'twere mixt
With subtle falsehood. Whilst he stands, betwixt 90
High rage and grief distracted, doubtful yet
In what new dress to wear revenge, the fit
Forsakes Janusa ; who, not knowing she
Detected stood of lust's conspiracy
'Gainst honour's royal charter, from a low
Voice strains a welcome, which did seem to flow
From fickle discontent, such as the weak
Lungs breathe the thoughts in whilst their fibres break.
  To counterfeited slumbers leaving her,
He 's gone, with silent anger to confer ; 100
And, though rage lives in fire, the fury lies
Unseen through the false optics of his eyes.
With such a farewell as kind husbands leave
Their pregnant wives, preparing to receive
A mother's first of blessings, he forsakes
The room, and into strict inquiry takes
The wretched Manto ; who, ere she could call
Excuse to aid, surprised, discovers all
Her sin's black art, from whose dark theorems he
This method draws :—That night, designed to be 110

Lightened with lust's hot triumphs, he pretends
Commanded absence, yet the false stroke bends
But towards that guard, ere, by a swift reverse
Brought back, his soul's sly scouts had gained commerce
With all those enemies to honour, by
Whose aid Janusa ruins chastity.
   Placed by false Manto in a closet, which,
Silent and sad, had only, to enrich
Its roof with light, some few neglected beams
Sent from Janusa's room, which serve as streams   120
To waft intelligence ;—here he beheld,
Whilst she, who with his absence had expelled
All thoughtful cares, was with her joy swelled high
As captives are when called to liberty.
Her linen, like a princely bride's that meets
In the soft folds of her first nuptial sheets
Perfumed and costly ; her fair bed was more
Adorned than shrines, whose saints rich kings adore ;
Incense, in smoky curls, climbs to the fair
Roof, whilst choice music rarifies the air :   130
Each element, in more perfection here
Than in their first creation, did appear,
Yet lived in harmony ;—the winged fire lent
Perfumes to the air, that, to moist cordials pent
In crystal vials, strength ; and those impart
Their vigour to that ball of earth, the heart.
The nice eye here epitomized might see
Rich Persia's wealth, and old Rome's luxury.
   But now, like Nature's new made favourite,
Who, until all created for delight   140
Was framed, did ne'er see paradise, comes in
Deceived Argalia, thinking he had been
Called thither to behold a penitent
Arming for death, not heaven's choice blessings, spent
On th' vanities of life ; but mirth soon gives
That thought its mortal wound, and shows she lives
Beyond that dark sphere—where her joys did move
As if her eyes alone gave laws to love ;
Where beauty's constellations all did shine
As if no cross aspect could e'er untwine   150
Their clasped conjunctions, which did seem to guide
Old nature's steps, till from their zenith's pride,
By virtue, the soul's motion, which the world
In order keeps, into confusion hurled :
For here gay Vanity, though clothed in all
Her gaudy pageants, lets her trophies fall
Before bright virtue's throne. With such a high
Heroic scorn as aged saints, that die
Heaven's favourites, leave the trivial world, he slights
That gilded pomp ; no splendent beam invites   160

His serious eye to meet their objects in
An amorous glance: reserved as he had been
Before his grave confessor, he beholds
Beauty's bright magic, while its art unfolds
Great love's mysterious riddles, and commands
Captive Janusa to infringe the bands
Of matrimonial modesty. When all
Temptation fails, she leaves her throne to fall,
The scorn of greatness, at his feet: but prayer,
Like flattery, expires in useless air,   170
Too weak to batter that firm confidence
Their torment's thunder could not shake. From hence
Despair, love's tyrant, had enforced her to
More wild attempts, had not her Ammurat, who,
Unseen, beheld all this, prevented by
His sight the death of bleeding modesty.
    Made swift with rage, the ruffled curtain flies
His angry touch—he enters—fixed his eyes,
From whence some drops of rage distil, on her
Whose heart had lent her face its character.   180
Whilst he stood red with flaming anger, she
Looks pale with fear;—passion's disparity,
In such extremes as nature's laws require,
'Twixt earth's cold centre and the air's circling fire,
Dwelt in their troubled breasts; his wild eyes stood,
Like comets when attracting storms of blood,
Shook with portentous sadness, whilst hers sate
Like the dull earth, when trembling at the fate
Of those ensuing ills—heavy and fixt
Within their orbs. Passions thus strangely mixt,   190
No various fever e'er created in
The frenzied brain, when Sleep's sweet calm had been
From her soft throne deposed. This lightning past,
Thunder succeeds; as burning mountains cast
But horrid noise after their flaming smoke,
So having paused, his dreadful voice thus broke
The dismal silence:—'Thou prodigious whore,
The curse of my nativity, that more
Afflicts me than eternal wrath can do
Spirits condemned—some fiends instruct me to   200
Heighten revenge to thy desert; but so
I should do more than mortals may, and throw
Thy spotted soul to flames. Yet I will give
Its passport hence; for think not to outlive
This hour, this fatal hour, ordained to see
More than an age before of tragedy.'
    She that fell from a firmament of pride
To fortune's lowest region, and there died

207-220. A remarkable and almost unique example of a passage where poetry is
absolutely 'above grammar.'

A sad example to ensuing times—
That honour's altitude supports not crimes,   210
When in their stretched extensions reaching to
Justice, which can through reversed optics view
Giants, though pigmy sins do oft appear,
Like the dim moon, more great, because more near;
Sins that, till fear their guilt did aggravate,
Wore virtue's frontispiece, since now too late
To hope for life, in their own monstrous form
Encounter reason's guards, till the big storm
Of various passions all were settled in
Dregs of despair. When, fearing tears should win   220
The victory of anger, Ammurat draws
His cimetar, which had in blood writ laws
For conquered provinces, and with a swift
And cruel rage, ere penitence could lift
Her burthened soul in a repentant thought
Towards Heaven, sheathes the cold steel in her soft
And snowy breast. With a loud groan she falls
Upon the bloody floor, half breathless, calls
For his untimely pity; but perceiving
The fleeting spirits with her blood, were leaving   230
Her heart unguarded, she employs that breath
Which yet remained, not to bewail her death,
But beg his life that caused it—on her knees
Struggling to rise. But now calmed Ammurat frees
Her from disturbing death, in 's last great work,
And thus declares some virtue in a Turk.—
  'I have, brave Christian, by perusing thee
In this great act of honour, learnt to be
Too late, thy slow-paced follower: this ring (with that
Gives him his signet) shall, when questioned at   240
The castle-guards, thy safety be. And now
I see her blood's low water doth allow
Me only time to launch my soul's black bark
Into death's rubric sea—for to the dark
And silent region, though we here were by
Passion divorced, fortune shall not deny
Our souls to sail together. From thy eyes
Remove death's load, and see what sacrifice
My love is offering.' With that word, a stroke
Pierces his breast, whose speedy pains invoke   250
Death's opiates to appease them. He sinks down
By 's dying wife, who, ere the cold flood drown
Life in the deluge of her wounds, once more
Betrays her eyes t' the light; and though they bore
The weight of death upon their lids, did keep
Them so long open, till the icy sleep
Began to seize on him, and then she cries—
'Oh see, just Heaven! see, see my Ammurat dies,

(163)

To wander with me in the unknown shade
Of immortality—But I have made 260
The wounds that murdered both: his hand that gave
Mine, did but gently let me blood to save
An everlasting fever. Pardon me,
My dear, my dying lord! Eternity
Shall see my soul washed white in tears; but oh!
I now feel time's dear want—they will not flow
Fast as my stream of blood. Christian, farewell!
Whene'er thou dost our tragic story tell,
Do not extenuate my crimes, but let
Them in their own black characters be set 270
Near Ammurat's bright virtues, that, read by
The unpractised lover, which posterity,
Whilst wanton winds play with our dust, shall raise
On beauty's throne, the good may justice praise
By his example, and the bad by mine
From Vice's throne be scared to Virtue's shrine.'
    And here the speed Death's messengers did make
To hurry forth their souls, did faintly shake
Her words into imperfect accents. 'This,'
She cries, 'is our last interview'—a kiss 280
Then joins their bloodless lips—each close the eyes
Of the other, whilst the parting spirit flies
Mounted on both their breaths, the latest gasp
They e'er must draw. Whilst with stiff arms they clasp
Each other's neck, Argalia through a cloud
Of liquid sorrow did behold the proud
Triumphs of death in their untimely fate:
He sees great Ammurat for a robe of state
Grovelling in blood, the fair Janusa lie,
Purpled in death, like polished ivory 290
Dipped in vermilion; the bright crystals, that
Her soul in conquering flames looked thorough at,
Both quenched and cooled in death. But time did lend
His tears scarce passage, till a drop could end
Its journey o'er his cheeks, before a page,
Whose cruelty had far out-grown his age,
Enters in haste; and with an anger that,
Though indiscreet, at wrongs seemed kindled at,
In wounds did on the bassa's body vent
A spleen that death's discharge could not content. 300
    This seen, Argalia, to whom all must be
Offence that injures fair humanity,
Stops the vain torrent, and a nearer way
To just revenge directs the angry boy:
Who, by unfolded truth, now lets him know,
His rage to that uncivil height did grow,
Not from a childish spleen, but wrongs that he,
A Christian, suffered in captivity.

Assured by this confession that he might
Be useful, more than in a secret flight,   310
Argalia bids him, in his bassa's name,
A mandate write for some of worthiest fame,
'Mongst all the Christian citizens, and those
To send the guard for, ere the morning rose
On the black ruins of the night. This done,
Before that time the victory had won
Of opportunity; their warders slain,
Each Christian captive from his rusty chain
His bold hand frees, and by their happy aid,
The gates being first secured, with ease dismayed   320
The drowsy garrison, from whom they found
But weak resistance ;—some soft sleep had bound
To beds of ease, intemperate riot kept
Others more vainly waking; here one slept
Between a mistress' arms, and there another,
Stole to a private catamite, did smother
Delight in whispers; in which loose garb found,
Ere time rolls up what slow neglect unwound,
Even in security's soft lap surprised,
They met grim death in pleasure's shape disguised.   330
   All now being slain but feeble eunuchs and
Poor trembling maids, the new but valiant band
Of late, freed captives crown the walls, from whence
They saw the soldiers' wicked diligence
In finding those which the false mandate had
Designed for ruin general : as sad
The city's sorrows were ; a desolate
And silent horror unregarded sate
In the empty streets, which action had not filled
Yet with employment. But when day did gild   340
The ebony of night, to hear the rude
Murmur that did from the mixed multitude
Open together with their doors, assures
Argalia, that their fear, which yet secures
That handful of insulting tyrants, might,
With anger being charged home, be put to flight
With a reserve of hope ; whilst every breast
Was swelled with stifled spirits ; whilst, opprest
With silent grief, helpless spectators, they
Saw those they once for virtue did obey—   350
Their reverend senators, whose silvered heads
Age now made fit for ease, forced from their beds
By feverish power's rude fits, whose heat, not all
The juleps of their tears, though some drops fall
From Beauty's lovely blossoms, cool—Their rage
Neglected youth slights like unreverent age.

343 open] Orig. 'opened.'

But when the conquering captives, by the brave
Argalia rescued from the castle, gave
Bright victory's signal; when they saw each lance
The bleeding head of a grim Turk advance,   360
Anger, like unobstructed love, breaks forth
In flaming haste. Yet here the want of worth
And valour 'mongst the city herd, had drove
Them all to death's dark fields, if, whilst they strove
With that stout band of Janissaries, they
Had not been by Argalia taught the way
To victory; who in a sally meets
Retreating fear when creeping from the streets
T' the vain protection of their doors. And now,
His conquering sword having taught all to bow   370
Beneath its burnished splendour, since the high
Applause o' the loudest acclamations fly
Beneath his worth, a general vote elects
Him for their prince: but his brave soul affects
Not so sublime a burthen, knowing they,
Bred under a democracy, obey
Contracted power; but harshly he returns
All to their senate, who of late, like urns,
Nought but the useless ashes did contain
Of their own laws, which were by conquest slain.   380
    But his refusal, where acceptance not
Envy could say Ambition had begot,
But new plants virtue; who from thence did take
The deeper root, and 'mongst the throng did make
That choice so epidemical, that he,
For valour feared, loved for humility.
The people's prayer, those humble shrubs that owe
For safety to power's cedars, join to grow
Shadowed beneath his merit, and create
Him prince o' the senate; who, their doubtful state   390
Requiring strong allies, a fleet prepared,
To seek those princes who their danger shared.
Which ready, with a prosperous gale of wind,
He, though employed by honour, sails to find
Out Love's rich Indies; and, with 's white-winged fleet,
Hastens Palermo's nearest port to meet.

THE END OF THE FOURTH CANTO.

363 herd] Orig. 'heard.'

Canto V

THE ARGUMENT

With prosperous sails moved from Sardinia's shore,
  Argalia safe doth now from danger set
The Cyprian prince, who, though so large in score
  With noble friendship, soon repays the debt.

In Sparta's court they're now arrived, where he
  That life he saved ventures, to save him in
An act so great—it sets the princess free,
  Who for his sake had long a prisoner been.

WHILST with bent oars Argalia's squadrons move,
Like the light wings of Time's physician, Love,
Who steered his course, and now had safely drawn
Him through the Ionian waves, when by the dawn
Of a still morning, whose pale sickly light,
Yet bounded in the ebony of night,
Showed like a dull quicksilver foil spread o'er
The world's great glass, whose even surface bore
Within their view two galleons, whom they saw,
Like timorous hares base hunters give no law,   10
Chased by a nimble numerous fleet. Drawn near,
Christians the chased, the chasers Turks appear ;
Which, like a shoal of smaller fishes made
So bold by number that they durst invade
The big-bulked whale, on every side assails
The slow-paced fleet : who, since not strength prevails
Against such odds, their fiery spirits spent
In thunder, which had from their broadsides sent
The last great groan for power's decease, and they,
Not their foe's terror, but good fortune, lay.   20
    Whilst cramped in this convulsion of their fear,
Which honour gilding, made despair appear
The child of fortitude, they all prepare
Bravely to die, Argalia's squadrons bear
Up with the wind ; and ere the Turk's proud fleet,
Deceived by their own crescents, fear to meet,
A danger, like a hurricane, falls in
Destruction ; which was suffered whilst unseen.
So wealthy merchants, whose returning cost
A storm on the pacific sea hath lost,   30
Fall from the arms of hope : sudden and swift
As inundations, whose impetuous drift
Swallows a sleeping city up, had they
Lost the firm hold of victory, and lay
Sad captives in their own lost ship—for flight
Saves few, where all in hopes of conquest fight.
    Fair victory made more bright by accident,
(Even when despair hope's wasted stock had spent),

Those that were rescued from their soft prayers raise,
To pay Heaven's tribute in their louder praise : 40
Which oft-neglected debt discharged, they gave,
Allayed with thanks, to him, whose hand did save—
A miracle in their delivery—all
Deserved applause, that can when mounted, fall
I' the circle of humanity. To kiss
Those hands which plucked him from the black abyss
Of death, their brave commander goes ; where he
Discovered by majestic courtesy
Such real forms of worth, that he was grown
Rich in esteem before more fully known. 50
But long truth stands not veiled in a disguise
Of ignorance, ere they are taught to prize
His friendship at a higher rate, by seeing
Their active valour had been blest in freeing
The Cyprian prince ; for such he was, and then
Bound for Morea. This made public, when
Acquaintance had taught love more boldness, he,
All that discretion would permit to be
Lodged in the closet of a friendly breast,
Tells to Argalia : who, though in his best 60
Of hopes a rival knowing him, was in
Love too secure to harbour envious sin.
Their prosperous fleet, ere Time's short steps had trod
In hours a full day's journey, safely rode
At anchor in Gerenza's bay ; from whence,
When known, their cannons in a loud expense
Proclaim their welcome. The acquaintance that
The Cyprian's father, ere his youth staid at
Its summer solstice, with Cleander had,
Revives i' the son's embraces, which the glad 70
City i' the triumphs echoes, ere 'twas known
That his resolves were such—as love was grown
The wishes of the people's throng, who thought
That that unpolished prince Zoranza brought
Unequal strength of merit, ere to win
The fort Pharonnida lodged virtue in.
When first they entered the admiring court,
Fame (wise men's care, but the fools' busy sport)
Making the ear the eye's wise harbinger,
By learning first their virtues, did confer 80
More honour on their persons. They beheld
I' the Cyprian prince heroic worth, yet swelled
With no ambitious tumour ; calm and free
As wholesome air, when its ubiquity
Breathes healthful blasts, were his smooth thoughts—to all
Most sweetly affable, but few could call

69 Cleander] Cleander, seldom if ever *named* before, is the King, Pharonnida's father.

His love familiar; his youth had not
Yet learnt rough war, although from precept got
Its useful rudiments, and by valour shows
Future command may pay what action owes   90
To speculation : by the grave sad man,
Whose counsel could conspiracies unspan
When ready to give fire, he is beheld
As one whose virtues far his years excelled,
And might, when at maturity, afford
Length to the sceptre from 's victorious sword.
From this young prince, Heaven's hopeful blossom, they,
Pleased but not satisfied, their souls convey
On those winged messengers—their eyes, unto
Manly Argalia; finding there a new   100
And various form of worth :—on 's brow did sit
Reserved discretion reconciled to wit;
Serious and grave his carriage, yet a face
Where Love's fair shrine did Wisdom's temple grace;
His scars, those broad seals which protecting fate
His future safety signed in, on him sate
Not to deform, but until age remain,
Like maids of honour placed in Beauty's train.
True worth dwelt in the other, but in this
Brave hero's breast had her metropolis.   110
The Cyprian's safety and Sardinia's brave
Redemption, were the passports which fame gave
Unto his travelling praise ; which, fled in haste
Through the ears' short stages, in each breast had placed
A love of 's worth ; which wise men softly praise
Whilst the loud throng to acclamations raise.
    Not long these true-born sons of honour in
Palermo's court remain, ere, what had been
The cause which had the youthful Cyprian drew
From 's father's court, white fame presents unto   120
Busy inquirers. Which design from all—
Those swift but weak recruits, good wishes—call,
Except from some it most concerned ; 'mongst which
Cleander staggers unresolved. The rich
And powerful kingdom, which affinity
With Cyprus promised, was a prize to be
Valued before Epirus' wealth, who, though
Of late victorious, yet could never grow
Up to that glorious height. This thought, the most
Of all that e'er obstructed love, had crost   130
Zoranza's hopes, had not his wishes been,
Though covetously vast, confined within
The other's merits ; amongst which the chief
Opposes first itself, and, the relief,
Whispers in 's soul, that had been thence brought by
Him, when his state wept blood for liberty.

This in the scale of justice seemed as large
As love's dimensions, till a second charge
Of thoughts proclaim the Cyprian's power to do
The same if in necessity sought to;   140
Which blames becoming gratitude, as, in
Relation to servility, a sin
In the great soul of princes, who can be,
If they remain in debt for courtesy,
But captives in the throne — too oft the cause
Why meritorious subjects meet the law's
Harsh rigour for reward, when their deserts,
Many and great, o'erfill their princes' hearts.
    Before Cleander's gravity had laid
This tempest of his passions, fame betrayed   150
Their cause to the Epirot prince, who hears
The Cyprian's welcome; which his various fears
But briefly comment on, before, without
More slow delays than what were spent about
The swiftest preparations, he intends
To visit fair Pharonnida, and ends
His journey, ere a thought unwinged with love
Could lead him forth of 's court: which haste did prove
His passions stronger than the strength of age
Appeared to promise. What it might presage,   160
To see at once two royal strangers in
Their glorious court, which both employed had been
About one amorous errand, strangely did
Affect the citizens; whose fears, forbid
The public stage, in private whispers tells
What danger lay betwixt those parallels.
    Yet, in the opposition of those stars
That shine in passion's sphere, Love's civil wars
Had no field army; all his power did rest
Within the private garrisons o' the breast,   170
Which, though besieged by sly suspicion, made
No verbal sallies, but prepare to invade
Beauty's bright province. Yet, each only had
A single visit given unto the sad
Sweet object of their hopes, and thence received
A welcome, such as neither had bereaved
The other's hopes — both rather finding cause
Of cold despair. Cleander pleads the laws
Of nature and free choice, to wave his own
Engagements to Zoranza; which had blown   180
Love's sickly flame with the tempestuous breath
Of anger forth, had not those thoughts to death
I' the bud been doomed. Whilst thus his passions slept
In Love's soft arms, the noble Cyprian kept
A distance 'twixt his hopes and wishes by
The staid Epirot's interest :—both rely

On their own merits, and Love's doubtful fate
Makes subject to the monarchy of Fate.
　　But whilst this busy combat of the heart
On equal terms is fought, time bent to part   190
The royal champions.　Through the obscure ports
Of dark disguise into Love's field resorts
A third brave combatant, whose merit had
(Though not i' the armour of great titles clad)
By parley won that maiden fort, which they,
Although they scaled on golden mountains, lay
Before in vain.　Argalia, though within
Gerenza's court, had yet a stranger been,
More than in fame and big report, to her
Whose best of thoughts wore his soul's character: 200
And yet, although a virgin's bashful grace
Concealed her own, for to behold that face
So much in debt t' the people's praises, to
Her window oft the royal maid had drew;
Where, whilst his eyes did waste their beams in vain
To pierce those stubborn walls that did contain
Rich Love's unvalued treasure, she beholds
His brave deportment; which, since strange, unfolds
New volumes of unprinted joy, which she
(Sorrow affording so much liberty)   210
Oft with delight looks o'er, beholding in 't
Argalia's virtues in a different print.
　　But his wise fate, even when his prayer grew weak
In faith, did through hope's cold antarctic break
In a long summer's day.—His noble friend,
The princely Cyprian, did so largely spend
His stock of eloquence in 's praise, when he
Last saw divine Pharonnida, that she,
Although from no remoter cause than springs
From virtue's public love, tells him—he brings   220
His next best welcome with his friend : which, proud
To be observant in, when time allowed
A visit, he performs.　Now to the court,
Beauty's dull cloister, which no thronged resort
Of clients fill they're come ; the surly guard,
Those wakeful dragons, did without reward
Let in that danger in disguise, which had
Met death i' the entrance, if in that unclad.
　　The way that cleft the scowling rock being by
A thousand steps ascended, they i' the high   230
Clifts find the royal eaglet, trying that
Bright eye of her fair soul, discretion, at
The fiery beams of anger, which were shot
From her majestic father.　Being got

　187, 8 fate] The first 'fate' should of course be 'state.'

Once more to breathe his soul upon that hand
Where love's first vows, sealed with his lips, did stand,
(Knowledge inflaming passion's fever), like
Unpractised saints, which miracles do strike
Into a reverend zeal, he trembling takes
That holy relic, which a cold fear shakes   240
In that warm touch.   Her eyes' fair splendour shone
Like bright stars in heaven's trepidation,
Shook with the general motion, though betwixt
The spheres of love and wonder they stood fixt
In their own orbs, and their united beams
Centred on him; yet (like dead friends which dreams
Imperfectly present) his lovely form,
As mariners when land is through a storm
With doubtful joy descried, she sees: but yet
Knowledge had met with no prospective fit   250
To guide her through the dark disguise unto
The road of truth;—his valour was in new
Habiliments of honour clothed, and scars
Made her love's heaven adorned with unknown stars.
    But whilst her recollecting spirits were
All busied—his idea to compare
With what she saw, a sudden glance of the eye
Develops truth; that jewel, which was by
His first protector left, is seen, by which
Hope, near impoverished with despair, grows rich   260
In faith, heaven's tenure.   But the rushing tide
O'erflows so much, that love's fresh rivers glide
Over weak Nature's banks,—she faints, and in
A silent joy contracted what had been
By love dilated: from which giddy trance
To rescue her, Argalia doth advance
To charge those troops of passions, which o'er her
Had proved victorious; nor did Fate defer
The conquest long, ere she displays again
Beauty's fair banner in Love's ivory plain.   270
    The imprisoned spirits freed, the blood in haste,
Fearing her love had Wisdom's throne defaced,
To Beauty's frontiers flies; so mornings weep
And blush together, when they oversleep
Themselves in night's black bed.   Though fear's dull charms,
Whilst in the circle of Argalia's arms,
Like dream's fantastic visions, vanish in
Her waking joys; yet, knowing they had been
Betrayed into a stranger's view, they both
Stood mute with passion, till the Cyprian, loath   280
To add more weights unto affliction, by
Imping Love's wings with noble courtesy,
Fans off the southern clouds of fear, and thus
Calms the loud storm :—' Doubt not, because to us,

Fair princess, Love's mysterious riddles are
By accident resolved, the factious war
Shall be renewed; such base intelligence
Traitors and spies give, when the dark offence
Starts at discovery. If my service may   290
Be useful, know I sooner dare betray
My sins t' the world, than your intentions to
A smooth seducer. This rare interview
May be my wonder—-but shall never prove
My guilt, though all the stratagems of Love
Lay open to my heart, which, though unskilled
In his polemics, yet with truth is filled.'
    Since now too late to seek protection by
A faint denial, the wished privacy
Their room afforded, gives them leave to lead
His apprehension where conceit did read   300
The story of Love's civil wars: whose rage,
Since treaty could not calm, makes him engage
His stock of power in their defence, and end
His passion's progress to let Love attend
On Friendship's royal train; what not the force
Of earth's united beauties could divorce;
Nor wealth's, nor honour's strong attractions draw
To other objects; by that holy law
Informed, as hateful sacrilege, doth fly
The bold intrusion on love's hierarchy.   310
    With joy assured of such a powerful friend,
The hopeful lovers sadder cares suspend,
To lay the platform of their safety by
A fair escape. But fear doth oft untie
The golden webs of fancy. When they come
To name the means, invention, then struck dumb,
Startles into distraction; no smooth stroke
Of soft-palmed flattery could ere provoke
Sleep in her watchful dragons, nor no shower
Of ponderous gold pierce through her sable tower—   320
The harsh commander of her surly guard,
Wakeful as foaming Cerberus, and hard
As Parian quars, a heart that could not melt
In love's alembic; the slave never felt
His darts but when lust gave the wound, and then,
Seared with enjoying, the blood stops again,
And leaves behind the fever; which disease
Now in him raged. Amphibia, that could please
None but a sympathizing nature, in
His blood had both disease and medicine been,—   330
With lust's enchantments, thick loose glances, first
Breeding a calenture, whose sickly thirst
Consenting sin allays again. But long
This monster thrives not in the dark, ere, strong

By custom grown, with impudence he dares
Affront unveiled report, and boldly bears
Himself above those headstrong torrents, by
Whose streams harsh censure grew to calumny.
Which careless pride did unobstruct the way,
Through which to liberty love's progress lay.   340
   A short delay, which lets not fancy rest
In idle thought, their actions did disgest
Into a method. The succeeding night
To that great day, by whose triumphant light
Their annual feasts her birth did celebrate,
The time designed. Which done, to stroke rough fate
Into a calm, Argalia first finds out
Despised Florenza, then employed about
Coarse housewifery in the dull country, where
She soon became a partner of his care;   350
Prepares for safety with a diligence
Whose privacy pays lavish time's expense.
   Now from night's swarthy region rose that day,
'Gainst which Invention taught her babes the way
To level at delight, though she flew high
As monarchs' breasts. Beauty and valour vie
Each other in a conquering pride within
A spacious field, that oft before had been
The theatre of martial sports; each knight,
Whom the desire of honour did invite   360
By her swift herald, Fame, were met; and all,
Whom the respects of either part did call
To the Epirot's or young Cyprian's part,
Repair unto their tents, which, rich in art,
Adorned both sides o' the stately lists, and lent
Their beauties to be prospect's ornament.
   Near to the scaffold every seat was filled
With bright court beauties, ladies that did gild
Youth, Nature's throne of polished ivory, in
Pride—there but greatness, though low fortune's sin. 370
Ranged next to these the city madams, that
Came both to wonder and be wondered at,
Fine as on their first Lady-days, did sit
Comparing fashions, to commend their wit;
Besides the silk-worms' spoils, their husbands' gain,
Jewels they wore, like eyes in beauty's wane
Grown dim with age, so dim, that they did look
As if they'd been from plundered Delphos took;
Although that sprung from faction, yet each face
Was all set form, hardly affording place   380

342 disgest] *Sic in orig.*: and perhaps worth keeping, the pronunciation being even now hardly obsolete as a vulgarism.
   366 be] Singer 'the' for 'be.' It is not at all improbable, considering his system of versification, that Chamberlayne wrote 'be th'.'

For a stolen smile, save when some ticklish lord
Strikes sail, which they could wish should come aboard.
Below, near to the over-heated throng,
Sweet country beauties, such as ne'er did wrong
Nature with nicer art, were seated ; where
Though big rude pride cast them in honour's rear,
Yet in Love's province they appeared to have
Command from their acknowledged beauty gave ;
Humble their looks, yet Virtue there kept state,
And made e'en Envy wish to imitate   390
Their fashions—not fantastic, yet their dress
Made gallantry in love with comeliness.
    Whilst here the learned astronomers of love
Observed how eyes, those wandering stars, did move,
And thence with heedful art did calculate
Approaching changes in that doubtful state ;
The princess, like the planet of the day,
Comes with a lustre forth that did betray
The others' beams into contempt, and made
The morning stars of meaner beauties fade,   400
Sadly confessing by their languished light,
They shone but when her absence made it night.
Stately her look, yet not too high to be
Seen in the valleys of humility ;
Clear as Heaven's brow was hers, her smiles to all,
Like the sun's comforts, epidemical ;
Yet by the boldest gazer, with no less
Reverence adored, than Persians in distress
Do that bright power, who, though familiar by
An airy medium, still is throned on high.   410
    Lest the ungoverned multitude which raise
Their eyes to her, should in their lavish praise
From zeal to superstition grow, they 're now
Drawn off—the entered combatants allow
Their eyes no further leisure, but beginning
Their martial sports, with various fate were winning
Bright victory's laurels. But I here must let
Honour in their own stories live, the debt
I owe to promise but extends unto
The fortune of our royal lovers ; who,   420
Though both concerned in this, have actions far
More full of fate approaching. That bright star
Which gave Argalia victory here, scarce shows
Its spangled records, unto which he owes
Far more sublime protection, yet it lends
Vigour to that bright planet which attends
His future fortune, and discovers all
His astracisms in rising cosmical.
    Followed with acclamations, such as made
The troops of envy tremble to invade   430

(175)

His conquering fame, he leaves the field ; and by
Cleander, with rewards of victory
First honoured in the public view, is brought
From thence to meet delicious mirth in soft
Retired delights ; which in a spacious flood,
From princes' breasts to tenify the blood
Of the blunt soldiers, hastes ; whose dull souls swelled
With airy pleasures had from thought expelled
All sullen cares, and levelled paths unto
Designs which did to their neglect ensue.   440
   The black-browed night, to court the drowsy world,
Had put her starry mantle on, and hurled
Into the sea (their spacious-breasted mother)
Her dark attendants ; silent sleep did smother
Exalted clamours ; and in private meets
The busy whisperer, sporting 'twixt his sheets.
Veiled in which shady calm, Argalia, by
The noble Cyprian only in his high
Attempt assisted, now prepares to free
The great preserver of his liberty.   450
   Come to the bridge, that to secure the sleep
O' the careless guard, which slender watch did keep,
Finding it drawn, the depth and ugly look
O' the heavy stream had from the Cyprian took
All hopes of passage, till that doubt did end
In greater fear—the danger of his friend ;
Who, with a courage high as if in that
He 'd centred all the world did tremble at
In his precedent victories, had cast
Himself t' the mercy of the stream, and past   460
In safety o'er, though nets enough were spread
On her dark face to make his death's cold bed.
   Giving his spirits leave to fortify
His heart with breath, he then ascends the high
Opposing clifts, which in an ugly pride
Threatened beneath her ruined scales to hide
That rising flame of honour. Being come
To the other side, a sentry, but struck dumb
With sleep's prevailing rhetoric, he finds ;
Upon whose keys he seizes, and then binds   470
His sluggish limbs, ere full awake, conveys
Him to a place whence no loud cry betrays
The sounds of danger to his fellows, that
Revelled in louder mirth. Unstartled at

433, 4 brought] This couplet confirms the view of the pronunciation of ' brought,'
taken above.
   436 tenify] This unusual word should of course be ' tenuify' and was very probably
written so. Singer, in next line, ' haste.'
   466 scales] ' Scales ' no doubt in sense of ' staircase.'

The river's depth, the wondering Cyprian now
Crossed the united bridge, and, being taught how
By imitation to slight danger, goes
With his brave friend toward their careless foes.
    Not far were they advanced before they hear
Approaching steps; a soldier was drawn near,   480
Which to relieve the other came, but shared
In his misfortune ere he had prepared
To make resistance; which attempt succeeds
So equal to their wishes, that there needs
No more to strengthen faith.   By the command
O' the will's best leader, reason, both did stand
Awhile to view their danger;—through a way
Narrow and dark their dreadful passage lay;
The rugged rock upon each side so steep,
That, should they 've missed, no trembling hold could keep   490
Them from the grasp of death: to add to this
More forms of horror, from the dark abyss
Which undermined the rock's rough sides, they hear
A hollow murmur; the black towers appear
Flanked with destruction, every part did hold
Peculiar terror, but the whole unfold,
Through the black glass of night, a face like that
Which chaos wore, ere time was wakened at
The first great fiat—or, could aught appear
More dark and dreadful, know 'twas emblemed here.   500
    Safe passed through the first steps of danger, they
Now to the main guard come; whom they betray
By a soft knock—of all conceived 't had been
The voice their sentry called for entrance in.
Their errand undisputed, postern-gates
Are open thrown, at which the royal mates
Both rushing in, strangely amaze them; but
Now being entered, 'twas too late to shut
The danger forth, nor could confusion lend
Their trembling nerves a strength fit to defend   510
By opposition.   In base flight lay all
Their hopes of life, which some attempting fall
On the dark road of death, but few escape
To show their fellows danger's dreadful shape.
    Whilst here, like powerful winds that dissipate
Infectious damps, in unobstructed state
Their valour reigned, to tell them that the way
Which led unto the princess' freedom lay
Yet through more slippery paths of blood, with haste
Wild as their rage, Brumorchus' brothers, placed   520
That guard's commanders, enter.   Loose neglect,
Which drew them thence, since cause of that effect,
They now redeem with speed.   Riot had not
Unnerved their limbs; although their blood grew hot

With large intemperate draughts, the fever yet
I' the spirits only dwelt, till this rude fit
On the stretched heart lays hold in flames, which had
Scorched valour's wings if not in judgement clad.
Here, though their numbers equal were, yet in
A larger volume danger had not been   530
Often before presented to the view
Of the brave champions; as if she had drew
With doubtful art lines in the scheme of fate
For them and their proud foes, pale virtue sate
Trembling for fear her power should not defend
Her followers, 'gainst that strength which did attend
Those big-boned villains' strokes. Beneath whose force
The Cyprian prince had felt a sad divorce
Of Nature's wedlock, if, when sinking in
The icy sleep, Death's wide gorge had not been   540
Stopped by a stroke from fierce Argalia, sent
To aid him when in his defence he'd spent
His stock of strength. Freed by which happy blow
From Janus' guard, since now his friend lay low,
Near Death's dark valley, he contracts his power
To quench the other's lamp of life : a shower
Of wounds lets fall on 's enemy, which now
Clogged his soul's upper garments, and allow
His eyes' dim optics no more use of light,
Than what directs him in a staggering flight.   550
Yet in the darkness of approaching death,
In mischief's sables, that small stock of breath
That yet remains, to clothe, he suddenly
Gives fire unto a cannon that was by
Wise care ordained to give intelligence,
When big with danger fear could not dispense
With time's delays. The princess, that within
Her closet had that fatal evening been
Retired and sad, whilst strong-winged prayer acquaints
Her flaming zeal with Heaven's whole choir of saints,   560
Thus startled by the treacherous thunder, all
Her yet unnumbered stock of beads lets fall
'Mongst those that prayer had ranked, and did implore
In one great shriek deliverance; to her door
Hastes to behold the danger of those friends
On whose success love's fortress—hope, depends.
Where being come, her eyes' first progress met
Her prayers' reward, e'en whilst his sword was wet
With blood, the balm of victory. But long
The ecstasies of fancy, though more strong   570
Than sacred raptures, last not, all was now
Too full of noise and tumult to allow

544 Janus' guard] ' Janus' guard ' I suppose means that if he had had to face the
two, he would have had to look both ways at once, to prevent being attacked behind.

A room for passion's flow : disputes within
The schools of action, loud alarums in
The castle court and city raged ; all were
Huddled into confusion ; some prepare
To fly what others with an ignorance
As great (though bolder) to oppose advance.
 Here had our heaven-protected lovers lost
What such large sums of prayer and tears had cost,   580
Had not the torrent of the people's throng,
When rushing towards the castle, by a strong
Voice—danger, been diverted, to prevent
A hungry flame which, in the Cyprian's tent
Begun, had spread its air-dilated wings
Over the city : whose feared danger brings
On them a worse distemperature than all
Their last night's surfeits. Whilst proud turrets fall
In their own ashes, the discordant bells,
Ordained to call for aid, but ring their knells   590
That in a drunken fury, half-awake,
First their warm beds, and then their lives forsake ;
For to destruction here big pride had swelled,
Had not night's errors been by day expelled.
 With swift calls frighted, but more terrified
At their sad cause, fear being his doubtful guide,
The stout Epirot to Cleander's court
Repairs ; and there amongst a thick resort
Of subjects, finds the prince distracted by
Those epidemic clamours that did fly   600
From every part o' the city. To appease
Whose fury whilst he goes, the sharp disease
In flames feeds on her ruined beauty, and
Mounts on insulting wings ; which to withstand,
The mazed inhabitants did stop its flight
With the whole weight of rivers, till that light,
Which an usurper on the sooty throne
Of darkness sat, vanished, or only shone
From their dim torches' rays. The prince thus staid
In 's hasty journey till the flames allayed   610
Lent safety to the city, by it gave
The royal fugitives the time to save
Themselves by flight from those ensuing ills,
Whose clamorous scouts, rude sounds, the stirred air fills.
 Descended to the garden's postern gate,
A place where silence yet unruffled sate
(A night obscure and an unhaunted way,
Conspiring their pursuers to betray
To dark mistakes) with silent joy, which had
All fear's pale symptoms in love's purple clad,   620
Close as that bold Attempter, whose brave theft
Was sacred fire, the walks behind them left,

(179)

William Chamberlayne

Argalia hastes unto the castle moat
With his rich prize, there a neglected boat,
Half-hid amongst the willow beds, finds out;
In which Pharonnida, that nought could doubt
Whilst her successful lover steered, passed o'er
To meet the safety of a larger shore.

THE END OF THE THIRD BOOK.

BOOK IV. Canto I

THE ARGUMENT

Whilst noise and tumult fill the court, the sad
    Orlinda, to lament alone retired,
Finds the brave Captain in death's symptoms clad,
    Whose perfect health her friendly care acquired.

The scouts with an unwelcome emptiness
    Of news returned ; the princess' secret flight
Yet well succeeds, but now in sad distress
    Finds a black morning to that dismal night.

WHEN Fear, like an unskilful pilot in
A storm distracted, long in vain had been
Placed at the helm of Action, whilst those rude
Waves raised by greater winds, the multitude,
Swelled with uncertain counsels, all met in
A thick and dangerous confluence ; those within
The castle, by a hotter passion to
A high-wrought fury startled, did undo
Those links of counsel, which the other broke
With corrosives of fear, by the rude stroke   10
Of heedless anger; whose uncivil strife
Had robbed revenge of justice, and each life
That here was in death's inundations spilt,
Shed but to aggravate a private guilt,
Had not the prince, whose anger's flame they feared
More than grim death, to appease the storm appeared.
    Beat from the out-works of their hopes, all in
A busy tumult are employed within
The princess' lodgings; but there only find
Their knowledge by her secret flight struck blind,   20
Stumbled on errors. No characters, but what
The wasteful hand of death had scattered at
The guard, inform them; and even those seem left
The weak opposers of successful theft,
Dropt as their foe's victorious fate flew by,
To show his fortune and their loyalty.
Leaving which late warm tenements of breath,
Without once throwing up that bed of death,
Their grave-clothes o'er them, every active friend
Hastes toward her search, whilst suffering females spend   30
The hours (grown slow since burdened by their fears)
In prayers, whose doubts they numbered by their tears.

　　But amongst all of those that sacrificed
Tears to her loss, sorrow had most disguised
Lovely Orlinda, the fair sister to
The vexed Messenian; who, with love that grew
From equal attributes of honour, in
The parallels of beauty placed, had been
In ·this restraint of liberty so long
Her pleased companion, that her grief too strong　　40
For comfort grown, to mourn her absence she,
Forsaking all her friends' society,
Whilst seeking of some shady grove, is brought
To one whose veil, black as her darkest thought,
Appeared so much a stranger to the light,
That solitude did thither soon invite
The pensive lady : who, whilst entering, by
A deep groan's sound diverted, turns her eye
Toward one, who, near the utmost ebb of life
Disguised in 's blood, was with the latest strife　　50
Of death contending. At the dreadful view
Of which sad object she, retreating to
Some of her maids, who, fearing to intrude
Whilst she appeared intending solitude,
A distance kept ; made bold by number, now
Return to see if life did yet allow
A room for help, or, if his soul were fled,
To let their care entomb the helpless dead.
　　Arrived so near, that through the rubric veil
Of 's blood they saw how life did yet prevail　　60
O'er death's convulsions, they behold one lie,
Whose wounds, an object for their charity,
Soon drew them nearer in such trembling haste,
As if they feared those lavish springs would waste
Life's stock too fast. Where come, with linen soft
And white as were those hands that thither brought
That blessing, having gently wiped away
His blood, his face discovered did betray
Him to their knowledge. For the Cyprian prince
All soon conclude him, whose desert e'er since　　70
That court she knew, had to Orlinda proved
A dear delight ; yet she ne'er knew she loved,
Till her soft pity and his sad distress,
Conspiring to betray that bashfulness
Whose blushes scorched that tender plant, did now,
Even in their fortune's roughest storm, allow
It leave to grow safe, since yet passing by
No other name but noble charity.
　　By all the nimblest stratagems which Art
E'er learnt from Nature, striving to impart　　80
The best of mortal blessings, health, unto
Her royal patient, praised Orlinda grew

So high in his deserved esteem, that, though
Posterity doth to his friendship owe
For their most perfect copy, knowing she
Too ·much adored Pharonnida to be
Her base betrayer, when his health's advance
Gave way for language, every circumstance
Declares which was in that so fatal night
The sad preludiums to her secret flight.   90
By which when she, whose love (though full of fire)
Yet lay raked up in a remote desire,
Unstirred by hope, with joy had learned that he,
More than what friendship patronized, was free
From all affection to the princess; in
Her eyes, which unto then had clouded been,
Love, with as bright and pure a flame as e'er
Did in the shades of modesty declare
Passion, breaks forth. Which happy signs by him
Whose heart her eyes, e'en whilst they shone most dim,   100
With mutual flames had fired ;—that loyal love,
Which fate in vain shall struggle to remove,
Begins with flames as innocently bright
As the first rays of new-created light.
    But stay, rash reader ! think not they are led
Through these smooth walks unto their nuptial bed ;
But now, behold that their misfortune prove,
Which thou hast wept for if thou e'er didst love,
A separation. The suspicion, that
Sparta's vexed king (when first distempered at   110
His daughter's loss) did of this stranger prince
Justly conceive, persuades him now, that since
Not found within the Cyprian court, that he
Who had been vainly sought abroad might be
Yet lodged at home. Which supposition bred
So strict a search, that, though the silent dead
Not silenter than her attendants were,
Yet kind Orlinda, whom a pious care
Prompted to save what she did yet possess,
Whilst seeking with a lover's tenderness   120
How to secure him, doth at length convey
Her roving fancy to this hopeful way.—
    Not long before, though now 'twere silenced in
Domestic ills, report had busied been
In the relating of the sad distress
Of a brave Lybian prince; whom Heaven, to bless
With an eternal crown, in midst of all
His youth's fresh glories, by a powerful call
Summons to serve her : and that faith, which he
Had from the early dawn of infancy   130
Sucked from the great Impostor of the East,
Though now by time opinion's strength increast,

(183)

Spite of a people's prayers or father's threats,
Wholly forsaking; which revolt begets
So much aversion, pity could invent
Nought easier than perpetual banishment,
To punish what their faith, mistaken in
Its object, terms a black apostate's sin.

    Disguised in such a dress as pity might
Expect to encounter so distressed a wight   140
As was that wandering prince, attended by
No train but what becomes the obscurity
Of such a fortune, to the Spartan court
Amindor comes; where, though the thick resort
Of well-known friends might justly make him fear
Some treacherous eye, knowledge could ne'er appear
Through that black veil his happy art had took,
To make him like a sun-burnt Lybian look.

    Yet what engaged them more than safety in
Prayers to Heaven, his person had now been   150
Not long the wonder of the court, before
His fairer virtues, which adorned him more
Than the other could disguise, did justly prove
The happy object of the prince's love :
Whose influence, whilst it him to power did raise,
Taught by reflex the people how to praise
That fair election, till the pyramid,
Raised to his fame, had fixed its lofty head
Above the clouds of fortune. Yet not this
Fate's fairest smile, a lover's best of bliss—   160
A free commerce (which unsuspected might,
Though long and pleasant as the summer's light,
Be ne'er disturbed) with fair Orlinda, gives
Content such fullness, that although he lives
To all unknown but her alone, in that
Enjoyed more than ambition e'er aimed at.

    And now from all the fruitless diligence
Of inquisitions, and the vain expense
Of time, returned were every troop that had
Through forlorn hopes been active in the sad   170
Search of Pharonnida; which ending in
A just despair, some that till then within
The castle walls had (though as vainly) sought
Their sorrow forth, before the grieved prince brought
Brumorchus; whom they in a small lodge, where,
Secured by solitude, the household care
Of locks and bolts were vain, unsought, they found
In the soft bands of grief's best opiate bound,
Sleep; who, though throned within her ebon seat,
From lust's hot field appears but his retreat   180

150 now] Orig. 'not.'

When tired with action; for besides him they,
Where 's poison's antidote, Amphibia, lay
Locked up in 's arms, beheld. The air, with all
Their voices struck, at length had raised a call
That drowned their sleeping thunder; from the bed
Brumorchus starting struggles to have fled
The shameful danger, whilst Amphibia creeps
Beneath her sheets' protection, but nought keeps
Pursuing vengeance back. They 're took and brought
Before the prince; who, startled at the thought   190
Of such a complicated crime, refers
Their punishment to death's dire messengers.
   The yet successful lovers, long ere this
Safely arrived at their first stage of bliss,
Florenza's low and envied roof, did there,
Since speed was now the fairest child of care,
Stay only to exchange their horse, and take
With her a guide whose practic skill could make
Their untrod paths familiar. Through a low
Dark vale, where shade-affecting weeds did grow   200
Eternal strangers to the sun, did lie
The narrow path, frequented only by
The forest tyrants, when they bore their prey
From open dangers of discovering day.
   Passed through this desert valley, they were now .
Climbing an easy hill, where every bough
Maintained a feathered chorister to sing
Soft panegyrics, and the rude winds bring
Into a murmuring slumber; whilst the calm
Morn on each leaf did hang her liquid balm,   210
With an intent, before the next sun's birth,
To drop it in those wounds which the cleft earth
Received from 's last day's beams. The hill's ascent,
Wound up by action, in a large extent
Of leafy plains, shows them the canopy
Beneath whose shadow their large way did lie.
Which being looked o'er, whilst thankful praise did pay
Their debts to Heaven, they thence with a convey
Of prayers, those swift ambassadors, did send
A hopeful glance toward their large journey's end.   220
   These short surveys past, since the place assures
A safe repose, to cool the calentures
Of feverish action, down a way that led
From Pleasure's throne unto her fragrant bed,
A rank of laurels, spreading to protect
The flowery path which not unpruned neglect
Robbed of delight, they passed; the slow descent
Soon brings them where her richest ornament

218 'Convey' = convoy.

(185)

(Although with art unpleited) Nature in
A lovely landscape wore, that once had been   230
Sacred to the island's fruitful goddess. Here
Whilst they behold the infants of the year
I' the spring's unsullied livery clad, the fair
And large-limbed trees preparing to repair
Autumn's spent stock, from out a humble hill
A tributary fountain did distil
The earth's cold blood, and murmuring conveys
It on a bed of pebbles, till it pays
Her debts to the neighbouring river ; near to it
Full choruses of feathered heroes sit   240
Amidst their willow mansions, to whose ease
Their shrill notes call the sportive Dryades.
   Whilst by the brightest glories of that age
This royal robe, worn in a hermitage,
Is seen with such a silent sad delight
As smoothes the furrows of an anchorite,
Their solemn walk had brought them to a green
Skirt of that mantle, fairly spread between
Two mossy rocks, that near the crystal flood
Appendices to larger mountains stood.   250
Near which they saw, with mournful majesty
A heap of solitary ruins lie,
Half sepulchred in dust, the bankrupt heir
To prodigal antiquity, whose fair
Composures did, beneath time's pride sunk low,
But dim vestigia of their beauty show.
   Yet that it might unreverend gazers tell
It once was sacred, Ceres' image, fell
From a throne's splendour, did neglected lie,
Sunk with her temple to deformity.   260
Dark gloomy groves, which holy altars shade
With solitude, such as religion made
Full of an awful reverence, and drew
The ravishing soul from the world's wandering view,
Circled the sacred valley : into one
Of which our royal lovers were alone
Retired, in private solitude to pay
Sleep's forfeitures, whilst the bright bloomy day
Sweats the hydroptic earth ; but joy denies
That sullen guest an entrance in their eyes—   270
Their eyes, which now like wandering planets met
After a race of cross aspects, and set
Within a firmament of beauty, thence
On Love's cold region dropped their influence ;
Warmed by whose vigour, springs of pleasure had,
Watering their cheeks, those fields in roses clad.

229 unpleited] Singer 'unplighted.' But I should rather take the orig. as = ' un-
pleated,' i. e. not 'folded up in,' 'complicated with.'

Fear, that till now had made them languish in
A dangerous hectic, or at best had been
But eased with intervals, which did include
Ambiguous hopes in time's vicissitude,   280
Ceased to usurp; yet (though the throne expelled)
A large command in Reason's empire held,
Leading those parties which wise counsel sent
Close ambuscadoed dangers to prevent:
Nor could the conduct fail, assailed by aught
Within the circuit of extended thought;
Deliberation, the soul's wary scout,
Being still employed to lead fresh parties out
'Gainst the known enemies of hope. But here
Black troops of danger, undiscerned of fear,   290
Assaults unrallied Fortitude, whilst she
Slept 'mongst the rose-beds of security,
    Exalted far above the gross mistakes
Of vulgar love—clothed in such thoughts as shakes
Ripe souls from out their husks of earth to be
Picked up by angels, joy's stenography
In their embraces met; not with less strength
Of love (though yet not to be wrought at length)
Than that which meets in nuptial folds when they
Reap Heaven's first blessing, in their blood's allay   300
Met their full seas of passion; yet both, calm
As Virtue's brow, their blood but warmed like balm
To pour in sorrow's wounds, not boiled into
A scum of lust; the world's first man did woo
The blushing offspring of his side, the first
Unpractised virgin, with as great a thirst
Of blood as theirs, when, in the safe defence
Of paradise, each act was innocence.
    Here whilst their sweet employment was discourse,
Taught in the school of virtue, to divorce   310
Those maiden brides, their twisted eye-beams, Sleep,
Which flies the open gates of care, did creep
In at their crystal windows, to remove
The lamp of joy filled with the oil of love.
The princess' spirits, fled from the distress
Of action into forgetfulness,
Having the curtains drawn, Argalia's head
Softly reposing on her lap, that bed
Of precious odours, there receives awhile
A rest, for sweetness—such as saints beguile   320
Time [with] in their still dormitories, till
Heaven's summons shall their hopes on earth fulfil.
Removed from them, feeding his horses in
A well-fleeced meadow, which that age had seen

321 'with' is Singer's insertion, no doubt rightly.

Till then ne'er lose its summer robe before
Russet with age he put it off, and wore
A glittering tissue furred with snow, did lie
Their careful guide, secured ; till frighted by
A dreadful noise of horse, whose rushing wakes
Him to behold—what seen, with terror shakes   330
Off sleep's declining weights, in such a strange
Amaze as (forts surprised) the scared guards change
Their swords for fetters : flying he looks back
On the steel-fronted troop, till at his back
Approaching danger, gathering in a cloud
Of death, o'erwhelms him ; frighting with its loud
Exalted clamours from their then closed eyes—
Love's altars, sleep's intended sacrifice.
    Shook from their slumber with the first salutes
Of light to meet their ruin, thick recruits   340
Of brave resolves into Argalia's breast
Had swiftly summoned ; but the princess' rest
Exchanged for wild amazement : in which sad
Restraint of spirits, life with beauty had
Fled to the silent region, if not by
Her royal friend supported ; who, the high
Pitch of exalted anger, whilst he. draws
His sword to vindicate their righteous cause,
Descends to comfort her. Thinking those troops
Her father's messengers, his brave soul stoops   350
Not to request a favour ; but although
Their multitude, in hope's account outgrow
Life, more than those diseases which attend
On age's cold extreme, he dares defend
Love, though, by vigour of supreme commands,
Deprived of favour's mercenary bands.
    Prompted by power, that sovereign antidote
'Gainst Nature's poison, baseness, and by rote,
Not Art's fair rules, taught lessons of defence,
These dregs of men, not having more pretence   360
Than what from riot was extorted, in
Unwieldy throngs the conquest strive to win
From single valour. Not the powerful prayer
Of her, whose voice had purified the air
To a seraphic excellence, the sweet
Heaven-loved Pharonnida, could come to meet
Pity in this rude wilderness ; her words,
Losing their form in the wild air, affords
Their busy souls no heedful leisure, but
With wilder passions the soul's portals shut.   370
    That sober friend to happy solitude,
Silence, which long those blest shades did include,
By rude noise banished from her solemn throne,
Did in a deep and hollow echo groan ;

(188)

Whilst the brave champion, whose own worth did bring
Assistance, yet had in a bloody ring
Strewed death's pale triumphs, and in safety stands
The dangerous business of so many hands,
All which had in the grave joined palms, if by
One stroke, that index unto victory,   380
His sword, had not with sudden breaking proved
Traitor t' the strength by whose command it moved.
    Robbed of this safe defence, valour's brave flame
In vain is spent; that pyramid of fame,
Built by his hand o'er Love's fair temple, now
Even in the view of 's saint, is forced to bow
Beneath an earthquake. His commanding soul,
In this sharp conflict striving to control
Nature, rebellious to her power, lets fly
In vain the piercing lightning of the eye,   390
Whose dark lids, drooping in a death-like close,
Forbid high fury thundering on his foes.
He falls, and from each purple sallyport
Of wounds, tired spirits, in a thick resort,
Fly the approach of death ; in which wild trance,
His eyes did their declining lights advance
Above their gloom of darkness, to convey
The last faint beam of nature's falling day
To his distressed Pharonnida. But she;
In clouds of sorrow lost, was gone to be   400
Close mourner for his rigid fate beneath
A pale swoon's shady veil, and could not breathe
One sigh to welcome those sick guests, nor lend
A beam to light them to their journey's end.
Which being deprived of, in death's dark disguise
Forgetful shadows did obscure his eyes.
    Branded with an ignoble victory,
His base oppressors, staying not to try
Whe'er fire remain in life's dark lamp, forsake
Their bleeding shame, and only with them take   410
The trembling ladies ; whose amazement yet
Grief's flood-gates shuts in a distracting fit
Of wilder passions : circled in which cloud
She 's hurried thence ; and, ere that damp allowed
Light through her soul's prospectives, had passed o'er
Much of the desert, and arrived before
A barren rock's proud front ; which, being too steep
For the laborious traveller, a deep
Dark vault did pierce, whose dismal black descent
Safe passage to a distant valley lent.   420
    With slow ill-boding steps this horrid way
O'ercome, they meet the beauties of the day

---

409 'Whe'er' is Singer's reading, and very likely ; but the 'where' of the original
is not quite impossible.

Within the pregnant vale, a place that showed
Some art had pruned what nature's hand bestowed.
No earth-encumbering weeds, but wholesome plants,
Such as relieve the winter of our wants,
Were here in comely order placed; each tree,
Tired with his fruitful burden, stoops to be
Eased by the lowliest hand; for want of which
Their feeble stems had dropped them to enrich   430
Their pregnant mother. This civility,
Proclaiming more than art had meant to be
The dress of deserts, did at first appear
As if those useful blessings had, for fear
That wasteful man should ravish them to feed
His luxury, fled thither: none that need
Such thrifty joys, in the circumference
O' the valley seeming to have residence.
   All whose exalted pride did terminate
The levelled eye, was a round hill that sate   440
As centre to the golden vale; come near
To which, what did externally appear
A rock in ivy dressed, being entered, shewed
The beauties of a gorgeous palace, hewed
Out of the living stone, whose vaulted breast
Had by the union of each part exprest
The strength of concord. The black rock was all
Tinselled with windows, over which did fall
Thin ivy wreaths, like cobweb veils that shade
The sallyports of beauty, only made   450
To cool, not darken, and on those that sit
Within bestow a shady benefit.
   They being drawn near, a sad old man that sate
Unwilling porter, from the spacious gate
Withdrew the verdant curtain.—She is now
Entered the castle, where, could fear allow
Her eyes that liberty, she had surveyed
Buildings, whose strength with beauty joined, betrayed
Time's modern issues to contempt, and by
A lasting glory praised antiquity.   460
But pleasure spreads her baits in vain; she sate
Beneath the frozen arctic of her fate,
Whilst he, from whose aspect she only felt
Delightful heat, in's winter-solstice dwelt.
   More to depress her sinking spirits, she
Too soon finds cause to think that gravity
She met in the entrance but the reverend shade
Of injured worth, which accident had made
Stoop to that bondage;—virtue drooping in
His furrowed cheeks, as if disposed, she'd been   470
Thither confined within the walls, to let
Imperious vice her painted banners set.

A troop of wild bandits, villains whose guilt
Shunned public haunts, Heaven's private blessings spilt
There in luxurious riot, which grown bold
By toleration, durst t' the light unfold
Vice's deformedst issues ; nought b' the name
Of sin being known, but sin's betrayer, shame :
In such a loose intemperance as reigns
In conquered cities, when the soldier's pains   480
With spoils of peace is paid, they lived. 'Mongst these
Some few unhappy women, kept to appease
Lust's tumults, she beheld ; whose looks betrayed
A sickly guilt, and made the royal maid,
Amidst her grief's cold symptoms, blush to see
How pale they looked with lust's deformity.
    Whilst these are viewed, with such a change as that
Poor village drunkards are enforced to at
An officer's approach, when the night grows
Deep as their draughts, she sees them all compose   490
Their late wild looks ; nor was this dress of fear
In vain put on, Almanzor did appear—
Dreaded Almanzor, who on them had built
A power, which though by unsuccessful guilt
Banished t' the desert, forced their wants to be
The helpless sufferers of his tyranny.
    Passed through the fear-dispersèd throng, he 's to
The princess come ; where, startled at the view
Of majesty, shrinks back. Unsteady haste,
Which brought him there but to view beauties placed   500
Within the reach of 's lust, assaulted by
Objects that both to love and loyalty
Had proved him an apostate, to retreat
Within a blush attempts ; but that 's too great
A friend to bashful virtue, in that face,
Whose heart deposes her, to sprinkle grace.
    Ruffled with this recoil of spirits, in
Such troubled haste as novices begin
New conned orations, he himself applies
To the injured lady ; whose brave spirit flies   510
Not what see feared, but with the brave defence
Of scorn opposes blushless impudence,
Crushing the embryos of that language, in
Whose guilty accents he attempts to win
Opinion's favour, and by that redeem
What former guilt had lost in her esteem.
    Contemned with such a look as princes cast
On overbold usurpers, he is past
The first encounter of her eye, and she
Turned in disdain, to show her great soul free   520

473 bandits] Note the accent of *banditti* preserved in 'bandìts.'

From low submission; by which fired into
A sullen anger, he resolves to mew
The royal eaglet, until freedom grow
A favour, whose fair streams might overflow
Those barren fields of indesert, in which
His fortune pines—lest this fair prize enrich
The cursed soil, and on its surface place
The long-abstracted beams of princely grace.

   She to the narrow confines of a room
Restrained, to let his muffled thoughts resume   530
Their calm composture, counsel's throne, he goes
Aside, and on that doubtful text bestows
The clearest comment of his judgement; yet
Falls short of truth, and must contented sit
To know her there, though not the accident
Which from her father's glorious court had sent
Her so ill guarded: but referring that
To time's discovery, he, transported at
What was a truth confirmed, within the wide
Arms of his hope, grasps what aspiring pride   540
Or lust's loose rhetoric, when youth's vigorous fire
Beauty hath kindled, prompts him to desire.

   Yet by two several paths to tread that way,
His crimes' dark roads, lust and ambition, lay,
The poor Florenza, that long since had been
The trembling object of the baser sin,
To make his sly access to either free
From the other's thoughts, must from her lady be
In this dark storm removed; he fearing less
That counsel aiding virtue in distress,   550
Though wanting strength the battle to maintain,
Might countermine the engine of his brain.

   To this sad separation leaving them,
Whom innocence had licensed to condemn
Fortune's harsh discipline, Almanzor goes,
Fate's dark enigmas, by the help of those
That took her, to unveil; but 'twas a work
Too full of subtle mystery:—A Turk,
Her brave defender, by those garments which
Rash fear had only rifled to enrich   560
Nice inquisition, seemed. By which betrayed
To dark mistakes, his policy obeyed
Domestic counsels; and by subtle spies,
Whose ears were more officious than their eyes,
Soon from the love-sick lady's close complaints
His wiser knowledge with their cause acquaints.

THE END OF THE FIRST CANTO.

526 lest] Orig. 'least,' is here as not seldom = 'unless.'
541 vigorous] Orig. 'rigorous,' possibly.

Canto II

THE ARGUMENT

From all the hopes of love and liberty
  O'erwhelmed in the vast ocean of her grief,
The wretched princess is constrained to be
  A prisoner to her youth's first dreadful thief—

The cursed Almanzor; in whose dismal cell
  She comments on the various texts of grief
In every form, till from the tip of hell,
  When seeming darkest, just Heaven sent relief.

DISTRACTED in the agony of love,
Pharonnida, whose sad complaints did prove
Her sorrow's true interpreters, had made
Argalia's name, wrapped up in sighs, invade
The ears of an unseen informer; whence,
Almanzor's thoughts, delivered from suspense,
Shake off their doubtful dress of fears, and teach
Hypocrisy by paths untrod to reach
The apex of his hopes. What not the fear
Of ills, whilst her own interest did appear   10
The only sharer, could perform, he now
Presumes affection to her friend would bow
With low submission, if by that she might
Aid his dim stars with a reserve of light.
  With frequent visits, which on sin's dark text
Wrought a fair gloss, Almanzor oft had vext
The calmer passions of the princess in-
To ruffled anger; but when all could win
No entrance on her favour, fury tries
A harsher corrosive—Stern power denies   20
Her even of those poor narrow comforts which
Her soul's dark region, that was only rich
In sorrow's sables, could possess. Withdrew
Were all those slippery parasites that knew
To her no pity, but what did reflect
The rays o' the tyrant's favour, whose neglect
Taught them the lesson of disdain, whilst she
Her practised soul trained in humility.
  Pensive as an unpractised convert, in
A bath of tears she shadowed lies within   30
The unfrequented room; a curtain-bed
Her close retreat, till light's fair angel fled

Arg. 7 tip] 'lip?'
  20 denies] 'denies of' is a characteristic blending—'deprives *of*' and 'denies.'
  31 curtain-bed] Singer 'curtained,' but 'curtain-bed' (cf. 'arm-chair') is quite probable.

The swarthy region. But whilst here she lies,
Like in a dark lantern that in black disguise
Circles imprisoned light . . . .
Grief from the sullen world concealed: to turn
The troubled stream—as if the silent urn
Of some dead friend, to private sorrow had
Summoned her hither, entered was a sad
And sober matron ; in her hands she bore   40
A light, whose feeble rays could scarce restore
The sick successor of the day unto
A cheerful smile. Sad pilgrims, that renew
Acquaintance with their better angels by
Harsh penitence, have of humility
Less in their looks than she ;—her habit showed
Like costly ruins that for fashion owed
To elder pride, in whose reversion she
Appeared, the noble choice of charity.
   This shadow of religious virtue drawn   50
Near her disordered bed, a sickly dawn
Of light breaks through the princess' clouded eyes
To meet the welcome object ; the disguise
Of sorrow, which at first appearance sate
Fixed on her brow, a partner of her fate
Making her seem. Nor was the fancy crushed
In the infancy of faith, fair truth first blushed
For verbal crimes. Near to the bed reposed
Where the sad lady lay, she thus disclosed
Her cause of entrance :—'Cease, fair stranger, to   60
Monopolize a sorrow, which not you
Here share alone ; pity, instructed by
Experience in the rules of misery,
Hath brought me from complaining of my own
To comfort thine. This castle once hath known
Me for its mistress, though it now behold
Me (in the dress of poverty grown old)
Despised and poor, the scorn of those that were
Nursed into life by my indulgent care.'
   This, in her tears' o'erflowing language spoke,   70
Persuades the pensive princess to revoke
Depraved opinion's doom, confessing she
Wedded not grief to singularity.
But comfort in the julep of her words
Was scarce dissolved, ere a reply affords
Conceived requital, striving to prevent
The oft more forward thanks. 'Rise to content,
Fair soul, (she cries) ; be but so wise to let
Sick passion die with just neglect, I'll set
Thy dropped stars in their orbs again. I have,   80
Forced by command, a late attendance gave
Unto a wounded stranger, that remains

(194)

Within this castle in the heavy chains
Of cruel bondage; from whose weight unless
Your love redeem him, dark forgetfulness
Will draw the curtains of the grave about
His dull mortality, and the sick doubt
Of hope resolve in death.   This evening I
O'erheard his heavy doom, from which to fly
He hath no refuge but your mercy; which   90
Stripped of light passion, must be clothed in rich
But graver robes of reason, when it sits
In council how to reconcile the fits
Of feverish love—when, being most propense
To passion's heat, a frost of abstinence
Benumbs it to a lethargy.   In brief,
'Tis he, whose prosperous tyranny the chief
Command within this castle gave, that in
His swift destruction doth attempt to win
Free passage to enjoying you, then prove   100
He friend to him that begs you to change love
For now more useful pity, and so save
A life that must no longer live to crave,
If now denied.   This ring' (with that presents
A jewel, that, when love's first elements
The harmony of faith united, she
Gave to confirm her vows) ' he sends to be
A note that he denies whate'er was made
Authentic, when your mixed vows did invade
Unwilling Heaven, which in your sufferance shows   110
We may intend, but wiser powers dispose.'
　　Pharonnida, whose fears confirmed, did need
No more to wound a fancy that did bleed
At all the springs of passion, being by
The fatal present taught, whose liberty
Her love's exchange must purchase, with a sad
Reverse of the eye beholding it, unclad
Her sorrow thus:—'And did, oh, did this come
By thy commands, Argalia? no; by some
Unworthy hand thou'rt robbed of it—I know   120
Thou sooner wouldst be tempted to let go
Relics of thy protecting saint.—Oh, cease,
Whate'er you are, to wrong him; the calm peace
He wears to encounter death in, cannot be
Scattered by any storm of fear.   Would he,
That hath affronted death in every shape
Of horror, tamely yield unto the rape
Of's virgin honour, and not stand the shock
Of a base tyrant's anger?   But I mock
My hopes with vain phantasms; 'tis the love   130
He bears to me, carries his fear above

　　　101 He] So orig. and Singer. Emendation is not easy.

(195)

The orb of his own noble temper to
An unknown world of passions, in whose new
Regions ambitious grown, it scorns to fall
Back to its centre—reason, whither all
The lines of action until now did bend
From 's soul's circumference. Yet know, his end,
If doomed unto this cursed place, shall tell
The bloody tyrant that my passing bell
Tolls in his dying groans, and will ere long   140
Ring out in death—if sorrow, when grown strong
As fate, can raise the strokes of grief above
The strength of nature; which if not, yet love
Will find a passage, where our souls shall rest
In an eternal union—whilst opprest
With horror, he, by whose commands he dies,
Falls to the infernal powers a sacrifice.
    ' If that your pity were no fiction, to
Betray my feeble passions, and undo
The knots of resolution, tell my friend—   150
I live but to die his, and will attend
Him with my prayers, those verbal angels, till
His soul 's on the wing, then follow him, and fill
Those blanks our fate left in the lines of life
Up with eternal bliss, where no harsh strife
Of a dissenting parent shall destroy
The blooming springs of our conjugal joy.'
    Vexed by this brave display of fortitude
To sullen anger, with a haste more rude
Than bold intrusions, lust's sly advocate   160
Forsakes her seat, and though affronts too late
Came to create a blush, yet passion had
Her cheeks in red revenge's livery clad ;
Her eyes, like Saturn's in the house of death,
Heavy with ills to come ; her tainted breath
Scattering infectious murmurs : with a look
Oblique and deadly, the cursed hag forsook
That ebon cabinet of grief, and hastes
To tell Almanzor how his passion wastes
More spirits in persuasion's hectic, than   170
If power had quenched ambition's fever when
'Twas first inflamed with hope, whose cordials prove
Oft slow as opiates in the heat of love.
    This, with a heat that spoiled digestion, by
The angry tyrant heard, rage did untie
The curls of passion, whose soft trammels had
Crisped smooth hypocrisy ; from which unclad,
Developed nature shows her unfiled dress
Rough as an angry friend, by no distress
Of beauty to be calmed. Since sly deceit   180
Virtue had now unmasked, no candid bait

Conceals his thoughts, which soon in public shows
From what black sea those mists of passion rose.
· Day's sepulchre, the ebon-archèd night,
Was raised above the battlements of light;
The frenzied world's allaying opiate, sleep,
O'ertaking action, did in silence steep
The various fruits of labour, and from thence
Recovers what pays for her time's expense:
In which slow calm, whilst half the drowsy earth   190
Lay in the shade of nature, to give birth
Unto the burthen of sick fancy—fear,
Groans, deep as death's alarums, through her ear
Fly toward the throne of reason, to inform
The pensive princess, that the last great storm
Of fate was now descending, beyond which
Her eyes, o'erwhelmed in sorrow, must enrich
Their orbs with love no more, but in the dawn
Of life behold her friend's destruction drawn,
Since threatened danger sad assurance gives—   200
In those deep groans he now but dying lives.
    More swiftly to destroy the falling leaves
Of blasted hope, with horror she receives,
By a convey of wearied light, that strook
Through rusty gates, intelligence which shook
The strength of fortitude—There was a room,
Deep and obscure, where, in a heavy gloom,
The unstirred air in such a darkness dwelt
As masked Egyptians from Heaven's vengeance felt,
Till by the struggling rays of a faint lamp   210
Forced to retreat, and the quicksilver damp
Shed on the sweaty walls, which hid within
That glittering veil, worn figures that had been
The hieroglyphic epitaphs of those
Which charity did to the earth dispose
In friendship's last of legacies, except
What is to cure loose fame's diseases kept.
    Here, 'mongst the ruins of mortality,
In blood disfigured, she beholds one lie,
Who, though disguised in death's approach, appears   220
By 's habit, that confirmer of her fears
Her gentle love, alone and helpless, in
The grasp of death, striving in vain to win
The field from that grim tyrant; who had now
Embalmed him in his blood, and did allow
Him no more spirits, but what in that strife
Served to groan out the epilogue of life,
And then depart Nature's cold stage, to be
Sucked up from time into eternity.
When thus the everlasting silence had   230
Locked up his voice, and death's rude hand unclad

(197)

His hovering soul, whose elemental dress
Is left to dust and dark forgetfulness;
When Nature's lamps being snuffed to death, he lay
A night-pieced draught of once well-modelled clay:
With such a silent pace as witches use
To tread o'er graves, when their black arts abuse
Their cold inhabitants, his murderers were
Entered the vault, from the stained floor to bear
The cold stiff corpse; which having softly laid   240
In 's doomsday's bed, unto the royal maid,
Whose beauty, in this agony defaced,
Grief's emblem sat, with eager speed they haste.
   Either a guilty shame, or fear to be
Converted by her form's divinity,
Made them choose darkness for protection; in
Whose hideous shade, she of herself unseen
Is hurried thence unto that dreadful place
Where he entombed lay, whom she must embrace
In death's dark lodgings; and, ere life was fled,   250
Remain a sad companion of the dead—
Confining beauty, in youth's glorious bloom,
To the black prison of a dismal tomb:
Where, fast enclosed, earth's fairest blossom must
Unnaturally be planted in the dust;
Where life's bright star, Heaven's glorious influence,
Her soul, in labour with the slow suspense
Of lingering torments, must expecting lie,
Till famine Nature's ligatures untie.
   And can, oh, can we never hope to save   260
Her that 's in life a tenant to the grave!
Can aught redeem one that already lies
Within the bed of death, whose hot lust fries
In the enjoyment of all beauties that
The aged world ere had to wonder at!
To feed whose riot, the well-tempered blood,
That sanguine youth's smooth cheek mixed with a flood
Of harsh distemperatures, o'erflows, and brings
Some to their lodgings on the flaming wings
Of speedy fevers; whilst the others creep   270
On slow consumptions, millions from the steep
And dangerous precipice of war: some in
A stream of their own humours that have been
Swelled to a dropsy, being even pressed to death
By their own weight; whilst others part with breath
From bodies worn so thin, they seemed to be
Grown near the soul's invisibility.
   But whither strays our fancy? have we left
The woful lady in a tomb, bereft

   261 to] Singer, unnecessarily and I think unwisely, ' of.'

Of all society, and shall I let 280
My wandering pen forsake her? Such a debt
Would bankrupt pity. The undistinguished day,
Whose new-born light did but e'en then display
Its dewy wings, when first she was confined
To the dark tomb, was now grown almost blind
With age, when thus through Fate's black curtain broke
Unlooked-for light: that darkness—which did choke
All passages by which the thin air held
Commerce with neighbouring rooms, being now expelled
By the dim taper's glimmering beams—let fall 290
Part of the rays through an old ruined wall
That fenced an ugly dungeon, where the night
Dwelt safe as in the centre. By the sight
Of which unlooked-for guest, some prisoners, who
Had there been staid, even till despairing to
Be e'er released, in eager fury tries
To force their way, where their directing eyes,
Led by the light, should guide them; come at length
Where, with time's burden tired, the building's strength,
Losing its first firm union, was divorced 300
With gaping clefts, an easy strength enforced
Those feeble guards: but come into the room
Where, o'er the living lady's sable tomb,
Hung the directing light, they there in vain
For further passage seeking, were again
To the black dungeon, horror's dismal seat,
In sad despair making their slow retreat.
Now near departing, a deep doleful groan
Reversed their eyes, amazement almost grown
To stupefaction stays them, whilst they hear 310
New sighs confirm their wonder, not their fear;
Till thus Euriolus, whose bold look spoke
The braver soul, the dismal silence broke.
  'Whate'er thou art that hoverest here within
This gloomy shadow, speak what wrong hath been
Thy troubled ghost's tormentor? art thou fled
From woe to stir the dust o' the peaceful dead?
Or com'st from sacred shadows to lament
Some friend's dead corpse, which this dark tenement
Hath lodged in dust?' The trembling lady, hearing 320
A human voice again, and now not fearing
The approaches of a greater danger, cries:—
'Whate'er you are, fear mocks your faith; here lies
A woful wretch entombed alive, that ne'er
Must look on light again; my spirit were
Blest if resolved to air, but here it must
A sad companion, in the silent dust,
To loathed corruption be, until the pale
Approaching fiend, harsh famine, shall exhale,

In dews of blood, the purple moisture, that   330
Fed life's fresh springs :—but none shall tremble at
My doleful story, 'tis enough that Fate
Hath for this tomb exchanged a throne of state.'
    To active pity stirred, the valiant friends
Attempt her rescue, but their labour ends
In fruitless toils, the ponderous marble lies
With too much weight to let the weak supplies
Of human strength remove 't ; which whilst they tried
To weary sweats, kind fortune lends this guide
To their masked virtue—The informing ear   340
Proclaims approaching steps, which ushered fear
Into Ismander's breast ; but his brave friend,
The bold Euriolus, resolved to end
By death or victory their bondage, goes
Near to the gate, where soon were entered those
Which in Pharonnida's restraint had been
The active engines of that hateful sin,
With them, that hag whose cursed invention had
Revenge in such an uncouth dressing clad.
    Whilst her Ismander seized, and with a charm   350
Of nimble strength commands, the active arm
Of fierce Euriolus, directed by
Victorious valour, purchased liberty
By strokes whose weight to dark destruction sunk
His worthless foes, and sent their pale souls, drunk
With innocent blood, staggering from earth, to be
Masked in the deserts of eternity.
    This being beheld by her whose hopes of life
With them departed, she concludes the strife
Of inquisition by directing to   360
An engine, which but touched would soon undo
That knot which puzzled all their strength, and give
The captive princess hopes again to live
Within the reach of light ; whose beams, whilst she
Unfolds her eyes—those dazzled stars, to see,
Dark misty wonder in a cloud o'erspread
His faith that raised her from that gloomy bed,
Amazed Euriolus ; whose zeal-guided eyes
Soon know the princess through grief's dark disguise.
Could his inflamed devotion into one   370
Great blast of praises be made up, 't had gone
Toward heavenly bowers on the expanded wings
Of his exalted joy ; nor are the springs
Of life less raised with wonder in the breast
Of 's royal mistress, whose free soul exprest

331 none] Orig. 'now.'
  357, 378 masked] Both these passages illustrate, in the same word 'masked,'
Chamberlayne's curious locution.   The first passage looks quite wrong ; the second
helps to gloss the word as = ' bewildered,' ' out of themselves.'

As much of joy as, in her clouded fate,
With reason at the helm of action sate.
  Here had they, masked in mutual wonder, staid
To unriddle fate, had not wise fear obeyed
Reason's grave dictates, and with eager speed   380
Urged their departure; for whose guide they need
No more but her directions, who then lay
Taught by the fear of vengeance to obey
Their just demands. By whom informed of all
That might within the castle's circuit fall
With weights of danger, and taught how to free
Confined Florenza, to meet liberty
They march in triumph, leaving none to take
Possession there, but her whose guilt would make
The torment just, though there constrained to dwell   390
Till death prepared her for a larger hell.
Whilst sleep's guards, doubled by intemperance, reigned
Within the walls, with happy speed they gained
The castle's utmost ward; and furnished there
With such choice horses, as provided were
For the outlaws' next day's scouts, a glad adieu
Of their loathed jail they take. Ismander knew
Each obscure way that in their secret flight
Might safely promise; so that sullen night
Could not obstruct their passage, though, through ways   400
So full of dark meanders, not the day's
Light could assist a stranger. Ere the dawn
O' the wakeful morn had spread her veils of lawn
O'er the fair virgins of the spring, they're past
That sylvan labyrinth, and with that had cast
Their greatest terror off, and taught their eyes
The welcome joys of liberty to prize.
  And now the spangled squadrons of the night,
Encountering beams, had lost the field to light,
The morning proud in beauty grown, whilst they   410
With cheerful speed passed on the levelled way
By solitude secure; of all unseen,
Save early labourers that resided in
Dispersed poor cottages, by whom they're viewed
With humble reverence, such as did delude
Sharp-eyed suspicion, they are now drawn near
Ismander's palace; whose fair towers appear
Above the groves, whose green enamel lent
The neighbouring hills their prospects' ornament.
  A river, whose unwearied bounty brings   420
The hourly tribute of a thousand springs
From several fragrant valleys here, as grown
So rich, she now strove to preserve her own

          381 Urged] Orig. 'urge.'

Streams from the all-devouring sea, did glide
Betwixt two hills, which Nature did divide
To entertain the smiling nymph, till to
An entrance where her silver eye did view
A wealthy vale she came—a vale in which
All fruitful pleasures did content enrich;
Where all so much deserved the name of best,   430
Each, took apart, seemed to excel the rest.
   Rounded with spacious meads, here scattered stood
Fair country farms, whose happy neighbourhood,
Though not so near as justling palaces
Which troubled cities, yet had more to please
By a community of goodness in
That separation. Nature's hand had been
To all too liberal, to let any want
The treasures of a free inhabitant;
Each in his own unracked inheritance   440
Where born expired, not striving to advance
Their levelled fortunes to a loftier pitch
Than what first styled them honest, after rich;
Sober and sweet their lives, in all things blest
Which harmless nature, living unopprest
With surfeits, did require; their own flocks bred
Their homespun garments, and on that they fed
Which from their fields' or dairies' plenteous store
Had fresh supplies: what fortune lent them more
Than an indifferent mean, was sent to be   450
The harbingers of hospitality.
Fair virgins, in their youth's fresh April drest,
Courted by amorous swains, were unopprest
By dark suspicion, age's sullen spies,
Whose spleen would have the envious counted wise
Love was religious here, and for to awe
Their wilder passions, conscience was their law.
More to complete this rural happiness,
They were protected from the harsh distress
Of long-winged power by the blest neighbourhood   460
Of brave Ismander; whose known greatness stood
Not to eclipse their humble states, although
It shadowed them when injured power did grow
To persecution, by which means he proved—
Not feared for greatness, but for goodness loved.
Which gentle passion his unhappy loss
Had soured to grief, and made their joy their cross.
   But now their antidote approaches, he
From heavy bondage is returned to be

435 Which troubled cities] In another writer one might suspect '*In* troubled cities'
or 'Which *trouble* cities.' But it is quite like Chamberlayne to *attract* his verb into the
form of 'stood' and 'had.'

Their joyful wonder. At his palace gate   470
Being now arrived, his palace, that of late
With 's absence dimmed in her most beauteous age,
Stood more neglected than a hermitage,
Or sacred buildings, when the sinful times
To persecution aggravate their crimes :
But being entered, sadder objects took
Those outside wonders off ; each servant's look
Spoke him a sullen mourner, grave and sad
Their sober carriage, in no liveries clad
But doleful sable, all their acts like those   480
Of weeping wives, when they t' the grave dispose
Their youthful husbands. Yet all these were but
Imperfect shadows of a sorrow, put
In distant landscape, when to trial brought
Near his fair Ammida's ; whose grief had sought
As dark a region for her sad retreat
As desperate grief e'er made pale Sorrow's seat :
In sacred temples the neglected lamp
So wastes its oil, when heresies do cramp
Religion's beams ; with such a heavy look   490
Monarchs deposed behold themselves forsook
By those that flattered greatness ; shut from all
Those glorious objects of the world that call
Our souls in admiration forth, her time
Being spent in grief, made life but Nature's crime.
   The rough disguise of time, assisted by
The meagre gripe of harsh captivity,
Had now expunged those characters by which
Ismander once was known, and even the rich
In love and duty rendered strangers to   500
Their honoured master ; from whose serious view
Neglective grief withdraws them, so that he
An unknown pilgrim might have gone to be
Theirs and his own afflicter, had that fear
Not thus been cured :—A spaniel, being of dear
Esteem to Ammida, since the delight
Of her Ismander once, come to the sight
Of 's first protector, stays not till a call
Invites acquaintance, but preventing all
The guides of reason by the sleights of sense,   510
Fawning on 's master, checks the intelligence
Of 's more forgetful followers. Which being seen
By an old servant (whose firm youth had been
Spun out amongst that family, till by
Grave age surprised), it led his sober eye
To stricter observations, such as brought
Him near to truth, and on contracted thought
Raised a belief, which though it durst conclude
Nought on the dark text, yet, i' the magnitude

(203)

Of hope exalted, by his joy he hastes   520
To 's mourning mistress, tells her that she wastes
Each minute more she spends in grief, if he
Dares trust his eyes to inform his memory.
   Contracted spirits, starting from the heart
Of doubtful Ammida, to every part
Post through the troubled blood ; a combat, fought
Betwixt pale fear and sanguine hope, had oft
Won and lost battles in her cheeks, whilst she,
Leaving her sullen train, did haste to see
Those new-come guests. But the first interview   530
Unmasks Ismander ; winged with love she flew
To his embraces : 'twas no faint disguise
Of a coarse habit could betray those eyes
Into mistakes, that for directors had
Love's powerful optics ; nuptial joys unclad
In all their naked beauties—no delight
So full of pleasure, the first active night
Being but a busy and laborious dream
Compared with this—this, that had swelled the stream
Of joy to fainting surfeits ; whose hot strife   540
Had overflowed the crimson sea of life,
If not restrained by a desire to keep
What each had lost in the eternal sleep.
   But now, broke through the epileptic mist
Of amorous rapture, rallied spirits twist
Again their optic cordage ; whose mixed beams
Now separate, and on collateral streams
Dispersed expressions of affection bore
To each congratulating friend, that wore
Not out those favours with neglect, but by   550
A speedy, though unpractic sympathy,
Met their full tide of bliss. Glad Fame, which brings
Truth's messages upon her silver wings
In private whisper hovers for awhile
Within the palace ; every servant's smile
Invites a new spectator ; who from thence
(Proud to be author of intelligence
So welcome) hastes, till knowledge ranged through all,
Diffusive joy made epidemical :
For though that noble family alone   560
Afforded pleasure a triumphant throne,
Yet frolic mirth did find a residence
In every neighbour's bosom. They dispense
With their allegiance to their labour, and
Revel in lusty cups ; the brown bowls stand
With amber liquor filled, whose fruitful tears
Dropped loved Ismander's health, till it appears
In sanguine tincture on their cheeks. All now
Had if not calmed their passions, smoothed a brow

To temporize with pleasure. The sad story   570
Of his own fortune, and that age's glory,
Pharonnida, whilst each attentive dwells
On expectation, brave Ismander tells.

THE END OF THE SECOND CANTO.

Canto III

THE ARGUMENT

From the sad consort of her silent grief
    The princess doth with pleasing wonder hear
Poor Vanlore's fate, and the unjust relief
    Which his unworthy father freed from fear.

Whose hell-deep plots, the dregs of avarice
    Had so defiled, that whilst he seeks for aid,
His subtlety, masked on the road of vice,
    By his presumed assistant is betrayed.

COMPOSING time did now begin to slack
The reign of mirth ; exalted joy shrunk back
From pleasure's summer-solstice, and gave way
For more domestic passions to obey
An economic government ; which brought
Loose fancy on the wings of serious thought
Back to her sober home, in that to find
Those several burthens that were left behind
In the career of mirth ; amongst which number,
Pharonnida, that had let sorrow slumber,   10
In the high room of joy, awakes again
That clamorous elf, which she must entertain
At beauty's cost. Yet in this dark retreat,
From pleasure's throne to sorrow's dismal seat,
She finds a sweet companion ; one that had,
By fatal love opposed, with loss unclad
Delight of all his summer-robes, to dress
Her trembling soul in sables of distress.
    The sad Silvandra (for surviving fame
Hath on record so charactered her name)   20
Being sister to returned Ismander, in
This flourish of triumphant joy had been
So much eclipsed with grief, that oft her tears
Dimmed beauty's rays, whilst through them she appears
A fit companion for the princess to
Twist those discourses with, whose mourning clew
Led through the labyrinth of their lives. They oft,
In shades as secret as their closest thought

2 reign] Orig. 'rain,' Singer 'rein.' The curious thing is that both, as well as the text, are possible.

With pensive paces meeting, sit and tell
Stories so sad, that nought could parallel— 30
But love and loss; a theme they both had been
By rigid power made hapless students in.
 One eye-bright morning tempting them to take
The start of time, soon as the lark did wake,
Summons them from the palace to the side
Of a small wood, whose bushy crest, the pride
Of all the flowery plains, they chose to be
'Gainst the invading sun their canopy.
Reposed beneath a full-grown tree, that spread
His trembling arms to shade their fragrant bed, 40
They now are set; where for awhile they view
The distant vale, whilst contemplation grew
Pregnant with wonder, whose next prosperous birth
Had been delight, had they not sent their mirth
In sad exchange, whilst tears did usher in
Silvandra's fate; who, weeping, did begin,
With such a look as did command belief,
The late-past story of a present grief.
 'In yonder fields (with that directs her eye
To a black fen, whose heavy earth did lie 50
Low in a dark and dirty vale) is placed
Amarus's castle, which though now defaced
More by the owner's covetous neglect
Than time's rough strokes, that strength, which did protect
Once its inhabitants, being now but made
Use of when want doth with weak prayers invade
The gates, being thought sufficient—if they keep
The poor at bay, or, whilst his stiff hinds sleep,
Their labouring beasts secure. But I, alas,
Blush to discover that this miser was 60
Father to my dead Vanlore, and to her
Whose living virtues kind Heaven did confer
As blessings on my brother; but the sun
Ne'er saw two sweeter streams of virtue run
From such a bitter fountain. This accurst
And wretched man (so hated that he durst
Scarce look abroad, fearing oppression would
Be paid with vengeance, if he ever should
Fall into the hands of those whose faces he
Ground with extortion, till the injury 70
Fear clothed like justice), venturing once to view
A manor, whose intemperate lord outgrew
In debts the compass of a bond, besides
His common guard of clowns, fellows whose hides
Served for defensive armour, he commands
His son's attendance; who, since from his hands
Racked tenants hoped for ease, he thought that they
Would for that hope with reverent duty pay.

But vain mistakes betray opinion to
A fatal precipice, which they might view   80
I' the objects of each glance ; one side affords
Large plains, whose flocks—the wealth of several lords,
By him contracted, but the spoils appears
Of beggared orphans, pickled in their tears ;
Farms for whose loss poor widows wept, and fields,
Which being confined to strict enclosure, yields
To his crammed chests the starving poor man's food ;
For private ends robbing their public good,
With guilt enclosed those ways which now had brought
Him by some cottages, whose owners bought   90
Poor livelihoods at a laborious rate
From his racked lands ; for which pursuing Hate
Now follows him in curses : for in that
They yet take vengeance ; till arriving at
The thicker-peopled villages, where, more bold
By number made, the fire of hate takes hold
On clamorous women, whose vexed husbands thirst
I' the fever of revenge ; to these, when first
They kindled had the flame, swiftly succeeds
More active men, such as resolved their deeds,   100
Spite of restrictive law, should set them free
From the oppressors of their liberty.
   ' His son, the noble Vanlore, to appease
The dangerous fury of this rash disease,
Spends all his stock of rhetoric, but in
Fruitless attempts. His rustic guard had been
At the first onset scattered, and were now
Posting for safety ; whilst his son, taught how
By frequent injuries to entertain
Anger's unusual guests, shows it in vain,   110
Though brave attempts of valour, by whose high
Unhappy flame whilst circling foes did die
Unworthy hecatombs for him, at length
Engaged him had beyond the power of strength,·
Though backed by fortune to redeem ; which when
Beheld by those whose characters of men
In rage was lost, they wildly persecute
Revenge, till life, nature's harmonious fruit,
Was blasted to untimely death.'—And here
Her fatal story in its full career,   120
The memory of him, who died to be
The people's curse and crime of destiny,
Grief did obstruct, whilst liquid passion feeds
Her crystal springs ; which stopped, she thus proceeds :—
   ' His brave defender now retreating to
The road to death, whilst he did vainly sue

<hr>

90 owners] Orig. ' honours.'

For undeserved remorse, Amarus lies
Their fury's object; in whose wild disguise,
Whilst giddy clouds of dark amazement dwell
O'er his dim eyes, the exalted tumult fell   130
In a black storm of danger; in whose shade
They drag him thence,—that fury, being made
Wise by delays, might study torments great
As was their rage; but in their wild retreat
They thus are stopped :—A wandering knight that near
The place approached, directed by his ear
How to inform his eye, arrives to see
The wretched trophies of this victory ;—
A dying son, whose latest beams of light
Through death's dim optics bids the world good night,   140
With looks that did so black a sorrow limn—
He frowned on earth though Heaven did smile on him ;
Hurried from thence by unrelenting hate,
A living father of more woful fate.
    'Pity, that brave allay of manly heat,
Persuades the noble stranger to entreat
A parle with rage; which, being denied, he then
Attempts to force; and since their ablest men
Were wounded in the former conflict, soon
Successful proves. Like mists i' the pride of noon,   150
Being huddled into hurtless clouds, they fly
Before his fury, till from reach of the eye
Shrunk to the wood's protection ; where, whilst each,
With such a fear a sanguine guilt did teach
The world's first murderer, seeks for safety, he
Retreating leaves the scattered herd—to be
Their own afflicters ; and hastes thence to find
Him to whom fortune proved so strangely kind
In his approach, as by his sword to be,
When hope lost anchor, blest with liberty.   160
Come to the place where old Amarus lay
With fear so startled, that he durst betray
Life through no motion ; yet he's followed by
That train of cowards, which, though they did fly
The danger, when they saw their foes pursued,
On the reward—the victory, intrude ;
Whose easy spoils, those invitations to
A coward's daring, such a distance drew
Them from their homes, that they with labour were
Recalled from rifling enemies to bear   170
Their feeble masters off—Amarus lying
As weak with fear as Vanlore was with dying.
    'Before the black obstructions of the night
Did interpose, they were arrived i' the sight
O' the castle's ruined walls, a place whose hue,
Uncouth and wild, banished delight unto

(208)

Uncomely profit, and at distance gives
A sad assurance—that its owner lives
By men so hated, and by Heaven unblest,
As he enjoyed not what he there possest.   180
  'Come to the front of the house, whose dirt forbid
A cleanly entrance, he sees pavements hid
With heaps of rubbish—time's slow hand let fall
From the neglected ruins of the wall;
Green arbours, pleasant groves, all which were now
Swiftly dismantling to make way for th' plough;
Only his barns, preservers of that store
Detained with curses from the pining poor,
Their upper garments of warm thatch did wear
So thick to keep them dry, whilst thin and bare   190
E'en his own lodging stood; the hall, first built
To have that wealth, which he in sparing spilt,
Spent there in hospitality, ne'er by
More heat warmed than a candle gave, did lie
Moulded with lazy damps—the wall o'ergrown
With moss and weeds—unhaunted and alone
The empty tables stood; for never guess
Come there, except thin bankrupts, whom distress
Spurred on with sharp necessity to crave
Forbearing months, which he, when bribed, forgave.   200
Hence, by a rude domestic led, he goes
To view the cellar, where, like distant foes
Or buildings in a new plantation, stand
The distant barrels, yet from all command
But his own keys exempted. To bestow
A welcome on him, which he ne'er did show
To man before, led by a rusty slave,
Whose iron limbs, rattling in leather, gave
Alarums to the half-starved rats, he here
Is by Amarus visited; whose fear   210
That place should too much suffer, soon from thence
Sounds a retreat to supper, where the expense
Became a usurer's purse: yet what was by
Sparing defective, neatness did supply,
A virtue, where repining penury
Prepares, unusual; but he soon did see
Whence it proceeds—The sad sweet Ammida
Whom shame and grief attempted to withdraw
From public view, was by her father's call,
To crown that entertainment, brought; whose all   220

---

178 owner] Orig. again 'honour.' The constant occurrence of this suggests not merely dictation, as observed before, but a probably Irish dictater.

197 guess] Singer boldly prints 'guests,' which the sense of course requires. But 'guess' is in original, and I leave it to the reader to decide whether the sense, or the rhyme, or the pronunciation is to yield the place.

Was else so bad, it the first visit might
Repented make, not to the next invite.
  'Here, with afflicted patience, he had spent
Some few, but tedious days, whose slow extent
Behind his wishes flagged, ere he had seen
Vanlore interred, whose obsequies had been
In secret huddled up, but then prepares
To take his leave ; when adverse fate, that shares
Double with man's intentions, in the tart
Of 's full resolves opposing, claims her part   230
By harsh command :—A dangerous fever, that
Threatened destruction ere arriving at
Its distant crisis, and on flaming wings,
Posts through the blood ; whose mass infected brings
Death's banners near the fort of life, which in
Acute distempers it attempts to win
From Nature's guards, had not the hot assault
By youth sustained, made Death's black army halt
Whilst marching to the grave—the swift disease
Like a proud foe repulsed, forced to give ease   240
By slow retreats ; yet of those cruel wars
Left long remaining bloodless characters.
  'But ere the weak Euriolus (for he
This hapless stranger was) again could be
By strength supported, base Amarus, who
Could think no more than priceless thanks was due
For all his dangerous pains, more beastly rude
Than untamed Indians, basely did exclude
That noble guest : which being with sorrow seen
By Ammida, whose prayers and tears had been   250
His helpless advocates, she gives in charge
To her Ismander—that till time enlarge
Her then restrained desires, he entertain
Her desolate and wandering friend.   Nor vain
Were these commands, his entertainment being
Such as observant love thought best agreeing
To her desires.   But here not long he staid,
Ere fortune, prompted by his wit, obeyed
That artful mistress, and reward obtains
By fine imposture for firm virtue's pains.   260
The gout, that common curse of slothful wealth,
With frequent pain had long impaired the health
Of old Amarus, who, though else to all
Griping as that, for ease was liberal.
From practised physic to the patient's curse—
Poor prattling women, or impostors worse—
Sly mountebanks, whose empty impudence
Do frequent murders under health's pretence,

261. Although I have barred myself from frequent annotation on matter, the
following passage may deserve an invitation to observe the poet's professional spirit.

He all had tried, yet found he must endure
What, though some eased, none perfectly could cure.   270
Oft had his judgement, purse, and patience been
Abused by cheats, yet still defective in
The choice of men ; which error known unto
My brother and Euriolus, they drew
Their platform thus :—Euriolus, clad in
An antic dress, which showed as he had been
Physician to the Great Mogul, first by
Ismander praised at distance, doth apply
Himself unto Amarus ; where, to enhance
The price of's art, he first applauds the chance   280
That had from distant regions thither brought
Him to eclipse their glory, who had sought
For't in his cure before, then seconds that
With larger promises ; which, tickled at,
Amarus vies with his, threatening to break
His iron chests, and make those idols speak
His gratitude, though, locked with conscience, they
To his own clamorous wants had silent lay.
  'Some common medicines which the people prize,
'Cause from their knowledge veiled in slight disguise,   290
Applied to's pain, and those assisted by
Opinion, whose best antidotes supply
The weak defects of art, he soon attains
So much of health, that now his greatest pains
Had been the engaged reward, had he not been
By future hopes kept from ungrateful sin
So far, that in performing action he
Exceeds his passion's prodigality—
Large promises, with such performance, that,
Whilst his deluders smile and wonder at,   300
Thus speaks its dark original. To show
Euriolus how fortune did outgrow
Desert in his estate, he was one day
From th' castle walls taking a pleased survey
Of spacious fields, whose soils, made fertile by
Luxurious art, in rich variety
Still youthful nature clothed ; which, whilst he views,
An old suspicion thus his tongue renews :—
  ' " How blest, my worthy friend, how blest had I
Been in my youth's laborious industry   310
T' have seen a son possessed of this ! But now,
A daughter's match a stranger must endow
With what I've toiled to get ; and what is more
My torment, one that, being betrothed before
My son's decease, wants an estate to make
Her marriage blest. But knew I how to shake
This swaggerer off, there lives, not far from hence,
One that to match her to were worth the expense

Of my estate; his name is Dargonel—
A wary lad, who, though his land do swell   320
Each day with new additions, yet still lives
Sparing and close, takes heed to whom he gives,
Or whom he lends, except on mortgage, by
Whose strength it may securely multiply.
This worthy gentleman, with wise foresight
Beholding what an object of delight
Our linked estates would be, hath, since I lost
My heir, been in 's intention only crost
By this Ismander, whom though I confess
A braver man, yet since a fortune less,   330
Ne'er must have my consent; only since by
Her contract I have lost the liberty
Of second choice, unless I vainly draw
Myself in danger of the o'erbusy law,
I want some sound advice that might inform
Me how to rid him, yet not stand a storm
Broke from his rage. Although my daughter love
Him more than health, I shall command above
Her feeble passions, if you dare impart
So much of aid from your almighty art   340
As to remove this remora."—And here
He stopped, yet lets a silent guilt appear
In looks that showed what else the theme affords
He'd have conceived, as being too foul for words.
Which seen by him whose active wit grew strong
In friendship's cause, as loath to torture long
His expectations, thus their streams he stays
With what at once both comforts and betrays :—
' " Raise up your spirits, my blest patron, to
Sublime content, Heaven sent me to renew   350
Your soul's harmonious peace; that dreadful toy
Of conscience wisely waived, you may enjoy
Uninterrupted hopes. Yet since we must
Be still most wary where we 're most unjust,
Let 's not be rash; swift things are oft unsure,
Whilst moles through death's dark angles creep secure.
Then, since it 's full of danger to remove
Betrothed Ismander, whilst his public love,
By your consent raised to assurance, may
A granted interest claim—first let us stay   360
His fury and the people's censures by
A nuptial knot, whose links we will untie,
Ere the first night confirms the hallowed band,
By ways so secret, that death's skilful hand
Shall work unknown to fate, and render you
To the deluded world's more public view,

---

329 whom] Singer ' who,' obliterating attraction and not quite conciliating the more rigid grammar.

A real mourner, whilst your curtained thought
Triumphs to be from strict engagements brought.
Besides the veiling of our dark design
Like virtue thus, this plot will sink a mine   370
Whose wealthy womb in ample jointure will
Bring much of dead Ismander's state, to fill
The vast desire of wealth.   This being done,
I with prevailing philtres will outrun
Sorrow's black bark, which whilst it lies at drift,
I'll so renew her mirth, no sigh shall lift
Its heavy sails, which in a calm neglect
Shall lie forgot ; whilst what 's not now respect
To Dargonel, shall soon grow up to be,
Like Nature's undiscovered sympathy,   380
A love so swift, so secret, all shall pause
At its effects, whilst they admire the cause."
  ' This by Amarus, with belief which grew
Into applause, heard out, he doth renew
With large additions what he'd promised in
His first attempts.   Then hasting to begin
The tragic scene, which must in triumph be
Ushered to light, his known deformity
Of wretched baseness for awhile he lays
Aside, and by a liberal mirth betrays   390
Approaching joy; which, since incited by
His wishes, soon lifts Hymen's torches high
As their exalted hopes.   The happy pair,
Dear to indulgent Heaven, with omens fair
As were their youthful paranymphs, had been
In the hallowed temple taught without a sin
To taste the fruits of paradise ; and now
The time, when tedious custom did allow
A wished retirement, come, preparing are
To beautify their beds, whence that bright star,   400
Whose evening's blush did please the gazers' eyes,
Eclipsed in sorrow, is ordained to rise.
But such whose superficial veil opprest
Only her friends, whose knowledge were not blest
With the design, which to our proscript lovers
Euriolus with timely zeal discovers.
The morning opens, and the wakened bride,
By light and friends surprised, attempts to hide
Her bashful beauty, till their hands withdrew
The curtains, which betrayed unto their view   410
Ismander cold and stiff.   Which horrid sight,
Met where they looked for objects of delight,
At first a silent sad amazement spread
Through all the room, till Fear's pale army fled
In sad assurance ; Sorrow's next hot charge
Began in shrieks, whose terror did enlarge

Infectious grief, till, like an ugly cloud
That cramps the beauties of the day, grown proud
In her black empire, Hymen's tapers she
Changes to funeral brands, and, from that tree   420
That shadows graves, pulls branches, which, being wet
In tears, are where love's myrtles flourished set.
Their .nuptial hymns thus turned to dirges, all
In sad exchange let cloudy sable fall
O'er pleasure's purple robes, whilst from that bed,
Whence love oppressed seemed, to their sorrow, fled
To death for refuge, sadly they attend
T' the last of homes—his tomb—their sleeping friend:
Who there, with all the hallowed rights that do
Betray surviving friendship, left unto   430
Darkness and dust, they thence with sober pace
Return ; whilst shrouded near that dismal place
Euriolus conceals himself, that so,
When Sleep, whose soft excess is Nature's foe,
Hath spent her stupefactive opiates, he
Might ready to his friend's assistance be.
  'And now that minute come, which, to comply
With Art's sure rules, gives Nature leave to untie
Sleep's powerful ligatures, his pulses beat
The blood's reveille, from whose dark retreat   440
The spirits thronging in their active flight,
His friend he encounters with the early light ;
By whose assistance, whilst the quiet earth
Yet .slept in night's black arms, before the birth
O' the morn, whose busy childhood might betray
Their close design, Ismander takes his way
Toward a distant friend's, whose house he knew
To be as secret as his love was true.
  There whilst concealed e'en from suspicion he
In safety rests, Euriolus, to free   450
Her fear's fair captivè, Ammida, hastes back
To old Amarus ; who, too rash to slack
Sorrow's black cordage by degrees that might
Weaken mistrust, lets mirth take open flight
Into suspected action, whilst he gives
To Dargonel, who now his darling lives,
So free a welcome that he in 't might read,
If love could not for swift succession plead,
Power should command ; yet waives the exercise
Of either, till his empiric's skill he tries.   460
Who now returned, ere Dargonel, that lay
Slow to attempt since certain to betray,
Had more than faced at distance, he pretends
To close attempts of art, whose wished-for ends,
Ere their expecting faith had time to fear,
In acts which raised their wonder did appear.—

'Love, which by judgement ruled, had made desert
In her first choice the climax to her heart,
By which it slowly moved; now, as if swayed
By heedless passion, seems to have betrayed   470
At one rash glance her heart, which now begins
To break through passion's bashful cherubins,
Spreading, without a modest blush, the light
Of morning beauty o'er that hideous night
Of all those dull deformities that dwell,
Like earth's black damps, o'er cloudy Dargonel.
Who, being become an antic in the mask
Of playful love, grows proud, and scorns to ask
Advice from sober thought, but lets conceit
Persuade him how his worth had spread that bait;   480
Which sly Amarus, who presumed to know
From whence that torrent of her love did flow,
With a just doubt suspecting, strives to make
His thoughts secure, ere reason did o'ertake
Passion's enforced career. Nor did his plot
Want an indulgent hope; like dreams, forgot
In the delights of day, his daughter shook
Off grief's black dress, and in a cheerful look
Promised approaching love, no more disguised
Than served to show strict virtue how she prized   490
Her only in applause; whose harmony
Still to preserve, she is resolved to be,
If secret silence might with action dwell,
Swift as his wish, espoused to Dargonel.
   'More joyed than fettered captives in the year
Of Jubilee, Amarus did appear
Proud with delight; in whose warm shine, when's haste
Had with officious diligence embraced
Euriolus, he, waving all delays,
To Dargonel the welcome news conveys;   500
Who, soon prepared for what so long had been
His hope's delight, to meet those joys within
The sacred temple, hastes. The place they chose
For Hymen's court, lest treacherous eyes disclose
The bride's just blushes, was a chapel, where
Devotion, when but a domestic care,
Was by his household practised; for the time—
'Twas ere the morn blushed to detect a crime.
   'All thus prepared, the priest conducting, they
With sober pace, which gently might convey   510
Diseased Amarus in his chair, they to
The chapel haste: which now come near, as through
The ancient room they pass, a sad deep groan
Assaults their ears; which, whilst with wonder grown
Into disease they entertain, appears
A sad confirmer of their doubtful fears—

Ismander, whom but late before they had
Followed t' the grave, his lively beauty clad
In the upper garments of pale death. Which sight
The train avoiding by their speedy flight,   520
Except the willing bride, behind leave none
But lame Amarus; who, his chair o'erthrown
By his affrighted bearers, there must lie
Exposed to fear, which, when attempts to fly,
Through often struggling, proved his labour vain,
He grovelling lies unseen to entertain.
  'Thus far successful, blest Ismander, thence
Conveys his lovely bride, whilst the expense
Of time being all laid out in fear, by none
He was observed. Amarus long alone   530
Lying tormented with his passions, ere
His frighted servants durst return to bear
Their fainting master off; but being at length,
When greater numbers had confirmed the strength
Of fortitude, grown bold, entering again
The room, which yet fear told them did retain
The scent of brimstone, there they only found
Their trembling master, tumbling on the ground.
Horror, augmented by internal guilt,
Had in his conscience's trepidations spilt   540
Both prayers and tears, which, since Heaven's law they crost,
For human passions in despair were lost.
Obscured in whose black mists, not daring to
Unclose his eyes, fearing again the view
Of that affrighting apparition, he
Is hurried from that dreadful place, to be
Their mirth, whom he (for fiends mistaking) cries
For mercy to, scarce trusting of his eyes,
When they unfolded had discovered none
But such whom long he'd for domestics known.   550
  'Yet to torment him more, before these fears
Wholly forsake him, in his room appears
Some officers; whose power, made dreadful by
The dictates of supreme authority,
As guilty of Ismander's death, arrest
Him for his murderer. By which charge opprest
More than before with fear, he, who now thought
On nought but death, to a tribunal brought,
Ere asked, confesses that foul crime, for which
He this just doom receives:—Since to enrich   560
What had before wealth's surfeit took, this sin
Was chiefly acted, his estate, fallen in
T' the hands of justice, by the judge should be
From hence disposed of; then, from death to free

556 charge] Orig. 'change.'

His life, already forfeited, except
Murdered Ismander, whom he thought had slept
In 's winding sheet, his hopeless advocate
Should there appear. In which unhappy state
The wretch, now ready to depart, beholds
This glorious change ;—Ismander first unfolds   570
Himself and her, who, bound by Nature's laws,
Implore his pardon ere they plead his cause ;
Which done, the judge, that his lost wealth might be
No cause of grief, unmasking, lets him see
Euriolus, by whom from th' worst of sin
To liberal virtue he 'd deluded been.'

THE END OF THE THIRD CANTO.

Canto IV

THE ARGUMENT

Whilst we awhile the pensive lady leave
  Here a close mourner for her rigid fate,
Let 's from the dark records of time receive
  The manner how Argalia waived the hate

Of his malignant stars ; which, when they seem
  To threaten most, through that dark cloud did lead
Him to a knowledge of such dear esteem,—
  He his high birth did there distinctly read.

FREED from the noise o' the busy world within
A deep dark vale, whose silent shade had been
Religion's veil, when blasted by the beams
Of persecution, far from the extremes
Of solitude or sweaty labour, were
Some few blest men, whose choice made Heaven their care,
Sequestered from the throngs of men to find
Those better joys, calms of a peaceful mind.
Yet though on this pacific sea, their main
Design was Heaven, that voyage did not restrain   10
Knowledge of human arts, which as they past
They safely viewed, though there no anchor cast ;
Their better tempered judgements counting that
But hoodwinked zeal, which blindly catches at
The great Creator's sacred will, without
Knowing those works that will was spent about ;
Which being the climax to true judgement, we
Behold stooped down to visibility
In lowliest creatures, Nature's stock being nought
But God in 's image to our senses brought.   20
  In the fair evening of that fatal day,
By whose meridian light love did betray

(217)

Engaged Argalia near to death, was one
Of these, Heaven's happy pensioners, alone,
Walking amongst the gloomy groves, to view
What sovereign virtues there in secret grew,
Confined to humble plants; whose signatures
Whilst by observing, he his art secures
From vain experiments.   Argalia's page,
Crossing a neighbouring path, did disengage   30
His serious eye from Nature's busy task,
To see the wandering boy, who was to ask
The way; for more his youth's unprompted fear
Expects not there, to the blest man drawn near.
But when, with such a weeping innocence
As saints confess those sins which the expense
Of tears exacted, he had sadly told
What harsh fate in restrictive wounds laid hold
Of 's worthy master, pity, prompted by
Religious love, helps the poor boy to dry   40
His tears with hopes of comfort; whilst he goes
To see what sad catastrophe did close
Those bloody scenes, which the unequal fight
Foretold, before fear prompted him to flight.
   Not far they'd passed ere they the place had found
Where, grovelling in a stream of blood, the ground
His purple bed, the wearied prince they see
Struggling with death: from whose dark monarchy
Pale troops assail his cheeks, whilst his dim eyes,
Like a spent lamp, which, ere its weak flame dies,   50
In giddy blazes glares, as if his soul
Were at those casements flying out, did roll,
Swifter than thought, their blood-shot orbs; his hands
Did with death's agues tremble; cold dew stands
Upon his clammy lips; the springs of blood,
Having breathed forth the spirits, clotted stood
On that majestic brow, whose dreadful frown
Had to death's sceptre laid its terror down.
   The holy man, upon the brink o' the grave
Finding such forms of worth, attempts to save   60
His life from dropping in, by all his best
Reserves of art; selecting from the rest
Of his choice store an herb whose sovereign power
No flux of blood, though falling in a shower
Of death, could force; which gently bruised, and to
His wound applied, taught Nature to renew
Her late neglected functions, and through short
Recruits of breath, made able to support
His blood-enfeebled body, till they reach
The monastry, where nobler art did teach   70

70 monastry] Chamberlayne probably meant this spelling.

Their simple medicines to submit to those
Which skill from their mixed virtues did compose.
  Life, which the unexpected gift of Fate
Rather than Art appeared, in this debate
Of death prevailing, in short time had gained
So much of strength, that weakness now remained
The only slothful remora that in
His bed detained him. Where, being often seen
By those whom art alike had qualified
For his relief, as one of them applied   80
His morning medicines to a spacious wound
Fixed on his breast, he that rare jewel found
Which, in his undiscerning infancy
There hung by 's father, fortune had kept free
From all her various accidents, to show
How much his birth did to her favour owe.
  Shook with such silent joy as he had been
In calm devotion by an angel seen,
The good old man, his wonder rarified
Into amazement, stands : he had descried   90
What, if no force had robbed him of it since
'Twas first bestowed, none but his true-born prince
Could wear, since Art, wise Nature's fruitful ape,
Ne'er but in that had birth which bore that shape.
Assured by which, with unstirred confidence
He asks Argalia—Whe'er he knew from whence,
When Nature first did so much wealth impart
To earth, that jewel took those forms of art?
But being answered—That his infancy,
When first it was conferred on him, might be   100
The excuse of 's ignorance ; that voice alone
Confirms his aged friend : who, having known
As much of fortune, as in Fate's dark shade
His understanding legible had made,
From weak Argalia, to requite him leads
Knowledge where he his life's first copy reads
Dressed in this language : . . . .
  . . . .'Twas, unhappy prince !
(For such this story must salute you, since
Told to confirm 't a truth) my destiny   110
When youth and strength rendered me fit to be
My dearest country's servant, placed within
Mantinea's glorious court ; where, having been
Made capable by sacred orders, I
Attained the height of priestly dignity,
Being unto him, whose awful power did sway
That crown, in dear esteem ; but honour's day,
Which gilded then the courtly sphere, sunk down,
I lost my mitre in the fall o' the crown.
Sad is the doleful tale ; yet, since that in   120

Its progress you may find where did begin
Your life's first stage, thus take it.—When the court,
Stifled with throngs of men, whose thick resort
Plenty and peace called thither, being grown
Sickly with ease, viewed, as a thing unknown,
Danger's stern brow, which even in smiling fates
Proves a quotidian unto wiser states ;
Whilst Pride grew big, and Envy bigger, we,
Sleeping i' the bed of soft security,
Were with alarums wakened.—Faction had,   130
To show neglect's deformities, unclad
That gaudy monster, whose first dress had been
The night-pieced works of their unriper sin ;
And those that in contracted fortunes dwelt,
Calmly in favour's shadow, having felt
The glorious burthen of their honour grown
Too large for all that fortune called their own,
Like fishes which the lesser fry devour,
Pride having joined oppression to their power,
Preyed on the subject, till their load outgrew   140
Their loyalty, and forced even those that knew
Once only to obey, in sullen rage
To mutter threats, whose horror did presage
That blood must in domestic jars be spilt,
To cure their envy, and the people's guilt.
  'These seeds of discord, which began to rise
To active growth, by the honourable spies
Of other princes seen, had soon betrayed
Our state's obscure disease, and called, to aid
Ambitious subjects, foreign powers ; whose strength,   150
First but as physic used, was grown at length
Our worst disease, which, whilst we hoped for cure,
Turned our slow hectic to a calenture.
  'A Syracusan army, that had been
Against our strength often victorious in
A haughty rebel's quarrel, being by
Success taught how to ravish victory
Without his aid, which only useful proved
When treason first for novelty was loved,
Seizing on all that in 's pretended cause   160
Had stooped to conquest, what the enfeebled laws
In vain attempted, soon perform, and give
The traitor death from what made treason live :
This done, whilst their victorious ensigns were
Fanned by Fame's breath, they their bold standards bear
Near to our last hopes ;—an army which,
Like oft-tried ore, disasters made more rich

133 ' Night-pieced,' 'secretly combined,' is quite Chamberlaynian ; but the word
may have been that odd ' night-*peeked* ' which we have had before.

In loyal valour than vast numbers, and
By shaking fixed those roots on which did stand
Their well-elected principles; which here,   170
Opprest with number, only did appear
In bravely dying, when their righteous cause,
Condemned by Fate's inevitable laws,
Let its religion—virtue—valour—all
That Heaven calls just, beneath rebellion fall.
  'Near to the end of this black day, when none
Was left that durst protect his injured throne;
When loyal valour, having lost the day,
Bleeding within the bed of honour lay;
Thy wounded father, when his acts had shown   180
As high a spirit as did ever groan
Beneath misfortune, is enforced to leave
The field's wild fury, and some rest receive
In faithful Enna; where his springs of blood
Were hardly stopped, before a harsher flood
Assails his eyes:—Thy royal mother, then
More blooming than Earth's full-blown beauties when
Warmed in the ides of May, her fruitful womb
Pregnant with thee, to an untimely tomb,
Her fainting spirits, in that horrid fright   190
Losing the paths of life, from time, from light,
And grief, steals down: yet ere she had discharged
Her debts to death, protecting Heaven enlarged
Thy narrow lodging, and that life, which she
Lost in thy fatal birth, bestowed on thee—
On thee, in whom those joys, thy father prized
More than loved empire, are epitomized.
  'And now, as if the arms of adverse fate
Had all conspired our ills to aggravate
Above the strength of patience, we are by   200
Victorious foes, before our fear could fly
To a remoter refuge, closed within
Unhappy Enna; which, before they win,
Though stormed with fierce assaults, the restless sun
His annual progress through the heavens had run;
But then, tired with disasters which attend
A slow-paced siege, unable to defend
Their numbers from resistless famine, they
With an unwilling loyalty obey
The next harsh summons, and so prostrate lie   210
T' the rage or mercy of their enemy.
But ere the city's fortune was unto
This last black stage arrived, safely withdrew
T' the castle's strength thy father was, where he,
Though far from safety, finds the time to be
Informed by sober counsel how to steer
Through this black storm; love, loyalty, and fear,

Had often varied judgements, but at last
Into this form their full resolves were cast.
   'To cool hot action, and to bathe in rest   220
More peaceful places, darkness dispossest
The day's sovereignty; to usher whom
Into her sable throne, a cloud's full womb,
Congealed by frigid air, as if that then
The elements had warred as well as men,
In a white veil came hovering down—to hide
The coral pavements; but forbid b' the pride
O' the conqueror's triumphs, and expelled from thence
As that which too much emblemed innocence—
Since that the city no safe harbour yields,   230
It takes its lodging in the neighbouring fields;
Which, mantled in those spotless robes, invite
The prince through them to take his secret flight.
   'In sad distress leaving his nobles to
Swallow such harsh conditions as the view
Of danger candied o'er, from treacherous eyes
Obscured in a plebeian's poor disguise,
His glorious train shrunk to desertless I—
The sad companion of his misery;
He, now departing, thee, his infant son,   240
Heir to his crown and cares, ordained to run
This dangerous hazard of thy life before
Time taught thee how thy fortune to deplore
When venturing on this precipice of fate,
We slowly sallied forth, 'twas cold and late;
The drowsy guard asleep, the sentries hid
Close in their huts did shivering stand, and chid
The whistling winds with chattering teeth. When now
A leave as solemn as haste would allow,
Of all our friends, our mourning friends, being took,   250
We, like the earth, veiled all in white, forsook
Our sallyport; whilst slowly marching o'er
The new-fallen snow, thee in his arms he bore.
Whilst this imposture made the scared guards, when
They saw us move—then make a stand again,
Either to think that dallying winds had played
With flakes of snow, or that their sight betrayed
Their fancy into errors; we were past
The reach of danger, and in triumph cast
Off, with our fears, what had us safety lent,   260
When strength refused to save the innocent.
The eager lover hugs himself not in
Such roseal beds of joy, when what hath been
His sickly wishes is possessed, as we,
Through watchful foes arrived to liberty,

---

263 roseal] Singer again 'rose*ate*,' which is even worse than before, because it
would simply mean a 'pink' bed, not a 'bed of roses.'

Embrace the welcome blessing. First we steer
Our course towards Syracuse, whose confines near
The mountain stood, upon whose cloudy brow
Poor Enna did beneath her ruins bow.
  ' The stars, clothed in the pride of light, had sent   270
Their sharp beams from the spangled firmament,
To silver o'er the earth, which being embost
With hills, seemed now enamelled o'er with frost ;
The keen winds whistle in the justling trees,
And clothed their naked limbs in hoary frieze ;
When, having paced some miles of crusted earth,
Whose labour warmed our blood, before the birth
O' the sluggish morning from his bed had drawn
The early villager, the sober dawn
Lending our eyes the slow salutes of light,   280
We are encountered with the welcome sight
Of some poor scattered cottages, that stood
I' the dark shadow of a spacious wood
That fringed an humble valley. Towards those,
Whilst the still morn knew nought to discompose
Her sleepy infancy, we went ; and now,
Being come so near, we might discover how
The unstirred smoke streamed from the cottage tops ;
A glimmering light from a low window stops
Our further course : we're come to a low shed,   290
Whose happy owner, ne'er disquieted
With those domestic troubles that attend
On larger roofs, here in content did spend
Fortune's scant gifts ; at his unhaunted gate
Hearing us knock, he stands not to debate
With wealthy misers' slow suspicion, but
Swift, as if 'twere a sin to keep it shut,
Removes that slender guard. But when he there
Unusual strangers saw, with such a care
As only spoke a conscious shame to be   300
Surprised, whilst unprovided poverty
Straitened desire, he starts ; yet entertains
Us so, that showed by an industrious pains
He strove to welcome more. Here being by
Their goodness and our own necessity
Tempted awhile to rest, we safely lay
Far from pursuing ill ; yet since the way
To danger by suspicion lies, we still
Fear being betrayed ·by those that meant no ill,
Since oft their busy whispers, though they spring   310
From love and wonder, slow discoveries bring.
  ' Being now removing, since thy tender age
Threatened to make the grave its second stage,

291 owner] Here again in orig. the misprint, or misprision, of ' honour.'

If thence conveyed by us, whose fondest love
Could to thy wants but fruitless pity prove :
T' enlarge thy commons though increase our fears,
To those indulgent rurals, who for tears
Had springs of milk to feed thee, thou remain'st
An infant tenant ; for thy own name gain'st
What since thou hast been known by; which when we   320
Contracted had to the stenography,
Some gold, the last of all our wealth, we leave
To make their burden light ; which they receive
With thankful joy, amazed to see those bright
Angels display their strange unwonted light
In poverty's cold region, where they had
Been pined for want, if not by labour clad.
    ' When age should make thee capable to tell
Thy wonder how thy infancy had fell
From honour's pyramids, a jewel, which   330
Did once the splendour of his crown enrich,
About thy neck he hangs ; then breathing on
Thy tender lips a parting kiss, we're gone—
Gone from our last delight, to find some place
Dark as our clouded stars, there to embrace
Unenvied poverty, in the cold bed
Of sad despair ; till on his reverend head,
Once centre to a crown, grief makes him wear
A silver frost, by frequent storms of care
Forced on that royal mount, whose verdure fades,   340
Ere Time—his youth's antagonist, invades.
    ' Not far, through dark and unknown paths we had
Wandered within those forests, which, unclad
By big winds of their summer's beauteous dress,
Naked and trembling stood, ere fair success,
Smiling upon our miseries, did bring
Us to a crystal stream, from whose cold spring,
With busy and laborious care, we saw
A feeble hermit stooping down to draw
An earthen pot, whose empty want supplied   350
With liquid treasure, soon had satisfied
His thirsty hopes : who now returning by
A narrow path, which did directing lie
Through the unfrequented desert, with the haste
Of doubtful travellers in lands laid waste
By conquering foes, we follow, till drawn near
To him whom innocence secured from fear,

319 gain'st] Orig. ' against,' which Singer duly corrected, as he did nearly all such
things.   And I should like to observe that the notes in which I have sometimes
differed with him imply no slight to the very great care and intelligence which he
bestowed on our text.
    341 This is Singer's reading.   The orig. has ' Time *by*,' and I am not sure that, as in
some other cases, it is not right.   If it is, ' youth's antagonist' would be *Age*, Time's
general in the attack.   I do not think this is unlike Chamberlayne.

Disburthening of his staff, he sits to rest
What was with age and labour both opprest.
'Our first salutes when we for blessings had   360
Exchanged with him; being set, we there unclad
All our deformed misfortunes, and, unless
A kingdom's loss, developed our distress.
Which heard with pity, that he safely might
Be the directing Pharos, by whose light
We might be safely guided from the rocks
Of the tempestuous world, his tongue unlocks
A cabinet of holy counsel; which
More than our vanished honour did enrich
Our souls (for whose eternal good was meant   370
This cordial) with the world's best wealth, content,
Content, which flies the busy throne, to dwell
With hungry hermits in the noiseless cell.
'More safe than age from the hot sins of youth,
Peaceful as faith, free as untroubled truth,
Being by him directed hither, we
Long lived within this narrow monastry;
Whose orders, being too strict for those that ne'er
Had lost delight i' the prosecuting care
Of unsuccessful action, suited best   380
With us whose griefs compared taught the distrest
To slight their own, as guests that did intrude
On reason in the want of fortitude,
That brave supporter, which such comfort brings,
That none can know but persecuted kings.
'The purple-robe, his birth's unquestioned right,
For the coarse habit of a carmelite
Being now exchanged; and we retired from both
Our fears and hopes, like private lovers, loath
When solved from the observant spy, to be   390
Disturbed by friends, from want or greatness free,
Secure and calm, we spent those happy days,
In nought ambitious, but of what might raise
Our thoughts towards Heaven, with whom each hour acquaints,
In prayer more frequent than afflicted saints,
Our happy souls; which here so long had been
Refining, till that grand reward of sin,
Death, did by Age, his common harbinger—
Proclaim's approach, and warned us to defer
For the earth's trivial business nought that might   400
Concern eternity, lest life and light,
Forsaking our dark mansions, leave us to
Darkness and death, unfurnished of a clew
Which might conduct, when time shall cease to be,
Through the meanders of eternity.'

        362 Here, as elsewhere, 'unless' = 'except.'
        391 from] Orig. 'for.'

(225)

'Thy pious father, ere the thefts of age,
Decaying strength, should his stiff limbs engage
In an uneasy rest, to level all
Accounts with heaven, doth to remembrance call
A vow, which though in hot affliction made,   410
Whilst passion's short ephemeras did invade
His troubled soul, doth now, when the disease
Time had expunged, from solitary ease
Call him again to an unwilling view
Of the active world, in a long journey to
Forlorn Enna ; unto whose temple he
Had vowed, if fortune lent him liberty,
Till tired with the extremes of weary age,
The cheap devotion of a pilgrimage.

THE END OF THE FOURTH CANTO.

Canto V

THE ARGUMENT

To the grave author of this happy news
    The pleased Argalia with delight did hear,
Till, whilst the fatal story he pursues,
    He brings his great soul near the gates of fear

By letting him in full discovery know
    The dreadful danger that did then attend
His royal sire ; who to his sword must owe
    For safety, ere his sad afflictions end.

'FORSAKING now our solitary friends,
Whose prayers upon each slow-paced step attends,
From danger by a dress so coarse exempt,
As wore religion to avoid contempt,
Through toils of many a tedious day, at last
We Enna reach ; where when his vows had past
The danger of a forfeiture, and we,
That debt discharged to heaven, had liberty
To look abroad, with sorrow-laden eyes
We view those ruins in whose ashes lies   10
Sad objects of our former loss, not then
Raked up so deep, but old observant men,
When youths were in procession led, could tell
Where towers once stood, and in what fights they fell ;
Which to confirm, some in an aged pride
Show wounds, which then though they did wisely hide
As signatures of loyal valour, they,
Now unsuspected, with delight display.
    'Hence when commanded by the wane of light,
We sought protection from approaching night   20

(226)

In an adjacent monastry; where we,
The wandering objects of their charity,
Although by all welcomed with friendly zeal,
Found only one whose outside did reveal
So much of an internal worth, that might
To active talk our clouded souls invite
From grief's obscure retreats; his grave aspect,
Though reverend age dwelt with unpruned neglect,
Seemed dressed with such a sacred solitude,
As ruined temples in their dust include.   30
　'My royal master, as some power divine
Had by instinct taught great souls how to twine,
Though 'mongst the weeds of poverty, with this
Blest man consorting; whilst their apt souls miss,
In all their long discourse, no tittle set
For man's direction in Heaven's alphabet;
Whilst controverted points, those rocks on which
Weak faiths are shipwrecked, did with gems enrich
Their art-assisted zeal, a sudden noise,
Clamorous and loud, in the soft womb destroys   40
That sacred infant;—The concordant bells
Proclaim a joy, which larger triumph tells
To be of such a public birth, that they
In quiet cells for what they late did pray
In tears—the soul's o'erflowing language, now
(Being by example's common rule taught how)
They vary passions, and in manly praise
Their silent prayers to hallelujahs raise.
By swift report informed that this day's mirth
From the proclaiming of their prince took birth,   50
These private mourners for the public faults
Of busy nations, by the hot assaults
Of triumph startled from their gravity,
Prepare for joy; all but grave Sophron: he
Then with the pilgrim prince, who both were sate
Like sad physicians when the doubtful state
O' the patients threatens death:—the serious eye
Of Sophron as a threatening prodigy
Viewing that flattering smile of Fate, which they
Of shallower souls praised as approaching day.   60
　'When both, their souls from active words retired
Awhile had silent sat, the prince desired
To know the cause why in that triumph he
Of all that convent found the time to be
With thoughtful cares alone; whom Sophron gave
This satisfaction:—"Worthy sir, I have
In the few hours of our acquaintance found
In you such worth, 'twould question for unsound
My judgement, if unwilling to impart
A secret, though the darling of my heart.—   70

(227)

Know then, this hapless province, which of late
Faction hath harassed, a wise prince, whom Fate
Deprived us of, once ruled ; but so long since,
That age hath learned from time how to convince
The hot enormities of youth, since we
With such a ruler lost our liberty.
For though at first, (as he alone had been
Our evil genius, whose abode brought in
All those attendant plagues), our fortune seemed
To calm her brow, and captive hope redeemed   80
In the destruction of our foes, which by
A hot infection were enforced to fly
From conquest near obtained : yet we, to show
That only 'twas our vices did o'erthrow
The merits of his weaker virtues, when
Successful battles had reduced again
Our panting land from all external ill,
Domestic quarrels threatened then to kill
What foreign powers assailed in vain, and made
Danger surprise, which trembled to invade.   90
For many years tossed by the uncertain wind
Of wild ambition, we had sailed to find
Out the Leucadian rocks of peace ; but in
A vain pursuit : for we so long had been
A headless multitude, the factious peers
Oppressing the injured commons, till our fears
Became our fate, few having so much left
Unsequestered, as might incite to theft
Even those whom want makes desperate ; all being spent
On those that turn to th' worst of punishment   100
What wore protection's name—villains that we,
Enforced, maintained to Christian tyranny
I' the injured name of justice, such as kept
Litigious counsels, for whose votes we wept,
From punishment so long, till grown above
The blinded people's envy or their love.
  ' " But lately these prodigious fires, that led
Us through the night of anarchy, being fled
At the approach of one, who since hath stood
Fixed like a star of the first magnitude,   110
Diffusive power, which then was only shown
In faction's dress, being now rebellion grown,
By the uniting of those atoms in
One haughty peer, ambitious Zarrobrin ;
Whose pride, that spur of valour, when 't had set
Him in the front of honour's alphabet,
The sole commander of those forces whence
Our peace distilled, and in as large a sense
As subjects durst, whilst loyal, hope to have
Adorn their tombs, the highest titles gave   120

(228)

Of a depending honour ; to repay
Their easy faiths that levelled had the way
Unto his greatness, that command he made
The steps by which he struggled to invade
A throne, and in their heedless votes include
Unnoted figures of their servitude.
    ' " When with attempts, frequent as fruitless, I
With others, whose firm love to loyalty
Time had not yet expunged, had oft in vain
Opposed our power ; which found too weak to gain   130
Our country's freedom, we, as useless, did
Retire to mourn for what the Fates forbid
To have redressed. Since when, his pride being grown
The people's burthen whilst he urged his own
Ambitious ends, he hath, to fix their love
On principles whose structure should not move,
Unless it their allegiance shook, brought forth
Their prince, whose father's unforgotten worth
Did soon command their full consent, and he,
For treason feared, made loved for loyalty.   140
But since that 'mongst observant judgements, this
So sudden change might stand in doubt to miss
A fair construction, to confirm 't he brings
An old confessor of their absent king's,
The reverend Halophantes ; one whose youth
Made human hearts submit to sacred truth
So much, that now, arrived to graver age,
He (like authentic authors) did engage
The people's easy faith into a glad
Belief—that, when his youth's afflictions had   150
Unthroned their prince, he in that fatal night,
Wisely contracting his imagined flight,
As roads unto destruction leaving all
Frequented paths, did in the night's silence call
At 's unfrequented cell ; where, entertained
With all the zeal that subjects, which have gained
From gracious sovereigns, study to express
A virtue in, which thrives by the distress
Of an afflicted patron's, he betrays
Inquiring scouts, till some expunging days   160
Make them forsake their inquisition in
Despair to find : which vacancy did win
Time to bestow his infant burthen where
Some secret friends did with indulgent care
Raise him from undiscerning childhood, to
Be such as now exposed unto their view."
    ' Thy father, who with doubtful thoughts had heard
This story, till confirmed in what he feared,
Starts into so much passion as betrays
Him, through the thick mask of those tedious days   170

Time had in thirty annual journeys stept,
To Sophron ; who, when he awhile had wept
A short encomium to good fortune, in
Such prostrate lowliness as seemed—for sin
To censure guiltless ignorance, he meets
His prince's full discovery ; whom he greets
With all the zeal, such whose uncourtly arts
Make tongues the true interpreters of hearts,
To those wise princes whom they know to start
At aguish flattery, as if indesert   180
Ushered it in :—Those that know how to rate
Their worth, prize it by virtue, not by fate.
     ' With arguments, which to assist he made
Reason's firm power Passion's light scouts invade,
He had so oft the unwilling prince assailed,
That importunity at length prevailed
On his resolves ; from peaceful poverty,
His age's refuge, hurrying him to be
Once more an agent unto fortune in
Uncertain toils. Whose troubles to begin,   190
Leaving his prince to so much rest as those
Whose serious souls are busied to compose
Unravelled thoughts into a method, now
Sophron forsakes him, to discover how
His fellow-peers of that lost party stand
Disposed for action, if a king's command
Should give it life ; all which he finds to be
So full of yet untainted loyalty,
That in a swift convention they prepare
By joining judgements to divide their care.   200
From distant places, with such secret haste
As did declare a flaming zeal, though placed
In caution's shadow, old considerate peers,
Such whose light youth the experienced weight of years
Had long since ballast with discretion, met
To see their prince, and to discharge the debt
Of full obedience. Each had with him brought
His state's surviving hope, snatched from the soft
Hands of lamenting mothers, that to those,
If fit for arms, they safely might dispose   210
The execution of those councils, which
Their sober age with judgement did enrich.
     ' In Sophron's palace, which being far removed
From the street's talking throngs, was most approved
For needful privacy, these loyal lords,
Whose faithful hearts—the infallible records
The heedless vulgar (whose neglective sin
Had lost the copies of allegiance in

179 To those] Singer ' Do,' of which I fail to make sense.

This interregnum) trust to—being met,
To shun delays, man's late-repented debt,   220
The prince with speed appears; whom no disguise
Of youth's betrayer, time, could from their eyes
Long undiscovered keep : through the rough veil
Of age, or what more powerful did prevail
On beauty's ruins, they did soon descry
The unquenched embers of a majesty,
Too bright for time to hide with curtains less
Dark than that mansion of forgetfulness,
The grave, which man's first folly taught to be
The obscure passage to eternity.   230
  'That their example might be precept to
Unknowing youth, with all the reverence due
To awful princes on their thrones, the old
Experienced courtiers kneel ; by which grown bold
In their belief, those of unriper age
Upon their judgements did their faith engage
So far, that they in solemn vows unite
Their yet concordant thoughts, which, ere the flight
Of time should leave the day behind, desired
To live in action. But this rising fire   240
Of loyal rage, which in their breasts did burn,
The thankful prince thus gently strives to turn
Into a milder passion, such as might
Not scorch with anger, but with judgement light.—
  ' " How much 'tis both my wonder and my joy,
That we, whom treason studied to destroy
With near as much of miracle, as in
The last of days lost bodies, that have been
Scattered amongst the elements, shall be
Convened i' the court of immortality.   250
Depressed with fortune, and disguised with age,
(Sad arguments, brave subjects, to engage
Your loyal valour !) I had gone from all
My mortal hopes, had not this secret call
Of Heaven, which doth with unknown method curb
Our wild intention, brought me to disturb
Your peaceful age, whose abler youth had in
Defending me exposed to ruin been.
I had no more, my conscience now at rest,
With widows' curses, orphans' tears opprest ;   260
No more in fighting fields, those busy marts
Where honour doth for fame with death change hearts,

---

246 we] Left entirely ' in the air,' for the reader to supply ' are now convened ' or
something similar.
259 had] Similarly deprived of 'been.' I note these two because, little as Cham-
berlayne seems to have revised the earlier books, he appears to have left this last part
even more in ostrich-fashion.

Beheld the sad success of battles, where
Proud victors make youth's conquest age's care;
But, hid from all a crown's false glories, spent,
Like beauteous flowers, which vainly waste the scent
Of odours in unhaunted deserts, all
My time concealed till withered age should fall
From that short stem of nature—life, to be
Lost in the dust of death's obscurity.   270
 ' "When in the pride of youth my stars withdrew
Their influence first, I then had stood with you
Those thunderbolts of fate, and bravely died,
Contemning fortune, had that feverish pride
Of valour not been quenched in hope to save
My infant son from an untimely grave.
But he, when from domestic ills conveyed
In safety, being by treacherous fate betrayed,
Either by death or ignorance, from what
His stars, when kindled first, were pointed at,   280
Either lives not, or else concealed within
Some coarse disguise, whose poverty hath been
So long his dull companion, till he's grown
Not less to us than to himself unknown.
 ' "All this being weighed in Reason's scale, is there
Aught in't can tempt decrepit age to bear
Such glorious burthens, which if fortunate
In the obtaining of, in Nature's date
Can have no long account, ere I again
What I had got with danger, kept with pain,   290
Summoned by Death—the grave's black monarch, must
With sorrow lose? Yet since that Heaven so just,
And you so loyal I have found, that it
Might argue fear, if I unmoved should sit
At all your just desires, I here, i' the sight
Of Heaven declare, together with my right,
To prosecute your liberties as far
As justice dares to patronize a war."
 ' This, with a magnanimity that showed
His youth's brave spirits were not all bestowed   300
On the accounts of age, had to so high
A pitch of zeal inflamed their loyalty,
That in contempt of slow-paced counsels they
Did, like rash youth, whose wit wants time's allay,
Haste to unripe engagements, such as found
The issue weak, whose parents are unsound.
 ' All, to those towns where neighbourhood had made
Them loved for virtue, or for power obeyed,
Whilst each with his peculiar guard attends
His honoured prince, employ their active friends;   310
Who having with collecting trumpets made
Important errands ready to invade

The people's censure, for a theme to fame—
Their long-lost prince's safe return proclaim:
Which, though at first a subject it appeared
Only for faith, when circumstance had cleared
The eye of reason, from each nobler mind
The embraces of a welcome truth did find.
In public throngs, whilst every forward friend
Spoke his resolves, his sullen foes did spend   320
Their doubts in private whispers; by exchange
Of which they found hate had no further range
Than close intelligence, whose utmost bounds
Ere they obtain, the useful trumpet sounds
No distant summons, but close marches to
His loyal friends; whom now their foes might view
In troops, which if fate favour their intents,
Ere long must swell to big-bulked regiments.
Through country towns, and cities' prouder streets,
The murmuring drum in busy marches meets   330
Such forward valour—husbandmen did fear
The earth would languish the succeeding year
For want of labourers; nor could business stop
The straitened 'prentice, who, the slighted shop
Left to his angry master (who must be
Forced to abridge his seven years' tyranny),
Changes the baser utensils of trade
For burnished arms, and by example made
More valiant, scorns those shadows which they feared
More than rough war, whilst 'mongst the city's herd.   340
    'To regiments from scattering bands being grown,
From that to armies, whose big looks made known
Those bold designs, which justice feared to own,
Though her's till placed in Power's imperial throne,
They now toward action haste. Which to begin,
Whilst castles are secured, and towns girt in
With armèd lines, whose palisadoes had
Whole forests of their whispering oaks unclad;
The prince, his mercy willing to prevent
Approaching danger, by a herald sent   350
To Zarrobrin, commands him to lay down
His arms, and, as he owed unto his crown
A subject's due allegiance, to appear,
Before a month was added to that year,
Within his court; which now, since action gave
Life to that body whose firm strength did save
His life—by treason levelled at, was in
His moving camp. But this too weak to win

---

358 this] Here either 'is' might be absorbed or 'being' left out. Singer apparently
thought the former was the case and put a semi-colon at 'rebel.' I think the latter
more Chamberlaynian, and prefer a comma. Cf. 'But come' *infra*, l. 365.

The doubtful rebel, since his lawful right
Swords must dispute, the prince prepares to fight.   360
  'Proud Zarrobrin, who had by late success
Taught Syracuse how to avoid distress
By seeking peace, like a black storm that flies
On southern winds, which in a tumult rise
From neighbouring seas, was on his march.   But come
So near the prince, that now he had by some
Of 's spreading scouts made full discovery where
His army lay, whose scarce discovered rear
Such distance from their well-armed van appeared,
That such, whose judgements were with numbers feared,   370
Making no further inquisition, fled—
By swift report their pale disease to spread.
Disturbing clouds, which rather seemed to rise
From guilt than fear, spread darkness o'er the eyes
O' the rebels, who, although by custom made
To death familiar, wish their killing trade
In peace concluded; and with murmurs, nigh
Grown to the boldness of a mutiny,
Question their own frail judgements, which so oft
Had life exposed to dangers, that had brought   380
No more reward than what preserved them still
The slaves unto a proud commander's will.
To stop this swift infection, which, begun
In lowly huts, to lofty tents had run,
Sly Zarrobrin, who to preserve the esteem
Of honour, least liberality might seem
The child of fear, with secret speed prevents
What he appears to slight—their discontents,
As if attending, though attended by
Their young mock-prince, whose landscape royalty   390
Showed only fair when viewed at distance, he
Passing with slow observant pace to see
Each squadron's order, he confirms their love
With donatives, such as were far above
Their hopes if victors ; then, to show that in
That pride of bounty he'd not strove to win
Assistance by unworthy bribes, he leads
Them far from danger, since his judgement reads
In long experience—that authentic story,
Whose lines have taught the nearest way to glory—   400
That soft delays, like treacherous streams, which by
Submitting let the rash intruder try
Their dangerous depth, to an unwilling stay
His fierce pursuers would ere long betray :
Whose force, since of the untutored multitude,
By want made desperate and by custom rude,
Would soon waste their unwieldy strength ; whilst they,
Whom discipline had taught how to obey,

By pay made nimble and by order sure,
Would war's delays with easier wants endure.   410
  'This sound advice meeting with sad success
From the pursuing army, whose distress,
From tedious marches being too clamorous grown
For 's friends' estates to quiet, soon was shown
In actions such, which though necessity
Enforced on virtue, made their presence be
To the inconsiderate vulgar, whose loose glance
For virtue takes vice glossed with circumstance,
Such an oppression, that comparing those
Which fled with mildness, they behold as foes,   420
Only their ruder followers, whom they curse—
Not that their cause, but company was worse.
  'When thus their wants had brought disorder in,
And that neglect whose looser garb had been
At first so shy, that what was hardly known
From business then, was now to custom grown;
This large-limbed body, since united by
No cement but the love to loyalty,
Loses those baser parts, such as to please
Unworthy ends turned duty to disease,   430
Retaining only those whose valour sought
No more reward than what with blood they bought.
But here,—to show that slumbering Justice may,
Oppressed with power, faint in the busy day
Of doubtful battle—when their valour had
So many souls from robes of flesh unclad
Of his brave friends, that the forsaken prince,
Whose sad success taught knowledge to convince
The arguments of hope, unguarded, left
Unto pursuing foes, was soon bereft   440
Of all that in this cloud of fortune might,
By opposition or unworthy flight,
But promise safety; and, when death denied
Him her last dark retreat, to raise the pride
Of an insulting foe, is forced to see
The scorn of greatness in captivity.
  'Yet with more terror to limn sorrow in
His mighty soul, such friends, as had not been
By death discharged in fatal battle, now
Suffered so much as made even fear allow   450
Her palest sons to seek in future wars
Brave victory, got by age's honour—scars,
Or braver death—that antidote of shame,
Whose stage none pass upon the road of fame;
Those that fared best being murdered, others sent
With life to more afflicting banishment.'

436 flesh] Orig. 'fresh.'   447 limn] Orig. 'limb.'

When thus by him, whose sacred order made
The truth authentic, from his fortune's shade
Argalia was redeemed; the prelate, to
Confirm his story, from his bosom drew   460
The jewel, which having by ways unknown
To him that wore it opened, there was shown
By wit contracted into art, as rare
As his that durst make silver spheres compare
With heaven's light motion, an effigies, which
His royal sire, whilst beauty did enrich
His youth, appeared in such epitome,
As spacious fields are represented by
Rare optics on opposing walls, where sight
Is cozened with imperfect forms of light.   470
   When with such joy as Scythians, that grow proud
Of day, behold light gild an eastern cloud,
Argalia long had viewed that picture, in
Whose face he saw forms that said his had been
Drawn by that pattern, with such thanks, as best
The silent eloquence of looks exprest,
The night grown ancient ere their story's end,
With solemn joy leaves his informing friend.

465–467 which . . . appeared] 'In which' or 'displayed' would of course be required
by precisians.

THE END OF THE FOURTH BOOK.

BOOK V. Canto I

THE ARGUMENT

Tired with afflictions, in a safe retreat
  From the active world, Pharonnida is now
Making a sacred monastry her seat;
  Where, near approaching the confirming vow,

A rude assault makes her a prisoner to
  Almanzor's power; to expiate whose sin,
The subtle traitor swiftly leads her to
  The court, where she had long a stranger been.

HERE harsh employments, the unsavoury weeds
Of barren wants, had overrun the seeds
Of fancy with domestic cares, and in
Those winter storms shipwrecked whate'er had been
My youth's imperfect offspring, had not I,
For love of this, neglected poverty—
That meagre fiend, whose rusty talons stick
Contempt on all that are enforced to seek
Like me a poor subsistence 'mongst the low
Shrubs of employment; whilst blest wits, that grow   10
Good Fortune's favourites, like proud cedars stand,
Scorning the stroke of every feeble hand,
Whose vain attempts, though they should martyr sense,
Would be repulsed with big-bulked confidence:
Yet blush not, gentle Muse! thou oft hast had
Followers, by Fortune's hand as meanly clad,
And such as, when time had worn envy forth,
Succeeding ages honoured for their worth.
  Then though not by these rare examples fired
To vain presumption, with a soul untired   20
As his, whose fancy's short ephemeras know
No life—but what doth from his liquor flow,
Whose wit, grown wanton with Canary's wealth,
Makes the chaste Muse a pandress to a health,
Our royal lovers' story I'll pursue
Through Time's dark paths; which now have led me to
Behold Argalia, by assisting Art
Advanced to health, preparing to depart
From his obscure abode, to prosecute
Designs, which, when success strikes terror mute   30
With pleasing joy, shall him the mirror prove
Of forward valour, glossed with filial love.
  But let us here with prosperous blessings leave
Awhile the noble hero, and receive

From Time's accounts the often varying story
Of her whose love conducted him to glory,
Distressed Pharonnida; whose sufferings grown
Too great for all that virtue ere had known
From human precepts, flies for refuge to
Heaven's narrowest paths, where the directing clew   40
Of law, to which the earth for order owes,
Lost in zeal's light, a useless trouble grows.
  Returned were all the messengers, which she
Had at the first salutes of liberty
To seek Argalia sent : but since none brought
Her passion's ease, sick Hope no longer sought
Those flattering empirics ; but at Love's bright fires
Kindling her zeal, with sober pace retires
From all expected honours, to bestow
What time her youth did yet to Nature owe,   50
A solemn recluse, by a sacred vow
Locked up from action, whilst she practised how,
By speculation safely to attain
What busier mortals doubtfully do gain.
  Within the compass of the valley, where
Ismander's palace stood, the pious care
Of elder times had placed a monastry,
Whose fair possessors, from life's tumults free,
In a calm voyage towards Heaven—their home, there spent
The quiet hours, so sweetly innocent,   60
As if that place, that happy place, had been
Of all the earth alone exempt from sin ;
Some sacred power ordaining (when 'twas given)
It for the next preparing school to heaven,
From whence those vestals should, when life expires,
Be for supplies advanced to heavenly choirs.
Lost to the world in sorrow's labyrinths, here
Pharonnida, now out of hope to clear
This tempest of her fate, resolves to cast
Her faith's firm anchor : but before she passed   70
The dangerous straits of a restrictive vow,
She, to such friends as judgement taught her how
To prize, imparts it ; 'mongst which few, the fair
Silvandra, whom lost love had taught despair,
With sad Florenza, both resolve to take
The same strict habit, and with her forsake
The treacherous world. But to disturb this clear
Stream of devotion, soon there did appear
Dissuading friends—Ismander, loath to lose
So loved a guest, whilst she 's of power to choose,   80
Together with the virtuous Ammida,
Spend their most powerful arguments to draw
Her from those cold thoughts, that her virtue might,
Whilst unconcealed, lend weaker mortals light.

Long had this friendly conflict lasted, ere
Her conquered friends, whom a religious care
Frighted from robbing Heaven of saints, withdrew
To mourn her loss; yet ere they left her to
Her cloistered cell, Ismander, to comply
With aged custom, calls such friends whom nigh   90
Abode had made familiar, to attend
His royal guest. Some hasty days they spend
In solemn feasting, where each friend, although
Clothed as when they at triumphs met, did show
A silent sadness, such as wretched brides,
When the neglected nuptial robe but hides
The cares of an obstructed love, before
Harsh parents wear. The mirthless feast passed o'er,
The noble virgins, in procession by
The mourning train, unto the monastry   100
Slowly conducted are; each led by two
Full-breasted maids, whom Hymen, to renew
The world's decaying stock, his joys to prove
By contracts summoned to conjugal love.
These as they passed, like paranymphs which led
Young beauties to espouse a maidenhead,
With harmony, whose each concording part
Tickled the ear, whilst it did strike the heart
With mournful numbers, rifling every breast
Of their deep thoughts, thus the sad sense exprest.   110

I.

To secret walks, to silent shades,
To places where no voice invades
The air, but what's created by
Their own retired society,
Slowly these blooming nymphs we bring
To wither out their fragrant spring;
For whose sweet odours lovers pine,
Where beauty doth but vainly shine:
CHO. Where Nature's wealth, and Art's assisting cost,
Both in the beams of distant Hope are lost.   120

II.

To cloisters where cold damps destroy
The busy thoughts of bridal joy;
To vows whose harsh events must be
Uncoupled cold virginity;
To pensive prayers, where Heaven appears
Through the pale cloud of private tears;
These captive virgins we must leave,
Till freedom they from death receive:
CHO. Only in this remote conclusion blest,
This vale of tears leads to eternal rest.   130

III.

Then since that such a choice as theirs,
Which styles them the undoubted heirs
To Heaven, 'twere sinful to repent;
Here may they live, till beauty spent
In a religious life, prepare
Them with their fellow-saints to share
Celestial joys, for whose desire
They freely from the world retire:
CHO. Go then, and rest in blessed peace, whilst we
Deplore the loss of such society.   140

Through all the slow delays of love arrived
To the unguarded gate, Friendship, that thrived
Not in Persuasion's rhetoric, withdraws
Her forces to assist that juster cause—
Prayers for their future good—with which whilst they
Are taking leave, the unfolded gates give way
For the blest votaries' entrance, whom to meet,
A hundred pair of maids, more chastely sweet
Than flowers which grow untouched in deserts, were
Led by their abbess; to whose pious care   150
These being joined, with such a sad reverse
Of eyes o'erflowing, (as the sable herse
Close mourners leave, when they must see no more
Their coffined dead), their friends are from the door
With eager looks, woe's last—since now denied
A further view—departs unsatisfied.
  This last of duties, which the dearest friend
Ought to perform, brought to successful end;
For here no custom with a dowry's price
At entrance paid, nursed slothful avarice;   160
They 're softly led through a fair garden where
Each walk was by the founder's pious care,
For various fancies, wanton imagery,
To catch the heart, and not to court the eye,
Adorned with sacred histories. From hence
T' the centre of this fair circumference,
The fabric come, the roving eye, confined
Within the buildings, to enlarge the mind
In contemplation, saw where happy art
Had on the figured walls the second part   170
Of sacred story drawn, in lines that had
The world's Redeemer, from His first being clad
In robes of flesh, presented to the view
Through all His passions, till it brought Him to

. 156 departs] Singer, on general grammatical principles as usual, 'depart.' But he
does not seem to have noticed that, if any alteration is made, a *participle* is required for
'are.' Chamberlayne would not have hesitated to write 'are departed' and I am not
sure that he would have hesitated to scan 'depart'd.'

The cross, that highest seal of love, where He
A sinless offering died, from sin to free
The captived world, which knew no other price
But that to pay the debts of paradise.
    Passed through this place, where bleeding passion strove
Their melting pity to refine to love,   180
They 're now the temple entered; where, to screen
Their thoughts yet nearer Heaven, whom they had seen
I' the entrance scourged, contemned, and crucified,
They there beheld, though veils of glory hide
Some part of the amazing majesty,
In His .ascension, as when raised to be,
For them that hear His death freed from the hate
Of angry Heaven, the powerful advocate.
    Besides these bold attempts of art that stood
To fright the wicked, or to prompt the good,   190
Something more great, more sacred, than could by
Art be expressed, without the help of the eye
Reached at the centre of the soul; from whence
To Heaven, our raised desires' circumference,
Striking the lines of contemplation, she,
Wrapped from the earth, is, in an ecstasy
Holy and high, through faith's clear optic shown
Those joys which to departed saints are known.
    Before those prayers, which zeal had tedious made,
With their last troops did conquered Heaven invade,   200
The day was on the glittering wings of light
Fled to the western world, and swarthy night
In her black empire throned; from silver shrines
The kindled lamps through all the temple shines
With dappled rays, that did to the eye present
The beauties of the larger firmament.
In which still calm, when all their rites were now
So near performed, that the confirming vow
Alone remained, a sudden noise, of rude
And clamorous sound, did through the ear intrude   210
On their affrighted fancies, in so high
A voice, that all their sacred harmony,
In this confusion lost, appeared so small,
As if that whispered which was made to call.
    Although the awful majesty that here
Religion held, the weak effects of fear
With faith expelled, yet when that nearer to
Their slender gates the murmuring tumult drew,
The abbess sends not to secure, but see
Who durst attempt what Heaven from all kept free   220
By strictest law, save those unhallowed hands
That follow curses whilst they fly commands:
But they being entered, ere the timorous scout
Could notice give, fear, which first sprung from doubt,

Being into wild confusion grown, from all
Set forms affrights them; whilst at once they call
For Heaven's protecting mercy, to behold
That place where peaceful saints used to unfold
Heaven's oracles, possessed with villains that
Did ne'er know aught but want to tremble at,　　　230
Which looked like those that with proud angels fell,
And to storm Heaven were sent in arms from Hell;
Converts that scene, where nothing did appear
But calm devotion, to distracting fear.
Amazed with horror, each sad vot'ress stands,
Whilst sacred relics drop from trembling hands;
Here one whose heart with fear's convulsions faint,
Flies to the shrine of her protecting saint;
By her another stands, whose spirits spent
In passion, looks pale as her monument:　　　240
One shrieks, another prays, a third had crossed
Herself so much, ill angels might have lost
The way to hurt her, if not taught to do 't,
'Cause she t' the sign too much did attribute.
　The royal stranger, by her fear pursued,
To the altar fled, had with mixed passion viewed
This dreadful troop, whilst from the temple gate
They passed the seat where trembling virgins sat
Free from uncivil wrongs, as if that they
That entered had been men prepared to pray,　　　250
Not come to ravish; from which sight her fear
Picks flowers of hope, but such as, they drawn near,
From fancy's soft lap, in a hurricane
Of passion dropped her prayers and tears in vain,
As words in winds, or showers in seas, when they
Prepare for ruin the obstructed way
To pity, which her stock of prayers had cost,
In the dark shade of sudden horror lost.
　Seized on by two o' the sacrilegious train,
Whose black disguise had made the eye in vain　　　260
Seek to inform the soul, she and the poor
Florenza, whilst their helpless friends deplore
With silent tears so sad a loss, are drew
From the clasped altar in the offended view
Of their protecting saints; from whose shrines in
A dismal omen dropped whate'er had been
With hopes of merit placed.　Black sulphury damps
With swift convulsions quenched the sacred lamps,
The fabric shakes, and, as if grieved they stood
To circle guilt, the walls sweat tears of blood.　　　270
Shrieks, such as if those sainted souls, that there
Trod Heaven's straight paths, in their just quarrel were

271 sainted] Orig. 'fainted'—of course a mere 'literal' for the long *s*.

Rose from their silent dormitories to
Deter their foes, through all the temple flew.
  But here in vain destroying angels shook
The sword of vengeance, whilst his bold crimes struck
'Gainst heaven in high contempt ; with impious haste,
Snatched from the altar, whilst their friends did waste
Unheard orisons for their safety, they
Unto the fabric's utmost gate convey   280
Their beauteous prizes, where with silence stood
Their dreadful guard, which, like a neighbouring wood,
When vapours tip the naked boughs in light,
With unsheathed swords through the black mists of night
A sparkling terror struck, with such a speed
As scarce gave time to fear what would succeed
To such preceding villanies. Within
Her coach imprisoned, the sad princess, in
A march for swiftness such as busy war
Hastes to meet death in, but for silence far   290
More still than funerals, is by that black troop,
With such a change as falling stars do stoop
To night's black region, from the monastry
Hurried in haste ; by whom, or whither, she
Yet knows no more than souls departing, when
Or where to meet in robes of flesh again.
  The day salutes her, and uncurtained light
Welcomes her through the confines of the night,
But lends no comfort ; every object that
It showed her, being such as frighted at,   300
The prince of day, grieved he'd no longer slept,
To shun, shrunk back beneath a cloud, and wept.
When the unfolded curtains gave her eyes
Leave to look forth, a troop, whose close disguise
Were stubborn arms, she only saw, and they
So silent, nought but motion did betray
The faculties of life ; by whom being led,
In such a sad march as their honoured dead
Close mourners follow, she, some slow-paced days
'Mongst strangers passing, thorough stranger ways   310
At both amazed, at length, unfathomed by
Her deepest thought, within the reach of the eye
Her known Gerenza views ; but with a look
From whence cold passion all the blood had took,
And in her face, that frozen sea of fear,
Left nought but storms of wonder to appear.
  Convened within the spacious judgement-hall
Of Reason, she ere this had summoned all
Her weaker passions to the impartial bar
Of moral virtue, where they sentenced are   320

310 thorough] Orig. ' through,' contrary to contemporary practice where this metrical
value is required.

Only to an untroubled silence; in
Which serious act whilst she had busied been,
She is, unnoted, ere the fall of day
Brought by her convoy to a lodge that lay
Off from the road, a place, when seen, she knew
Ere his rebellion had belonged unto
Her worst of foes, Almanzor; which begins
At first a doubt, whose growing force soon wins
The field of faith, and tells her timorous thought,
Her father's troops would ne'er have thither brought   330
Her, if designed to suffer, since that he
Knew those more fit for close captivity.
    But long her reason lies not fettered in
These cross dilemmas; the slow night had been
With tedious hours passed o'er, whilst she by none
But mutes, no less unheard than they're unknown,
Is only waited on; by whom, when day
To action called, she veiled, is led the way
To the attending convoy, who had now
Varied the scene;—Almanzor, studying how   340
To court compassion in his prince, dares not
At the first view, ere merit had begot
A calm remission of rebellious sin,
Affront an anger which had justice been
In his confusion; his arms he now behind,
As that which might too soon have called to mind
His former crimes, he leaves, and for them took,
To gain the aspect of a pitying look,
A hermit's homely weed: his willing train,
By that fair gloss their liberties to gain,   350
Rode armed; but so, what for offence they bore,
Was in submission to lay down before
The throne of injured power, to cure whose fear
Their armèd heads on haltered necks appear.
    Near to the rear of these, the princess in
A mourning litter, close as she had been
In a night-march unto her tomb, is through
The city's wondering tumults led unto
The royal palace, at whose gates all stay,
Save bold Almanzor; whom the guards obey   360
For his appearing sanctity so much,
That he unquestioned enters, and, thought such
As his grave habit promised, soon obtained
The prince's sight; where with a gesture feigned
To all the shapes of true devotion, he
By a successful fiction comes to be
Esteemed the true converter of those wild
Bandits, which, being by their own crimes exiled,

345, 347 he] One of these is of course superfluous and the first is not even necessary
for the metre.

In spite of law had lived to punish those
Which did the rules of punishment compose.   370
   These being pardoned, as he 'd took from thence
Encouragement, veiled under the pretence
Of a religious pity, he begins,
In language whose emollient smoothness wins
An easy conquest on belief, to frame
A sad petition; which, although in name
It had disguised Pharonnida, did find
So much of pity as the prince, inclined
To lend his aid for the relief of her
Whose virtue found so fair a character   380
In his description, it might make unblest
That power which left so much of worth distrest.
   Though too much tired with private cares to show
In public throngs, how much his love did owe
To suffering virtue; yet since told that she
Was too much masked in clouds of grief to be
The object of the censuring court, he to
The litter goes, whose sable veil withdrew,
With wonder, that did scarce belief admit,
Shadowed in grief, he sees his daughter sit,   390
His long-lost daughter, whom unsought, to be
Thus strangely found, to such an ecstasy
Of joy exalts him, that his spirits by
Those swift pulsations had been all let fly
With thanks towards Heaven, had not the royal maid
With showers of penitential tears allayed
Those hotter passions, and revoked him to
Support her griefs, whose burthen had outgrew
The powers of life, but that there did appear
Kind Nature's love to cure weak Nature's fear.   400
   In this encounter of their passions, both
With sorrow silent stood, words being loath
To intrude upon their busy thoughts, till they
In moist compassion melted had away
His anger's fever and her frozen fears
In nature's balm, soft love's extracted tears:
Like a sad patient, whose forgotten strength
Decayed by chronic ills, hath made the length
Of life his burthen, when near death, meets there
Unhoped-for health; so from continual care,   410
The soul's slow hectic, elevated by
This cordial joy, the slothful lethargy
Of age or sorrow finds an easier cure
Than the unsafe extreme, a calenture.
   Nor are these comforts long constrained to rest
Within the confines of his own swelled breast,
Ere its dismantled rays did in a flight,
Swift as the motions of unbodied light,

Disperse its epidemic virtues through
The joyful court ; which now arrived unto   420
Its former splendour, Heaven's expected praise
Doth on the wings of candid mercy raise :
Which spreading in a joyful jubilee
To all offenders, tells Almanzor he
Might safely now unmask; which done, ere yet
Discovered, at the well-pleased prince's feet,
Humbled with guilt, he kneels ; who, at the sight
As much amazed as so sublime a flight
Of joy admitted, stands attentive to
What did in these submissive words ensue.   430
  'Behold, great sir, for now I dare be seen
An object for your mercy, that had been
Too dreadful for discovery, had not this
Preceding joy told me no crime could miss
The road of mercy, though, like mine, a sin
The suffering nation is enveloped in.
Sunk in the ocean of my guilt, I'd gone,
A desperate rebel, waited on by none
But outlaws, to a grave obscure, had not
Relenting Heaven thus taught me how to blot   440
Out some of sin's black characters, ere I
Beheld the beams of injured majesty.'
  This, in his passion's relaxation spoke,
Persuades the prince's justice to revoke
Its former rigour. By the helpful hand
Of mercy raised, Almanzor soon did stand
Not only pardoned, but secured by all
His former honours from a future fall,
Making that fortune, which did now appear
Their pity's object, through the glass of fear   450
With envy looked on ; but in vain, he stood
Confirmed in love's meridian altitude,
The length of life from Honour's western shade,
Except in new rebellion retrograde :
Which plotting leave him, till the winding clew
Of fancy shall conduct your knowledge to
Those uncouth vaults ; and mounting the next story,
See virtue climbing to the throne of glory.

THE END OF THE FIRST CANTO.

426 prince's] Singer, nodding, 'princess'.' In orig. these words are often inter-
changed.

Pharonnida

Canto II

THE ARGUMENT

Leaving Pharonnida to entertain
  The various passions of her father, we
Must now return to see Argalia gain
  That power by which he sets his father free.

From the command of haughty rebels, who
  By justice sent to a deservèd death,
Argalia takes the crown, his merits' due,
  And the old prince in peace resigns his breath.

RETURNED to see what all the dark records
Of the old Spartan history affords
I' the progress of Argalia's fate, I found
The chained historian here so strictly bound
To follow truth, although at danger's cost,
No silent night, nor smoky battle lost
The doubtful road ; which often did appear
Through floods of faction filled with storms of fear,
Obscure and dark to the belief of that
Less guilty age ; though then to tremble at   10
Rome's bold ambition, and those prodigies
Of earth, their tyrants, to inform their eyes,
Left mourning monuments of ill, but none
Like what they now attempt, a sin unknown
To old aspirers, which should have been sent
Some ages forward for a precedent
To these, with whom compared, their crimes had been,
Though past to act, but weak essays of sin.
  With such a speed as the supplies of air,
Fearing a vacuum, hasten to repair   20
The ruptures of the earth, at our last view
We left revived Argalia posting to
Ætolia's distant confines ; where arrived,
He found their army, whose attempts had thrived,
Since he Epirus had forsook, so far
Advanced, that now the varied scene of war,
Transferred to faithless Ardenna, was there
Fixed in a siege, whose slow approaches were
The doubts of both. The city pines for fear
Remote supplies might fail, which drawn so near,   30
The circling army knows, that either they
Must fly from conquest near obtained, or stay
To meet a danger, which by judgement scanned,
Their strength appears unable to withstand.
  Whilst thus their pensive leaders busied are
In cross dilemmas, as by public war
He meant to meet revenge in private, to
Their camp Argalia comes ; a camp which knew

Him by the fair wrought characters of fame
So well, that now he needs no more than name   40
Himself to merit welcome, all mistrust
Being cleared by them which left, as too unjust
To be obeyed, the false Epirot's side,
When by his loss made subject to the pride
Of stranger chiefs ; these for their virtue praised,
For number feared, to such a height had raised
Applauding truths of him, that Zarrobrin,
Conjoined to one he trembled at whilst seen
In opposition, slights what did of late
Appear a dreadful precipice of fate.   50
   Lest poor employments might make favour show
Like faint mistrust, he doth at first bestow
On the brave stranger the supreme command
Of some choice horse, selected to withstand
The fierce Epirot's march ; whose army, ere
The slow Ætolians could their strength prepare
Fit to resist, if not by him withstood,
With ease had gained a dangerous neighbourhood.
But he, whose anger's thunderbolts could stay,
Though hurled from clouds of rage, if the allay   60
Of judgement interposed, here finding nought
More safe than haste, ere his secure foes thought
Of opposition, strongly had possessed
A strait in which small troops had oft distressed
Large bodied armies, until brought so low,
Those they contemned did liberty bestow.
   Whilst stopped by this unlooked-for remora,
The baffled army oft had strove to draw
Argalia from his safe retreats, but found
His art of more advantage than his ground ;   70
In the dead age of unsuccessful night
A forward party, which had learned to fight
From honour's dictates, not commands, being by
Youth's hasty guide, rash valour, brought so nigh
Argalia's troops, that in a storm which cost
Some lives, they many noble captives lost :
Amongst which number, as if thither sent
By such a fate as showed Heaven's close intent
Pointed at good, Euriolus appears
First a sad captive : but those common fears   80
Soon, whilst in conflict with his passions, rest
On the wished object of his long inquest—
Admired Argalia, to whose joy he brings
As much of honour, as elected kings
Meet in those votes, which so auspicious prove,
They light to honour with the rays of love.
   Having from him in full relation heard
Pharonnida yet lived, whom long he feared

Beyond redemption lost, they thence proceed
To counsels, whose mature results might breed   90
Their heedless foes confusion ; which, since they
That now were captives bore the greatest sway
In the opposing army, proves a task
So free from danger, death did scarce unmask
The face of horror in a charge, before
Argalia's name, echoed in praises o'er
The rallied troops, summons from thence so large
A party, that the valour of a charge
In those that stood were madness, which to shun,
Base cowards taught brave fighters how to run.   100
     This easy conquest gained, ere Zarrobrin
Was with his slower army drawn within
The noise o' the battle, to such vast extent
Of fame, high virtue's spreading ornament,
Had raised Argalia's merits, that the pride
Of his commander wisely laid aside
For such advantage, to let Honour stand
On her own basis, the supreme command
Of all the strangers in his camp to him
He freely gives ; a power which soon would dim   110
His, if ere by some harsh distemper placed
In opposition, but his thoughts embraced
In all suspicion's darkest cells no fiend
So pale as fear ; fixed on the sudden end
Of high designs, he looks on this success
As the straight road to future happiness.
     With such a speed as prosperous victors go
To see and conquer, when the vanquished foe
Retreats from honour, the Ætolian had
Followed success, till that fair hand unclad   120
The sunk Epirot of his strength ; and now,
Secured from foreign ills, was studying how
To cure domestic dangers : which since he
The weak foundation of his tyranny
Had fixed in sand but only cemented
With loyal blood, such just contempt had bred
In the age's deep discerning judgements, that
The unsettled herd, ere scarcely lightened at
Those sober flames, like ill-mixed vapours break
In blustering murmurs forth ; which, though too weak 130
To force his fortune on the rocks of hate,
With terror shook the structure of his fate.
     Like wise physicians, which, when called to cure
Infectious ills, with antidotes make sure
Themselves from danger ; since hypocrisy
Could steal no entrance to affection, he
Leads part of 's army for his guard, that they,
Where mines did fail, by storm might force a way.

But since he doubts constrained domestics, though
Abroad obedient, might, when come to know   140
From burthened friends their cause of grief, forsake
Unjust commands, his wiser care did take
Argalia and his stranger troops, as those
Which, unconcerned, he freely might dispose
To wind up all the engines of his brain,
So guilt was gilded with the hopes of gain.
  By hasty marches being arrived with these
Within Ætolia, where his frowns appease
Those bubbles that, their Neptune absent, would
Have swelled to waves ; ere his hot spirits cooled   150
Were with relaxing rest, he visits him,
The weak reflex of whose light crown looks dim
T' the burnished splendour of his blade, that set
Him only there to be the cabinet
Of that usurpèd diadem ; which he,
Whose subtle arts in clouded brows could see
The heart's intended storms, beheld without
His unstrained reach, until the people's doubt,
Which yet lived in the dawn of hope, he saw
O'ershadowed with the forms of injured law.   160
  Though Time, that fatal enemy to truth,
Had not alone robbed the fresh thoughts of youth
O' the knowledge of their long lost prince, but been,
Even unto those that had adored him in
His throne, Oblivion's handmaid ; yet left by
Some power occult, that in captivity
Forsakes not injured monarchs, there remained
In most some passions, which first entertained
At Pity's cost, at length by Reason tried
Grew so much loved, that only power denied   170
Them to support his sinking cause. Which seen
By Zarrobrin, whose tyranny had been
At first their fear, and now their hate, he brings
His army, an elixir, which to kings
Transforms plebeians, by the strength of that
To bind those hands that else had struggled at
Their head's offence ; which wanting power to cure,
They now with grief's convulsions must endure.
  A court convened of such whose killing trade
The rigid law so flexible had made,   180
That their keen votes had forced the bloodiest field
To the deep tincture of the scaffold yield ;
Forth of his uncouth prison summoned by
The rude commands of wronged authority,
An object which succeeding ages, when
But spoke of, weep, because they blushed not then,
The prince appears—a guarded captive in
That city where his morning star had been

Beheld in honour's zenith; slowly by
Inferior slaves, which ne'er on majesty,   190
Whilst uneclipsed, durst look, being led to prove
Who blushed with anger, or looked pale with love.
   By these being to a mock tribunal brought,
Where damned rebellion for disguise had sought
The veil of justice, but so thinly spread,
Each stroke, their envy levelled at his head,
Betrayed black Treason's hand, couched in that vote
Which struck with law to cut Religion's throat.
From a poor pleader, whose cheap conscience had
Been sold for bribes, long ere the purple clad   200
So base a thing, their calm-souled sovereign hears
Death's fatal doom; which when pronounced, appears
His candour, and their guilt: the one exprest
By a reception, which declared his breast
Unstirred with passion; the other struggling in
Their troubled looks, which showed this monstrous sin,
That this damned plot did to rebellion bear,
Even frighted those that treason's midwives were.
   Hence, all their black designs encouraged by
The levelled paths of prosperous villany,   210
High-mounted mischief, stretched upon the wing
Of powerful ill, pursues the helpless king
To the last stage of life, a scaffold; whence,
With tears, cheap offerings to his innocence,
Such of his pitying friends as durst disclose
Their passions, view him; whilst insulting foes,
Exalted on the pyramids of pride
By long-winged power, with base contempt deride
Their sorrow, and his sufferings whom they hate,
Had followed near the period of his fate;   220
Which being now so near arrived, that all
With various passion did expect the fall
Of the last fatal stroke, kind Heaven, to save
A life so near the confines of the grave,
Transcends dull hope by so sublime a flight,
That dazzled faith, amazed with too much light,
Whilst ecstasies of wonder did destroy
Unripe belief, near lost the road of joy.
   Even with the juncture of that minute when
The axe was falling, from those throngs of men   230
Swayed by 's command, Argalia, with a speed
That startled action, mounts the stage, and freed
The trembling prince from death's pale fear; which done,
To show on what just grounds he had begun
So brave, so bold an action, seizes all
That knowledge or suspicion dares to call

235 action] Singer reads 'act, he.' But the nominative is quite easily supplied from
'mounts.'

The tyrant's friends. The guilty tyrant, who,
Whilst he doth from his distant palace view
This dreadful change, with a disdain as high
As are his crimes, being apprehended by   240
Argalia's nimble guards, is forced to be
Their sad conductor to a destiny
So full of horror, that it hardly lies
In 's foes to save him for a sacrifice
From their wild rage, who know no justice but
What doth by death a stop to fury put.
    From noiseless prayers and bloodless looks being by
The bold attempters of his liberty
Raised to behold his rescue; heedless fear,
Hatched by mistake, from those that bordered near,   250
Had with such swiftness its infection spread,
That the more distant, knowing not what bred
The busy tumult, in so wild a haste,
As vanquished troops which at the heels are chased
Fly the pursuing sword, they madly run
To meet those dangers which they strove to shun:
In which confusion none o' the throng had been
Left to behold how justice triumphed in
Revenge's throne, had not a swift command,
By power enabled, hastened to withstand   260
That troubled torrent which the truth outgrew,
Until their fears' original they knew.
    The onset past, Argalia, having first
Secured the tyrant, for whose blood the thirst
Of the vexed people raged, he mounted on
That scaffold whence his father should have gone
A royal martyr to the grave, did there
By a commanded silence first prepare
The clamorous throng to hear the hidden cause
Which made him slight their new-created laws.   270
Then, in that mart of satisfaction which
With knowledge doth the doubtful herd enrich,
The public view, he freely shows how far
Through Fortune's deserts the auspicious star
Of Heaven's unfathomed providence had led
Him—from the axe to save that sacred head;
Whose reverend snow his full discovery had
In the first dress of youthful vigour clad,
Could constant Nature sympathize with that
Reviving joy his spirits panted at.   280
    His son's relation, seconded by all
That suffering sharer in his pitied fall,
Mantinea's bishop, knew, joined to the sight
Of that known jewel, whose unwasted light
Had served alone to guide them, satisfies
The inquisition e'en of critic eyes

(252)

With such a fullness of content, that they,
Each from his prince being lightened with a ray
Of sprightly mirth, endeavoured to destroy
Their former grief in hope of future joy :   290
Which to attain to, those whose counsels had
The land in blood, and then in mourning clad,
Called forth by order to confession, there
Are scarce given time the foulness to declare
Of their past crimes, before the people's hate,
That head-strong monster, strove to anticipate
The sword of vengeance, and in wild rage save
The labour of an ignominious grave
To every parcel of those rent limbs that,
When but beheld, they lately trembled at.   300
Such being the fate of falling tyrants, when
Conquering, the fear, conquered, the scorn of men.
But here lest inconsiderate rage should send
Their souls to darkness, ere confession end
Their tragic story, hated Zarrobrin,
With that unhappy boy whose crown had been
Worn but to make him capable to die
A sacrifice to injured liberty,
Rescued by order from the rout, is to
A public trial brought ; where, in the view   310
Of all the injured multitude, the old
Audacious traitor did t' the light unfold
His acts of darkness, which discovered him
They gazed on, whilst unquestioned power did dim
Discerning wits, but a dull meteor—one
By hot ambition mounted to a throne,
By an attractive policy, which when
Its influence failed, back to that lazy fen,
His fortune's centre, hurling him again,
The only star in honour's orb would reign.   320
    This sly impostor, seconded by that
Rebellious guilt his actions offered at
In all its bold attempts, had kindled in
The late supporters of unprosperous sin
So high a rage, that in wild fury they,
Their anger wanting what it should obey—
A sober judgement, stands not to dispute
With the slow law, but with their strength confute
All tending to delay ; like torrents broke
Through the imprisoning banks, to get one stroke   330
At heads so hated, all rush in, until
Their severed limbs want quantity to fill
A room in the eyes' receiving beams. This done,
With blood and anger warmed, they wildly run
To search out such whom consanguinity
Had rendered so unhappy, as to be

Allied to them : all which, with rage that styled
Beasts merciful, and angry soldiers mild,
They to destruction chase ; whilst guiltless walls,
In which they dwelt, in funeral blazes falls ;   340
Where burns inviting treasure, as they saw
In the gold's splendour an anathema
So full of horror, as it seemed to be
A plague beyond unpitied poverty.

    Impetuous rage, like whirlwinds unopposed,
Hushed to a calm, as hate had but unclosed
The anger-blinded eyes of love, the bold
Flame, like a fire forced from repulsive cold,
Breaks through the harsh extreme of hate, to show
How much their loyal duty did outgrow   350
Those fruits of forced obedience, which before
They slowly to intruding tyrants bore.
In which procession of their joy, that he
Might meet their hopes with a solemnity
Large as their love, or his delight, the prince,
Taught by informing age how to convince
Ambition's hasty arguments, calls forth
His long-lost son, whose late discovered worth
Was grown the age's wonder, to support
The ponderous crown, whilst he did tread the short   360
And sickly step of age, untroubled by
The burthen of afflicting majesty.

    His coronation passed, in such a tide
Of full content, as to be glorified
Blest souls in the world's conflagration shall
From tombs their reunited bodies call,
The feeble prince, leaving the joyful throng
Of his applauding subjects, seeks among
Religious shades, those cool retreats, to find
That best composer of a stormy mind—   370
A still devotion ; on whose downy bed
Not long he 'd laid, before that entrance led
Him to the court of Heaven, though through the gate
Of welcome death, a cross, which though from fate,
Not accident, he being instructed by
Age and religion to prepare to die
On Nature's summons, yet so deep a strain
Spreads o'er those robes that joy had died in grain,
That his heroic son, to meet alone
So fierce a foe, leaving the widowed throne,   380
Retreats to silent tears ; whose plenteous spring,
By the example of their mourning king,
From those small clouds there first beheld to rise,
Begets a storm in every subject's eyes.

353 procession] Singer ' profession,' by no means necessarily, I think.

Betraying Time, the world's unquestioned thief,
Intending o'er obliterated grief
Some new transcription, to perform it brings
A ravished quill from Love's expanded wings,
Presenting to Argalia's willing view
Whate'er blind chance rolled on the various clew   390
Of his fair mistress' fate, unfolded by
Euriolus; who was, when victory
First gave him freedom, by Argalia sent
With speed that might anticipate intent,
The unconfined Pharonnida to free
From ·her religious strict captivity.
But being arrived where, contrary to all
His thoughts, he heard how first she came to fall
Into Almanzor's hand, by whom conveyed
Thence to her father's court, his judgement stayed   400
Not to consult with slow advice, but hastes
On the pursuit of her; whom found, he wastes
Few days before fair opportunity
Was so auspicious to his prayers, that he
Not only proves a happy messenger
Where first employed, but in exchange for her
Returns the story of what had been done
Since first this tempest of their fate begun.—
How she forsook the monastry, and in
What agonies of passion thence had been   410
Forced to her father's court, where all her fears
Dissolve in pity, he related hears
With calm attention; but when come to that,
Whose first conceptions he had trembled at,
The Syracusan's fresh assaults unto
That virgin fort, whose strength although he knew
Too great for storm, yet since assisted by
Her father's power, the wreaths of victory,
Rent by command from his deserts, might crown
Another's brows. To pull those laurels down,   420
Ere raised in triumph, he prepares to move
By royal steps unto the throne of love.

THE END OF THE SECOND CANTO.

Canto III

THE ARGUMENT

From the Ætolians' late victorious king
   Ambassadors in Sparta's court arrive;
Where slighted, back they this sad message bring,
   That force must only make his just claim thrive.

Which to confirm, the Epirot's power invades
   His land, in hopes for full reward to have
Pharonnida; but close Almanzor shades
   His glorious hopes in an untimely grave.

AN unripe rumour, such as causes near
Declining catch at, when betraying fear
Plunges at hope, had through Gerenza spread
The story of Argalia's fate, but shed
From such loose clouds of scattered fame, as by
Observant wits were only thought to fly
In the airy region of report, where they
Are forced each wind of fancy to obey;
Whose various blasts, when brought unto the test
Of judgement, rather the desires exprest,   10
Than knowledge of its authors. Here, 'mongst those
Of various censure, sly Almanzor chose
To be of the believing part, since that
Might soonest crush all hopes that levelled at
Affection to Pharonnida, whom he
Strove to preserve in calm neutrality.
   But here he fails to countermine his plot,
This seeming fable soon appears begot
By solid truth; a truth which scorns to lie
Begging at th' gates of probability: 20
Which to avoid, she from Argalia brings
Ambassadors, those mouths of absent kings,
To plead her right; at whose unlooked-for view,
Almanzor, whose fallacious schemes were drew
Only for false phenomena, is now
Forced to erect new figures, and allow
Each star its influence; but declared in vain,
Since pride did lord of the ascendant reign—
Pride, which, conjoined to policy, had made
All other motions seem but retrograde.   30
   His black arts thus deceived, since nought could make
The dull spectator's ignorance mistake
This constellation for a comet, he
Attempts with fear of its malignity
To fright each busy gazer; and since all
The circles of opinion were to fall

(256)

Like spacious azimuths in that zenith, to
Settle the prince, through whom the people view
All great conjunctions, where the different sign
Should force those aspects, which might 'mongst that trine 40
Of love else hold a concord, to dispense
On him its most destructive influence.
   The court being thus prepared, he boldly now
Dares the delayed ambassadors allow
A long expected audience, which in brief
Makes known their master's fate in the relief
Of 's injured father; thence proceeds to show
How much of praise his thankful friends did owe
To Heaven for his own restored estate, which he
Desires to join in calm confederacy   50
With them, his honoured neighbours; hence they past
To what concerned Pharonnida, their last
And most important message. Which, when heard
In such a language as the rivals feared;
A language, which, to prove his interest
In her unquestioned, come but to request
The freedom of a father's grant, a high
But stifled rage began to mutiny
In all their breasts, such as, if not withheld
B' the law of nations, had her father swelled   60
To open acts of violence; which seen
By some o' the lords, they calm his passion in
A cool retreat, such as might seem to be,
Though harsh contempt, wrapped in civility.
   Fired with disdain, the ambassadors, in such
A speed which showed affronts that did but touch
Their master's honour wounded theirs, forsook
Gerenza; whilst Euriolus betook
Himself to some more safe disguise that might
Protect him, till the subject of delight,   70
The course his royal master meant to steer
In gaining her, his story makes appear
Unto distressed Pharonnida: who, in
That confidence secure as she had been
From all succeeding ills protected by
A guard of angels, in a harmony
Of peaceful thoughts, such as in dangers keep
Safe innocence, rocks all her cares asleep.
   But here she rests not long before the fall
Of second storms proves this short interval   80
But lightning, which in tempests shows unto
Shores, which the shipwrecked must no more than view.
Anger, Ambition, Hate, and jealous Fear,
Had all conspired Love's ruin, which drew near

54 the] Singer 'their.'

From hasty counsels' rash results, which in
His passion's storm had by her father been,
Like rocks which wretched mariners mistake
For harbours, fled to, when he did forsake
That safer channel of advice that might,
From free conventions, like the welcome light   90
Of Pharos, guided his designs, till they
At anchor in the road of honour lay.
  As if his fears by nothing could have been
Secured, but what proved him ungrateful in
Argalia's ruin, all discourses are
Distasteful grown, but what to sudden war
Incites his rage : which humour, though it needs
No greater fire than what his envy feeds,
Besides those court tarantulas whose breath
Stings easy princes, till they dance to death   100
At the delightful sound of flattery, there
Were deeper wits, such whom a subtle care,
Not servile fear, taught how to aggravate
His anger's flame, till their own eager hate,
Though burning with a mortal fury, might
Pass unobserved, since near a greater light.
Amongst those few whose love did not depend
So much on fortune, but the name of friend
Was still preserved, the faithful Cyprian prince
Durst only strive by reason to convince   110
Their wilder passions ; but each argument
With which affection struggled to prevent
A swift destruction, only seemed to prove
His friendship more effectual than his love.
From which mistake, such as did strive to please
The angry prince's passionate disease,
With what might feed the sickly humours, draw
A consequence that proves Pharonnida
A blessing which was to his merits due
Who most opposed the bold aspirer to   120
That throne of beauty, which before possest,
Whole armies must dispute their interest.
  The slighted Cyprian, since their fear could trust
None but confederates, from their counsels thrust,
Those swift conclusions, which before to stay
Their violence had reason's cool allay,
Hurried to action, strict commands are sent
From fierce Zoranza through each regiment
Which stooped their ensigns to his power,—that, by
Such marches as they'd follow victory,   130
They reach Ætolia, ere its new-crowned king,
Warned by report, had liberty to bring

     91 guided] The omission of ' have' is characteristic.

Opposing strengths,—a task too hard to be
Performed with ease in power's minority.
Nor fails this counsel, for their army draws
No sooner near, but such as in the cause
Of unsuccessful rebels late had been
Exposed to danger, seek for refuge in
A fresh revolt; and, since their ulcerous guilt
Was so malignant, that e'en mercy spilt   140
Its balm in vain, their injured prince forsake,
To strengthen his proud enemies, who make
Those poisons up in cordials, and compound
Them with their army: which being thus grown sound,
Whereas it lately fainted, durst provoke
Unto the trial of another stroke
His late victorious forces; which, though yet
Faint with the blood lost in the last great fit
Of honour's fever, when the crisis proved
To cure's prognostic, had with ease removed   150
The proud invaders, had Morea been,
As heretofore, a hurtful neuter in
That war; which now, since double strengths oppose,
Brave fortitude like base oppression shows.
    So long both parties with variety
Of fortune fought, that fearing whose might be
The sad success, that old Cleander, in
Such speed as if his crown engaged had been,
Raises an army; whose command, since he
Base flattery takes for brave fidelity,   160
Waiving those peers to whose known faith he owes
The most of trust, in hoodwinked hope bestows
On false Almanzor; who by power advanced
Near to those hopes at which ambition glanced,
But like weak eyes upon the dazzling sun,
From that last fatal stage his plots begun
Mischief's dark course, which, ere concluded, shall
Crush the Epirot in Morea's fall.
    In this, the hot distemper of their state,
Amindor, whom the destinies of late,   170
To double-dye his honour's purple thread,
Robbed of a father, most disquieted
Their secret counsels; since they knew the love
He bore Argalia, propped with power, might prove
A sad obstruction to their plots, if he,
Urged by distastes, shook their confederacy
Off to assist his friend. Which to oppose,
With flattery—fleeting as the gourd that rose
But to discover his just wrath that made
The plant to cover, when it could not shade,—   180
They all attempt; though he engage not in
Their party, yet his easy youth to win

By honour's moths, by time's betrayers, soft
And smooth delights, those serpents which too oft
Strangle Herculean virtues : but they here
In age's April find a wit appear
Of such full growth, that by his judgement they
Are undermined, who studied to betray.

Being thus secured from foreign fears, they now
Employ that rage, whose speed could scarce allow   190
Advice from counsel, to extirpate those
New planted laurels victory did compose
To crown Argalia. But before they go
To ravish conquest from so cheap a foe,
Whose valour by o'erwhelming power was barred
From lying safe at a defensive guard,
Till old Cleander, that their league might be
Assured by bonds whose firm stability
Death only could divorce, intends, though she,
With such aversion as their destiny   200
Wretches condemned would shun, attempt to fly
The storm of fate ; yet countermanded by
His power, the fair Pharonnida, although
He not to love, but duty, seemed to owe
For such a blessing, should Zoranza's be,
Confirmed by Hymen's high solemnity.

This resolution, whose self-ends must blame
Her father's love, once registered by fame,
Submits to censure ; whilst Pharonnida
Laments her fate, some, prompted by the law   210
Of love and nature, are to entertain
So much of freedom, as they prove in vain
Her advocates ; others, whose cautious fear
Dares only pity, in that dress appear
Silent and sad ; only Almanzor, in
This state distemper, by that subtle sin,
Dissimulation, so disguises all
His black intentions, that whilst truth did call
Him treason's agent, its reflected light,
Appearance, spoke him virtue's proselyte ;   220
So much a convert, as if all those hot
Crimes of his youth ambition had begot,
Discreeter age had either cooled, or by
Repentance changed to zeal and loyalty.

Whilst thus i' the court the most judicious eyes
Deluded were by faction's false disguise,
By rumours heavy as the damps of death
When they fly laden with the dying breath
Of new-departed souls, this fatal news
Assaults the princess ; which whilst reason views   230
With sad resentments, to support her in
This storm of fate, Amindor, who had been

In all her griefs her best adviser, now
Enters, to tell her fainting sorrows how
They 'd yet a refuge left, from whom she might
Reap hopes of safety. The first welcome sight
Of such a friend, whose former actions had
Enhanced his worth, encountering with her sad
And serious thoughts, so rarifies that cloud
Of grief, that ere dissolving tears allowed　　　　240
A vocal utterance, as intended words
Something contained too doleful for records,
Both sighed, both wept : at length the princess broke
Silence, and thus her dismal passions spoke.
　' Dare you, my lord, approach so near unto
A factious grief, in this black storm to view
Distressed Pharonnida ! Have either I
Or my Argalia's slighted memory
Yet in Morea a remaining friend,
Whose virtue dares by its own strength contend　　　250
Against this torrent of court factions? Now,
Now, royal sir, that doom which will allow
My soul no more refreshing slumbers, by
My father's passed—my father, sir, whom I
Must disobey with all the curses due
To black rebellion, or else prove untrue
Those vows, those oft repeated vows, which in
Our love's full growth hath to Argalia been
Sealed in the sight of Heaven.'—About to speak
Her passions fuller, sorrow here did break　　　　260
The sad theme off, and to proclaim her fears,
Except the o'erflowing language of her tears,
No herald left. In which sad silent fit
The valiant Cyprian, who at first did sit
His passion's prisoner, from that bondage free,
To her disease prescribes this remedy.
　' . . . . . . Cease, madam, ...
Cease to eclipse illustrious beauty by
Untimely tears ; your grief's deformity
Frights not Amindor from his friendship. When　　270
I first beheld that miracle of men,
Adored Argalia, pluck from victory
His naval laurels, honour told me I
Was then so much his virtue's captive, that
Not all the dangers mortals tremble at
Can make me shun assisting of him in
Retaining you ; though my attempts have been
Employed in vain, in public council to
Procure your peace, there 's something left to do,
By which our private plots may undermine　　　　280
Their public power, and unperceived, decline
That danger which, without this secret friend,

It lies not in our fortune to defend.'
　From grief's cold swoon to living comforts by
This cordial raised, Pharonnida's reply
Owns this pathetic language : 'If there be
In all the dark paths of my destiny
Yet left a road to safety, name it, sir.
What I'll attempt, no danger shall deter,
So brave Amindor be my conduct through   290
The dismal road ; but my wild hopes outgrow
Whate'er my reason dictates.　No, my lord,
Fly that sad fate whose progress can afford
Nought but disasters, and live happy in
Orlinda's love.　Should I attempt to win
You from so fair a virtue, 't were a wrong
Too full of guilt to let me live among
The number of your friends, 'mongst whom let me
In all your future thoughts remembered be
As the most wretched—to whom rigid fate   300
All hope's weak cordials hath applied too late.'
　Here ceased the sorrowing lady, to suspend
Whose following tears, her charitable friend
Prescribes this comfort :—'Though my zeal hath been,
When serving you, so unsuccessful in
My first attempts, it gives just cause to doubt
My future actions ; yet to lead you out
Of this dark labyrinth, where your sorrow stands
Masked with amazements, not the countermands
Of my affection to Orlinda, though   310
Confirmed by vows, shall stop ; let Grief bestow
But so much time, unclouded by your fear,
To look Hope's volumes o'er, there will appear
Some lines of comfort yet ; which that we may
Not in a heedless horror cast away,
Prepare for speedy action ; to prevent
Ensuing ills, no time is left unspent,
But only this approaching night ; by which,
To fly from danger, you must stoop to enrich
A coarse disguise, whose humble shadows may   320
Inquiring eyes to dark mistakes betray.
　'Our first retreat, which is designed to be
No further than the neighbouring monastry,
Where I of late did lie concealed, I have
Thus made secure :—There stands an ancient cave,
Close hid in unfrequented shadows, near
Your garden's postern-gate ; which, when the fear
Of bordering foes denied a free access
To the old abbey, they, from the distress
Of threatening scouts were safe delivered by   330
A vault that through it leads ; which, though so nigh
Unto the city, careless time, since not

Forced to frequent, hath wholly left forgot
By busy mortals. In this silent cell,
Where nought but light's eternal strangers dwell
In the meridian depth of night, whilst all
Are robed in rest, you none encounter shall
Except myself, but him, who may with us
This secret share, esteemed Euriolus;
With whom, and your endeared Florenza, we,   340
Within the unsuspected monastry
Protected by some secret friends, may stay
Till fruitless searches waste their hopes away,
Whose watchful spleen, by care conducted, might
Stop our intentions of a further flight.'
  Raised from the cold bed of despair from this
Mature advice to hopes of future bliss,
The heavenly fair Pharonnida had now
Withdrawn the veil of grief, and could allow
Some smiles to wait upon those thanks which she   350
Returned her friend; who, that no time might be
Lost by neglect from needful action, in
A calm of comforts, such as had not been
Her late associates, leaves the princess to
Pursue those plots, which Fortune bent to undo,
Whilst Hope on Expectation's wings did hover,
Did thus by fatal accident discover.
  That knot in her fair thread of destiny,
That lurking snake, the purgatory by
Which Heaven refined her, cursed Amphibia, had,   360
Whilst mutual language all their thoughts unclad,
Close as an unsuspected plague that in
Darkness assaults, an unknown sharer been
Of this important issue; which with hate
Her genius met, soon strives to propagate
A brood of fiends. Almanzor, whose dark plots,
Like images of damned magicians, rots
Themselves to ruin others, like in this
Last act of ill by too much haste to miss
The road that led through slippery paths of sin,   370
From pride's stupendous precipice falls in
A gulf of horror; in whose dismal shade
A private room his dark retreat is made.
  Here, whilst his heart is boiled in gall, his brain
O'erwhelmed in clouds, whose darkness entertain
No beam of reason; whilst ambition mixed
Examples of the bloodiest murders fixed
Upon the brazen front of time, all which
Lends no unfathomed policy to enrich

346 from this] Singer ' *by* this,' probably, according to expectation, and still more
probably in consequence of the previous ' from ': but not, I think, Chamberlayne being
Chamberlayne, quite certainly.

His near impoverished brain, he hears one knock,   380
Whose sudden noise soon scattering all the flock
Of busy thoughts, him in a hasty rage
Hurries t' the door; where come, his eyes engage
His tongue to welcome one whose cursed advice
His tortured thoughts turned to a paradise
Of pleasing hopes, on whose foundation he
Prepares to build a future monarchy.
    A slow-consuming grief, whose chronic stealth
Had slily robbed Palermo's prince of health,
In spite of all the guards of art had long   390
Worn out his strength, and now had grown too strong
For age to bear. Each baffled artist in
A sad despair forsaking what had been
Tried but to upbraid their ignorance, except
An aged friar, whose judgement long had slept
From watchful practice, but i' the court of arts
Been so employed, that the mysterious parts
Of clouded theorics, which he courted by
High contemplation, to his mind's clear eye
Lay all undressed of that disguise which in   400
Man's fall, to afflict posterity, they'd been
By angry Heaven wrapped in; so that he knew
What astral virtues vegetables drew
From a celestial influence, and by what
Absconded magic Nature fitted that
To working humours, which they either move
By expulsive hate, or by attractive love.
This art's true master, when his hope was grown
Faint with delays, to the sick prince made known,
A swift command calls from his still repose   410
The reverend sire: who come, doth soon disclose
That long concealed malignity which had
The feeble prince in sickly paleness clad:
Nor stays his art at weak prognostics, but
Proceeds to practise whatso'er may put
His prince in ease—cordials abstracted by
A then near undiscovered chemistry,
Such as in single drops did all comprise
Nature e'er taught Art to epitomize:
Such as, if armed with a Promethean fire,   420
Might force a bloodless carcass to respire;
Such as curbed Fate, and, in their hot assault
Whilst storming Life, made Death's pale army halt.
This rare elixir by the prince had been,
With such success as those that languish in
Consuming ills, could wish themselves, so long
Used, that those fits, which else had grown too strong

389 Palermo's] Observe that we are once more hovering between the Morea and Sicily.

For Nature to contend withal, were now
Grown more remiss; when Fate, that can allow
No lasting comforts, to declare her power   430
O'er Art itself, arrests that conqueror
Of others' ills with a disease that led
Him a close prisoner to an uncouth bed.
Which like to prove Nature's slow chariot to
The expecting grave, loath to the public view
To prostitute a secret, yet bound by
The obligation of his loyalty
To assist his prince, he to Pharonnida
That sovereign secret, which could only awe
Her father's threatening pain, declares; which she   440
Hath since composed, whene'er 's extremity
Suffered those pains: whose progress to prevent
She'd by Amphibia now the cordial sent,
The sly Amphibia, who did soon obey
What lent her hate a freedom to betray.

His first salutes being past, with such a speed
As did declare the guilt of such a deed
Might doubt discovery, she unfolds that strange
Amazing truth, which from the giddy range
Of wild invention soon contracts each thought   450
Into resolves, such as no object sought
But the destruction of whate'er might stop
Ambition's progress; towards the slippery top
Of which now climbing, on Conceit's stretched wings,
He silent stands, whilst teeming Fancy brings
That monster forth, for whose conception he
Long since deflowered his virgin loyalty.

Few minutes, by that auxiliary aid
Which her discovery lent, his thoughts conveyed
Through all the roads of doubt; which safely past,   460
Strictly embracing her who in this last
And greatest act of villany must have
A further share, he thus begins :—'Oh save,
Save, thou that art my better genius now,
What thou alone hast raised; my hopes must bow
Beneath impossibilities, if not
By thee assisted. Fortune hath begot
The means already; let this cordial be
With poison mixed—Fate knows no enemy
Dares grapple with me—Do not start, there's here   470
No room for danger, if we banish fear.'
His thoughts thus far discovered, finding in
Her various looks, that apprehended sin,
The soul's mercurial pill, did penetrate
Her callous conscience, in whose cell this sat
With gnawing horror, whilst all other lives
Whom her fraud spilt, proved hurtless corrosives,

From the cold ague of repentance he
Thus rouses her:—'Can my Amphibia be
By fear, that fatal remora to all   480
That's great or good, thus startled? Is the fall
Of an old tyrant grown a subject for
This soft remorse? Let thy brave soul abhor
Such sickly passions: when our fortune stands
Fixed on their ruin, the unwilling hands
Of those that now withstand our glorious flight,
Will help enthrone us; whilst unquestioned right,
Which is for power the world's mistaken word,
Is made our own b' the legislative sword.'
   Raised from her fear's cold trepidations by   490
These hot ingredients, in an ecstasy
Of flatuous hopes, she casts herself into
This gulf of sin; and being prepared to do
An act, which not the present times could see
With sense enough, whilst in the extremity
Of wonder lost, through all his guards' strict care
Death to the unsuspecting prince doth bear.
Freed from this doubt, Almanzor, to avoid
That storm of rage, which, when their prince destroyed
The court should know, might rise from fear, pretends   500
Haste to the army; but being gone, suspends
That speedy voyage, and being attended by
A wretch whose guilt assured his privacy,
Through paths untrod hastes to the cave wherein
Those habits, which had by Amindor been
(Whilst he his beauteous charge did thence convey)
Prepared to cloud illustrious beauty, lay:
Of which, in such whose size did show they were
For th' largest sex, they both being clad, with care
Secret as swift, haste to augment the flood   510
Of swelling sins with yet more royal blood.
The Epirots' constant prince, by custom had
Made known a walk, which, when the day unclad
Of glittering tissue in her evening's lawn
Sat coolly dressed, to court the sober dawn,—
He often used. Near this, Almanzor, by
Hell made successful in his villany,
Arrived some minutes ere the other, lies
Concealed, till darkness and a close disguise,
Those safe protectors, from his unseen seat   520
Call him to action; where, with thoughts replete
With too much joy to admit suspicion, he
Finds the Messenian, whom no fear to be
Assaulted there had armed, his spacious train
Shrunk into one that served to entertain
Time with discourse. Upon which heedless pair
The armed Almanzor rushing unaware,

Ere strength had time their valour to obey,
In storms of wounds their senses lose the way
To external objects ; in which giddy trance   530
The other lord, whose spirits' re-advance
To life they fear not, lies secure, whilst by
Redoubled wounds his prince's spirits fly
From the most strong retreats of life ; which now,
Battered by death, no safety could allow.
   Revenge's thirst being in this royal flood
Quenched for awhile, that from the guiltless blood
His honour might not yet a stain receive,
First hasting to the cave, he there doth leave
Those injured habits, which by him were meant   540
For the betrayers of the innocent.
This done, that he e'en from suspicion might
Secure his guilt, before the wasted night
Looks pale at the approach of day, he flies
T' the distant army ; there securely lies,
Till all those black productions of his brain,
Now ripening to perfection, should attain
Maturity, and in the court appear
In their most horrid dress ; knowing the fear
Of the distracted city soon would call   550
Him and his army, to prevent the fall
Of such distracting dangers, as might be
Attendants on the eclipse of majesty.

THE END OF THE THIRD CANTO.

Canto IV

THE ARGUMENT

Now, as if that great engineer of ill,
   Accursed Almanzor, had accomplished all
Those black designs, which are ordained to fill
   The Spartan annals, by his prince's fall ;

With secret spite, yet such as seemed to be
   From an advised protector of the state,
Pharonnida's ill fate assisting, he
   Toward her destruction prosecutes his hate.

THAT dismal night, which in the dark records
Of story yet so much of fate affords
In the Morean annals, had to day
Resigned its reign, whose eastern beams display
Their morning beauties ; by whose welcome light,
The early courtier, tired with tedious night,

(267)

Rises to meet expected triumphs in
Their princess' nuptials, which so long had been
The joyful business of their thoughts, that now
Sallying to action, they 're instructed how   10
To court observance from the studied pain
Of best inventions—by attractive gain,
Joined to the itch of ostentative art,
Were thither drawn from each adjacent part.
   In this swelled torrent of expected mirth,
Which all conclude must make this morning's birth
To future ages celebrated by
An annual triumph, the disparity
Of passion, sorrow, first breaks forth among
The slain Epirot's followers; who so long   20
Had missed their master, that they now begin
To doubt his safety. Every place had been
By strict inquiry searched, to which they knew
Either affection or employment drew
His frequent visits; but with an effect
So vain, their care served only to detect
Their love, not him its object; who might have
Lain till corruption sought itself a grave,
Had not an early forester so near
The place approached, that maugre all that fear   30
Alleged to stop a full discovery, he
Beheld so much as taught him how to free
His friends from further fruitless searches, in
Discovering what beneath their fears had been.
   In sorrow, such as left no power to vent
Its symptoms, but a deep astonishment,
The amazed Messenians, whom a sad belief
Deprived of hope, did entertain their grief.
Whose swift infection to communicate—
Their murdered prince, as if pale death kept state   40
Clad in the crimson robes of blood, is to
The city brought; where, whilst the public view
In busy murmurs spread her sable wings,
Pale terror to the court, grief's centre, brings
The dreadful truth; which some officious lord,
Whom favour did the privilege afford
Of easy entrance, through the guards of fear
In haste conveys, to assault the prince's ear.
   With such a silence as did seem to show
Unwelcome news is in its entrance slow,   50
Entered the room, he 's with soft pace unto
The bed approached; whose curtains when withdrew,
Discovered Horror in the dismal dress
Of Death appears—Freed from the slow distress
Of Age, that coward tyrant which ne'er shows
His strength till man wants vigour to oppose,

(268)

Through Death's dark gates fled to the gloomy shade,
Whose fear, or hope, not knowledge doth invade
Our fancies yet, he man's material part
There only sees; which Form, whose heavenly art   60
Tunes motion into th' faculties of life,
Had now forsook; the elemental strife,
Which had so long at concord aimed, was now
Silenced in death; on his majestic brow
No awful frown did sit; the blood's retreat
From life and action left his cheeks the seat
Of Death's cold guest, which, summoned by his fate,
There in a pale and ghastly horror sat.
  Whilst the astonished courtier did behold
This, with such trembling as, when graves unfold   70
Their doomsday's curtains, sinful bodies shall
Rise from their urns, eternally to fall—
His stay, caused from restrictive fear, had drew
In more spectators; to whose wondering view
This ghastly object when opposed had strook
So swift a terror, that their fears forsook
The safe retreats of reason. Seeing life
Had now concluded all the busy strife
Of Nature's conflicts, by delivering those
Time-shaken forts unto more powerful foes,   80
Outcries in vain attempt for pity to
Scale Heaven; whose ear when from their prayers withdrew,
The court, now of her royal head bereft,
In a still calm of hopeless sorrow left.
  Infectious grief, disdaining now to be
Confined within the brief stenography
Of first discoverers, spreads itself among
The city herd; whose rude unsteady throng
Raised grief, which in the mourning court did dwell
In such a silence as an anchorite's cell   90
Ne'er knew a heavier solitude, into
Exalted outcries: whose loud call had drew
From their neglected arts so many, that
What first was choler, now being kindled at
Their rage, like humours grown adust, had been
The open breach to let rebellion in;
Had not the wiser nobles, which did know
That vulgar passions will to tumult grow
When backed with power, by a new-modelled form
Of counsel soon allayed this rising storm.   100
  Their tears, those fruitless sacrifices to
Unactive grief, wiped off, whilst they did view
The state's distempered body, to supply
The wants of that departed majesty,
Which, when their prince from life's horizon fell,
Fled from their view, before report should tell

This fatal story to the princess, they
A council call; by whose advice she may,
Whilst floating in this sea of sorrow, be
Saved from those unseen rocks, where Treachery,⠀⠀110
Rebellion's subtle engineer, might sit
To wreck the weakness of a female wit;
Which, though in her such that it might have been
The whole world's pilot, could, since clouded in
Such a tempestuous sea of passions, see
No star that might her safe director be.
⠀⠀A messenger, whose sad observant wit
By age allayed, seemed a conveyer fit
For such important business, with the news
Hastes towards the princess. Whom whilst Fear pursues⠀120
On wings of Pity, being arrived within
The palace, he, as that alone had been
The only seat where rigid Sorrow took
Her fixed abode, beholds each servant's look
Obscured with grief; through whose dark shades whilst he
Searches the cause, the strange variety
Explains itself—As families that have
Led their protecting ruler to the grave,
Whose loss they in a heedless sorrow mourn
So long, till care doth to distraction turn,⠀⠀130
Her servants sat; each wildly looking on
The other, till even sense itself was gone
In mourning wonder; whose wild flight to stay,
Its cause they to the pitying lord display
In such a tone, as, whilst it did detect
The princess' absence, showed their own neglect.
⠀⠀When this he'd heard, with such a sympathy
Of sorrow, as erected Grief to be
The mourning monarch of his thoughts, to those
Returned that sent him, he that transcript shows⠀⠀140
Of this obscure original—the flight
Of the absent princess, whilst the veil of night
Obscured her passage, tells: but, questioned—how,
With whom, or whether knowledge did allow
No satisfaction, all inquiry gained
From her amazed attendants, but explained
Their grief; whose troubled rivulet flowed in
To that vast ocean, where before they'd been
By sorrow shipwrecked, in the general flood
Mixed, wants a language to be understood⠀⠀150
In a peculiar character, and so
Conjoined, makes up one universal woe.
⠀⠀Only, as if Love knew alone the art

114 pilot] Orig. as elsewhere 'Pilate.'
120 Whom] Singer 'Who,' not only unnecessarily, but, I think, wrongly.

That taught his followers how to mourn apart,
Sad, sweet Orlinda, whose calm innocence
Had fostered passion at her health's expense;
Whilst wet with grief's o'erflowing spring, she to
Her brother's ghost did pay soft Nature's due,
In sorrow of such sad complexion, that
Others might lose their own to wonder at;   160
Yet when, as in the margin placed, she hears
Amindor lost, with new supplies of tears
Grief sallying forth, as if to be betrayed
Love now did fear, he draws the bashful maid
From those that did the mourning concert keep,
Where she unseen for Love's decease doth weep;
Frail woman's faith, and man's neglect doth blame,
And softly then sighs out Amindor's name—
Her lost Amindor, whose supposed disdain
Destroyed those spirits grief could ne'er have slain.   170
    And now before that power's decay engage
Too many hands in a vindictive rage,
The wise supporters of the state, to stay
Increasing factions, which can ne'er obey
Lest Fear commands, unto Almanzor send
A mandate, which enjoins him to attend
Their councils in this interregnum, till
Their joint consent had found out one to fill
The empty throne. Which summons, prompted by
A care which they interpret loyalty,   180
Though truly called ambition, he obeyed
With such a speed as Love would fly to aid
A ravished lady; having to impede
His march no more than what his care could lead—
Even with a winged speed, yet that a strength
Enough to make his will confine the length
Of their desires, who soon in council sit
But to bewail the abortion of their wit.
    The frighted city having entered in
A mourning march, as if his thoughts had been   190
A stranger to the sad events of this
So dismal night, he by relation is
Informed of each particular : which he
Seeming to hear in grief's extremity,
From silent sorrow which appeared to wait
On still attention, his prepared deceit
Disguised in rage appears; a rage which, in
Its active flight to find what hearts had been
Defiled with thoughts of such foul crimes, did seem
So full of zeal, its actions did redeem   200

185 winged] This is Singer's ingenious emendation for the orig. *vox nihili*
'singes.'

The lost report of loyalty in those
His former crimes made his most constant foes.
By guarded gates, and watchful parties that
Surround the walls, till th' people, frighted at
Their fury, shrink from public throngs. They now
Assured of safety, whilst inquiring how
Hell hatched these monsters—whose original
Whilst searching, they, by the consent of all
His best physicians, whose experienced skill
From outward signs knew what internal ill   210
Death struck the prince, informed the cause could be
From nought but such a subtle enemy
As poison; which, when every accident
They had examined, all conclude was sent
Mixed with that cordial, whose concealed receipt
Unknown to art, their envy termed the bait
To tempt the easy prince's faith into
That net which Death, allured by Treason, drew.
    With power, from this embraced suspicion sprung,
Almanzor, whom not envy's spotted tongue   220
Durst call profane, though rudely forcing those
Weak gates, which need no greater strength to oppose
Unclean intruders, than the reverence they,
Enforced by zeal, did with religion pay
Unto that place's sanctity; which he
Contemning, ere the wronged society
Expecting such injurious visits, in
Rude fury entering, those whose power had been
Employed by noble pity to attend
The suffering princess, in such haste did send   230
Them to her close and dark abodes, that now
Their doubts confirmed, they're only studying how
To shun that danger which informing fear
Falsely persuades towards them alone drew near.
Which dark suspicion, ere unclouded by
Seizing on him whose innocence durst fly
To no retreat, the royal fugitives
Back to the vault where first they entered, drives.
    Now, at the great'st antipathy to day,
The silent earth oppressed with midnight lay   240
Vested in clouds, black as they had been sent
To be the whole world's mourning monument;
When through the cave's damp womb, conducted by
A doubtful light that scarce informed the eye
To find out those unhaunted paths, they, in
A faint assurance, with soft pace begin
To sally forth; where, unsuspected, they
Are seized by guards that in close ambush lay:
Which, ere amazement could give action leave
To seek for safety, did their hopes deceive   250

By close restraint.   Awed by whose power, they're to
Almanzor brought; who from that object drew
Such joy as fills usurpers, when they see
Wronged princes struggling with captivity.
  From hence in such disdainful silence led
As taught their fear, from just suspicion bred,
To tremble at some unknown ill ; about
That sober time when light's small lamps go out
At the approach of day's bright glories, brought
Back to the court, they there not long had sought   260
Their sorrow's sad original, before
A court convened of such whose power had bore
(Whilst God's own choice, a monastry, had lent
Their dictates law) the weight of government.
They, hither called by summons that did sound
Like bold rebellion, in sad omen found
More than they feared :—A mourning train of lords
Placed round a black tribunal, that affords
To the spectator's penetrated eye
A dismal horror clothed in majesty.   270
Like hieroglyphics pointing to that fate
Which must ensue, all yet in silence sate—
A dreadful silence ! such as unto weak
Beholders seemed to threaten, when they speak,
Death and destruction dictates.   When they saw
Their princess entered, as if rigid law
To loyal duty let the sceptre fall,
In an obedient reverence raised, they all
Lowly salute her ; but that compliment
To bribe their pity, fear in vain had spent.   280
When all resuming now their seats, command
The royal captives, whose just cause did stand
On no defence but unknown truth, to be
Summoned t' the bar ; where, that they first might see
What rigour on the royal blood was shown,
From no unjust conspiracy had grown,
A sable curtain from their herses drawn,
Betrays her eyes, then in the sickly dawn
Of grief grown dim, unto that horrid place
Where they met death drawn in her father's face ;   290
By whom, now turned into well-modelled clay,
Fitted for 's tomb, the slain Epirot lay.
  At this, as if some over-venturous look
For temperate rays, destructive fire had took
In at her soul's receiving portals, all
Life's functions ceased ; sorrow at once lets fall

---

269 penetrated] Singer, with less than his usual judgement, 'penetrating.' 'Pene-
trated' of course means, as it does in French and did in English as late as Madame
d'Arblay, 'strongly moved.'

The burthen of so many griefs, which in
A death-like slumber had forgotten been,
Till human thoughts, obliterated by
The wished conversions of eternity,   300
Oppressed no more, had not injurious haste,
Before this conflict could those spirits waste,
Which had, to shun passion's external strife,
Fled to the *primum mobile* of life,
Recalled with them her sorrows to attend
Their nimblest motions, which too fast did spend
Her strength, to suffer weakness to obey
The court's intentions of a longer stay.
    From ruffled passions which her soul opprest,
By the soft hand of recollecting rest   310
Stroked to a calm, which settled Reason in
Her troubled throne; by those that first had been
Her guards, the princess—that fair pattern whence
Men drew the height of human excellence,
Is now returned, to let her proud foes see,
That the bright rays of magnanimity,
Though envy like the ungrateful moon do strive
To hide that sun, except what's relative
Ne'er knows eclipse, the darkness taking birth
From what's below, whilst that removed from earth,   320
Her clear unclouded conscience, ever stays
Amongst bright virtue's universal rays.
    The mourning court, those ministers of fate,
In expectation of their prisoners sate:—
They now appear in those disguises which
They first were took, being habits, though not rich
Enough to gild their rare perfections, yet
Such as did seem by sorrow made to fit
Their present sufferings:—both the men clothed in
Monastic robes, black as their threads had been   330
Spun from Peruvian wool; the women, clad
Like mournful votaries, showed so sweetly sad,
As if their virtues, which injurious fate
Did yet conceal, striving to anticipate
The flights of time, had to the external sense
Showed these as emblems of their innocence.
    But love, nor pity, though they both did here
Within their judges' sternest looks appear,
Durst plead for favour; their indictments read,
So guilty found, that those whose hearts e'en bled,   340
Disdained their eyes should weep, since justice did
In such foul crimes mercy as sin forbid.
Yet more to clear what circumstance had made
Level with reason, from the approaching shade
Of death redeemed, that lord, whose wounds had been
But slumbers to recover safety in,

(274)

When the Messenian murdered was, did now
Declare, as .far as reason could allow
The eyes to judge, those habits, which they then
Did wear, the same which clothed the murderers when   350
His prince was slain; which open proof appears
So full of guilt, it stops her friends' kind fears,
Ere. raised to hope, and in appearance shows
A guilt, which all but pity overgrows.
   The vexed Epirots, who for comfort saw
Revenge appearing in the form of law,
Retired, to feed their spleen with hope, until
The extent of justice should their vengeance fill.
When now, by accusations that denied
Access to pity, for a parricide   360
The princess questioned, whose too weak defence,
Being but the unseen guards of innocence,
Submits to censure. Yet to show that all
Those scattered pearls, which from her eyes did fall,
Dropped not to attempt their charity, but show
That no injurious storm could overflow
Her world of reason—which exalted stood
Above the surface of the spacious flood,
(Her tears for grief, not guilt, being shed), whilst in
The robes of magnanimity, not sin   370
Grown impudent, her brave resolved soul sate
Unshaken in this hurricane of fate.
   To meet her calm, which like religion drest
Doth all become, but female virtues best,
The rough Amindor, whose discoloured face
Anger did more than native beauty grace,
Since justly raised, disdaining thus to be
By a plebeian base captivity
Forced to submit his innocence unto
Their doubtful test, had from his anger drew   380
A ruin swifter than their hate intends,
Had not his rage, while it toward danger bends,
Been taught by her example to exclude
Vain passions with a princely fortitude;
Whose useful aid, like those good works which we
For comforts call in death's necessity,
Brought all their better angels to defend
Them from those terrors which did death attend.
   In busy whispers, which discovered by
Their doubtful looks the thoughts' variety,   390
Long in sad silence sat the court; until
Those noiseless streams of fancy which did fill
Each several breast, united by consent,
Want only now a tongue so impudent
As durst condemn their sovereign; which being in
Theumantius found, a lord whose youth had been

By favours nursed, till power's wild beast, grown rude,
Repays his foster with ingratitude.
This bold, bad man, love's most unhappy choice,
From flattery's treble now exalts his voice,   400
Without the mean of an excuse, into
The law's loud bass, and what those feared to do
That had been favoured less, that black decree
Pronounced, which discords all the harmony
Of subject fear and sovereign love, by what
Succeeding ages justly trembled at
Whilst innocent, but have of late been grown
So bad to show such monsters of their own.
   This sentence passed, which knew no more allay
Of mercy, than what lets their judgement stay   410
From following life to death's obscure retreat,
Till twenty nights had made their days complete,
The court breaks up; yet ere from public view
To close restraint the royal captives drew,
Grant them this favour from their rigid laws—
That if there durst, to vindicate their cause,
In that contracted span of time appear
Any whose forward valour durst endear
The people's love and prayers so much—to be
Their champion, that his victory should free   420
Them from that doom's strict rigour; to oppose
Which brave attempter they Almanzor chose,
Since high command that honour did afford
To him alone, to wield the answering sword.
   Now near departing, whilst the Cyprian in
A brave disdain, which for submissive sin
Looks on an answer, as his haste would show
An anger that did scorn to stoop so low
To strike with threats, stands silent; whilst that she,
Whose temper Heaven had made too calm to be   430
By rage transported, with a soul unmoved
By stormy passions, thus their sin reproved :—
   'Should I, my lords, here with a female haste
Discharge my passions, 'twere, perhaps, to waste
My prayers or threats, whilst one you would not fear,
Nor the other pity : but when Heaven shall clear
This curtained truth, wrapped in whose cloudy night,
Unjustly you, from my unquestioned right
By birth, obedience, into faction stray,
Then, though too late, untimely sorrow may   440
Strive by repentance to expunge these stains
Cast on your honour. These exhausted veins,
Fixed eyes, pale cheeks, death's dismal trophies, in
This royal face I now could not have seen

398 foster] 'forester' which Singer prints, is of course a result of confusion with
the form of that word common in Malory, &c.

With a less sorrow than had served to call
Me to attend him, had not the rude fall
Of your injustice, like those dangerous cures
Performed by turning into calentures
Dull lethargies, upon my heart laid hold
In such a flame of passion, as the cold   450
Approach of death wants power to quench, until
You add that crime to this preceding ill.
'Yet, though no fear can prompt my scorn to crave
A subject's mercy for myself, to save
This noble stranger, whose just acts, being crost
By misconstruction, have their titles lost,
I shall become your suppliant, lest there be
A sin contracted by his serving me;
And only in such noble ways as might
Unveil themselves t' the sun's meridian light.   460
Sure he unjustly suffers; which may cause
You want more swords to vindicate your laws,
Than his you late elected to make good
Your votes, ere scarce cleansed of that loyal blood
He in rebellion shed :—but I am now
Too near my fatal period, to allow
Disturbing passion any place within
My peaceful soul.   Whate'er his crimes have been
In public war, or private treason, may
Kind Heaven, when with the injustice of this day   470
Those shall be quickly questioned, to prevent
Their doom, conceal them in the large extent
Of Mercy's wings, which there may prove so kind
To you, though here I can no justice find !'
This spoken, in a garb that did detect
A sorrow which was ripened to neglect,
She silent stands ; whilst through the thick resort
Of thronged spectators, toward the rising court
Orlinda comes, with such a haste as showed
That service she by Love's allegiance owed—   480
Love, which had Sorrow's sable wings out-fled,
To mourn the living, not lament the dead.
Come where her fears' now near lost object she
Within the shadow of the grave might see
By sentence shut, neglecting death that lay
In ambush there her reason to betray
To hate, when, by the false informing law,
Her friend she as her brother's murderer saw,
In actions such as Scythian tyrants feel
Some softness from, she that ne'er used to kneel   490
To aught but Heaven, a lowly suppliant falls
Before the court; from whose stern breast she calls
So much of sorrow as perhaps had strook
Them all with horror, if a sudden look

Obliquely on her murdered brother cast,
Had not, ere Love assaulted with her last
And powerfullest prayers, whilst hot with action, in
A cool retreat of spirits silenced been.
    She, fainting fallen, as an addition to
Their former grief, is from the throng withdrew   500
Into the free untainted air—where, by
Assisting friends, which gently did apply
Their needful aid, heat, which was then grown slack
In Nature's work, antipathy calls back
To beauty's frontiers ; where, like bashful light,
It in a blush meets the spectators' sight,
But such an one, as, ere full blown, is by
Her friend's disasters forced again to fly
Beneath those clouds of grief, whose swelling pride,
Spread by report, did now not only hide   510
The court or city, but to bear a part
Of that sad load summons each subject's heart.
    Whilst now the prisoners, ere the people's love
To anger turn, the active guards remove,
To still the clamorous multitude, who, swayed
By various passions, did, whilst each obeyed
Opinion's dictates, but in darkness rove
At shadowed truth, whence now they boldly strove
To pluck the veil from declarations that
Contained those falsehoods, which whilst wondering at,   520
They wept to force upon their faith, are sent
Through th' land's each town, and army's regiment ;
By which Almanzor, who attempted in
This plot to join security with sin,
Doubting, if e'er this story reach his ear,
Argalia might their combatant appear,
Besides those stains which common fame did take
For sin's just debts, slily attempts to shake
The heaven-erected fabric of his love
By closer engines, such as seemed to move   530
On noble pity, which with grief engrost
That faith which envy in disdain had lost.
    Black rumour, on the wings of raised report
Flying in haste, had soon attained the court
Of the amazed Aetolian prince ; who hears
The dreadful story with such doubtful fears
As shook his noble soul, but not into
An easy faith each circumstance was true ;
He knew Almanzor's villainy to be
Of that extent, so foul a progeny   540
As all those horrid murders, might from thence
Take easy birth : but when the innocence
Of's virtuous princess, and his honoured friend,
The noble Cyprian prince, come to contend

With oft confirmed report, that strikes a deep
And solemn grief, yet such as must not keep
A firm possession in his soul, until
A further inquisition either kill
His yet unfainting hopes, or raise them to
Joy by confirming those reports untrue.   550

THE END OF THE FOURTH CANTO.

Canto V

THE ARGUMENT

Through royal blood to level that dark way
    Which rebels pass unto the injured throne,
Pharonnida is now condemned to pay
    A debt for crimes that none durst call her own.

When near the last step, brave Argalia, who
    In close disguise Truth's secrets had betrayed,
When most did doubt 'twas now too late to sue
    To Heaven for pity, brings a timely aid.

IF on those vanished heroes that are fled
Through the unknown dark chasms of the dead,
To rest in regions so remote from hence—
'Twixt them and life there's no intelligence,
Whene'er thou look'st through Time's dim optics, then
Brave emulation of those braver men
Rouses that ray of heaven—thy soul, to be
A sharer in their fame's eternity;
Thou'st then a genius fit to entertain
A muse's flight: which may be raised again   10
To sing thy actions, when there's left no more
Of thee, but what by life, whilst passing o'er
Nature's short stage, had either scattered been
By careless youth, or firmly planted in
Maturer age; whose wasted talent spent,
Those were his friends—This is his monument
Is all, except some muse thy life records,
That to thy worth the unthankful world affords.
    But if thy uninspirèd soul do bear
A lower sail, which, flagging with the care   20
Of humid pleasures, ne'er is swelled into
Sublimer thoughts than such as only view
Earth for its object, which ne'er yet did lend
Her favourites more than what they here do spend
To improve her barren wants, may none rehearse
Thy name—beneath the dignity of verse,
But trivial flatterers, such as strive to gain
Thy favour from ephemeras of the brain,

Unsalted jests ! Pleased at whose painted fire
I leave fond thee in vapour to expire,   30
Whilst from thy living shadow I return
To crown the dust in brave Argalia's urn.
    From common Fame, that wild impostor, he
Had often heard what Love denied should be
For truth admitted—his Pharonnida ˙
Accused for sins which envy strove to draw
Objects for Heaven's severest wrath ; and now,
Ere his considerate judgement would allow
Report for real, secret messengers
To Corinth sends ; who, ill-informed, transfers   40
His further trouble, in confirming what,
Whilst others wept for, he, transported at
So sad a change in her whose virtue had
Inflamed his thoughts, by passion near unclad
His soul of all his robes of flesh, which now
So loosely hung, as if she practised how
To strip herself, should unexpected death
To Heaven's hard course call forth the nimble breath,
    Could earth here conquer, or had it within
The power of whatsoe'er is mortal been,   50
T' have wrought disorders of amazement, where
The noble soul such true consent did bear
With the harmonious angels, (he in all
His acts like them appears, or, ere his fall,
Perhaps like man, that he could only be
Distinguished from some hallowed hierarchy,
By being clothed in the specific veil
Of flesh and blood), this grief might then prevail
Over his perfect temper, but he bears
These weights as if unfelt ; on his soul wears   60
The sable robes of sorrow, whilst his cheek
Is dressed in scarlet smiles ; no frown his sleek
And even front contracts—like to a slow
And quiet stream, his obscured thoughts did flow,
With greater depths than could be fathomed by
The beamy lines of a judicious eye.
    Whilst those good angels, which fond men call wit
Reformed by age, did all in council sit,
To steer those thoughts by which he did attend
Pharonnida's escape, they to this end   70
At length reduced his counsels :—That he must,
To succour her, leave grovelling in the dust
His kingdom, which being by domestic strife
Late wounded, was but newly rubbed to life :
Yet since that there to her redemption lay
In all the progress of his thoughts no way
Less full of danger, such of 's lords as he
Honoured for age, and praised for loyalty,

Called to a secret council, he discovers
His fixed resolves; which they, though now no lovers,   80
With such consenting souls did hear, that though
They knew his danger might e'en fear outgrow,
They, to oppose that score of cowards, brings
His vows, his sacred vows, those sceptred kings
Which justly rule the conscience, that awed by
Usurping fear submits to tyranny.
   Their first proposals, whence their judgement sought
To hide his absence, to conclusion brought,
They thence proceed to level him a way
Through that thick swarm of enemies that lay   90
Circling the walls; where reason stays awhile
In various censure, ere 't could reconcile
Their differing judgements; but at length in this,
As that which in this danger's dark abyss
Seems to lend fear most of the helpful light
Of hope, concludes—That when succeeding night
With strength of age was grown so gravely staid,
That dark designs feared not to be betrayed
B' the wanton twilight, he in close disguise,
Whilst some of 's troops diverted by surprise   100
His watchful foes, might pass their guards; which done,
Their care might be with 's further march begun.
In dismal darkness—that black throne of fear,
Night's silent empress awed the hemisphere;
When now Argalia's ready troops with slow
And noiseless marches issued through their low
Close sallyports, are swiftly rallied by
Such as had long taught Valour how to die
For Honour's rescue—captains that had been,
From youth's first bud till age was reverenced in   110
Her honoured scars, such strict disciples to
War's hardest precepts, that their fame outgrew
Their power, which that had so authentic made,
Where fear was scorned, they were for love obeyed.
   By these brave heroes, which had often led
Armies to sleep in Honour's purple bed,
The prince assisted, was with secret haste,
By ways where fear no sentinel had placed,
Drawn near the leaguer; which, the alarum took
From a stormed fort, had with such speed forsook   120
Their huts, that haste, which was intended to
Preserve, being now to wild confusion grew,
Helps to destroy. In undistinguished sounds,
Which not inform, but frighted sense confounds
With wild amazement, the unnoted words
Even of command are lost; no ear affords
Room for advice, nor the most serious eye
A place for order; ensigns vainly fly,

Since unperceived, through the dark air, which in
A storm ne'er knew more tumult than had been,   130
Since first their fear on this alarum fled
From reason, through the troubled leaguer spread.
   In this loud horror, whilst they need no lamp
To guide them more than their own flaming camp,
His frighted foes, fled from their quarter, lend
The prince some hope this sudden charge might end
Their slow-paced siege ; yet since approaching day,
Persuading haste, denies his longer stay,
The power to those commanders left, which he
For valour knew might force from victory   140
Unwilling laurels, though their judgement such,
Those hallowed wreaths they ne'er durst rashly touch,
He leaves (when first his sword, which none did spare
Within its reach, had of his being there
Left bloody marks) the conquered foes, to find
Out sterner foes in his afflicted mind :
Which, since usurping doubt with peaceful love
For empire strove, taught passion how to move
In spheres so differing from his reason's right
Ascension, that his cares' protracted night   150
From this oblique position caused, had made
His sorrow tedious as those nights which shade
Cold arctic regions, when the absent sun
Doth underneath the antarctic tropic run.
   This passage forced through his obstructed foes,
That now the treacherous day might not disclose
Him, whilst unguarded, to their view that might
In larger troops pursue a baser flight,
Through deep dark paths, which ne'er t' the sun had shown
Their uncouth shades, being to all unknown   160
Save neighbouring rurals, he, conducted by
A faithful guide, directs his liberty
Towards stately Corinth. Near whose confines, ere
Six morning dews had cooled the hemisphere,
Arrived in safety, that kind Heaven might bless
His future actions with desired success
To seek to them, he first sought those that in
The wane of 's blood had life's supporters been,
Those holy hermits, to whose art he owed
For life, next Heaven, which first that gift bestowed   170
   Come to their quiet cell, where all receive
Him with a wonder that did hardly leave
A room for welcome, till their fear had, in
A full relation of his fortune, been
Changed for as much of sanguine mirth as they
Could know, that had religion's cool allay
To check delight. He being retired with him,
Whose first discoveries in his fortunes' dim

Imperfect light directed him to know
His royal offspring, lets his language flow   180
With so much freedom as discovers what,
Whilst he by active war was aiming at
His kingdom's safety, called him thence to save
Sweet virtue from an ignominious grave.
    The fatal story heard by him, whose love
Fixed by religion, passion could not move,
Although he pitied all the afflicted, to
More softness than what had its offspring drew
From Heaven's strict precepts, which are then misspent
When easy man mistakes the innocent;   190
Since what permits hypocrisy to win
Remorse, by mercy doth but cherish sin.
Which to avoid, ere his consent approve
Of the design, neglecting all which love,
Prompted by pity, could allege to draw
Him to the combat, though he in it saw
Nought to defend but innocence, since in
That shape deluded, charity hath been
Too oft deceived; that his victorious sword
Might not, but where fair Justice could afford   200
Victory, be drawn, he, like a Pharos placed
'Mongst rocks of doubt, thus rectifies his haste :—
    ' Take heed, brave prince, that, in this doubtful way
'Twixt love and honour, thy bright virtues stray
Not from religion's latitude into
More dangerous stations ; reason's slender clew
Is here too short to guide thee, and may in
Its conduct but obliquely lead to sin.
Be cautious then, and rashly venture not
On unknown depths, where valour seems begot   210
By vain presumption.   Mortal beauty, that
Imperfect type of Heaven, though wondered at,
Yet may not be so much adored to make
Our passions Heaven's directing road mistake.
    ' Though thy affections were legitimate
As man's first choice, since in that happy state
Of innocence frail woman then found out
A way to fall, still let thy reason doubt
The same deceit, since that affected she
Which thou ador'st, yet wears mortality ;   220
A garment which, since man first wore, hath been
But once cast off without some spots of sin.
Yet, know, my counsel strives not to prevent
Thy sword's assisting of the innocent ;
As much of mercy on neglect being spilt,
As there 's got vengeance from presumptuous guilt.
Only, before thy valour dares to tread
This rubric path, whose slippery steps have led

So oft to ruin, let religion be
Thy prompter unto so much policy   230
As may secure thy conscience ; which to do,
Claim my assistance as thy virtue's due.'
   The grateful prince with lowly looks had paid
His thankful offerings, when, that promised aid
Might not fall short of expectation, he,
Whose words, like vows that hold affinity
With Heaven, breathed nought but constant truth, did thus
Proceed towards action :—' Whilst, loved prince, with us
Of this poor convent, you, by wounds restrained
From action, lived ; you know that what's contained   240
In our calm doctrine, gives us leave to be
So intimate with each society,
No secret, though masked in the clouds of sin,
Flies those discoveries which informs us in
Their last confessions ; by which means you may
Know whether justice calls your sword to pay
These bloody offerings, as a victim to
The appeasing of an inward virtue due.'
   By this advice instructed to convince
What love suggests, the apprehensive prince,   250
Since this includes nothing but what's too just
To disobey, although he all mistrust
Of her, like sin, avoids, consents to be
Ruled by his counsel, whose assistance he
So oft successful found. Which, that delay,
That slow-paced sin, might not obstruct the way
With time's too oft neglected loss, he now
So fast toward action hastes, they could allow
The night scarce time to steal a dark retreat,
Ere, having left that melancholy seat,   260
Devotion's dark retiring place, he goes
To see how much her frowns did discompose
That city's dress, of whom he'd ne'er a sight
Before, but when 'twas polished with delight.
   His arms, bright Honour's burnished robes, into
Such weeds as showed him to the public view
A coarse monastic, changed ; attended by
His aged friend, soon as the morning's eye
Adorned the east, the prosperous prince began
His pious journey ; which, before the sun   270
Blushed in the west, found a successful end
In clouded Corinth. Where arrived they spend,
The hours of the succeeding night to find
How, in that factious troubled sea, inclined
The city stood ; whose shallow sons dare vent
By nothing but their tongues, that discontent
Their hands might cure, were not those useful parts
Restrained from action by unmanly hearts,

Which being at once with grief and fear oppressed,
Durst do no more but pity the distressed; 280
Which gentle passion, since so general, lends
Some light of hope to her inquiring friends.
　　To usher in that dismal day, whose light
Designed to lead into eternal night
As much of beauty as did e'er give place
To death, the morning shows her gloomy face
Wrapped up in clouds, whose heavy vapours had
Hung Heaven in black; when, to perform the sad
And serious office of confessors to
Those royal sufferers whom harsh Fates pursue 290
To Death's dark confines, through their guard of foes
Argalia and his grave assistant goes.
Where he, whose love to neither did surmount
His zeal, to take the Cyprian's last account
Himself addressed; whilst his kind passions lead
Argalia from Pharonnida, to read
Her life's last story, made authentic by
The near approach of her eternity.
　　Entered the room, which to his startled sight
Appeared like sorrow sepulchred in night, 300
So dismal sad, so silent, that the cold
Retreat of death, the grave, did ne'er unfold
A heavier object; by a sickly light,
Which was e'en then to the artificial night
That filled the room resigning 'ts reign, he saw
Grief's fairest draught, divine Pharonnida,
Amidst her tears, fallen like a full-blown flower,
Whose polished leaves, o'erburthened with a shower,
Drops from their beauties in the pride of day
To deck the earth.—So sadly pining lay 310
The pensive princess, whom an ecstasy
Of passion led to practise how to die,
In such abstracted contemplations, that
Angels forsook their thrones to wonder at.
　　Wet with those tears, in whose elixir she
Was bathing of the lilies' nursery,
Her bloodless cheeks—her trembling hand sustained
A book, which, what Heaven's mercy hath ordained
For a support to human frailty in
Storms of·affliction, lay; which, as she'd been 320
Now so well in repentant lectures read,
That Faith was on the wings of Knowledge fled
To Meditation, her unactive grief
Lets softly fall, whilst Time, wise Nature's thief,
That all might look like Sorrow's swarthy night,
Is stealing forth of the neglected light;
Whose sullen flame, as it would sympathize

318 which] for ' *in* which.'

With those quenched beams that once adorned her eyes,
After a feeble blaze, that spoke its strife
But vain, in silence weeps away its life.   330
   Come to behold this beauteous monument
Of mourning passion, his great spirits spent
On love and wonder, the astonished prince
Here silent stands, valour could not convince
His wild amazement. To behold her lie,
By rigid laws restrained from liberty,
To whom his soul was captive, troubles all
His reason's guards : but when, how she must fall
From beauteous youth and virtuous life, to be
One of the grave's obscure society,—   340
Must fall no martyr, whose lamented death
Grows pity's object, but depart with breath
'Mongst ignominious clouds of guilt, that must
Stick an eternal odium on her dust—
That thought transports him from his temper to
Passions, in which he had forgot to do
His priestly office : and, in rage as high
As ever yet inflamed humanity,
Sent him to actions, whose attempt had been
The road his valour must have perished in,   350
Had not her sorrow's agony forsook
The princess. By whose first unsteady look,
He, being as far as his disguise gave leave
Discovered, is invited to receive
Those last confessions, in whose freedom she
Seeks by absolving comforts how to free
Her soul of all which a religious fear
Like spots on her white conscience made appear.
   Having from her unburthened soul learned how
To ease his own, the priestly prince had now,   360
As far as bold humanity durst dive
Into remission, Heaven's prerogative,
Pronounced that pardon for whose seal there stood
The sin-polluted world's redeeming blood :
By which blest voice raised from what did appear
Like sorrow, till her faith had banished fear,
The princess, in such gentle calms of joy
As souls that wear their bodies but to cloy
Celestial flights can feel, to entertain
Her fatal doom with a resolved disdain   370
Of death, prepares. Whilst he, whom Heaven to her
Had made their mercy's happy messenger,
Forsaking her, repairs to him that had
With the same hand the Cyprian's thoughts unclad.
By whom informed, how that in their defence
His sword protected nought but innocence ;

338 when] 'he thinks' has of course to be supplied from 'that thought' below.

Armed with those blessings which so just a cause
Proclaimed his due, he secretly withdraws
To change those emblems of religious peace,
Monastic robes, for such as might increase   380
Their joy and wonder, whose contracted fear
Despaired to see a combatant appear,
Although they knew his sword defended then
The best of causes 'gainst the worst of men.
   Whilst he prepares, with near as much of speed
As incorporeal substances that need
But will for motion, to defend her in
The assaults of death, that hour, which long had been
The dreadful expectation of those friends
That pitied her, arrived, in sorrow ends   390
Fear's cold disease. Those ministers of fate,
The props to all that's illegitimate,
The army, to suppress the weak essays
Of love or pity, guarded had the ways
By which illegal power conducted her
From that dark room, grief's curtained theatre,
To be beheld upon the public stage,
The glory, yet the scandal of the age;
Which two extremes met on the scaffold in
A princess' suffering, and a people's sin.   400
Which now, joined to the dreadful pomp that calls
His subjects to attend the funerals
Of her loved father, whose life's virtues won
Tears for his death, thus solemnly begun.
   Removed no farther from the city then
An hour's short walk, though undertaken when
Sol raged in Cancer, might with ease convey
Scorched travellers, a dismal temple lay,
In a dark valley, where more ancient times
Had perpetrated those religious crimes   410
Of human offerings to those idols that
Their hands made, for their hearts to tremble at.
Yet this, since now made venerable by
Those reverend relics of antiquity,
The Spartan princes' monuments, by those
Of latter times, though altered faith, is chose
For their retreat, when life's extinguished glory
Sought rest beneath a silent dormitory.
Nor stood this fabric all alone; long since
A palace, by some melancholy prince   420
Which hated light, or loved the darkness, built
To please his humour, or conceal his guilt,
So near it stood, to distant eyes which sent
Thither their beams, it seemed one monument;
Whose sable roof 'mongst cypress shadows fills

<hr>

393 Another of the interesting Royalist flashes.

The deep dark basis of those barren hills
With such a mournful majesty, as strook
A terror into each beholder's look,
Awful as if some deity had made
That gloomy vale to be the sacred shade,　　　430
Where he chose in enigmas to relate
The dark decrees of man's uncertain fate.
　Betwixt this temple and the city stood,
In squadrons thick as shows an ancient wood
To distant sight, the army, placed to be
In this sad march their guilt's security;
Whose glittering swords shone, as if drawn to light
Day's beauties to the palace of the night.
Toward which the prisoners, yet detained within
The city, in this dreadful pomp begin　　　440
Their mournful march, led by that doleful call
By which loud war proclaims a funeral.
Those that had been the common guards unto
The murdered princes, to the people's view
Are first presented; on an ebon spear
Each bore a scutcheon, where there did appear
The arms which once adorned those princes' shields,
Sadly displayed within their sable fields.
　Next these, some troops, whose prosperous valour in
Their courts had steps unto preferment been,　　　450
Come slowly on; but slowlier followed are
By elder captains, such whom busy war,
Whose victories had their youth in honour died,
As useless now for council laid aside.
I' the rear of these, the officers of state,
Grave as they'd been of council unto Fate,
I' the purple robes of royal mourners clad,
With heavy pace conducted in a sad
And dismal object—two black chariots, drawn
Like hideous night when it assaults the dawn　　　460
In dreadful shadows; where, to fright the day
With sadder objects, on black herses lay
The effigies of the murdered princes; in
Whose form those spots of treason that had been
Fate's agents to unravel Nature's law,
In bloody marks the mourning people saw.
At which sad sight, from silent sorrow they
Advanced, had let external grief betray
Their love and loss, if not diverted by
Succeeding objects, which assault the eye　　　470
With what, though living, yet more terror bred
Than what they found for the lamented dead.
　In such a garb as sorrow strives to hide
The hot effluviums of a sullen pride,

　474 effluviums] Singer, most improperly, ' effluvia.'

Almanzor next, with slow portentous pace,
Follows the herses; his discovered face
So subtly dyed in sorrow, as it had
Strove to outmourn the sable arms which clad
His falser breast; whose studied treason knew
No such disguise, as first to meet the view   480
O' the censuring people, in a dress that shows
Him by their state's maturer council chose,
'Gainst whoe'er durst maintain the prisoners' cause,
By 's valour for to vindicate their laws.
    But now, to lose these rivulets of tears
In the vast ocean of their grief, appears
Their last and most lamented object, in
The royal captives; whose sad fate had been
Not so disguised in attributes of guilt,
But that the love their former virtue built   490
In every breast, broke through their fear, to show
How much their duty did to sorrow owe.
In that black train they had beheld before,
Though full of sadness, wearied life passed o'er
The stage of Nature, is their darkest text
To comment on; which, since good men perplexed
With life's cares are, finds less regret than now
To living sufferers justly they allow:
Friends, though less near, since death is but that rest
They vainly seek that are in life distrest,   500
Being pitied more than those whose worst of fate
We have beheld destruction terminate.
    That nought might in this scene of sorrow be
Wanting to perfect grief's solemnity,
The kingdom's marshal—who supported in
His hand a sword, which, glittering through a thin
Wreathed cipers, through the sad spectator's eye
Struck such a terror, as if shadowed by
Death's sooty veil—conducting, after goes
The undaunted Cyprian, with a look that shows   510
A soul whose valour was of power to light
Such high resolves as by their splendour might
Make death look lovely; on his upper hand
Her sex's glory, she whose virtues scanned
Her actions by Heaven's strictest rules, the sweet
Pharonnida, unmoved, prepares to meet
The ministers of death, her train being by
Florenza, who must in that tragedy
Act her last part, sustained. The garment which
The beauteous princess did that day enrich,   520

507, 528 cipers] Singer, with more excuse perhaps, 'cyprus.' But where an antique
spelling definitely indicates pronunciation and the modern obscures it, it is probably
better to keep the former.

Was black, but cut on white, o'er which the fair
Neglected treasure of her flowing hair
Hung loosely down; upon her head she wore
A wreath of lilies, almost shadowed o'er
With purple hyacinths, on which the stains
Of murder yet in bloody marks remains;
Over all this, a melancholy cloud
Of thick curled cipers from the head did shroud
Her to the feet, through which those spots of white
Appeared like stars, those comforts of the night,   530
When stole through scattered clouds; in her right hand
She held a watch, whose next stage should have spanned
The minutes of her life; her left did hold
A branch of myrtle, which, as grown too old
To live, began to wither;—for defence
O' the falling leaves, as death and innocence
Had both conspired to save 't, the bough was round
In mystic wreaths of black and silver wound.
    Near to the royal prisoners, many peers
Of either kingdom, men o' the gravest years   540
And loyalest hearts, did with a doleful pace
Bring up the rear; each melancholy place
Through which they passed being with those pensive flowers
That wait on funerals strewed. The lofty towers
Of chequered marble had their stately brows
In sables bound, their pinnacles with boughs
Of dismal yew adorned, as if their knell
Should next be rung; a solemn passing bell
In every church was tolled, whose doleful sound,
Mixed with the drum and trumpet's Dead March, drowned 550
The people's cries, whose grief can ne'er be shown
In 'ts native dress, till loud and clamorous grown.
    In this black pomp the mourning train had left
The sable city, which, being now bereft
Of all her sad and solemn guests, did bear
The emblem of an empty sepulchre,—
So full of silence, all her throng being gone
With heavy pace to be attendants on
Those funeral rites, which ere performed must have
More virtue for attendants to the grave   560
Than e'er they could again expect to see,
Whose hopes of life lay in minority.
    Come to the desert vale, which yet had kept
A solitary loveliness—that slept
There in untroubled rest, a levelled green,
Chose for the lists, which nature lodged between
Two barren hills; upon whose bare front grew,
Though thinly scattered, here a baleful yew,
And there a dismal cypress, placed as they
Had only chose that station to display   570

The people's passions; who, with eyes fixed in
Full orbs of tears, ere this had sorrowing seen
The pitied prisoners to those scaffolds brought,
Where those lamented lives whom treason sought
To ruin, must be sacrificed to please
Ambitious man, not angry Heaven appease.
This curds their bloods, which soon inflamed had grown,
Had not the varied scene of sorrow shown
The murdered princes; who, produced as they
Had been reserved as opiates to allay   580
Their anger's flame, are both exposed unto
The satisfaction of the public view,
Mounted on herses, which, on either side
O' the temple gate, with death's most dismal pride
On ebon pillars stood, as raised to show
What justice did to their destruction owe.

   Placed near to these, their sorrows' sad records,
Almanzor's tent, to show that it affords
For red revenge a close reception, stood
Like a black rock; from whence in clouds of blood   590
The sanguine streamers through the thickened sky
Did waving with unconstant motion fly.
In view of which, though at the other end,
If any durst appear that could defend
Their cause, whom Heaven alone knew innocent,
There to receive him stood an empty tent;
Whose outside, as if fancied to deter
His entrance, there appeared a sepulchre.
Over whose gate her false accusers had
Transcribed those crimes which so unjustly clad   600
In purple sins those candid souls; which seen
In their bright virtue's spotless robes, had been
The hated wonders of those foes, whose ends
Now find success i' the pity of their friends.

   Near this black tent, on mourning scaffolds, where
Death did to encounter Innocence prepare
His heaviest darts, such as were headed by
That more than mortal plagues, foul infamy,
The prisoners mounted. At the other gate,
Almanzor, like the messenger of Fate,   610
Fraught with revenge, appears; his dreadful form,
More full of terror than a midnight storm,
To straitened fleets, appearing to the view
O' the multitude; who, whilst their prayers pursue
The prisoners' safety on the flagging wings
Of sickly hope, his sure destruction brings,

---

577 curds] This is Singer's reading for orig. 'curls' which is not quite impossible
and even rather vivid—for passion meeting and *ruffling* the blood as wind does water.
And if one begins guessing, why not 'cools'?

Since from their knowledge more remote to cure,
Unto their hates' impatient calenture.
  Thrice had their trumpet sadly sounded been,
And thrice a herald's voice had summoned in   620
Some bold defendant; but both yet so vain,
As if just Heaven neglected to maintain
That righteous cause: which sadly seen of all,
The sorrowful but helpless people fall,
Since hopes of life was shrunk into despair,
To be assistant by their private prayer
At death's distracting conflict. In a brief
Effectual speech, which answered to the chief
Heads of 's indictment, in those powerful words
Conceived his last, the Cyprian prince affords   630
Their sorrow yet a larger theme. Which done,
Being first to die, having with prayer begun
That doubtful road, he now a short leave takes
Of all his mourning friends, then calmly shakes
Off each terrestrial thought; and, heightened by
The speculations of eternity
Above those damps, which Nature's hand did weave,
Of human fear, submitting to receive
The fatal stroke, that centre to a crown,
But orb of wit—his sacred head, lays down.   640
  Fled to the dark cell of their utmost fears,
With eyes whose lids were cemented in tears,
Each still spectator's thoughts did now repair
To the last refuge of a silent prayer;
In which close parl, from that deep lethargy
They are to joy and wonder wakened by
A trumpet's voice, which from the other gate
Sounds a defiance. 'Twas not yet so late
In Hope's dim twilight, but they once more may,
In expectation of a glorious day,   650
Dare look abroad; which done, unto their view,
A Cyprian herald being designed unto
That office, they, leading a stranger knight
Into the lists, behold; whose welcome sight
Was entertained with acclamations that
Raised thunder for his foes to tremble at.
  This valiant hero, whose brave gesture gave
Life to that hope which told them Heaven would save
Such suffering virtue, now drawn near unto
The tent, is taking a disdainful view   660
Of that accursed inscription; whilst all eyes,
Centred on him, see through his steel disguise
A goodlier shape, though not so vastly great
As that cursed lump Nature had made the seat
Of 's enemy's black soul. The armour which
He wore, they knew not whether for more rich

(292)

Or rare to prize. The ground of it, as he
For those had mourned which now from infamy
His sword sought to redeem, was black, but all
Enamelled o'er with silver hearts, let fall   670
From flaming clouds ; which hovering above
Them, looked like incense fired by heavenly love :
'Mongst these, in every vacant place, was found
A death's head scattered ; some of which were crowned
With laurel, others on their bare fronts wore
A regal diadem. In's shield he bore,
In a field argent, on the dexter side,
A new-made grave, to which a lamb, denied
Succour on earth, to shun the swift pursuit
Of a fierce wolf, was fled ; but ere one foot   680
Was entered there, from a red cloud, that charged
The field in chief, a thunderbolt, enlarged
By Heaven's just wrath, from's sulphury seat was sent
So swiftly, that what saved the innocent
The guilty slew ; which now in's blood doth lie,
A precedent for powerful tyranny.
   Those short surveys o' the people hardly took,
Ere, having now the unuseful tent forsook,
The brave defendant with a loud salute
Had passed the scaffold in the bold pursuit   690
Of glorious victory ; whom his angry foe,
Whose valour's flame ne'er an allay did know
So cold as fear, in that wild flame which rage
Opposed had kindled, hastens to engage
Him with so high a storm of fury, that,
Each falling stroke, others did tremble at
What they sustained. Strength, valour, judgement, all
Which e'er made conquerors stand, or conquered fall,
Here seemed to meet. As if to outrun desire,
Each nimble stroke, quick as aethereal fire   700
When winged by motion, fell ; yet with a heft
So full of danger, most behind them left
Their bloody marks, which in this fatal strife
Seemed like the opened sallyports of life.
   Sadly expecting whom by Fate would be
This day chose favourite unto destiny,
The people in such silent ecstasies,
As if their souls only informed their eyes,
Sat to behold the combat ; when, to give
Their faith assurance, justice yet did live   710
Unchained by faction, from a fatal blow
Struck near his heart, Almanzor fallen so low
From hopes of victory they beheld, that in
His ruin, what before their fear had been,
Grew now their comfort. When, that speedy death
Might not transport his soul ere his last breath

(293)

Confessed his guilt, the noble champion stays
His just raised rage, whilst his own tongue displays
His thoughts' black curtains, by discovering all
Those crimes, beneath whose burthen he did fall,   720
Heavy as curses which from Heaven are sent
For th' people's plague, or prince's punishment.
In which short close of life, to ease the grief
Of late repentance, that successful thief,
Whose happiest hour his latest proved, being took
For precedent, he in a calm forsook
That world, which, whilst his plots did strive to build
Ambition high, he had with tempests filled.
    The multitude, whose universal voice
Had taught even such, though distant to rejoice,   730
As age or sickness had detained within
The city walls, forced those that yet had been
Her foes, converted by the general votes
For joy, to change their envy's ill-set notes
To calm compliance; in whose concord they,
With as much speed as duty did convey
Her best of subjects, to congratulate
Her freedom hastes. Who, in this smile of fate,
Whilst all her friends strove to forget those fears
Whose form they lately trembled at, appears   740
Shadowed in grief; on whose joy could reflect
No beam of comfort, the supposed neglect
Of her Argalia, whose victorious sword
Did in her fears' extremity afford
Some hopes of comfort, which to opinion lost,
More sorrow than the assaults of death had cost;
Had not, whilst she did in dark passion stray,
His full discovery glorified the day.
    Amidst the people's acclamations, she,
Though from a scaffold now conveyed to be   750
Raised to a crown, all that vain pomp beholds
With eyes o'ercast in grief, till he unfolds
Her further comfort, by discovering what,
Whilst each spectator was admiring at,
Becomes to her so much of joy, that in
This calm, that courage which before had been
Unshook in tempests, now begins to move;
And what scorned hate, submits to powerful love.
From whose fixed centre, with as swift a flight
And kind a welcome, as the nimble light   760
Salutes the morning, Pleasure now imparts
Her powerful beams, until those neighbouring hearts
That lived by Hope's thin diet, drew from hence
Substantial lines to Joy's circumference.
    Her innocence unveiled by his success,
And both by that black foil of wickedness,

Almanzor's guilt, more glorious made, is now
The only volume wonder could allow
Those that before her worst of foes had been,
Sadly to read repentant lectures in.   770
Which seen by her observant peers, that all
Succeeding discords in that tyrant's fall
Might find a tomb, him, being their princess' choice,
The Spartan army's universal voice
Salute their chief. Which precedent affords
A pattern to the wise Epirot lords ;
Who had a law, age made authentic, which
Prohibited their diadem to enrich
A female brow : on him, whose title stood
Nearest of all collateral streams of blood,   780
They wisely fix a choice, which proves to be
Their glory and their state's security.
    And now raised from that lowly posture in
Which fear had left them, the vast rout begin
Their motion toward fair Gerenza ; where
The varied scene did such proportion bear
With joy's exalted harmony, which in
Their rescued princess dwelt, all that had been
Their sorrow's dismal characters they now
Obliterate, and her late clouded brow   790
Crown with delights. The solemn bells, whose sad
Toll, when they left your mourning city, had
Frighted the trembling hearer, now are all
Rung out for joy, as if so loud a call
Only became a love which could not be
Expressed until the full solemnity
Of their approaching nuptials did unite
Their hearts or crowns, not with more full delight
Than what did near as great a blessing prove,
Discording subjects, in your bonds of love.   800
    Thus, after all the wild variety
Through Fate's dark labyrinths, now arrived to be
Crowned with as much content as e'er was known
By any that death did enforce to own
The frailties of mortality, we leave
Our celebrated lovers to receive
Those blessings which Heaven on such kings showers down,
Whose virtues add a lustre to the crown.

792 your] Singer, obviously, 'their' : but strangely enough he leaves 'your' in 800.
The *double* oddity suggests that Chamberlayne originally meant this to form part
of a speech ; then changed his mind, and with his usual equanimity omitted the
necessary adjustment.

806 celebrated] A vivid instance of the correct use of the word as opposed to
the modern vulgarity.

ENGLAND'S JUBILE[E]

[I do not know why Singer did not complete his edition by reprinting this Poem—but perhaps he had not seen it. To me, the tedium of copying it has been not a little alleviated by the interest of its prosody, and of the comparison with Dryden's. As we might expect, both from the fact of its being an address, not a narrative, and from its composition being later than at least the earlier part of *Pharonnida*, the stopped, or nearly stopped couplet is much more in evidence than the enjambed, though this latter is also common enough. And the good side of the change has sufficient exemplification—there are some couplets, and more lines, of the new stamp, of which Dryden himself need not have been ashamed. The older side is not so well shown : for the flowing similes and conceits which it so well suited would have been out of place. But the poem has vigour, adequacy, and not more than a proper share of exaggeration, where required. It is certainly the best of the poems on the Restoration next to Dryden's[1].—ED.]

[1] The British Museum copy has no title-page.

ENGLAND'S JUBILE :

OR, A POEM ON THE HAPPY RETURN OF
HIS SACRED MAJESTY, CHARLES THE II

To the King's Most Sacred Majesty.

Pardon, great Prince, for all our offering here,
But weak discoveries of our wants appear.
No language is commensurate with thee,
Our loftiest flights but plain humility.
Yet since we may, our frailty to conceal,
Be guilty of a crime in smothering zeal,
That bids thy blest returns more welcome then
Plenty to the starved, or land to shipwrackt men.
For such were we, or if there's ought can more
Demonstrate ill, that wo was ours before.   10
Heaven, to restore our lost light, sent us him,
Without whose raise our sphere had still been dim.
Dim as in that dark interval, when we
Saw nothing but the clouds of anarchy,
Raised by the witchcraft of Rebellion, to
So vast a height, none durst pretend to view,
Whilst they lay curtained in that black disguise,
Majestic beams, but 'twas with bloodshot eyes.
   Then if such of necessity must pine,
Who 're robbed of food, both human and divine,   20
How could we thrive, when those that did pretend
To feed did all on their ambition spend.
Who with the sword, not reason, did convince,
And rackt the subject to unthrone the Prince.
The doleful years of thy exile have been
At once our Nation's punishment and sin :
Tost in a storm of dark afflictions we
Floated at random, yet still looked on thee
As our safe harbour, but had none to guide
Us to 't; False pilots with the winds complied.   30
We saw what crime drenched the amazèd rout,
Yet wanted strength to cast that curst thing out.

---

7 then] then = than.   12 raise] raise = rise.
30 pilots] Orig. 'Pilates,' with a possible play (?), though, as we have seen in
Pharonnida, the mere misprint is common.

Though oft 'twas vainly struggled for, yet we—
Who were exiled from nought but Liberty,
Who durst live here spectators of those times,
Do now in tears repent our passive crimes,
And with one universal voice allow
We all deserve death, since we live till now.
    But this is England's Jubilee, nor must
Thy friends doubt mercy, where thy foes dare trust.   40
Thou art our great Panpharmacon, which by
Its virtue cures each various malady,
Giving their pride a cool allay of fears,
Whilst to restore our hectic, Hope appears :
And these began the cure, which to complete
Expansive Mercy makes thy throne her seat :
So that there now (except the guilt within)
No sign remains there hath a difference been.
    The giddy rout, who in their first address,
Cried Liberty, but meant licentiousness,   50
When depraved judgements, not content to see
A heaven of stars their *primum mobile*,
Did change the system, and i' th' spite o' th' love
Or fear of Heaven, taught earth's base dregs to move
In the bright orb of Honour, where to all
That's great, or good, they were eccentrical—
Having long found their direful influence
In nought but plagues descended—did from thence
Learn sad repentant lectures, and dare now
Present the sword, where late the knee did bow :   60
Dare tell their damn'd impostors they but made
False Zeal the light, whilst Treason cast the shade :
Dare curse their new discoveries which placed in
Hell's geography Americas of sin.
    But these, like dust raised 'twixt two armies, do
Hurt or assist, as they are hurried to
Either by levity ; and therefore must
By none be held an object of their trust ;
For though they are Usurpers' Lands, they've found
They rent at night, what they i' th' morning crowned.   70
    But you, great Sir, whose fate has been so mixt
As to behold these volatile and fixt,
May, since the offspring of their sufferings, be
More certain of their future loyalty.
And though your title, and heaven-settled state,
Needs not, usurper-like, measure your fate
By such vain love, yet may you still be sure
They'll ne'er again a rebel's scourge endure.
    These past years of infatuation, which
Hath drained their coffers, did their hearts enrich   80
With so much eager loyalty that when
With wonder—like those new recovered men,

Who, by Our Saviour's miracles escaped
From darkness, thought men had like trees been shaped—
They only through mist rarefied, gazed at
Those glimmering beams, whilest they knew not what
Th' event would be, now, winged with hope, did they
Each feeble· glance praise as approaching day.
　But when, with such advantage as the light
Gains, by succeeding the black dress of night,　　　　90
Through all the fogs of their preceding fear,
They from the North saw loyal Monk appear,
How in petitions did their prayers exhale
To waft him on, until the gentle gale
(Although by ways so wisely intricate
They raised our fear whilst they did calm our fate)
Brought him at length through all our doubts to be
The great assertor of our liberty!
Then did we think that modest blush but just,
Whose present dye displayed our late mistrust.　　　　100
And to requite those injuries we'd done
To myriads raised what single praise begun.
　　Through all the devious paths which he did tread,
From the base Rump unto the glorious Head,
We scanned his actions, which did nought comprise
That might offend, but that he was too wise
For vulgar judgements, whose weak fancies guessed
By present actions what would be the rest.
　But when their eyes unveiled, discovered who
Had, to destroy the monster, found the clew,　　　　110
How did they praise his wisdom, valour, all
That could within the name of subject fall,
And to complete whate'er his due might be,
Knit up those laurels with his loyalty—
That noble virtue, without which the rest
Had only burdened, not adorned, his crest.
Then since we now by this heaven-guided hand
Once more behold the glory of our land,
Whom midnight plots long studied to exclude
Again fixed in 's meridian altitude,　　　　120
Let's cease to mourn, and whilst those fogs attend
Such miscreant wretches as dare still offend
By flying mercy, raise our souls, deprest
E'er since this Star set in the gloomy West—
For then begun that dreadful night, which we
Have since with terror seen, brave Loyalty
Being so opprest by a prevailing fate
'Twas only known by being unfortunate.
　　Yet, though Rebellion in unnatural wars
So far did thrive, to prove us falling stars,　　　　130

　　　88 glance] one might expect ' glimpse.'

The wiser world saw those that did aspire,
Not as Heaven's lamps, but Hell's impetuous fire.
As monsters of ambition, such whose wild
Chimeras since Rebellion first defiled
Our English annals, only were advanced;
But Fortune's light ephemeras, to be glanced
A while with secret envy on, and then
Hurled from the ill-managed helm to be by men
Pursued with such a just deservèd hate
As makes each curse add weights unto their fate,   140
Horrid as are their names, which ne'er shall be
Mentioned without adjuncts of infamy
So full of guilt, all ages to ensue
Shall weep to hear what this ne'er blushed to do.
   Whilst we were in these uncouth shades o'ercast
To tell what wild meanders hath been past
By thee, our Royal Sovereign, is a task
That would the tongues of inspired angels ask:
Yet since domestic miseries hath taught
Us part of the sad story's ruder draught,   150
We may, by weak reflection, come to see
With what dire weight these dark storms fell on thee:
Who, whilst thou didst, from hence excluded, stand
The pitied wonder of each foreign land,
Learnd'st, by commanding passions, how to sway
A nation more rebellious far than they.
So that the school which thou wert tutored in,
Though thy disease, our antidote hath been—
We suffering not our crime's desert, because
From hence you learned to pity, and the laws'   160
Just harness with such candour mitigate
As once you bore the rigour of your fate.
   What earthquakes breeds it in our breasts, when we
But think o'er thy progressive misery!
How thou, our restless dove, seeing no mark
Of land, wert hurried from our floating ark,
And, whilst those villains, that exposed thee, lay
Forced every wind of faction to obey,
Wert long with billows of affliction beat
Ere thou didst with thy olive-branch retreat.   170
How by poor friends and powerful enemies,
By flattering strangers, and by false allies,
Were thy afflictions varied, for all these
Shared in the complicating thy disease.
   Like doleful mourners that surround the bed
Of a departing friend, those few that fled

---

161 harness] Orig. 'harnesse': but it is almost certainly a misprint for 'har*d*ness.'
candour] With the sense of 'mildness.' Thus 'a *candid* critic' used to mean, what it
scarcely does now, a favourable and polite censor.

Hence on the wings of Loyalty, to be
Partakers of whate'er attended thee—
Whilst they did mourn, but could not lend relief
Did by their sorrow but increase thy grief.　　　180
　　Such was the power of thy prescribing foes,
No place afforded safety, some of those
Whom poverty sent to attend thy train
To cure that malady, did entertain
Infectious counsels, which did festering lie
Till rebels' gold outweighed their Loyalty,
And from the black pernicious Embryo bred
Monsters whose hands strove to destroy their head.
　　Nor whilst these secret sorrows sunk a mine
Which, if not hindered by a power divine,　　　190
Had blown up all thy patience, wert thou free
From public injuries—that amity,
Which former leagues, or the more sacred ties
Of blood could claim, veiled in the base disguise
Of policy starts back, and doth give way
For treason to expel or else betray.
Great birth and virtues which did that excel
As the meridian doth each parallel,
Are but weak props : a rebel's threats convince
And all avoid a persecuted Prince.　　　200
　　When after these big storms of ill abroad
Some loyal subjects had prepared the road
Unto thy throne, and thou didst once more here
Armed for redemption of thy crown appear,
Whilst all our hearts, whose distant Lands could not
Come to assist thy righteous cause, waxed hot
With loyal hopes—how were we planet-strook
When Fortune, with pretended friends forsook
Thy side at fatal Worcester, and to raise
A rebel's trophies, robbed thee of thy bays !　　　210
How dismal sad, how gloomy was each thought
Of thy obedient subjects, whilst they sought
Their flying Sovereign, curtained from their eyes,
In the dark dress of an unsafe disguise !
All wished to know, what all desire should be
A secret kept, such strange variety
Of contradictions did our passions twist :
We would behold the Sun, yet praised the mist.
But whilst Desire thus shot at rovers, that
More powerful sacrifice our prayers being at　　　220
Heaven's penetrated ear directed, found
Our hopes by thy deserting us near crowned.

192 that] = ' so that.'   Orig. has 'amit*ies*,' which is obviously wrong and easily
accounted for.
222 crowned] Orig. absurdly, 'Crown.'

For though to want thee was our great'st distress,
Yet now thy absence was our happiness.
    Then, though we ne'er enough can celebrate
The praise of this, yet thy mysterious fate,
Great favourite of Heaven! so often hath
Advanced our wonder that the long trod path
Directs us now without more guides to see
Those miracles wrought in preserving thee   230
Were God's immediate acts, to whose intents
Were often fitted weakest instruments,
From whose success faith this impression bore,
He that preserved thee would at length restore,
Which now through such a labyrinth is done,
We see the end, ere know how 'twas begun.
    That big-bulked cloud of poisonous vapours in
Whose dismal shades, our liberty had been
Long in amaze of errors lost, was by
A wholesome northern gale enforcèd to fly   240
Easy as morning mists, so that the fate
Seem'd not more strange, which did at first create,
Than what did now destroy in it, did appear
As far from Hope, as was the first from Fear.
    When a rebellious tyranny had been
So strengthened by a prosperous growth in sin
That the contagious leprosy had left
None sound but what were honest by their theft—
Then to behold that hydra, which had bred
So many, in an instant, her last head   250
Submit to justice, is a blessing we
Must praise i' th' raptures of an ecstasy,
Till from the pleasing trance, being welcomed by
Loud acclamations, raised from Loyalty,
We come, we come, with all the reverence due
To Heaven's best gifts, great Prince, to welcome you—
You, who by suffering in a righteous cause
Safely restored that Liberty, those Laws,
Which after long convulsive fits were now
Expiring, so that future times, told how   260
This great work was performed, shall wonder most
To see the fever cured, yet no blood lost.
    But these are mercies fit to usher in
Him to a throne, whose virtuous life hath been
Beyond detraction good: therefore attend
Those joys which Heaven to us, by you, did send:
Whose sacred essence, waited on by all
The most transcendant blessings that can fall,
Within the sphere of human virtue, still
Surround your throne! May all imagined ill   270

243 in it] If the poem were less badly printed, the extended form 'in it' for the usual 'in 't' would have prosodic interest: but it is probably mere accident.

Die in the embryo! May no dark disguise
Of seeming friends, or foes that temporize,
E'er prejudice your peace! May your foes prove
All blushing converts! May all those that love
You do 't for zeal, not gain ; and though that we
(What was of late your mark) our poverty
Are still enforced to wear, oh may there thence
Ne'er spring a thought to take or give offence!
May all toward you be fraughted with desires
That may in flaming zeal outblaze the fires   280
That you were welcomed in with! May delight
Within your royal breast no opposite
E're find, but so let gentle pleasure grow,
That it may kiss the banks, but ne'er o'erflow!
When Hymen leads you to the temple, let
It be to take that gem which Heaven hath set
The world's adorning ornament—that we
May by that blest conjunction's influence see
Such hopeful fruit spring from our royal stem
As may deserve the whole world's diadem.   290
May Peace adorn your throne! Yet if the sword
Must needs be drawn, may it no sound afford
But victory, until extended power
Adds weight unto your sceptre! May no hour
E'en set a seal to the records of Time,
But what still makes your pleasure more sublime,
Till they, being grown too pure for earth, shall be
Called to the triumphs of Eternity!

By WILL. CHAMBERLAINE.

London, Printed for Robert Clavell
at the Stags-head in St. Pauls
Church yard, 1660.

292 sound] So in orig.
299 Chamberlaine] So *here* in orig.   In *Pharonnida* 'Chamberlayne.'

THEOPHILA,

OR

LOVES SACRIFICE.

A

Divine Poem.

WRITTEN BY *E. B.* Esq;

Several *Parts* thereof set to fit *Aires* by M*r* *J. JENKINS*.

Longum Iter per Præcepta, *breve & efficax per* Exempla,
Si Præceptis *non accendimur, saltem* Exemplis *incitemur, atq̃ in*
Appetitu Rectitudinis *nil sibi* Mens *nostra difficile æstimet,*
quod perfectè peragi ab Aliis *videt.* Greg.Mag. l. 9. c. 43.
Id peragas Vitâ, *quod velles* Morte *peractum.*

LONDON,
Printed by *R. N.* Sold by *Henry Seile* in *Fleetstreet,* and
Humphrey Moseley at the Princes Arms in S. *Pauls*
Church-yard. 1652.

INTRODUCTION TO
EDWARD BENLOWES

THE fate of Benlowes has been one of the hardest in the history of English poetry. Such approval as he met with, in his own time and from persons likely to sympathize with his general way of writing, was chiefly interested; he was savagely though very amusingly satirized by the greatest satirist, save one, of his own later day; he came in, long after his death, for sneers, suppressed and not suppressed, from Pope, as well as for a gratuitous salutation from Warburton's bludgeon[1]; and at the Romantic revival he was almost entirely passed over. Neither Ellis nor Campbell, who were both pretty equitable to the Caroline poets, gave him admission: even Southey, so far as I remember, lets him alone, which is a pretty clear sign that he did not know him. Of late he has received more attention. But most of it has been of the unsatisfactory bibliographical character, little calculated to allay the thirst of the clear spirit in life or after death: and most, even of this, has been due to the very cause which (it may be more than suspected) has made Benlowes so rare. At one time (see biographical note[2]), he was a rich man or at least well-to-do, and with the nascent interest in art which distinguished the Cavalier party, from the King downwards, he

---

[1] Notices of Benlowes have been apt to dwell only on Warburton's note at *Dunc.* iii. 21 which hits our poet's *titles*. But Pope himself, probably from some traditional Roman Catholic grudge at the convert-revert, had set the example. The actual passage just cited is not crushing:

> Benlowes, propitious still to blockheads, bows.

But he had thought of including in *Prol. Sat.* the couplet:

> How pleased I see some patron to each scrub;
> Quarles had his Benlowes, Tibbald has his Bubb.

with the note, at l. 250,—A gentleman of Oxford who patronized all bad poets of that reign.

[2] Information about Benlowes is mainly derived from Anthony Wood, with some slight supplements. According to it, he was born about 1603, the son and heir of a man of fortune who owned Brent Hall, in Essex. He was sent to St. John's College, Cambridge, in 1620; and after leaving the University, made the grand tour. Some say that he was brought up a Roman Catholic; others that he adopted Roman Catholicism abroad; but it is agreed that he died a faithful Anglican. According to Butler he served in the Civil War, which may have assisted his lavishness to friends and relations, and his expenditure on collecting and otherwise, in producing that exhaustion of his fortune which is also agreed upon. He spent the last eight years of his life at Oxford, making good use of the Bodleian, but (according to Wood) in a state of great poverty, which (on the same authority) even shortened his life by insufficient provision of food and firing during a severe winter. At any rate he died in December, 1676, aged seventy-three, and was buried in St. Mary's. Hazlitt attributes to him eight other works besides *Theophila*, and the *Dictionary of National Biography* ten with a possible eleventh; but all of these are short and most of them are in Latin.

set himself to embellish his principal work, *Theophila*, in a manner very uncommon before his time. An uncertain number (for hardly any two copies agree, and the tale seems to vary from six-and-thirty downwards) of illustrations—sometimes separate, sometimes in the text, and ranging from more than full folio plates to two-inch-square vignettes—decorate the poem. These have in most instances been ruthlessly ravished from it—often, in the case of those backing matter, to the mutilation of the text, and almost always to the danger and disintegration of the book. It is also probable that no very large number of copies was printed, while the poem was never reissued : so that its rarity is not surprising.

But rarity is very far from being always or necessarily a cause of neglect. On the contrary, it notoriously, and very often, serves as a direct attraction and stimulant to reprinters. It is more difficult to know whether to admit or disallow as a *vera causa* of Benlowes' obscurity, the fantastic ingenuity (as 'metaphysical' in reality as its prey) of Butler's attack. A similar combination of rarity and satire has had no doubt much to do with Shadwell's practical occultation : but this was never so complete as that of Benlowes, and moreover Dryden's consummate art had contrived to kill even curiosity about his victim. For few people care to explore simple and unmitigated dulness. There was something—at least after the eighteenth century was over—which might have excited, instead of quenching, this curiosity in Butler's 'Character of a Small Poet' where, after several pages of general ridicule, Benlowes is gibbetted by name. The woes of Mr. Prynne— when having put a new hat in a hat-box which had been unfortunately lined with leaves from *Theophila*, or something else of its author's, he suffered from singing in the head, vertigo, and even after blood-letting, a tendency to write harsh poetry ; the poet's mastery of high-rope 'wit' and low-rope wit alike ; his improvement on altars and pyramids by frying-pans and gridirons in verse ; his troop-horse's furniture 'all in beaten poetry' ; the fatal effect of his printed sheets even upon tobacco ; his Macaronic Latin and so forth :—these are things which might rather tempt at least a slight exploration than discourage it. One does not object to a glimpse, at any rate, of the extravagant and absurd ; though one may have a holy horror of the merely dull. And as for Warburton nobody, even in his own time, took him for much of an authority on poetry : while his condemnation was rather likely to serve as a commendation, after the beginning of the nineteenth century, to anybody except the neoclassic remnant, whether the individual took his ideas of poetry from Coleridge or from Wordsworth, from Southey or from Byron, from Shelley or from Keats.

We shall hardly be epigrammatic out of season if we solve or evade the difficulty by saying that accident probably assisted rarity, and that Benlowes himself certainly assisted Butler. He has done (except in the

Introduction

matter of the sculpturesque embellishments which have so often disappeared) almost everything he could to 'fence his table' against at least modern readers. Some (let it be hoped not too many) would drop off at once on perceiving that 'Theophila' is but a name for the soul, in its mystical status as the bride of Christ. More might faint at the prospect before them on coming to the information in the Preface that 'The glorious projection and transfusion of ethereal light, both in the Sun and the six magnitudes, constitute, by astronomical computation, more than 300 suns upward to the Empyrean Heaven. A star in the Equator makes 12,598,666 miles in an hour, which is 209,994 miles in a minute, a motion quicker than thought.' For even Dante, though he may double Theology with Astronomy, does not cumulate both with Arithmetic in this fashion. And of those who still hold their course, across prefaces and prefatory poems, to the actual text, not a few more may break down at or a little past the gateway.

Benlowes has chosen one of the most awkward stanzas (if it is to be called a stanza) possible—a triplet composed of decasyllable, octosyllable, and alexandrine—the jolt of which only after long familiarity becomes rhythmical even to the most patient and experienced ear, and never reaches a perfect charm. These triplets are monorhymed : but the author begins with three on the same sound, and never expresses the slightest consideration as to symphonic or symmetrical effect in rhyme. He showers italics and capitals in a fashion which might give pause to the sternest stickler for literal typographic reproduction. But undoubtedly the most serious objects of distaste are likely to be found, where Butler long ago found them, in his style—taking that word in the wide sense which admits both diction and expression of thought.

Even before arriving at these one may quarrel (far from captiously) at his general plan and *ordonnance*. Despite more than one declaration of the author's design, explicit enough in intention, it is very difficult to put this design with any intelligible brevity : and his introductory panegyrists in verse take very good care not to attempt it. The Praelibation, Humiliation, Restoration, Inamoration, Representation, Contemplation, Admiration, Recapitulation, Translations, Abnegation, Disincantation, Segregation, Reinvitation, and Termination—as the several Cantos are headed— refuse reduction to any common denomination except perhaps this :—'a very discursive treatise on mystical theology and passions of the soul, succeeded by an equally discursive comment on the sins of the flesh.' The author adopts as his vehicle sometimes English, sometimes Latin, sometimes both in face-to-face translation. The mere lexicon of the vernacular parts is distinctively Caroline : out-of-the-way catchwords such as 'remora' and 'enthean,' both of which he shares with Chamberlayne, being alternated with extremely familiar phrases and archaisms, as well as with the hideous abbreviations ('who's days' for 'who his days' and the like), which are the greatest blot upon the poetry of this time. He coins pretty freely (e. g. 'angelence' in a very early and by no means bad stanza) and one of the things which shocked Butler was the certainly tremendous Macaronic invention of *hypocondruncicus* : while one can imagine the almost stuttering rage of some critics to-day at such another word as ' Proteustant,' for the Covenanters. But, on the whole, his licences this way, though considerable and no doubt excessive, are certainly less frequent, if perhaps to the grave and precise more shocking, than the irresponsible and irrepressible libertinism of his composition as regards clause and sentence, material and contexture.

The late Greek rhetoricians, in that mania for subdividing and labelling figures which Quintilian soberly ridicules, might have lost themselves in endeavouring to devise tickets for the subdivisions of Benlowes' indulgence in good, or hectic, or horse-playful, conceit. Already the twentieth couplet of the ' Praelibation ' provides us with this :—

> Each gallon breeds a ruby ;—drawer ! score 'um—
> Cheeks dyed in claret seem o' th' quorum,
> When our nose-carbuncles, like link-boys, blaze before 'um.

But an even less dignified use of ' the *blushing* grape of *western* France ' occurs later :—

> War hath our lukewarm *claret* broach'd with spears

where it would be really interesting to know whether there is an earlier instance of the 'fancy' use of the word. It would not be easy to find a wilder welter of forced metaphors than here :—

> Betimes, when keen-breath'd winds, with frosty cream,
> Periwig bald trees, glaze tattling stream :
> For May-games past, white-sheet *peccavi* is Winter's theme [1].

And he surpasses even his usual quaintness when he concludes a long interruption of Theophila's address to him on heavenly things in the Fifth Canto :—

> Fond that I am to speak. Pass on to bliss,
> That with an individual kiss
> Greets thee for ever ! Pardon this parenthesis.

[1] Of course Benlowes, though he added the absurdity of 'cream,' borrowed this from the famous *locus* of Sylvester which Dryden ridicules in the Dedication to *The Spanish Friar*. But what is even more noteworthy, and to my knowledge has never yet been noted, is that Dryden himself, in the error which Scott has detected in quoting 'And periwig with *snow* the bald-pate woods' for Sylvester's 'wool' has been anticipated by Benlowes in another passage of *Theophila*,

> When periwigg'd with snow 's each bald-pate wood.

Now, Dryden, who was twenty-one when *Theophila* came out, and was probably not past the stage when he wrote the ' Lines on Lord Hastings,' may very likely have read Benlowes himself.

Introduction

He does not hesitate to rhyme 'Hades' to 'Shades' and will draw
attention in the margin, with modest pride, to a *versus cancrinus* (it is in
Latin), that is to say one which reads the same with the letters taken
backwards or forwards. I have thought it well to make no secret or
'abscondence' of these absurdities. They are such, and there are many others;
indeed, the man who could commit some of them evidently could not have
guarded himself against others if he would, and perhaps would not if he
could. If any be of the mood of Butler on this particular occasion (for as
I have hinted above his own method is often only that of Benlowes
changed from unconscious indulgence to conscientious and deliberate
utilization for comic effect), or of Boileau always, he had better abstain from
Benlowes. For 'awful examples' of the metaphysical gone mad are on
record plentifully already, and there is no need to do again what Johnson
did sufficiently more than a hundred years ago in the *Life of Cowley*.
Indeed, I do not know, despite the greater sureness of Crashaw's command
of poetical expression, that Benlowes has ever gone beyond Crashaw when
he pictured the eyes of St. Mary Magdalen as walking baths and portable
oceans, though modern practice has brought out an extra whimsicality
for us in this. But the arguments which have been sketched in the
General Introduction apply here with special force. We know that
Crashaw was not a fool; and, though there is no reason for adopting the
opinions of parasites and pensioners [1] about Benlowes, there is nearly as
little for agreeing with Butler that our poet was one. We come in him
to one of the most remarkable examples provided by English literature of
the extreme autumn of the Elizabethan *annus mirabilis*. The belief in
conceits is as strong as ever : and though the power of producing them poeti-
cally is dying down, and except for flickers has almost died, a fresh, deliberate,
critical, belief in *furor poeticus* has come to blow the embers. There is still
a too exclusive reliance on one of the great pair of poetic instruments—
the method of making the unfamiliar acceptable, of procuring a welcome for
the strange. But the exercise and employment of this is forced, mechanical,
what was called two hundred years later, in a fresh though only momentary
revival of the circumstances, 'spasmodic.' One perfectly understands how,
in presence of such things, men, especially not feeling any particular
enthusiasm themselves, turned to the *other* method—the method of raising
and inspiring the familiar, the ordinary, the common-sense. And one
understands with scarcely less fulness and ease why men like Butler felt
their own sense of the ridiculous stimulated and, as it were, exacerbated by
the consciousness (half-conscious as it might be) that it was their own
method which was thus caricatured and brought into contempt—that their
own matters were at stake, or at least one side of them. Meanwhile the

[1] Who anagrammatized his name into 'Benevolus,' and swallowed up his fortune.

other side—that which leant to the new dispensation of Prose and Sense—
was wholly and genuinely hostile to all the works, all the spirit, all the
tastes, methods, intellectual habits of persons like the author of *Theophila*.
The opportunity of such understanding is not fully provided till we know
these persons in their own work—in that 'horse-furniture of beaten poetry'
in which they ambled and jingled across the stage.

But we are, or ought to be, more disinterested now than Butler or even
Dryden, though it is unnecessary to repeat what should have been said on
this head before. And Benlowes, besides his interest of absurdity—his
mere helotry which, though it might almost suffice for some, cannot be
expected to do so for all—has other and less dubious claims. The earlier,
larger, and better part of his poem is a really remarkable, and beyond all
reasonable doubt a perfectly genuine, example of that glowing intensity of
mystical devotion which plays, like a sort of Aurora, on the Anglican
High Churchmanship of the seventeenth century, and has made it, to some,
one of the most attractive phases of religious emotion to be found in all
history. It may be prejudice or partisanship, but there seems to me some
reason for connecting Benlowes' return to Anglican orthodoxy, as contrasted
with Crashaw's permanent estrangement, with the freedom from over-
lusciousness which is remarkable in the lesser poet. Benlowes is afraid
of no metaphor, however extravagant and however doubtful in point of
taste : but his metaphors are not, to use the Persian criticism,

> Limber in loin and liquid on the lip

like those of some others. His 'Clevelandisms,' his astonishing contortions
and bizarrenesses of thought and phrase, are not more incompatible with
true and intense piety than some to be found in the poetical books of
the Bible, and even no doubt, to some extent, owe suggestions to them.
Those who insist upon 'sanity' as the first and last distinction of religion
cannot like him ; but they will find (and as is notorious enough have found)
not very much less difficulty with a rather formidable body of Prophets,
Saints, Apostles, Fathers, Divine Poets, from the earliest and the latest
days of Christianity.

Coming to still closer quarters, the eccentricity of *Theophila* does not
prevent it from containing not a few passages, sometimes of length, that
require very little allowance or apology from any tolerably catholic-tasted
reader of poetry. There is a fine outburst, justifying its own pretty phrase,

> The opal-coloured dawns raise fancy high,

beginning at stanza LXIII of the 'Praelibation' itself ; another, fantastic
enough but not uncharming, on Theophila in penance, at Canto II. LXX sq.
Theophila's Love-Song, in the six-lined stanza, shows at once the relief from

the stricture of the blood caused by the 'cross-gartered' triplet which Benlowes has perversely used elsewhere ; the address to the Ancient of Days at vi. LII sq. is really impressive (one rather likes the idea of Blake illustrating Benlowes anew) and at the end there is a delightful country-and-evening piece to match the opal-coloured dawns of the opening.

But (as was once said in a phrase which, as it happens, chimes in with the Latin anagram that cost Benlowes part of his fortune), apologies are things which *lectori benevolo supervacanea, nihil curat malevolus.* It is at any rate open to the former, as well as to the latter, to treat this poet each after his own kind.

In the setting up of *Pharonnida* Singer's reprint, already modernized in spelling, was utilized ; but as *Theophila* is printed directly from the original it may be desirable to explain the principles of orthography which have been observed here, and will be observed in similar cases. I am, of course, well aware that there is, as there has long been, a habit of demanding adherence to original spelling, and of regarding those editions which comply with this demand as ' scholarly,' and those which do not as ' slovenly.' I disagree with the opinion and decline to comply with the demand. As a matter of fact, the retention of the old spelling gives the editor very little trouble, and the alteration of it a very great deal. But this is nothing. In the first place there is no real reason, in the case of any writer at any rate later than the beginning of the seventeenth century, for throwing in the way of the modern reader an unnecessary obstacle to enjoyment. In the second place, and in the case of such authors as those with whom we are now dealing, the advantage of the original spelling, even to the severest reader for knowledge and not enjoyment, is almost infinitesimally small. I have before writing these words carefully gone over a page, selected at random, of the text which follows. It contains twenty-six lines, and in round numbers over two hundred words. Of these (putting some classes of typographical peculiarity, to be mentioned presently, aside) exactly *eight* and *eight* only are spelt differently from our present system, and these differences supply us with the immensely important and interesting knowledge that 'less' was spelt ' less*e* (twice), that adjectives like ' natural' were spelt with two *l's* (twice), that ' obey ' was sometimes spelt ' obay,' that ' wild ' and ' find ' had a final *e* ; and that the contraction of ' over ' was carelessly written ' o're ' [1]. Of the *general* variations, the habit of beginning nouns with a capital can be neither surprising nor instructive to any one who has interest enough in English literature to open such a book as this : and it frets the eyes of some who have a good deal of such interest. The other habit of frequent

---

[1] By no means always. Those who think that each spelling should be registered, may also regret evidence that ' gem ' and ' jem ' were used according to the taste and fancy of the moment and the person ; and that ' to Day ' with a capital, and ' to morrow ' without, occur in the same line.

italicizing (*without* personification or the like) has a still more fretting effect, and is very difficult to reduce to any logical system ; while though the presence of apostrophes in such words as ' pow'r ' is undoubtedly important as showing metrical theory, and is therefore kept here, the absence of it in the genitive case is again fretting and sometimes confusing, so that it is worth correction. The same is not quite the case with Benlowes' frequent habit of printing whole words in capitals : and this is therefore frequently retained. But in those other things, general and particular, nothing is gained by the reproduction of what were in most cases mere arbitrary printers' caprices or fashions. And even putting aside, as a question not to be disputed, the question which makes the prettier page, there can be little dispute that retention of such things prevents that *horizontal* study of English poetry—that taking it all on equal terms—which some think the great *desideratum* and *desiderandum*. We want these things to be regarded as poems, not as curiosities and *bric-à-brac*. You cannot modernize Chaucer without loss, because his language itself is not modern: you cannot modernize Chatterton without unfairness, because his archaism was part of his deliberate method. But Chamberlayne and Benlowes lose (except in the very rarest instances) nothing at all and may gain something : while innumerable instances—whole lines, whole stanzas, whole passages, present not a single actual variation from modern practice except the initial capital. And the extraordinary 'harlequin' effect of the original printing of *Theophila*, of which a specimen is given, emphasizes unduly, for modern readers, the already sufficient eccentricity of the text. In every case where there is the slightest direct or indirect interest, historical, phonetic in the good sense, prosodic, grammatical, or other, attention will be drawn in the notes to the original spelling. Elsewhere, that method will be adopted which will give the poetry the best chance of producing any poetical effect of which it is capable.

After examining the minor poems attributed to Benlowes, I have decided to add only *two*, to *Theophila*. Most, as said above, are wholly in Latin ; and though I did not think it fit to exclude the Latin parts of his *magnum opus* there is no reason for including these. Some are very doubtfully his :—the initials E. B. being treacherous. The *Summary of Wisdom*, however, in a hundred triplets of the *Theophila* stamp, though it duplicates that poem largely does not do so wholly, and should therefore be given ; while the little musical piece which follows it is fresh, pleasing, and very characteristic [1].

---

[1] I may perhaps refer to an article of mine on Benlowes in *The* [American] *Bibliographer* (New York, Jan. 1903) at the end of which is an elaborate collation, text and plates, of an unusually complete copy of *Theophila* by Miss Carolyn Shipman.

Mens Authoris [1]

TE, mi CHRISTE, Tuæq̃ canam Suf-piria SPONSÆ;
ARDORESq̃ pios, & GAUDIA cælica, Mundo
Abdita; divinæ pandam MYSTERIA Mentis,
Accenfasq̃ Faces CŒLO! Fuge, cæca Libido,
Et Faftus populator Opum, Livorq̃ secundis
Pallidus, & rabidis violenta Calumnia Dictis,
Diraq̃ pacatas lacerans Difcordia Mentes,
Et Scelerum male-fuada Cohors. TE, mitis IESV,
Da mihi velle fequi! Greffus alato fequentis!
DIVINÆ fum tefta ROTÆ; Vas obline fido

Rimofum Gypfo, fic Vas ego reddar Honoris:
Sum tenebrofa Tui radiantis LUMINIS umbra,
Quod, veniente Die, quod, decedente, viderem!
Cujus nec VISUS Spatium, nec GLORIA Laudem,
Nec VOX ulla capit MERITUM, nec TERMINUS Ævum!
Unius est in Verba fatis juraffe MAGISTRI,
Et TE præfentem Causæ petiiffe PATRONUM!

Thema fit Æthereo facranda THEOPHILA TEMPLO,
Pura repurgato folvens LIBAMINA Corde.

The Author's Design

OF CHRIST, and of the SPOUSE'S sighs, I sing,
And of the joys that from those ardours spring,
The world ne'er knew; of her soul's mystic sense,
And of her heav'nly zeal. Blind Lust, pack hence,
Hence Pride, exhausting Wealth; hence, Envy, fly,
Pal'd at success; hence foul-mouth'd Calumny,
And savage Discord, striving to divide
United minds; with all Sin's troop beside.
JESUS! grant I may follow THEE, my feet
Wing THOU, and make them in pursuance fleet!

Close up my cracks by faith, so shall I be
A vessel made of honour unto THEE.
I'm but a faint resultance from Thy light,
Which, at Sol's rise and set, encheers my sight.
No space Thy view, no glory bounds Thy praise,
No terms do reach Thy worth, no age Thy days!
May I but swear obedience to Thy laws,
And crave THEE PATRON to my present cause!
My subject's THEOPHIL, for Heav'n design'd,
Off'ring pure Sacrifice with sacred Mind.

---

[1] Printed exactly from original as a specimen.

LADIES,

We jangle not in schools, but strain to set
Church-music, at which saints being met,
May warble forth Heav'n's praise, and thence Heav'n's blessing get.

Church-anthems irksome to the factious grow;
In what a sad case were they, trow,
Should they be penn'd in Heav'n, where hymns for ever flow?

As, fir'd affections to your beauties move—
So, stillatories be of love;
That, what was vapour, may, by virtue, essence prove.

Survey THEOPHILA; her rules apply,
That you may live, as you would die:
Virtue enamels life; 'tis Grace does glorify.

O, may those fragrant flow'rs that in her grew,
Blown by such breath, drench'd by such dew,
Spring, and display their buds, ladies elect, in you!

To this Spring-Garden, virgins, chaste and fair,
Coacht in pure thoughts, make your repair,
To recreate your minds, and take fresh heav'nly air.

Ye snowy fires, observe her in each grace;
So, may you, bright in soul as face,
Have in the Gallery of Heroic Women place.

Nay, when your days and piety shall sum
Up their completeness, may ye come
To endless Glory's Court, and with blest souls have room!

THE PREFACE

SAD Experience confirms, what the Ancient of Days foretold; that the last times shall be worst: for, in this dotage of the world (where Atheism stands at the right hand of Profaneness, and Superstition on the blind side of Ignorance; where there is unmerciful oppression, and overmerciful connivence, her beloved favourites (who are of past things mindless, of future regardless, having different opinions, yet but one Religion, Money, one God, Mammon) do laugh at others, who fall not down, and worship the Golden Image that secular Nabuchodonosors have set up; but let them, who think themselves safe in the herd, being night-wildered in their intellects, prosecute their sensuality, which will soon, like Dalila, put out their eyes; for earthly complacencies and exterior gaieties are not only chaff in the hand, Vanity, but also chaff in the eye, Vexation of Spirit. How art thou, foolish World, loaden with sin, fond of trifles, neglecting objects fit for Christians, fit for men! Could thy minions consider, that thou canst give but what thou hast, a smoke of Honour, a shadow of Riches, a sound of Pleasure, a blast of Fame, which can neither add to length nor happiness of life; that thy whole self art an overdear bargain, if bought of the Devil, at the expense of a deadly sin, when as sudden chance or sickness may snatch and rend them hence in a moment, they would not then so madly *rant* it as they do, but court sobriety, being aware of the dangers that proceed from, and wait upon the abused opulency of an indulgent fortune, whose caresses are apt to swell into exorbitances of spirit, and run wildly into dissoluteness of manners. But, for want of circumspection, men grow covetous as Jewish merchants, ambitious as Eastern potentates, factious as the giddy multitude, revengeful as jealousy, and proud as usurpers ; though soon such swallowed baits dissolve into a gally bitterness ; wherefore, it were highly to be wished, that in the midst of their extravagancies they would ponder, that nothing is more unhappy than the felicity of sinners, who prosper as if they were the beloved of GOD, when, indeed, by His patience they are only (probably) hardened to their more dreadful destruction ! How, how will eternal anguish be aggravated by temporary past happiness ! If we contemplate what unspeakable torments are for ever there, we should have no cause to envy *Worldlings* prosperity, but rather wonder that their portion on earth is not greater, and that ever they should be sensible of sickness, affront or trouble ; since, if their fortunateness should far exceed their ambition, it could not any way recompense that torture for an hour, which yet shall hold to the duration of an infinite Eternity ! when as all the play and pageantry of earth is ever changing, and nothing abides but the stage of the world, and the Spectator GOD. That bliss is not true of whose Eternity we may doubt. View then, Christian reader, the folly of ill counsel unmasked ; and demonstrated that all policy is wretched without piety, without Scriptural wisdom, without CHRIST the Essential Wisdom ; and that all iniquity has so much of justice in it, that it usually condemns, yea leads itself to execution ; witness Absolon's head, Achitophel's hands, and the surrender of Caesar's citadel, (summoned by Judgement's herald, and all his glory's cobweb-guard yielded to the storm) just before the statue of Pompey, whose ruin he had so ambitiously pursued. Would then any wise man choose to be Caesar for his glory, Absolon for his beauty, Achitophel for his policy, Dives for his wealth, or Judas for his office ? Seeing then that happiness consists not in the affluence of exorbitant possessions, nor in the humours of fickle honour, all external splendours being unsatisfactory, let Christians neglect terrestrial vanities, and retire into the recesses of Religion, nothing being so great in human actions as a pious

knowing mind, which disposeth great things, and may yield such permanent monuments, as bring felicity to mankind above the founders of empires ; being an Antepast to the overflowing Feasts of Eternity. Man endued with altitude of wisdom, in the sweetness of conscience and height of virtue, is of all creatures sub-angelical the Almighty's masterpiece, the image of his Maker, a candidate of Divinity, and model of the universe ; who, in holy colloquies, whisperings, and secret conferences with GOD, finds Him a torrent of pleasure, a fountain of honour, and an inexhaustible treasure ; whose divine life is a character of the Divine Nature, by taking GOD for the text, Truth for the doctrine, and Holiness for the use,. without which the highest endowments of the most refined wit are but the quaint magic of a learned lunacy. Most wretched therefore are they, beyond all synonyms of misery, whose undisciplined education leaves them unfurnished of skill to spend their time in anything, but what in the prosecution of sin tends to death ; wealth and greatness rendering them past reproof, even ready to tempt their very tempter ; whereby they are wholly inclined to sensualities, being in their entertainments commonly intemperate, in their drink humorous, their humours quarrellous, their duels damnable, concluding a voluptuous and brutish life in a bloody and desperate death, preferring the Body before the Soul, Sense before the Spirit, Appetite before Reason ; temporary fooleries, fantastic visits, idle courtships, gay trifles, fascinating vanities (as if the pleasure of life were but the smothering of precious time in those things, which are mere puffs in expectation, vanity in enjoyment, and vexation of spirit in departure) before solid goodness, and eternal exultations. To divert thee, therefore, from such shelves of indiscreet vice, and to direct thee to the safe and noble channel of virtue, even to faith with good works, to piety with compassion, to zeal with charity, and to know the end which distinguisheth thee from a beast, and to choose a good end, which differenceth thee from an evil man, be so much thine own friend as to peruse seriously this spiritual poem which treateth on Sub-cœlestials, Cœlestials, and Supercœlestials, whereby a delightful curiousness may steal thee into the pleasure of Goodness. Know then that Sub-cœlestials, or Sublunaries, have their assignment in the lowest portion of the universe, and being wholly of a corporeal nature do enjoy spiritual gifts, the chief of which is life, by loan only ; where there is no generation without corruption, no birth without death. From the surface of the earth to the centre is 3,436 miles, the whole thickness 6,872 miles, the whole compass 21,600 miles ; from its centre to the moon is 3,924,912 miles. Now Cœlestials, or aethereal bodies, are seated in the middle, which, participating of a greater portion of perfection, impart innumerable rare virtues, and influential efficacies to things below, not enduring a corruption, only subject, having obtained their period, to change. The glorious projection and transfusion of aethereal light, both of the sun and of the stars of the six magnitudes, constitute, by astronomical computation, more than 300 suns upward to the Empyrean Heaven. A star in the Equator makes 12,598,666 miles in an hour, which is 209,994 miles in a minute, a motion quicker than thought. Super-cœlestials are intelligencies, altogether spiritual and immortal, excellent in their beings, intuitive in their conceptions ; such as are the glorious quire of the Apostles, the exulting number of the Prophets, the innumerable army of crowned Martyrs, triumphing Virgins, charitable Confessors, &c., or the blessed hierarchy of Angels, participating somewhat of GOD and man ; having had a beginning as man, and now being immortal with GOD, having their immortality for His sempiternity ; void of all mixture, as is GOD, and yet consisting of matter and form as doth man ; subsisting in some subject and substance as doth man, yet being incorporeal, as is GOD ; they having charity, impassibility, subtility, and agility, having understanding without error, light without darkness, joy without sorrow, will without perturbation, impassibility without corruption ; pure as the light, ordained to serve the Lord of Light. They are local and circumscribed by place, as is man ; yet are they in a place not properly by way of circumscription, but by way of definition ; though they cannot be in several places at once, yet are they able in a moment to be anywhere, as GOD always is everywhere ; of admirable capacity and knowledge, resembling GOD ; yet ignorant of the Essence of GOD, much less see they all things in It, in that like man. Even these incorporeal substances would pine and starve, if an all-filling, and infinitely all-sufficient and superabundant GOD were not the object of their high contemplation, whose bliss of theirs is the nearest approach to that Divine Majesty, Who is a true, real, substantial, and essential Nature, subsisting of Himself, an eternal Being, an infinite Oneness, the radical Principle of all things ; whose essence is an incomprehensible light, His power is omnipotency, and his beck an absolute act ; Who, before the Creation, was a book rolled up in Himself, having light only in Himself ; Who is a Spirit existent from everlasting to everlasting ; One Essence, Three Subsistencies ; whose Divine Nature is an essential and infinite Understanding, which knows all things actually always ; which cannot possibly be comprehended by any finite creature, much less by Man grovelling on earth in the mud of error and gross ignorance, who are unable by any art or industry to find out the true nature, form and virtue of the least fly or gnat. The whole universe is the looking-glass of GOD'S power, wisdom, and bounty ; He loves as Charity, knows as Truth, judges as Equity, rules as Majesty, defends as Safety, works as Virtue, reveals as Light, &c. He is a never deficient Brightness, a never weary Life, a Spring ever-flowing, the Principle of Beginning, &c. If any creature knew what GOD is, he should be GOD ; for none knoweth HIM but HIMSELF, Who is good without quality, great without quantity, present without place, everlasting without time ; Who by a body is nowhere, by energy everywhere, above all by power, beneath all by sustaining all, without all by compassing all, within all by penetrating all, being absent seen, being present invisible; of Whom to speak, is to be silent, Whom to value is to exceed all rate, Whom to define, is still to increase in definition; Infiniteness being the right Philosopher's stone, which turns all metals into gold, and one dram of it being put, not only to a Seraphin, or to a whole element, but even to the least' gnat in the world, or the least mote in the sun, is of force to make it true and very GOD: For, first, It maketh it to be the first Essence, derived from none other. 2. It maketh it to be but One, because there cannot be two Infinites; where there are two, there is division; where division, there is end of one, and beginning of another, and so no Infinite. 3. It maketh the subject to be immaterial, for no matter can be infinite; for, a body is contained, and, if contained, not infinite; being without matter, it is also without passion; for, *sola materia patitur*; and so becometh also immutable, for there can be no change without passion. 4. It maketh a thing to be immoveable, for whatsoever moveth hath bounds, but in Infinite there is no bounds. 5. The Infinite Thing is simple, for in composition there is division and quality, and so by consequent limits. Thus, Infiniteness distinguisheth from all creatures, and is first primary without cause, but existing absolutely in Himself, and of Himself, and is to all other things the cause and beginning, yet not diminishing Him, having all their essence, but no part of His Essence from Him. But oh, here the most superlative expressions of eloquence are no other than mere extenuations. I tread a maze, and thread a labyrinth on hills of ice, where, if I slip, I tumble into heresy; I am with St. Peter in the deep, where, without the Hand of Power, I should sink eternally, and be swallowed up by the bottomless gulf. The prosecution of this argument were fitter for the pens of Angels, than for the sons of corruption; whereof we may say, that if all should be written of Infiniteness, not only the whole world, but even Heaven itself would not suffice to hold the books which should be written. I satisfy my incapacity with rejoicing in GOD's incomprehensibility. And

now, descending from these amazing heights, know, reader, that Divine Poesy is the internal triumph of the mind, rapt with St. Paul into the third heaven, where she contemplates ineffables: 'tis the sacred oracles of faith put into melodious anthems that make music ravishing, no earthly jubilation being comparable to it. It discovers the causes, beginnings, progress, and end of things, it instructeth youth, comforteth age, graceth prosperity, solaceth adversity, pleaseth at home, delighteth abroad, shorteneth the night, and refresheth the day. No star in the sphere of Wisdom outshines it: Natural Philosophy hath not anything in it which may satisfy the soul, because that is created to something more excellent then all Nature; but this divine rapture chains the mind with harmonious precepts from a divine influence, whose operations are as subtle and resistless as the influence of planets; teaching mortals to live as in the sight of GOD, by whom the coverts of the thickest hypocrisy (that white Devil) are most clearly seen through. Now 'tis Judgement begets the strength, Invention the ornaments of a poem; both these joined form Wit, which is the agility of spirits: vivacity of Fancy in a florid style disposeth light and life to a poem, wherein the masculine and refined pleasures of the understanding transcend the feminine and sensual of the eye: From the excellence of Fancy proceed grateful similes, apt metaphors, &c. Sublime poets are by Nature strengthened, by the power of the mind inflamed, and by divine rapture inspired; they should have a plentiful stock to set up, and manage it artfully, their conceptions should be choice, brief, perspicuous, well-habited. In Scripture Moses, Job, David, Solomon, and others, are famous for employing their talents in this kind. St. Paul likewise cited three of the heathen poets (whom he calls *prophets*) as evident convictions of vice, and demonstrations of Divinity: viz. Epimenides to the Cretians, *Tit.* i. 12 Κρῆτες ἀεὶ ψεῦσται, κακὰ θηρία, γαστέρες ἀργαί. Menander to the Corinthians, 1 *Cor.* xv. 33 Φθείρουσιν ἤθη χρῆσθ' ὁμιλίαι κακαί. And Aratus to the Athenians,

Edward Benlowes

Acts xvii. 28 Τοῦ γὰρ καὶ γένος ἐσμέν. From these results I fell in love with our more divine and Christian poesy, observing that in the sayings and writings of our Blessed SAVIOUR and His disciples, there are no less than sixty authorities produced from above forty of David's Psalms. Hence from that high Love, which hath no weapons but fiery rays, my spirit is struck into a flame to enter into the secret and sacred rooms of *Theology*, and, reader, if thou wilt not prejudice thine own charity by miscrediting me, I dare profess, thou wilt neither repent of thy cost or time in reviewing these interval issues of spiritual recreation, which may thus, happily, prove a pleasant lure to thy pious devotion. May likewise thy charity suggest to thy belief, that I have done my best to that end, and if thou thinkest that I have wanted salt to preserve them to posterity, know that the very subject itself is balsam enough to make them perpetual. Delightest thou in a Heroic Poem? If actions of magnanimity and fidelity advancing moral virtue merit the title of heroic, much more may THEOPHILA, a combatant with the world, hell, and her own corruptions, gain an eternal laurel ; whose example and precepts, well followed, will without doubt bring honour, joy, peace, serenity, and hopes full of confidence. The Composer hath extracted out of the even mixture of theory and action this cordial water of saving wisdom, by distilling them through the limbeck of Piety, whereof they drink to their soul's health, who not only take it in, as parched earth does rain, but turn it into nourishment by a spiritual digestion, being made like it Divine. This metrical Discourse of his serious day, to which he was led by instigation of conscience, not titillation of fame, inoculates grafts of reason on the stock of religion, and would have all put upon this important consideration, that the life of Nature is given to seek the life of Grace, which bringeth us to the life of Glory; the obtainment of which is his only aim, being fully persuaded, that as every new star gilds the firmament, and increaseth its first glory : so those, who are instruments of the conversion of others, shall not only introduce new beauties, but, when themselves shine like other stars in glory, they shall have some reflexions from the light of others, to whose fixing in the orb of Heaven they themselves have been instrumental. He would not run thee out of breath by long-winded strains ; for in a poem, as in a prayer, 'tis vigour not length that crowns it ; Οὐκ ἐν τῷ μεγάλῳ τὸ εὖ, ἀλλ' ἐν τῷ εὖ τὸ μέγα.

Tædia ut Ambages pariant, nervosa Favorem
Sic Brevitas ; Labor est non brevis esse brevem.

He wisheth it might be his happiness to meet with such readers, as discern the analogy of Grounds, as well as the knowledge of the letter, and have as well a system of Reason, as the understanding of Words : yea, such as have judgement and affections refined, and with THEOPHILA be love-sick too, which love is never more eloquent, than when ventilated in sighs and groans, Heaven's delighted *music* being in the broken consort of hearts and spirits, the will there accepted for the work, and the desire for desert. Behold here in an original is presented an example of life, with force of precepts, happy who copy them out in their actions ! Indeed examples and precepts are as poems and pictures ; for, as poems are speaking pictures, and pictures are silent poems : so example is a silent precept, and precept a speaking example. And as musick is an audible beauty, and beauty a visible music : so precepts are audible sweets to the wise, and examples silent harmony to the illiterate, who may unclasp and glance on these poems, as on pictures with inadvertency ; yet he who shall contribute to the improvement of the author, either by a prudent detection of an error, or a sober communication of an irrefragable truth, deserves the venerable esteem and welcome of a good Angel; and he who by a candid adherence unto, and a fruitful participation of what is good and pious confirms him therein, merits the honourable entertainment of a faithful friend. But he who shall traduce him in absence, for what in presence he would seem to applaud, incurs the double guilt of flattery and slander; and he who wounds him with ill reading and misprision, does execution on him before judgement.

Now He who is the Way, *the* Truth, *and the* Life, *bring those to everlasting* Life, *who love the* Way, *and* Truth *in sincerity!*

The several Cantos

The
{
Praelibation.
Humiliation.
Restoration.
Inamoration.
Representation.
Association.
Contemplation.
Admiration.
}

The
{
Recapitulation.
Translations [1].
Abnegation.
Disincantation.
Segregation.
Reinvitation.
Termination.
}

Be pleased, Reader, first to correct these Typographical Errours.

Acres circumfert centum licet Argus *Ocellos,*
Non tamen errantes *cernat ubique* Typos.

At the bottom B 4. Line 20. Read *Ecstasies,* Pag. 1. Stanza 1. *Strains.* p. 54. St. 23. *Condescent,* p. 76. St. 71. *Unbounded.* p. 84. St. 25. *Thee.* p. 106. St. 86. *doth most.* 132. 31. *non.* p. 144. rectifie the Figures. p. 169. St. 60. *repurgat.* 173. 90. *eversis,* 203. 82. *For.* 214. l. 12. *exanimes.* 217. l. 7. *splendet.* 239. 29. *didst.* 268. l. 25. *Nectare, &c.*

Pneumato-Sarco-Machia : or

Theophila's Spiritual Warfare

The life of a true Christian is a continual conflict; each act of the good fight hath a military scene; and our blessed SAVIOUR coming like a Man of War, commands in Chief, under the FATHER, who hath laid help upon One that is mighty, by anointing Him with the HOLY GHOST and with power. This world is His pitched field; His standard the cross; His colours Blood; His armour Patience; His battle Persecution; His victory Death. And in mystical Divinity His two-handed sword is the Word and Spirit, which wounds and heals; and what is shed in this holy war is not blood but Love; His trumpeters are Prophets and Preachers; His menaces Mercies; and His arrows Benefits. When He offers Himself to us, He then invades us; His great and small shot are volleys of sighs and groans; when we are converted we are conquered; He binds when He embraceth us. In the cords of love He leads us captives; and kills us into life, when He crucifies the old, and quickens in us the new man. So then here is no death, but of inbred corruptions: no slaughter, but of carnal affections, which being mortified the soul becomes a living sacrifice, holy and acceptable unto GOD.

[1] Plural in *orig.*

(321)

WHEN that great Gen'ralissimo of all
Infernal janissaries shall
His legions of temptations raise, enroll,
And muster them 'gainst thee, my
Soul ;
And ranks of pleasures, profits, hon-
ours bring,
To give a charge on the right wing :
And place his dreadful troops of deadly
sins
Upon the left, with murth'ring gins :
And draw to his main body thousand
lusts,
And for reserve—wherein he trusts,
Shall specious Sanctity's Brigade pro-
vide,
Whose leader is Spiritual Pride :
And having treacherously laid his trains
In ambush, under hope of gains
By sinning, as so many scouts, to find
Each march and posture of thy mind:
Then, Soul, sound an alarm to Faith,
and press
Thy Zeal to be in readiness ;
And levy all thy faculties to serve
Thy CHIEF. Take Pray'r for thy
reserve
Under the conduct of His SPIRIT; see
Under the banner that they be

Of thy Salvation's CAPTAIN. Then be
sure
That all thy outworks stand secure.
Yet narrower look into th' indenting
line
Of thy ambiguous thoughts. Design
With constant care a watch o'er every
part ;
Ev'n at thy Cinque-ports, and thy
heart
Set sentinels. Let Faith be captain
o'er
The life-guard, standing at the door
Of thy well-warded breast : disloyal
Fear
That corresponds with Guilt, cashier.
Nor let Hypocrisy sneak in and out
Thy garrison, with that spy, Doubt.
The watchword be IMMANUEL. Then
set
Strong parties of thy tears ; and let
Them still to sally forth prepared stand,
And but expect the Soul's command;
Waiting until a blest recruit from High
Be sent, with Grace's free supply.

Thus where the LORD of hosts the van
leads, there
Triumphant palms bring up the rear.

To My Fancy upon Theophila

FLY, Fancy, Beauty's arched brow,
Darts, wing'd with fire, thence spark-
ling flow.
From flash of lightning eye-balls turn ;
Contracted beams of [1] crystal burn.
Waive [2] curls, which Wit gold-tresses
calls,
That golden fleece to tinsel falls.

Evade   thou   peach-bloom   cheek-
decoys,
Where both the roses blend false joys.
Press not the two-leav'd ruby gates,
Which fence their pearl-portcullis
grates.
Suck not the breath, though it return
Fragrant, as Phoenix' spicy urn.

Lock up thine ears, and so disarm
The magic of enamouring charm.
The lilied breasts with violets vein'd
Are flow'rs, as soon deflowr'd as
gain'd.
Love-locks, perfume, paint, spots dis-
praise ;
These by the black-art spirits raise.

Garnish no Bristows [3] with rich mine,
Glow-worms are vermin, though they
shine.
Should one love-knot all lovelies tie,
This one, these all, soon cloy and die.
Cupid, as lame as blind, being gone,
Live one with HIM, Who made thee
one.

---

[1] Corrected to ' on ' in my copy.
[2] Orig. ' Wave ' : but this is the common spelling for ' waive,' which seems to be
required to match ' Fly ' and ' Evade.'
[3] Bristol being famous as a stronghold and also for ' diamonds.'

Avoid exotic pangs o'th' brain,
Nor let thy margent blush a stain.
With artful method misc'line[1] sow :
May judgement with invention grow.
Profit with pleasure bring to th' test,
Be ore refin'd, before imprest.

Pass forge and file, be point and edge
'Gainst what severest brows allege.
Mix balm with ink ; let thy salt heal :
T' each palate various manna deal.
Have for the wise strong sense, deep
    truth :
Grand-sallet of choice wit for youth.

Cull metaphors well-weigh'd and clear,
Enucleate mysteries to th' ear.
Be wit stenographied, yet free ;
'Tis largest in epitome.
Fly through *Art's* heptarchy, be clad
With wings to soar, but not to gad.

Thy pinions raise with mystic fire,
Sometimes 'bove high-roof'd sense as-
    pire.
So draw THEOPH'LA, that each line,
Cent'ring in Heav'n, may seem divine.
Her voice soon fits thee for that quire ;
W' are cind'red by intrinsic fire.

Magnetic Virtue's in her breast
Impregn'd with Grace, the noblest
    guest.
Who in Love's albo[2] are enroll'd,
Unutterable joys behold.
Geographers Earth's globe survey,
Fancy, Heav'n's astrolabe display.

Six hast thou view'd of Europe's
    Courts,
Soon, as Ideas, pass'd their sports.

Sense, canst thou *parse* and *construe*
    bliss ?
Only souls sanctified know this.
Then hackney not, to toys, life's span.
The Saint's rear tops the Courtier's van.

In *Hope's* cell holy hermit be :
Let ecstasies transfigure thee.
There, as *Truth's* champion, strive
    always,
To storm Love's tower with hosts of
    praise.
Keep strong *Faith's* Court of Guard.
    The stars
March in battalia to these wars.

Zealous in pray'r besiege the sky,
Conquests are crown'd by constancy :
Stand sent'nel at the BRIDEGROOM'S
    gates ;
Who serve there, reign o'er earthly
    states,
Rais'd on *Devotion's* flaming wings
Disdain the crackling blaze of things.

No music courts spiritual ears
Like high-tun'd anthems ; this up-
    rears
Thee, Fancy, rapt through mists of
    fears,
And clouds of penitential tears ;
Eagling 'bove transitory spheres,
Till ev'n the INVISIBLE appears.

Divorc'd from past and present toys,
'Spouse New Jerus'lem's future joys ;
Be re-baptiz'd in Eye-dew-Fall,
Of all forgot, forget thou all.
    These acts well kept, commence, and
    prove
Professor in Seraphic Love.

A Friend's Echo, to his Fancy upon Sacrata

I

WHEN Fancy bright SACRATA courts,
It is not with accustom'd sports ;
'Tis not in prizing of her eyes,
To the disvalue of the skies ;
Nor robbing gardens of their hue,
To give her flow'ry cheeks their due.

II

'Tis not in stripping of the sea
For coral, to resign that plea
It hath to the vermilion dye,
If that her ruddy lips be nigh,
Or that I long to see them ope,
As if I thence for pearl did hope.

---

[1] ' Misc'line ' in various forms = ' mixed seed.'   [2] ' Album ' declined.

III

Nor is't in promising my ears
Rather to her than to the spheres ;
Or that a smile of hers displays
As much content as *Phoebus'* rays,
Or that her hand for whiteness shames
The down of swans on silver Thames.

IV

Let such on these Romances dwell,
Who do admire Love's husk and shell.
Hark, wanton fair-ones, all your fawns
Are Happiness's hapless pawns :
With these alone the mind does flag ;
Beauty is oft the soul's black bag.

V

Pure flames that ravish with their fire,
Ascend unmeasurably higher ;
Which, after search we find to be
In virtue link'd with piety.
The radiations of the soul
All splendours of the flesh control.

VI

Fond sense, cry up a rosy skin,
SACRATA rosied is within :
But brighter THEOPHIL behold,
Whose vest is wrought with purfled gold.
LOVE'S self in her his flame em-beams,
LOVE'S sacrifice ZEAL'S rapture seems.

VII

Of Paradise before the Fall
This Saint is emblematical.
Then, *Fancy*, give her due renown,
She 's Queen of Arts ; this book, her crown.

SACRATA turns CASTARA unto us,
And BENLOWES (anagramm'd) BENE-VOLUS.

> JER. COLLIER[1], *M.A. and Fell. of S. John's Coll., Camb.*

Non me Palma negata Macrum, data reddet Opimum

A SMOOTH clear vein should have it[2] source
From Nature, and have Art but nurse :
Which, though it men at Athens feasts,
May fight at Ephesus with beasts.

Wits, rudely hal'd to *Momus'* bar,
By braying beasts condemnèd are.
Reason ! How many brutes there be
'Mong men, 'cause not inform'd by thee ?

Vates Poet-Prophet is ; if good,
Alike both scorn'd, and understood.
Though readers' censure 's writers' fate,

Spleen sha'nt contract, nor praise dilate.

Or clap, or hiss. The moon sails round,
Though bark'd at by each yelping hound.
The brighter she, the more they bark ;
But slumb'ring quetch[3] not in the dark.

Deign him, bright souls, your piercing glance,
(Art's foes are sons of Ignorance)
So, freed from Night's rude overseers,
The Poet may be tried by his Peers.

---

[1] This is not the famous Jeremy, who was born only two years before *Theophila* appeared.

[2] 'It' for 'it's,' as so often.

[3] 'Quetch,' more usually 'quitch,' 'to move,' 'stir.'

Commendatory Poems

A Verdict for the Pious Sacrificer

To shine, and light, not scorch, thy
Muse did aim ;
And so hath rais'd this quintessential
flame.
By th' salt, and whiteness of her lines,
we think
With holy water (tears) she mixt her ink ;
And both the fire and food of this chaste
Muse   [use.
Is more what Altars, than what Tables

Who does not pray with zeal thy Faith
may move,
Rightly concentric with thy Hope and
Love ?
So, in the Temple these religious
hosts
From Hecatombs may rise to Holo-
causts.

WALTER MONTAGUE [1],
Com. Manch. Filius.

A Glance at Theophila

WHO sacrificèd last ? The hallow'd
air
Seems all ensoul'd with sweet per-
fume,
Which pleased *Heav'n* deigns to
assume,
The smiling sky appeareth brightly
fair ;
Was't not THEOPHILA's fam'd sire,
Say, sacred *Priest*, obtain'd the holy
fire
To bless, and burn his victim of sub-
lime desire ?

Know, curious mortal, this rare
sacrifice,
Scarce known to our now-bedrid
age,
Was got by *Zeal*, and holy *Rage*,
And offer'd by *Benevolus* the wise :
For, speckled *Craft*, and a loose
fit
Of aguish knowledge, glimm'ring
acts beget ;
Chaste *Piety* bears fruit to *Wisdom*,
not to *Wit*.

No tiger's whelp with blood-be-
smearèd jaws,
No cub of bears, lick'd into shape,
No lustful offspring of the ape,
No musky panther with close guileful
claws,

No dirty gruntling of the swine,
No lion's whelp of e'er so high
design,
Is offer'd here : keep off, Unclean !
Here's all divine.

The chosen wood (as harbinger to all
Those future then, now passed
rites)
Was Laurel, that guards lightning
frights,
The weeping Fir, sad Yew for funeral,
The lasting Oak, and joyful Vine,
The fruitful Fig-tree billets did con-
sign ;
The peaceful Olive with cleft Juniper
did join.

On knees in tears think altar'd
THEOPHIL,
Incensed with sweet *Obedience*,
Who makes LOVE'S life in death
commence,
Scaling with heart, hands, eyes,
Heav'n's lofty hill :
Her circled head you might behold
Was glorified with burnish'd crown
of gold,
Embost with gems ; embrac'd by
Angels manifold.

Thus in a fiery chariot up SHE flies,
Perfuming the forsaken earth

---

[1] A rather remarkable person, born about 1603, who died in 1677 after becoming a Roman Catholic, being imprisoned for Royalism in the Tower, and enjoying the abbacy of St. Martin, at Pontoise.

(The midwife orbs do help her birth),
Into the glory of the Hierarchies.
   Where ecstasies of joys do grow,
   Which they themselves eternally do
      sow,

But 'tis too high for me to think, or thee
    to know.
Priests thus by hieroglyphic keys
Unlock their hidden mysteries.

              W. DENNIE, *Baronet* [1].

To the Author, upon his Divine Poem

TILL now I guess'd but blindly to what
   height
The Muses' eagles could maintain their
   flight !
Though poets are, like eaglets, bred to
   soar,
Gazing on stars at Heav'n's mysterious
   pow'r ;
Yet I observe they quickly stoop to
   ease
Their wings, and perch on palace-pin-
   nacles :
From thence more usefully they Courts
   discern ;
The Schools where greatness does
   disguises learn ;
The stages where *She* acts to vulgar
   sight
Those parts which statesmen as her
   Poets write ;
Where none but those wise poets may
   survey
The private practice of her public play ;
Where kings, GOD'S counterfeits, reach
   but the skill
In studied scenes to act the Godhead
   ill :
Where cowards, smiling in their closets,
   breed
Those wars which make the vain and
   furious bleed :
Where Beauty plays not merely
   Nature's part,
But is, like Pow'r, a creature form'd by
   Art ;
And, as at first, Pow'r by consent was
   made,
And those who form'd it did themselves
   invade :
So harmless Beauty (which has now far
   more
Injurious force than States' or Mon-
   archs' power)

Was by consent of Courts allow'd
   Art's aid ;
By which themselves they to her sway
   betray'd.
'Twas Art, not Nature, taught excessive
   power ;
Which whom it lists does favour or
   devour :
'Twas Art taught Beauty the imperial
   skill
Of ruling, not by justice, but by will.
And, as successive kings scarce seem
   to reign,
Whilst lazily they empire's weight sus-
   tain ;
Thinking because their pow'r they
   native call
Therefore our duty too is natural ;
And by presuming that we ought [t']
   obey,
They lose the craft and exercise of sway :
So, when at Court a native Beauty
   reigns
O'er Love's wild subjects, and Art's
   help disdains ;
When her presumptuous sloth finds
   not why Art
In Pow'r's grave play does act the
   longest part ;
When, like proud gentry, she does
   level all
Industrious arts with arts mechanical ;
And vaunts of small inheritance no less
Than new States boast of purchas'd
   provinces ;
Whilst she does every other homage
   scorn,
But that to which by Nature she was
   born :
Thus when so heedlessly she lovers
   sways,
As scarce she finds her pow'r ere it
   decays ;

[1] Author of *The Shepherd's Holiday*, 1653, and other Poems, which might be included in this Collection if we had room. This piece strikes one as above the ordinary commendatory work.

Which is her beauty, and which un-
supplied
By what wise Art would carefully pro-
vide,
Is but Love's lightning, and does hardly
last
Till we can say it was ere it be past;
Soon then when beauty's gone she
turns her face,
Asham'd of that which was erewhile her
grace;
So, when a monarch's gone, the chair
of State
Is backward turn'd where he in glory
sate.
   The secret arts of Love and Pow'r;
how these
Rule courts, and how those courts rule
provinces,
Have been the task of every noble Muse;
Whose aid of old nor Pow'r nor Love
did use
Merely to make their lucky conquests
known
(Though to the Muse they owe their
first renown;
For she taught Time to speak, and ev'n
to Fame,
Who gives the great their names, she
gave a name),
But they by studying numbers rather
knew
To make those happy whom they did
subdue.
   Here let me shift my sails! and
higher bear
My course than that which moral poets
steer!
For now (best poet!) I divine would be,

And only can be so by studying thee.
Those whom thy flights do lead shall
pass no more
Through dark'ning clouds when they to
Heav'n would soar;
Nor in ascent fear such excess of light
As rather frustrates than maintains the
sight;
For thou dost clear Heav'n's darken'd
mysteries,
And mak'st the lustre safe to weakest
eyes.
Noiseless, as planets move, thy numbers
flow,
And soft as lovers' whispers when they
woo!
Thy labour'd thoughts with ease thou
dost dispense,
Clothing in maiden dress a manly sense;
And as in narrow room Elixir lies,
So in a little thou dost much comprise.
Here fix thy pillars! which as marks
shall be
How far the soul in Heav'n's discovery
Can possibly advance; yet, whilst they
are
Thy trophies, they but warrant our
despair:
For human excellence hath this ill fate,
That where it virtue most doth elevate
It bears the blot of being singular,
And Envy blasts that Fame it cannot
share:
Ev'n good examples may so great be
made
As to discourage whom they should
persuade.   WILL. DAVENANT.

TOWER, May 13, 1652.

For the Author, truly Heroic, by Blood, Virtue, Learning

Scholar, Commander, Traveller com-
mixt;
Schools, Camps, and *Courts* raise FAME,
and make it fixt.
Your fame and feet have Alps and
   Oceans past: [Envy blast.
Fam'd feet! which Art can't raise, nor

Beaumont and *Fletcher* coin'd a golden
way,   [play.
T' express, suspend, and passionate a

Nimble and pleasant are all motions
there,
For two intelligences rul'd the sphere.

Both sock and buskin sunk with them,
and then
Davenant and *Denham* buoy'd them up
agen.
Beyond these pillars some think
nothing is:
Great Britain's wit stands in a precipice.

But, Sir, as though Heav'n's Straits
    discover'd were,
By science of your card, Unknowns
    appear:
Sail then with prince of wits, illustrious
    Dunne[1],
Who rapt earth round with Love, and
    was its sun.

But your first love was pure: whose
    ev'ry dress
Is inter-tissu'd *Wit* and *Holiness*;
And mends upon itself; whose streams
    (that meet
With *Sands'*[2] and *Herbert's*) grow more
    deep, more sweet.

I, wing'd with joy, to th' PRAELIBA-
    TION fly;
Thence view I Error's Tragi-comedy:
With THEOPHIL from fear to faith
    I rise,
The mystic Bridge, 'twixt Hell and
    Paradise.

Hell scap't seems double Heav'n:
    Renew'd, with bands
Of pray'rs, vows, tears, with eyes, and
    knees, and hands,
I see her cope with Heav'n, and
    Heav'n does thence,
As in the *Baptist's* days, feel violence.

But her ecstatic SONGS OF LOVE
    declare,
To *Jedidiah* she's apparent heir.
Be those then next, The SONG OF
    ᾽SONGS. Love styles
Her *fourth*, The *Second* Book of CAN-
    TICLES.

But with what dreadful yet delightful
    tones
She sings when GLORIFIED! then,
    stingless drones
Are Death and Hell: Joy's crescent
    then's increast,
To fullest lustre, at her Bridal Feast.

Sixth, sev'nth, and eighth such ban-
    quets' frame would make
Wisdom turn Cormorant; my spirits
    shake
I' th' reading. Soul of joy! thy ravish-
    ing sp'rit
Draws bed-rid minds to longing
    appetite.

Fame, write with gold on diamond
    pages; treat
Upon the glories of a work so great.
*Be't then enacted, that all Graces
    dwell
In Thee* THEOPH'LA, *Virtue's Chro-
    nicle:*

Who gemm'st it in Jerusalem above,
Where all is Grace and Glory, Light
    and Love.
To that Unparallel this comes so
    near,
That, 'tis a glimpse of Heav'n to read
    thee here.

O, blest Ambition! Speculations high
Enchariot thee, Elijah-like, to the
    sky!
What state worth envy, like thy sweet
    abode,
That overtops the world, and mounts
    to GOD?

Walkt through your Eden stanzas, you
    invite
Our ravisht souls to recreate with
    delight,
In bow'r of compt discourse: great
    verse, but prose
Such, none but our great MASTER could
    compose.

For bulk, an easy Folio is this all;
Yet we a volume may each Canto
    call,
For solid matter: where we should
    consult
On paragraphs, mark what does thence
    result:

For, every period's of DEVOTION
    proof,
And each resolve is of concern'd be-
    hoof.
Peruse, examine, censure; oh, how
    bright
Does shine RELIGION, chequer'd with
    delight!

Diffusive Soul! your spirit was soar-
    ing, when
This manna dew'd from your inspirèd
    pen.
Such melting passions of a soul divine,
Could they be cast in any mould but
    thine?

---

[1] Donne.

[2] George Sandys.

Wonder arrests our thought ; that you
  alone
In such combustions, wherein thousands
  groan,
(And when some sparkles of the public
  flame
Seiz'd on your private state, and scorcht
  the same)
Could warble thus.   Steer ships each
  pilot may

In calms ; but whoso can in stormy
  day
May justly dominere.   But what may
  daunt
Him, who, like mermaids, thus in
  storms can chant ?
Grace crowns the suff'ring, Glory the
  triumphing Saint.
                    TH. PESTIL,
                    Regi quondam à Sacris.

THOSE ladies, Sir, we virtuosas
  call,
But copies are to this original ;
Whose charming empire of her grace
  does sense
Astonish by a super-excellence.
  And, like as *Midas'* touch made gold :
  so, thus
  THEOPHILA'S touch may make
  THEOPHILUS.

Zeuxes cull'd out perfections of each
  sort
For his *Pandora* ; yet did all come
  short
As far of this embellishment as she

Had been limn'd out in Painting's
  infancy.
  For, magisterial virtue draws no
  grace
  From corp'ral limbs, or features of the
  face.

Here Heav'n-born SUADAS [1], star-like,
  gild each dress
Of the Bride Soul espous'd to Happiness.
Here Piety informs poetic art ;
As all in all, and all in every part.
  For all these died not with fam'd
  Cartwright, though
  A score of poets join'd to have it so.
              T. BENLOWES, *A. M.*

For the much honoured Author

THE winged Intellect once taught to fly
By *Art* and *Reason*, may be bold to pry
Into the secrets of a wand'ring star,
Although its motions be irregular :
And from the smiles and glances that
  those bright
Corrivals cast, that do embellish night,
Guess darkly at, though not directly
  know,
The various changes that fall here be-
  low.
And perching on the high'st perimeter,
May find the distances of every sphere,
Which in full orbs do move, tunicled so
That the less spheres within the greater
  go,
As cell in cell, spun by the dying fly ;
Or ball in ball, turn'd in smooth ivory.
Each hath a prince circled upon a
  throne,
In a refulgent habitation.

Only the constellations seem to be
Like nobles, in an aristocracy.
Their Milky Way like *Innocence*, and
  thus
Should all great actions be diaphanous.
But the great Monarch, *Light*, dis-
  poses all :
His stores are magazine, and festival :
And by his pow'r Earth's epicycle may
Move in a silver sphere, as well as they.
Else, her poor little orb appears to be
A very point to their immensity.
Thus strung, like beads, they on their
  centres move ;
But the great centre of this all, is LOVE.
  Though the brute creatures by the
  height of sense
Foretell their calm and boisterous
  influence,
Yet to find out their motions is man's
  part,

---

[1] 'Suada' or 'Suadela,' one of the subsidiary goddesses of Love and Marriage, who 'persuades' the Beloved.

Not by the help of Nature, but of Art,
Which rarefies the soul, and makes it rise,
And sees no farther than *that* gives it eyes.
And by that prospect will directly tell
What regions stoop to every parallel.
Which cities turrèd are with snow, which lie
Naked, and scorch'd under Heav'n's canopy.
How men, like cloves stuck in an orange, stand
Still upright, with their feet upon the land.
And where the seas oppos'd to us do flow,
Yet quench they not that heat where spices grow.
It sees fair Morning's rising neck beset
With orient gems, like a rich carcanet.
Who every night doth send her beams to spy
In what dark caves her golden treasures lie:
And there they brood and hatch the callow race,
Till they take wing, and fly in every place.
It sees the frozen Fir shrouding its arms,
While Cocus trees are courted with blest charms,
That swell their pregnant womb: whose issue may
Sweeten our world, but that they die by th' way.
It sees the Seasons lying at the door,
Some warm and wanton, and some cold and poor;
And knows from whence they come, both foul and fair,
And from their presence gilds, or soils the air.
It sees plain Nature's face, how rude it looks
Till it be polishèd by men and books:
And most of her dark secrets can discover
To open view of an industrious lover.
Whatever under Heav'n's great throne we prize
Or value, in Art's chamber-practice lies.
But when before the ALMIGHTY JUDGE he come
To speak of HIM, my Orator is dumb.
Go then, thou silenced Soul, present thy plea

By the fair hand of sweet THEOPHILA.
Hap'ly thy harsh and broken strains may rise
In the perfume of her sweet sacrifice;
And if by this access thou find'st a way
To th' highest THRONE, alas! what canst thou say?
What can the bubble (though its breath it bring
Upon the gliding stream) say of the spring?
Can the proud painted flow'r boast that it knows
The root that bears it, and whereon it grows?
Or can the crawling worm, though ne'er so stout,
With its meand'rings find the centre out?
Can Infinite be measur'd by a span?
And what art thou, less than all these, O man?
Man is a thing of nought! yet from above
There beams upon his soul such rays of love,
As may discover by *Faith's* optic, where
The Burning Bush is, though not see HIM there.
The meekest man on earth did only see
His shadow shining there, it was not HE.
And if that great soul, who with holy flame,
And ravish'd spirit to the Third Heav'n came,
Saw things unutterable, what can we
Express of those things that we ne'er did see?
The Senses' strongest pillars cannot bear
The weight of the least grain of glory there.
No more than where to bound, or comprehend
Infinity, they can begin, or end.
Since then the Soul is circumscrib'd within
The narrow limits of a tender skin;
Let us be babes in innocence, and grow
Strong *upwards*, and more weak to things *below*.
By sacred chemistry, the spirit must
Ascend and leave the sediment to dust.
This cordial is distilled from the eyes,
And we must sprinkle 't on the sacrifice:

Offer'd i' th' virtue of THEOPH'LA'S
name.
Which must be to it holocaust and
flame.
Then, wing'd with *Zeal*, we may aspire
to see

The hallow'd Oracles exprest by THEE,
Who art LOVE'S *Flamen*, and with
Holy fire
Refin'st thy Muse, to make her mount
the higher.

ARTH. WILSON.

For the Renowned Composer

A POET'S ashes need nor brass, nor
stone
To be their wardrobe; since his name
alone
Shall stand both brass and marble to
the tomb.
Nor doth he want the cere-cloth's
balmy womb
T' enwrap his dust, until his drowsy
clay
Again enliven'd by an active ray,
Shot from the last day's fire, shall
wake, and rise,
Attir'd with Light. No; when a
Poet dies,
His sheets alone wind up his earth.
They'll be
Instead of Mourner, Tomb, and Obse-
quy;
And to embalm it, his own ink he
takes:
Gum Arabic the richest mummy
makes.
Then, Sir, you need no obelisk, that
may
Seclude your ashes from plebeian
clay.
For, from your mine of Fancy now we
see
Y' have digg'd so many gems of Poesy,
That out of them you raise a glorious
shrine,
In which your ever-blooming name
will shine;
Free from th' eclipse of age, and
clouds of rust,
Which are the moths to other com-
mon dust.
Then, could we now collect th' all-
worshipt ore,

With which kind Nature paves the
Indian shore;
And gather to one mass that stock of
spice,
Which copies out afresh old Paradise,
And in the *Phoenix'* od'rous nest is
pent,
All would fall short of this rich monu-
ment.
About the surface of whose verge,
you stick
So many fragrant flow'rs of Rhetoric
That lovers shall approach in throngs,
and seek
With their rich leaves t' adorn each
beauty's cheek;
So that these sacred trophies will be-
come
In after-times your altar, not your tomb.
To which the poets shall in well-dressed
lays,
Offer their victims, with a grove of bays.
For here among these leaves, no
speckled snake,
Or viper doth his bed of venom make:
No lust-burnt goat, nor looser Satyr
weaves
His cabin out, among these spotless
leaves.
A virgin here may safely dart her eye,
And yet not blush for fear, lest any by
Should see her read. These pages do
dispense
A julep, which so charms the itch
of sense,
That we are forc'd to think your guilt-
less quill
Did, with its ink, the turtle's blood
distil.

T. PHILIPOT.

Pietatis, Pöeticesque, Cultori

IGNE cales tali, quali cum Nuncius Ora
Seraphicus sacro tetigit Carbone Prophetæ.
Macte DEI plenum Pectus ; Te his dedito Flammis,
Sancte Pöetarum Phœnix ! Reparabilis Ignis
Te voret hîc Totum ; Quo plus consumeris Illo,
Hoc magis Æterno Tu consummaberis Ævo.

Incipe Censurâ major, qui Fonte Camænas
Idalias tingis casto ; Tua Metra Sionem
Parnasso jungunt celebri ; tam digna Lituris
Nulla canis, quàm sunt omni dignissima Laude.
Theiophilam resonare docens Modulamine diam,
Impia priscorum lustrâsti Carmina Vatum.

Perge, beatifico correptus NUMINE, Perge,
Vivida felici fundendo Pöemata Flatu,
Pectore digna tuo, COELI penetrare Recessus :
Et, quæ densa tegit Nubes, Mysteria claro
Lumine perlustra, solito non concite Plectro,
Quælibet altisono prosterne Piacula Versu.

Perfice, terrenum transcende, Pöeta, Cacumen :
Conversus converte Vagos ; Quos decipit Error
Incautos, Meliora doce ; Britonesque bilingues
Lingua fac erudiat Britonum, sit quanta superbi
Pectoris Ambitio et Veri Caligo ; Camænis
Subdola vesani depinge Sophismata Secli. JO. GAUDENTIUS, *S.T.D.*

In Sanctos Theophilæ Amores

VIX mihi Te vidisse semel concessit Apollo,
Inque tuo pictam Carmine Theiophilam :
Quum gemino Ipse miser, sed fortunatus Amore
Deperii ; dubius sic Ego factus Amans.
Cur Dubius ? Fallor. Nam, quamvis partibus æquis,
Igne simul duplici me novus urat Amor,
Afficitur tamen Objecto, atque unitur in uno,
Totaque divisis una Favilla manet.
Ne, Lector, mirêre ; Novum est. Sed protinus Ignes,
Si sine felle legas, experiêre meos.
Theiophila ! In cunctis Præcellentissima Nymphis ;
Nominis ad Famam quot Tibi Corda cadent !

Corporis, Ingeniique Bonis dotata triumphas,
Binaque cum summa Laude, Trophæa geris.
Docte, Tibi æternæ quales Spectacula Chartæ,
Quotque Illi efficient Pagina docta Procos !
Sexus uterque pari, visâ Hac, ardebit Amore ;
Hacque frui ex æquo Sexus uterque volet.
Ne vereare tamen, Cuncti licet Oscula figant
Theiophilæ, ne sit casta, vel una Tibi.
Famæ Ejus nil detrahitur si publica fiat ;
Hanc ut ament Omnes, Nil Tibi, Amice, perit.
Tu solus Domina dignus censeberis Illâ,
Illam qui solus pingere dignus eras.
P. DE CARDONEL.

In celeberrimam Theophilam, feliciter elucubratam

ANNE novi, veterisve prius Monumenta revolvam
Ingenii: et Tragicos superantia Scripta Cothurnos,
Atque Sophoclæis numerari digna Triumphis?
  Quàm bene vivificis depingitur Artibus Echo?
Quàm bene monstriferas Vitiorum discutis Hydras?
Carminibusque in doces quantum peccaverit Ævum?
Quanta Polucephalis repserunt Agmina Sectis?
Sphinge Theologica quæ dia Poemata pangis?
Mira et Vera canens, nodosa Ænigmata solvis.
  Nec vitæ pars ulla perit, nec transigis unam
Ingratam sine Luce Diem; dum pervigil Artes
Exantlas, avidisque bibis Permessida Labris.   [catus Eoo,
Jamque, velut primo Phœnix revo-Apparet nostris nova Sponsa Theophila Terris.
Illius è roseis flammatur Purpura malis;
Et Gemmis Lux major adest, et blandius Aurum

A Calamo, Benlose, tuo; dum Dotibus amplis
Excolis, Ingeniique Opibus melioribus ornas.
Lactea Ripheas præcellunt Colla Pruinas;
Fronte Decor radiat, sanctoque Modestia Vultu;
Suada verecundis et Gratia plena Labellis
Assidet, et casti Mores imitata Poetæ,
Te Moderatorem fusis amplectitur Ulnis.
  Hisce Triumphatrix decorata Theophila Gemmis,
Celsior assurgit, Mundumque nitentior intrat
Virgineis comitata Choris; Quam Tramite longo
Agmina Cecropiis stipant Heliconia Turmis.
Non aliter quoties adremigat Æquoris Undas
Frænatis Neptunus Equis, fluit ocyùs Antris
Nereidum Gens tota suis, Dominumque salutant,
Blandula cæruleo figentes Oscula Collo.

P. F.

Qui Virtutes Theo[p]hilæ prædicat, Religioni non Gloriæ studeat. Noverim Te, Domine, noverim me

LAUDIS in Oceano me submersistis, Amici: [patet.
  Maxima pars Decoris me nihil esse,
Laus, famulare DEO, submissi Victima Cordis
  Est Hecatombæis anteferenda Sacris.
CHRISTE, meæ da par ut sit mea Vita Camænæ;
  Sim neque Laus Aliis prodiga, parca TIBI.

O'ercome me not with your perfumes, O Friends!
  My greatest worth, to show I'm nothing, tends.
Praise, wait on Heav'n. Th' Host of an humble heart
  Excels the sacred hecatombs of *Art*.
Grant, LORD, my life may parallel my lays!
  They me too much, I THEE too little, praise.

(333)   z

Edward Benlowes

In Divinos Poetas

Sancto Sancta Columba Musa Vati.
Parnassus superæ Cacumen Æthræ.
Christi Gratia Pegasus supremus.
Vati Castalis Unda Dius Imber.
Pennam dat Seraphin suis ab
    Alis.
Agni scribitur Optimi Cruore.

Vati Bibliotheca Sphæra Coeli.
Vitæ è Codice fœnerans Medullam,
Internos penetrat Poli Recessus.
O, Conamina fructuosiora !
O, Solamina delicatiora !
Per Quæ creditur Angelus Poeta,
Patronusque pio Deus Poetæ !

On Divine Poets

A hallow'd Poet's Muse is th' Holy
    Dove.
Parnassus th' Empyrean Height above.
His lofty-soaring Pegasus Christ's Love.
Heav'n's Show'r of Grace is his Casta-
    lian spring.
A Seraphin lends pen from his own
    wing.
His ink is of the best Lamb's purple
    dye.
To Him Heav'n's sphere is a vast
    library.

Rais'd by th' advantage of th' Eternal
    Book,
His piercing eye ev'n into Heav'n
    does look.
O, what endeavours can more fruitful
    be !
What comforts can we more delightful
    see !
By which the poet we an Angel
    deem ;
Yea, God to's sacred Muse does
    Patron seem.

Ergo brevi stringam Cœlestia Cantu

Aiming to profit, as to please, we
    bring
No usual hawk to try her wing.
Come, come Theoph'la, fresh as
    May :
Hark how the falc'ner lures ! This is
    Love's Holy-Day.

Her stretch is for Devotion's quarry,
    which
Mounts up her Zeal to eagle-pitch :

Cheer thou her present tim'rous flight,
Whilst she thus cuts with wing the
    driving rack of height.

From thence, 'bove sparkling stars,
    she'll spritely move,
Her plumes of Faith being prun'd
    by Love.
As Grace shall imp her pinion, more,
Or less, she will, or flag, or 'bove
    what's mortal, soar[1].

---

[1] Of these later pieces Davenant's has not only the most famous author but the most striking interest from contrast of style. Pestil (-ell) was a Cambridge man who contributed to *Lacrymae Musarum*. If Arthur Wilson is the A. W. who died in the year of our book he was a man of some mark. T. Phil[i]pot was a 'miscellaneous writer'; 'Gaudentius' the famous 'editor' of *Eikon Basilike*; Cardonel probably the father of Marlborough's secretary. Of T. Benlowes and P. F. I know nothing.

THEOPHILA

THE PRELIBATION TO THE SACRIFICE

Canto I

THE ARGUMENT

Spes alit occiduas qui Sublunaribus hæret;
  Rivales Jesus non in Amore sinit.
Quid mihi non sapiat Terrâ, mihi dum sapit Æther?
  Sed sapiet, sapias nî mihi, Christe, nihil.

Awake, arise, Love's steersman, and first taste
  Delight; sound that; ere anchor's cast
On Joy; steer hence a pray'rful course to Heav'n at last.

STANZA I

Might souls converse with souls, by Angel-way,
  Enfranchis'd from their pris'ning clay,
What strains by intuition, would they then convey!

II

But, Spirits, sublim'd too fast, evap'rate may,
  Without some interpos'd allay;
And notions, subtiliz'd too thin, exhale away.

III

The Gold (Sol's child) when in Earth's womb it lay
  As precious was, though not so gay,
As, when refin'd, it doth itself abroad display.

IV

Mount, Fancy, then through orbs to Glory's sphere   10
  (Wild is the course that ends not there):
You, who are Virtue's friends, lend to her tongue an ear.

V

Let not the wanton love-fights, which may rise

From vocal fifes, flame-darting eyes
  (Beauty's munition), hearts with wounds unseen surprise:

VI

Whose basilisk-like glances taint the air
  Of virgin pureness, and ensnare
Entangled thoughts i' th' trammels of their ambush-hair.

VII

Love's captive view, who's days in warm frosts spends;   19
  On's idol dotes, to wit pretends;
Writes, blots, and rends; nor heeds where he begins or ends.

VIII

His stock of verse in comic fragments lies:
  Higher than Ten'riff's Peak he flies:
Sol's but a spark; thou outray'st all diamonds of the skies.

IX

'Victorious flames glow from thy brighter eye;
  Cloud those twin-lightning orbs (they'll fry
An ice-vein'd monk), cloud them, or, planet-struck, I die.

X

'Indians, pierce rocks for gems;
 negroes, the brine
For pearls; Tartars, to hunt com-
 bine
For sables; consecrate all off'rings
 at her shrine. 30

XI

'Crouch low, O vermeil-tinctur'd
 cheek! for, thence
The organs to my optic sense
Are dazzled at the blaze of so
 bright angelence.'

XII

Does Troy-bane Helen (friend)
 with angels share?
All lawless passions idols are:
Frequent are fuco'd cheeks; the
 virtuosa's rare:

XIII

A truth authentic. Let not skin-
 deep white
And red, perplex the nobler light
O' th' intellect; nor mask the soul's
 clear piercing sight.

XIV

Burn odes, Lust's paperplots; fly
 plays, its flame; 40
Shun guileful courtisms; forge
 for shame
No chains; lip-traffic and eye-
 dialogues disclaim.

XV

Hark how the frothy, empty heads
 within
Roar and carouse i' th' jovial sin,
Amidst the wild Levaltos on their
 merry pin!

XVI

Drain dry the ransack'd cellars, and
 resign
Your reason up to riot, join
Your fleet, and sail by sugar-rocks
 through floods of wine:

XVII

Send care to Dead Sea of phleg-
 matic age; 49
Ride without bit your restive rage;
And act your revel-rout thus on
 the tippling stage.

XVIII

'Swell us a lusty brimmer,—more,—
 till most;
So vast, that none may spy the
 coast:
We'll down with all, though therein
 sail'd Lepanto's host:

XIX

'Top and top-gallant hoise; we
 will outroar
The bellowing storms, though
 shipwrackt more
Healths are, than tempting'st sirens
 did enchant of yore.

XX

'Each gallon breeds a ruby;—
 drawer, score 'um;
Cheeks dyed in claret seem o' th'
 quorum,
When our nose-carbuncles, like link-
 boys, blaze before 'um.' 60

XXI

Such are their ranting catches, to
 unsoul,
And outlaw man; they stagger, roll,
Their feet indent, their sense being
 drunk with *Circe's* bowl.

XXII

Entombed souls! Why rot ye thus
 alive,
Melting your salt to lees? and strive
To strangle Nature, and hatch Death?
 Healths, health deprive.

XXIII

The sinless herd loathes your sense-
 stifling streams,
When long spits point your tale:
 ye breams
In wine and sleep, your princes
 are but fumes, and dreams.

41 courtisms] = 'ceremonies of courtship.'
68 breams] = 'fish' chosen for rhyme merely; see the Latin, p. 411, l. 68, which is different.

XXIV

I'd rather be preserv'd in brine, than
    rot   70
  In nectar. Now to dice they're got:
Their tables snare in both; then
    what can be their shot?

XXV

Yet blades will throw at all, sans
    fear, or wit;
  Oaths black the night when dice
    don't hit;
When winners lose at play, can
    losers win by it?

XXVI

Egypt's spermatic nurse, when her
    spread floor
  Is flow'd 'bove sev'nteen cubits o'er,
Breeds dearth: and spendthrifts
    waste, when they inflame the
    score.

XXVII

Tell me, ye piebald butterflies, who
    poise
  Extrinsic with intrinsic joys; 80
What gain ye from such short-liv'd,
    fruitless, empty toys?

XXVIII

Ye fools, who barter gold for trash,
    report,
  Can fire in pictures warm? Can
    sport
That stings, the mock-sense fill?
    How low's your Heav'n! how
    short!

XXIX

Go, chaffer Bliss for Pleasure; which
    is had
  More by the beast, than man;
    the bad
Swim in their mirth (CHRIST wept,
    ne'er laugh'd): the best are sad.

XXX

Brutes covet nought but what's
    terrene; Heav'n's quire
  Do in eternal joys conspire;
Man, 'twixt them both, does inter-
    mediate things desire.   90

XXXI

Had we no bodies, we were angels;
    and
  Had we no souls, we were un-
    mann'd
To beasts: brutes are all flesh, all
    spirit the heav'nly band.

XXXII

At first GOD made them one, thus;
    by subjecting
  The sense to reason; and directing
The appetite by th' spirit: but sin,
    by infecting

XXXIII

Man's free-born will, so shatters
    them, that they
  At present nor cohabit may
Without regret, nor without grief
    depart away.

XXXIV

Go, cheating world, that dancest
    o'er thy thorns;   100
  Lov'st what undoes; hat'st what
    adorns:
Go, idolize thy vice, and virtue
    load with scorns.

XXXV

Thy luscious cup, more deadly than
    asp's gall,
  Empois'neth souls for hell: thou all
Time's mortals dost enchant with
    thy delusive call.

XXXVI

Who steals from Time, Time steals
    from him the prey:
  Pastimes pass Time, pass Heav'n
    away:
Few, like the blessed thief, do steal
    Salvation's Day.

XXXVII

Fools rifle Time's rich lott'ry: who
    misspend   109
  Life's peerless gem, alive descend;
And antedate with stings their
    never-ending end.

XXXVIII

Whose vast desires engross the
    boundless land

---

72 Probably 'table's' should be read: and possibly 'share.'

By fraud, or force; like spiders
stand,
Squeezing small flies; such are their
nets, and such their hand.

XXXIX

When Nimrod's vulture-talons par'd
shall be,
Their house's name soon changed
you'll see;
For their Bethesda shall be turn'd
to Bethany.

XL

Better destroy'd by law, than rul'd
by will;
What salves can cure, if balsams
kill?
That good is worst that does de-
generate to ill.   120

XLI

Had not GOD left the Best within
the power
Of persecutors, who devour;
We had nor martyrs' had, nor yet
a SAVIOUR.

XLII

SAINTS melt as wax, fool's-clay grows
hard at cries
Of that scarce-breathing corse,
who lies
With dry teeth, meagre cheeks, thin
maw, and hollow eyes.

XLIII

GOD made life; give 't to man; by
opening veins,
Death 's sluic'd out, and pleuretic
pains:
Make GOD thy pattern, cure thyself,
alms are best gains.

XLIV

HEAV'N'S glory to achieve, what
scantling span   130
Hath the frail pilgrimage of man!
Which sets, when risen; ends, when
it but now began.

XLV

Who fight with outward lusts, win
inward peace;

Judgements against self-judges
cease:
Who face their cloaks with zeal do
but their woes increase.

XLVI

The mighty, mighty torments shall
endure,
If impious: hell admits no cure.
The best security is ne'er to be secure.

XLVII

Oaks, that dare grapple with Heav'n's
thunder, sink
All shiver'd; coals that scorch do
shrink   140
To ashes; vap'ring snuffs expire in
noisome stink.

XLVIII

Time, strip the writhell'd witch;
pluck the black bags
From off Sin's grizzly scalp; the
hag's
Plague-sores show then more loath-
some than her leprous rags.

XLIX

'Twas she slew guiltless Naboth;
'twas she curl'd
The painted Jezebel; she hurl'd
Realms from their centre; she un-
hing'd the new-fram'd world.

L

Blest then who shall her dash 'gainst
rocks (her groans,
Our mirth), and wash the bloody
stones
With her own cursed gore; repave
them with her bones.   150

LI

By Salique law she should not reign:
storms swell
By her, which halcyon days dispel:
Nought 's left that 's good where she
in souls possest does dwell.

LII

'Twas her excess bred plagues! in-
fecting stars,
Infesting dearth, intestine wars
Surfeit with graves the earth, 'mongst
living making jars.

128 'Pleuretic' *sic. in orig.* but should be of course 'pleur*i*tic.'

LIII
My soul, enlabyrinth'd in grief,
  spend years
  In sackcloth, chamleted with
  tears,
Retir'd to rocks' dark entrals, court
  unwitness'd fears.

LIV
There pass with Heraclite a gentler
  age,   160
  Free from the sad account of rage,
That acts the toilsome world on its
  tumultuous stage.

LV
There, sweet Religion strings, and
  tunes, and screws
  The soul's the orb, and doth infuse
Grave *Doric* epods in th' enthusiastic
  Muse.

LVI
There, Love turns trumpets into
  harps, which call
  Off sieges from the gun-shot wall;
Alluring them to Heav'n, her seat
  imperial.

LVII
Thence came our joy, and thence
  hymns eas'd our grief;   169
  Of which th' angelical was chief;
' Glory to GOD ; earth peace ; good
  will for man's relief.'

LVIII
Quills, pluck'd from Venus' doves,
  impress but shame :
  Then, give your rhymes to Vulcan's
  flame ;
He'll elevate your badger feet : he 's
  free, though lame.

LIX
Things fall, and nothings rise ! Old
  Virtue fram'd
  Honour for Wisdom : Wisdom
  fam'd
Old Virtue: such times were ! wealth
  then Art's page was nam'd.

LX
Lambeth was Oxford's whetstone :
  yet above
  Preferment's pinnacle they move,

Who string the universe, and
  bracelet it for love.   180

LXI
Virtue's magnific orb inflames their
  zeal ;
  By high-rais'd anthems plagues
  they heal ;
And threefork'd thunders in
  Heav'n's outstretch'd arm repeal.

LXII
Shall larks with shrill-chirpt matins
  rouse from bed
  Of curtain'd night Sol's orient head?
And shall quick souls lie numb'd,
  as wrapt in sheets of lead ?

LXIII
Awake from slumb'ring lethargy ;
  the gay
  And circling charioteer of day,
In 's progress through the azure
  fields sees, checks our stay.

LXIV
Arise ; and rising, emulate the rare
  Industrious spinsters, who with fair
Embroid'ries checker-work the
  chambers of the air.   192

LXV
Ascend ; Sol does on hills his gold
  display,
  And, scatt'ring sweets, does spice
  the day,
And shoots delight through Nature
  with each arrow'd ray.

LXVI
The opal-colour'd dawns raise fancy
  high ;
  Hymns ravish those who pulpits
  fly ;
Convert dull lead to active gold
  by love-chemy.

LXVII
As Nature's prime confectioner, the
  bee,   199
  By her flow'r-nibbling chemistry,
Turns *vert* to *or* : so, verse gross
  prose does rarefy.

LXVIII
Pow'rs cannot poets, as they pow'rs
  up-buoy ;

Whose soul-enliv'ning charms decoy
Each wrinkled care to the pacific sea of joy.

LXIX
As, where from jewels sparkling lustre darts,
Those rays enstar the dusky parts :
So, beams of poesy give light, life, soul to arts.

LXX
Rich poesy ! thy more irradiant gems
Give splendour unto diadems,
And with coruscant rays emblaz'st Honour's stems.   210

LXXI
Thee, Muse (Art's ambient air, Invention's door,
The stage of wits) both rich and poor
Do court. A prince may glory to become thy wooer.

LXXII
Poets lie entomb'd by kings. Arts gums dispense ;
By rumination bruis'd, are thence
By verse so fir'd, that their perfume enheav'n's the sense.

LXXIII
Its theory makes all wiser, yet few better ;
Practice is spirit, art the letter ;
Use artless doth enlarge, art useless does but fetter.

LXXIV
Sharp sentences are goads to make deeds go ;   220
Good works are males, words females show :
Whose lives act precedents, prevent the laws, and do.

LXXV
So far we know, as we obey GOD; and
He counts we leave not His command,
When as our interludes but 'twixt our acts do stand.

LXXVI
Honour's brave soul is in that body shrin'd,
Which floats not with each giddy wind
(Fickle as courtly dress), but Wisdom's sea does find :

LXXVII
Steering by *Grace's* pole-star, which is fast
In th' apostolic Zodiac plac'd   230
Whose course at first four evangelic pilots trac'd :

LXXVIII
The Theanthropic Word ; that mystic glass
Of revelations ; that mass
Of oracles ; that fuel of pray'r ; that wall of brass ;

LXXIX
That print of Heav'n on earth ; that *Mercy's* treasure
And key ; that evidence and seizure ;
Faith's card, *Hope's* anchor ; *Love's* full sail ; abyss of pleasure.

LXXX
Such saints' high tides ne'er ebb so low, to shelf
Them on the quicksand of their self-
Swallowing corruption : Sin 's the wrack, they fly that elf,   240

LXXXI
Gloomier than west of death ; than north of night ;
Than nest of triduan blacks, with fright
Which Egypt scar'd when He brought darkness who made light.

LXXXII
Compar'd to whose storm, thund'ring peals are calm :
Compar'd to whose sting, asps yield balm :
Compar'd to whose loath'd charm, death is a mercy-psalm.

222 Orig. ' Presidents ' as often.   236 seizure] In the legal sense.
242 triduan blacks] Characteristic for ' three days' darkness,' or ' mourning,' cf. II. 211.

LXXXIII

Her snares escap'd, soar, Muse, to
   Him, whose bright
Spirit-illuminating sight
Turns damps to glorious days; turns
   fogs to radiant light.

LXXXIV

Religion's Wisdom's study; that
   display,   250
   Lord, countermand what goes
   astray;
And smite the ass (rude Flesh) when
   it does start or bray.

LXXXV

Soul, thou art less than Mercy's
   least; three ne'er
Depart from sin: Shame, Guilt,
   and Fear:
Fear, Shame, Guilt, Sin are four;
   yet all in one appear.

LXXXVI

Crest-fall'n by sin, how wretchedly
   I stray!
Methinks 'tis pride in me to pray:
Heav'n aid me struggling under this
   sad load of clay.

LXXXVII

No man may merit, yet did One,
   we hold;
Who most do vaunt their zeal,
   are cold: 260
Thus tin for silver goes with these,
   and brass for gold.

LXXXVIII

Renew my heart, direct my tongue,
   unseal
My hand, inspire my faith, reveal
My hope, increase my love, and my
   backslidings heal!

LXXXIX

Let language (man's choice glory)
   serve the mind:
Thy Spirit on Bezaleel shin'd:
Help, Blood, by faith applied! Thy
   spittle cur'd the blind.

XC

Turn sense to spirit; Nature's
   chang'd alone

By grace; that is the chemic-stone:
And Thy all-pow'rful Word is pure
   projection;   270

XCI

Truth's touchstone, surest rule that
   ere was fram'd
(Tradition, man's dark map, 's
   disclaim'd),
The paper burns me not, yet I am
   all inflam'd:

XCII

For, as I read, such inward splendour
   glows;
Such life-renewing vigour flows,
That all, what's known of Thy most
   righteous will, it shows:

XCIII

Whose spells make Enoch's walk
   with Thee; withhold
Corruption, and translate ere old:
All Vaticans are dross; this magi-
   sterial gold.

XCIV

Thus, poor numb'd Tartars, when
   they're brought into   280
   Warm Persia's gem-pav'd court,
   are so
Reviv'd, that then they live; till
   then half dead with snow.

XCV

Good thoughts from Thee infus'd I
   do derive;
Good words effus'd Thou dost me
   give;
Good works diffus'd by Thee, in
   Thee do live and thrive.

XCVI

Nerve-stretching Muse, thy bow's
   new strung; shoot
Hymns to the Best, from worst
   of men;
Make arts thy tributaries, twist heart,
   tongue, and pen.

279 magisterial] In the alchemical sense 'pure' 'precipitated from an admixture.'
280 bow's] The metre requires *is* in full but the habit of contraction prevailed.

XCVII

But how can Eve's degenerate issue, bent
To sin, in its weak measures vent
Thy praise: Unmeasurable! and
Omnipotent? 291

XCVIII

Shrubs cannot cedars, nor wrens
eagles praise;
Nor purblind owls on Sol's orb
gaze:
What is a drop to seas, a beam to
boundless rays?

XCIX

Yet Hope and Love may raise my
drooping flight;
And faith in Thee embeam my
night:
Great Love, supply Faith's nerves
with wingèd hope—I WRITE.

C

My spirit, LORD, my soul, my body, all
My thoughts, words, works, hereafter
shall 299
Praise Thee, and sin bemoan.
JESU, how lov'dst Thou me!
Me blessed, Thy Love make!
Me raised, Thy Love take!
JESU, my precious One!
May this, LOVE'S OFFERING, be!
My heart, tongue, eye, hand, bowèd
knee,
As all came from, let all return to Thee!

NUNC sacra primus habet Finem, mea
Cura, Libellus;
Jam precor impellat sanctior Aura
ratem!
I felix, rapidas diffindas Cærula
Syrtes;
Te Divina regit Dextera; Sospes
abi.

NON NOBIS DOMINE.

THEOPHILA'S LOVE-SACRIFICE

The Summary of the Poem

THEOPHILA, or Divine Love, ascends to her Beloved by three degrees: by Humility, by Zeal, by Contemplation. In the first she is sincere, in the second fervent, in the third ecstatical. In her humiliation she sadly condoles her sin, in her devotion she improves her grace, in her meditation she antedates her glory, and triumphantly congratulates the fruition of her Spouse. And by three Ways, which divines call the Purgative, Illuminative, and Unitive, she is happily led into the disquisition of sin by man; of suffering by CHRIST as Sponsor; of salvation by Him as Redeemer. In the Purgative Way she falls upon repentance, mortification, self-denial; helped in part by the knowledge of herself, which breeds contrition, renunciation, and purpose of amendment: in the Illuminative she pursues moral virtues, theological graces, and gospel promises, revealed by CHRIST, as the great Apostle, which begets in her gratitude, imitation, and appropriation. In the Unitive she is wholly taken up with intuition of super-celestial excellences, with beatifical apprehensions and adherences, as to CHRIST in body, to the HOLY GHOST in spirit, to GOD the FATHER in a bright resemblance of the Divine Nature. All which are felt by the knowledge of CHRIST as Mediator; whence flow admiration, elevation, consummated in glorification. And were mysteriously

Stanza c] This, which even as printed has the *shape* of an altar, is in orig. framed with an actual altar outlined and shaded. See Introduction for Butler's flings at our poet's indulgence in this not uncommon nor uncomely freak.

intimated in the symbolical oblations of the star-led *Sophies*[1], who by their myrrh signified faith, chastity, mortification, the purgative actions; by their incense implied hope, prayer, obedience, the illuminative devotions; by their gold importing charity, satiety, radiancy, the unitive eminences: and it is the only ambition of THEOPHILA to offer these presents to her Beloved; by whom her sin is purged, her understanding enlightened, her will and affections inflamed to the communion of all His glories. Thus she, by recollecting past creation, present corruption,. and future beatifical vision, endeavours to rouse us up from hellish security, worldly solicitude, and carnal concupiscence, that, being raised, we may conform to the will, submit to the power, and sympathize with the Spirit of CHRIST, by a total resignation of self-comforts, abilities, ends; and by the internal acts of love, devotion, contemplation, she makes Sense subservient to Reason, Reason to Faith, and Faith to the written Word. By Faith she believes what He has revealed, and yields Him up all her understanding: by Hope she waits for His promises, and refers to Him all her will. By Charity she loves His excellences, and resigns to Him all her affections. And by all these she triumphs over sin, death, hell, in the sensual world, and by His virtue, grace, favour, enjoys an eminent degree of perfection in the intellectual.

The Author's Prayer

O THOU most High, distinct in Persons, undivided in Essence! Eternal Principle of all substances, essential Being of all subsistences, Cause of all causalities, Life of our souls, and Soul of our lives! Whose DEITY is as far beyond the comprehension of our reason as Thy omnipotency transcends our impotency: We, wretched dust, acknowledge that Adam's fall, as it *deprived* us of all good, so hath it *depraved* us with all evil; for, from our production to our dissolution, our life, if strictly discussed, will be found wholly tainted, always tempted with sin. We discover our condition to be more corrupt than we can fully discover: the sense of our sin stupefies us, the sight of it reveals our blindness, and the remembrance thereof doth put us in mind of our forgetfulness of Thee. The number of our transgressions surpasseth our skill in arithmetic; their weight is insupportable, depressing us even to the abyss; their guilt more extense than anything but thy mercy. O LORD, we have loved darkness more than light, because our deeds were evil! therefore, Thou hast showed us terrible things; we have sucked out the dregs of deadly wine! Our national crimes have extorted from Thy justice national judgements! Our hellish sins inflame Thy wrath, and Thy wrath inflames hell-fire against us! We want so much of happiness as of obedience (our beatitude consisting in a thorough submission of our determinations unto Thy disposings, and our practice to Thy providence), which causeth us, with humbly-pressing importunity, to implore Thy goodness (for His sake, who of mere love took upon Him a nature of infirmities to cure the infirmities of our nature) that Thou wouldst give us a sense of our senselessness, and a fervent desire of more fervency; and true remorse and sorrow for want of remorse and sorrow for these our sins. Oh, steer the mystical ship of Thy Church safe amidst the rocks and quicksands of schism and heresy, superstition and sacrilege, into the fair havens of Peace and Truth! Give to Thy disconsolate Spouse, melting in tears of blood, the spirit of sanctity and prudence! May the light which conducts her to Thy celestial Canaan be never mocked by new false lights of apostatizing

---

[1] i. e. the Wise Men or Three Kings: to whom Benlowes extends the form commonly reserved for the Persian monarch.

hypocrisy, nor extinguished by barbarism! Thou, our FATHER, art the GOD of Peace; Thy SON, our SAVIOUR, the Prince of Peace; Thy SPIRIT, the Spirit of Peace, Thy servants, the children of Peace, whose duty is the study of Peace, and the end of their faith the Peace of GOD which passeth all understanding! Let all submit to Thy sceptre, adore Thy judgements, revere Thy laws, and love Thee above all, for Thine own sake, and others (even their enemies) for Thy sake, having Thee for our pattern, Thy precepts for our rule, and Thy Spirit for our guide.

And now, in particular, I throw myself (who have unmeasurably swerved from Thy statutes) upon Thy mercies; beseeching Thee to give me a deep sense of my own unworthiness, and yet withal sincere thankfulness for Thy assistances: grant that my sorrow for sin may be unfeigned, my desires of forgiveness fervent, my purpose of amendment steadfast; that so my hopes of Heaven may be advanced, and, what Thou hast sown in Thy mercy Thou mayst reap from my duty! Let religion and right reason rule as sovereign in me, and let the irascible and concupiscible faculties be their subjects! Give me an estate balanced between want and waste [1], pity and envy; give me grace to spend my wealth and strength in Thy service; let all my melancholy be repentance, my joys spiritual exultations, my rest hope, my peace a good conscience, and my acquiescence in Thee! In Thee, as the principle of truth, in Thy Word as the measure of knowledge, in Thy law as the rule of life, in Thy promise as the satisfaction of hope, and in Thy union as the highest fruition of glory! Oh, Thou Spring of Bounty, who hast given Thy SON to redeem me, Thy HOLY SPIRIT to sanctify me, and THYSELF to satisfy me: give me a generous contempt of sensual delusions, that I may see the vanity of the world, the deceitfulness of riches, the shame of pleasures, the folly of sports, the inconstancy of honours, the danger of greatness, and the strict account to be given for all! Oh, then give me an un-

daunted fortitude, an elevated course of contemplation, a resignation of spirit, and a sincere desire of Thy glory! Add, O LORD, to the cheerfulness of my obedience, the assurance of faith, and to the confidence of my hope, the joys of love! Oh, Thou who art the fountain of my faith, the object of my joy, and the rock of my confidence, guide my passion by reason, my reason by religion, my religion by faith, my faith by Thy Word; be pleased to improve Thy Word by Thy SPIRIT; that so, being established by faith, confirmed in hope, and rooted in charity, I may be only ambitious of Thee, prizing Thee above the delights of men, love of women, and treasures of the world! Nothing being so precious as Thy favour, so dreadful as Thy displeasure, so hateful as sin, so desirable as Thy grace! Let my heart be always fixed upon Thee, possessed by Thee, established in Thee, true unto Thee, upright toward Thee, and entire for Thee! that being thus inebriated with the sweet and pure streams of Thy sanctuary, I may serve Thee to the utmost of each faculty, with all the extension of my will, and intention of my affections, till my love shall ascend from earth to Heaven, from small beginnings to the consummation of a well-regulated and never-ceasing charity! O GOD, who art no less infinite in wisdom than in goodness, let me, where I cannot rightly know Thee, there reverently admire Thee, that in transcendencies my very ignorance may honour Thee. Let Thy HOLY SPIRIT inflame my zeal, inform my judgement, conform my will, reform my affections, and transform me wholly into the image and imitation of Thy only SON! Grant that I may improve my talent to Thy glory, who art the imparter of the gift, the blesser of the action, and the assister of the design! So that having sown to the Spirit, I may by Thy mercies and Thy SON'S merits (who is the Son of Thy love, the anchor of my hope, and the finisher of my faith) reap life everlasting! And now, in His only Name vouchsafe to accept from dust and ashes the oblation of this weak, yet willing service; and secure the pos-

---

[1] There is humorous pathos in this, considering what we are told of Benlowes' fortunes.

session to Thyself, that sin may neither pollute the sacrifice, divide the gift, nor question the title. Fill my mouth with praises for these happy opportunities of contemplation, the managing of public actions less agreeing with my disposition; and though my body be retired, yet let my soul be enlarged (like an uncaptived bird) to soar in the speculation of divine mysteries! Oh, be praised, for that, in this general combustion of Christendom, Thou hast vouchsafed me a litttle Zoar, as refuge, in which my soul doth yet live to magnify Thee; but above all for my redemption from the execution of Thy wrath by the execration of the SON of Thy love, having made innocence to become guilty, to make the guilty innocent, and the Sun of Righteousness to suffer a total eclipse to expiate the deeds of darkness. Be Thou exalted for the myriads of Thy mercies in my travels through Europe, as far

transcending my computation as compensation; but chiefly for the hope Thou hast given me, that when I have served Thee in humbly strict obedience to the glory of Thy Name, Thou art pleased that I shall enter into the glory of my LORD to all eternity; where I shall behold THEE in Thy majesty, CHRIST Thy SON in His glory, the SPIRIT in His sanctity, the Hierarchy of Heaven in their excellency, and the saints in their rest; in which rest there is perfect tranquillity, and in this tranquillity joy, and in this joy variety, and in this variety security, and in this security immortality, with Thee, who reignest in the excellences of transcendency, and in the infinite durations of a blessed eternity. To whom, with the image of Thy goodness, and the breath of Thy love, O most glorious TRINITY and ineffable UNITY, be all sanctity and adoration sacrificed now, and for evermore. *Amen, Amen.*

INTO the most Holy Treasury
Of the ever-glorious praises
Of the MEDIATOR between
GOD and man, CHRIST JESUS;
The empyraean flame of the Divinity,
Indefinable, interminable, ineffable;
The immaculate earth of the Humanity,
Inseparable, inconfusible, inconvertible;
Mysterious in an hypostatical Union,
Who is,
The true Light enlightening the World
The Eternal WORD,

By Energy incarnated,
{ Embrightening our knowledge,
{ Enlivening our Faith,
{ Quickening our Hope,
{ Enflaming our Love:
Prostrated dust and ashes,
With an adoring awfulness and trembling veneration.
To his Infinite Majesty
Doth humbly cast this mite
(Acknowledging from GOD all opportunities of good) to be improved
by His grace, to His glory[1].

[1] The matter of these two cols. is in orig. continuous and arranged pedestal-fashion. But there is no *frame* as in the former case, and it is therefore not certain that Benlowes intended the shape.

Canto II. The Humiliation

THE ARGUMENT

Unde superbit Homo? cujus Conceptio, Culpa;
  Nasci, Pœna, Labor, Vita; necesse mori.
Totus homo pravus; Caro, Mens, Natura, Voluntas;
Cœlicus ast Hominis Crimina tollit AMOR.

The Deiform'd soul, deformed by sin, repents;
  In pray'rs and tears, her grief she vents,
And, till faith cheer her by CHRIST's love, life, death, laments.

STANZA I

ALMIGHTY Power, who didst all souls
    create;
  Who didst redeem their fall'n
    estate;
Who still dost sanctify, and them
    redintegrate.

II

Source, river, ocean of all bliss,
    instil
  Spring-tides into my low-ebb'd
    quill:
Each graceful work flows from (what
    works all grace) Thy Will.

III

LORD! Thou, before time, matter,
    form, or place,
  Wast all; ere nature's mortal race:
Thyself, host, guest, and palace,
    nature's total space.

IV

When yet (though not discern'd)
    in that abyss   10
  Creator, Word, and Spirit of bliss,
In Unity the Trine, one GOD, ador-
    ed is.

V

Ere Thou the crystal-mantled
    Heav'n didst rear,
  Or did the earth, Sol's bride,
    appear,
First race of intellectuals mad'st,
    Thee to revere.

VI

Praise best doth Inexpressibles
    express:

Soul, th' Architect of wonders
    bless;
  Whose all-creating Word embirth'd
    a nothingness.

VII

Who, brooding on the deep, produc-
    tion
  Dispos'd, then call'd out Light,
    which on   20
The formless world's rude face was
    all dispers'dly thrown.

VIII

When callow Nature, pluck'd from
    out her nest
  Of causes, was awak'd from rest,
Her shapeless lump with fledg'd
    effects He trimly drest.

IX

Then new-born day He gilt with
    glittering sun
  (Contracted light); with changing
    Moon
He night adorn'd, and hung up
    lamps, like spangled bullion.

X

The earth, with water mixed, He
    separates:
  Earth plants brought forth, and
    beasts all mates;
The waters fowl, and fish to yield
    man delicates.   30

XI

Then did of th' elements' dust man's
    body frame
  A perfect microcosm, the same
He quickened with a sparkle of
    pneumatic flame.

XII

More heav'nly specified by life
  from th' Word;
  That, Nature doth, this, Grace
  afford;
And Glory from the Spirit design'd,
  as threefold cord.

XIII

Man, ere a child; by infusion wise;
  though He
  Was of, yet not for earth, though
  free
Chanc'llor install'd of Eden's Uni-
  versity.

XIV

His virgin-sister-wife i' th' grove he
  woo'd   40
(Heav'n's nursery); new fruit his
  food,
Skin was his robe : clouds wash'd,
  winds swept his floor.

XV

Envy, that GOD should so love man,
  first mov'd all good.
  Satan, to ruin Heav'n's belov'd:
The serpent devill'd Eve, she's dam
  to Adam prov'd.

XVI

Both taste, by tasting, tasteless
  both became;
  Who all would know, knew nought
  but shame:
They blush for that which they,
  when righteous, could not name.

XVII

Still in our maw that apple's core
  doth stick,
  Which they did swallow, and the
  thick   50
Rind of forbidden fruit has left
  our nature sick.

XVIII

Now serves our guiltiness as winding
  sheet,
  To wrap up lepers; cover meet;
While thus stern vengeance does
  our wormships sadly greet.

XIX

' Disloyal slaves, look out, see, Mis-
  chief revels;
  Look in, see your own den of evils;
Look up, see Heav'n's dread Judge;
  look down, see Hell's fierce
  devils.

XX

' Created in GOD's image to look high;
  Corrupted, like to brutes, you lie:
Perdition's from yourselves: no cure
  for those will die.   60

XXI

'Your beauty, rottenness skinn'd o'er,
  does show
  Like to a dunghill, blanch'd with
  snow,
Your glorious nature's by embasing
  sin brought low.

XXII

' Hence you the heavy doom of
  death do gain,
  Enforc'd unto laborious pain;
And th' Angel's flaming sword doth
  you, expuls'd, restrain.'

XXIII

Thus she reproach'd; yet more (alas)
  remain'd;
  Man's issue in his loins is stain'd:
Sin set his throne in him, and since
  o'er all has reign'd.

XXIV

Black sin! more hideous than green
  dragon's claws,   70
  Dun gryphon's talons, swart bear's
  paws,
Than chequer'd panther's teeth, or
  tawny lion's jaws.

XXV

Forfeit to the Creator's thus man's
  race,
  And by the Word withdrawn is
  grace,
From him the Spirit of Glory turn'd
  His pleasing face.

---

45 dam] Of course as a play on *damnum* and perhaps with reminiscence of the
actual French word. Benlowes often shows Fr. influences.

XXVI

Yet that this second race, in fallen
plight,
  Might not with the first be ruin'd
  quite,
The Word doth interpose to stop th'
incensèd Might.

XXVII

Then undertakes for man to satisfy,
  And the sad loss of Grace supply
That us He might advance to Glory's
hierarchy.   81

XXVIII

Then Peace is preach'd i'th'woman's
Seed ; but then
  As men increase, so, sins of men,
And actual on original heap'd, God's
vex'd again.

XXIX

Till drench'd they were in Deluge,
had no shore ;
  And burnt in Sodom-flames, of
  yore ;
Plagued in Egypt, plung'd into the
gulf of Core ;

XXX

And gnawn by worms in Herod :
sin's asp's womb,
  Plotter, thief, plaintiff, witness,
  doom,
Sledge, executioner, hell's inmate,
horror's tomb.   90

XXXI

Misgotten brat ! thy trains are
infinite
  To ruin each entangled wight ;
Mischiefs ne'er rest in men, th' have
everlasting spite.

XXXII

Spite wageth war, then war turns
law to lust ;
  Lust crumbles faith into distrust ;
Distrust by causeless jealousy betrays
the just ;

XXXIII

The just are plunder'd by thy rage ;
thy rage

Bubbleth from envy ; envy's page
  To thy misdeeds ; misdeeds their
  own misfate engage.

XXXIV

Thus link'd to Hell's thy chain !
Curs'd be that need   100
  Makes sinners in their sins pro-
  ceed :
Shame, to guilt's forlorn hope, leads
left-hand files.   Take heed.

XXXV

God's fort (the conscience) in the
worst does stand ;
  Though sin the town keeps by
  strong hand,
Yet lies it open to the check at
Heav'n's command.

XXXVI

Hence Hell surrounds them : in
their dreams to fall
  Headlong they seem, then start,
  groan, crawl
From furies, with excessive frights
which them appal.

XXXVII

Ne'er was more mischief, ne'er was
less remorse ;
  Never Revenge on his black horse
Did swifter ride ; never to God so
slow recourse !   111

XXXVIII

The age-bow'd earth groans under
sinners' weight ;
  While guiltless blood cries to
  Heav'n's height,
Justice soon takes th' alarm, whose
steelèd arm will smite.

XXXIX

Inevitable woes a while may stay,
  Vengeance is God's, who will
  repay
The desperately wilful nor will
long delay.

XL

'Tis darkest near daybreak.   He will
o'erturn
  Th' implacable, who mercy spurn

87 Cf. A. V. Ep. S. Jude ver. 11 'the gainsaying of Core.'   Benlowes obviously has
the context in mind.
102 left-hand files] Perhaps one of the *military* passages which drew Butler's fire.

Superlative abuses in th' abyss shall
  burn.   120

XLI

Death's hell Death's self out-deaths !
  Vindictive place !
Deep under depths ! Eccentric
  space !
Horror itself, than thee, wears a
  less horrid face !

XLII

Where pride, lust, rage (sin treble-
  pointed) dwell ;
Shackled in red-hot chains they yell
In bottomless extremes of never-
  slaking Hell !

XLIII

Riddle ! Compell'd, at once, to live
  and die !
Frying they freeze, and freezing fry!
On helpless, hopeless, easeless,
  endless racks they lie !

XLIV

And rave for what they hate !
  Cursing in vain,   130
Yet each curse is a pray'r for pain,
For, cursing still their woe, they woo
  GOD's curse again !

XLV

Devils and shrieks their ears, their
  eyes affright !
There 's blazing fire, yet darkest
  night !
Still paying, ne'er discharg'd. Sin's
  debt is infinite !

XLVI

Angels by one sin fell ; so, man :
  how then
May sinners stand ! Let 's quit
  sin's den :
This moment 's ours ; life hastes
  away ; delays gangrene.

XLVII

Conviction ushers Grace ; fall to
  prevent
Thy fall, Time's forelock take ;
  relent.   140
Shall is to come ; and *Was* is past;
  then, *Now* repent.

XLVIII

Before the sun's long shadows span
  up night ;
Ere on thy shaking head snows
  light ;
Ere round thy palsied heart ice be
  congealèd quite ;

XLIX

Ere in thy pocket thou thine eyes
  dost wear ;
Ere thy bones serve for calender ;
Ere in thy hand 's thy leg, or silver
  in thy hair ;

L

Preventing physic use. Think, now
  ye hear
The dead-awakening trump ; lo ;
  there
The queasy-stomach'd graves dis-
  gorge worms-fat'ning cheer 150

LI

Sin's sergeants wait t' attach you ;
  then make haste,
Lest you into despair be cast :
The JUDGE unsway'd : take days at
  best, count each your last.

LII

Time posts on loose-rein'd steeds.
  The sun ere 't face
To west, may see thee end thy race :
Death is a noun, yet not declin'd
  in any case.

LIII

The cradle 's nigh the tomb. That
  soul has woe,
Whose drowsy march to Heav'n
  is slow,
As drawling snails, whose slime
  glues them to things below.

LIV

Anathema to lukewarm souls. Lo,
  here   160
Theophila 's unhing'd with fear,
Clamm'd with chill sweat, when as
  her rankling sins appear.

LV

Perplex'd in crime's meand'ring maze,
  GOD's law,

XLVIII-XLIX] The poetry and the grotesque of the 'metaphysical' style are well
shown in this pair of stanzas.

And guilt, that does strict judge-
ment draw,
And her too carnal, yet too stony
heart she saw.

LVI

'Yet rocks may cleave,' she cries.
Then weeps for tears,
And grieves for grief; fears want
of fears;
She hell, Heav'n's prison, views;
distress, for robe, she wears.

LVII

Deprav'd by vice, depriv'd of grace;
with pray'r,
She runs Faith's course; breaks
through Despair,   170
O'ertakes Hope. Broken legs by
setting stronger are.

LVIII

Shame, native Conscience, views that
Holy One,
Who came from GOD to man un-
done,
Whose birth produc'd a star, whose
death eclips'd the sun.

LIX

She sees Earth-Heav'n, Flesh-spirit,
Man-God in stamp
Of Him who shakes, but does not
cramp
The bruised reed; snuffs puts not
out the sputt'ring lamp.

LX

She sees for creatures the Creator
came
To die; the Shepherd prov'd the
lamb
For sacrifice, when Jews releas'd
a spotted ram.   180

LXI

She sees defamèd Glory, wrongèd
Right,
Debasèd Majesty, crush'd Might,
Virtue condemn'd, Peace robb'd,
Love slain! and all by Spite.

LXII

She streaming sees, like spouts,
each broachèd vein
With gore, not to be match'd
again!

(350)

Her grief thence draws up mists to
fall in weeping rain.

LXIII

Vast cares, long dumb, thus vent.
'Flow tears, Soul's wine,
Juice of an heart opprest; incline,
LORD, to this heart-broke altar
cemented with brine!

LXIV

'Remorseful clouds, dissolve in
show'rs; 'tis blood   190
Turns rocky hearts into a flood:
Eyes, keep your sluices ope; Heav'n
best by tears is woo'd.

LXV

'Thou, who one shoreless sea of all
didst make,
Except one floating isle, to take
Vengeance on guilt; my salt flood
rais'd, drown sin i' th' lake.

LXVI

'Oh, how these words, "Arise to
judgement," quell!
On wheels in torments broke I'd
dwell,
So as by grace I might be sav'd
from endless Hell.

LXVII

'To Angel-intercessor, I'm forbid
To pray; yet pray to One that
did   200
Pray to Another for Himself when 's
blood-drops slid.

LXVIII

'Father! Perfection's self in CHRIST
does shine;
Thy justice then in Him confine;
Through 's merits make Thy mercies,
both are endless, mine!

LXIX

'See not, but through 's abstersive
blood, my sin;
By which I being cleans'd within,
Add perseverance. 'Tis as hard to
hold as win.'

LXX

Her eyes are sentinels to pray'r, to
moans
Her ears, her nose courts charnel-
bones;

Her hands breast-hammers are, her
  constant food is groans. 210

LXXI

Her heart is hung with blacks, with
  dust she cloys
  Her golden tresses ; weds annoys,
Breeds sighs, bears grief, which,
  ibis-like, sin-snakes destroys.

LXXII

Thus mounts she drizzling Olivet ;
  the plains
  Of Jericho she leaves. (While rains
The farmer wet, they fully swell his
  earing grains.)

LXXIII

She, her own farmer, stock'd from
  Heav'n, is bent
  To thrive; care 'bout the pay-day's
  spent.
Strange ! She alone is farmer, farm,
  and stock, and rent.

LXXIV

The porcupine so's quiver, bow, and
  darts 220
  To herself alone ; has all war's
  arts ;
Her own artillery needs no aid from
  foreign parts.

LXXV

Sad votaress ! thy earth, of late o'er-
  grown
  With weeds, is plough'd, till'd,
  harrow'd, sown.
The seed of grace sprouts up when
  Nature is kept down.

LXXVI

Thy glebe is mellow'd with faith-
  quick'ning juice ;
  The furrows thence hope-blades
  produce ;
Thy valley cloth'd with Love will
  harvest joys diffuse.

LXXVII

Live, Phœnix, from self-death. I' th'
  morn who dies
  To sin, does but immortalize : 230
Who study death, ere dead, ere th'
  Resurrection rise.

(351)

LXXVIII

Rachel, thy children goal and crown
  have won,
  Ere they had skill or will to
  run.
Blest, who their whole day's work
  in their life's morn have done.

LXXIX

Like misty morn, she rose in dew ;
  so found
  She ne'er was, till this sickness,
  sound ;
Till sin, in sorrow's flowing issue
  (tears) lay drown'd.

LXXX

Soul's life blood tears, prevailing
  pleaders, tame
  Such rebels, as by Eve did shame
Man's glory ; only these the old
  fall'n world new frame. 240

LXXXI

Lust causeth sin, sin shame, shame
  bids repent,
  Repentance weeps, tears sorrow
  vent,
Sorrow shows faith, Faith hope,
  Hope love, Love soul's content.

LXXXII

Thus, from bruis'd spiceries of her
  breast, doth rise
  Incense, sweet-smelling sacrifice :
Whilst she lifts up to Heav'n her
  heart, her hand, her eyes.

LXXXIII

' I'm sick with trembling, sunk with
  mourning, blasted
  With sinning, and with sighing
  wasted ;
New life begins to breathe ; O joy,
  too long untasted !

LXXXIV

' Twice didst new life (by breath,
  by death) bestow 250
  On man prevaricating, who,
By yielding to a woman, made man
  yield to woe.

LXXXV

' Then didst his soul *restore* (as first
  inspire)
  With second grace, renewing fire ;

Whence he hath part again in Thy
    celestial quire.

LXXXVI

' Once more for this Heav'n-denizen
    didst get
A never-fading coronet,
Which was with two bright jewels,
    Grace and Glory, set.

LXXXVII

' 'Twas at my blood-stain'd birth
    Thy Love said, *Live* :
Links of Thy previous chain re-
    vive   260
Ev'n crumbled dust : so, thou my
    soul from death reprieve !

LXXXVIII

' CHRIST, th' unction art, Salvation
    JESUS ; in
Thy death redemption, blood for
    sin
Gives satisfaction, Thy Ascension
    hope does win ;

LXXXIX

' Thy session comfort.   Though I
    did offend,
LORD, fears disband, give grace
    t' amend,
That, hope, which reaps not shame,
    may rise, and peace descend.

XC

' My pardon sign. The spear pierc'd
    Thee 's the pen,
Thy blood the ink, Thy Gospel then
The standish is, Oh, let my soul
    be paper clean !   270

XCI

' Kind, angry LORD, since Thou dost
    wound, yet cure ;
I'll bear the yoke, the cross endure ;
Lament, and love ; and, when set
    free, keep conscience pure.'

XCII

Thus mourns she, and, in mourning
    thus, she joys ;
Ev'n that adds comfort which
    annoys ;
Sighs turn to songs, and tears to
    wine, fear Fear destroys.

XCIII

As holy flame did from her heart
    arise,
Dropt holy water from her eyes,
While pray'r her incense was, and
    Love her sacrifice.

XCIV

Arm ! arm ! she breaks in with
    strong zeal ; the place   280
Sin quits, now garrison'd by Grace ;
Illustrious triumphs do the steps of
    victors trace.

XCV

When the loud volleys of her pray'rs
    begin
To make a breach, they soon
    take in
The parapets, redoubts, and counter-
    scarps of sin.

XCVI

At once she works and fights : with
    lamp she waits,
Midst virgins, at the Bridegroom's
    gates,
With Him to feast her with His
    bridal delicates.

XCVII

To Heav'n now goes she on her
    knees ; which cry
Loud, as her tongue ; much speaks
    her eye :   290
Heav'n, storm'd by violence, yields.
    Eyes, tongue, and knees scale
    high.

XCVIII

' My last crave pardon for my first
    extremes ;
Be prais'd, who crown'st my morn
    with beams ;
Converted age sees visions, erring
    youth dreamt dreams.

XCIX

' Religion 's its own lustre ; who this
    shun,
Night-founder'd grope at midday
    sun.

---

256 denizen] Original ' denison.'

(352)

Rebellion is its own self-tort'ring
  dungeon.'

C

Man's restless mind, GOD's image,
  can't be blest
Till of this One, this All, possest.
Thou our Soul's Centre art, our
  everlasting REST!   300

Pars superata Freti, Lucem præ-
  bentibus Astris;
Longior at nostræ Pars superanda
  Viæ.
Da, DEUS, ut Cursus suscepti nostra
  propinquet
Meta, laboranti grata futura Rati.

MAGNIFICAT ANIMA MEA DOMINUM.

Canto III.   The Restoration

THE ARGUMENT

Lætior una Dies, JESU, tua Sacra Canenti;
  Quàm sine Te, melicis Secula mille Lyris.
Ut paveam Scelus omne, petam super Omnia Cœlum;
  Da mihi Fræna Timor, Da mihi Calcar Amor!

The author's rapture; Grace is prais'd; a flood
  Of tears is pour'd for Albion's blood,
Shed in a mist; for smot[e] Micaiahs, Peace is woo'd.

STANZA I

MUSE, twang the pow'rful harp, and
  brush each string
O' th' warbling lute, and canzons
  sing
May ravish earth, and thence to
  Heav'n in triumph spring.

II

Noble Du Bartas, in a high-flown
  trance,
Observ'd to start from 's bed and
  dance;
Said: 'Thus by me shall caper all
  the realm of France.'

III

As vicious meteors, fram'd of earthly
  slime,
By motion fir'd, like stars, do
  climb
The woolly-curdled clouds, and
  there blaze out their time,

IV

Streaming with burnish'd flames;
  yet those but ray   10

To spend themselves, and light
  our way;
And panting winds, to cool ours,
  not their own lungs, play.

V

So [when] enliven'd spirits ascend
  the skies,
Wasting to make the simple wise,
Who bears the torch, himself shades,
  lightens others' eyes.

VI

As Lust for Hell, Zeal sweats to build
  for Heav'n,
When fervent aspirations, driv'n
By all the soul's quick pow'rs, to that
  high search are giv'n.

VII

High is the sphere on which Faith's
  poles are hinged:
Pure Knowledge, thou art not
  restringed,   20
Thy flames enfire the bushy heart,
  yet leave 't unsinged.

13 when] This is not in orig., but there is a space before 'enlivened' (not to mention the sense), and the metre requires something. The clash of '*when en-*' probably puzzled the compositor. I have altered the full stop at 'wise' to a comma: but this is not necessary now if 'when' be inserted.

VIII

Suburbs of Paradise! Thou saintly
    land
  Of visions, woo'd by Wisdom's
    band;
By dull mules in gold-trappings how
    dost slighted stand!

IX

Whose world's a frantic sea; more
    cross winds fly
  Than sailor's compass knows;
    saints ply
Their sails through airy waves, and
    anchor still on high.

X

'Tis Holiness landst here; where
    none (distasted)
  Rave with guilt's dread, nor with
    rage wasted;
Nor beauty-dazzled eyes with female
    wantons blasted.   30

XI

No childish toys; no boiling youth's
    wild thirst;
  No ripe ambition; no accurst
Old griping avarice; no doting
    sloth there's nurst:

XII

No glutt'ny's maw-worm; nor the
    itch of lust;
  No tympany of pride; nor rust
Of envy; no wrath's spleen; nor
    obduration's crust:

XIII

No canker of self-love; nor cramp
    of cares;
  No schism-vertigo; nor night-
    mares
Of inward stings affright; here lurk
    no penal snares.

XIV

Hence earth a dim spot shows;
  where mortals toil   40
  For shot-bruis'd mud-walls (child-
    ish broil);
For pot-gun cracks 'gainst ant-hill
    works; oh, what a coil!

XV

Where Glutt'ny is full gorg'd; where
    Lust still spawns;
  Where Wrath takes blood and
    Avarice pawns;
Where Envy frets, Pride struts, and
    dull Remissness yawns.

XVI

Where Mars th' ascendant's: how
    realms shatter'd lie
  With scatter'd courts, beneath
    mine eye;
Which show like atoms chas'd by
    wind's inconstancy.

XVII

Here, th' Universe in Nature's frame
    doth stand,
  Upheld by Truth and Wisdom's
    hand: 50
Zanzummims show from hence as
    dwarfs on Pigmy-land.

XVIII

How vile's the world! Fancy, keep
    up thy wings
  (Ruffled in bustle of low things,
Toss'd in the common throng), then
    acquiesce 'bove kings.

XIX

Thus, thou being rapt, and struck
    with enthean fire,
  In sky's star-chamber strike thy
    lyre:
Proud Rome, not all thy Caesars
    could thus high aspire.

XX

Man's spiritual state, enlarg'd, still
    widening flows,
  As th' Helix doth : a circle shows
Man's nat'ral life, which Death soon
    from its zenith throws.   60

XXI

Heav'n's perspective is over-reas'n-
    ing Faith,
  Which soul-entrancing visions
    hath;
Truth's beacon, fir'd by Love, Joy's
    empire open lay'th.

---

24 mules] A reminiscence possibly of Philip's 'ass laden with gold.' I note this as
one of a thousand things that might be noted if the plan of this edition were different.

XXII

This all-informing Light i' th' preg-
nant mind,
The babe Theophila enshrin'd :
Grace dawns when Nature sets :
dawn for fair day design'd.

XXIII

Breathe in thy dainty bud, sweet
rose ; 'tis Time
Makes thee to ripened virtues
climb,
When as the Sun of Grace shall
spread thee to thy prime.

XXIV

When her life's clock struck twelve
(Hope's noon) so bright   70
She beam'd, that queens admir'd
her sight,
Viewing, through Beauty's lantern,
her intrinsic light.

XXV

As, when fair tapers burn in crystal
frame,
The case seems fairer by the flame :
So, does Heav'n's brighter love
brighten this lovely dame ;

XXVI

Her soul the pearl, her shell out-
whites the snow,
Or streams that from stretch'd
udders flow ;
Her lips rock-rubies, and her veins
wrought sapphires show.

XXVII

Attractive graces dance about her
lips ;
Spice from those scarlet portals
skips ;   80
Thence Gilead's mystic balm
(Grief's sov'reign balsam) slips.

XXVIII

Such precious fume the incens'd
altar vents :
So, gums in air breathe compli-
ments :
So, rose's damask'd robe, prank'd
with green ribbons, scents.

XXIX

Her eyes amaze the viewers, and
inspire
To hearts a warm, yet chaste desire
(As Sol heats all), yet feel they in
themselves no fire.

XXX

Those lights, the radiant windows
of her mind,
Who would portray, as soon
may find
A way to paint the viewless, poise
the weightless wind.   90

XXXI

But, might we her sweet breast,
Love's Eden, see ;
On those snow-mountlets apples
be,
May cure those mischiefs wrought
by the forbidden tree.

XXXII

Her hands are soft, as swanny
down, and much
More white ; whose temperate
warmth is such,
As when ripe gold and quick'ning
sunbeams inly touch.

XXXIII

Ye sirens of the groves, who, perch'd
on high,
Tune gutt'ral sweets, air-minstrels,
why
From your bough-cradles, rock'd
with wind, to Her d'ye fly ?

XXXIV

See, lilies, gown'd in tissue, simper
by her ;   100
With marigolds in flaming tire ;
Green satin'd bays, with primrose
fringed, seem all on fire.

XXXV

Th' art silver-voic'd, teeth-pearl'd,
thy head 's gold-thatch'd,
Nature's reviver, Flora 's patch'd,
Though trick'd in May's new raiment,
when with thee she 's match'd.

91] This and the following stanzas give us (I say this not to say it again) one of the
passages for which those who love poetry cannot spare Benlowes. It is one of the
finest.

XXXVI
Thou, chaste as fair, Eve ere she
blush'd ; from thee
The lib'ral arts *in capite*,
The virtues by knight-service, Graces
hold in fee.

XXXVII
A gracious soul, figur'd in beauty, is
Best portraiture of heavenly bliss,
Drawn to the life : wit-feign'd Pan-
dora vails to this.   111

XXXVIII
So, Cynthia seems Star-chamber's
President,
With crescent splendour from Sol
lent,
Rallying her starry troop to guard
her glittering tent.

XXXIX
(Pearl'd dews add stars) Yet earth's
shade shuts up soon
Her shop of beams ; whose cone
doth run
'Bove th' horned moon, beneath the
golden-tressèd sun.

XL
Wh' on sky, clouds, seas, earth,
rocks doth rays disperse,
Stars, rainbows, pearls, fruits,
diamonds pierce ;
The world's eye, source of light,
soul of the universe.   120

XLI
Who glows like carbuncles, when
wingèd hours
Dandle the infant morn, which
scours
Dame Luna, with her twinkling spies,
from azure tow'rs.

XLII
Thee, Theophil, Day's sparkling eye
we call ;
Thy faith 's the lid, thy love the
ball,
Beautying thy graceful mien with
form angelical.

XLIII
That lady-prioress of the cloister'd
sky,
Coach'd with her spangled vestals
nigh,
Vails to this constellation from
divinity.

XLIV
Virtue 's her spring of honour, her
Allies   130
Are saints, Guard angels, Heav'n
her prize ;
Whose modesty looks down, while
thus her graces rise.

XLV
Eugenia wit, Paidia art affords,
Eusebia truth for her uphords.
(Poets have legislative pow'r of
making words.)

XLVI
Her heart 's a court, her richly-
temper'd breast
A chapel for Love's regent Guest :
Here feasts she sacred poets, she
herself a feast.

XLVII
Ye bay-crown'd Lords, who dig from
Wisdom's pits
The ore of arts, and with your
wits   140
Refine't, who prop the doting world
in stagg'ring fits ;

XLVIII
And in Fame's court raise obelisks
divine ;
Such symphonies do ye combine,
As may inspirit flesh with your soul-
ravishing wine.

XLIX
While Winter Autumn, Summer
clasps the Spring ;
While tenter'd Time shall pæans
sing,
Your eagle-plumes (that others
waste) shall imp Fame's wing.

112 The political historian is sometimes severe on the Star-chamber : the literary
could collect a set of plays on the word which more than save it.
133 Note the correct quantification of Paidia as compared with her sisters.
134 Benlowes' note in the next line dispenses one from correcting ' uphoards.'

L

The rampant juice of Teneriffe re-
    cruits
Wildly the routed spirits: so, lutes,
Harps, viols, organs; ah! and trum-
    pets, drums, and flutes!   150

LI

Though Art should humour grum-
    bling basses still,
Tort'ring the deep-mouth'd cat-
    lins, till
Hoarse-thund'ring diapasons should
    the whole room fill;

LII

Yet those but string this lady's
    harp; she'll try
Each chord's tun'd pulse, till she
    descry
Where most harmonious Music's
    mystic soul does lie.

LIII

Now grace with language chimes:
    'Thrice blest, who taste
Their Heav'n on earth, in Life's
    book grac'd;
Who leaving sense with sense, their
    spirit with spirits have plac'd.

LIV

'With those divine patricians, who
    being not   160
Eclips'd with sense, or body's spot,
Are in the spring of living flame
    seraphic hot.

LV

'One taste gives joys! joys at which
    words but rove;
Schools, purblind, grope at things
    above,
Cimmerian-like, on whose sun's
    brow clouds darkly move.

LVI

'Heav'n's paths are traceless, by
    excess of light;
O'er fulgent beams daz'd eyes be-
    night.
Say Ephata, and clay's collyrium for
    my sight!

LVII .

'Transported in this ecstasy, be-
    friend
Me, like the Stagirite, to end
My thoughts in that Euripus, none
    can comprehend!'   171

LVIII

This mystic chain, oh, lengthen'd
    still! imparts
Links, fett'ring 'bove all time-
    born arts;
Such sweet divisions from tun'd
    strings may ravish hearts.

LIX

Best tenure holds by th' ear: in
    Saul, disguis'd,
When Satan oft tarantuliz'd,
The psalming harp was 'bove the
    swaying sceptre priz'd.

LX

This Hymn, Zeal's burning fever,
    does refine
My gross hydropic soul; Divine
Anthems unbowel bliss, and angels
    down incline.   180

LXI

Angels shot forth the happiest
    Christmas news;
Ev'n CHRIST to warble hymns
    did use;
When Heav'n's high'st DOVE does
    soar, He wings of verse doth
    choose.

LXII

No verse, no text. Since verse
    charms all, sing on;
Let sermons wait till Psalms be
    done;
Soul-raisers, ye prevent the Resur-
    rection.

LXIII

But, ah! in war (Wrath's midwife)
    which does tire,
Yet never fills the jaws of ire
(Keen as the evening wolf), can
    she yet use her lyre?

152 catlins] So in orig., and better for 'catgut' than 'catlings,' which suggests
'kittens.' For Benlowes' interest in music see the subjoined poem on the subject.

LXIV
Yes.   She's unmov'd in earthquakes,
     tun'd in jars   190
(Fear argues guilt) ; she stands
     in wars,
And   storms of thund'ring brass,
     bright as coruscant stars.

LXV
Virtue's a balsam to itself.   Invoke
     She Mercy did to oil steel's yoke:
Thus, in an iron age, this golden
     Virgin spoke.

LXVI
' Dread GOD ! black clouds sur-
     charged with storms, begin,
When purple robes hide scarlet
     sin,
Ingrain'd from that life-blood, which
     moated their souls in.

LXVII
' Our sea-girt world (once Fort'nate
     Isle, oh, change
Deplorable !) t'itself seems strange ;
Unthrifty Death has spread where
     thriving Peace did range.   201

LXVIII
' War hath our lukewarm claret
     broach'd with spears :
LORD, save Thy ark from floods
     of fears,
Or Thy sad spouse may sink as deep
     in blood, as tears !

LXIX
' She chaws bread steep'd in woes,
     gulp'd down with cries ;
She drinks the rivers of her eyes ;
Plung'd in distress for sin, to Thee
     she fainting flies.

LXX
' Tune th' Irish harp from sharps
     to flats !   Compose
Whatever vicious harshness grows
Upon the Scottish thistle, or the
     English rose !   210

LXXI
' No ramping lion its own kind
     does fear,

No tuskèd boar, no rav'ning bear :
Man, man's Apollyon, doth CHRIST'S
     mystic Body tear.

LXXII
' Ye sons of thunder, if you'll needs
     fight on,
     Lead your fierce troops 'gainst
     Turkish moon,
Out of the line of Faith's com-
     munication.

LXXIII
' The large-commanding Thracian
     force defy :
     Like   gun-stocks, though your
     corps may fly
To earth, your souls, like bullets,
     will ascend on high.

LXXIV
' If GOD be then i'th' camp, much
     more will He   220
     In's Militant Church (His Temple)
     be,
To chasten schism, and pervicacious
     heresy.

LXXV
' LORD ! rent's Thy coat, Love's type !
     This sads the good !
     Though Presters, rudely fierce,
     fain would
Be heard ; Thou hat'st uncivil pray'r,
     and civil blood.

LXXVI
' Ah, could dissembling pulpiteers
     cry 't good
     To wade through seas of native
     blood,
Break greatest ties, play fast and
     loose, beneath Smect's hood !

LXXVII
' By such were Catechisms, Com-
     munions, Creeds
     Disus'd !   As March spawns frogs ;
     so, weeds   230
Sprung hence.   Worst Atheist from
     corrupted Churchman breeds.

224 Presters] Benlowes wanted a disyllabic form of ' Presbyter,' but one may be sure
that he was not sorry to suggest ' *Prester* John.'
228 Smect] Of course = ' Smectymnuus.'

LXXVIII

'Use the LORD's Pray'r, be th'
  Publican; recant
The Pharisee; or else, avant
With your six-hundred-sixty-six-word
  Covenant.

LXXIX

'LORD, they, through faithless
  dreams, the Feast disown
Of Thy SON's Incarnation!
(Then whether will such Proteus-
  tants at last be blown?)

LXXX

'That Feast of Feasts, Archangel's
  joy, Heav'n here
Espous'd to earth, Saints' bliss,
  most dear
Prerogative o' th' Church, the grand
  day of the year.   240

LXXXI

'Man, first made good, himself un-
  made, and then
The Word, made flesh, must
  dwell with men,
That, man, thus worse than nought,
  may better'd be again.

LXXXII

'Dare to own truth. Drones seiz'd
  the bees' full bow'r;
All's paint that butterflies deflow'r;
As ants improve, so, grasshoppers
  impair their hour.

LXXXIII

'When pirate-wasps sail to the
  honey'd grot,
They'll find a trap-glass, death
  i' th' pot:
Levites, slight not your breast-
  work for vain outworks got.

LXXXIV

'We ken Kirk interest; Draco's laws
  recall;   250
Repair the old Church; Saints the
  wall,
True Pastors conduits, Grace the
  font, Love cements all.

LXXXV

'Pass freely would we of oblivion
  An Act, and pardon all bygone,
Would you smite hand on thigh, and
  say, What have we done!

LXXXVI

'Truth's pensioners! your flocks
  bleat; food they need;
CHRIST's flesh, their meat; blood,
  drink indeed:
View Glory's crown; in season, out
  of season, feed.

LXXXVII

'Ye friends to th' Bridegroom,
  stewards to the Bride,
With oracles of truth us guide; 260
Truth blesseth Church and State;
  faithful, till crown'd, abide.

LXXXVIII

'So, when the Judge with His reward
  appears,
You'll reap in joy what's sown in
  tears:
Moist seed-times crown the fields
  with golden-bearded ears.

LXXXIX

'Judge-Advocate to th' wrong'd!
  sure, Thou to guilt,
Which would unmake Thy crea-
  tures, wilt
Be just, when inquisition's made for
  blood that's spilt.

XC

'At our ear's port land Peace and
  Truth! Oh, then,
Welcome, as Sol to th' Russ in's
  den!
As shore to shipwreck'd, as to towns
  dismantled, men!   270

XCI

'Oh, might a second angel-choir
  ne'er cease
To worms, worn out with War's
  distress,
To sing, in all men's hearing, their
  blest song of Peace!

234 The number of the Beast.   237 Proteustants] See Introduction.
250 ken] Sardonically as well as alliteratively, no doubt.

XCII

'Peace! Home of pilgrims, first song
at Christ's birth ;
Peace, His last legacy on earth ;
Peace, gen'ral preface to all good ;
Peace, saints' true mirth.

XCIII

' Love, thou support to martyrs ! as
jet straw,
So us to our Belov'd dost draw ;
Thou art gold's true elixir, thou
summ'st up the law.

XCIV

' Who can Divine Love speak in
words of sense ?   280
Since, man, as ransom'd, angels
thence
Transcends ! Such is Christ's pas-
sion's high pre-eminence ! '

XCV

Here did she seal her lips, unsluice
her eyes
To flowing rhet'ric, and descries
The world 's a cask, its wine false
mirth, its lees fool's prize.

XCVI

And now, by limpid spring of life-joy,
where
Crystal is limbeck'd all the year,
To God she would her Heav'n-
ascending raptures rear.

XCVII

Taught hence, misguided Zeal,
whom heats dispose
To animosities, may close ;   290

And bloody Fury's converts be, by
pond'ring those.

XCVIII

Harmonious Beauty, feast our ear !
They're kings
At least, who hear when Love
thus sings :
Love, to high Grace's key screws up
low Nature's strings.

XCIX

Love, thou canst ocean-flowing
storms appease ;
And such o'ergrown Behemoths
please,
As tax the scaly nation, and excise
the seas.

C

If, Theophil, thy Love-Song can't
assuage
The fate incumbent on this age,
No time to write, but weep ; for we
are ripe for rage !   300

Ite sacrosanctæ Tabulata per Alta
Carinæ ;
Non opus est Fluviis, Lintea pan-
do Mari.
Ite Rates Ventis, quo vos rapit Aura,
secundis :
Brittica Cymba pias findat Amoris
Aquas.

ANIMARUM SPONSUS IESUS.

Canto IV.   The Inamoration

THE ARGUMENT

O, Deus, aut nullo caleat mihi Pectus ab Igne!
Aut solo caleat Pectus ab Igne Tui!
Languet ut Illa Deo, mihi Mens simul æmula languet!
Cœlitùs ut rapitur, me Violenta rapit!

She onset makes, first with love-darts aloof;
Then, with Zeal's fireworks, storms Heav'n's roof;
Whose Faith's shield, and Salvation's helmet are hell-proof.

THEOPHILA'S SOLILOQUY [1]

STANZAS I, II

When Heav'n's Love paramount,
Himself reveals,
And to the suppliant soul, her pardon
seals,
At fear'd-Hope's doubtful gate, which
trembling fell,
(Who heav'nward sails, coasts by the
Cape of Hell,)
That her He deigns to take, she joys
in woes,
To have in labour pass'd the partu-
rition throes.

III, IV

All travail-pangs, all new-birth heart-
deep groans,
All after-births of penitential moans,
Are swallow'd up in living streams of
bliss;
When as the Heav'n-born heir, the
new man is,   10
By th' quick'ning Spirit of the High'st
re-born:
Time past hath pass'd her night,
present presents her morn.

V, VI

See joy in light, see light in joy; oh,
see,
Poor worthless maid, fruit brought
thee from Life's tree,
By th' Spouse and Spirit, saints' sole
supporters! Rise

Then, Hell's apostate, and be heav'n
ly wise:
Thou art (let's interpledge our souls)
my One,
My All, though not by unity, by
union!

VII, VIII

Ineffably mysterious knot begun;
Saints mount, as dew allur'd by
beck'ning sun: 20
Love's faithful friends, what parallels
your guard,
Where Truth is sentinel, and Grace
the ward?
The way is flow'r-strown, where the
guide is Love:
His Spirit with you below, your
spirit with Him above.

IX, X

Reciprocal excess of joy! Then, soar
My soul to Him, who man became;
nay more,
Took sin itself, to cleanse thy sullied
clay,
But took it, only to take it away.
O Self-Donation! peerless Gift, un-
known!
Now since that He is thine, be never
thou thine own!   30

XI, XII

O prodigy of great and good! Faith,
sound
This Love's abyss, that does so
strangely bound

---

[1] The arrangement in orig. is curious. The stanzas are printed as here, and as they clearly must be, in six-line groups. But only the odd numbers (1, 3, &c.) are put at the heads, and the even (2, 4, &c.) accompany the fourth line of each stanza at the side.

Almightiness Itself! From whose
veins, see,
Unsluic'd, Love's purple ocean, when
His free
Red-streaming life did vanquish
Death and Hell!
That thou might'st live, He died!
That thou might rise, He fell!

XIII, XIV

God so lov'd man, that naturalists
may deem
God to set man before Himself did
seem!
When man, with seeing blind, 'gainst
GOD arose,
And slew his only Friend, GOD
'   sav'd his foes!   40
Sol mourn'd in blacks! Heav'n's
Viceroy, Nature, swounded!
Excess Love's reason was, Immensity
Love bounded!

XV, XVI

Ye twins of light, as sunflow'rs be
inclin'd
To th' Sun of Righteousness; let
Taste, refin'd,
Like nothing as Love's Heav'nly
Manna; and
Let all but CHRIST feel rough, as
Esau's hand;
Let nought like 's garment smell;
let ears rejoice,
But in expressless dictates of Love's
whisp'ring voice!

XVII, XVIII

He's thy bright sun; 'twixt whom,
and thy soul's bliss,
Thy earthy body interposèd is;   50
Whereby such dread eclipses causèd
are,
As fam'd astronomers can ne'er
declare:
Yet oft He shines; then, vanish ser-
vile fears;
Then, heav'nward filial hopes dry up
thy trickling tears.

XIX, XX

Spiritual light spirituals clears: in
Heav'n

Thou'lt view that full, what now by
glimpse, like Steph'n,
Thou canst but spy; there, shalt
thou face to face,
His light, His joy, His love, His
pow'r, His grace,
And His all-filling glory clearly see
In optic emanations from Eter-
nity!   60

XXI, XXII

I' th' ring of boundless lustre, from
whose ray
This petty world gleaneth its peep of
day:
Thou shalt be crown'd with wreaths
of endless light:
Here, oft's an interview in heat, and
might,
By inter-lucidations from above,
Twining embraces with 's ensphering
arm of love!

XXIII, XXIV

Most blessed souls, to whom He
does appear,
Folded within your ' arms, chaste
Hemisphere!
Oh, condescend! How 's lips shed
love! life! merit!
He makes His angels court of guard!
By 's Spirit   70
He crowns you with His grace! So,
with His blood,
When He redeem'd you, and con-
sign'd His Flesh for food!

XXV, XXVI

Meat came from th' eater, from the
strong did dew
Sweetness; when as, incomparably
true,
Omnipotency's Self did largely shed
His mystic oil of joy upon thy head:
Then, trample sin in Babylon's gold-
en cup;
Treasures away she trifles, trifles
treasures up.

XXVII, XXVIII

Oil of this lamp, obsequious soul,
lights thee
To thine approaching Heav'n! In
sanctity   80

Be actuated then ; being up assum'd
By this bright sun, with this rich oil
    perfum'd,
Th' art prepossess'd with heav'nly
    comforts, which,
With their soul-cheering sweets, both
    ravish and enrich.

XXIX, XXX

Poor, panting heart, Love's seat,
    yearn for Joy's pith !
To have (thy highest bliss !) com-
    munion with
The Father and the Son, one Spirit
    with CHRIST !
And one in Them, as They are One !
    Thou fly'st
Through grace to glory ! Vision shall
    sublime
Thy faith, Fruition hope, Eternity
    thy time !   90

THEOPHILA'S LOVE-SONG

XXXI, XXXII

Self ! oh, how mean an harmony it
    breeds !
JESUS ! All names this Name of
    names exceeds !
This Name 's GOD's mercy at full
    sea, 'tis Love's
High tow'r, Joy's loadstone; this, my
    spirit moves.
Hark : ' Rise, my love, my fair one,
    come away ;
Ling'ring breeds loss ; I am thy
    Leader, Light, and Way.'

XXXIII, XXXIV

What speed Speed's self can make,
    soul, fly withal ;
Greatness and goodness most mag-
    netical !
Shoot, like a flash of fire, to th' ruby
    wine,
His precious blood, transcendently
    Divine !   100
(How poor those costly pearls were,
    drunk by some)
My LORD, drink Blood to me ! Let
    It to th' world's health come !

XXXV, XXXVI

All hope 's unanchor'd but in That.
    Thou art,
'Bove Indies' womb, rich to my love-
    sick heart !
Flesh-fair endowments are but skin-
    deep brags,
Varnish'd corruption ; wealth is but
    Care's bags ;
The bag imposthumed chokes. Gold,
    Beauty, Fame
Are sublunary mists to Saints' sera-
    phic flame.

XXXVII, XXXVIII

JESUS ! This fans my fire, which has
    at best
But grains of incense, pounds of
    interest.   110
Go, int'rest; take the principal, Thine
    own :
Divine Love loves Thy loveliness
    alone !
What flames to Thine proportionable
    be !
LORD, hadst not first lov'd man, man
    could not have lov'd Thee !

XXXIX, XL

Why lov'st us, but because THOU
    wouldst ? Oh, why
For lepers would the Undefilèd die?
That pen was dipt i' th' standish of
    thy Blood,
Which wrote th' indenture of our
    termless good !
O Love, 'bove wish! Never such Love
    enroll'd !
Who think their utmost flames
    enough for Thee, are cold. 120

XLI, XLII

Whose Highness did not to be low
    disdain,
Yet, when at lowest, highest did
    remain !
Who bow'dst Heav'n's altitude, re-
    fresh with flow'rs,
With JESSE's sov'reign flow'r, my
    fainting pow'rs,

107 imposthumed] Orig. ' impostom'd.'

Which sink (as shaft-struck hart em-
    boss'd) twixt grief,
And joy: grief for my sin, joy for Thy
    free relief.

XLIII, XLIV

Wrack'd is with bitter-sweet extremes
    my mind,
Shell'd, sheath'd, cag'd, coffin'd in
    her treacherous friend ;
Her always tempting mass of flesh
    she bears,
Her hopes, did they not sprout from
    Thee, were fears :   130
Hope, Thou perfume of lovers, for
    Thy sake
Love's generous, throws at all : life's
    but a petty stake ;

XLV, XLVI

Scarce worth the prize. Love makes
    two spirits but one ;
Me, counterpart to Thy indenture,
    own ;
I, active then as light, tread air and
    flame,
Without or wing, or chariot; and
    disclaim
All the faint sweets of earth.   Thy
    Spirit views
How in Love's torrid zone Thy swel-
    t'ring martyr stews.

XLVII, XLVIII

Row me, ye dove-wing'd oars, whom
    Hope does buoy,
To wish'd-for hav'n, flowing with
    tides of joy !   140
Yet wish I not, my Joy, Thy joys
    above,
Merely for joy; nor pleasures of Thy
    Love,
Only for love of pleasure.   No, let
    free
Spiritual languors teem ! fruitful, yet
    virgins be !

XLIX, L

Give, give me children, or I die !
    Love, rest
Thy head upon the pillows of my
    breast !
When me Thou shalt impregn'd with
    virtues make

(364)

A fruitful Eden, all the fruitage take !
Thy passion, Jonathan, below did
    move ;
Rapt spirits, in high excess, flame
    with intensest love !   150

LI, LII

My life is hid with Thee in GOD !
    Descry
Thyself, O Thou, my plighted
    Spouse, that I
May ever glorious be ! That my joy'd
    soul
With Thee may make up marriage !
    and my whole
Self Thee for Bridegroom have ! My
    hope still sends
Up ' Come,' that I may enter with
    Thy feasted friends !

LIII, LIV

Oh, that long-long'd for Come ! oh,
    Come ! mine eyes,
Love's sentinels, watch, like officious
    spies !
Strike sparks of joy t' inflame Love's
    tinder ! make
The exile view her home, the
    dreamer wake !   160
Tears raise the fire of Love ! Ease
    sighs of air,
Fire's passion, wat'ry tears, and earthy
    self-despair !

LV, LVI

My sighs, condens'd to drops, com-
    pute hours spent !
Cancel the lease of my clay-tenement,
Which pays dear rent of groans ! oh,
    grant a writ
Of ease ! I languish out, not live !
    Permit
A pass to Sion's Mount ! But, I re-
    sign
My green-sick will, though sick of
    Love, to that of Thine !

LVII, LVIII

Waitings, which ripen hopes, are not
    delays ;
Presence how great, how true's Love,
    absence says :   170
While lungs my breath shall organ,
    I'll press still

Th' exinanition of my o'ergrown will.
'Behold, I quickly come.' O'erjoy'd
I'm here !
Oh, Come ! Till then, each day 's an
age, each hour a year.

LIX, LX

JESU ! (That Name's Joy's essence !)
hasten on !
Throng amorous sighs for dissolution !
Fastidious earth, avaunt ; with love-
plumes soar,
My soul, to meet thy Spouse. Canst
wish for more ?
Only come ! give a RING ! Re-echo
then,
'Oh, Come. Even so, LORD JESU,
Come ! Amen. Amen.'   180

LXI

Who 's this inamor'd vot'ress ? Like
the morn
From mountain unto mountain
born ?
Who first, with night-drops dew'd,
seem'd turtle-dove forlorn ?

LXII

But now, ere warpèd body, near
decay,
Stands, bow-like, bent, to shoot
away
Her soul, ere prone looks kiss her
grave, ere her last day,

LXIII

She (Love-fill'd) wants no mate, has
rather one
Body too much. I' th' Spirit's
throne
CHRIST's peace is fullest quire ! Such
loneness, least alone !

LXIV

When soft-flying Sleep, Death's sister,
wings does spread   190
Over that curtain'd grave, her bed,
Then, with prophetic dreams the
Highest crowns her head.

LXV

Behold, a comely Person, clad in
white,
The all-enlight'ning sun less
bright
Than that illustrious Face of His,
which blest her sight.

LXVI

To her, in Majesty, His way HE
broke,
And, softly thus to her HE spoke,
'Come, come away.' 'My JESUS'
says she. So, she woke.

LXVII

Her pray'rs, more passionate than
witty, rise,
As Sol's postilion, bright ; her
eyes,   200
Wrestling with GOD for grace, bedew
Love's Paradise.

LXVIII

Betimes, when keen-breath'd winds,
with frosty cream,
Periwig bald trees, glaze tattling
stream :
For May-games past, white-sheet
peccavi is Winter's theme.

LXIX

Those daybreaks give good morrows,
which she takes
With thanks, so, doubly good
them makes.
Who in GOD's promise rests, in GOD's
remembrance wakes.

LXX

Saints nothing more, saints nothing
less regard,
Than LOVE's SELF, than self-love ;
unscar'd,
Though rack'd into an anagram, their
souls being spar'd.   210

LXXI

Through virtuous self-mistrust they
acted move

---

190 Death's sister] The substitution of ' sister ' for the usual ' brother ' though obvious
is not trivial, and still less unpoetical. Grammar prevented it in the classical languages :
our happy freedom therefrom allows it. And the attributes of Sleep are certainly
more feminine than masculine.
194 sun] I should like to read ' sun 's.'

Like needle, touch'd by th' stone
of Love.
Blest magnet, which attracts, and
souls directs Above !

LXXII

Were she but mortal, she were satis-
fied,
So GOD liv'd in her, till she died ;
His Word, her deed ; His Will, her
warrant ; both, her guide.

LXXIII

Thus, this Devota breathes out
yearning cries.
' Let not dust blind my sensual
eyes,
When as my spirit's energy trans-
cends the skies !

LXXIV

' Virtues raise souls. All 's filial to
Above ;   220
Low'st step is mercenary love ;
Fraternal are the sides that Saint's
ascent improve.

LXXV

' Manna to my enamour'd soul, art
THOU !
The Spirit of Heav'n, distill'd,
does flow
From Thy aspect ; by that, from
brutes, we angels grow.

LXXVI

' Had I, oh, had I many lives, as
` years ;
As many loves, as love hath fears ;
All, all were Thine, had I as many
hearts, as hairs !

LXXVII

' From THEE my joy-extensions
spreading flow ;
Dilating, as leaf-gold ! be n't
slow,   230
O, THOU, my All, and more ! Love-
lorn, THEE still I woo !

LXXVIII

' The widow press'd, till THEE to grant
she bound ;
The virgin sought Thee, till she
found ;
The publican did knock, till opening
knocking crown'd.

(366)

LXXIX

' Though nought but dross I in my-
self can spy,
Yet melted with Thy beaming Eye,
My refuse turns to gold, by mystic
alchemy ;

LXXX

' Then, whet thy blunt scythe, Time,
and wing thy feet :
Life, not in length, but use, is sweet :
Come, Death (the body brought abed
o[f] th[e] soul), come, fleet ! 240

LXXXI

' Be pulse, my passing-bell ; be skin,
my hearse :
Night's sable curtains that disperse
The rays of day, be shroud : dews,
weep my funeral verse !

LXXXII

' Pity me, love-sick virgins !' Then,
she swoon'd ;
O'ercome with zeal, she sunk to
th' ground :
Darts of intolerable sweets her soul
did wound.

LXXXIII

She lay with flaming Love impierc'd
to th' heart :
Wak'd, as she bled, she kist the
dart ;
Then sigh'd. ' Take all I am, or
have ! All, All Thou art !'

LXXXIV

Then, sunk again. Reviv'd, Love's
bow she bent,   250
And married string to shaft, and
sent
Ejaculations, which the skies, like
lightning, rent.

LXXXV

Piercing them through (feather'd
with sighs) to show
She little paid, yet much did owe :
The feathers sung, and fir'd, as they
did upward go.

LXXXVI

No ice-fring'd cloud may quench
Love's soaring flame :
Love is more strong than death,
or shame.

Grown up all soul, the flesh sinks in
   a triple qualm.

LXXXVII

'I charge ye, Sion Virgins, let her still
   Enjoy her disencloister'd fill 260
In these high ecstasies of Union and
   Will.

LXXXVIII

'Do not with claps of hands, or noise
   of feet,
Awake her from what is more sweet,
Till the bright rising day-star light her
   to Heav'n's street.

LXXXIX

'Yield her, what her unfetter'd
   rapture gives,
Since she's more where she loves,
   than lives :
Transanimations, scaling Heav'n,
   break carnal gyves.

XC

'In Love's triumphant chariot plac'd
   she is ;
Concentric are her joys with his;
Enchariotedin fire, her spirit Heav'n-
   ripe for bliss.' 270

XCI

They're only found, who thus are lost
   in trance ;
Transported to the high'st advance,
With him, who was in spirit rapt to
   expressless glance.

XCII

Return'd, she cried : 'Oh, slay me
   thus again !
Ne'er lives she who thus ne'er is
   slain !
How sweet the wounds of Love ! No
   pleasure to Love's pain !

XCIII

'In furnac'd heat, Pyrausta-like, I
   fry !
To live is faith ! 'tis gain to die !
One life's enough for two ! Thou
   liv'st in me, not I !

XCIV

'How, midst regalias of Love's ban-
   quet, I 280
Dissolve in Sweet's extremity !
O languors ! Thus to live is in pure
   flames to die !

XCV

'Three kings three gifts to th' King
   of kings did bring ;
Myrrh, incense, gold, to Man, GOD,
   King :
For myrrh, tears ; incense, pray'rs ;
   gold, take Love's offering !

XCVI

'Oh, take Love's hecatomb !' Then,
   through her eyes
Did Love enamouring passions rise :
High'st Glory crowns Theophila's
   love-sacrifice.

XCVII

Not she, Mortality alone did die ;
Death's but translation to the
   sky : 290
All virtues fir'd in her pure breast
   their spicery.

XCVIII

As, when Arabia's wonder spices
   brings,
Which fann'd to flames by her own
   wings,
She, from the glowing holocaust in
   triumph springs :

XCIX

So, Virtue's pattern (priestess, altar,
   fire,
Incense, and victim) up did spire ;
'Victoria, Victoria,' sung all Heav'n's
   quire.

C

She echoing (echo, which does all
   surpass !
GOD'S sight is Glory's looking-
   glass !) 299
Magnificats, Hosannas, Halleluiahs!

---

277 Pyrausta] πυραύστης 'a moth that is singed in a flame,' and thus a sort of salamander.

287 Love] So in orig. 'Love-enamouring' 'making Love Himself love' seems very like Benlowes.

300 Halleluiahs] Five syllables.

Pars Cursûs emensa mei, Pars restat
    aranda :
  Ex æquo Metam Vesper & Ortus
    habent.

Ergo per immensos properent cava
    Lintea Fluctus :
  Jactatam capiant Littora sancta
    Ratem !

AMANS ANIMÂ SATIATUR AMANTIS.

Canto V. The Representation

THE ARGUMENT

Mundus Opes, Animam Cœlum, Terramque resumpsit
  Terra : Deus, Vitam cúm tulit, Ipse dedit.
Solus Amor facit esse Deum ; Quem, Mente capaci,
  Si Quis conciperet, posset et esse Deus.

The Author's vision, her ascent, Heav'n's place
  Descried, where reigns all glorious Grace,
Where 's all-sufficient Good, the sum of Bliss she has.

STANZA I

I'm vile, a thing impure, Corruption's son,
  Earth-crawling worm, by sin un-done,
Whose suppliant dust doth own its shame, and t' Heav'n doth run.

II

Grace, intervene 'twixt sin and shame, and tie
  A hopeful bliss to misery !
Lord, pardon dust and ashes : both, yea worse, am I !

III

Though dust, Thy work : though clay, Thy Hand did turn
  This vessel ; and, though ashes, th' Urn
Thou art, them to restore when sky and earth shall burn.

IV

Whilst that my Heav'n-allied soul does stay   10
  Wholly on Thee, not Europe's sway
Can elevate my wish, like one grace-darted ray.

V

Meet, meet my prison'd Soul's address ! oh, might
  She view, through mould'ring earth, Thy Sight !

Grace perfects Nature's want : say here, ' Let there be light ! '

VI

Then, though in flesh my spirit prison'd be,
  She may by Faith ascend to Thee,
And up be rais'd, till she shall mount to liberty.

VII

Clear-sighted Faith, point out the way ; I will
  Neglect curl'd Phrase's frizzled skill :   20
Humble Devotion, lift thou up my flagging quill ;

VIII

Which faints at first approach ; my faith 's too light
  To move this mountain, reach this height :
Can squeaking reeds sound forth the organ's full delight ?

IX

I'm mute, for only light can light declare ;
  A diamond must a diamond square ;
Yet, where I dare not speak, there yet adore I dare.

X

Ear has not heard, nor eye has seen, nor can

(368)

Man's heart conceive (vast heart of
   man)
The riches treasur'd up in Glory's
   ocean!   30
          XI
Tomes full of mystic characters
   enfense
Those seas of bliss! To write to
   sense
Heav'n's chronicle, would ask a
   Heav'n'd intelligence.
          XII
How, then, from flood of tears may
   an ark'd dove try
Its vent'rous pinions, to descry
That land, unknown to Nature? Vast
   Eternity!
          XIII
Fear gulfs unfathomable; nor desire,
   Ere of GOD's court thou art, t' as-
   pire
To be of 's council; pry not, but with
   awe admire.
          XIV
Dwarf-words do limp, do derogate,
   do scan   40
Nor height, nor depth. Since Time
   began,
What constitutes a gnat was ne'er
   found out by man.
          XV
Dares mortal slime, with ruder tongue,
   express
What ev'n Celestials do confess
Is inexpressible? Thou clod of earth,
   first guess
          XVI
In like degrees from equinoctial
   track,
   Why men are tawny, white, and
   black?
Why Bactria's camel two? Arab's one
   bunch on 's back?
          XVII
Canst lead Leviathan with a silken
   string?
   Canst cover with a hornet's wing 50
Behemoth? Canst thou seas into a
   nutshell bring?

          XVIII
Canst motion fix? count sands? recall
   past day?
   Show height, breadth, length o' th'
   spreading ray?
Discardinate the spheres? and rapid
   whirlwinds stay?
          XIX
Tell, tell how pond'rous Earth's huge
   propless ball
   Hangs poisèd in the fluent hall
Of fleeting air? how clouds sustainèd
   are from fall?
          XX
How burnt the Bush, when verdure
   cloth'd its fire?
   How from the rock, rod-struck in
   ire,
Did cataracts gush out? How did the
   sea retire?   60
          XXI
Canst thou take post-horse with the
   coursing sun,
   And with him through the zodiac
   run?
How many stages be there ere the
   race be done?
          XXII
Then, tell how once he shot his beams
   down-right
   From the same zenith, while for
   night,
Mortals stood gazing at a doubled
   noonday's light?
          XXIII
Tell, how that planet did in after-days
   Turn Cancer, shooting Parthian
   rays,
Ten whole degrees revers'd, which
   did the world amaze.
          XXIV
Poor thingling man! Propitious
   Heav'n, assign   70
   Some angel for this high design!
Heav'n's history requires at least a
   Seraphin.
          XXV
Oh, might some glorious Spirit then
   retire,
   And warble to a sacred lyre

The Song of Moses and the Lamb in
    Heav'n's full quire !
XXVI
'Twas at Night's noon, when sleep th'
    oppress'd had drown'd ;
    But sleepless were oppressors
      found ;
'Twas when Sky's spangled head in
    sable veil was bound :
XXVII
For thievish Night had stole, and
    clos'd up quite,
    In her dark lantern, starry light :
No planet seen to sail in that dead
    ebb of Night : 81
XXVIII
When, lo, all-spreading rays the room
    surround !
    Like such reflections, as rebound,
Shooting their beams to th' sun, from
    rocks of diamond.
XXIX
This, to a wonder, summonèd my
    sight,
    Which dazzled was at so pure light !
A Form angelic there appear'd
    divinely bright !
XXX
I wish'd myself more eyes to view this
    gleam ;
    I was awake, I did not dream ;
Too exquisite delight makes true
    things feignèd seem. 90
XXXI
Model of Heav'n it was ; I floated long
    'Twixt joy and wonder ; passion
      strong,
Wanting due vent, made sight my
    speech, and eyes my tongue !
XXXII
Oft, my rapt soul, ascending to the eye,
    Peep'd through upon Angelity,
Whose blaze·did burnish'd plate of
    sparkling Sol outvie !
XXXIII
If gracious silence shin'd forth any-
    where

With sweet aspect, 'twas in this
    sphere ;
The soul of sweetness, and the spirit
    of joys mix'd here
XXXIV
From out Love's wing he must a
    pencil frame, 100
    Who, on Time's cloth, would paint
    this flame :
None can portray this glorious draft
    but who 's the same.
XXXV
Veil then, Timanthes-like, this guess'd
    at face,
    (The curtain of that inward grace),
Whose forehead with diaphanous
    gold impalèd was.
XXXVI
For, starry knobs, like diamonds, did
    attire
    That front with glory, and conspire
To lavish out their beams, to radiate
    that fire.
XXXVII
Whose amber-curling tresses were
    unbound,
    And, like a glittering veil, spread
    round, 110
And so about the snowy shoulders
    sweetly wound.
XXXVIII
Whose robe shot forth a tissue-
    waving shine,
    Which seem'd loose-flowing, far
    more fine
Than any interwoven silk with silver
    twine.
XXXIX
With gracious smile, approaching
    nearer, sat
    This glorious thing : oh, humble
    state !
Yet, on the Vision inexpressive rays
    did wait.
XL
'Twas glorified Theophila sat there.
    I, mute, as if I tongueless were,

---

103 Timanthes] Orig. 'Timantes.' The story of the picture of the sacrifice of
Iphigenia is well known.

Till her voice-music drew my soul
  into mine ear: 120

XLI

'Twas 'bove lute's sweetest touch,
  or richest air !
' I bring thee things (says she)
  are rare :
All subcelestial streams drops to
  this ocean are.

XLII

' Hear, first, my progress. Loos'd
  from Nature's chain,
And quit from clay, I did attain,
Swift as a glancing meteor to
  th' aerial plain :

XLIII

' Where, passing through, I did
  perfume the air
With sacred spice, and incens'd
  pray'r ;
While grateful clouds their liquid
  pearl, as gift, prepare.

XLIV

' I spare t' unlock those treasuries of
  snow ; 130
Or tell what paints the rainy bow ;
Or what cause thunders, lightnings,
  rains ; or whence winds flow.

XLV

' Those regions pass'd, where beard-
  ed comets light
The world to fatal woes; a bright
Large orb of harmless fire enflam'd
  my heav'nward flight.

XLVI

' To azure-archèd sky ascends my soul
  (Thence view I North and South-
  ern Pole),
Where globes in serpentine yet
  order'd motions roll.

XLVII

' Thence by the changing Moon's
  alternate Face,
Up, through unweari'd Phosphor's
  place, 140
I mount to Sol's diurnal and his
  annual race :

XLVIII

' By whose propitious influence things
  are

Quicken'd below, this monarch
  star,
Making his progress through the
  signs, unclouds the air ;

XLIX

' And, eight-score times outbulks the
  earth ; whose race
In four and twenty hours' space
'Bove fifty millions of Germanic
  leagues does pace.

L

' This giant with as many tongues as
  rays,
Speaks out, so oft as he displays
His beams, which gild the world ;
  that man his LORD should praise.

LI

' Through spheres I pass'd to stars,
  that nail Heav'n's court, 151
  (My stay was with sky-wonders
  short,)
Which, by first Mover's force, are
  whirl'd about their fort.

LII

' Through the blue-spangled frame,
  my psalming tongue
Made th' orbs suspend their usual
  song,
To hear celestial hymns the glist'ring
  quires did throng.

LIII

' Chime out, ye crystal spheres, and
  tune your poles ;
  Skies, sound your bass ; ere ye to
  coals
Dissolve, and tumble on the bonfire
  world in shoals.

LIV

' The *Primum Mobile* does seem
  immense, 160
  And doth transfusèd influence
Through all inferior orbs, as swift as
  thought, dispense.

LV

' Suppose, a millstone should from
  thence be hurl'd
Unto the centre of this world,
'Twould make up sixscore years, ere
  it could down be whirl'd.

LVI

Now, enter'd I Heav'n's suburbs,
    pav'd with gems ;
No orient jewels cast such beams ;
(Oh, might this verse be wreath'd
    but with such diadems !)

LVII

'Sol's radiant fulgence in meridian
    skies   169
Seem'd shade unto those clarities ;
Where Beauty's self might beautify
    her fairest eyes.

LVIII

''Tis 'bove high'st verge, where
    reason dares be bold ;
That Heav'n of GOD is of such
    mould,
That eyes, till glorified, cannot the
    same behold.

LIX

''Tis purely spirit'al, and so must be,
    Above compare in all degree,
With aught that draws its line from
    th' six days' pedigree.

LX

''Tis immaterial, 'bove the highest
    sphere,
Doth brighter than the rest appear ;
Than orbs of fire, moon, sun, or
    crystalline more clear.   180

LXI

''Tis space immense, from whence
    apostates driv'n,
    Their rooms might so to men be
    giv'n
With those confirmèd sons, th'
    indigenae of Heav'n.

LXII

'Absurdly some philosophers did
    dream,
    That Heav'n's an uncreated beam
Which forth eternally from GOD
    HIMSELF did stream.

LXIII

''Tis but a creature, though its
    essence be
    To change unsubject, standing
    free
On never-shaken pillars of Infinity.

LXIV

' Ocean of Joys ! Who can thee fully
    state ?   190
    For clearer knowledge man must
    wait ;
First shoot Death's Gulf, thy soul may
    then arrive thereat :

LXV

' For no one enters there, till he
    hath trod
    Death's path, then, from that period
Elected souls ascend to Heav'n, to
    bliss, to GOD !'

LXVI

(Zeal through me fires its way to
    speak, that I
    Would thither, like wing'd light-
    ning, fly,
Were my flesh-curtain drawn that
    clouds my spirit's eye !

LXVII

What heights would souls affect,
    could they undress
    Themselves of rags, that them
    depress !   200
How beautiful 's the form of naked
    Holiness !

LXVIII

New light, life, love, joy, bliss there
    boundless flow !
There shall my soul thy glory know,
When she her robe of clay shall to
    earth's wardrobe throw !

LXIX

Fond that I am to speak. Pass on
    to bliss,
    That with an individual kiss
Greets thee for ever ! Pardon this
    parenthesis.)

LXX

' Faith 's the Soul's eye ; as nothing
    were between,
    They that believe, see things
    unseen :
Close then thy carnal, thy spiritual
    eyes unscreen.   210

LXXI

' For, my transplanted spirit shall
    emblaze

Words, may make wonder stand at
  . gaze :
Unboundless bliss doth ev'n the
  sep'rate spirit amaze.

LXXII

' Oh, fleet of intellectuals, glory-
  fraught, .
(Inestimable arras, wrought
With heart-o'ercoming colours,) how
  ye pass all thought ! '

LXXIII

Thou All-comprising, uncompris'd
  Who art
Ever, yet never made, impart
Thou (Love's abyss, without or ebb
  or shore) a heart

LXXIV

Of Wisdom to attempt, proceed, and
  end   220
What never was, is, can be penn'd !
May spots in maps (dumb teachers)
  empires comprehend ?

LXXV

' The sky-enchasèd diamonds lesser
  show
Than July's hairy worms that glow,
Sampled with those rebounds un-
  bounded glories throw.

LXXVI

' That Vessel of Election, rapt to
  th' soil
Of highest bliss, did here recoil :
I' th' same attempt 'tis honour to
  confess a foil.

LXXVII

' Sense knows not 'bove court-
  triumphs, thrones, or kings,
Gems, music, beauties, banquet-
  ings,   230
Without such tropes it can't unfold
  spiritual things.

LXXVIII

' Oh, how that most unutterable
  blaze
Of Heav'n's all-luminating rays
Does souls (disrob'd of flesh) both
  brighten, and amaze !

LXXIX

' That boundless solstice, with trans-
  parent beams,
Through Heav'n's triumphant
  arches streams,
And, gliding through each spirit with
  intrinsic gleams,

LXXX

' Pierceth to th' little world, and doth
  dispel
The gloomy clouds of sin, that
  swell
The soul, decoying it to ever-burn-
  ing Hell !   240

LXXXI

' By glory, how are spirits made
  divine !
How super-radiantly they shine
From th' ever-flowing spring of the
  refulgent TRINE !

LXXXII

' Beyond report of high'st discourse
  they dart
Their radiations, 'bove all art !
This cath'lic bliss o'erflows the most
  capacious heart !

LXXXIII

' Conceive a court, where all joys
  domineer,
Where seas of sweets o'erflow, and
  where
Glory's exhaustless mines, sport's
  endless springs, appear :

LXXXIV

' Where infinite excess of sweets
  ne'er cloys !   250
Where, still fruition's feast em-
  ploys
Desire ! where who enjoy the least
  can't count their joys !

LXXXV

' One may t' a glimpse, none to a
  half can rise,
Had he more tongues, than heav'n
  has eyes !
Such, nothing see, as would in words
  this sight comprise !

213 Unboundless] So in my copy, but corrected to ' unbounded,' which is of course
obvious.

LXXXVI

' Can measures such Unmeasurables
  hold ?
  Can time Infinity unfold ?
Superlative Delights may be admired,
  not told.

LXXXVII

' When Glory's Heav'n is all one
  sunny blaze,
  That flowing radiance doth amaze,
While on that inconceivable result
  we gaze !   261

LXXXVIII

' What king would not court martyr-
  dom, to hold
  In capite a city of gold,
Where, look how many gates, so
  many pearls are told !

LXXXIX

' The structure's square ; a firm
  foundation,   [stone,
  Twelvefold, for each a precious
The LAMB's Apostles' names en-
  graven thereupon.

XC

' There sparkles forth the verdant
  emerald,
  The blue-ey'd sapphire therein
  wall'd,
The topaz too, with that stone which
  from gold is call'd :   270

XCI

' There, jasper, chalcedon, chryso-
  prase shine,
  There sardonyx, and sardius join,
There beryl, hyacinth, and amethyst
  combine.

XCII

' No sympathizing turkise there, to
  tell
  By paleness th' owner is not well,
For, grief's exil'd to earth, and
  anguish groans in hell !

XCIII

' The streets with gold perspicuous
  are array'd,
  With blazing carbuncles inlaid ;

271] Read ' chrysoprase, chalcedon ' ?

Yet, all seem night, to glories from
  the LAMB display'd.

XCIV

' For, thousand suns make an eclipse
  to those !   280
  The diamond there for pavement
  grows,
As on its glitt'ring stock, and all its
  sparkles throws.

XCV

' And there, on every angel-trodden
  way
  Loose pearls, instead of pebbles,
  play,
Like dusky atoms in the sun's em-
  bright'ning ray.

XCVI

' Had I a quill sent from a Seraph's
  wing,
  And skill to tune 't ! I could not
  sing
The moiety of that wealth, which that
  all-glorious King

XCVII

' Of Heav'n enstates those in, who
  follow good,
  And prize 't above their vital blood!
Heav'n may be gain'd on earth, but
  never understood !   291

XCVIII

' As, when the sun shakes off the veil
  of night,
  And scatters on the dawn his light,
He soon takes pris'ner to himself th'
  engagèd sight :

XCIX

' So, when I view those indeficient
  beams,
  Oh, they in overfulgent gleams,
Like diamonds, thaw'd to air, em-
  bubble forth in streams !

C

' Ev'n spirits, who have disrob'd their
  rags of clay,
  Laid up in wardrobe till that day,
O'ercome, they dazzled are by each
  imperious ray ! '   300

286] Note this.

<table>
<tr><td>Sexta repercussi, Pars antepenultima, Ponti,
Imparibus restat perficienda Modis;</td><td>Quam (si præstiterit Mentem DEUS OPTIMUS) addam
Flammiferos Phœbus cum jugat ortus Equos.</td></tr>
</table>

EX OBSCURO SPECTABILE CŒLUM.

Canto VI.   The Association

THE ARGUMENT

Panduntur Cœli, juvat hinc invisere Divûm
  Atria, mortali non adeunda Pede:
Hic, Animæ pennis advecta THEOPHILA, cernit
  Agmina Cœlicolûm ducere sancta Choros.

Heav'n's order, beauty, glory is descried:
  Here, read the state o' th' Glorified,
Which THEOPHIL i' th' heraldry of Heav'n had eyed.

STANZA I

'THOSE happy mansions, glorious
   Saint, discover,
   Where the bright Host of Spirits
   hover!
Bring down all Heav'n before the
   eyes o' th' Heav'nly Lover.'

II

Frail man, with zeal and wonder here
   behold
Clay cast into a heav'nly mould:
Faith did, now Vision does Beatitude
   unfold.

III

· The tenants in this splendid frame
   are they
Whose grosser and unpolish'd clay,
Calcin'd in graves, now robes of
   glory do array.

IV

Here martyrs sit enthron'd, who late
   did bleed   10
Sap from their fertile wounds, to
   feed
With oil the Church's lamps, and
   with red dew her seed.

V

These ovant souls, Knights of Saint
   Vincent are,
   For high achievements gain'd,
   each scar,
To make a golden constellation,
   seems a star.

VI

Not by inflicting, but receiving blows,
   By suff'ring, they o'ercame their
   foes:
How long, LORD, ere Thou dost
   avenge their blood on those?

VII

These own their bliss, sprung from
   the word and will
O' th' LAMB, by whom they con-
   quer'd still   20
Themselves, and that revolted band
   that Hell does fill.

VIII

Therefore, each prostrate casts, with
   th' elders, down
At the LAMB's feet their palm and
   crown,
Beholding round all eminences, but
   their own.

8 unpolish'd] Orig. 'unpolish,' an obvious oversight.
13 Knights of St. Vincent] i. e. 'conquerors.'

IX

Th' Apostles here, with him, in
    whose sweet tongue
  The lute of high-tun'd Love was
    strung,
When through so many regions he
    the Gospel sung.

X

The loving, lov'd Evangelist here lives
  On Love's pure influence, and gives
No bounds to 's flaming love, but how
    to heighten 't strives.   30

XI

Love was his only theme. She, here
    is crown'd,
  Who near Death's tomb, Life risen
    found ;
Whose eye-bowl was tear-brimm'd,
    whose towel hair unbound.

XII

Parch'd Afric's glory, born in 's
    mother's eyes
  (A happier offspring of her cries,
Than of her womb), here to ecstatic
    Love does rise.

XIII

The bounds are boundless of divine
    Amour ;
  Love hopes, and yet hath all
    things, for,
In Heav'n's eternal heraldry, true
    Love is *Or*.

XIV

Fruition Love enfires, thence Zeal 's
    renew'd ;   40
  Love hath the SPIRIT's plenitude,
Burning with flames in splendour of
    Beatitude !

XV

Love caus'd the SON of GOD from 's
    throne dismount,
  And make Himself of no account,
Become a Man of Sorrows, who of
    Joy 's the fount !

XVI

This Love, by quire of Heav'n scarce
    understood !

Could so much ill cause so much
    good,
For man's redemption that GOD's
    SON should shed His blood ?

XVII

Thou, Love, when as my guilty soul
    did dwell
  In nest of ruin, didst unshell   50
My spirit (fledg'd with Grace) from
    that disorder'd cell.

XVIII

And, having crush'd the outward film
    of earth,
  Gav'st her, new form'd with Glory,
    birth
That she might sty to th' Seat of
    Beatific Mirth !

XIX

And praise Thee, with those virgin-
    souls, who in
  The cloisters of their flesh have
    been
Wash'd in their SAVIOUR's bath of
    blood from spots of sin.

XX

Flow'rs on our heads, as on their
    stems, do grow,
  Which into fadeless colours flow,
Nor cold to blast, nor heat to scorch,
    nor age they know.   60

XXI

Scenting 'bove thousand precious
    ointments, shed
  On consecrated Aaron's head ;
Above pearl'd dew on Hermon's ever-
    fragrant bed.

XXII

How far, immaculate flames, do you
    excel
  All that in thought's high turret
    dwell !
What then can optics see ?   What
    then can volumes tell ?

XXIII

If Beauty's self we could incarnate
    see

---

34 The promotion of St. Augustine to special company with St. John and St. Mary
Magdalene is noteworthy.
  54 sty] Benlowes probably took this rare but good word (= ' rise ') from Spenser.

Teeming with youth and joy, yet
    she
Would not so beauteous as the Virgin-
    Mother be.

XXIV

Who, like a full-orb'd moon, our stars
    outshin'd   70
In glorious fulgurance of mind !
For whose surpassing splendour I
    this Ode design'd.

XXV

' Hail, blessed Virgin-Spouse, who
    didst bequeath
    Breath unto Him, who made thee
    breathe !
And gav'st a life to Him, who gave
    thee life from death !

XXVI

'Who bor'st Him in thy womb, whose
    hands did stack
    The studded orbs with stars, and
    tack
The glowing constellations to the
    Zodiac !

XXVII

' And, what improves the mystery
    begun,   79
New mysteries from thee were spun,
He did, at once, become thy Father,
    Spouse, and Son !

XXVIII

' Conceiving HIM, as by the womb,
    so th' ear !
    By th' Angels' tongue Heav'n cast
    seed there !
Thou heard'st, believ'dst, and thence
    didst breed, and thence didst
    bear !

XXIX

' Thou only may'st (so it be humbly)
    boast
    To have brought forth the Eternal
    Host
By mystic obumbration of the HOLY
    GHOST !

XXX

' By thee did GOD and man embrace
    each other !
    Thus, Heav'n to Earth became a
    brother !

(377)

Thus, thou, a Virgin, to thy MAKER
    wast a Mother !   90

XXXI

' Thy fleece was wet, when all the
    ground lay dry !
Dry, when all moist about did lie !
As Aaron's rootless rod, so didst
    thou fructify !

XXXII

' Thou art, from whence Faith's
    burgeon sprang, the ground !
Before, in, after birth was found
Pureness untouch'd, with Virgin-
    Mother's Honour crowned !

XXXIII

' Thou, shrine of Glory, ark of Bliss,
    thou high
    Fair Temple of Divinity,
In thee, the masterpiece of Nature
    I descry ! '

XXXIV

' My ravish'd Soul,' said she, ' extols
    His Name,   100
    Who rules the Heav'n's expansèd
    frame,
Whose mercy rais'd me up to mag-
    nify the same.'

XXXV

Who can anatomize the glorious list
    Of heirs to GOD, coheirs with
    CHRIST,
Who royalize it there by Grace's high
    acquist ?

XXXVI

Whose several glories admirable are !
    And yet as infinite, as fair !
Where all 's enjoyed at full ; where
    everything is rare !

XXXVII

The joy of each one is the joy of all !
    Beatitude 's reciprocal !   110
They drink CHRIST's cup of flowing
    wine, who pledg'd His gall !

XXXVIII

Silence most rhet'ric hath, and glories
    best
    Do portray forth that royal feast,
At which each blessed saint is an
    eternal guest !

XXXIX

Nor can a thought of earthly friend's
    annoys
  Extenuate one grain of joys,
While Mercy saves the wise, while
    Justice fools destroys !

XL

Strangely their intellects enlighten'd
    be !
  Nature's compendium did not see
One half ; yea, ere he tasted the
    Forbidden Tree !   120

XLI

If, that sea-parting Prince, from cleft
    rocks' space
  Viewing GOD's back-parts, thought
    it grace,
What honour is it then to see Him
    face to face !

XLII

Who doth inspirit th' indeficient ray,
  Not dimm'd with a minute allay ;
Where, though no sun e'er rose, yet
    'tis eternal day !

XLIII

Where all are fill'd, yet all from food
    abstain !
  Where all are subjects, yet all reign !
All rich, yet have no bags that stifled
    wealth contain !

XLIV

Where each saint does a glorious
    kingdom own ;   130
  Where each king hath a starry
    crown ;
Each crown a kingdom, free from the
    rude people's frown.

XLV

Where each hath all, yet, more than
    all, they owe ;
  All subjects, yet no kings they
    know,
Save King of kings, and Lord of lords,
    who quell'd their Foe.

XLVI

Where highest joy is their perpetual
    fare ;
  Their exercise Hosannas are ;
Spirits the choristers, the subject
    Praise and Prayer.

XLVII

The laureate King his Psalming voice
    doth raise,
  And sings to 's solemn harp high
    lays,   140
Being himself the organ to his
    MAKER's praise.

XLVIII

Enflam'd with holy zeal, and high
    desire,
  Encircled with the enthean quire,
Warbles this epinician canzon to his
    lyre.

XLIX

' Thou, Crown of Bliss, whose foot-
    stool 's Earth, whose throne
  Outshines ten thousand suns in
    one,
Who art the radical life of all true joy
    alone !

L

' Royal PROTECTOR ! when in THEE,
    Light's sun,
  Mortals would deem the last hour
    run,
We find no wane of day, but a
    solstitial noon !   150

LI

' When we Time's volumes of past
    thousands scan,
  Thy origin with time to span,
We find no track in infant age when
    it began !

LII

'Ancient of Days ! to whom all times
    are now ;
  Before whom, Seraphims do bow,
Though highest creatures, yet to their
    CREATOR, low !

LIII

' Who art by light-surrounded powers
    obey'd
  (Heav'n's host Thy minist'ring
    spirits made),
Cloth'd with UBIQUITY, to whom all
    light is shade !

LIV

' Whose thunder-clasping Hand does
    grasp the shoal   160
  Of total Nature, and unroll

The spangled canopy of Heav'n from
  pole to pole !

LV

'Who, on the clouds and winds, Thy
  chariot, rid'st ;
  And, bridling wildest storms, them
  guid'st ;
Who, moveless, all dost move; who,
  changing all, abid'st !

LVI

'The ocean Thou begirt'st with misty
  shrouds ;
  That monster wrap'st in swathing
  clouds,
And, with Thy mighty Word controll'st
  tempestuous floods !

LVII

'Earth-circling oceans Thy displeas-
  ure flee ;
  Mountains dismounted are by
  Thee ;   170
Those airy giants smoke if Thou
  incensèd be !

LVIII

'Innumerable troops of Joys do
  stand
Before Thy boundless Presence, and
Uncessantly attend Thy ever-blissful
  Hand !

LIX

'Thou, LORD, good without quality,
  dost send
  Bliss to all Thine ; great, without
  end ;
Whose magnitude no quantity can
  comprehend !

LX

'What's worthless man ? what his
  earth-crawling race ?
  That Thou shouldst such a shadow
  grace,
And in unspeakable triumphant glory
  place !   180

LXI

'Who may thy Mercy's height, depth,
  breadth extend ?
  In height it does to Heav'n ascend,
Confirms the Angels, and in depth
  doth low descend,

LXII

'Lessening the pains o' th' damnèd
  ev'n in Hell ;
  In breadth, from East to West does
  swell
And over all the world, and all Thy
  works excel !

LXIII

'Immense EXISTENCE !   Heav'n's
  amaz'd at Thy
  INCOMPREHENSIBILITY !
Intelligences dread Thine all-com-
  manding Eye !

LXIV

'Ye wingèd heroes, whom all bliss
  embow'rs,   190
  To HIM in anthems strain your
  pow'rs,
Whose sea of goodness has no shore,
  whose age, no hours ! '

LXV

Then, o'er the trembling cords his
  swift hand strays,
  And clos'd all with full diapaze ;
As, in a sounding quire the well-
  struck concert plays.

LXVI

Victorious jubilees, when echo'd clear
  From the Church Militant, are
  dear
To Heav'n's triumphing quire ; such
  no gross ear can hear.

LXVII

Music's first martyr, Strada's night-
  ingale,   199
  Might ever wish (poor bird) to fall
On that excelling harp, and joy i' th'
  funeral !

LXVIII

Had it but heard those airs, where
  Music meets
  With raptures of voice-warbled
  sweets,
Flowing with ravishing excess in
  Sion's streets.

LXIX

All, what symphonious breaths in-
  spire, all, what

194 diapaze] The *z* is a little interesting.

Quick fingers touch, compar'd,
sound flat :
Could I but coin a word beyond all
sweets ! 'Twere that.

LXX

What orders in New-Salem's Hier-
archy,
In what degrees they' enstated be,
Are wings that mount my thoughts
to high discovery.   210

LXXI

Blest sight to see Heav'n's order'd
Host to move
In legions glist'ring all above,
Whose armour is true Zeal, whose
banner is pure Love !

LXXII

Bright-harnessed Intelligences ! Who
Enucleate can your Essence so,
As men may both your mighty pow'r
and nature know !

LXXIII

Invisible, impassive, happy, fair,
High, incorporeal, active, rare,
Pure, scientific and illustrious spirits
you are.

LXXIV

Guess at their strength, by One ; was
not almost   220
Two hundred thousand of an host
By an Angel slain, when Assur's chief
'gainst Heav'n did boast ?

LXXV

In brightness they the morning star
outvie ;
In nimbleness the Winds outfly ;
And far surpass the sunbeams in
subtility.

LXXVI

Archangels, those superior Spirits, are
GOD's legates, when He will declare
His mind to 's chosen ; Gabriel did
thus prepare

LXXVII

GOD's embassy, when His Belov'd
did tie
Our flesh to His Divinity ;   230

Grace was the kiss, the Union was
the ring from high ;

LXXVIII

Angels the posy sung : this, made
our clay
O'er empyrean courtiers sway,
Whenas the SPOUSE His mystic
nuptials did display.

LXXIX

No sooner shall that great Archangel
sound
His wakeful trump of doom to th'
ground,
And echo shall, as banded ball, make
quick rebound ;

LXXX

But, pamper'd graves, with all their
jaws, shall yawn ;
And seas, floods' nurse, strange
shoals shall spawn
Of men, to wait o' th' dreadful Judge
at 's judgement's dawn.   240

LXXXI

To incorruption then corruption's
night
Shall turnèd be ; for that strange
sight
Inebriates souls with deepest woes,
or high'st delight !

LXXXII

Then shall my ear, my nose, my hand,
tongue, eye,
Always hear, smell, feel, taste, espy,
Hosannas, incense, off'rings, feasts,
felicity !

LXXXIII

To act GOD's will, o'er sublunary
things,
The Dominations sway, as kings ;
He curbs aerian potentates, by th'
Pow'rs He wings ;

LXXXIV

The Principates, of princes take the
care,   250
T' enlarge their realms, or to
impair ;
Virtues in acting of His will have
their full share ;

209 they'] So in orig. : the apostrophe evidently indicating a slur.
237 banded] = ' bandied.'

(380)

LXXXV

Thrones Him contemplate, nor from's
presence move ;
To Cherubs He reveals above
Hid things ; He Seraphins inflames
with ardent love.

LXXXVI

Precelling Seraphs show God's ardour
still ;
Wise Cherubs His abyss of skill
In governing of all; beatious Thrones
instil

LXXXVII

To us His steadiness in 's 'blessed
throne,
Ever unalterably One ;   260
Pow'rs, virtues, principates to His
commands are prone ;

LXXXVIII

Dominions own His regal sway ;
and so
Archangels, Angels swiftly show
Agility that from the Deity does flow.

LXXXIX

Their number's numberless, not half
so few
As orient pearls of early dew ;
Like aromatic lamps they in Heav'n's
Temple show :

XC

And yet of them though vast the
number be,
The thing that most does glorify
Their Maker's this, they differ
specifically.   270

XCI

Of the first machine they the parcels
are ;
Yet, if we them with God compare,
Then with their wings they screen
themselves, though else most
fair.

XCII

Lawless Desire does never pierce
their breast ;
Th' Almighty's face is still their
feast ;

Their bliss in service lies, in messages
their rest :

XCIII

They speak with thought, achieve
without a fee ;
Silence they hear, Ideas see ;
Still magnifying Him, who cannot
greater be!

XCIV

Thus, they, with one fleet glance in-
tuitive,   280
Into each other's knowledge dive ;
And, by consent, thoughts, else in-
scrutable, unrive.

XCV

Each one in Psalms Eternity employs ;
Where use nor tires, nor fullness
cloys ;
Enjoying God, their end, without an
end of joys !

XCVI

Each ravishing voice, each instru-
ment, each face
Compos'd such music, that I was
In doubt, each so in tune, which did
precede in grace :

XCVII

The spritely instruments did sweetly
smile ;
The faces play'd their parts; mean-
while   290
The voices, with both graces, did
them both beguile.

XCVIII

The Ninefold Quire such heav'nly
accents there
In sweets Extension still do rear,
As overpow'r the windings of a mortal
ear.

XCIX

Who Music hate, in barb'rous discord
roll ;
In Heav'n there is not such a
soul ;
For, there's all-harmony. Saints sing,
the damnèd howl.

258 beatious] This, though an ugly word, no doubt intentionally connects with
'beatific' and 'beatitude.'
xciii–xciv] *Cf.* Dante, *De Vulg. Eloq.* I. ii.

C

Celestial sweets did this discourse excite ;
Firm joy, fast ove, fix'd life, fair sight !
But may a creature, its CREATOR'S glory write?   300

Nunc alti Plumbum scrutatur Viscera Ponti,
Viscera Navarchæ non repetenda Manu !
Hinc. procul optatam divino Lumine Terram
Cernimus, optatum perficiamus Iter !

TE DEUM LAUDAMUS.

Canto VII. The Contemplation

THE ARGUMENT

Pango nec humanis Opus enarrabile Verbis,
  Quæ meliùs possem Mira silendo loqui !
Da, DEUS, Illa canam, quæ Vox non personet ulla,
  Metiar ut minimis Maxima Mira modis !

She launcheth into shoreless Seas of Light,
  Inexplicable, infinite !
Whose beams both strike her blind, and renovate her sight !

STANZA I

WERE all men Maros, were those Maros all
  Evangelists, met in Earth's Hall
For grand-inquest of that which we Eternal call :

II

Draw Time from 's cradle (Innocence) could they,
  And pilèd heaps of ages lay
Amassèd in one scale ; those would they find to weigh,

III

Balanc'd with THEE, no more (when all is done)
  Than, if they vainly had begun
To poise minutest atoms with the mighty sun.

IV

Could they Earth's ball with numbers quilted see ;   10
  Yet, those throng'd figures sum not THEE,
They were but ciphers to immense ETERNITY !

(382)

V

Should every sand for thousand ages run,
  When emptied shores of sands were done,
That glass no more THEE measures, than if now begun !

VI

Had tongues Heav'n's mint, to coin each Angel-grace
  In dialect ; they'd fail o' th' space,
Where all to come is one with all that ever was !

VII

Faith, stretch thy line, yet that's too short, to sound
  Sea without bottom, without bound ;   20
As circular, as infinite, O shoreless round !

VIII

Immense ETERNITY ! What mystic art
  Of THEE may copy any part,
Since THOU an indeterminable CIRCLE art !

IX

Whose very centre so diffus'd is found,
That not Heav'n's circuit can it bound,
Then what, what may the whole circumference surround?

X

Heav'n's heroes, can ye find for th' ENDLESS end?
Can pow'r's IMMENSITY extend?
UBIQUITY enclose? The BOUNDLESS comprehend? 30

XI

JEHOVAH's zone to this uncentred BALL,
Ecliptic, and meridional,
Who was before, is with, and shall be after all!

XII

But now behold its height, above all height!
Plac'd beyond place! Above light's light!
Rapt were the three Apostles by a glimpse o' th' sight!

XIII

Oh, thou all-splendent, all transcending Throne!
Compact of high'st Dominion!
That 'bove the super-eminence of lustre shone!

XIV

From each of thine ineffably bright sides 40
Diffusion of such splendour glides,
As rolls 'bove thousand seas of joys in flaming tides

XV

With such refulgence, that, if Cherubs might,
With face unveil'd gaze on that sight,
Straight their spiritual natures would be nothing'd quite.

XVI

Nature, put on thy most coruscant vest;

Thy gaieties show, brought to this test,
As a crude jelly dropt from dusky clouds at best.

XVII

Couldst thou impov'rish every Indian mine,
And, from each golden cell, unshrine 50
Those beams, that with their blaze outface day's em'lous shine:

XVIII

Couldst find out secret engines to unlock
The treasuring casket of each rock,
And reap the glowing harvest of that sparkling shock:

XIX

Couldst thread the stars (fix'd and erratic) here,
That stud the luminated sphere,
That all those orbs of light one constellation were:

XX

Couldst join mines, gems, sky-tapers, all in one;
Whose near-immense reflection
Might both outrival, and outvie the glorious sun: 60

XXI

Could all thy stones be gems, seas liquid gold,
Air crystal, dust to pearl enroll'd,
Each star a sun, that sun more bright a thousandfold:

XXII

Yet would those gems seem flints, those seas a plash,
Those stars a spark, that sun a flash;
Pearl'd islands, diamond rocks, gold mines, all sullied trash:

XXIII

Yea, were all eyes of earth, sky, Heav'n combin'd,
And to one optic point confin'd,

59 near] Orig. 'neer.'

This super-radiant object would ev'n
    strike that blind !

XXIV

Blind, as the sable veil of gloomy
    night   70
    (The Gospel's self but hints this
    Sight) :
All seem obscurer shades to this non-
    pareil Light !

XXV

Amazing ! Most inexplicably rare !
    Oh, if, but those who worthy are,
None may this light declare—none
    may this light declare !

XXVI

Best eloquence is languid, high'st
    thoughts vail,
    To think, to speak, wit, language
    fail ;
'Tis an abyss, through which no
    Spirit's eye can sail !

XXVII

Here Glory dwells, with lustres so
    surrounded,
    That brightest rays are quite con-
    founded,   80
When they approach this radiant
    eminence unbounded !

XXVIII

Forth from this fulgurance such
    splendours fly,
    As shall draw up frail dust on
    high ;
Which, else, would in its lumpish urn
    still bedrid lie.

XXIX

Before the Almighty's throne my
    soul I throw,
    Whence all, that's good and great,
    does flow.
Lord, I that grace implore, which
    may this glory show !

XXX

Great God ! Thou all-beginning, un-
    begun !
    Whose hand the web of Nature
    spun !
At once the plenitude of all, and yet
    but One !   90

(384)

XXXI

Parent of beings, Entity's sole stud !
    Spirit's eternal spring and flood !
Sprung of Thyself, or rather no way
    sprung ! Chief Good !

XXXII

Abstract of joys, whose Wisdom an
    abyss !
    Whose Pow'r Omnipotency is !
Whose soul-enlivening sight's the
    universal bliss !

XXXIII

Thou dost descend on wings of air
    display'd,
    'Bove majesty itself array'd,
Curtain'd with clouds, the Host of
    Heav'n attendants made !   99

XXXIV

Essence of glory, Summity of praise !
    Abash'd at Thy all-piercing rays,
Heav'n's quire does chaunt unces-
    sant Alleluiahs !

XXXV

Diamonds than glass, than diamonds
    stars more bright ;
    Than stars the sun, than sun
    Heav'n's light ;
But infinitely purer than Heav'n's
    self 's Thy Sight !

XXXVI

Great is the earth, more large the
    air's extent :
    Planets exceed ; the firmament
Of stars outvies ; unlimited 's the
    Heav'nly Tent :

XXXVII

But, as my tenter'd mind its spirits
    still
    Strains forth, from less to more
    (Lord, fill   110
My outspent raptures by Thy all-re-
    pairing skill !)

XXXVIII

When I above air, stars, Heav'n, on
    would press
    Rack'd thoughts to spheres beyond
    excess ;
Myriads of spheres seem motes to Thy
    Immense Oneness !

XXXIX
Eternity is but Thine hour-glass!
Immensity but fills Thy space!
Whole Nature's six days' work took
up but six words' place!

XL
One word did th' all-surrounding sky-
roof frame,
With all its starry sparkling flame!
Not all created wisdom can spell out
THY NAME!   120

XLI
Supreme COMMANDER of the rolling
stars!
Thy law sets to their progress bars,
Does epicycle their obliquely gliding
cars!

XLII
No lines, poles, tropics, zones can
Thee enthrall,
First MOVER of the spheric ball,
Above, beneath, without, within, be-
yond them all!

XLIII
What could, but thy all-potent Hand,
sustain
Those magazines of hail, snow, rain,
Lest they should fall at once, and
deluge all again?

XLIV
By them Thou plenty dost to earth
distil;   130
And man's dependent heart dost
fill:
Winds are van-couriers, and posti-
lions to Thy Will!

XLV
'Tis that the ominous cause of earth-
quakes binds
In subterranean grots; that finds
Strange ruptures to enfranchise th'
ever-struggling winds!

XLVI
Thy sandy cord does proudest surges
bound;
And seas, unfathom'd bottoms
sound;

Thy semi-circling bow i' th' clouds
thy covenant crown'd!

XLVII
Earth's hinges hang upon thy fiat; set
Midst air-surrounding waters, yet
Stand fix'd on that, like which, what
is so firm, so great?   141

XLVIII
Yet earth's fast columns at Thy frown
do quake;
And oceans dreadful horrors
make;
Flints melt, the rocks do roll, the
airy mountains shake!

XLIX
Yea, Heav'n's self trembled, and the
centre shook,
With Thy amazing Presence strook,
When Power of pow'rs on Sina's
Mount His station took!

L
Each Ens (as link'd to Providence,
Thy chain)
Is govern'd by Thy fingers' rein!
Thou seeing us, we grace; we, Thee,
do glory gain!   150

LI
Who hast no eyes to see, nor ears to
hear;
Yet see'st, and hear'st, all eye, all
ear!
Who nowhere art contain'd, yet art
Thou everywhere!

LII
The optic glass we of Thy prescience
may
Call th' Ark, where all ideas lay,
By which each entity Thou dost at
first portray!

LIII
Future events are pre-existent here,
As if they lately acted were;
Than any new-dissect anatomy more
clear!

LIV
Each where, at once, Thou totally
art still   160

132 couriers] Orig. 'curriers.'
160 Each where] So in orig., but the word, which is Spenserian, should be revived
as one, i. e. 'eachwhere,' for 'everywhere' is not synonymous.

The same unchang'd; yet, at Thy
will,
Thou changest all; who, though
Thou art unmov'd, dost fill

LV

Things that are most remote; in
whose forecast
Contingencies do crowd so fast,
As if past things were now, and
things to come were past!

LVI

Though acts on earth cross to Thy
will are done,
Besides Thy will yet acteth none;
Preceding and succeeding will, in
Thee are one!

LVII

Of whose vast Manor all the Earth's
domains!
Though Earth, nor air, nor Heav'n
contains,   170
Yet each obscurer grot Thy OMNI-
PRESENCE gains!

LVIII

Though nought accrues to Thy
unbounded state
From spirits, which Thou didst
create,
Yet they Thy goodness and Thy love
shall still dilate!

LIX

Thou, who mad'st all, mad'st neither
sin, nor death;
Man's folly first gave them their
breath;
That did abase whole Nature with
itself beneath.

LX

But sin to cure, Thou in a crib gav'st
man
EMANUEL! Divine-humane!
Who diff'ring natures join'd; whose
reign no ages scan!   180

LXI

And Thou, O MEDIATOR! Thou,
whose praise,
Like morning dews, to first of
days
Was sung by heav'nly choristers in
seraph lays!

LXII

GOD, by the Holy Ghost, begat Thee,
Lord! .
Flesh took by the Eternal Word!
Whose self-eternal EMANATION none
record!

LXIII

As Thy eternal EMANATION's past;
So to Eternity shalt last!
In the beginning was the Word,
shows still THOU wast;

LXIV

There God in Essence, one in
Persons Three!   190
Here Natures two in One agree!
Thou, sitting in the midst of TRINAL-
UNITY

LXV

At Heav'n's high council-table, dart'st
such rays,
As strike ev'n cherubs with amaze!
Of which the school, disputing all,
it nothing says.

LXVI

Search we the ages past so long ago,
None, none this Mystery could
show,
Till in that maiden-birth, 'twas acted
here below!

LXVII

A Dove hatch'd in that nest Thyself
did build!
A Lamb that Thine own flock does
shield!   200
A winter Flow'r that fram'd, from
whence it sprung, the field!

LXVIII

The Jewish shepherds all affrighted
are,
When heralds THEE proclaim'd
i' th' air!
Yea, Magi came t' adore, led by a new-
born star!

LXIX

Yet, though thus wond'rously begot,
thus born,
Sponsor for us, fall'n race, forlorn,
T' ingratiate us with GOD, becam'st
to man a scorn!

LXX

The Grace Self wast, th' Honour t'
  evangelize !
The sacred Function, as a prize,
Thou took'st, yet that not on, till
  call'd in Aaron's guise !   210

LXXI

Which GOD t' apostolize did bring
  to pass,
By th' HOLY GHOST'S descent, at
  face
Of Jordan's then blest streams, of
  which John witness was !

LXXII

Thence, led by th' HOLY GHOST to
  th' wilderness,
There tempted by the Fiend's
  address,
Him overcam'st by *Scriptum est* ;
  hence our release !
Then forth Thou went'st.—

LXXIII

Thy sermons, oracles ; acts, wonders
  were !
Those Faith begot, these others
  Fear !
By both, thus wrought in us, to THEE
  ourselves we rear !   220

LXXIV

Thou gav'st the lame swift legs, the
  blind clear eyes !
Thou heal'dst all human maladies !
Thou mad'st the dumb to speak !
  Thou mad'st the dead to rise !

LXXV

And art to dead men Life, to sick
  men Health !
Sight to the blind, to th' needy
  Wealth !
A Pleasure without pain ! a Treasure
  without stealth !

LXXVI

LORD, in, not of this world, Thy
  Kingdom is ;

Thy chos'n Apostles preach'd Thy
  bliss,
That none of all Thy creatures might
  salvation miss.

LXXVII

Abraham, long dead before, yet saw
  Thy day,   230
In Isaac born, and vows did pay !
Type first, then antitype, and quick-
  'nest every way !

, LXXVIII

Thy Gospel Wisdom's Academy
  show'd ;
Thy Mercy, Justice calm'd ; Life,
  view'd
Is Temperance ; Thy Death the flag
  of Fortitude !

LXXIX

Thou, altar, sanctuary, sacrifice,
  Priest, bread of life dost all suffice !
Ne'er-cloying feast, where appetite
  by food doth rise !

LXXX

And, Son of Man, dost sin of man
  forgive !   239
To be Thy victims hearts do strive,
Who liv'dst that life might die, and
  di'dst that death might live !

LXXXI

Yet di'dst Thou not, but that (Spirit
  quicken'd) free
Thou might'st saints paradisèd see,
Rejoic'd assurance give to them
  rejoic'd in Thee !

LXXXII

And that, from thence, to Satan's
  gloomy shades,
Made prison for the damnèd
  Hades,
Thou might'st Thy conquest show,
  Thy glory that ne'er fades !

LXXXIII

Thence loos'd Death's chains from
  body, up to rear it,

217] This extra hemistich is printed in orig. level with the number LXXIII of the next
stanza as a kind of aside, a parenthetic ejaculation.
232 quick'nest] This, which is without apostrophe in orig., is rather hard to adjust
even to Benlowes' singular stenography. I should like to read 'thou' for 'and.'
246 Hades] Rhyme noted in Introd.

That, when rais'd state THOU dost
  inherit,
THOU might'st become to us an ever-
  quick'ning SPIRIT !   250

LXXXIV

The FATHER to reveal gives to His
  SON
Thee, HOLY GHOST (thus Three
  in One)
Of all peculiar Sanctifier, yet not
  alone !

LXXXV

The Father's love, and Son's;
  Adoption's seal,
The Spring of sanctity, the Weal
O' th' Church : Thyself in light of
  fiery tongues reveal !

LXXXVI

O Light unscann'd ! Of wisdom
  every glance
Beams only from Thy countenance;
Whose store, when emptied most
  itself doth most advance !

LXXXVII

Whose fruits are Gentleness, Peace,
  Love, and Joy,   260
All crown'd with bliss, freed from
  annoy ;
Which neither Time, World, Death,
  Hell, Devil can destroy !

LXXXVIII

Thou art a feast, fram'd of that fruit-
  ful fare,
Which hungers waste not, but
  repair !
A rich perfume, no winds can winnow
  into air !

LXXXIX

A light unseen, yet in each place
  dost shine !
A sound no art can e'er define !
A pure embrace, that Time's assault
  can ne'er untwine !

XC

Floods of unebbing joys from Thee
  do roll !
Which, to each sin-disdaining soul
Thou dost exhibit in an unexhausted
  bowl !   271

XCI

This Wine of Ecstasy, by th' SPIRIT
  giv'n,
Doth raise the ravish'd souls to
  Heav'n !
Affording them those comforts are
  of Earth's bereav'n !

XCII

Thy union is as strict, as large thy
  merit !
No Heav'n but THEE, which
  Saints inherit
Through grace, divinest sap, deriv'd
  by th' Holy Spirit !

XCIII

When souls enflamèd by that highest
  light,
Fix on Thy glorifying sight,
All glories else, compar'd to that, are
  dusky night !   280

XCIV

When high'st infusions pass our
  highest sense,
Amazement is high eloquence,
'Bove all hyperboles which fall to
  exigence.

XCV

Blest TRINITY, Th' art all; above
  all, Good !
Beatitude's Beatitude !
Which swallows us, yet swim we in
  this Living Flood !

XCVI

TH' art King of kings, of lords Lord !
  None like THEE !
Who, for Thy style hast Majesty !
And for Thy royal robes hast
  Immortality.

XCVII

Mercy for throne ! for sceptre Justice
  hast !   290
Immensity 's for kingdom plac'd !
And for Thy crown such glory as
  doth ever last !

XCVIII

For peace, what passeth understand-
  ing's eye !
Pow'r, irresistibility !
For holiness, all what's most sacred,
  pure, and high !

XCIX

For truth, Thy Word ! Wisdom for
  counsellor !
  Omnipotence does guard Thy
    tow'r !
Thou minist'ring angels hast to act
  Thy sovereign pow'r !

C

Omniscience Thine intelligencer is !
For treasure Thou hast endless
  bliss !   300

For date eternity ! Oh, swallow me,
  ABYSS !

Ite, pii Cantus, Cantus quibus arduus
    Æther
  Est Portus ; Portus, quem videt
    alma Fides.
Visuram Littus Navem, sacra Serta
    coronent,
  Serta per innumeros non peritura
    Dies !

GLORIA IN EXCELSIS DEO.

Canto VIII.   The Admiration

THE ARGUMENT

Cœli trina MONAS, TRIAS una, faveto precanti !
  PERSONAS unâ Tres DEITATE colo !
Sunt tria, sunt et idem, Fons, Flumen, Gurges aquarum :
  Sic tria sunt unum, Sol, Jubar, atque Calor.
Th' Elixir centuplies itself. But, oh,
  Myriads of myriads must she so,
T' express GOD's Essence which no intellect can show !

STANZA I

PROJECTION to my soul ! Thy sight's
  a wreath
Of glory ; thou dost virtue breathe ;
Thy words, like sacred incense, fuel
  and flame bequeath.

II

Thou Maid of Honour in Heav'n's
  Court ! to break
Thy gold-twist lines shows judge-
  ment weak ;
Yet deign to hear my suit ; of GOD's
  hid Nature speak !

III

Can counters sum up infinite ? Fond
  man,
  Couldst grasp whole oceans in thy
    span,
And Phœbus couldst outface in his
  meridian ;

IV

Tear rocks of adamant, and scale the
  wall   10

O' th' glorious empyræan hall ;
And worms to super-eminence of
  Seraphs call !

V

Yet this, ev'n then, thou couldst nor
  learn, nor teach :
  The World, unravell'd, cannot
    stretch
To sound th' Abyss.   Itself alone it-
  self can reach.

VI

Of all intelligences not all Light
  Muster'd into one optic sight,
Can speak what each where is, yet no
  where seen to th' height !

VII

Who out of nothing all things did
  compact ;
  Whose will's His work, whose word
    His act :   20
Of whom, who says the most, must
  from His worth detract ?

VIII

How from the Essence the Creator
  flows !
  Or how the Word, what creature
  knows !
How th' Spirit, all in 't, all from 't, does
  Heav'n's assembly pose !

IX

Here they, who leave the Church's
  ship, are tost
  Till irrecoverably lost !
Whose rudder is GOD's Word, steers-
  man, th' HOLY GHOST.

X

Archessence ! Thou, self-full ! self-
  infinite !
  Residing in approachless light !
In the Incomprehensibilities of
  Height !   30

XI

Thy peerless uncreated NATURE is
  The super-excellence of BLISS !
Where Holiness and Pow'r ; where
  Truth and Goodness kiss !

XII

Who only in THYSELF subsists, with-
  out
  Or form, or matter ! yet, no doubt,
Inform'st the matter of the universe
  throughout !

XIII

No need compels THEE, no disasters
  sad
  Disturb thy state, no mirth makes
  glad ;
Oblivion takes not from THEE, nor
  can mem'ry add !

XIV

With prudent rev'rence, thus. What-
  e'er 's in GOD,   40
  His Essence is ; there's His abode ;
Whose will His rule, whose Heav'n
  His court, whose hell His rod.

XV

He exists an active ENS, upholding
  both
  Itself, and everything that doth

Exist ; without distinction or of parts,
  or growth !

XVI

Not made by nothing (nothing no-
  thing makes) ;
  Nor birth from anything HE takes ;
For, what gives birth, precedes :
  springs usher in their lakes.

XVII

Were HE material, then HE local were ;
  All matter being in place ; so, there
Th' Incircumscriptible would circum-
  scrib'd appear.   51

XVIII

HE's so diffusive, that HE's all in all !
  All in the universal ball !
All out of it ! The only WAS, the IS,
  the SHALL.

XIX

To help thy reason, think of air ;
  there see
  Ubiquity unseen, and free
From touch ; inviolable, though it
  piercèd be.

XX

Mere air corrupts not, though con-
  vey'd unto
  All lungs ; for, thither it does go
To cool them ; quick'neth all, as the
  world's soul doth show :   60

XXI

Moisture and heat, its qualities, are
  cause
  Of all production : yet, because
This element 's a creature, GOD
  Creator, pause.

XXII

Self-life the attribute of 's Being is !
  His Will, of governing ! and His
Command of execution ! and His
  love of bliss !

XXIII

All's tied in this love-knot : JEHOVAH's
  love.
  Time's birth the Trinity does prove :
Creator made, Word spake, and
  Spirit of GOD did move :   69

27 th'] So in orig.: if correctly, Benlowes must have made 'steērsman' trisyllabic.
63 Creator,] No comma in orig., but required. 'Pause' corresponds to 'think' in 55.

XXIV
'Let us in our own image man create.'
  Which Solomon does explicate ;
Remember the Creators in thy youth-
  ful state.

XXV
The Father spake, the Son i' th'
  stream did move
At His baptizing ; from above
The Holy Ghost descended in the
  form o' th' Dove.

XXVI
Of Him, to Him, and through Him
  all things be :
  Of, through, and to declare the
  Three ;
And in the HIM, the Unity of GOD we
  see.

XXVII
Thus Holy, Holy, Holy 's nam'd, to
  show
A Ternion we in Union know : 80
The notions issuing from the Trine,
  int' One do flow.

XXVIII
Whilst that I think on THREE, I am
  confin'd
To One ! while I have One in mind,
I am let forth to Three ! Yet Three
  in One combin'd !

XXIX
Oh, inconceivable IDENTITY !
  In One how may a Plural be !
Coequal both in attributes, and
  majesty !

XXX
The FATHER is true GOD i' th' Ternion:
  The WORD unborn, yet after Son:
The SPIRIT GOD coessential ; Three,
  cause Three from One !   90

XXXI
The Father and Word are One !
  One, shows their power :
Are, distinct Persons. *One* does
  show'r
On Tritheists vengeance : *Are*, does
  Arians devour.

XXXII
One, yet not one ! The Father and
  the Son
In Persons two, from Father one
By th' SPIRIT ; Son is one by resigna-
  tion !

XXXIII
The Word is what He was ; yet, once
  was not
  What now He is ! for, He hath got
A Nature more than once He had,
  to cleanse our spot !

XXXIV
For, ne'er had man from earth to
  Heav'n attain'd,   100
  Had GOD from Heav'n to earth
  not deign'd
His Son ! now unto GOD man's way
  by Man is gain'd !

XXXV
EQUAL, and Son, the form of servant
  takes !
  The world, unmade by sin, new
  makes !
EQUAL, Son, servant ! All are mys-
  teries, not mistakes !

XXXVI
Thus, by free grace is man's defection
  heal'd :
  Behold the mystery reveal'd.
WORD, equal ; shadowing, Son ;
  Unction is servant seal'd !

XXXVII
Because GOD'S EQUAL, serpent's
  tempts are quell'd :
  Yet He, as Son, to death must
  yield   110
For us ; by resurrection to regain the
  field.

XXXVIII
The SPIRIT is true GOD ; from ever He
  Did reign with Both ! The TRINITY
Coequal, Coeternal, Coessential be !

XXXIX
The FATHER 's full, though th' SON
  hath all engross'd !
  Nor yet is aught of this all lost,

90 cause] So in orig., and possible, Benlowes often having comma between noun
and verb. But it may, as often also, be 'cause = ' because.'
93 Tritheists] Orig. ' Tritheits.'

(391)

Though th' FATHER give Himself
  to th' SON by th' HOLY GHOST!
XL
For, though He freely thus give all
  His store ;
Yet hath He Infinite, as before !
Conceive for glimpse some endless
  spring, or mine of ore !   120
XLI
What soul will have this TRIAD for
  his book,
  With faith must on the back-parts
  look,
For, with His glorious FACE, blind
  are ev'n Seraphs strook !
XLII
By speculation from Sol's substance,
  we
  The FATHER ; from its splendour
  see
The SON ; from's heat the HOLY
  GHOST. Here, One is Three.
XLIII
The intellect, the memory, the will
  Resemblance make o' th' TRINE ;
  these fill
One soul, yet are distinct in outward
  workings still !
XLIV
Thus, to restore from fall, we may
  descry   130
  THE TRINITY in UNITY !
Inscrutable ABYSS rebates our weaker
  eye !
XLV
Be ever-ever-ever blest, O TRINE !
  Ever Unitedness divine !
Who dost as well in ants, as in Arch-
  angels shine !
XLVI
The Principats, Thrones, Domina-
  tions, all
  Archangels, Pow'rs celestial
Are ministers attending on thy
  sovereign call !
XLVII
The government 'bove star-embroi-
  der'd hall,

Thus truly is monarchical,   140
Where all are kings, and yet one King
  does rule them all !
XLVIII
Less than the thousand part I have
  express'd ;
  Man's weakness cannot bear the
  rest.
For Thy expressless Nature, LORD, be
  ever blest !
XLIX
Soul of all sweets ! my love, life, joy
  and bliss !
  To enjoy Thee's Heav'n ! Hell
  Thee to miss !
What's Earth's ? Ev'n Heav'n hath
  its beatitude from this !
L
Remove the needle from the pole-
  star, and
  'Tis still with trembling motion
  fann'd,
Till it returns. No fixture but in
  GOD does stand.   150
LI
To saints all other objects prizeless be ;
  In GOD, the All of All, we see :
Feast to the taste, all beauty to the
  sight is He !
LII
Music to th' ear ; and those whom
  He unites,
  Partake with Him in high'st
  delights !
Springtides of pleasures overwhelm
  their ravish'd sprites !
LIII
But, contraries, when opposite, best
  show.
  (As foils set diamonds off, we know),
See Hell, where caitives pine, yet still
  their tortures grow !
LIV
As metals fiery waves in furnace
  swell,   160
  That founders run, to cast each
  bell ;

139] Allusions to the Star-chamber (see note, p. 356) are not uncommon at this time :
the special play of thought here is pretty obvious.

This, not endur'd ; more rage ten
  thousand times is Hell !

LV

Where souls still rave, adust with
  horrid pain !
They tug, they tear, but all in vain,
For, them from raging smart, Hope
  never shall unchain !

LVI

Oh, that for trash these Esaus sold
  their bliss !
For sin, that worse than nothing is !
This desperates their rage ! How they
  blaspheme at this !

LVII

This viper clings, corrodes, 'gainst
  which no ward !
God's beatific sight debarr'd,   170
Renders their case 'bove all the pains
  of sense more hard !

LVIII

Oh, never-sated worm ! unpitied woes !
Unintermitted ! what Sin owes,
Hell pays ! The damn'd are anvils to
  relentless blows !

LIX

Fiends forfeit not their energy.
  There Cain
Fries, but for one lamb by him slain !
Oh, what flames then shall butchers
  of Christ's flock sustain ?

LX

Earth's fatal mischief, prosp'rous thief,
  that thunder
Which tore the nations all asunder,
Whom just Fate slew i' th' world's
  revenge, that conqu'ring wonder,

LXI

That ghost of Philip's hot-brain'd son
  may tell   181
Heart-breaking stories of his Hell !
Too late he finds one soul did his
  whole world excel !

LXII

There, curs'd oppressors dreadful
  rackings feel !
Whose hearts were rocks, and
  bowels steel !

Oh, scorching fire ! (cries Dives) for
  one drop I kneel !

LXIII

Oblig'd is man, God's steward, to
  supply
Brethren, in Christ coheirs, who
  lie
Gasping in stiff'ning frosts, no cov'ring
  but the sky :

LXIV

Whose wither'd skins, sear as the
  sapless wood,   190
Cleave to their bones, for want of
  food,
Seem Nature's monsters thrown
  ashore by Mis'ry's flood.

LXV

Though all their physic 's but a diet
  spare ;
Have no more earth, than what
  they are,
Nor more o' th' world, than graves, yet
  in Heav'n's love they share.

LXVI

Inestimable Love, from none be-
  reav'n !
Heav'n sunk to earth, earth mounts
  to Heav'n !
Just Judge ! to Dives Hell, to Laz'rus
  Heav'n is giv'n !

LXVII

Love, disengage us of ourselves !
  Love has
Nor bit, nor reins ! Rich, 'bove
  earth's mass !   200
Fix'd in ideas of Love's soul-enliv'n-
  ing grace !

LXVIII

O Love ! O Height, above all height,
  to Thine !
Thy favour did to foes incline !
Unmeasurable Measure ! endless End
  of line !

LXIX

Love darts all thoughts to its Belov'd ;
  doth place
All bliss in waiting on His grace ;
It languisheth with Hope to view
  Him face to face !

194 Have] Apparently short for ' *though they* have.'

LXX

And ushers in that Beatific Love,
  Which so divinely flames above,
And doth to vision, union, and frui-
  tion move ! 210

LXXI

Ice is a thing distinct from th' ocean
  wide ;
But, melted by the sun, does glide
Into 't, becomes one with 't, and so
  shall e'er abide.

LXXII

Desire 's a tree, whose fruit is love,
  the show'rs
That ripen it are tears, the flow'rs
Are languors, leaves afflictions,
  blossoms pray'r-spent hours.

LXXIII

O mental Pray'r, thy joys are high !
  Resort
  By thee 's to GOD ! Thou art the
  port
Of inward peace from storms ! The
  path to Sion's Court !

LXXIV

By pray'r GOD 's serv'd betimes ;
  remember who 220
  The blessing got by wrestling so ;
Who early pray, they healthy, holy,
  happy grow.

LXXV

Then pray, before Light's rosy blush
  displays
I' th' Orient Sol's encheering rays,
When he from 's opal East to West
  obliquely strays :

LXXVI

Before the cock, Light's herald, day-
  break sings
  To 's feath'ry dames ; ere roost-lark
  springs,
Morn's usher ; when the dawn its
  mongrel hour forth brings.

LXXVII

Pray'r, thou art life's best act, soul's
  silent speech,
  The gate of Grace ; saints GOD
  beseech 230

By prayer, but join'd with alms and
  fasts they HIM besiege !

LXXVIII

Fasting, the soul's delicious banquet,
  can
  Add strength to pray'r, feast th'
  inner man,
And throw up to Eternity the body's
  span !

LXXIX

Fasts, sackcloth, ashes, grovelling on
  the ground
  Saints studied have with pain ;
  and found
With joy, that what degrades the
  sense, in Heav'n is crown'd !

LXXX

Prize Faith, the shield of martyrs,
  Joy's confection,
  Soul's light, the Prophet's sure
  direction,
Hope's guide, Salvation's path, the
  pledge of all perfection ! 240

LXXXI

In Faith's mysterious Eden make
  abode ;
  With Jacob's staff, and Aaron's rod
Frequent its grove, where none are
  but the lov'd of GOD !

LXXXII

The radiations of Faith's lamp excite
  Such a Colosse of sparkling light,
That saints through worldly waves
  may steer life's course aright.

LXXXIII

Being in, not of this world, they
  comforts rear
  Above the pitch of servile fear :
Terrestrial blossoms first must die,
  ere fruit they bear.

LXXXIV

No clogging fetters of impris'ning clay,
  No wry-mouth squint-ey'd scoff
  can stay 251
Their swift progression, soaring in
  their heav'nly way !

LXXXV

Thoughts on the endless weight of
  glory shall

238 confection] Used, it would seem, in the sense of 'completion,' familiar in *conficere*.

Render ev'n crowns, as dung, and
all
Afflictions light, as chaff chas'd on
Earth's empty ball.

LXXXVI

The torch that shines in night, as
eye of noon,
Is but as darkness to the sun :
Run after shades, they fly; fly after
shades, they run.

LXXXVII

All worldly gays are reeds, without
support,
Fitly with rainbow gleams they
sort,   260
Want solidness ; when gain'd, they
are as false, as short.

LXXXVIII

While fools, like silly larks, with
feathers play,
And stoop to th' glass, are twitch'd
away,
Amidst their pleasing madness, to
Hell's dismal bay !

LXXXIX

Oh, could embodied souls sin's bane
view well,
Rather in flames they'd choose to
dwell !
Not so much ill, as sin, have all the
pains of Hell !

XC

A smiling conscience (wrong'd) does
sweetly rest,
Though starv'd abroad, within
doth feast ;
Has Heav'n itself for cates, has GOD
Himself for Guest !   270

XCI

May call Him FATHER ; His Vice-
gerent be !
An atom of DIVINITY !
Redeem'd by 's SON, by the SPIRIT
inspir'd, blest by ALL THREE !

XCII

His judge becomes His advocate !
hath care
To plead for Him ! The Angels
are

His guardians ! from his GOD him
heights nor depths may scare.

XCIII

Oh, blest, who in His courts their
days do spend !
And on that Sovereign Good de-
pend !
His Word their rule ; His Spirit their
light ; Himself their end !

XCIV

While pride of life, and lust o' th' eye
do quite   280
Dazzle the world, saints out of
sight
Retire, to view their bliss : on which
some cantos write :

XCV

For, souls, sincerely good, in humble
cell
Encloister'd, near Devotion's bell,
By Contemplation's groves and
springs near Heav'n do dwell.

XCVI

Bright-gifted soaring minds (though
fortune-trod)
Are careless of dull Earth's dark
clod ;
Enrich'd with higher donatives ;
their prize is GOD !

XCVII

'Farewell.' As vanish'd lightning
then she flies.
Oh, how in me did burnings rise !
The only discord was 'Farewell.'
Hearts outreach eyes.   291

XCVIII

The air respires those quintessential
sweets
From whence she breath'd, and
whoso meets
With such, the tuneful orbs he in
that zenith greets.

XCIX

Dwell on this joy, my thoughts,
react her part ;
Such raptures on thy shuddering
heart
Make thee all ecstasy by spirit-seizing
art !

(395)

c

Chewing upon those Heav'n-enchanting strains,
My soul Earth's giddy mirth disdains ;
Fleet Joy runs races in my blood through thousand veins ! 300

Contingit gratam victrix Industria Metam ;
Et mea nunc Portu fessa potire Ratis.
Est Opus exactum, Cujus non pœnitet Acti :
Me juvat at Cæpti Summa videre mei.

OMNIA IN UNO, ET IN OMNIBUS UNUS.

MIRA mihi inter Authorem & Opus occurrit Symphonia : Ille Cælebs, Hoc Virgineum ; Ille Philomusicus ; Hoc, ipsum Melos ; Ille Dilectus, Hoc ipsa Dilectio : Quis enim ad Vim Amoris explicandum vel copiosiùs dixit, vel impensiùs Opere perfecit, quàm Autor hîc in sua THEOPHILA ? quæ tantâ Florum Varietate conspersa est, ut quid priùs legam, aut laudem, vix mihi post

repetitam Lectionem constare possit. Quid etiam Jucundiùs Animi Oculis, quàm sitientem tam cœlesti Nectare Animam adimplere ? Sine me Deliciis igitur istis inebriari ; & me Epulis, hisce, Mel & Amorem spirantibus, jugiter accumbere. Modus amandi DEUM non habet modum ; nullus planè in hoc Genere Excessus datur. Scripserunt De Arte Amandi Varii, sed imperfectè admodum, & impurè ; ac si, non tam Amandi quàm Peccandi Artem edocere professi essent : Quia hujusmodi illecebræ, dum sensìm sine sensu Venenum hauriunt, Morbo sine Medelâ afficiunt. Hîc autem sunt Dictu honesta, Lectu jucunda, Scitu utilia, Observatu digna, & Factu præstantissima. Eximium ergo hoc felicis Ingenii Specimen, propter Multiplices Aculeos in Legentium Animos suavitèr penetrantes, & penitiorem æternæ Veritatis Cognitionem instillatam, Auresque harmonicè demulcentem, in Lucem emitti, non possum non lætari.

M. G. S.T.D.

Jam satìs expertus Briticum Mare, contraho Vela ;
Naviget Ausonio Musa Latina Salo.
Fallor, an externo venit Aura secundior Orbe ?
Portus in Latios versa Triremis eat.

Ad piæ Poesios Cultum Invitatio

VOS, Eruditionis Candidati, quibus Crux DOMINI Gloriæ, Religio Cordi, Integritas Honori, Doctrina Ornamento, Poesis sacra Oblectamento, qui Cupiditates Rationi, Rationem Religioni, ut Christiani, subjugâstis, cum Musis convivamini devotioribus, ut perpetuâ Posterorum vigeatis Memoriâ. Non ad Mundi deliria, vos, Animæ piè anhelantes, sed, fulguris more, ad Sublimia nascimini. Credite Vosmetipsos DEI Filios, respondete Generi, vivite Cœlo, PATREM Similitudine referte ; Quid enim evidentius cœlestis Originis Indicium, quàm humano Corpore Mentem Angelicam circumferre ? Vosmetipsos ergo erigite, Dictatores, Magna loquimini, Magna vivite ; Cæteros, ad inferiora depressos, Quadrupedes non esse natos, pœniteat. O, quàm divina Res est Mens variis

ornata Disciplinis ! Acquisitio Sapientiæ Carbunculos, & pretiosissimas Orientis Gazas antecellit : Nihil, Vobis o Animæ, DEI insignitæ Imagine, desponsatæ Fide, dotatæ Spiritu, redemptæ Sanguine, deputatæ cum Angelis, capaces Beatitudinis, æquè sit Curæ, quàm ut omnes altiores Animi vestri Vires in summum Illius Honorem, qui primum Illum Vobis inspiravit Æstum exeratis. Tanti enim est Quisque quanti Mens, quæ, præter DEUM, nihil excelsius in Terris Seipsâ complecti potest. Ad Se igitur revocetur, Secum versetur, in Se abeat, Sibi tota intendat, deque sua Sublimitate, & Autore semper adorando, cogitet. Hoc autem præstare non possit, nisi Vitia Corporis ableget, nisi Avaritiæ & Ambitioni renuntiet, nisi sui Juris sit, nisi Se denique a Sensibus separata, penitiùs perfruatur; tunc enim ad DEUM, Objectum suum, libera assurgat ; Hæc autem, ipsius in Seipsam Conversio ac Defixio, tantæ est Voluptatis, ut excogitari nulla in hac Vita possit, quæ vel ad aliquam ejus particulam accedat. Ut igitur ad summum hoc Bonum, summis Ingeniis Propositum, perveniatis, Votis & Vocibus cohortamur: Imo DEUS in Vobis & velle, &

perficere operetur; Ipse Autor, Ipse Remunerator, Ipse Causa effectiva & finalis ; Cui soli, Nobilissimi, incumbite, & Unum Hoc agite, ut vos, DEO & Davidicæ Pietati consecratos, Sedes in GLORIÆ Templo æternæ excipiant. Sed, quia Heroes alloquimur, heroico nostram hanc Pa ænesin Carmine substringemus.

Vos, sacra Progenies CŒLI, celsique capaces,
Pectoris, HEROES, salvete ; Poemata Mundo
Sancta triumphato diffundite; Versibus Orbis
Ultimus applaudat: Spargant Præconia Musæ ;
Frivola Vesani Crepitacula spernite Sêcli.
Excelsos Excelsa decent: Mens una Beatos

Reddit : præ Sanctis sordescant Cuncta Triumphis.
Davidicæ Decori Vos aspirate Camœnæ.
Felix Vena sacros potiùs prorumpat in Hymnos,
Quàm micet eois Caput aspectabile Gemmis.
Sic, celebretur Opus, donec Formica Profundum
Ebibat, & vastum Testudo perambulet Orbem.

I. G. Sculp.

Hecatombe IX
Recapitulatio

ANIMÆ PIÉ ANHELANTIS DE-
SCRIPTIO.

Beato THEOPHILÆ Virginis Incendio
Quisquis flagrare gestis,
In quo felicior Salamandrâ triumphes,
Et instar Pyraustæ nascaris, instar
Phœnicis moriaris ;
Ut ÆVITERNITATI resurgas,
Non tam vitam deferens, quam
conferens :
Sanctioris Ovidii Carmina
Cordis Oculis, & Oculorum Corde
perlustres :
Debuissent Incendia dia Adamantino Stylo
In Tabula IMMORTALITATIS
incîdi ;   10
Sed, quoniam pennæ ductibus
scribenda fuêre,

Canto IX
The Recapitulation

AND PORTRAIT OF A HEAV'NLY
BREATHING SOUL.

Whoso delights to burn in holy fire
Of Virgin fair THEOPHILA,
Joy, Salamander, in that flame ;
Thou so, Pyrausta born, may'st like
the Phoenix burn,
That to Eternity thou rise,
Not losing life, but sowing well
the same :
A holier Ovid's smoothed
verse
With eyes of heart, with heart all
eyes, behold :
Such sacred flames by adamantine hand
Ought to be plac'd in lasting
urns ;   10
But, 'cause these writings needed
aid of pens,

3 Pyrausta] See note *sup.* p. 367.
5 Æviternitati] It is very like Benlowes to show his knowledge of the uncontracted form.

Pennas porrigat Scribenti Pietas pennatior Ave,
Et centum Oculos Legenti oculatior Argo.

Virtue, than birds more swift, unto the scribe lend wing,
And let the reader's care more eyes than Argus bring.

PORTICUS

Amor erga Magistrum, & Sodalem
Languidiùs se movet, & quodamodo vegetat ;
Erga Parentem & Conjugem
Expansiùs se exerit,&quasi sentit ;
Erga Patriam, & Patriæ Patrem
Elatiùs se erigit, & Rationem induit :
At erga DEUM
Totus Ecstasin patitur, Sese transcendit,
Nec Modi, nec Limitis capax ;
Sed, separatarum instar Animarum,
Cupit, æstuat, ebullit, anhelat !
Finitus INFINITATEM ambit, ac suspirat !   12

THE PORTICO

Love to the master, and the mate
Stirs itself feebly in Life's lowest sphere ;
That to our parent, and the bed
More large extends, and breathes a life of sense ;
That to our country, and its sire
Self raises loftier in Reason's air :
But, that to GOD,
Ravish'd with ecstasy, itself transcends,
Nor bounds, nor limits would it own ;
But, narrow'd that (like lovers, kept apart)   10
Warms, heats, yea boils, boils up and over !
Longs for th' Eternal, sighs for HIM, beyond that lover !

ARGUMENTUM

Musa sacrata struens Aras, ut NUMEN honoret,
Calcat, & odit haras, Musa peligna, tuas :
Est Hæc, ut Clytie, studiosa Pedissequa Solis ;
Sol DEUS est, Solis Lumen AMANTIS amat.

THE ARGUMENT

Blest Muse the Altar builds, where Love's ador'd ;
And throweth down, loose wit, thy nest abhorr'd :
She, Clytie-like, to th' Sun of Glory turns ;
GOD is her Sun, with light of Zeal she burns.

DISTICHON I

Musa, silere potes, vaga dum Citharistria Sylvæ
Crispillat tremulo gutture mille Sonos?

DISTICH I

Muse, canst be silent, when each charmèd grove
Harbours a thousand warbling notes of Love?

II

Ars acuit Concepta, Poesis acuminat Artem ;
Spicula jactet Epos; jacta coronet Eros :

II

Art whets the mind, and hymns set edge on art :
Dart up an epod ; Zeal, crown thou the dart.

Arg. 2] It is rather odd that Benlowes in his Englishing softens *haras*, 'styes,' to 'nest'; and omits the direct reference (*Peligna*) to Ovid altogether.

4] Here one has to choose between 'Epos' for 'Epode' in the Latin, and 'Epod' for 'Epic' in the English.

III

Spes Arcus, sit Amor tibi Dextra,
  Fidesque Sagitta ;
A Spe missa Fides, NUMEN Amore
  petit.

IV

Est sacrum quod conor Opus : DEUS,
  annue Cœptis !
Seminat Ista Fides, Spes alit, auget
  Amor.

V

Mundus Ager, Semen Verbum, DEUS
  Ipse Colonus,
Latro Satan, Lolium Gens mala ;
  Sancta, Seges.   10

VI

Da mihi Cœlipetæ Fastigia, NUMEN,
  Alaudæ ;
Mens, ut Avis, pennâ remige sulcet
  Iter !

VII

Nôsse DEUM, bene posse Bonum,
  sunt Vota Piorum :
Da mihi nôsse Bonum, da mihi
  posse, DEUS !

VIII

Notio non Cœli, sed habet Dilectio
  Palmam :
Tu mihi nôsse dabas Cœlica, velle
  dabis.

IX

Quod volo, quod possum, quod sum,
  Tibi debeo, CHRISTE :
Quod sum, quod possum, quod
  volo, CHRISTE, cape.

X

Nil video sine Te, sapio nil, nil queo ;
  Solus
Sol meus es, meus es Sal, mea sola
  Salus.   20

XI

Lux, Via, Vita pio, DEUS ; hac Face,
  Tramite, Corde,
Qui videt, it, vivit, non cadit, errat,
  obit.

XII

Da cumulem tua centenis ALTARIA
  Donis !
Victima sint Versus, Ara Cor, Ignis
  Amor.

III

Hope be thy bow, thy hand Love,
  Faith the shaft ;
Let Hope shoot Faith to GOD with
  Love's strong draft.

IV

Sacred's my theme ; may my first-
  fruits Him please !
Faith plants, Hope nourishes, Love
  ripens these.

V

This world's the field, GOD sows, His
  Word the seed,
Satan the thief, the good, corn, th'
  ill, the weed.   10

VI

LORD, mount me to the pitch of
  larks on high ;
That I, as birds' wing'd oars, may
  cut the sky !

VII

Saints would know GOD, so, as they
  good may do :
Let me both know this good, and
  act it too !

VIII

Heav'n's love, not knowledge doth
  the palm acquire :
Who heav'nly knowledge gave, will
  give desire.

IX

That aught I will, can, am, is, CHRIST,
  from thee :
CHRIST, what I am, can, will, accept
  from me !

X

No light, taste, strength without
  Thee ; Thou alone
Art health unto my soul, my salt,
  my sun.   20

XI

Thou, Light, Way, Life ; who sees,
  walks, liveth by
That flame, path, strength, does not
  fall, fail, nor die.

XII

Upon Thy altars let my verses
  prove
The victim, heart the altar, the fire
  love !

XIII

Thura Preces, Lachrymæ Myrrhæ,
　　Pietasque sit Aurum :
Mentis Opus, Clysmus Cordis,
　　Amoris Opes.

XIV

Hoc Hecatombæi Tibi Carminis
　　offero Libum :
Ut tu millenos, Nate Davide,
　　Boves.

XV

Vult pia Musa DEUM ! Quoties volat
　　altiùs, Alas
Flagitat assiduè, SANCTA Co-
　　LUMBA, Tuas ! 　　　　30

XVI

Ferre per Æthereas volitante Vigore
　　Phalanges,
Fulgida Chrysolithûm Lux ubi
　　stellat Iter.

XVII

Carmine ducat Amor, quos terret
　　Concio ; Mentes
Elevet in Cœlum, quò nequit ire
　　Fides !

XVIII

Grata repercussi referant Modulamina
　　Nervi ;
Unica nec nostræ sit Synalæpha
　　Lyræ.

XIX

Umbra mihi DEUS. ──I, patulæ,
　　Maro, tegmine fagi ;
Tu, Siloame, veni ; Castalis Unda,
　　vale.

XX

Vana profanorum calcando crepundia
　　Vatum,
Spirituale pius parturit Author
　　Opus. 　　　　40

XXI

Vita quid est ? Fumus. Quid Forma ?
　　Favilla. Quid Aurum ?
Idolum. Quid Honos ? Bulla.
　　Quid Orbis ? Onus :

XXII

Vita repentè fugit, citò Forma polita
　　recedit,
Aurum fallit, Honor deficit, Orbis
　　hebet.

XIII

Pray'r frankincense, tears myrrh, be
　　gold, soul's health :
The mind's best work, heart's laver,
　　and love's wealth.

XIV

I this verse-hecatomb to Thee do
　　bring ;
As Solomon his numerous offering.

XV

The pious Muse courts Heav'n ;
　　when highest things
She soars for, still she craves, BLEST
　　DOVE, Thy wings ! 　　　　30

XVI

With active plumes fly up to th'
　　angel-quire,
Where chrysolites to gild thy way
　　conspire.

XVII

Love may them lead by verse, whom
　　sermons fright ;
Bring them, where Faith comes not,
　　into Heav'n's light.

XVIII

Oh, may our numbers in sweet
　　music flow ;
Nor the least harshness of elisions
　　know !

XIX

Shade me, O LORD ! I seek not
　　Virgil's tree ;
Hence, springs profane ; glide, Si-
　　loam, by me !

XX

Trampling vain labours, with loose
　　wits defil'd,
The hallow'd brain brings forth a
　　spritely child. 　　　　40

XXI

What 's life ? a vapour ; beauty ?
　　ashes ; gain ?
An idol ; honour ? bubble ; the
　　world ? vain :

XXII

Life flits away, and beauty wanes at
　　full,
Gold cheats, and honour fades, the
　　world is dull.

XXIII

Vita Voluptatis brevis est, Vitæque
    Voluptas;
  Non capit illa Deo quid sit
    Amante capi.

XXIV

Illa maritali quæ Tæda parata
    Leandro,
  Illa Sepulturæ Tæda parata
    fuit.

XXV

Mille Viæ Morti, proh, mille! sed
    unica Vitæ :
  Crimina qui non hîc eluet, ille
    luet.   50

XXVI

Bellica fædifragos pessundabit Ira
    Tyrannos :
  Non Vobis, Sceleri vincitis; Ultor
    adest.

XXVII

Peccantûm Limen, Peccati linquite
    Semen ;
  Contagem ducit Proximitate Pecus.

XXVIII

Hinc, Josephe, fugis, fugis hinc sine
    Veste, Johannes ;
  Proh Dolor ! Ipse manes, Petre,
    manendo negas !

XXIX

Conscia Mens Noctesque, Diesque,
    Domique, Forisque
  Pungitur : In Sese Verbera Tortor
    agit !

XXX

Jussa decem, bis sex Credenda,
    Sacratio Cænæ,
  Heu, nimis in Templis, Lege
    loquente, silent !   60

XXXI

Grex perit hinc ! Veniet, quâ non
    speratur in horâ,
  Judex : Terribilis Sontibus Ultor
    adest !

XXXII

Nec Prece, nec Pretio, nec Fraude,
    nec Arte, nec Irâ
  Vincitur ! In Pænas Flamma
    perennis erit !

XXIII

Life's pleasure's short, and pleasure's
    life is vain ;
  It knows not highest bliss, God's
    love, to gain.

XXIV

That torch which flam'd so bright in
    Hero's room,
  Did light her lov'd Leander to his
    tomb.

XXV

To death a thousand ways, to life
    but one :
  For sin who groans not, he for sin
    shall groan.   50

XXVI

Arm'd wrath perfidious tyrants throws
    from high ;
  They conquer Right, Sin them ; th'
    Avenger 's nigh.

XXVII

Sinner's first steps, sin's seed, and
    fruit avoid ;
  Many by near infection are destroy'd.

XXVIII

Kill vice i' th' egg : John, Joseph,
    robeless fly ;
  Peter, thou stay'st, and stay'st but to
    deny !

XXIX

By night and day, at home, and
    when abroad,
  Guilt stings the soul, and thereon
    lays its load !

XXX

Of Decalogue, Creed, Supper of the
    Lord,
  Though laws speak loud, our Church
    hath scarce a word !   60

XXXI

Hence flocks are pin'd. The Judge
    in time will come
  Unthought of : near to guilt 's the
    Avenger's doom !

XXXII

Nor pray'r, nor price, nor fraud, nor
    rage, nor art
  Can help ; ah, fear then flames'
    eternal smart !

XXXIII

Imbre rigante Genas, quoties Tibi
  CHRISTE, querebar,
  Nocte vigil, nullo Teste, Medela,
  veni !

XXXIV

Aspicis, & Pateris ? Scelus omne
  repelle, Colonus
  Nec gerat Arma suâ quâ serit Arva
  Manu !

XXXV

Vis, Amor, est exorsa DEO ; data
  Gratia gratis ;
  Hanc Vim THEIOPHILÆ Nomine
  Musa vocat.   70

XXXVI

Ureris ignifluis confossa THEOPHILA
  Telis !
  Sacra beatificans si cremet Ossa
  Calor,

XXXVII

Quo magìs ardescis, magis, hoc, sis
  Follis ad Ignes ;
  Omnibus exundet, qui calet intus,
  Amor.

XXXVIII

Ure Tepescéntes, Viresque Calen-
  tibus adde ;
  Igne crema, recrea Lumine, Mente
  bea.

XXXIX

Et Mare tentanti Pharos esto,
  Benigna, Poetæ,
  Dum pandit Vento Lintea plena
  sacro !

XL

Vela pius Genius, Tu Sidus, Acumina
  Remi,
  Vates Nauta, Salum Vena, Poema
  Ratis.   80

XLI

Consecro Fræna tuæ moderanda
  Poetica Dextræ ;
  Sunt Donantis Honor, sed Ca-
  pientis Amor.

XLII

Stringe soluta, recude proterva, revelle
  prophana,

XXXIII

Wet-cheek'd, how oft I've moan'd
  to Thee, my Dear,
  All night awake, alone, O cure,
  appear !

XXXIV

See'st Thou, and suff'rest ? Stop
  sin's course, and birth ;
  Let not that hand bear arms, that
  sows the earth.

XXXV

Love's pow'r 's infus'd from GOD, a
  free-giv'n grace ;
  THEOPHILA from Love takes name
  and race.   70

XXXVI

Thou burn'st, pierc'd THEOPHIL,
  with fiery dart ;
  If blessed heat enflames thy vigorous
  heart.

XXXVII

The more thou burn'st, the more be
  bellows still ;
  As thy flames grow, let those flames
  others fill !

XXXVIII

Heat the luke-warm, to those, more
  hot, give fire ;
  Bless GOD ; refresh with grace,
  enflame desire.

XXXIX

The poet's Pharos be that sets forth
  sail,
  While he steers sheet-fill'd with a
  holy gale.

XL

Pure wit's the sails, quick judgement
  oars, thou th' star,
  Pilot the scribe, sea vein, the ship
  hymns are.   80

XLI

I give wit's tackling to thy guiding
  hands :
  Honour in giving, love in taking
  stands.

XLII

Bind up what 's loose, what 's rash
  new-mould, refell

70 Theiophilæ] Benlowes takes the liberty of this form, to get the long syllable, after the analogy of θειολόγος, &c. In next line Theophila is more daring.

Supple manca, poli scabra, superba preme.

XLIII

Irrita sulphurei rides Crepitacula Mundi ;
Regnaque pro Nidis, quæ fabricantur, habes.

XLIV

Despicis Orbis , Opes, opulentior Orbe, minorque
Orbis, majori pulchrior Orbe, micas.

XLV

Congestas effundis Opes, releventur ut Ægri :
Sic ab Amante tuo semper amere Deo.   90

XLVI

Scisque Deum, notumque doces, doctumque vereris ;
Praxis habet Cultum ; Quæ canis, illa facis.

XLVII

Osa Malis, pretiosa Piis, Lyra viva Poetis,
Casta Fide, Genio candida, chara Deo.

XLVIII

Sylva Smaragdicomas quæ ventilat, invidet Auro
Crinis, & ad Cirros Gratia trina rubet.

XLIX

Gaudia tot spargunt splendentia Sidera Vultus,
Quot fovet Attis Apes, quot gerit Æthra Faces.

L

Invidet igniparis Adamantinus Ardor Ocellis,
Vibrat abinde sacras Pupula casta Faces.   100

LI

Emula puniceis Tinctura Corallina Labris ;
Livet ad Ambrosias pensilis Uva Genas.

LII

Mirarer Labrique Rosas, & Lilia Malæ,

What 's ill, lame help, smooth rough, depress what swell.

XLIII

Thou slight'st earth's rattling squibs, with sulphur fill'd :
Kingdoms such nests are as the birds do build.

XLIV

Above all worldly wealth thy riches rise ;
Thy microcosm the macrocosm outvies.

XLV

Thou lay'st out hoarded gold the poor to aid ;
So, with God's love, thy love to God 's repaid.   90

XLVI

Thy sacred skill imparted reverence breeds ;
Thy worship 's practice, and thy words are deeds.

XLVII

Fiends hate, saints prize, whence lyric strings sound clear,
Of spotless faith, pure mind, to th' Highest dear.

XLVIII

The emerald grove envies thy golden hair,
Whose curls make Graces blush themselves more fair,

XLIX

As many joys thy starry beauties shed,
As bees in Attis, gems in skies are spread.

L

The diamond sparkleth rage at thine eyebeams,
Whose chaste orbs brandish thence their sacred gleams.   100

LI

The coral die is blank'd at lips so red,
And livid grapes at rosy cheeks hang head :

LII

I'd gaze o' th' lilied cheek, and the lips' rose,

(403)

Mala sed exuperat Lilia, Labra
    Rosas.

LIII

Suavia mellifluo dimanant Verba
    Palato,
    Verbula Nectareis limpidiora Ca-
      dis.

LIV

Quas non Delicias, radiantibus ebria
    Guttis,
    Psaltria dia, creas! Ore Mel, Aure
      Melos.

LV

Spiras Tota Crocos, Violas, Opobal-
    sama, Myrrhas,
    Bdellia, Thura, Cedros, Cinnama,
      Narda, Rosas.   110

LVI

Ruris Aroma Rosas. Quot Cantica
    sacra profundis,
    Tot paris Ore Favos, tot jacis Ore
      Faces.

LVII

Dum jaciuntur ab Ore Favi, superæ-
    que Favillæ,
    Pascor, ut incendar; Flamma dat
      ipsa Dapes!

LVIII

Languet Olor dum spectat Ebur
    Cervicis: Ad Agnum
    Hæc Via susceptum Lactea mon-
      strat Iter.

LIX

Ningit in Alpinis mansura Pruina
    Papillis;
    Anser es His Cornix, Nix nigra,
      sordet Olor.

LX

Vellera cana Nivis, Manibus collata,
    lutescunt;
    Figis ubi Gressum pressa resultat
      Humus.   120

LXI

Lilia Lacte lavet, Violas depurpuret
    Uva,
    Ære Crocos tingat, Murice, Flora,
      Rosas;

LXII

Nec potis est meritam Tibi texere
    Flora Corollam;

But oh, thy cheek, thy lip surpasseth
    those!

LIII

Grace pours sweet-flowing words from
    charming lips,
    Sparkling 'bove nectar which i' th'
      crystal skips.

LIV

Rare Psaltress, with Heav'n-drops
    inebriate,
    What sweets to mouth, and ear dost
      thou create?

LV

Sweet violets, saffron, balm, myrrh
    from thee flows,
    Bdell, incense, cedar, cinnamon,
      nard, the rose—   110

LVI

The rose, swain's spice: such heav'n-
    dew'd verse dost frame,
    As sweet as honeycomb, as bright
      as flame.

LVII

While combs, and flames divine from
    thee are cast,
    I'm fed, as fir'd; ev'n flames do nurse
      my taste!

LVIII

The swan pines at thy neck; this
    Milky Way
    Doth steps, begun to th' Holy LAMB,
      display.

LIX

There falls on thine Alp-breasts a
    lasting snow,
    To which snow's black, swans foul,
      the goose a crow.

LX

The hoary frost turns dirt, vied with
    thy hand,
    And, where thy foot does tread, it
      prides the land.   120

LXI

On lilies milk, on violets purple
    throw,
    On saffron gold, scarlet o' th' rose
      bestow;

LXII

Wreaths, worthy thee, fair Flora ne'er
    can weave;

Te, nec hyperbolicus, dum cano,
  Cantor ero.

LXIII
Floribus omnigenis, Gemmisque
  nitentibus ardens,
Tu Paradisiaci Præda videris
  Agri.

LXIV
Quælibet in Vitâ Virtus sic æqua
  relucet ;
Ut dubitetur an hæc, illa, vel ista
  præit.

LXV
Desuper extat Amor ; Tibi Mens
  contermina Cœlo,
Regnat Honor, radiat Forma,
  triumphat Amor.   130

LXVI
Illud es Elixir, Chymicâ quod pro-
  tinus Arte,
Mutet in auratas me, rude Pondus,
  Opes.

LXVII
Igne Cinis fit agente Vitrum ; micat
  Igne Metallum ;
Corpus & hoc fieri Spiritus Igne
  potest.

LXVIII
Magneti salit e Ferro celer Ignis
  Amoris ;
Imo Silex faculas, quis putet ?
  intus alit.

LXIX
Durius at Saxo nil est, nil mollius
  Igne :
Dura sed ignitus Saxa resolvit
  Amor.

LXX
Hæc meditans, quis non Facibus
  solvatur Amoris ?
Tu Charis es, Studiis Tu Cynosura
  meis.   140

LXXI
Gemmula Mentis, Ocella Sinûs, pia
  Flammula Cordis :
Incepi Duce Te, Te Duce cœpta
  sequar.

LXXII
Sponsa creata Deo, Virtutum fulgida
  Cœtu,

Nor can our highest strains thee
  higher heave.

LXIII
With all-bred flow'rs, and glitt'ring
  buds thou beam'st ;
As if t' have cropt all Paradise thou
  seem'st.

LXIV
Each virtue 's in thy life so pois'd, so
  fine ;
What 's first ? This ? That ? or
  'T'other ? since all shine.

LXV
Love to thy soul deriv'd is from
  above,
Where Honour reigns, sparks beauty,
  triumphs Love.   130

LXVI
In chemic art thou my elixir
  be ;
Convert to gold the worthless dross
  in me.

LXVII
Fire makes of ashes glass, makes
  metals shine ;
This fire my body may to spirit cal-
  cine.

LXVIII
Enamour'd iron does to the magnet
  fly ;
Yea, sparks in hardest flints conceal'd
  lie.

LXIX
Nothing more hard than stone, more
  soft than fire ;
Yet stones are melted by inflam'd
  desire.

LXX
Is 't so? Who'd not dissolve in flames
  of Love ?
Be thou the grace, thou my thought's
  loadstar prove.   140

LXXI
Mind's gem, eye's apple, heart's in-
  tenser flame ;
Thou show'dst the way, I'll prosecute
  the same

LXXII
For God created, bright in Virtue's
  train,

Jus colis, Affectus supprimis, Acta regis.

LXXIII

Est Tibi Vita DEUS, Pietas Lex, Gloria CHRISTUS,
Expetis Hunc, Tibi Qui semper Amore præit.

LXXIV

Quid Te, CHRISTE, Crucem perferre coegit ? Amoris
Ardor ! Amaroris Pignus Amoris erat !

LXXV

Factus Amans, fit & Esca DEUS ! Te nutrit IESUS :
O Bonitas ! Quales Hoc in Amante Dapes ! 150

LXXVI

Est mihi Christus (ais) Laus, Splendor, Aroma, Triumphus,
Musica, Vina, Dapes, Fama, Corona, DEUS.

LXXVII

Omnia Tu JESUS ! præ TE, nihil Omnia ! Coelum
Exploraturæ, quàm mihi sordet Humus !

LXXVIII

Orbis es Exilium, Mors Janua, Patria Coelum ;
Dux sit Amor, Baculus Spes, Comes alma Fides.

LXXIX

Diffluat in Gemmas Oriens, in Carmina Coelum ;
Nec Meritis Oriens, nec Polus æqua ferat.

LXXX

Fac timeam, fac amem ; Quæ Te timet, acriùs ardet ;
Nempe tui Cultûs Fons Timor, Amnis Amor. 160

LXXXI

Vox tua Norma mihi ; Tibi Palmes adhæreo Viti ;
Totus es Ipse mihi, sim tua tota DEUS !

Weigh'st right, quell'st passions, and o'er deeds dost reign.

LXXIII

GOD is thy life, Law virtue, Glory CHRIST ;
Him, who leads thee by love, thou lov'st Him high'st.

LXXIV

CHRIST, to endure the cross, what did Thee move ?
The pledge of bitterness was pledge of Love !

LXXV

Is GOD both meat and lover? CHRIST thy food ?
What banquet is this Lover ! As sweet, as good ! 150

LXXVI

CHRIST's spice (thou say'st) light, triumph, praise to me ;
Music, wine, feast, fame, crown, GOD ; all to thee.

LXXVII

LORD, Thou art all in all ! Thou lost, all 's nought ;
How base seems muddy earth, where Heav'n is sought !

LXXVIII

Earth 's exile, Death the gate, my home 's above ;
My staff's *Hope, Faith* companion, leader *Love*.

LXXIX

Turn Indie into jewels, Heav'n to verse,
Nor Indie can Thy worth, nor Heav'n rehearse.

LXXX

Let me Thee fear, and love ; fear Love's heat blows ;
Fear is Devotion's fount, whence love o'erflows. 160

LXXXI

Thy word's my rule, I cleave to Thee, my Vine ;
LORD, Thou are all to me, I'm wholly Thine.

157 Indie] As we have kept the plural why not the singular ?

LXXXII
Comprecor, exaudi; patior, succurre;
    molestor,
Auxiliare; premor, protege; flagro,
    fave !

LXXXIII
Te voco, laudo, rogo, colo, diligo,
    quæro, Redemptor,
Affectu, Prece, Re, Spe, Pietate,
    Fide !

LXXXIV
Si Te contueor, liquefio, perusta
    Favillis ;
Ni Te contueor, sum glaciata
    Gelu !

LXXXV
O, Facibus superadde Faces, ut Tota
    liquescam !
Sim vel Mortis Odor, sim vel
    Amantis Amor.   170

LXXXVI
Grata Procella, jugum mihi gratum,
    gratus & Ignis,
Me quibus immergit, deprimit,
    urit Amor !

LXXXVII
Non mea sum, sed Amore DEI
    languesco ! Sorores,
Me stipate Rosis, languet Amore
    Sinus!

LXXXVIII
Nil Animantis habet, quæ Pectore
    vivit Amantis :
Hoc in Amore mihi sit mora nulla
    mori !

LXXXIX
Unio sit Nobis, Animamque liqua-
    mur in unam !
Unaque Vita Duos stringat Amor-
    que Duos !

XC
Tu super Omne places ! Tua sum,
    Tu noster, & Ambos
Mutuus Ardor agit, possidet unus
    Amor.   180

XCI
Uror, Io; Redamatur Amor! Voto-
    que fruiscor !
Dum quod Amans redamor, dum
    quod Amante fruor.

LXXXII
Oh, hear my pray'r, my suff'rings
    bear, my task
Take off, redress my wrongs, grant
    what I ask !

LXXXIII
With pray'r, desire, faith, zeal, hope,
    deed I call,
Laud, seek, love, pray, worship Thee
    all in all.

LXXXIV
If I behold Thee, I'm all flaming
    spice ;
If not behold Thee, I'm congeal'd
    to ice !

LXXXV
Add flames to flames, that I may
    melt away !
Be I belov'd of Thee, or else Death's
    prey !   170

LXXXVI
Sweet seas, light yoke, a friendly
    flame I find,
Which me with love doth drown, and
    burn, and bind.

LXXXVII
I'm not mine own, but faint for GOD
    above !
Rose-deck me, Virgins, for I'm sick
    of Love !

LXXXVIII
Nought of a liver, hath a lover's
    heart !
Or live belov'd, or life-bereft
    depart !

LXXXIX
Let us be one ! In one, two melted
    flow !
Let one life, as one love, inform us
    two !

XC
My only joy, I'm Thine; Thou mine;
    and both
The like flame burns ; th' one loves,
    as t' other doth.   180

XCI
Fire ! Fire ! Love is beloved ! My
    Maker's mine !
Loving, I'm lov'd ! while with my
    Spouse I twine !

(407)

XCII

O, quid Amare ! Quid est Redamari !
        Gaudia nacta
    Tanta, stupendo tacet ! Tanta,
        tacendo stupet !

XCIII

Vivo Deo, morior Mundo, moriendo
        resurgo ;
    Inde, catenato Dite, triumphat
        Amor.

XCIV

Sic amet omnis Amans, sic immo-
        riatur Amanti :
    Ut Lyra Lusciniæ Vitaque Mors-
        que fuit.

XCV

Si mea Lumen habent, si Nomen
        Carmina ; Lumen
    Ex Oculo Sponsi, Nomen ab Ore
        venit.   190

XCVI

Argus eat, qui Talpa venit, radiatus
        Amore ;
    Vates Sperati fidus Amoris ero.

XCVII

Cingant Theiophilæ potius mea
        Tempora Lauri,
    Quam gemmans Capiti sit Dia-
        dema meo.

XCVIII

Nam, quid erunt, animæ Damno,
        Diademata Mundi ?
    Celsa ruunt, fugiunt blandula,
        prava necant.

XCIX

Ut præsens novit, sic postera noverit
        Ætas,
    Sive premamus Humum, Sive
        premamur Humo.

C

Finis Fine caret, nec Terminus ullus
        Amantem
    Terminat ; Hîc Modus est non
        habuisse Modum.   200

. XCII

O Love, belov'd ! Her, who such
        joys partakes,
    Silence makes wonder, wonder silence
        makes !

XCIII

To Heav'n I live, to Earth I die ;
        dying rise !
    So, Hell being chain'd, Love takes
        the victor's prize.

XCIV

Lovers so love, as for the lov'd to
        die !
    As Strada's lute was life and des-
        tiny.

XCV

If these my lays have either light, or
        name,
    Name from thy word, light from thy
        grace doth flame   193

XCVI

Who came a mole, goes Argus hence
        by Love ;
    I shall Faith's priest to hopeful Charis
        prove.

XCVII

Theophila's bays to me more honour
        brings
    Than gems that blaze on the proud
        heads of kings.

XCVIII

For what boot worldly crowns with
        soul's loss bought,
    Heights fall, spruce courtship fades,
        vice brings to nought.

XCIX

We may hereafter, as we now have
        found
    The voice of Fame above, so, under
        ground.

C

The last shall last ; Term can't Vaca-
        tion lend
    To th' Lover ; here 'tis end to have no
        END

188 Strada's lute] Benlowes merely alludes to what Ford and Crashaw had elaborately
handled. And the piecing together of the allusion by the Latin and English is note-
worthy.

Imus in Albionis, Freta per Latialia, Littus ;	To see, not know, is not to see :
Siste Britannales, Hâc Vice, Musa, Pedes.	Then, let our English reader be Warn'd, not on Latian Alps to roam ;
Anglica num præstent Latiis, Briticisve Latina	
Scire velim : Placeant quæ magis, Illa dabo.	The next vale's path will lead him home.

PRÆLIBATIO
AD THEOPHILÆ AMORIS HOSTIAM

QUÆ UNICA CANTIO A DOMINO ALEX. ROSSÆO IN CARMEN LATINUM CONVERSA EST[1].

Cantio I

ARGUMENTUM

Evigiles, surgas, divini Rector Amoris ;
Delicium priùs explores, quàm Gaudia tentes :
Ad Cœlos Cursum tandèm pia Vota gubernent.

TRISTICHON I

MUTUA si Mentes agerent Commercia Secum,
Angelicum in Morem, terrenâ Mole solutæ,
Intuitu quales possent effundere Cantus !

II

Spiritus ut subitô si sublimetur, abibit
In Fumum, nimium chymicus nisi temperet Æstum ;
Haud alitèr perit omne nimîs subtile Noema.

III

Aurum, Sole satum, Terræ inter Viscera clausum,
Non pretio cessit, quamvis non splenduit æquè,
Qualiter excoctum flagranti fulgurat Igne.

IV

Mens age, nunc Famæ Sphæram conscende per Orbes ;   10
Errat enim quisquis non Cursum dirigit illuc :
Virtutis Comites, Aures adhibete Docenti.

V

Ergò, nè Veneris lascivæ Prælia, Cornu
Vocali accensa, aut Oculis flammantibus Igne,
(Formæ Armis) cedant inopinis Pectora Plagis.

VI

Quarum pestiferis Oculis, jaculantibus Ignem,
Virginitatis Honos purus maculatur, & ipsa
Mens capitur Laqueis fictarum incauta Comarum.

[1] The 'English reader,' after the broad hint given to him *not* to 'read Alexander Ross over' in the last stanza above, may be emboldened to ask why this Latin duplication is even given here ? But the original of *Theophila* is too rare for the reproduction to be mutilated.

VII

Aspice Captivum Veneris, qui trans-
igit Ævum
In fervente gelu, colit Umbram;
atque Ingeniosum 20
Se credens, scribit, delet, laceratque,
furitque.

VIII

Ejus Opes Fragmenta quidèm sunt
Comica, quorum
Præsidiò superat Tenariffæ Verticis
auram.
'Sol Tibi scintilla est, Tu Lumine
Sidera vincis.

IX

'Victrix Flamma tuis Oculis micat
acribus, Orbes
Obnubas geminos lucentes, nàm-
que rigentem
Accendent Monachum, vel fiam
Morte Bidental.

X

' Ob Gemmas Indi penetrant Saxa,
Æthiopesque
Oceanum ob Conchas, pretiosis
Pellibus instat
Tartara Gens; Omnes ejus dant
munera Templo. 30

XI

' Flagrantes dimitte Genas, quæ
fulgure nostras
Perstringis Oculorum Acies, non
ferre valentes
Tales Angelico radiantes Lumine
Vultus.'

XII

Estne Helene, Trojana Lues, atque
Angelus idem?
Passio non domita est insanæ Men-
tis Idolum:
Multæ se fucant, Paucæ Virtutibus
ornant.

XIII

Veriùs hoc nihil est; Cutis alba,
rubore Rosarum
Permista, eximium Lumen ne Men-
tis obumbret,

Nevè Animæ Visum penetrantem
obnubulet unquam.

XIV

Ure Odas, Veneris Stratagemata
chartea; Ludos 40
Effuge, sunt Flammæ; fabrices ne
Vinc'la, Dolosque
Neve loquare Oculis; Oris Commer-
cia vita.

XV

Spumea nonne audis Cerebella, &
inania, ut intùs
Et rugeant, nec non Joviali in
Crimine Potu
Luxurient, saltentque furentes, atque
cachinnent?

XVI

Prædatas Cellas siccate, & mox
Rationem
Luxuriæ Vinclis submittite; per
Freta Vini, &
Mellis arundinei Scopulos date vela
furentes.

XVII

Ad Senii Mare mortiferum transmit-
tite Curas:
Quadrupedem effrænem defessi agi-
tate Furoris 50
Bacchantes, Rabiem in Vini mon-
strate Theatro.

XVIII

'Turgescant Vino Carchesia, donec
in altum
Provehimur Bacchi, Terræque Urbes-
que recedant:
Omnia sorbemus, sit ibi Naupactia
Classis.

XIX

'Aplustrum simul & Carchesia
pandite, Fluctus
Horrisonos Fremitu superemus;
Plura Salutis
Naufragia hìc, quàm cùm cecinerunt
Monstra marina.

XX

' Amphora quæque; parit (signato,
Prome,) Pyropum;

23 Tenariffae] Orig. has the *a*.
50 effrænem; 55 Aplustrum] Note Ross's preference for unusual forms as against
effraen*us*, and in the other aplustr*e*. Also in l. 68 *aci*, 'garfish,' for 'breams.'

Et tinctæ Baccho Buccæ, mihi
  sæpè videntur
Tediferæ, quoties Gemmis micat un-
  dique Nasus. 60

XXI

Cantibus alternis Homines sese esse
  negantes,
Exleges fiunt. Titubant, seseque
  volutant,
Atque Pedes sinuant, potant Cir-
  cæa Venena.

XXII

O, tumulatæ Animæ, vivæ putresci-
  tis ! usque
Ad Fæces Vester liquefit Sal : Quis-
  que coercet
Naturam, & Mortem accelerat,
  Spernitque Salutem.

XXIII

Insontes Pecudes vestros odêre
  Liquores
Cum Nugas Vomitu & Punctis
  distinguitis : Aci,
In Vino & Somno ; Proceres nisi
  Fumus & Umbra.

XXIV

Mallem condiri Muriâ, quàm Nectare
  dulci 70
Putrere. Invitatmiseros nunc Alea,
  Mensæ
Illaqueant, nunquam felix datur
  Exitus illis.

XXV

Sed sine Mente uno jactu Patrimo-
  nia perdunt :
Obscurant Noctem cum decipit Alea
  Diris.
Vincitur en Victor ; num Victus vin-
  cere posset ?

XXVI

Denis & septem Cubitis si Nilus
  inundat
Fertilis Egypti Campos, miseranda
  sequetur
Esuries, Tabes sequitur sic sæva
  Nepotes.

XXVII

Dicite vos pictæ, vos, dicite, Papi-
  liones,

(411)

Gaudia quæ Veris pensatis falsa, quid
  estis 80
Lucratæ, ex infrugiferis Nugisque
  caducis ?

XXVIII

Stulti qui propter Nugas divenditis
  Aurum,
Dicite, num caleat quæ Flamma est
  picta ? Voluptas
Num stimulans juvat ? ô, angustum
  Cœlum, inferiusque !

XXIX

Ite, & Deliciis (fruitur queîs Bestia
  sola)
Gaudia mutetis vera ; at Gens impia
  turget
Deliciis ; CHRISTUS flevit ; Gens
  optima luget.

XXX

Nil nisi terrenum cupiunt Animalia
  Bruta ;
Cœlestes Animæ cœlestia Gaudia
  quærunt ;
Ast Homines mediæ Naturæ Dona
  requirunt. 90

XXXI

Gens humana foret si moles Corpo-
  ris expers,
Angelicæ Naturæ esset ; si Mente
  careret,
Brutiginæ : Caro Brutorum est,
  Mens Angelicorum.

XXXII

Principio Deus Hos univit, subji-
  ciendo
Sensum Judicio Rationis, tùm
  moderando
Affectum Arbitrio Mentis, verum in-
  ficiendo

XXXIII

Libertatem Animæ, Crimen concus-
  sit, ut Ipsæ
Jam nequeunt habitare simul, nisi
  Lucta sequatur ;
Nec sine Tristitiâ divelli posse vide-
  mus.

XXXIV

Jam valeat Mundus fallax, spinosa
  Voluptas 100

Cui Cordi est, quod perdit amat,
quod Nobile spernit.
I, Cole nunc Vitium, ride Virtutis
Amantes.

XXXV

Mellito Cyatho, at Felle Aspidis
haud meliore,
Inficis incautas Animas ad Tartara,
semper
Mortales Magico & fallaci decipis
Ore.

XXXVI

Dum Tempus fallis, Tempus te fal-
lit, & aufert
Prædam, dum Tempus perdis,
Cœlestia perdis,
Sed, cum Fure bono, pauci furantur
Olympum.

XXXVII

Projiciunt Stulti pretiosum Temporis
Aurum :
Qui Vitæ Gemmam generosam pro-
digit, ille   110
Ad Barathrum graditur, Stimulisque
agitatur Averni.

XXXVIII

Cui Terram amplecti vastam furiosa
Cupido est,
Vique Doloque simul ; Muscis hic
Retia tendit,
Ut foribus laxos suspendit Aranea
Casses.

XXXIX

Cum Mors præscindet Nimrodi
Vulturis ungues,
Nomina cernemus subito mutata
Domorum :
Bethesda his fiet tandem Bethania
tristis.

XL

Arbitrio subdi pejus, quàm Lege
perire ;
Pharmaca quæ curare valent, si
Balsama perdunt ?
Namque Bono quod degenerat, nil
pejus habetur.   120

XLI

Sique Tyrannorum arbitrio non
traderet ullos

Omnipotens Sanctos, crudeli Morte
premendos,
Nullum Martyrium foret, aut Salva-
tor Iesus.

XLII

Stulti durescunt, sed Sancti, ut
Cera, liquescunt :
Corporis ad gemitum morientis,
jamque jacentis
Nudo Dente, Genis macris, Oculis-
que cavatis.

XLIII

Vitæ Author Vitam præbet, largire
Misellis ;
Dissectis Venis præclusa est Janua
Lethi :
Sit Deus Exemplar ; te cura ; pasce
Famentes.

XLIV

Ut Cœlum obtineas, heu, quantula
Portio Vitæ   130
Hic peregrinantis superest ! namque
excipit Ortum
Occasus subito, Finisque ab Ori-
gine pendet.

XLV

Cum Vitiis cui Bella forìs, Pax per-
manet intùs :
Cessat Judicium, quùm sese judicat
ullus :
Extrà vestiri Zelo est augere Dolores.

XLVI

Magnates, Vos magna manent Tor-
menta, Tyranni
Si sitis.   Infernus Medicinam haud
exhibet ullam :
Securus nè sis, securus si cupis esse.

XLVII

Robora franguntur quæ Cœli Mur-
mura temnunt ;
Ardentem in Cineres Prunam consi-
dere cernes ;   140
Nec non in fumos clarum vanescere
Lychnum.

XLVIII

Exue rugosam Sagam, jam Tempus,
& aufer
Peccati Achanis velamina nigra,
Magarum

Leprosis pannis superabunt Ulcera fœda.

XLIX

Insontem hoc Naboth Ferro superavit, idemque
Jezabelis pinxit Faciem, Centroque removit
Tot Regna, atque novum dimovit Cardine Mundum.

L

Felices hujus qui spargent Saxa Cerebro,
Quiqueea loturi maledicto Sanguine, sternetque
Osse Vias: Cujus Gemitus sunt Gaudia nostra.   150

LI

Non debet Salicâ regnare Hæc Lege, Procellas
Excitat, Halcyonumque Dies dispellit, in Aula
Mentis nil habitat Bonitatis, si regit Illa.

LII

Luxuries ejus quot Morbos edidit? Astra
Inficit, Esuriemque auget, Vivisque molesta est
Dum crapulantur humum Tumulis civilia Bella.

LIII

Mens mea, Mæstitiæ Labyrinthis septa, quot Annis
In sacco, Lachrymis baccato, transige Vitam!
Clàm nigris in Speluncis ambito Timores!

LIV

Cumque Heraclito pacatum transige Tempus,   160
A Turbis procul, & procul à Discordibus Armis,
Quæ Mundum insanum turbato in Pegmate versant.

LV

Illic Relligio dulcis vel Pectine pulsat,
Vel Digitis Cytharam, vel Cantu personat Antra,

Divinæ inspirat vel Dorica Carmina Musæ.

LVI

Proque Tubis resonabit Amor Testudine, solvens
Obsidione Urbes, quassatas Marte, vocansque
In Cœlum, Imperii Sedem, mortalia Corda.

LVII

Nostra hinc Lætitia, hinc Hymni Solatia nostra,
Præcipuè Angelici.   Summo sit Gloria Patri,   170
Pax Terris, Hominum succedat prompta Voluntas!

LVIII

Pennæ quas Veneris Volucres dant, Dedecus addunt;
Ergò, Vulcano Versus committite; tollet
Ille pedes Melis; liber, sed claudicat Ille.

LIX

Tollitur en Nihil, ast Aliquid cadit! ô, ubi Merces
Antiquæ Virtutis Honos! Sapientia quondam
Virtutem evexit; coluisti, Plute, Minervam.

LX

Cos fuit Oxonii Lambeth! tamen Ille Volatu
Exuperat longè Pinnacula Divitiarum,
Qui Virtutem ambit, puro Virtutis Amore.   180

LXI

Virtutis Radiis accenditur Illius Ardor,
Et Pestes omnes Modulis fugat ille canoris,
Fulminaque extinguit per Cœli Expansa trisulca.

LXII

An matutinæ Volucres cantando citabunt
Solem ex nocturnis Tenebris, tectoque Cubili?

Atque Animæ vivæ in Tenebris &
   Morte jacebunt?

LXIII

Evigilate ergò de Somno, & Nocte
   soporâ;
Increpat ecce Moras nostras Auriga
   Diei,
Sol dum cæruleos moderatur in
   Æthere Currus.

LXIV

Jamque experrecti, Textrices mille
   Laborum   190
Conspicite aerias, quæ fingunt Arte
   stupendâ
Mæandros, texuntque suis per inania
   Telis.

LXV

Surgite, Sol Aurum per summa
   Cacumina spargit,
Condit Aromatibus Lucem, dum
   spargit Odores,
Cuncta sagittiferis Radiis Dulcedine
   replet.

LXVI

Erigit in Cœlum Mentes Lux aurea
   Phœbi:
Pulpita qui fugiunt, Hymnis capiun-
   tur.   In Aurum
Vertit Amor Plumbum, Chymico
   præstantior omni.

LXVII

Utque Opifex Naturæ Apis est, Tra-
   gemata fingens
Mellea, dum sugens chymicè trans-
   format in Aurum   200
Flores; ditatur sic plumbea Carmine
   Prosa.

LXVIII

Nullus Rex Vatem, sed Regem Car-
   mine Vates
Evehit, Ille Animas languentes
   excitat, Ille
Ad Mare Pacificum Curas trans-
   mittit edaces.

LXIX

Ut Gemmæ radiant, atque æmula
   Lumina Stellis,
Per Loca transmittunt tenebrosa:
   ita docta Poesis

(414)

Et Lucem, ac Animam, Vitamque
   dat Artibus ipsam.

LXX

O dives, ridens, radiansque Poetica
   Gemmis,
Nobilitas Splendore tuo Diademata
   Regum!
Tu Gentilitium Clypeum depingis
   Honoris.   210

LXXI

Te, (quæ circundas Artes velut Aere)
   Teque
Rerum inventarum Portam, Scenam
   Ingeniorum,
Tam dives, quàm pauper amat,
   Regesque procando.

LXXII

Vates & Reges Tumulo conduntur
   eodem;
Ruminat Ars quodcunque accenditur
   Igne Poetæ,
Sensibus ut nostris divinum exhalet
   Odorem.

LXXIII

Prudentes reddit Speculatio, non
   meliores:
Littera solum Ars est, sed Praxis
   Spiritus; Usus
Arte valet, sic Ars usu; qui seperat,
   aufert.

LXXIV

Languida Facta quidem Dictis
   stimulantur acutis,   220
Verba ut Femellis, Maribus sic Facta
   probantur:
Sit Vita Exemplar, fac, Leges præ-
   veniantur.

LXXV

Maxima Cognitio nostra est servire
   Tonanti,
Tunc nos morigeros Mandatis æsti-
   mat, Actus
Excipiunt quandò quædam Inter-
   ludia nostros.

LXXVI

Illorum Mentes sola ad Sublimia
   tendunt,
Quorum non quovis agitantur Pectora
   Vento,

Utque Aula instabiles, sed in Æquore
   nant Sapientis.

LXXVII

Non alia his Cynosura nitet quàm
   Gratia, quamque
Portat Apostolicus collustrans Sig-
   nifer Orbem :   230
Hâc Evangelici Cursum rexere
   Magistri.

LXXVIII

Hicque Theanthropos Sermo, tum
   mystica Vitra
Oris fatidici, nec non Oracula tanta,
Fomentumque Precum, tum Murus
   Aheneus hîc est ;

LXXIX

Cœli Sculptura hîc, Pietatis Clavis,
   & ipsa
Gaza, Instrumentum, Spesque An-
   chora, Charta fidelis,
Atque Voluptatis Gurges, sic Navis
   Amoris.

LXXX

Nunquam sic refluit Sanctorum
   Fluctus, ut ipsos
Urgeat in Syrtes Errorum cuncta
   vorantes,
Peccati Clades fugiunt, ut naufraga
   saxa.   240

LXXXI

Ut Casus Mortis, Noctis Septentrio,
   Non tam
Obscuri, aut Tenebræ triduanæ,
   quas super omnem
Egyptum induxit, qui Lucem &
   Sydera fecit.

LXXXII

Tempestati hujus collata Tonitrua
   languent ;
Si Stimulos spectes Aspis fert Bal-
   sama, Mors est
Vel Pietas, hujus cùm Carmina
   fæda videbis.

LXXXIII

Hujus cùm laqueos mea Musa eva-
   seris, illuc
Tende Alis, ubi Lux Mentes quæ
   luminat, ardet ;
Et Nebulas abigit, tenebrasque Nitore
   resolvit.

(415)

LXXXIV

Sit tibi Relligio curæ, quam discute,
   meque   250
Errantem cohibe, Deus alme, &
   percute Carnis
Ignavæ (si quando salit vel rudet)
   asellum.

LXXXV

Mens minor es minimo Cœli indul-
   gentis Amore :
Peccatum haud linquunt Terror,
   Pudor, atque Reatus ;
Quatuor hi Comites Cœtum glome-
   rantur in unum.

LXXXVI

Peccato defectus ego, nunc perditus
   erro ;
Namque orare mihi vesana Superbia
   visa est.
Luctantem, Deus alme, leva sub
   Pondere Terræ.

LXXXVII

Nemo merere potest, meruit tamen
   Unus, & horum
Qui jactant Sese, Zelum frigescere
   cernis,   260
His stannum, Argentum est, æs
   Aurum sæpè videtur.

LXXXVIII

Cor renova, Linguam mihi dirige,
   porrige Dextram,
Inspiresque Fidem, Spem velo detege
   tectam :
Erige collapsum, crescat Vis semper
   Amoris.

LXXXIX

Lingua, Decus nostrum, Menti ser-
   vire memento.
Spiritus ille tuus Bezaliel illustravit.
Mors Fide me salvat, Cæcis das
   Lumina sputo.

XC

Spiritus ex sensu fiat, nam Gratia
   sola
Naturam vertit, chymichus Lapis
   ecce repertus,
Et Verbum omnipotens sola est
   Projectio pura.   270

XCI

Verbum, Cos veri, nec Regula certior
ulla :
Rejicimus Mappam tenebrosam
Traditionum.
Non urit me Charta, tamen Mens
ignibus ardet.

XCII

Dum lego, Mens intùs magno Splen-
dore coruscat,
Et novus ecce Vigor penetrat Præ-
cordia, namque
Omnia describit Placitorum Arcana
tuorum.

XCIII

Hujus Carminibus tecum versantur
Enochi ;
Avertit Mortem, transfert nos ante
Senectam :
Dat Vaticanus Scoriam, purum hîc
nitet Aurum.

XCIV

Sic cùm pigra gelu Gens Tartara,
splendida Gemmis   280
Tecta subit Sophiæ, subito Fervore
refecta,
Quæ nive semianimis fuerat, se
vivere sentit.

XCV

Infundis mihi Tu Meditamina sancta,
meoque
Effundis pia Verba Ore, & laudando
per Orbem
Diffundis mea Facta, tuo quæ Munere
vivunt.

XCVI

Musa, mihi Chordas tendens, cane
Facta Bonorum
Hymnis, sed pravos taceas ; Artesque
Tributum

Dent tibi, tu Cordi Linguam, Pen-
namque ligabis.

XCVII

Degener at Soboles Evæ, pollutaque
Culpis,
An Te Mensurâ tenui comprêndere
posset,   290
Omnipotens quum sis, nec mensu-
rabilis unquam ?

XCVIII

Arbustum Cedros, Aquilam non
regulus effert
Laudibus, aut cernit Phœbeas noctua
Flammas,
Gutta quid Oceano ? Radiis Jubar
infinitis ?

XCIX

Languentem sed Spes & Amor per
inane volatum
Ferre valent, in Te noctem Fiducia
lustrat ;
Grandis Amor, suppleto Fidem, Spêi
scribimus Alis.

C

Spiritus, alme DEUS, Mens, Corpus, &
omnia Facta,
Et Verba, & Mentis Meditamina,
postea discent
Et Laudes celebrare tuas, &
Crimina flere.   300
O, quantum JESU me diligis !
Ergo Beatum
Me tua jam reddat Dilectio,
suscipiatque
Erectum rursus Dilectio
MAXIME JESU !
Hæc ara est, atque hæc mea
victima dulcis amoris.
Cor, Oculus, Lingua, atque Manus,
Poplesque reflexus
A te sunt Cuncta hæc, ad te sint Cuncta
vicissim [1].

Post Homerum Iliada, post Vossæum
Grammaticen, post Rossæum, celeber-
rimum illum Virgilii Evangelizantis
Autorem, Carmen Heroicum con-
scribere audax planè videatur Facinus.
Tenuitatis quippe meæ, & imparis longè

in Poesi venæ conscius, cùm non possum
quod vellem, volo tamen quod possum
effundere.

Est aliquid prodire tenus si non datur
ultra.

[1] This is again, in the original, arranged and framed altar-wise.

THEOPHILÆ AMORIS HOSTIA

Cantio III.   Latino Carmine donata.   Restauratio

ARGUMENTUM

Authoris Raptus, laudatur Gratia ; fusæ
Sunt Lachrymæ charo Britonum pro Sanguine fuso
Obscurè, petitur Pax ictis prisca Michaiis.

TRISTICHON I

SOLLICITES mea Musa Lyram, digi-
  toque pererra
Argutæ Chelyos Chordas, & Cantica
  psallas
Quæ rapiant Terras, & scandant
  Astra Triumphis.

II

Ecstatico raptus Motu Bartæius
  Heros,
Lecto subsiliens, alacres ducensque
  Choræas,
Dixit ; In hunc Morem saltabunt
  Gallica Regna.

III

Seu Meteora Soli viscoso Semine
  facta,
Quæ, motu succensa suo, super
  ardua tendunt
Nubila, Stellarum nec non de More
  coruscis

IV

Effulgent Flammis ; Duntaxat at illa
  relucent   10
Ut Sese absumant, & nos per
  Compita ducant ;
Nec pro se Venti, sed Nobis, Flamina
  spirant :

V

Enthea sic superas mea Mens
  ascendit ad Arces,
Sese dispendens, Stolidos ut reddat
  Acutos :
Qui Tædam præfert Aliis, Se Lumine
  privat.

VI

Qualitèr Inferno sudat vesana
  Libido :

Sic Cœlo aspirat divini Zelus Amoris ;
Scrutari Hoc Mentis contendit tota
  Facultas.

VII

Cardinibus subnixa Fides conver-
  titur altis ;
Purior haud ullis præclusa Scientia
  Metis ;   20
Flamma, Cor accendens, non Ignis
  Signa relinquit.

VIII

Horti florentis blandùm Po[i]mæria,
  sancta
Visorum Tellus, Sapientum grata
  Cohorti,
Auratis Asini Phaleris Ludibria
  prostas.

IX

Huic Mare fit rabidum Mundus,
  Discordia major
Est ubi Ventorum, quàm Pyxis
  nautica nôrit :
Incumbit Sanctus Velis, tenet An-
  chora Cœlum.

X

Appulit hîc Pietas, ubi non confracta
  Dolore
Conscia Mens fremitat, Rabie aut
  consumpta malignâ ;
Lumina lascivæ Veneris nec Fulgure
  tacta.   30

XI

Non Nugæ Hîc Pueri ; Juvenis non
  fervidus Æstus ;
Ambitus Ætatis maturæ nullus ;
  Avari
Grandævi haud Vitium ; non Otia
  pigra coluntur

22 Po*i*mæria] *Sic* in orig.

XII

Non Gula, lascivi aut Pruritus turpis
    Amoris,
Turgidus haud Fastus, non invi-
    diosa Rubigo,
Ira nec ardescens, aut Obduratio
    Cordis.

XIII

Non Amor invadit proprius, vel
    Pectora Curæ
Scindentes, Schisma aut Doctrinæ
    mobile flatu,
Non cæci pungunt Stimuli, nec Pœna
    Latebris.

XIV

Hinc macula apparet Tellus obscura,
    ubi certant   40
Pro vanis Homines, puerilis more
    tumultûs ;
Formicæ, veluti peterent, munimina,
    scloppis.

XV

Est ubi Luxuries satiata, Libidoque
    spumat,
Sanguis ubi Irato, petiturque ubi
    Pignus Avaro,
Turget ubi Ambitio, Livor fremit,
    Otia torpent.

XVI

Imperio Martis remanent quàm
    Regna revulsa,
Dispersis Aulis ! sub nostro Lumine
    quæ sunt
Pulvis ut exiguus Ventorum Flatibus
    actus.

XVII

Hic stat formosi polydædala Machina
    Mundi,
Sustentata Manu Veri, summique
    Jehovæ.   50
Apparent instar Nanorum exindè
    Gigantes.

XVIII

Quàm vilis Mundus ! pia Musa,
    innitere Pennis
Firmis, (terreno fueras detenta
    Tumultu,
Jactatâ & Turbâ) demùm transcende
    Monarchas.

(418)

XIX

Raptus in hunc morem divino con-
    citus Igne,
Ætheris in Camerâ stellatâ percute
    Chordas :
Aspirare tui nequeunt huc, Roma,
    Regentes.

XX

Sese dilatans Animus fit latior usquè
Sicut Helix ; Hominis status at
    Nativus, ut Orbis,
Quem subitò à Zenith deturbant
    Fata superno.   60

XXI

Perspiciens Ratione Fides oculatior
    Aulam
Sideream, Mentes rapiunt sua Visa
    serenas ;
Veri accensa Pharos per Amorem
    Gaudia pandit.

XXII

Hæc Lux quæ Radiis conuestit
    singula claris,
Theiophilam, inclusit Prægnanti
    Mente decoram ;
Excipit occiduum Naturæ, Gratia,
    Solem.

XXIII

Fundat Aroma Calyx, Rosa quam
    dulcissima, Virtus
Illustris matura siet tua Tempore
    justo,
Explicet ac Radius divinus Floris
    Honorem.

XXIV

Anni Procursu duodeni sic sua
    Forma   70
Enituit, Formam Dominæ stupuêre
    potentes ;
Spectantes Animæ Lucem per
    Corporis Umbram.

XXV

Ardet Crystallo veluti Lucerna polito,
Cujus transparens decoratur Fabrica
    Flammis ;
Hæc ita divino splendescit Virgo
    Nitore.

XXVI

Mens Gemmam superat, superat sua
    Concha pruinam,

Flumina vel Lactis manantia ab
Ubere pleno :
Venæ Saphiros præcellunt, Labra
Rubinos.

XXVII

Circùm Labra volant Charites sua
mille venustæ,
Suavia Puniceis labuntur Aromata
Portis,   80
Indè fluunt cunctos medicantia
Balsama Morbos.

XXVIII

Emittunt tales Altaria Sancta
Vapores ;
Tales Blanditias halant Fragrantia
Gummi ;
Sic Rosa coccineâ spirat præflorida
Veste.

XXIX

Attonitos reddunt Spectantûm
Lumina Vultus,
Afficiunt quamvis Præcordia fervida
castis,
Attamen Ardoris sunt ipsa immunia,
Flammis.

XXX

Lampadas hasce volet quisquis de-
pingere, quisquis
Exprimeret clarâ radiantes Luce
Fenestras,
Pingeret Aspectum fugientem, pon-
deret Austrum.   90

XXXI

Suave videremus Pectus, micat Eden
Amoris,
Illis Monticulis nascuntur Mala
decoris,
Quæ Mala de vetitâ sanarent Arbore
nata.

XXXII

Mollities, Candorque Manûs tran-
scendit Oloris
Plumas ; est talis cujus moderatior
Ardor,
Qualis cùm coeunt Radius Phœbeus
& Aurum.

XXXIII

Jucundæ Nemoris Syrenes, Musica
turba,

Gutturibus quarum dimanat dul-
cior Aer,
Illam quid petitis cunabula vestra
perosæ ?

XXXIV

Ecce Latus claudunt Argentea Lilia
castum,   100
Calthæ fulgentes Auri flammantis
amictu,
Ignes evibrat cùm Lauro Primula
Veris.

XXXV

Margaron excellunt Dentes ; Tegmen,
Caput, Auri,
Vox præit Argento, de Te Natura
Vigorem
Sumit, Panniculis est præ Te squal-
lida Flora.

XXXVI

O, Formosa, Pudica tamen, seu
Chava, priusquàm
Candida purpureo suffuderat Ora
Rubore
A Te Virtutes, Artes, Charitesque
profectæ.

XXXVII

Ad vivum depicta manet non
Pulchrior Icon
Quàm pia Mens pulchro quæ
splendet Corpore clausa :   110
Hujus Cœlesti cedit Pandora Decori.

XXXVIII

Aulæ Sideribus pictæ sic Cynthia
Præses
Apparet, Phœbi Splendoribus aucta
refractis,
Fulgida Stellarum dum stipant
Castra Phalanges.

XXXIX

(Astra Pruina refert) subitò Telluris
at Umbrâ
Objectâ Lucem retrahit, cui Conus
opacus
Falcatam supra Lunam, sub Lumine
Solis.

XL

Qui Cœlum, Nubes, Terras, Mare,
Saxaque lustrat,
Qui penetrat Gemmas, Fructus,
Stellas, Adamantas ;

Mundi Oculus, claræ Promus Con-
dusque Diei.   120

XLI

Cujus gliscentes imitatur Flamma
  Pyropos,
Purpureas Aurora Fores dum
  pandit Eoo,
Noctis lucentem Dominam, Famu-
  lasque repellens.

XLII

Theiophilam radians Lumen Te
  appello Diei,
Palpebra quippè Fides tua fit, seu
  Pupula Fervor,
Vultus Angelico speciosos More
  venustans.

XLIII

Ætheris illa potens, casta & Regina,
  reclusi,
Plurima vestalis quam cingit Virgo
  propinqua,
Disparet, dia hæc si Constellatio
  splendet.

XLIV

Nobilitas vera est Virtus, Cognatio
  Sancti,   130
Tutela Angelicus Chorus est,
  Cœlumque Brabium ;
Cujus demissus, dum surgit Gratia,
  Vultus.

XLV

Eugenia Ingenium, Paidia ministrat
  Acumen ;
Thesauros Veri charos Eusebia
  præbet.
(Cudendi Voces Vati concessa
  Potestas.)

XLVI

Aula Cor est formosa sibi, divinius
  Ejus
Pectus, Sacrati Penetralia candida
  Amoris ;
Hîc Sibi Delicio est, Sanctos reficitque
  Poetas.

XLVII

Illustres Domini, quos Laurea Serta
  coronant,
Artes qui eruitis, qui cultas reddi-
  tis Artes,   140

Estis & infirmi qui Sustentacula
  Mundi ;

XLVIII

Qui struitis Famæ Monumenta
  perinclyta Templo,
Mellea de Vobis Modulamina talia
  manent,
Qualia divino mulcerent Pectora
  Succo.

XLIX

Dum succedit Hyems Autumno, Ver
  premit Æstas,
Dum recitat Modulis Tempus
  Pœana vetustis,
Vestris Vos Famæ Plumis repara-
  bitis Alas.

L

Illud quod præbent sublimia Tænera
  Vinum,
Insanè Vires poterit reparare
  fugatas ;
Sic Citharæ, atque Tubæ, sic Organa,
  Tympana, Sistra.   150

LI

Conciliat quamvis reboantia Mur-
  mura Basso
Ars, torquens Nervos graviores
  usque, sonoro
Fulmine dum complent Aulam
  Diapasona totam ;

LII

Ista parùm valeant ; Dominæ Testu-
  dine tensâ
Hujus, Chordarum Pulsum tenta-
  verit Omnem,
Dum Mens Harmoniæ pertracta est
  Pollice docto.

LIII

Gratia inest Verbis ; O, terque
  quaterque beati,
Queîs Cœlum Terris, æterno
  Codice scripti !
Qui, Sensu amoti, cupiunt Com-
  mercia Mentis !

LIV

Inter Eos qui divino de Semine
  creti,   160
Non obscurati Sensu nec Corporis
  Umbrâ,

Seraphicè exardent vivacis Origine
Flammæ.

LV

Gaudia dat Gustus, non exequanda
Loquelis !
Ritu Cimmerioque Scholis pal-
panda superna,
In quorum Solis Frontem sunt
Nubila densa.

LVI

Callis inaccessus nimio fit Lumine
Cœli ;
Splendidior Radius teneros per-
stringit Ocellos :
Ephata fare, Lutum Visu me reddet
acuto.

LVII

Hoc Raptu emotus divino, fac mihi
talis
Contingat Finis, Stagaritæ qualis,
in illo   170
Euripo, quem non ullus comprêndere
posset !

LVIII

Mystica præbeat hæc (ô sit protensa !)
Catena
Nexus, qui stringat vel quavis
fortiùs Arte !
Talia lenitos rapiant Modulamina
Sensus.

LIX

Musica pervadit Mentes, cum per-
citus Oestro
Insano Saulus, Genio fremuitque
maligno,
Gemmea præ Plectris sordebant
Sceptra Tyranni.

LX

Hujus inardescens Hymni me
Flamma repurgat
Fœcibus à Terræ : Cantus Pene-
tralia Cœli
Divini reserant, deducunt Agmina
pura :   180

LXI

Agmina pura Dei celebrant Natalia
læta ;
Hymnos vel Christus modulatur ;
Sancta Columba

Cœli, summa petens, Numerorum
deligit Alas.

LXII

Nî Versus, non sit Textus, quia
quælibet Hymni
Incantant ; actis famuletur Concio
Psalmis,
Antè Diem summum, per Vos
demortua surgunt !

LXIII

Ast ubi grassatur Furiis Bellona
tremendis,
Stragibus, heu, lassato, sed haud
satiata recedens,
Prædatrice Lupâ truculentior, Or-
gana pulset ?

LXIV

Est equidèm non Mota Solo, pacata
Tumultu :   190
Degeneres trepidant ; manet illa
invicta Catervis,
Displosi metuit nec rauca Tonitrua
Scloppi.

LXV

Insunt Virtuti sua Balsama ; sollici-
tavit
Intensè Numen Gladii mollire
Rigorem :
Ætatis Ferro sic Aurea Virgo profatur.

LXVI

Ingruit, O, Numen Venerandum !
dira Procella,
Coccina purpureæ cum velant
Crimina Vestes,
Effuso tinctæ pretioso Sanguine
Vitæ !

LXVII

Orbis Aquis cinctus, fortunatissimus
olim,
O, deplorandum ! quantum muta-
tus ab illo !   200
Pax ubi floruerat pia, Mors ibi pro-
diga regnat !

LXVIII

Rubrum deprompsit Vinum Mavor-
tius Ardor !
Conserves Arcam, Deus, in Tor-
rente Timorum,

170 Stagaritæ] *Sic* in orig.

Aut tua subsidat Lachrymis, tum
  Sanguine, Sponsa !

LXIX

Est Panem Lachrymata suum,
  Gemitusque resorbet :
Lumina pro Potu sua sunt in
  Flumina versa !
Ipsa, immersa Malis, ad Te Se lan-
  guida confert.

LXX

Ad Modulos Compone graves, Pater
  Orbis, acutos
Hybernæ Chelios ! quævis Dis-
  cordia Concors
Esto, Scoti fuerit super, aut Insigni-
  bus Angli !   210

LXXI

Non inter Socios sævo Formido
  Leoni ;
Vel prædabundis inter se con-
  venit Ursis ;
Mutua Pernicies, lacerat, Vir, Corpus
  Iesu !

LXXII

Si modò fert Animus, pugnetis Ful-
  mina Martis,
Turcico & invisam Labaro dedu-
  cite Lunam,
Sacra relinquentes Fidei Confinia
  rectæ.

LXXIII

Agminibus Thracum densis conten-
  dite ; quamvis
Sclopporum seu Truncus iners,
  Caro vestra deorsùm
Tendat, summa petent Animæ de
  more Globorum.

LXXIV

Numinis in mediis si sit Præsentia
  Castris,   220
In Templo resident multò magis
  Ille sacrato,
Hæresin ut pellat, perversaque Schi-
  smata purget.

LXXV

Hæc Tunicam rupêre Tuam, Dolor
  undè Bonorum !
Zelotæ quamvis raucâ Te Voce
  fatigant,
Voto indignaris civili Sanguine mixto.

LXXVI

Fallaces potuêre Bonum suadere
  fuisse
Præcones, per Diluvium vadare
  Cruoris ?
Præstigiis uti, Summosque resolvere
  Nexus ?

LXXVII

Inde Catechismi neglecti, & sacra
  Synaxis !
Herbæ hinc sylvestres, seu Ranæ
  Vere Palustres !   230
Athea Schismatici Corruptio pessima
  Cleri.

LXXVIII

Prætextus fugiant speciosos, sunto
  fideles ;
Cultu divino repetantque Precamen
  Iesu ;
Fœderis aut valeant Mysteria dira
  trisexti.

LXXIX

Sic seduxerunt illos Insomnia vana,
Vilescant illis adeô ut Natalia Christi !
(Nemo tenet Nodis mutantem Protea
  Vultum.)

LXXX

Festum Festorum, supremæ dulce
  Cohorti ;
Inclinat Cœlum hîc Terris, hinc
  Gaudia Sanctis ;
Judice Relligione Dies primarius
  Anni.   240

LXXXI

Factus Homo bonus est primum,
  tum degener ; Ipse
Sermo Caro Factus, nostra haud
  Commercia vitans,
Pejor ut is nihilo, meliori Sorte
  fruatur.

LXXXII

Audetis Verum profiteri ? Pabula
  pascunt
Fuci aliena ; merum Pigmentum
  Papiliones ;
Tettix deperdit, redemit sibi Tem-
  pora Myrmex.

LXXXIII

Mellea dum repetunt Vespæ Spelæa
  rapaces,

Illis Insidiis structis merguntur in Ollâ,
Corporis haud tanti sint ac Munimina Mentis.

LXXXIV

'Kirk-Int'rest kenimus'; Leges revocate Draconis,   250
Instaurate vetus Templum; Sunt Mœnia Sancti,
Seu Tubus est Pastor, Fons Gratia, Gluten Amorque.

LXXXV

Vobis præteritos ignoscat Musa Furores,
Singula propitio condant Oblivia Velo,
De Rebus moveat si Vos Metanœa peractis.

LXXXVI

Veri Cultores, balantes pascite Christi Agnos; quippè Merum Sanguis, Caro dapsilis Esca:
Illos pascentes semper, spectate Coronam.

LXXXVII

Dispensatores Sponso, Sponsæque fideles,
Nos sacra divini ducant Oracula Veri,   260
Relligione Status floret, data Gloria Fidis.

LXXXVIII

Cùm Judex veniet, Merces erit ampla Labori,
Pro Lachrymis Vobis manabunt Gaudia Rivis,
Auratæ surgunt Spicæ sementibus udis.

LXXXIX

Læsis, Omnipotens Vindex! certò æqua rependes
Illis, qui sese fœdo maculâre Reatu,
Sanguinis innocui cum sit Detectio fusi!

XC

Aurea Pax aures, Verumque appellat amicum!
Lumina non Phœbi latebris tam grata Borusso,

Urbibus eversis Homines, vel Littora Fractis.   270

XCI

O, si cœlestis vel tandem Turma secunda,
Nobis, Bellorum diris Cruciatibus haustis,
Grata salutiferæ resonaret Cantica Pacis!

XCII

Pax Domus est fessis, Pax ad Natalia Christi
Cantio prima fuit, Terris suprema Voluntas,
Pax Bonitatis amans, Pax Sanctis vera Voluptas.

XCIII

Martyribus fulcimen Amor, ceu stramen Achates
Attrahit; ad nostrum sic nos perducis Amantem,
Elixir Auri verum, Compendia Legis!

XCIV

Ullanè Divinum narret Facundia Amorem?   280
Quippè redemptus Homo Naturas nobiliores
Angelicas superat; Tanti sit Passio Christi!

XCV

Hîc demùm tacuit; Lachrimarum Flumina manant
Ex oculis, illi Mundus Cadus esse videtur,
Gaudia falsa Merum, Stultorum portio Fæces.

XCVI

Et nunc Lætitiæ vivæ de Fonte micanti,
Pura ubi perpetuo Chrystalla fluentia Cursu,
Mens erit æthereas conscendere Raptibus Oras.

XCVII

Hinc Documenta sibi Zelus malesanus habebit,
Ardores Cujus tradunt in Prælia sævi,   290

250 kenimus] Cf. Introd. on Butler's wrath at Benlowes' macaronics.

Hinc fera depositis mitescant Secula
  Bellis.

XCVIII

Auribus exhibeas Epulum, selecta
  Venustas !
Dum sic cantat Amor, Reges dulce-
  dine capti :
Gratia Naturæ Nervos intendit
  Amore.

XCIX

Horrisonas Amor ipse potes sedare
  Procellas,
Cantibus & placare tuis immania
  Cete,
Quæ Dominatrici diverrunt Marmora
  Caudâ.

C

Si tua, Virgo, nequit compescere
  Erotica Musa
Incumbens Ævo Fatum miserabile
  nostro,
Pro Scriptis Lachrymæ ; Nam Gens
  est danda Furori !   300

Provecti, tandèm Latiales linqui-
  mus Oras,
Te petimus Patrium, Terra Bri-
  tanna, Solum.
Hîc ubi Nemo citis designet Lit-
  tus Ocellis :
Egressæ faveant Fluctus, & Aura
  Rati.

Upon the Vanity of the World

Long have I sought the wish of all
To find ; and what it is men call
True Happiness ; but cannot see
The world hath it, which it can be,
  Or with it hold a sympathy.

He that enjoys what here below
Frail elements have to bestow,
Shall find most sweet bare hopes at first ;
Fruition by fruition's burst,
  Sea-water so allays the thirst.   10

Whoever would be happy then,
Must be so to himself ; for, whēn
Judges are taken from without,
To judge what we are, fenc'd about,
  They do not judge, but guess, and
    doubt.

His soul must hug no private sin ;
For, that 's a thorn conceal'd i'th' skin ;
But Innocence, where she is nurst
Plants valiant Peace ; so, Cato durst
  Ev'n then be best, when Rome was
    worst.   20

God-built he must be in his mind ;
That is, Divine ; whose faith no wind
Can shake ; when firmly he relies
Upon the Almighty, he outflies
  Low chance, and fate of destinies.

As fountains rest not till they lead,
Meand'ring high, as their first head :
So, man rests not till he hath trod
Death's height : then, by that period,
  He rests too, rais'd in soul to God 30
              Owen Feltham.

POTESTAS Culminis est Tempestas
Mentis, Splendorem habet Titulo,
cruciatum Animo ; desuntque Inopiæ
multa, Avaritiæ omnia. Ne petas
igitur, devota Anima, esse qualis in
Anglia Dux Buckingamiæ, & in Aula
Cæsaria Princeps ab Eggenberg, &
in Hispania Comes D'Olivares, & in
Imperio Ottomanico Mustapha Bassa
fuere ; nec tibi magis arrideant cerus-
satæ Laudes, & calamistrata Encomia,
quàm sinceræ & sacrosanctæ Amoris
Anhelationes. Seculi delectatiunculas
devita, & Cœlorum Jubilo recreaberis :
delicatula nimis es, si velis gaudere cum
Mundo, & postea regnare cum CHRISTO :
Amarescat Mundus, ut dulcescat DEUS.
Quamdiù est in te Ægypti Farina,
Manna cœleste non gustabis ; Gustat
DEUM cui Libido Seculi Nauseam parit :
Exinanitio nostra plenitudinis Cœli
capaces reddit. Si vis frui Sole, verte

Owen Feltham] **Not the worst verses of the author of the** *Resolves.*

dorsum Umbræ : nec amaris à Mundo, nisi à CHRISTO repulsa, nec à CHRISTO, nisi à Mundo spreta. Dejicit se de Culmine Majestatis qui à DEO ad Consolatiunculas Creaturulæ confugit. O quâm contempta recula[1] est homo nisi supra humana se erexerit! Beatum nil facit Hominem, nisi qui fecit Hominem; minimum enim Dei omnis Orbis Magnitudine est magnificentius. Paucis, nec tibi ignominiosum sit pati quod passus est CHRISTUS, nec gloriosum facere quod fecit Judas. Morere Mundo, ut vivas Deo. Quicunque cum DEO habet Amicitiam, Felicitatis tenet Fastigium. Hæc unica Laus, hic Apex Sapientiæ est, ea viventem appetere, quæ morienti forent appetenda : Mortis ergò Meditationi, & Æternitatis Contemplationi Lucernulæ tuæ Oleum impendas. Vale.

STORMS on the mind from Honour's hill descend;
Titles external beams add not to bliss :
The poor wants much, the covetous all. My soul,
No painted praise, nor flow'r'd encomiums prize
Equal to pious breathings of pure love:
Eschew the petty pleasures of the time,
And Heav'n's refreshments make thy jubilee:
Imagine not to swim in worldly pomp,
And afterwards to reign with Christ in bliss :
Earth must be gall, that God may honey prove :   10
He the best relish hath of Heav'n, who most
Disdains the base licentiousness o' th' age ;
We must be emptied of ourselves, before
We can have entrance into th' heav'nly court :
If we desire fruition of the sun,
Then must our backs upon the shade be turn'd ;

Disclaim'd by Christ are those the world doth love,
And those whom Christ does love, the world contemns :
He of his greatness doth himself divest,
Who goes from God, and creature-comforts seeks.   20
Oh, what a mean despised thing is man,
Unless he raise himself above the earth,
Since nought but his Creator makes him high !
Let's think 't no shame t' endure what Christ endur'd,
Nor glory to do that which Judas did ;
Dead to the world, let's be alive to God,
Who gain His favour are supremely blest :
This is the height of wisdom, to desire
Those things in life, which thou wouldst dying crave :
Then on the thoughts of death thy lamp's oil spend,   30
And muse upon that state which ne'er shall end [2].

Mundo immundo

NON possum, non Arte loqui ; Furor addit Acumen :
Crimina taxantur, Nomina salva latent.
Munde, quid hoc sibi vult ? tantò longinquiùs erras,
Quantò plùs graderis ; Te Cacoethes habet.
In quos Schismaticas torsisti sæviùs Hastas,

Quàm quos Virtutis cœlitùs Umbo tegit.
Protege me, Cœlum ! Quis adest ? Oppressor avarus,
Cui prior est Nummus Numine, Libra Libro.
Numme, potens Deus es ! Sic undique supplicat Auro,
Omnipotens veluti Numen inesset Ei ;   10

[1] *recula*] For *this* diminutive ('thinglet,' 'trifle') B. might quote Plautus and Apuleius : *creaturula* and *consolatiuncula* must be ecclesiastical if he did not coin them.
[2] This blank verse translation (with couplet-tip) of the preceding Latin prose paragraph is curious : and it might, at the time, have been much worse.

AurumNequitiæ Pater est,& Filius Orci;
  Os promit Nectar ; Mens Aconita
    vomit.
Hic vorat, utque rapax ruit in nova
  frusta Molossus ;
    Vasta Sitim pariunt Æquora, Terra
      Famem ;
Tota nec explerent Pellæas Æquora
  Fauces,
    Terraque sat tantæ non erit una
      Fami.
Perfida quisquis amat, se perdit, & odit
  amando :
    Plus habet Ille Dei, qui minus Orbis
      habet.
Dum captat, capitur; Dæmon licèt
  Omnia spondet,

Dat Mundus, magnum præter inane,
  nihil.   20
Plena Fames, mellita Lues, Persuasio
  fallax,
    Gloria Flos, Pulvis Gaza, Tiara cinis.
Tendiculas, Pigmenta, Dolos, Crepita-
  cula, Fumos ;
    Has rauco Merces Gutture laudet
      Anus.
Insatiata Fames rapto superincubet
  Auro,
    Porcus & aggestas grunniat inter
      Opes.
Littera R hebræa, pelasga, latina no-
  tabunt
    Quòd, malus, eR-RO-RESh nil nisi,
      Mundus habet [1].

THE VANITY OF THE WORLD

Canto X. The Abnegation

THE ARGUMENT

What's potent Opulency ? What's remiss
Voluptuousness ? World, what's all this,
To that the Soul's created for, Eternal Bliss ?

STANZA I

VARIOUS are poets' flames ; some,
  eclogues write,
    Others describe a horrid fight,
Some lyric strains, and some the
  epic do delight :

II

But, here my sharpen'd Muse shall
  entertain
    The scourges of satiric vein,
To lash the world, in which such
  store of vices reign.

III

No grandee patron court I, nor
  entice
    Love-glances from enchanting
      eyes,
Nor blandishments from lisping
  wanton's vocal spice.

IV

No such trite themes our fired genius
  fit,   10

Of which so many pens have writ :
Prudential souls affect sound Reason,
  not slight wit.

V

Blest talents which the Gospel's
  Pearl do buy :
    Frail hopes that on the world rely,
Where none are sav'd by faith, but
  by' infidelity.

VI

The way to gain more ground, is to
  retreat ;
    Our flight will be our foe's defeat ;
Minds conqu'ring great delights,
  triumph in joys more great :

VII

Pull me not, *World* ; nor can, nor
  will I stay :
    Juggler, I know what thou canst
      say :   20
Thy magic spells charm easy sense
  but to betray.

[1] Observe the most Benlowesian eccentricity of the subscribed *h* to get the Hebrew *resh*.
15 by'] Cf. note on ' they' ' *supra*, p. 380.

VIII
Wits toil to please thee, sables yield
  their skins;
  The silkworm to thy wardrobe
    spins;
Rocks send their gems, seas pearls,
  to purvey for thy sins.

IX
Thou bright'nest cupboards with
  throng'd massy plate;
  Heap'st ermin'd mantles of estate;
Shew'st rich caparison'd champing
  coursers at thy gate.

X
Thou cull'st of Nature's spoil from
  air, earth, seas,
  The wing'd, hoof'd, finny droves,
    to please
Gluttons, who make themselves
  spittles of each disease.   30

XI
And shall, like Dives, a sad reck'ning
  pay;
  Feasts hasten'd on his fun'ral
    day;
Death brought the voider, and the
  Devil took away.

XII
Tell me no more, th' art sweet, as
  spicy air;
  Or, as the blooming Virgin, fair;
And canst with jovial mirth resusci-
  tate from care.

XIII
Boast not of ruby lips, and diamond
  eyes,
  Rose cheeks, and lily fronts, made
    prize,
With dimpled chins, the trap-pits
  where a fondling lies.

XIV
Death's serjeant soon thy courted
  Helens must   40
  Attach, whose eyes, now orbs of
    lust,
The worms shall feed on, till they
  crumble into dust.

XV
Boast, *World*, who unto revels dost
  decoy
  Thy fav'rites, that they're bath'd
    in joy;
Disdaining saints, who precious time
  in pray'r employ:

XVI
Who, where they come, with purer
  rays of light,
  Dazzle thy bat-ey'd legions quite,
Rage, *Impudence*, and *Ignorance*,
  the imps of Night.

XVII
Fool, thy attractives, in no limits
  pent,
  Indulge to surfeits, not content, 50
And but illude the mind, not give it
  ornament.

XVIII
Gild o'er thy bitter pills with guileful
  arts;
  Sweet potions brew for frolic
    hearts:
When most thou smil'st, thou actest
  most perfidious parts.

XIX
With thee dwells fawning *Craft;* and
  glozing *Hate*,
  Th' allurements of imperious state,
Which barks, like calms, invite unto
  a shipwreck'd fate.

XX
Guile, rule the world, that doth in
  madness roll:
  Great things the better oft con-
    trol,
Where *Pride* is coach'd, *Fraud*
  shopp'd, and taverns drown the
  soul.   60

XXI
Folly in ruffling storms with *Frenzy*
  meets,
  Ebbing, and flowing o'er the
    streets
O' th' care-fill'd pompous city, which
  exiles true sweets.

30 spittles] Of course = ' spitals.'

XXII

Oh, fretting broils in populous bustle pent,
  Where still more noise than sense they vent,
And, now as much to gold, as late to battles bent!

XXIII

World, reason if thou canst. Thy sports leave stings;
  Thy scenes, like thee, prove empty things;
Thou glorious seem'st in paint, from whence all falsehood springs.

XXIV

So, rainbow colours on doves' necks have shone   70
  In hue so diverse, yet so one,
That fools have thought them all, the wiser knew them none.

XXV

I'll countercharm thy spells, that souls, ere thee,
  May trust wild Irish seas; who flee
Distress'd to thy relief, thou say'st;
  'What 's that to me?'

XXVI

Fawn, and betray, and Treason's self outdare,
  T' o'erthrow by raising is thy care,
But I'll ungull thy minions, undisguise thy ware.

XXVII

Thy gold 's dross, glitt'ring troubles are thy bliss,
  By pomp thou cheat'st, thy all 's amiss: 80
Thou art Sin's stage, the Devil prompts, Flesh actor is.

XXVIII

Spectator *Sense* applauds each witching gin,
  But, unto *Reason's* eye within,
Thou seem'st Hell's broker, and the servile pimp of Sin.

XXIX

Thus peaches do rough stones in velvet tire;

Thus rotten sticks mock starry fire;
Thus quagmires with green emeralds crown their cheating mire.

XXX

So, Mermaids lovely seem in beauty's guise,
  With voice, and smiles, draw ears, and eyes,
But whom they win, they sink; those never more shall rise. 90

XXXI

Thy shop 's but an exchange of apish fashion,
  Thy wealth, sports, honours are vexation,
Thy favours glist'ring cares, sweet surfeits, woo'd damnation.

XXXII

Base proverbs are thy counsels to enthral.
  'Each for himself, and God for All':
'Young saints' (I dread to speak it) 'to old devils fall.'

XXXIII

Rain on thy darling's head a Danaen shower,
  Let him be drench'd in wealth, and power;
What then? Th' hast storm'd, and seiz'd on all in one short hour.

XXXIV

Oh, thou Pride's restless sea! swoln fancies blow   100
  Thee up, dost blue with envy grow,
Brinish with blood, like the Red Sea, with lust dost flow.

XXXV

Remorseless *Rage*! thou in thy fifth act's breath,
  When blood does freeze to ice of death,
And life 's jail'd up for Nature's debt, where art? Beneath.

XXXVI

World, ev'n thy name a whirling storm implies,

102 blood—lust] The suggestion to transpose these is obvious: and is supported by a minute ² and ¹ over the words in my copy.

Where men in generations rise,
Like bubbles, dropsied bladders of
  the rainy skies.

XXXVII

Some straight sink down, whom
  waters' sheet does hide ;
Some, floating up and down,
  abide ;   110
The longest are so circumvolv'd, as
  rest 's denied.

XXXVIII

So, have we rid out storms, when
  Eol's rave
Plough'd up the ocean, whose
  each wave
Might waken Death with noise, and
  make its paunch a grave.

XXXIX

The sick ship groan'd, fierce winds
  her tacklings rent ;
The proud sea scorn'd to be shore-
  pent ;
We seem'd to knock at Hell, and
  bounce the firmament.

XL

Clouds then ungilt the skies, when
  lightning's light
Flash'd thousand glimmering
  days t' our sight,
But thunder's cannons soon turn'd
  those flash'd days to night. 120

XLI

Thus art thou, *World*, life's storm,
  at death distress ;
Starving 's the bottom of excess :
Thyself a piteous creature, how
  can'st me redress ?

XLII

No : hadst less cruel been, th' hadst
  been less kind ;
Oil 's in thy gall to heal my mind :
Thus Hell may help to Heav'n,
  Satan a soul befriend :

XLIII

A good cause with good means
  some use, yet fare
But ill, when others, of thy care,
Whose cause is bad, and means ill
  us'd, successful are.

XLIV

No wonder Sin's career, uncheck'd,
  runs on,   130
Since here life's joy it hath alone,
Which, though thou bragg'st is giv'n,
  no sooner 's giv'n, than gone.

XLV

Pomp, Pleasure, Pelf, idolatriz'd by
  fools,
Dispute we now in Wisdom's
  schools :
Ambition's quenchless fire i' th'
  spring of judgement cools.

XLVI

Pride bladders tymp'nous hearts, till
  prick'd by fear,
Soon they subside by venting
  there :
Unsafe ascents to pow'r do watching
  dangers rear.

XLVII

Fearful, and fear'd is Pomp ; Ambi-
  tion steep
Does Envy get, and Hatred
  keep ;   140
High state wants station ; honour-
  thirsting minds can't sleep.

XLVIII

Summon Aspiro, with his looms of
  state
To weave Pride's web, in spite of
  fate ;
Who, once got up, throws down
  the steps did elevate.

XLIX

He hates superiors, 'cause superiors,
  and
Inferiors, lest they 's equals stand ;
And on his fellows squints, that are
  in joint command.

L

Th' ambitious treach'rous are, and
  hoodwink'd quite ;
Their giddy heads have dazzled
  sight,
For Jealousy clothes Truth in
  double mists of spite.   150

LI

His eye must see, and wink ; his
  tongue must brave,

And flatter too ; his ear must have
Audience, yet careless be : thus acts he king and slave.

LII

So, brightest angel blackest devil hides ;
High'st rise to lowest downfall slides ;
A mathematic point thus East and West divides.

So what?

LIII

Bright Wisdom sends dark Policy to school,
Proves the contriver but a fool,
Who builds his maxims on a precipice, or pool.

LIV

Great ones, keep realms from want; they'll you from hate :   160
Life 's not so dear as wealth ; for, that
Holds single bodies, this the body of the State.

LV

Who bad desires conceive, they soon wax great
With mischief, then bring forth deceit,
So, brood they desolation, till it grows complete.

LVI

Let such as sail 'gainst Virtue's wind, use skill
To tack about ; for, what 's first ill,
Grows worse by use, and worst by prosecution still.

LVII

Ev'n that to which Pride's tow'ring project flies,
When grasp'd, soon by fruition dies :   170
Great fears, great hopes, great plots, great men make tragedies !

LVIII

Achitophel and Absalom prov'd this,

Whose brains of their designs did miss ;
Teaching deep Machavels ; 'Fraud worst to th' Plotter is.'

LIX

Fallacious they, and fallible have been,
Who made Religion cloak their sin :
Man's greatest good, or greatest ill is from within.

LX

Those policies that hunt for shadows so,
As let at last the substance go,
Which ever lasts, make wretched end in endless woe.   180

LXI

Hadst for thy household stuff the spoil of realms,
Couldst thou engross Cathaiah's gems,
And more then triplicate Rome's triple diadems ;

LXII

Couldst with thy feet toss empires into air,
And sit i' th universal chair
Of State ; were pageants made for thee, the whole world's Mayor ;

LXIII

Yet those but pageants were ; thou, slave to sense ;
To him, not 's own, all things dispense
But storms ; thou happier wast i' th' preterperfect tense.

LXIV

Steward, give up th' account, the audit 's near   190
To reckon how, and when, and where ;
Where much is lent, there 's much requir'd : Doomsday 's severe.

LXV

Thus, proud Ambition is by Conscience peal'd ;
Vapours sent up, awhile conceal'd,

169 tow'ring] Orig. ' touring.'
174 Machavels] The *i* is often missed at this time in various forms ' Matchavil,' &c.

In thund'ring storms pour down at
  length, when all's reveal'd.

LXVI

Though Pride's high head doth
  brush the stars, yet shall
Its carcass, like a sulphur ball,
Plunge into Flames' abyss. Pride
  concav'd Satan's hall.

LXVII

The mighti'st are but worms ; pale
  cowards they
Abash'd shall stand at that Great
  Day,   200
When Conscience, King of Terrors,
  shall their crimes display.

LXVIII

Giants of earth, avisos may you
  tell,
  That though with envied state you
  swell,
Yet, soon within Corruption's charnel-
  house you'll dwell.

LXIX

Sceptres are frail, as reeds : who had
  no bound,
  Are clasp'd within six foot of
  ground ;
Whose epitaphs next age will be
  oblivion found.

LXX

Such yesterday, as would have been
  their slave,
  To-day may tread upon their
  grave,
That flats the nose : best lectures
  dust-seal'd pulpits have.   210

LXXI

Who toss'd the ball of Earth, in dark
  vaults rest :
All what that gen'ral once possest
Was but a shirt in 's tomb, who van-
  quish'd all the East.

LXXII

Invading Cyrus in a tub of gore,
  Might quaff his fill, who evermore

Had thirsted blood : him timeless
  Fate midst triumphs tore.

LXXIII

Weigh things ; Life's frail, Pomp
  vain ; remember Paul,
(The way to rise will be to fall,)
In 's high commission, low, in 's low
  conversion, tall.

LXXIV

Soul, wou'dst aspire to th' High'st ?
  clip Tumor's wing ;   220
To th' test of Heav'n thy axioms
  bring :
Best politic David was. Who con-
  quers Sin 's the King.

LXXV

Let raisèd thoughts, Elijah-like,
  aspire
To be encharioted in fire :
Faith, Love, Joy, Peace, the wheels
  to saints' sublime desire.

LXXVI

Avaro cite, as void of grace, as stor'd
  With gold, the GOD his soul
  ador'd ;
Wealth twins with fear: why start'st ?
  Unlock thy unsunn'd hoard :

LXXVII

I'll treble't by the philosophic stone;
  This makes thee stare. Why, thus
  'tis done,   230
To passives actives join in due
  proportion.

LXXVIII

Behold vast sums unown'd ! Thou
  hutch-cramm'd chink,
Art made as nothing with a wink,
Thou, bred from Hell, with Hell-
  deeds souls to Hell dost sink

LXXIX

Gold is the fautress of all civil jars,
  Treason's reward, the nerve of
  wars,
Nurse of profaneness, suckling rage
  that kingdoms mars.

?

---

202 avisos] In the abstract sense of the original Spanish, which we have more gener-
ally Englished into ' advice-*boat*.'
220 Tumor] So in orig. The context supports ' Timur' or Tamerlane. But 'tumour'
(= ' swelling pride ') or ' rumour ' would make sense.

LXXX

Thou potent Devil, how dost thou
  bewitch
  The dreggy soul, spot'st it with
    itch !
This slave to thee, his slave, was
  never poor, till rich.   240

LXXXI

Now chest th' all worshipp'd ore
  with rev'rend awe ;
  Sol's gold, and Luna's silver draw
(Should Hell have these, 'twould
  plunder'd be) to sate thy maw.

LXXXII

While gripes of famine mutiny
  within,
  And tan, like hides, the shrivell'd
    skin
O' th' poor, whose pining want can
  not thy pity win :

LXXXIII

Having their gravestones underneath
  their feet,
  Breathe out their woes to all they
    meet,
While thou to them are flintier than
  their bed, the street.

LXXXIV

Blinded with tears, with crying
  hoarse, forlorn   250
They seem to be of all, but scorn:
Death than delay (Want's bloodless
  wound) is easier borne.

LXXXV

Thy dropsy breeds consumption in
  thine heir ;
  Who thus t' himself : ' I'll ease
    your care,
Measure not grounds, but your own
  earth : Die now to spare.

LXXXVI

' What 's rak'd by wrong, and kept
  by fear, when mine,
  Shall spread, as I'm—then
    brood the shine,
Penurious wretch, till thou by empty
  fullness pine.

LXXXVII

' Thy care 's to lessen cost ; how
  slow thy pays !
  How quick receipts ! Lov'st fast-
    ing-days,   260
But 'tis to save ; thus starv'st in
  store, thee plenty slays.

LXXXVIII

' When shall I rifle every trunk and
  shelf
  Of this old mucky wretched elf,
Who turns, as chemists do, all that
  he scrapes, to pelf ? '

LXXXIX

Oh, sordid frenzy ! Anxious maze
  of care !
  Oh, gripple covetize to spare,
And dream of gold ! The miser's
  heav'n, the Indian's snare.

XC

Oppression is the bloodshot in their
  eyes ;
  Bribes blanch Gehazi till he dies :
Fool, read, this night Death may thy
  dunghill soul surprise.   270

XCI

Think not for whom thou dost thy
  soul deceive,
  And injur'd Nature so bereave ;
But still thy knotty brain with wedge-
  like anguish cleave.

XCII

Struck blind with gold, brood on
  thy rapines, till
  Thou hatch up stinging cares to
    th' fill :
The heaviest curse on this side
  Hell 's to thrive in ill.

XCIII

Go, venture for 't with sharks ; haste,
  miser old
  To th' hook, because the bait is gold:
Pawn thy soul for 't, as Judas did,
  when 's LORD he sold.

XCIV

Possessors are, as Saul, possess'd,
  who cross   280

257 I'm—shine⟩ This is one of several places where B.'s oddities leave almost any
room for conjecture. We may *suppose* that ' I'm ' is the familiar half-completed oath and
' shine ' has the slang sense of ' shiner ' = ' money.'

Heav'ns law ; gain, got by guile,
proves loss ;
Getting begets more itch ; Lust's
specious ore is dross.

XCV

Who sow to sin shall reap to judge-
ment ; train
To Hell is idolizèd gain.
Canst death, or vengeance bribe ?
If not, dread ceaseless pain.

XCVI

Why so fast posted by thy struggling
cares,
And self-slaying fraud, with all
their snares ?
Stay, view thyself ; Destruction her
crack'd glass prepares.

XCVII

His pursy conscience opens now.
' I've run
On rocks ' (he howls) ' too late to
shun,   290
Lost use, and principal ! Gold, I'm
by thee undone ! '

XCVIII

If, to exhort be not too late, attend
The wholesome counsel of a friend,

Renounce thy idol, and prevent thy
wretched end.

XCIX

Sound for Faith's bottom with Hope's
anch'ring cord ;
Repent, restore, large alms afford,
The dismal fraught of sinking sins
cast overboard.

C

He who returns to 's avarice left, his
sore
Grows desp'rate, deadlier than
before,
His hopes of Heav'n much less, his
fears of Hell much more.   300

Oceani Monstrum natat infrænabile,
Lingua ;
Naves sæpè pias hæc Echeneis
habet ;
Cui paro Naumachiam, Freta con-
turbata pererrans,
Sit Remoque meo, Lis, Remoræ-
que tuæ.

SPES REBUS AFFIXA FUGACIBUS,
UNO
FRANGITUR AFFLATU.

THE VANITY OF THE WORLD

Canto XI.   The Disincantation

THE ARGUMENT

Crispulus hic, nulli Nugarum Laude secundus,
Cui Mens Lucis inops, Stulta Ruina Domûs ;
Qui Cereri, Bromioque litat, Luxuque liquescit;
Huic ne putrescat, pro Sale Vita datur.

Volupto, crown'd with bliss of fools, is bent
To wine, feasts, gauds, loose merriment ;
Runs on in Lust's career, till Grace stops with ' Repent.'

STANZA I

O headless, heady age ! O giddy toys !
As humble cots yield quiet joys ;
So prouder palaces are drums of
restless noise.

II

'Twas in the blooming verdure of the
year,
When through the twins Sol's
course did steer,

That a spruce gallant did, on sum-
mons, straight appear.

III

Glitt'ring in brav'ry, like the Knight
o' th' Sun ;
Whose nags in Hyde-park races run
This ev'n. 'Tis sure <u>Volupto, old
Avaro's son.</u>

IV

Hot shows the day, by th' dust upon
his head,   10
And all his clothes so loosely
spread,
He's so untruss'd, as if it were not
long to bed :

V

His hands keep time to th' tune of 's
feet, his pace
Is dancèd measures, and 'tis
grace
Enough, o'er 's shoulder to afford
a quarter-face.

VI

Act, 'bove French monkeys, anti-
masks he might
Before the apes (spectators' right)
Such dops, shrugs, puppet-plays show
best by candle-light.

VII

How mimic hum'rous garbs in
various kind
Do chequer whimsies in the
mind !   20
As diff'ring flow'rs on Peru's Wonder
gard'ners find.

VIII

Hast thou black patches too ? for
shame, forbear ;
Smooth chins should not have
spots, but hair :
But thou art modish, and canst
vapour, drink, and swear.

IX

How blazing tapers waste Life's
blink away
In socket of their mould'ring clay !
How powder'd curls do sin-polluted
dust bewray !

X

As Prudence fram'd Art to be
Nature's ape ;
So Pride forms Nature to Art's
shape :
Corrupted wine is worst that's
press'd from richest grape.   30

XI

Wilt Reason's sense dissolve in
senseless wine ?
And sing, while Youth's frail gem
does shine,
' Come, Laughter, stretch our spleen ;
come sack in crystal shrine !

XII

'First, wine shall set, next shall
a wanton dame
Our blood on fire, then quench
our flame.'
But, brute, Repentance shall, or
Hell thy wildfire tame.

XIII

Now, with the gallon ere thou try'st
a fall,
Think o' th' handwriting on the
wall :
If Bacchus th' inturn gets, down
Conscience goes and All.

XIV

Shouldst thou but once the swinish
drunkard view,   40
Presented in a mirror true,
Quite sous'd in tavern juice; in him,
thyself thou'dst rue.

XV

A nobler birth, with an ignoble
breast,
Rich corpse without a mind's
a beast :
He's raz'd from Honour's stem, who,
Riot, is thy guest ;

XVI

Thy guests swoln dropsies, and dull
surfeits are:
The gluttons' teeth their graves
prepare ;
They're sick in health, and living
dead, whose maw's their care.

18 dops] Low bows or courtesies.

XVII

Go, corm'rants, go, with your luxu-
  rious flock,
  Rap'd from three elements; we
    mock   50
Your musky jelly, pheasant, candid
  apricock.

XVIII

To Arabs, that they send their Phœ-
  nix write;
  In 's spice nest be cook'd it might:
Far fetch'd, dear bought, best suits
  the Apician appetite.

XIX

Go, with thy stags embalm'd, en-
  tomb'd in paste;
  On tenants' sweat feeds rampant
    waste:
We prize 'bove wild intemp'rance a
  Carthusian fast.

XX

Excess enhanceth rates: thou, on
  this score,
  Grind'st 'twixt thy teeth the
    starving poor,
Who beg dry crumbs, which they
  with tears would moisten o'er. 60

XXI

Laz'rus, thy skin 's Death's sheet,
  'twixt that and bone
  There's no parenthesis! be-
    moan,
Dives, CHRIST'S members now, or
  thou shalt ever groan.

XXII

Prance, pamper'd stallions, to the
  grave y' are driv'n:
  Nought satisfies the soul but
    Heav'n,
Th' art empty, World, from morn,
  through noon to doting ev'n.

XXIII

In twice-dyed Tyrian purple thou
  dost nest,

Restless, with heaving fumes op-
  prest,
Which cause tumultuous dreams,
  foes to indulgent rest.

XXIV

From hence the Spark (what pity
  'tis!) is ill,   70
  Grown crop-sick. Post for phy-
    sic's skill;
Phlebotomize he must, and take the
  vomit pill.

XXV

Doctor, the cause of this distemper
  state us.
  ' His cachexy results from flatus
Hypocondrunkicus ex crapulâ crea-
  tus.'

XXVI

School him, whose Heav'n is sense,
  whose reason dim;
  Who wastes his time, as Time
    wastes him:
Give o'er his soul, Divine; Tailor,
  make 's body trim.

XXVII

Now, sheath'd in rustling silks, new
  suits display;
  Thy Clothes outworth thee: wise
    men say,   80
Hedge-creeping glow-worms never
  mount to starry ray.

XXVIII

Yet, who 's born under Jupiter shall
  move
  I' th' sphere of Honour, Riches,
    Love;
Say wizards. Under Jove w' are all
  born, none above.

XXIX

Still to be pounc'd, perfum'd, still
  quaintly drest,
  Still to be guarded to a feast
By fawning looks, and squinting
  hearts, like an arrest.

51 candid] *sic* in orig.
53 spice] The metre wants 'spicy.'
75 Hypocondrunkicus] See Introd. Some timid person has altered this tremendous
coinage where it appears in the *Summary of Wisdom* (*v. inf.*), to *hypocondriacus* in the
B. M. copy.

XXX

Still to have toting waits unseal
    thine eyes,
  In bed, at board, when sit, when
    rise :
Such, Card'nal-like, their Paris prize
  'bove Paradise.   90

XXXI

Know, worldlings, that Prosperity 's
    a gin,
  If wantoniz'd, breeds storms
    within :
To torture turns the metamorphosis
  of sin.

XXXII

Pomp its own burthen is, whose
    slippery state
  Oft headlong, by too rash debate,
Tumbles for value of a straw, pulls
  on its fate.

XXXIII

His heart-blood seethes ; that blood
    sends up in heat
  Fierce spirits ; those, i' th' eye,
    their seat,
Fires kindle ; fiery eyes, like comets,
  ruin threat.

XXXIV

Fierce Balaam, hold thy hand, and
    smite no ass   100
  But him i' th' saddle ; he, alas !
Wounds through her sides himself :
  wrath through the soul doth pass.

XXXV

Duels for blood, like Moloch's idol,
    gape.
  Thou, turn'd a swine out of an ape,
First put'st on peacock's pride, at
  last the tiger's shape.

XXXVI

They 're gross, not great, who serve
    wild laws of blood ;
  Such, only great, who dare be
    good :
Grace buoys up Honour, which,
  without it, sticks in mud.

XXXVII

Make thorough search : as hard to
  find thy cure,

As circle's puzzling quadrature, 110
Or, next way by North Sea to sail to
  China sure.

XXXVIII

Lo, idle sloth in lap of Sodom plac'd.
  'Here lies he '—did occasions
    waste,
Invaluable now, irreparable past.

XXXIX

Go, wanton with the wind : misus'd
    hours have
  A life, no other than the grave :
Most, for life's circumstance, the
  cause of living waive.

XL

The privy council of the glorious
    TRINE
  Did in creating man combine ;
Angels look'd on, and wonder'd at
  the soul divine !   120

XLI

Which storehouse of three living
    Natures is,
  Doth the vast world epitomize,
Of whom, ev'n all we see 's but a
  periphrasis !

XLII

Now, to what end can we conceive
    man's frame,
  Save to the glory of GOD's name,
And His eternal bliss, included in the
  same.

XLIII

Fools, living die ; saints, dying live :
    seeds thrive
  When earth'd ; who die to sin
    survive ;
So, to come richer up, pearl-fishers
  deeper dive.

XLIV

Now 's courtesan appears, who blows
    Love's fire,   130
  Her prattling eyes speak vain
    desire ;
To catch this art-fair fly the follow-
  ing trouts aspire.

XLV

The gamesome fly that round the
  candle plays,

88 toting] 'Observing,' 'watching carefully.'   Cf. Langland, *P. P.* (B text), xvi. 22.

Is scorch'd to death i' th' courted
　　blaze :
Thus is the amourist destroy'd by
　　lustful gaze.
XLVI
This dame of pleasure, does, to seem
　　more bright,
　　Lattice her day with bars of night;
Spots this fair sorceress cloud, more
　　to enforce delight.
XLVII
This Helen, who does Beauty counter-
　　feit,
　　And on her face black Patches set
(Like tickets on the door) shows that
　　she may be let.　　　　141
XLVIII
She'd coach affection on her cheek :
　　but why
　　Wou'd Cupid's horses climb so
　　high
Over her alpine nose, t' o'erthrow
　　it in her eye?
XLIX
Truth's apes, beware ; such wheels
　　your earth do wear ;
　　Horses with rugged hoofs will tear;
Who living's coach'd with pride, shall
　　dying fall with fear.
L
(But, noble ladies, virgins chaste, as
　　fair ;
　　Sweet modest sex, that virtuous are,
Ye first, my honour ; my respect, ye
　　second, share.　　　　150
LI
Angelic forms, far be it to perplex,
　　Or cast aspersion on your sex :
Loose art in those, your native beam-
　　ing lustre decks.
LII
So, have I seen the limner's hand
　　design
　　A ruder piece, near one Divine,
With this coarse face, to make that
　　other beauty shine.)

LIII
Her eyes spread nets, her lips baits,
　　and her arms
　　Enthralling chains : Sense hugs the
　　charms
Of Idleness and Pride, while Reason's
　　free from harms.
LIV
Tempestuous whirlwinds revel in the
　　air　　　　160
　　Of her feign'd sighs : her smile's
　　a snare,
Which she as slyly sets, as subtly does
　　prepare.
LV
Scarce is the toy at noon to th' girdle
　　drest ;
　　Nine pedlars need each morn be
　　prest
To launch her forth : a ship as soon
　　is rigg'd to th' West.
LVI
At length she's built up with ac-
　　coutred grace ;
　　The spark's inflam'd with her set
　　face,
Her glancing eye, her lisping lip, her
　　mincing pace.
LVII
On those, his optic faculties do play,
　　Like frisking motes in sunny day,
Like gaudy nothings in the Trigon
　　glass that ray.　　　　171
LVIII
On her, profusely now he spends his
　　ore ;
　　Scarce the Triumvir lavish'd more
When he did costly treat his stately
　　Memphian whore.
LIX
Thou, inconsid'rate flash, spend'st
　　precious days
　　In dances, banquets, courtisms,
　　plays,
To gain the shade of joy, which,
　　soon as gain'd, decays.

141 and 195] See note below for the illustration of this.
171 Trigon] I confess myself puzzled as to which of the various senses of this word
—'game of ball,' 'harp,' 'triangle,' &c.—applies here.
176 courtisms] 'Ceremonies of courtship' as above, p. 337.

LX

Which, barely tasted makes thee
 long the more;
 Enjoy'd, 'tis loath'd, was lov'd
 before:
Thus, nor Mirth's flood, nor ebb can
 please, nor sea, nor shore. 180

LXI

His pulse beats Cupid's march, and's
 itching vein
 Must vent loose lines, whence
 souls are slain;
Which, by augmenting lust, will but
 augment his pain.

LXII

Ah, might too forward Sin be check'd
 by Fear!
 But, what may cure that eye, that
 ear,
Which, being blind and deaf, brags
 best to see and hear!

LXIII

Thy Juno's but a cloud: she is not
 she
 Thy fond esteem makes her to be;
Her basilisk's double eyesight kills
 with viewing thee.

LXIV

She murthers poisons, thence com-
 plexion's found 190
 To murther hearts. Oh, joys
 unsound
From light-bred daughters, though
 they weigh ten thousand pound!

LXV

Tell me not, simp'ring Lais, that
 thy ray
 Can blood, turn'd ice, unfreeze,
 like May;
Whose spotted face to Virtue does
 soul-spots betray.

LXVI

Ceruse, not lilies there; thy blush-
 ing rose
 Its tincture to vermilion owes:
Curs'd be those civil wars Love's
 royalty oppose.

LXVII

Say not, a noble love to thee he
 bears;
 While's hand writes odes, his eye
 drops tears; 200
That tim'rously he's bold, burns,
 freezes, dares, and fears.

LXVIII

Nor tell me, Nymphadoro, that
 Love's throes
 For her, rob thy repast, repose:
Thou pul'st not to repent, but to
 bebrine thy woes:

LXIX

Woes, worse than waitings at the
 five men's trade;
 Worse than, when sick, through
 sloughs to wade
In stormy night, hard jolted on a
 dull tir'd jade.

LXX

Shake off these remoras would thee
 undo:
 The virtuous loveliest are. Grace
 woo;
What jeweller for glass will orient
 pearl forgo? 210

LXXI

The soul, that beauteousness of
 Grace exquires,
 And to decline By-path's desires,
Must inward bend the rays of his
 selected fires.

LXXII

Unmuffle, ye dim clouds, and dis-
 inherit
 From black usurping mists his
 spirit;
From rocks, that split vain hopes, to
 heav'nly comforts rear it.

LXXIII

B' entrench'd ere midnight larums;
 undergo
 The penance of repentant snow,
Which, melting down, will quench,
 and cleanse, as it doth flow.

190] = (again *I suppose*) 'she makes herself look killing with cosmetics compounded
of poisons, which are drugs made more murderous' or 'destroyed *as* poisons.'
205] What was this trade?

LXXIV

Repentance health is, giv'n in bitter
    pill ;   220
Best rectifier of the will ;
The joy of angels, love of GOD, the
    hate of ill.

LXXV

Action's the life of counsel ; bathe
    thy soul,
I' th' LAMB's red Laver ; in dust
    roll,
Before Despair ; Hell's serjeant
    comes, drink Sorrow's bowl.

LXXVI

Ere th' icy mantle of a wrinkled skin
Candies the bristles of thy chin,
Repent ; ere chap-fall'n door shall
    let Death's terrors in.

LXXVII

Never too late does true Repentance
    sue ;   229
Yet, late repentance seldom's true :
Who would not, when they might,
    may, when they would, it rue.

LXXVIII

For minutes of impertinent delight,
Lose not, oh, lose not Infinite !
Scorn to be vassal to base Sin, and
    hellish Spite.

LXXIX

Why dost outsin the Devil ? He
    ne'er soil'd
With lust, or glutt'ny was ; ne'er
    foil'd
With drink, ne'er in the net of sloth-
    fulness entoil'd.

LXXX

I may persuade, yet not prevail !
    Sin-charms
Bewitch him, till Wrath cries to
    arms :
Sin's first face smiles, her second
    frowns, her third alarms.   240

LXXXI

Sinners are fondly blind when they
    transgress ;
All woes are, than such blindness,
    less :
That wretch most wretched is, who
    slights his wretchedness.

LXXXII

Presumption slays her thousands !
    too late then
For to advise of danger, when
Vengeance, that dogs their steps,
    shall worry them in 's den.

LXXXIII

Gallants, should Trophies Cæsarize
    your power,
Should beauty Helenize your
    flower,
Should Mammon Danaize ye with
    his golden shower ;

LXXXIV

Yet, when Revenge shall inward
    thunders send,   250
And Sodom-storms on souls
    descend,
Salvation scorn'd, what rests but every
    tort'ring fiend !

LXXXV

That GOD refus'd, who you from
    depth of nought
To being, nay, well-being brought !
Ingrate, for talents lent, return your-
    selves sin-fraught.

LXXXVI

Bad great ones are great bad ones :
    foul defect
It is, when pow'r doth Shame
    protect ;
Such, will do what they will, but,
    what they ought, neglect.

LXXXVII

Virtue by practice to her pitch does
    soar ;
But they, who such a course give
    o'er,   260
Shall sadly wish for Time, when Time
    shall be no more.

LXXXVIII

Ye, brittle sheds of clay, resolve ye
    must
Into originary dust,
When swift-heel'd Death o'ertakes
    you. Where 's then all your
    trust ?

LXXXIX

Men in their generations live by
    turns ;

Their light soon to its socket
  burns ;
Then to converse with spirits they
  go, and none returns.

XC

Tomb-pendant scutcheons, pompous
  rags of state,
Those gorgeous bubbles but relate
The thing that was, ne'er liv'd : 'tis
  Goodness gildeth Fate. 270

XCI

Grace outlasts marble vaults ; that
  crowns expense ;
Brass is shortliv'd to innocence :
Time's greedy self shall one day
  find its preter-tense.

XCII

When heav'ns that had their deluge-
  dropsy, shall
Their burning fever have ; when all
Is one combustion ; when Sol seems
  a black burnt ball :

XCIII

When Nature's laid asleep in her
  own urn ;
When, what was drown'd at first,
  shall burn ;
Then, sinners into quenchless flames,
  Sin's mulct, shall turn !

XCIV

Ne'er shall a cooling julep such
  appease, 280
  Whom brimstone torrents without
  ease
Enrage, i'th' dungeon of dark flames,
  and burning seas !

XCV

In centre of the terrible abyss,
  Remotest from supernal bliss,
That horrid, hideous, gloomy, end-
  less dungeon is !

XCVI

Fools, who hath charm'd you ? Sue
  betimes divorce
From your vain world ; where
  power did force
A rape, there let not choice make
  marriage, which is worse.

XCVII

Man is a world, and more ; for this
  huge mass
  Shrunk, as a scroll, away shall
  pass ; 290
Whilst his pure substance is as ever-
  lasting glass.

XCVIII

The world is like the basilisk's fell
  eyes ;
  Whose first sight kills ; first seen,
  it dies :
Man, by a brave disdain, its pois'n-
  ing venom flies.

XCIX

Gay World, who thee adores, thou
  great wilt make ;
  Pearl may he quaff, and pleasures
  take
Of sense, but must descend into the
  sulph'ry lake !

C

Is Hell the upshot thou to thine
  canst lend ?
  Crawl, grovelling trifles, to your
  end ;
Vanish beneath my scorn. Go,
  World, recant, amend. 300

Provehimur Portu, Terramque relin-
  quimus illam
  Quæ natum Gremio prima rigente
  tulit.
O felix Oculus Portum visurus
  Amantis,
  Sit licet in Lacrymas naufragus
  ipse suas !

DEDIGNOR INDIGNA [1].

---

[1] Here, in orig., is the illustration referred to above—a very fine plate engraved by Hollar, representing in half-length a lady with a fan in her hands, her face and neck spotted with sign-patches as in the Latin verses *inf.* and the English *sup.* st. xlvii. In these Latin verses *Venerilla* and *Lanissa*, if not classical, are also not ugly.

In lenocitantes hujus Tempestatis Venerillas, Juvenum Scrobes, Animarum Voragines

In nova fert Animus mutatas dicere Formas
Spectra, salax quarum Mente Libido furit.
Ludicra depicti jam prodit Imago Theatri,
En hìc Scena vafris insidiosa Dolis.
Ergò mihi nunquam nisi Personata videnda es?
Si vis Personam sumere, sume tuam.
Cui loquor? Ipse tuâ deludor Imagine; Vera
Quid facies, cùm vel fallere picta potes?
Picta Genas, discincta Sinus, nudata Papillas;
Albor Cerussâ fit, Minioque Rubor. 10
Vendere si non vis Carnem, conclude Macellum;
Nec Lupa mentitâ decipe Carne Procos.
Nunc emere haud fas est, quia Quadragesima, Carnes;
Venales Mammas ergò, Lanissa, tege.
Affigis Maculas dum Signa loquacia Malis,
Mercandum Pretio Corpus adesse notas.
Quæ primam extenuat Culpam, rea sæpè secundæ est;
Sæpiùs è primâ Labe secunda venit.
Plurima compositos conservat capsa Colores;
Sic Faciem tibi, cum cætera vendis, emis. 20
Suavia viscosis renuo libare Labellis,
Ne teneat Fucus fixa Labella tuus.
Quàm levis Incessus! quàm Lumina pæta vagantur!
Verbula quàm molli Gutture fracta fluunt!
Quid me blanda tuis fallacibus obruis Hirquis?

Serpentem Gremio, Virus in Ore geris.
Non amat, hamat Amor tuus, ò Trivenefica, nostro
Non opus est Cultu, Te nimis ipsa colis.
Sidera contendas Oculi sint, Purpura Malæ,
Electrum Crines, Dens Ebur, Ora Favi. 30
Consulto Speculo geris Omnia; fallet Imago:
[1] Te nam (an jurares) sera Ruina manet.
Sed quorsum in miseras labuntur Carmina Nugas?
Præsens, est absens, pars minor illa sui.
Quid velit hæc Pictura loquens?. quem postulat Usum?
Ut suspendatur nonnè Tabella nitet?
Quid tunc è tanto restabit Amantibus Igne?
Fumus iners, tristis Fæx, inamœnus Odor.
Ne jactes igitur Formam, fucata; Megæram 39
Formosam fieri sicquoque posse reor.
Dicite, Doctores, huic quæ Complexio? Quinta.
Quis placet huic Sensus, dicite? Sextus erit.
Sub quo signo orta? Opposito sub Virginis Astro.
Edita sub caudâ, credo, Draconis erat.
Quænam illi fuerit Mens? Subdola. Lingua? dolosa.
Quæ Metamorphôsis? Prodigiosa sibi.
Naso, suam Metamorphôsin quî scribere possit,
Quotidiè Formas cùm novet ista Venus?

[2] Insceleratissimam Seculi Licentiam, cujus in melius commutandi exilis admodùm supersit Spes

Totus adeò in Maligno (mali ligno) positus est Mundus, ut vehementer hujusmodi Satyris egeat. Ubiquè nunc locorum damnosa Malorum Vitia, noxiarum instar herbarum, citissimè pullulescunt. Perjuria, Superbia, Te-

---

[1] Versus cancrinus quoad Literas [*author's note*].
[2] Above this in orig. is a map of the two hemispheres inscribed *Typus Orbis Terrarum*.

mulentia, &c. Terram sub Mole Pec-
catorum non ruere admirabile, cùm
Cœli, qui ingentia illa Corpora Solis,
Lunæ, Stellarum, præter suam Vasti-
tatem non solùm ferunt, sed circum-
ferunt, absque Ruinæ Periculo ; unicum
tamen Peccatum ferre nequiverunt, sed
statim per solidas illas Machinas, pec-
catum, cum suo Authore Lucifero, delap-
sum, etiam Terram penetrans, ad Fun-
dum Abyssi infernalis descendit.

ACTOR Homo, Cœlum Spectator, grande
Theatrum   [Dies.
  Mundus, Vita frequens Fabula, Scena
Undè ego, sublimi positus, Deliria
  Mundi   20
Defleo, dum Vitij Pondere tristè
  gemit.
Esse quid hoc dicam, perversa quod
  Omnia cerno !

Densis quàm Tenebris mergitur
  Orbis iners !
Talia tartareo crevere Piacula Seclo,
  Vix Terris Scelerum mox Modus
  ullus erit.
Luxus ovans, impurus Amor, maculosa
  Libido,
Persica Mollities, Spes levis, Ira
  gravis.
Carnificina Boni, sed Iniqui sedula
  Nutrix,
Orbis es, Illecebras nil nisi turpis
  habes.
Fraus juvat, hinc justa est, fallique &
  fallere gaudes ;   30
  Mors Jocus, Infernus Fabula, Sanna
  Polus.
Heu, Pietas ubi prisca ! Profana ò
  Tempora ! Mundi
  Fæx, Vesper, propè Nox ; ô, mora !
  CHRISTE, Veni !

---

[1] TE rapit aerio ventosa Superbia Curru ;
Siste rotas, Currus ferventes siste ;
  Loquamur.
Nunc opus est leviore Lyrâ. Tu,
  Cyprie Bubo,
Ore procax, Novitatis amans, Veneris-
  que Satelles,
Callidus incautas Philtris mollire
  Puellas,
Splendida rimaris petulanti Lumine
  Spectra,
Et Mala quæque Bonis præfers, Deliria
  Veris,   40
Frivola vaniloquo Mendacia gutture
  jactas,
Mentis inops, Ratione carens, Virtutis
  inanis,
Volveris effuso suadente Libidine Luxu,
Lauta coronatis ambis Convivia Mensis,
Sunt tibi Deliciæ, Risus, Jocularia
  Cordi,
Futilibus fatuus Garritibus Aera pulsas,
Quique ciet Nugas, Donaria summa
  reportat,
Illicitumque putas nihil ; Omne, quod
  officit, optas ;

Expetis ut fulvum Mundus vertatur in
  Aurum ;
Auritâ de Gente Midæ reor esse Ne-
  potem :   50
Stulte, tuas Vestes, Avis ut Junonia
  plumas,
Aspicis ; in Cute curandâ malè con-
  teris Ævum.
O, Genus insipidum ! sani tibi mica
  Cerebri ?
Auscultet tumido Gens implacabilis
  Ore.
Luxuries prædulce Malum, blanditur,
  & angit :
Innumeras parit ipsa Cruces, nutritque,
  Voluptas :
Vita vices morientis habet, morerisque
  superstes.
Sed, quid ago ?   Surdis cantatur
  Fabula. Fati
Vespera mox veniet ! quid inexorabilis
  hæres ?
Cuncta tenere putes ; tu percipis omnia ;
  Solùm   60
Hoc nescis, Pantων quod es insanissi-
  mus Andρων.

In strenuos hujus Seculi Compotores,
& Gulones Perditissimos [1]

QUALIS hîc Boatus? quæ Vociferatio?
Auscultemus.   Aut bibite, aut hunc

Cantharum, quantus quantus est, in
Capita impingam vestra.   Sic enim

---

61 We need not suppose that Benlowes put in the Greek for anything but metre's sake.
[1] Above these passages respectively the orig. has two little vignettes in text, one

assuefacti (à sue facti) sunt ; Qui tamen
Ipsi nondum hesternam edormiverunt
Crapulam. Heu, quàm petitis perituri
peritura ! Labantes ad Præcipitium
impellitis, & ad Infernum proruentibus,
calcar subditis ! Interim tamen vos ac-
cusat Conscientia, Testis est Memoria,
Ratio Judex, Voluptas Carcer, Timor
Tortor, Oblectamentum Tormentum !
Undè, hi vorando, bibendo, ludendo,
dormiendo, moriendo, justè oblivi-
scantur sui, qui vivendo (nisi jurando)
semper obliti sunt Dei.

TURGIDUS iste quis est ? ambas per-
    potus ad Aures,
Qui tradit rabidæ Fræna soluta
    Gulæ;
Qui plures avido Calices ingurgitat
    haustu ;   20
Cui Venus in Vinis, Ignis in Igne furit ;
Cui Venter Deus est, & lauta Culina
    Sacellum ;
Orgia cui madidi grata profana Dei ;
Cui sunt Liba Dapes, & Compotatio
    Festum ;
Et Pietas plenâ Lance litare Gulæ ;
Plurima qui spondet, perfusus Tem-
    pora Baccho ;
Omnia quæ Sociis, cras, sine fronte
    negat ;
Cujus Lingua vomit spumantia Vota
    Salutis,
Obrutus est nimio dum sine Mente
    Mero.
' Vivamus liquidi, potemus, edamus,
    ovemus ;   30
Nulla Sepultorum nascitur Uva Cavis:
Mordaces Curas solvamus Vociferando,
Sic permittamus lætiùs ire Dies :
Falle Diem, strue Serta, Scyphum rape,
    tingere Nardo ;
Si tibi Cura mei, sit tibi Cura Meri :
Prome Falerna, remitte Pavenda, pro-
    pellito Nubes :
Leviathæ Os utinàm nunc mihi
    grande foret !

Gemmatis si Musta bibam flammantia
    Poclis,
Inde frequens Naso Gemma repentè
    micet.'   39
Plurima sic olidis epotat Vina Tabernis,
Ut referat brutas sordida Vita Sues :
Immersus Vitii Barathro, Scelerisque
    Profundo,
Ebrius Errorum Nectare, Porcus
    ovat.
Immemor ipse sui, nimiùm memor ipse
    Suorum,
Carneus iste Cadus, Viva Culina
    cluat.
Nocturno reboat dum cæca Platæa
    Tumultu,
Quodvis ex animo suavè peregit
    Opus.
Una Salus tibi sit nullam potare Salu-
    tem :
Te Puer in triviis erudiisse potest.
Qui mihi Discipulus, Bibo sis, cupis
    atque doceri ;   50
Huc ades, Abdomen spernere disce
    tuum.
Pondus iners, Carnis Cumulus, Vini-
    que Culullus,
Progenies Grylli, Dux Epicurus
    haræ ;
Cœnum, non Cœlum sapis, Ingluviem-
    que saginas,
Non Mentem ; solùm pro sale Vita
    datur.
Ditia sorbebit subitò Patrimonia
    Guttur ;
Quod tua peccarunt Guttura, Vitra
    luunt.
Quæ Mare, Terra, Polus, Pisce, Alite,
    Vite ministrant,
Desidis alta Gulæ Cuncta Bara-
    thra vorant.
Effera Tempestas Cellæ, Barathrum-
    que Macelli !   60
Exanimes tumulet mortua Turba tuos!
Hoc verbo concludo, nec os tibi sub-
    lino : Nequam es :
Exitio, nisi te corrigis, Ipse tibi.

EHEU, quàm Magnificus iste jam
ægrotat miserè ! ecce, Linteola Manu
contrahit, distorto Ore & distento
Labia dispandit, anhelis Pulmonibus
difficile spirat, longum Vale Mundo
dicit, tenebrescentes Oculos circum-
volvit, & suburbia Mortis intrat. Lec-
tores, clarum hîc Speculum Fragilitatis
cernite. Gregor. Magnus Lib. 4. Cap.
38. Dialogorum, de Chrysorio Ro-
mano tradit Historiam, de quo, an
Divitiis, seu Vitiis magis abundaverit,

representing a Caroline dandy in full dress standing ostentatiously, and the other the
same person sitting drinking—and drunken.

incertum fuit. Cum, quasi expirans, anxiaretur, apparuere illi teterrimi, Dæmones, ipsum certatim prensantes, trahereque ad Inferna annixi; Ille, Horrore tremuit, seque super Lectum huc atque illuc vertere miseris cœpit Modis. Nec dubitaret Quisquam Spiritus sibi apparuisse, qui probè illius Gestus, & Lamenta consideraret. Postremò, ipse, cùm jam Amicorum Auxilio desperasset, ad Hostes conversus, Inducias, oro, Inducias, inquit, Inducias, vel tantùm usque ad mane! cui, Dæmones; Stulte, hac nocte eripietur tibi Anima. Dum hoc poscendo ingeminat, Animam exhalavit! Væ vobis miseris, qui in ipsis Voluptatum Blandimentis, sævis Pauperum Oppressionibus, & iniquis Præliandi Ardoribus subitò auferimini! 95

INSTARE, heu, summum, Mens, tibi crede Diem,
Actus Fabellæ jam tibi quintus adest,
Namque stat ad Mortis Limina Vita tremens;
Quid modò, dum Muris imminet Hostis, agas? 99
Te rapiet subitò Mors inopina Gradu!
An non supremi Judicis Ora times?
Mente soporatâ Cuncta quieta fluunt,
Exagitat sævis evigilante Minis!
Stat vinctum rigido sons Adamante jecur,
Undique constrictum Crimine, Lege, Nece!
Stare tamen nullo mens queat ægra Loco!
Afflictum Pectus quis tolerare potest!
Me Tremor, Impietas, Flagra, Gehenna rotant!
Totus in Aspectu sum rea Massa Dei!
Heu, quàm terribilis Sontibus Ultor adest! 110
Qui Flagellorum millia mille parat!
Quis dabit hisce Modum, quêis Modus omnis abest!
Supplicium Æternum! Dirus ut ille Sonus!
Nullis Inferni Flamma domatur aquis!
Æstus at infusæ Gurgite crescit Aquæ!
Nunc, Mundi quid Honos, Gaza, Jocusque, valent!
Vos, speciem fumi, quicquid habetis, habet;
Perfidiosa sequi Ludicra Mundus amat;
Tristia sub placido melle Venena latent;
Quo magis arrident, sunt metuenda magis; 120

Turgida ventoso Pectora Folle replent.
Inter Acidalias, ceu Sybarita, Rosas
Crevi, Præda feris discrutianda Rogis!
Prædonum Paphiâ mitior Ira face;
Cultorem perdis; qui tibi vivit, obit;
Arbore seu Chavæ, prima Venena necis,
Arbore sic CHRISTI Vita secunda fluit.
Hac, hac sit nostrâ Meta terenda rotâ!
Jam nunc Justorum Fata subire velim!
Pro Te, CHRISTE, pati, est vincere, Vita mori: 130
Te peto dum superest Halitus; Oro, fave.
Hanc, DEUS, ex magno mittis Amore Crucem:
Sum miser, ah, misero fer miseratus Opem!
Nunc opus est Precibus, nunc Ope, CHRISTE, tuâ!
Unus Opem, Vulnus qui dedit, Ille ferat!
Pœnitet admissi Criminis; oro DEUS, Sanguinis inspergat, Gutta vel una tui!
Sperem, vix ullam Spes ubi cernat Opem!
Singula baptizem Corporis Acta mei!
Sint Lachrymæ Mentis Gaudia sola meæ! 140
Quæ suaves aliquid, Nectaris instar, habent;
Tristia qui spargit, Gaudia abindè metet;
Lætitiæ Segetem flebilis Unda parit:
Langueo, sola sones Lachryma! Lingua sile.

HÆC, LECTOR, SICCIS QUÌ TUEARE GENIS!

Mundi Contemptus

DELICIÆ, Luxus, laqueata Palatia, Gemmæ,
Incautos, veluti blanda Venena, necant ;
In Trabea Livor, Gemmâ Timor, Ira sub Auro ;
Bullatum his Pectus plurima Pestis agit.
Est Honor umbra Rei. Quid Honoris Spes ? minus umbrâ ;
Umbram finge umbræ, spes id Honoris erit ;
Dum placet, illudit ; dum splendet, fallit ; amœnam
Sic referens bullam, frangitur illa micans :
Aurea pacatam turbant Laquearia Mentem,
Et Vigiles Noctes Purpura sæpè trahit ;   10

Oblongas videt ire vigil sua Tædia Noctes,
Præque ipsis longas Noctibus ire Dies :
Sæpè Equitem excussit, fractâ Cervice Sedentis,
Ad Titulos properans Ambitionis Equus :
Illis, sceptrigeri quos lactat Gloria Mundi
Auratis Tectis, fit peregrina Salus.
Divitias Avidus per aperta Pericula Ponti,
Retia quæ Mentis, concumulare studet.
Hæc, mihi ne noceant cauto, cretata facessat   19
Ambitio, & fulvi sordida Cura Luti.
Felix qui streperi Ludibria rideat Orbis,
Aspernans Ævi luxuriantis Opes.

THE SWEETNESS OF RETIREMENT

OR THE HAPPINESS OF A PRIVATE LIFE

Canto XII.   The Segregation

ARGUMENT

TU, mihi Thema, Quies Animæ, sanctusque Recessus ;
Rores dum saturant me, Deus alme, tui.
Vera Quies, Paucos nosti, notissima Paucis ;
Dum fugio Plures, te peto, vera Quies.
Carmina Secessum ? Potiùs Devotio quærit :
Sic quadrant Modulis Pectora sancta suis.
Turbat Apollineas clamosa Molestia Musas ;
Christicolæ Modulos sed magìs illa gravat.
Sit procul Urbs, prope Vota mihi ;
mihi reddar, & intùs
Plena Fide perstet Mens mea, plena Deo !   10
Hoc Nemus est Templum, patuli Laquearia Rami ;
Fit sacræ Truncus quisque Columna Domûs :
Pervia Sylva patens est Porta, Cacumina Pinnæ ;
Baptismi Pignus Rivulus omnis habet :

Dat Mensam Collis sacram mihi Cespite tectus ;
Pectoris Ara Fides, Zelus Amorque focus.
Si quis Baptistes in Eremo prædicet, Ecce
Pulpita, in arboreâ Sede locata, patent.
Hìc licet elatâ dare Verba precantia Voce ;
Et sine Teste, Deo nec nisi Teste, loqui.   20
Ipsa monent tremulas quatientia Flamina frondes,
Per nos fundendas Corde tremente Preces.
Antevolansque cavo Suspiria nostra Susurro,
Dum gemit Aura levis, Tu geme, Cultor, ait.
Voce Deum celebro ; Concordes sponte Choristæ,
Sunt Præcentores, dum modulantur, Aves.
Amen subijcio ; dat Amen, quasi Clericus, Echo.
Sylva placet, Luxus Desidiose, Vale.

THE ARGUMENT

True Bliss! Thou know'st but few, to few art known;
While we shun many, thee alone
We court, and all enjoy in thee, when all are gone.

STANZA I

WASTE not another word on fools; forsake
　What grates the ear, pure notions take;
Know, that the smoothest hones the sharpest razors make.

II

Ill suits it with a russet life, to write
　Court-tissue: swains, by threshold's sight,
Observe, as well as lords by clocks of gold, Time's flight.

III

Whose crystal shrines, like oysters, gape each hour,
　Discov'ring Time by figures' pow'r:
That is the nobler watch, foreshows the threat'ning show'r.

IV

While cumb'rous gain does various cares obtrude, 10
　The richer mind courts solitude,
And does guile (subtle to beguile itself) exclude.

V

More than high greatness humble goodness draws;
　Elm rafters, mantled o'er with straws,
Outbless Escurial tow'rs that seem Heav'n's cupolas.

VI

Each city-shop's a trap; each toy, a yoke;
　What wise man willingly would choke
Himself in thicker clouds of griping care, than smoke?

VII

Who would not fly that broil, whence Bliss is flown;

Where, in Time's dregs, Religion's grown 20
　From best, to all (flow tears of blood!), from all, to none.

VIII

LORD, guide Thy Church, which interests impair;
　Who, without knowledge, factious are,
They little mind the flock, so they the fleece may share.

IX

Why climb'd they else the pulpit, as Lot's brother,
　With fire in one hand, knife i' th' other?
'Twas vip'rous Nero slew his own indulgent mother.

X

As Peace Heav'n's blessing; so is War His rod,
　Man-hunting beast, a scourge from GOD,
Which doth unhinge the world; fierce grapes in Wrath's press trod. 30

XI

Let me, in Grief's prerogative, be bold
　To question such, as dare to hold
That they the SHEPHERD lov'd, when they forsook the fold.

XII

Such scramblers at the shearing feasts, I shun;
　Forgetting, and forgotten, run
To fraudless swains. I have a Friend compliant won;

XIII

By his example may my life be penn'd,
　May he read, like himself, his friend:

21 This is a puzzling line. One would expect 'From best to all . . . to best to none,' or 'From best to worst . . . from all to none.' Cf. *Summary* version *inf*.

Souls in conjunction should, like
    stars, kind influence send.

XIV

Us Sympathy, the mind's true priest,
    does join ;   40
  'Tis Grace makes social love
    divine ;
Tun'd octaves unisons are, duos in
    one combine.

XV

When two enweav'd are in one high
    desire,
  They feel, like angels, mutual fire;
Flames intellective live, material
    flames expire.

XVI

Vain World, thy friends are thieves
    of Time ; twice they
  Are robb'd ; for, Time's self steals
    away,
Leaving a dull December for a
    sportive May.

XVII

Fools' chat is built on sand ; but
    blest who hives
  Discourse, that on Heav'n's sweet-
    ness lives,   50
Such, as to raise the fire to high-born
    Virtue strives.

XVIII

For birds of Paradise the proper
    fare
  Is purest vapour of the air;
Souls nourish'd from the influ'nce
    of GOD'S SPIRIT are.

XIX

Dew fattens earth, the earth yields
    plants, and then
  The plants feed beasts, the beasts
    feed men ;
Man on His WORD should feed, who
    gave him origin.

XX

From public roads, to private joy 's
    our flight ;
  To view GOD'S love, we leave
    man's sight ;
Rich in the purchase of a Friend,
    who gilds delight.   60

XXI

Thus go we, like the heroes of old
    Greece,
  In quest of more than golden
    fleece,
Retreating to sweet shades, our shat-
    ter'd thoughts we piece.

XXII

So, when the Sun, commander of
    the day,
  Muffles with clouds his glorious
    ray,
He clearer afterwards doth his bright
    face display.

XXIII

Kings, too much seen, grow mean.
    Renown does dawn
  From cots, unsightly hang'd, and
    drawn
With spider-woven arras, and their
    cobweb-lawn.

XXIV

Victorious Charles the Fifth, who
    had acquir'd   70
  Fame, wealth, and what could be
    desir'd
By greatest emperors, left all, to live
    retir'd.

XXV

That sea-dividing Prince, whose
    sceptred rod
  Wrought freedom to the Church
    of GOD,
Made in the Mount of Horeb forty
    days' abode.

XXVI

In wilderness the Baptist shin'd more
    clear,
  In Life's night starry souls appear:
They who themselves eclipse, are to
    Heav'n's court more dear.

XXVII

But, now what need we cite examples
    more,   79
  This by our SAVIOUR heretofore
Was practis'd, who, whole nights
    retir'd, did GOD implore.

XXVIII

Examples are best precepts. Sweet
    Secess,

The nurse to inbred Happiness,
How dost thou intellects with fuller
knowledge bless !

XXIX

Waft us, all-guiding Pow'r, from wild
resort,
By Cape of Hope, to Virtue's
Port,
Where Conscience, that strong cham-
pion, safely guards the fort.

XXX

Here, Liberty, ev'n from suspicion
free,
Does terminate our fears ; by
Thee
We conquer lusts : each sense wears
Reason's livery.   90

XXXI

With Thee, like cloister'd snails, is
better state,
Than to be lions in a grate :
The world hers, coop'd like Bajazet,
does captivate.

XXXII

But, here (the type of ever-smiling
joys,
Without disturbing fears, or noise),
We bright-ey'd Faith, with quick-eyed
Art, in Truth's scale poise.

XXXIII

Religious Mary's leisure we above
Encumber'd Martha's cares ap-
prove ;
Uncloister'd, we this course beyond
Court's splendour love.

XXXIV

Seated in safe repose (when circling
Earth   100
Suffers by rage of war, and dearth),
Secure from plagues and angry seas,
we manage mirth.

XXXV

The low-built fortune harbours Peace,
when as
Ambitious high-roof'd Babels pass
Through storms ; content with
thankfulness each blessing has.

XXXVI

So fragrant vi'lets, blushing straw-
berries,

(448)

Close-shrouded lurk from lofty
eyes,
The emblem of sweet bliss, which
low and hidden lies.

XXXVII

No maskèd fraud, no tempest of
black woes,
No flaunting pride, no rage of
foes,   110
Bends hitherward, but soon is laid,
or overblows.

XXXVIII

We rule our conquer'd selves ; what
need we more ?
To gadding Sense we shut the
door ;
Rich in our mind alone.   Who wants
himself, is poor.

XXXIX

Slander is stingless, Envy toothless
here ;
The russet is well lin'd we wear ;
Let cits make chains the ensigns of
their pomp appear.

XL

Faith link'd with Truth, and Love
with Quiet too,
O'er pleasant lawns securely go ;
The Golden Age, like Jordan's
stream, does here reflow.   120

XLI

For fields of combat, fields of corn
are here,
For trooping ranks, tree-ranks
appear ;
War steels the heart, but here we
melt heart, eye, and ear.

XLII

Oh, might a sacred Muse Earth's
frenzy calm !
On that we'd pour such suppling
balm,
As might vain trophies turn to an
unfading palm.

XLIII

Then should each He, who wears
the face of man,
Discern their emptiness, and span
The vulgar's trivial idols, and their
follies scan.

XLIV

Though in rough shells our bodies
  kernell'd are,   130
  Our roof is neat, and sweet our
  fare,
Banish'd are noisome vapours to the
  pent-up air.

XLV

No subtle poison in our cup we fear,
  Goblets of gold such horrors bear;
No palace-Furies haunt, O rich
  Content! thy cheer.

XLVI

How great are those who use, like
  gold, their clay;
  And who like clay, gold, great are
  they;
To grandeur, slighted titles are the
  ready way.

XLVII

Courts' amplest shine nor adds, nor
  takes from minds
  That pierce the world, true merit
  binds   140
Bright souls unto it, whilst a fog th'
  ignoble blinds.

XLVIII

Humble, not slav'd; without dis-
  comfort sad;
  Tim'rous, without despair; and
  glad,
Without wild freaks, we are. The
  world's or fool, or mad.

XLIX

From Taurus when Sol's influence
  descends,
  And Earth with verdant robe be-
  friends,
And richer showers, than fell on
  Danae's lap, dispends;

L

When early Phosphor lights from
  eastern bed
  The grey-eyed morn, with blushes
  red;
When opal colours prank the orient
  tulip's head: 150

LI

Then walk we forth, where twinkling
  spangles shew,
  Entinselling like stars the dew,
Where buds, like pearls, and where
  we leaves, like em'ralds, view:

LII

Birds by grovets in feather'd gar-
  ments sing
  New ditties to the non-ag'd
  spring;
Oh, how those traceless minstrels
  cheer up everything!

LIII

To hear quaint nightingales, the
  lutes o' th' wood,
  And turtle-doves, by their mates
  woo'd,
And smelling violet sweets, how do
  these cheer the blood!

LIV

While teeming Earth flower'd satin
  wears, embost   160
  With trees, with bushes shagg'd,
  with most
Clear riv'lets edg'd, by rocking winds
  each gently tost;

LV

The branching standards of the
  chirping grove,
  With rustling boughs, and streams
  that move
In murm'ring rage, seem Nature's
  consort, tun'd by Love.

LVI

We to their hoarse laments lend
  list'ning ears;
  And sympathize with them in tears,
Sadly rememb'ring British Sion's
  acted fears!

LVII

Then, our sad hearts are prick'd,
  whence spring forth cries;
  From those, drain'd through the
  bruis'd soul, rise   170
Faith-fumes, by Heav'n's fire drawn,
  which drop through melting
  eyes!

154 grovets] Rare.   162 rocking winds] Had Benlowes read Milton?
165 Rage] *Sic in orig.* but in my copy altered to 'base' = 'bass' which is probably right.

(449)

LVIII

'Cause hungry swords devour'd man's
flesh, like food,
And thirsty spears were drunk
with blood :
LORD, how Thy Spouse turns mum-
mied earth ! her gore a flood !

LIX

Edge-hill with bones look'd white,
with blood look'd red,
Maz'd at the number of the dead :
A theme for tears in unborn eyes to
be still shed !

LX

How many bound with iron, who
did 'scape
The steel ! and Death commits
a rape
On them in jails, who her defied in
warlike shape !   180

LXI

Cross-biasness to grace our ruin
spinn'd !
Harrow'd with woes, be Heav'n
our friend !
Sodom 'gainst Nature, we 'gainst
-    light of Truth have sinn'd !

LXII

This draws eye-tribute from Com-
punction's den ;
Grace, guard Thy prostrate sup-
pliant then,
Who am the chief of sinners, and
the worst of men !

LXIII

My guilt before Thy Mercy-seat I
lay,
For His sake save me, who gave
way
To die for sinners !   Ah, Sin kills
Him every day !

LXIV

Sin ne'er departs, till humbled in
deep fears,   190
Embalm'd in pray'rs, and drown'd
in tears,
The fragrant Araby breathes no per-
fume like theirs.

LXV

More fruitful those, unwitnessèd,
appear ;
Gems are too cheap for every
tear :
Deep Sorrow from itself doth its high
comfort rear.

LXVI

Salt tears, the pious convert's
sweetest sport,
To hopeful joys the ent'ring port,
Ye waft blest mariners to Sion's
glorious court.

LXVII

But whither stray'st thou, Grief ?
Pearl'd dew arrays
As yet the virgin-meads, whose
gays   200
Unbarb'd, perk up to prank the
curlèd stream that plays.

LXVIII

By rushy-fringèd banks with purling
rill,
Meand'ring underneath the hill :
Thus, stream-like, glides our life to
Death's broad ocean still.

LXIX

The pleasant grove triumphs with
blooming May,
While Melancholy scuds away ;
The painted quire on motley banks
sweet notes display.

LXX

Earth's flow'r-wov'n damask doth us
gently woo,
On her embroider'd mantle to
Repose, where various gems, like
constellations, shew.   210

LXXI

Ourselves here steal we from our-
selves, by qualms
Of pleasure, rais'd from new-
coin'd Psalms,
When skies are blue, earth green,
and meadows flow with balms.

LXXII

We there, on grassy tufted tapes-
tries,

199 whither] Orig. 'whether.'

In guiltless shades, by full-hair'd
trees,
Leaning unpillow'd heads, view
Nature's ants, and bees.

LXXIII

Justly admiring more those agile ants,
Than castle-bearing elephants ;
Where industry, epitomiz'd, no
vigour wants.

LXXIV

More than at tusks of boars we
wonder at   220
This moth's strange teeth ! Legs
of this gnat
Pass large-limb'd gryphons; then, on
bees we musing sat ;

LXXV

How colonies, Realm's hope, they
breed ; proclaim
Their king ; how nectar-courts
they frame ;
How they in waxen cells record
their prince's fame :

LXXVI

How kings amidst their bands in
armour shine ;
And great souls in small breasts
confine ;
How under strictest laws they keep
up discipline ;

LXXVII

How all agree, while their king lives,
in one ;
But dead, the public Faith's o'er-
thrown,   230
Their State becomes a spoil, which
was so plenteous grown.

LXXVIII

Abstruser depths ! here Aristotle's
eye
(That Ipse of philosophy,
Nature's professor) purblind was, to
search so high.

LXXIX

Thinking, which some deem idle-
ness, to me
It seems life's Heav'n on earth to
be ;

By observation GOD is seen in all we
see.

LXXX

Our books are Heav'n above us, air
and sea
Around, earth under ; Faith's our
stay,
And Grace our guide, the Word our
light, and CHRIST our way. 240

LXXXI

Friend, view that rock, and think
from rock's green Wound
How thirst-expelling streams did
bound :
View streams, and think how Jordan
did become dry ground.

LXXXII

View Seas, and think how waves,
like walls of glass,
Stood fix'd, while Hebrew troops
did pass ;
But clos'd the Pharian host in one
confusèd mass.

LXXXIII

These flow'rs, we see to-day, like
Beauty, brave,
At ev'n will be shut up, and have
Next week their death, then buried
soon in stalks, their grave.

LXXXIV

Beauty's a flow'r, Fame puff, high
State a gaze,   250
Pleasure a dance, and Gold a
blaze,
Greatness a load : these soon are
lost in Time's short maze !

LXXXV

As solemn statesmen slight mere
childish toil,
Framing card-structures : angels
smile,
And pity so, when life straight flits,
man's tearing broil.

LXXXVI

Search Empire's dawn, unwind
Time's ball again,
Unreel through ages its snarl'd
skein ;

222 sat] An unlucky word, in more than tense.

(451)

Run back, like Sol on Ahaz' dial ;
  see ' All 's vain.'

LXXXVII

This did I from THEOPHILA descry
  (Not her fair-feather'd speech
    could fly   260
To ground, but my ear's pitfall
  caught it instantly ;

LXXXVIII

Though her informing voice be
  parted hence,
Tides of impressive notions thence
Flow, soft as showers on balm, and
  sweet as frankincense).

LXXXIX

The conqueror who wades in blood
  for pow'r,
Cannot ensure th' ensuing hour ;
Death soon may his ovation's
  sweetest nectar sour.

XC

All 's vain. Th' Assyrian lion, Per-
  sian bear,
  Greek leopard, Roman eagle,
    where ?
Where is fam'd Troy, that did so
  proudly domineer ?   270

XCI

Troy 's gone, yet Simois stays. Oh,
  Fortune's play !
  That which was fix'd is fled away,
And only what was ever-flitting still
  does stay !

XCII

Vast pyramids uprear'd t' inter the
  dead,
  Themselves, like men, are sepul-
    chred ;
Ambitious obelisks, ostents of pride,
  dust wed.

XCIII

Heav'n sees the crumbling fabric of
  Earth's ball,
  That dust is man's original ;
To Him all nature is as wither'd
  leaves that fall :

XCIV

Terrestrials transient are.   Kings
  fight for clods ;   280

Heav'n's Heir is mightier Prince,
  by odds,
Ev'n all is his, and he is CHRIST's,
  and CHRIST is GOD's.

XCV

Thoughts, dwell on this.   Let 's be
  our own death's-head.
  The glorious Martyr lives, though
    dead,
Sweet rose, in His own fadeless
  leaves envelopèd :

XCVI

Heav'n was His watch, whose starry
  circles wind
  All ages up ; the hand that sign'd
Those figures, guides them ; World,
  thy clocks are false and blind.

XCVII

Time in Eternity's immense book is
  But as a short parenthesis ;   200
Man's life, a point ; GOD's day is
  never-setting bliss.

XCVIII

Could man sum up all times, so, as
  if there
  A moment not remaining were ;
Yet all those close-throng'd figures
  seem but ciphers here.

XCIX

Could calculators multiply Time's
  glass
  To myriads more of years ; alas,
Those sands, to this duration, as a
  minute pass.

C

Such mental buds we from each
  object take,
  And, for CHRIST's Spouse, of
    them we make
Spiritual wreaths, nor do we her
  own words forsake.   300

CI

' Arise, O North, and thou, O South-
  wind, blow ;
  Let scent of flow'rs, and spices flow,
That the BELOVED may into His
  Garden go.'

CII

Whose beauty flow'rs, whose height
  made lofty trees,

Whose permanence made Time, and these
Pay tribute by returns to Him, as springs to seas.

CIII

This steals our soul from her thick loom, t' aspire
To canzons, tin'd with enthean fire ;
Taking high wing to soar up to the angel-quire.

CIV

By suchlike speculations would we sty   310
To th' Sun of Righteousness ! though I
A star am less than least of all the galaxy.

CV

The burden to each hymn is this. 'Thy ways,
LORD, are inscrutable ! All days,
All tongues, are few, are weak, to sound Thy endless Praise !'

CVI

Oh, that a Voice more audible, and high'r
Than that shrill trump, when all 's on fire,
Might all men's hearts and tongues with Thy renown inspire !

CVII

Nature, bless GOD, His benefits be sung,
While that an ear can hear a tongue ;   320
Commerce with Him is th' only trade, all else but dung.

CVIII

'But dung'—the wild inhabitant repeats
From her inhospitable seats :
But, now 'tis noon ; prepare we for our costless meats.

CIX

'LORD of all grassy and all glassy plains !

Whose mighty hand doth wield Fate's reins,
Who dost embase the hills, emboss the woody veins.

CX

'By Thee, the pirate, who by Nile being bred
Has land for table, pool for bed,
Camels, Arabia's wand'ring ships, by Thee are fed ;   330

CXI

'Thou with Thy inexpressibly immense
Finger of active Providence,
The World's great Harbinger, dost all to each dispense.'

CXII

Strict temperance so cooks our mess, that we
With no brain-clouds eclipsèd be :
The driest clearness makes the brightest ingeny.

CXIII

The mount 's our table, grass our carpet, well
Our cellar, trees our banquet, cell
Our palace, birds our music, and our plate a shell.

CXIV

Nature pays all the score. Next fountain has   340
Bath, drink, and glass ; but our soul's glass
Presents Religion's face. Our meal 's as short as grace.

CXV

See, where the udder'd cattle find us food ;
As those sheep cloth ; these hedgerows wood.
See, now a present brought us from the neighbourhood :

CXVI

Ev'n th' herb that cramp and tooth-ache drives away,

308 tin'd] 'lighted.'   310 sty] as before ' rise.'
327] Embase = ' lower ' : ' emboss ' = ' raise ' obviously enough. But why ' woody veins '? Was he thinking of coal-mines ?

(453)

And bribes ear-minstrels not to play ;
And from arch'd roofs to spongy bellows dews does stay ;

CXVII

That makes quick spirits and agile fancy rove,
And genuine warmth i' th' brain does move,   350
'Bove furs or fires ; whose pipe's both ventiduct, and stove ;

CXVIII

That mounts invention with its active smoke ;
Draught of Promethean fir'd-air took,
Renerves slack joints, and ransacks each phlegmatic nook.

CXIX

That lust cloys which expectance swells ; but, here

Are dainties, that whet taste and ear ;
Where all are cheer'd with joy, and overjoy'd with cheer.

CXX

But, having travers'd more of ground to-day,
Let us, for our refreshment, stay,
And with next rising sun, complete next closing lay.   360

Irati sævas Maris evitare Procellas
  Quæ potuit, felix est nimìs illa Ratis ;
Littoris optati Prospectu Navita gaudet ;
  Gratulor emensam nec minùs ipse Viam.

ANIMI PABULUM CONTEMPLATIO.

THE PLEASURE OF RETIREMENT

Canto XIII. The Reinvitation

THE ARGUMENT

FELIX qui Suus est, Animi propriique Monarcha ;
  Laus est Imperii ponere Jura Sibi.
Felices Animæ, pulso Plutone Tyranno,
  Queìs datur Elysiis imperitare Plagis!
Maximus internum quisquis superaverit Hostem,
  Major Alexandro, Cæsare major erit.
Fabritium Æacidæ, Senecam præpono Neroni,
  Hic hiat Immenso, postulat Ille parùm.
Ecquid habent Reges, nisi Membris Tegmen & Escam ?
  Quæ vel Nobiscum vile Mapale tenet. 10

Ipse mihi Regnum, summâ dominabor in Aula
  Mentis, & hôc quod sum vel minor esse velim.
Rex est quem Ratio regit, & quem ducit Honestum :
  De Regno videas regia Sceptra queri.
Aspice quid Cineres sit Cæsaris inter, & Iri,
  Est unus Color his omnibus, unus Odor. Ergo.
Affectus superans, & qui superatur ab illis,
  Non nisi Victor ovat, non nisi Victus obit.

347 bribes &c.] It would probably be impossible to find a more characteristic conceit than this for the supposed virtue of stilling *tinnitus aurium*. The whole passage has, I think, in the general ignorance of our poet, escaped collectors of the Praise of Tobacco for the most part. If Lamb did not know it, it is a pity.

Who Chance, Change, Hopes, and Fears can under bring
Who can obey, yet rule each thing,
And slight Misfortune with a brave disdain, he's king.

STANZA I

WHEN lavish Phœbus pours out
    melted gold ;
  And Zephyr's breath does spice
    unfold ;
And we the blue-eyed sky in tissue-
    vest behold.

II

Then, view the mower, who with big-
    swoln veins,
  Wieldeth the crookèd scythe, and
    strains
To barb the flow'ry tresses of the
    verdant plains.

III

Then view we valleys, by whose
    fringèd seams
  A brook of liquid silver streams,
Whose water crystal seems, sand
    gold, and pebbles gems ;

IV

Where bright-scal'd gliding fish on
    trembling line   10
  We strike, when they our hook
    entwine :
Thence do we make a visit to a
    grave divine.

V

With harmless shepherds we some-
    times do stay,
  Whose plainness does outvie the
    gay,
While nibbling ewes do bleat, and
    frisking lambs do stray.

VI

With them, we strive to recollect,
    and find
  Dispers'd flocks of our rambling
    mind ;
Internal vigils are to that due work
    design'd.

VII

No puffing hopes, no shrinking fears
    them fright ;
  No begging wants on them do
    light ;   20
They wed Content, while Sloth feels
    want, and Brav'ry spite.

VIII

While swains the burth'ning fleeces
    shear away,
  Oat-pipes to past'ral sonnets play,
And all the merry hamlet bells
    chime holy day.

IX

In neighb'ring meads, with ermine
    mantles proud,
  Our eyes and ears discern a crowd
Of wide-horn'd oxen, trampling grass
    with lowings loud.

X

Next close feeds many a strutting-
    udder'd cow ;
  Hard by, tir'd cattle draw the
    plough,
Whose gallèd necks with toil and
    languishment do bow.   30

XI

Near which, in restless stalks, wav'd
    grain promotes
  The skipping grasshopper's hoarse
    notes ;
While round the aery choristers dis-
    tend their throats.

XII

Dry seas, with golden surges, ebb
    and flow ;
  The ripening ears smile as we go,
With boasts to crack the barn, so
    numberless they show.

XIII

When Sol to Virgo progress takes,
    and fields

6 barb] This verb in the sense of 'bar*ber*,' 'to clip,' has Elizabethan precedent.

With his prolongèd lustre gilds ;
When Sirius chinks the ground, the
    swain his hope then builds.

XIV

Soon as the sultry month has mellow'd
    corn, 40
    Gnats shake their spears, and
      wind their horn ;
The hinds do sweat through both
    their skins, and shopsters scorn.

XV

Their orchards with ripe fruit im-
    pregnèd be,
    Fruit that from taste of death is
      free,
And such as gives delight with choice
    variety.

XVI

Yet who in 's thriving mind improves
    his state,
    And Virtue steward makes, his
      fate
Transcends ; he 's rich at an inesti-
    mable rate.

XVII

He shuns prolixer law-suits ; nor
    does wait
    At thoughtful grandee's prouder
      gate ; 50
Nor 'larming trumpets him, nor
    drowning storms amate.

XVIII

From costly bills of greedy Emp'rics
    free,
    From plea of Ambidexter's fee,
From Vicar Any-Thing, the worst of
    all the three.

XIX

He in himself, himself to rule, re-
    tires ;
    And can, or blow, or quench his
      fires :
All blessings up are bound in
    bounding up desires.

XX

His little world commands the
    great : he there
    Rich Mem'ry has for treasurer ;

The tongue is secretary to his heart,
    and ear. 60

XXI

While May-Days London gallants
    take a pride,
    Coach'd through Hyde Park, to
      eye, be eyed,
Which day's vain cost might for the
    poor a year provide ;

XXII

He may to groves of myrrh in
    triumph pace,
    Where roots of Nature, flow'rs of
      Grace,
And fruits of Glory bud. A glimpse
    of Heav'n the place.

XXIII

This the Spring-Garden to spiritual
    eyes,
    Which fragrant scent of gums out-
      vies ;
Three kings had thence their triple
    mystic sacrifice.

XXIV

Oh, happier walks, where CHRIST,
    and none beside, 70
    Is journey's End, and Way, and
      Guide !
Where from the humble plains are
    greatest heights descry'd.

XXV

Heav'nward his gaze. Here does a
    bower display
    His bride-room, and SCRIPTURIA
Herself is bride; each morn presents
    his marriage-day.

XXVI

What ecstasy 's in this delicious
    grove !
    Th' unwitness'd witness of his love !
What pow'r so strongly can as
    flam'd affections move !

XXVII

The larks, wing'd travellers, that
    trail the sky,
    Unsoil'd with lusts, aloft do fly, 80
Warbling SCRIPTURIA, SCRIPTURIA
    on high.

---

42 shopsters] a good word. Indeed most things in these two cantos are 'good,'
either in the Polonian sense, or a better.

XXVIII

(T' have been affected by a virgin heir,
 Rich, young, and chaste, wise, good, and fair,
Was once his first delight, but Heav'n restrain'd that care !

XXIX

Thou, Providence, didst both their wills restrain ;
 Thou mad'st their losses turn to gain ;
For thou gav'st Heav'n to her, on him dost blessings rain !)

XXX

But stop, pleas'd thoughts ; A high'r love 's here design'd ;
 Fit in each breast to be enshrin'd ;
Bright angels do admit no sex, nor does the mind. 90

XXXI

To all her lovers thousand joys accrue ;
 And comforts, thicker than May's dew,
Show'r down on their rapt souls, as infinite as new !

XXXII

Her oracles directing rules declare,
 Unerring oracles, Truth's square ;
Her soul-informing light does Earth for Heav'n prepare.

XXXIII

All beatizing sweets, as in their hive,
 At her fair presence do arrive,
Which are to drooping spirits best restorative.

XXXIV

To whose sight eagles, parallel'd, are blind ; 100
 Had Argus thousand eyes, he'd find
Darkness, compar'd with her illuminating mind.

XXXV

The Sun does glean his splendour from her eyes ;
 Thence burn we' in sweets, as Phœnix lies
Glowing on Sol's ray-darted pile of spiceries.

XXXVI

From precious limbeck sacred loves distil
 Such sublimations, as do fill
Minds with amazèd raptures of their chemic skill.

XXXVII

That such soul-elevations still might stay,
 We'd bear and do, both vow and pay, 110
And serve the LORD of Lords by her directive way !

XXXVIII

Soon as our ear drinks in His [high] command,
 Be 't acted by our heart, and hand ;
Under His banner we shall Satan's darts withstand.

XXXIX

May He accept the music of our voice,
 While on His goodness we rejoice,
And while each melting Psalm makes on His Grace its choice.

XL

On feast-days from that bow'r to church we haste,
 Where Heav'n dissolves into repast,
When we regalios of the mystic Banquet taste. 120

XLI

Oh, delicacies, infinitely pure !
 To souls best nutriment and cure !
Where Knowledge, Faith, and Love beatitude ensure.

---

xxviii–xxix] These two apparently autobiographic stanzas are interesting, as adding a possible new detail to Benlowes' scantily known history.
103] Not quite a 'minor' line, this !
112 high] Written in above the line in my copy.

XLII

Poor Solomon's provision, poor to this,
  Manna, Heav'n-dewing banquet, is :
Who reigns in Heav'n becomes on earth our food and bliss.

XLIII

Oh, Sacramental cates, divinely drest !
  God the Feast-maker, Christ the Feast,
The Holy Ghost Inviter, and the Soul the guest !

XLIV

All joys await the blessed convives, knit   130
  All excellences are in it,
This overcomes our spirits, overpow'rs our wit !

XLV

For us, poor worms, that Glory's Sovereign died !
  Oh, let our fleshly barks still ride
At anchor in calm streams of His empiercèd Side !

XLVI

This is Heav'n's Antepast! By Union He 's One to All, and All to One
In Love's intrinsic Mystery to souls alone !

XLVII

Ecstatic raptures loose our héarts on high
  With Joy's ineffability !   140
Exub'rant sweets o'erwhelm, as torrents, tongue and eye.

XLVIII

Such life-infusing comforts, from above,
  Our souls with inward motions move,
That totally for God we quit all creature-love !

XLIX

Should He condemn us, yet would Love compel

Him down with us, and we would dwell
Rather than without Him in Heav'n, with Him in Hell.

L

Soul of my soul ! when I a joy receive
  Disjoin'd from Thee, let my tongue cleave
To 's palate !   Me of all, not of this Feast bereave !   150

LI

Not in the winter solstice of my years,
  When shivering snow surrounds deaf ears,
And dreary languishment Death's gashly vizard wears ;

LII

When they shall tremble that the house defend ;
  The columns which support it bend ;
The grinders fail, the watch through casements objects blend ;

LIII

Then shine, dear Lord ! when quivering Winter's dress
  Is icicled with hoary tress ;
When all streams frozen are, but tears, through Love's excess ;

LIV

When periwigg'd with snow 's each bald-pate wood,   160
  Bound in ice-chains each struggling flood ;
When North Seas bridled are, pris'ning their scaly brood.

LV

Then let those freezing hours be thaw'd by pray'r !
  As wells in winter warmer are
By circumsession of refrigerating air.

LVI

That, nipp'd with cold, or parch'd with heat, resign

136 Antepast] Nothing to do with time, but opposed to ' *re*past '—a foretaste. The word is Taylorian.
160] See Introd.

We may our will in each to Thine,
Be 't less or more, be 't low or high,
    be 't storm or shine.

LVII

After Night's soot smears Heav'n,
Day gilds its face ;
Wet April past, sweet May takes
    place ;   170
And calm air smiles, when ruffling
    winds have run their race.

LVIII

Who hope for mines, scorn dross ;
    such only get
Who lose a game to win the set :
Worldlings, he 's rich who 's good ;
    above 's his cabinet.

LIX

To well-tun'd tempers things that
    disagree
Have oft some likeness ; thus, we
    see
Wind kindles fire ; discord makes
    concord harmony.

LX

Affliction tunes the breast to rise, or
    fall,
Making the whole man musical ;
We may affliction Christians' second
    baptism call.   180

LXI

Who CHRIST for Spouse, His cross
    for jointure has ;
His hand supports, where 's rod
    doth pass :
The LORD of Angels, He the King
    of Suff'rings was.

LXII

Love's life took Death, that Death
    Love's life might gain !
The Sovereign died that slaves
    might reign !
The world can't books that should
    be writ of Him contain.

LXIII

Those have the greatest cross, who
    cross ne'er bore ;
They're rich in want, who GOD
    adore ;

Who does supply all emptiness with
    His full store.

LXIV

Saint Paul, the Gentiles' doctor, rich
    'bove kings,   190
And high 'bove Oratory's wings,
Rapt up to Heav'n, had nothing, yet
    possess'd all things.

LXV

The rav'n of birds proves caterer,
    and feasts
Elijah ; so the lion of beasts
Was Samson's purveyor ; quails to
    murm'ring Jews were guests.

LXVI

Midst thorns environ'd, Love sweet
    roses finds ;
Steep ways lie plain t' inamor'd
    minds ;
Love gilds all chains (surpris'd not
    thrall'd), with comfort binds.

LXVII

Then, threaten, World, a goal shall
    bolt me in ;
He 's free as air, who serves not
    Sin ;   200
Who 's gather'd in himself, his Self is
    his own inn.

LXVIII

Then let fierce Goths their strongest
    chains prepare ;
Grim Scythians me their slave
    declare ;
My soul being free, those tyrants in
    the face I'll stare.

LXIX

Man may confine the body, but the
    mind
(Like Nature's miracles, the wind
And dreams) does, though secur'd,
    a free enjoyment find.

LXX

Rays drawn in to a point more
    vig'rous beam ;
Joys more to saints, engoal'd, did
    stream ;
Linnets their cage to be a grove, bars
    boughs esteem.   210

199 goal] So in orig., of course = 'gaol.' So in 209 'engoaled.'

LXXI

Burnish'd to glory from Affliction's flame,
From prison to a sceptre came
The lov'd and fear'd ELIZA—titles vail t' her name.

LXXII

She pass'd the furnace to be more refin'd ;
From flames drew purity of mind,
Not heat of passion ; hence, being tried, she brighter shin'd.

LXXIII

Here wound, here lance me, LORD, thy Austin cries,
Dissect me here for Paradise !
The Cross the altar be, so Love be sacrifice !

LXXIV

Imprint Thy Love so deep into my heart,   220
That neither hunger, thirst, nor smart,
Gain, loss, nor thraldom, life nor death us ever part !

LXXV

Should foes rip up my breast with piercing blade,
My soul would but have passage made,
Through which to Heav'n she might in purple riv'lets wade.

LXXVI

Forbid the banns 'twixt soul and body join'd,
The corpse but falls to be refin'd,
And re-espous'd unto the glorified high mind.

LXXVII

Who makes th' Almighty his delight, he goes

To martyrdom, as to repose ; 230

The Red Sea leads to Palestine, where all joy flows.

LXXVIII

Steel'd 'gainst Affliction's anvil, let's become
Proud of the World's severest doom ;
No majesty on earth is like to martyrdom.

LXXIX

'Enter into thy Master's joy ' 's so great,
This thought is with such flames replete,
That from th' High Court of Mercy souls all deaths defeat !

LXXX

Who saith, ' Fear not,' Him must we fear alone ;
Blest, whom no fear makes Faith be gone ;
How many must they fear, who fear not only ONE !   240

LXXXI

We are but once to our grave's port brought in,
To which from birth w' have sailing been,
It matters not what way, so we 'scape rocks of sin.

LXXXII

But, hark, 'tis late ; the whistlers knock from plough ;
The droiling swineherd's drum beats now ;
Maids have their curtsies made to th' spongy-teated cow.

LXXXIII

Larks roosted are, the folded flocks are pent

213] Here is in text of orig. an engraving of Queen Elizabeth praying in her oratory with the following letterpress at the sides of the cut : ' Having reformed Religion : established Peace : reduced Coin to the just value : delivered Scotland from the French : revenged domestical Rebellion : saved France from headlong Ruine by Civil Warre : supported Belgia : overthrown the Spanish invincible Navie : expelled the Spaniards out of Ireland : received the Irish into Mercie : enriched England by her most prudent Government 45 Years : *Elizabeth* a vertuous and triumphant Queen : in the 70th year of her Age, in most happy and peaceable manner departed this Life : leaving here her mortal parts until by the last Trump she shall rise immortal.'

245 droiling] = ' drudging.' not very uncommon both as noun and verb in seventeenth century.   Note the conceit in next line.

In hurdled grates, the tir'd ox sent
In loose trace home, now Hesper
    lights his torch in 's tent.
LXXXIV
See glimmering light, the Pharos of
    our cot ;   250
By innocence protected, not
By guards, we thither tend, where
    Ev'nsong 's not forgot.
LXXXV
O, Pray'r ! thou anchor through the
    worldly sea !
Thou sov'reign rhet'ric, 'bove the
    plea
Of flesh ! that feed'st the fainting
    soul, thou art Heav'n's key.
LXXXVI
Blest season, when Day's eye is
    clos'd, to win
Our heart to clear th' account,—
    when Sin
Has pass'd the audit, ravishments of
    soul begin.
LXXXVII
Who never wake to meditate, or
    weep,
Shall sure be sentenc'd for their
    sleep ;   260
Night to forepassèd day should still
    strict sentry keep.
LXXXVIII
Oh, let them perish midst their
    flaring clay,
Who value treasures with a day
Devoutly spent ! Faith 's the true
    gem, the world a gay.
LXXXIX
So wasteful, us'rer, as thyself, there 's
    none,
Who losest three true gems for
    one
That 's counterfeit ; thy rest, fame,
    soul for ever gone !
XC
When dark'ning mists our hemi-
    sphere invade,
Of all the air when one blot 's
    made,
Mortals immantled in their silent
    gloomy shade,   270

XCI
Then for an hour (elixir of delight !)
We, Heav'n beleag'ring, pray and
    write,
When every eye is lock'd, but those
    that watch the night.
XCII
Saints fight on bended knees ; their
    weapons are
Defensive patience, tears, and
    pray'r ;
Their valour most, when without
    witness, Hell does scare.
XCIII
May whiter wishes, wing'd with Zeal,
    appear
Lovely unto Thy purest ear,
Where nothing is accepted but
    what 's chaste, and clear !
XCIV
Life's hectic fits find cordials in
    Pray'r's hive,   280
Transcendently restorative,
Which might our iron age to its first
    gold retrieve.
XCV
See, list'ning Time runs back to
    fetch the Age
Of Gold, when Pray'r does
    Heav'n engage ;
Devotion is Religion's lifeblood ;
    'tis GOD's page,
XCVI
Who brings rich bliss by bills of
    sure exchange ;
The blessings that the poor
    arrange
For alms receiv'd that day, beatifies
    our grange.
XCVII
Dance, Nabals, with large sails on
    smiling tides,
Till the black storm against you
    rides,   290
Whose pitchy rains interminable
    Vengeance guides !
XCVIII
But, LORD, let Charity our table
    spread ;
Let Unity adorn our bed ;

And may soft Love be pillow underneath our head!

XCIX

Enrich'd, let's darn up Want; what Fortune can
Or give, or take away from man,
We prize not much: Heav'n pays the good Samaritan.

C

Thus, Life, still blessing, and still blest, we spend;
Thus entertain we Death, as friend,
To disapparel us for Glory's endless end.   300

CI

Who, thus forgot, in graces grows, as years,
Loves cherish'd pray'r, unwitness'd tears,
Rescu'd from monstrous men, no other monster fears.

CII

They who their dwelling in Abdera had,
Did think Democritus was mad;
He knew 'twas so of them. The application's sad.

CIII

Knew but the World what comforts, tiding on,
Flow to such recollection,
It would run mad with envy, be with rage undone.

CIV

Oh, Sequestration! Rich, to worldlings' shame;   310
A life's our object, not a name:
Herostratus did sail, like witch, i' th' air of fame.

CV

Get long-breath'd chronicles, ye need such alms,
Sue from diurnal briefs for palms,
Injurious grandeur for its frantic pride wants balms.

CVI

In aery flatt'ries Rumour, not Fame lies;
Inconstancy, Time's mistress, cries

(462)

It up, which soon by arguing Time, Truth's parent, dies.

CVII

Fame's plant takes root from virtue, grows thereby;
Pure souls, though fortune-trod, stand high,   320
When mundane shallow-searchin breath itself shall die.

CVIII

Oh, frail applause of flesh! swoln bubbles pass.
Turf-fire more smoke than splendour has;
What bulwark firm on sand? what shell for pearl may pass?

CIX

But saints with an attentive hope from high,
On Heav'n's parole do live and die;
Passing from Life's short night to Day's Eternity.

CX

Who blessedly so breathe, and leave their breath,
Of dying life make living death;
Each day, spent like the last, does act a Heav'n beneath.   330

CXI

Death's one long sleep, and human life no more
Than one short watch an hour before:
World! after thy mad tempest 'tis the landing shore.

CXII

Mid point betwixt the lives of Loss, and Gain;
The path to boundless Joy, or Pain;
Saint's birthday, Nature's dread: Grace doth this bandog chain.

CXIII

When Moses from high Pisgah's top descried
Fair Canaan, type o' th' Heav'nly Bride,
He breath'd out his joy-ravish'd soul, so sweetly died.

CXIV

To Immortality the grave's a womb;
We pass into a glorious room 341
Thorough the gloomy entry of a
narrow tomb.

CXV

LORD, as THOU mad'st (most pow'rful
One in Three)
The world of nothing; so, let me
Make nothing of the world, but
make my all in Thee!

CXVI

Pardon the by-steps that my soul
has trod,
Most great, good, glorious, gracious
GOD!
Seal Thou the bill of my divorce to
Earth's dull clod!

CXVII

Thy boundless source of Grace the
scarlet spot
Scour'd white as wool, that first
did blot 350
Th' original in man, that was so
fairly wrote.

CXVIII

Check not my hope, but spur my
fear to Thee,

Virtue to court, and vice to flee!
Love, lend thou me thy spur; fear,
thou my bridle be.

CXIX

From hence, to run in heav'nly paths,
I'll strive;
My slender pen to th' world I
give;
My only study shall be how to live,
to *live*.

CXX

None blest, but those, who, when
last trump shall send
It summons, find the JUDGE their
friend.
The end doth crown the work;
great GOD crown thou my
END. 360

O, ter felicem, fortunatumque quieto
Cui natat in Portu nescia Cymba
Metûs!
O DEUS! optato sistant mea Carbasa
Cœlo!
Omnis ab æthereis Spes sit habenda
Plagis.

EST SUMMUS, JESU, TUA GRATIA
QUÆSTUS.

Vivitur exiguo—Facilè assentior sa-
pientissimo Aguri, DEUM obsecranti ut
nec Divitias sibi, nec Egestatem, sed
tantùm ad degendam Vitam donaret
Necessaria. Vita privata, quàm de-
lectas! Corporis spectem Valetudinem?

Nusquam salubrior Aer. Frugalitatem?
Nusquam minoris vivitur. Quæstum?
Nusquam Lucrum innocentius. Vitæ
Integritatem? Nusquam alibi minùs
Corruptelæ.

Navis es in Portu, tumidæ secura
Procellæ;
Mens Desideriis hîc vacat alta suis.
Liberiore Polum contemplor Corde,
quiescit
Hîc Mens tuta, sibi libera, plena DEO.
Quæ sibi multa petit, petit anxia multa,
Voluntas;
Et cui plura dedit Sors, Mala plura
dedit.
Alta cadunt, inflata crepant, cumulata
fatiscunt;

Crimine vixque suo plena Crumena
caret.
Celsior immundi Mens despicit Orgia
Mundi,
Indignabundo proterit illa Pede. 10
Munde, vale; quid me fallacibus allicis
Hamis?
Sophrosynen sacrâ Sobrietate colo:
Regia sit ramosa Domus, Rivusque
Falernum;
Arcta, sed ampla, DEUM si capit, illa
Domus.

(Prose) 2 Aguri] The Agur of Prov. xxx.
critic would be apt to suggest *auguri*.

I only note this because a certain class of

Florea gemmatâ subrident Pascua
  Veste,
  Fætaque nativas explicat Arbor Opes.
Caltha, Rosæ, Tulipæ, Violæ, Thyma,
  Lilia florent,
  Dum gravido Zephyrus rore maritat
  Humum.
Frugibus exultant Valles, Grege Pascua,
  Rupes
  Fontibus, intonso Crine triumphat
  Ager ;   20
Terra Famem, levat Unda Sitim, fugat
  Umbra Calorem ;
  Dat Togam Ovis, Lignum Sylva,
  Focumque Silex.
Quod satìs est Vitæ, satìs est ; Præste-
  tur Egenis
  Quod reliquum : Vitæ sat Toga,
  Panis, Aqua.
Non Mensis quæcunque Dapes cele-
  brantur in istis
  Prægustantis egent ; Vite Venena
  latent.
Hîc Parasitus abest, fugit hinc Gna-
  thonica Pestis ;
  Cura nec hîc Animos irrequieta
  coquit.
Cholica, Spasmus, Hydrops, Vertigo,
  Podagra recedunt ;

Grata Sapore beat Mensa, Sopore
              Thorus.   30
Pange DEO Laudes, positis Mens
  libera Curis ;
  Cætera si desint, Numine dives eris.
Sis modico contenta, gravis Nulli ;
  Ipsa Misellis
  Quas impendis Opes, has an habebis?
  habes.
Quod CHRISTUM decuit, deceat Te.
  Noverit uti
  Quisquis præsenti Sorte beatus erit.
Sic Abrahæ gaudebo Sinu ; dum,
  Dives, in Orco
  Æternùm diro deliciose peris.
Vita beata, tuas quî possim pangere
  laudes ?
  Mille cui Vitas, si mihi mille, darem !

Da, velut spero, bene, CHRISTE, spi-
  rem !
Da, velut credo, bene, CHRISTE, vivam !
Unus hac qui Spe fruitur, fruetur
              Mortuus Astris.

              Amico.
Si lenis tremulâ Quies in Umbra
Sit Cordi, huc propera, ferasque Tecum
Totum quicquid habes Libentiarum.

THEOPHILÆ AMORIS HOSTIA

Cantio VII

A DOMINO JEREMIÂ COLLIERO IN VERSUS LATIALES TRADUCTA

Contemplatio

ARGUMENTUM

Proripit in vastum Lucis se VIRGO Profundum,
Quam nullæ exequent Voces, nec Limite claudant ;
Obtundunt Radii Visum, renovantque Vigorem.

TRISTICON I

SI Maro Quisque foret, fierent si
  quique Marones
Præcones sacri, Conventus &
  Orbis apertus,
Quo scrutarentur Virtus Æterna
  quid esset.

II

Si vel ab innocuis possent deducere
  Cunis
Primævum Tempus, congestaque
  Secula mille
Inferrent Trutinæ ; tamen hæc sub
  Pondere justo

Title of Translation] The caution is perhaps once more advisable that this is a Jeremy
Collier *senior*, and not the Nonjuror.

III

Ponentes, norînt tandem non
    mominis esse
Majoris, frustrà quàm si cum Sole
    potenti
Exiles tentent atomos librare Bilance.

IV

Si Terræ Molem numeris spectare
    refertam   10
Possent, non istis tua constet
    Summa Figuris,
Æterno cyphræ comparent qualitèr
    Ævo !

V

Si Sabulum flueret, per Sæcula mille
    marinum,
Quando deficeret vacuatis Littus
    Arenis,
Æquè Te primò mensum est Clep-
    sammion illud.

VI

Cœlitùs impertita foret Facundia,
    Linguis
Aligeros referens, Spatium tamen
    haud æquarent,
Est ubi prorsus idem cum fluxis
    Omne futurum.

VII

Tende Fides bolidem, brevis at
    nimìs illa nequibit
Expertis Fundi Maris explorare
    Profundum,   20
Limite constricti nullo, nec Littore
    cincti.

VIII

Æterna haud unquam commensura-
    bilis Ætas,
Nulla Tui partem poterit de-
    scribere Penna ;
Circulus es siquidem cui non est
    Terminus ullus.

IX

Vel cujus Centrum tam se diffuderit,
    ipsum
Ambitus ingentis nequeat circun-
    dare Cœli,
Exterius poterit quid circumcingere
    Corpus?

X

Vos, quibus Æthereus Vigor est,
    num Fine carentem
Finem exquiratis ? num Immensum
    extendere fas est ?'
Claudere Ubique manens ? comprên-
    dere & INFINITUM ?   30

XI

Hujus Zona DEUS sine puncto,
    maximus, Orbis
Ante Mare, et Terras, et quod
    tegit omnia Cœlum,
Qui fuit, est, & erit cùm cuncta
    creata peribunt.

XII

Quin contemplemur suprà Sublimia
    quæque,
Ultra quemque Locum, super
    omnes Luminis Orbes !
Pectus Apostolicum rapuit Radiatio
    trinum.

XIII

Circumquaque micans Solium Præ-
    signe ! supremo
Imperio constans, & Majestate
    verendâ !
Cætera transcendens, quem nullus
    Fulgor adæquet !

XIV

Cingit utrumque Latus vel inenarra-
    bile Lumen !   40
Quod circumfusum tanto Splen-
    dore coruscat,
Æquora Lætitiæ superet flammantia
    mille.

XV

Quod sic Effulgens si conspectare
    liceret,
Detectâ Facie Cherubinis, Lumine
    tanto
Perculsi, in Nihilum remearent illicò
    primum.

XVI

Indue Te Tunicâ, dives Natura,
    coruscâ,
Ornamenta tamen, tanto collata
    decori,
Sunt tua, concretus seu lapsus
    Nubibus Humor.

---

7 mominis] Lucretian. Cf. Collier's fancy for spondaic endings, at least at first.

XVII

Indorum posses Opibus spoliare
 Fodinas,
Illos, auratis, Radiosque recludere,
 Cellis,   50
Qui collucentes cum Phœbi Lampade
 certant :

XVIII

Arcanâ posses reserare peritiùs
 Arte
Intima cujusvis ditis penetralia
 Rupis,
Illinc Thesauros nec non auferre
 nitentes :

XIX

Errantes, fixasque simul connectere
 Stellas
Posses, quæ rutilis exornant
 Æthera Bullis,
Luminis ut coeant cuncti Orbes
 Sydus in unum :

XX

Jungere si posses Gemmas, Aurique
 Fodinas,
Æthereasque Faces, radiata Reflectio
 quarum
Fulgida rivalis superaret Lumina
 Solis :   60

XXI

Si Lapides Gemmæ, riguum Mare
 funderet Aurum,
Margara si Pulvis fieret, Chrystallus
 & Aer,
Sol quodvis Sydus, plures Sibi mille
 Nitores ;

XXII

Gemmæ illæ Silices essent, Mare
 parva lacuna,
Stellæ istæ Scintilla forent, Fla-
 gratio Phœbus :
Aurum, Gemma micans, Adamantes,
 sordida Scruta :

XXIII

Si Terræ, complexa forent, & Lumina
 Cœli,
Optica & unius peterent Confinia
 Centri,
Hoc prius Objectum vel cæcum
 redderet illud.

XXIV

Cæcum, seu piceæ Velamen Noctis
 opacum,   70
(Innuitur Sacro duntaxat Visio
 Textu)
Hujus respectu Lucis sunt quælibet
 Umbræ.

XXV

O, planè infandam, summoque Stu-
 pore refertam !
Si Nemo nisi qui dignus describere
 possit,
Hanc sanè Lucem possit describere
 Nemo.

XXVI

Selecti Eloquii cujusvis languet
 Acumen,
Defecit Ingenium, Verborum hîc
 curta supellex ;
Hanc Lumen Mentis nullius tranet
 Abyssum.

XXVII

Hîc residet tantis circundata Gloria
 Flammis,
Quales confundant Aciem vel
 maxime acutam,   80
Huc tendat propiore nimis quæ
 improvida Gressu.

XXVIII

Splendor dimanat talis Fulgoribus
 istis,
Qualis pulveream sublimet in
 ardua Molem,
Urnâ quæ compôsta secùs remanêret
 inerti.

XXIX

Numinis ante Thronum Summi
 provolvo meipsum,
Profluit undè Bonum quodvis ut ab
 ubere Fonte :
Hoc Decus ut pandam faveat tua
 Gratia Cœptis.

XXX

Magne Deus, sine Principio, tamen
 omnis Origo,
Cujus Naturæ telam Manus inclyta
 nevit ;
Unâ qui Virtute tuâ Loca singula
 comples.   90

XXXI

Alme Parens rerum ; qui fulcis
quodque creatum,
Vitam Spiritibus qui præbes, con-
tinuasque,
Ortus es ipse Tibi, Bonitatis Origo
supremæ.

XXXII

Lætitiæ Summa es, cujus Sapientia
Abyssus,
Ad quodvis sese tendit tua vasta
Potestas,
Ac cunctos Facies reddet jucunda
beatos.

XXXIII

Aeris expansis puncto dilaberis
Alis,
Induis Augustæ Te Majestatis
amictu,
Te Nubes velant, Te stipant Agmina
Cœli.

XXXIV

Omnis Honoris Apex, Summæ es
Fastigia Laudis, 100
Ad Radios latè sparsos suffusa
Pudore
Hymnos decantat, cœlestis Turma,
perennes.

XXXV

Gemmæ quàm superant vitrum !
quàm Sidera Gemmas !
Sidera quam Phœbus ! quàm Phœ-
bum Gloria Cœli !
Purior ast ipsis longè est tua Visio
Cœlis

XXXVI

Magna quidem Tellus, se profert
latiùs Aer,
Planetæ excedunt, Stellarum Regia
major,
Supremi fines nec habent Tentoria
Cœli.

XXXVII

Mens mea dum Zelo conatur plura
referre
Fervida protenso, Pectus, DEUS alme,
repleto 110
Igne novo, nullum languorem Car-
mina noscant.

XXXVIII

Cum super Aerios tractus, & Sidera
Musæ
Urgeo Progressus, uni Tibi mille
videntur
Sphæræ, non secus ac atomi sub
Sole minuti.

XXXIX

Est Ætas æterna tibi seu clepsydra
tantum,
Immensum nisi sit Spatium complere
valet nil,
Cujus sex Verbis rerum Natura creata
est.

XL

Omnia complectens totius Fabrica
Cœli,
Cum Stellis rutilis, Verbo surgebat
ab uno,
Quomodò mortalis narret Sapientia
Nomen ? 120

XLI

Ætheris, Arbitrio, Crystalla micantia
volvis,
Illis consignat Virtus tua cœlica
Metas,
Obliquos horum moderatur Dextera
Currus.

XLII

Nullæ Te Zonæ, Tropicive, Polive
retardent,
Cum sis Sphæralis Motor Primarius
Orbis,
Intra, extra, supra, quìn ultrà singula
perstans.

XLIII

Ingentes Pluviæ atque Nivis susten-
tat acervos
Omnipotens tua sola Manus, quâ
nempè remotâ
Diluvium humanum perdat genus
omne secundum.

XLIV

Hisce ministratur stillatis Copia
Terris, 130
Et confisa Tibi mortalia Corda
replentur,
Flamina Ventorum peragunt tua
Jussa per Orbem ;

XLV

Hæc Tu, quando voles, cæcis in-
clusa cavernis
Constringis, validoque sinis pro-
rumpere motu,
Undè Tremore gravi Tellus concussa
dehiscit.

XLVI

Undarum furias Vinclis compescis
Arenæ,
Oceani arcanum vasti scrutare Pro-
fundum,
Te memorem pacti monstrat Thau-
mantias Iris.

XLVII

Cardinibus Verbi Tellus innixa
potentis,
Aer quam cingit, nec non circum-
fluus Humor,   140
Ponderibus librata suis immobilis
astat.

XLVIII

Ejus sed Frontem Te corrugante
Columnæ
Firmatæ trepidant, Fremitu Mare
Littora plangit,
Solvuntur Silicum Rupes, Montes-
que vacillant.

XLIX

Insuper intremuêre Poli, Centrum-
que recussum
Terræ, quæ Vultûs perculsa Stupore
verendi,
Accedit Montem Sina dum summa
Potestas.

L

Imbutum Vitâ quodvis tua Cura
focillat,
Divinis Cursum cujusvis flectis
Habenis,
Gratia de Vultu, de Vultu Gloria
manat.   150

LI

Non Tibi sunt Aures, non sunt Tibi
Lumina, verùm
Percipis Auditu quodvis, & cernis
acutè ;
Te Locus haud capiat, tamen Ipse
per Omnia præsens.

(468)

LII

Optica cœlestis dicamus Specla
Pronoias,
Arcam, quâ positas Idæas videris
omnes,
Ad quas conceptas formaveris Icona
quamvis.

LIII

Quippè præexistunt sic hîc Eventa
futura,
Sicut abhinc multo non tempore
gesta fuissent ;
Cernimus haud dissecta recèns tam
Corpora clarè.

LIV

Totus ubique semel remanes, Tu
semper es idem,   160
Attamen Arbitrio commutas omnia
solo,
Tu complêre remota soles Immo-
bilis Ipse.

LV

Sic interponunt se contingentia
Turmis
Sollerti Curæ, quæ mirè cuncta
gubernat,
Ac modò præteritum, sit præteritum-
que futurum.

LVI

Arbitrio quamvis malè sint conformia
quædam,
Nil tamen omninò citra hoc procedat
in Actum ;
Prævia, successura simul manet una
Voluntas.

LVII

Te penes ingentis sunt Climata
dissita Mundi,
Quamvis nec Tellus, nec Temet
continet Æther,   170
Obscurum lustrat Præsentia quod-
libet antrum.

LVIII

Quamvis ab istis quas tu formaveris
olim
Mentibus, accedat nil ad Præconia
clara,
Attamen æternùm celebrabunt
munera Amoris.

LIX

Præter Peccatum & Mortem tu
cuncta creasti,
Hæc sua Stultitiæ humanæ primor-
dia debent,
Illud Naturam conspersit Sordibus
omnem.

LX

Sed quò curares Peccati Vulnera,
Nobis
Donas IMMANUEL, sibi qui non
sumere nostram
Naturam renuit, qui non Præsepe
recusat.   180

LXI

O, dulcis noster Mediator! Munera
cujus
Laudis seu rores, Æterno, matutini
Sunt celebrata Choro cælesti Canti-
bus altis.

LXII

Concurrente, DEUS, genuit Te
Flamine Sancto,
Tu Verbo æterno contentus sumere
Carnem ;
Qualitèr emanas homini fas dicere
non est.

LXIII

Sicut ab Æterno fuit Emanatio mira;
Hæc sic æternum mirè durabit in
ævum :
Principio Verbum, monstrat Te
cuncta præisse.

LXIV

Unum est esse Tibi, paritèr Tu
trinus & unus ;   190
Et duplex Natura Tibi conspirat in
unâ,
Ipse trin-unius resides Deitatis
Honore ;

LXV

Deque tuo Radii Solio tot mille
refulgent,
Quales Aligerûm non possint Lumina
ferre ;
De quibus evolvunt Nil docta Noe-
mata Cleri.

LXVI

Ætatum, pateat, Monumenta legendo
priorum,

Hæc sacra quòd nullus potuit
Mysteria nobis
Pandere, Virgineo priùs ac sunt
edita Partu :

LXVII

Nido à Se structo fuit hîc exclusa
Columba,
Ille Gregem partus fuit hîc qui
protegat Agnus,   200
Se producentem, Flos, qui forma-
verat Agrum :

LXVIII

Agmine Cœlicolûm Te Concele-
brante corusco ;
Pectora Pastorum subito trepidâre
pavore ;
Te, monstrante Magi venerantur
Sydere Cursum.

LXIX

Cùm sis divinâ mirandus Origine
tali,
Vilia mortalis pateris Convitia Gentis,
Irato ut possis nos conciliare
Parenti.

LXX

Lætus Honoris erat proprii tua
Gratia Præco,
Es tu dignatus sacratum Munus
obire,
Ast Aaronis eras solito de more
vocatus.   210

LXXI

Ac ut divino constarent singula
Verbo,
In te de superis descendit Spiritus
auris,
Lenes propter aquas Jordanes, teste
Johanne.

LXXII

Hinc in Desertum perductus Flamine
sacro,
Dæmonis appulsu tentatus, Codice
verùm
Hunc superas Scripto, fluit undè
Redemptio nostra.
Protinùs egressus.

LXXIII

Actus Sermones, Oracula mira
fuêrunt,

Hæc genuêre Fidem, nec non
genuêre Timorem,
Erectas Animas ad Te tollamus
utrisque.   220

LXXIV

Firmatum claudis gressum tribuisti,
Lumina Cæcis,
Morbo languentes diro quocunque
levabas,
Defunctis Vitam, Mutis dederas-
que Loquelam.

LXXV

Defunctis Tu Vita, Salus mortalibus
ægris,
Tu cæcis Lumen, Tu rerum copia
egenis,
Thesaurus furtum spernens, sincera
Voluptas.

LXXVI

Non ex hoc Mundo Regnum Tibi,
RECTOR OLYMPI,
Nuncia Apostolico procedunt Pec-
tore læta,
Ut tua sit totum Miseratio nota per
Orbem.

LXXVII

Mortuus ante Diem conspexit fidus
Abraham,   230
Vota tibi pariter nato solvebat Isaco,
Antitypum atque Typus, versare per
omnia vivus.

LXXVIII

Est Evangelicus, Sapiens Academia,
Codex,
Justitiam vicit Clementia blanda
severam,
Sobrius ut Vitam ducebas, Fortis
obibas.

LXXIX

Es Tu, sacra Domus, Tu purum
Altare, Sacerdos,
Tu Vitæ Panis, citrà fastidia Festum,
Ex Escis ubi acuta novis exurgit
Orexis.

LXXX

Mortali natus mortalia Crimina
deles,
Victima grata foret Tibi quodvis
Pectus honestum,   240

(470)

Ob Genus humanum qui velles
fundere Vitam.

LXXXI

Non dedignatus, Crucis es tolerare
probrosæ
Tormina, quò nobis concessus sit
Paradisus ;
Quò pia Sanctorum Solentur Gaudia
Mentes.

LXXXII

Ferrea Tartarei diffringens Claustra
Tyranni,
Dira tenebrosi Phlegetontis Monstra
coerces :
Sic tua cuncta Tibi subigebat Dextera
victrix.

LXXXIII

Tu Virtute tuâ solvebas Vincula
Mortis,
Atque reviviscens superam contendis
in Arcem,
Inspirat Vitam Læthatis Spiritus
Oris.   250

LXXXIV

Te, Pater, electis ut signet Dona
Salutis
Spiritus Alme, dedit Nato (sic
Trinus in Uno)
Sanctificas Omnes propriè, non solus
at Omnes.

LXXXV

Patris Amor, nec non Nati, cœleste
Sigillum,
Præsidium Sanctis, felix Pietatis
Origo,
Alta salutiferæ pandas Mysteria
Linguæ.

LXXXVI

O Jubar immensum Radiis insigne
coruscis,
Omnis ab aspectu Sophiæ Radiatio
clara,
Non collata potest minui tua Copia
cunctis.

LXXXVII

Gaudia sunt Comites, Clementia,
Pacis Amorque ;   260
Quorum pacatum perturbant nulla
Tenorem

Tristia; Quem Mundus, nec Mors,
  nec destruat Orcus.

LXXXVIII

Festum ex selectis quod constet
  talibus Escis,
Qualitèr haud acris possit consumere
  Orexis,
Dives Odor quem non dispergat
  Ventus in Auram:

LXXXIX

Lux Oculos fugiens, tamen Ipse per
  Omnia splendes,
Tu Sonus es qualem non Musicus
  explicet ullus,
Arctus es Amplexus, quem Tempora
  nulla resolvant.

XC

Exindè irrefluo volvuntur Gaudia
  Cursu,
Qualia inexhaustis soleas præbere
  Culullis,   270
Cordibus, a fœdâ Peccati Labe
  remotis.

XCI

Ecstaticum hoc Vinum quod tradit
  Spiritus Almus,
Sidereum motas extollit ad Æthera
  Mentes;
Terrenis orbas Cœli Solatia mulcent.

XCII

O quàm sacrati connectit Gluten
  Amoris!
Ros fluit Ambrosiæ divino qualis
  ab Ore!
Sunt tua quæ solùm faciunt Com-
  mercia Cælum.

XCIII

Illustres Animæ, succensæ hoc
  Lumine summo,
Quando tuos Vultus radiantes Luce
  tuentur,
Quodque Decus reputant obscuræ
  Noctis adinstar.   280

XCIV

Sublimis nostros superans Infusio
  Sensus,

Tu stupor Eloquii Nomen mereare
  profundi,
Æquet hyperbolicus quem nullus
  Sermo superbus.

XCV

Sacrosancta Trias, complecteris
  Omnia solùm,
Exuperans quodcunque Bonum,
  super Omnia Felix,
Nos haustura, tamen vivo hoc in
  Fonte natamus:

XCVI

Imperio REX magne tuo par nulla
  Potestas,
Augusto cujus Majestas provenit Ore,
Pulchrâ es perpetui præcinctus
  Veste Decoris.

XCVII

Justitia est Sceptrum, Solium mise-
  ratio Mitis,   290
Regna perimmensos extendunt cœ-
  lica Tractus,
Gloria permansura, Tibi, per Sêcla
  Corona.

XCVIII

Pax Intellectûs tua quodvis præstat
  Acumen,
Obsisti poterit tua vasta Potentia
  frustrà,
Numen es Ipse sacrum, Sacro
  purgatius omni.

XCIX

Ore fluit Verum, Sapientia Pectore
  manat,
Ante tuam excubias agit Omni-
  potentia Turrim,
Aligeri peragunt tua Jussa verenda
  Ministri.

C

Perspicit Obtutu vel cuncta Scientia
  primo,
Thesauro frueris per Te sine Fine
  beato,   300
Tempus es Æternum; Quæ me
  demergat Abyssus!

Peroratio Eucharistica

Summas Tibi agit Grates, maxime Cœlorum Præses, æternùmque adorandum Numen, Servus tuus humillimus, quem post tot varias mundanarum Sollicitudinum Procellas, vastosque Curarum Fluctus, cùm olim Hollandiam, Brabantiam, Artesiam, Germaniam, Austriam, Hungariam, Styriam, Carinthiam, partem Italiæ, nec non Galliæ incolumem in Patriam reduxisti. Quàm gratum enim mihi placidum, post tot periculosas inter peregrinandum Agitationes, Quietis Pacisque Intervallum, ut devotæ Legum tuarum Observationi totus exindè vacem! Tu, benigne Deus, dulcissimum hoc mihi Otium concedis, quo Tibi Soli prompto libentique Animo inservire statui: sicut per Te vivo, sic Tibi viverem, & quicquid a Gratiâ acceperim, in Honorem refunderem! Hæc ergò Laudi & Gloriæ solius sapientis & immortalis Dei submissè consecrentur [1].

Conditor Omnipotens Cœlique
  Solique ! supremum
Cujus ad Arbitrium cuncta creata
  fluunt ;
Clementèr Finem lassis imponito
  Rebus,
  Nec plùs terrenis Mens operosa
    vacet :
Omnia solertèr sub utroque jacentìa
  Phœbo   [scio.
  Perpendens, tandem non nisi vana
Quà sese bifido Scaldis discriminat
  Alveo
  Vidi, Teque tuâ, Rhene palustris,
    Aqua :
Non iter excelsæ remoratæ Nubibus
  Alpes,
  Quæ nec in aeriis Nix sedet alta Jugis;
Vidimus oppositos vario sub Climate
  Mores ;   11
  Vidimus innumeras quas vehit Ister
    Aquas :
Diverso didici diversa Idiomata Tractu,
  Quæque Observatu sunt bene digna,
    scio :
Gallica Mobilitas, Fraus Itala, Fastus
  Iberi,
  Teutonica Ebrietas nota fuere nimis.
Quamlibet in Partem Regina Pecunia
  Mundum
  Flectit, acerba Meum Bella Tuumque
    gerunt.
Me conservanti per mille Pericula,
  Grates
  Quî possim meritas solvere, Christe,
    Tibi !   20

Cerno, detestans Vitium, lassusque
  Tumultu,
  Quod, non Vita, prior Vita, sed
    Error erat.
Velle Meum, sit velle Tuum, Regnator
  Olympi !
  Cui soli Grates Mens agit, egit, aget.
Si plures mihi Vita futura superstet
  in Annos,
  Huic sit juncta piâ Sedulitate Fides !
Nam nil contulerim benè docto sanus
  Amico,
  Spiritus ut sano Corpore sanus agat.
Nosse, & amare Deum ; Promissis
  credere Christi,   29
  Consulere Afflictis, edocuisse Rudes,
Accumulare Bonis Inopes, succurrere
  Lapsis,
  Obnixè Votis Ista petenda meis.
Vertam Bodleias, congesta Volumina,
  Gazas,
  Quæ Vaticano proxima, Roma, tuo :
Nocturnâ versanda tamen, versanda
  diurnâ,
  Præ cunctis aliis Biblia Sacra Manu :
Undè, ut Apis sese sùstentat Nectare
  Cellæ ;
  Sic vivam lectis Floribus hisce piis.
Talia fac, vives, Lector ; Quicunque
  beatus
  Esse cupis, tali Vita sit acta modo. 40
Me Vitam, atque Necem tibi proposuisse memento :
Elige sivè velis vivere, sivè mori.

FINIS.

---

[1] The reference to Benlowes' travels is interesting, though there seems to be something lost after *Galliæ*. Where was the country retreat so agreeably described in the last cantos ? He must probably have got rid of Brent Hall by this time : but it *may* be this. From the allusion to the Bodleian in the following lines he must already have been thinking of establishing himself at Oxford.

THE

SUMMARY

OF

WISEDOME.

BY

EDWARD BENLOWES, Esq.

Love not the World, neither the things that are in the World ; if any Man love the World, the love of the FATHER *is not in him : For all that is in the World, the Lust of the Eyes, the Lust of the Flesh, and the Pride of Life, is not of the* FATHER, *but is of the World ; and the World passeth away, and the Lust thereof. But He that doeth the Will of God abideth for ever.* I Joh. 2. 15, 16, 17.

LONDON,
Printed for *Humphry Mosely*, and are to be sold
at the *Princes Arms* in St. *Pauls* Church-
yard, 1657.

THE SUMMARY OF WISDOM[1]

Love not the world, neither the things that are in the world ; if any man love the world, the love of the Father is not in him, &c. 1 JOH. ii. 15, 16, 17.

I

WORLDLINGS we court not, envy not,
nor fear ;
  May friends to virtue lend their
  ear :
While sinners split on shelves, saints
to Heav'n's harbour steer.

II

Earthlings ! what's heap of wealth ?
what's Honour's height ?
  What's Pleasure's May ? can toys
  so slight
Bless Heav'n-descended souls with
life's eternal light ?

III

Riches from most men, swift as
eagles, fly ;
  Honours on popular breath rely ;
Pleasure's a flash ;—and All com-
bin'd, but Vanity.

IV

Why dot'st thou, World, on these ?
we will not stay :   10
  Juggler, we know thy tempting
  way ;
Which is, by charms to mock our
sense, and then betray.

V

Art toils to serve thee ; sables yield
their skins ;
  The silkworm for thy wardrobe
  spins ;
The rock with gems, the sea with
pearls, emboss thy sins.

VI

To bribe thy palate, Lust drains
earth, air, seas ;

Whence finny, wing'd, hoof'd
droves must please
The glutton, made thereby a spittle
of each disease.

VII

False World, asp's poison equals not
thy gall,
  Embittering souls to Hell.   Thus
  all   20
Thy darlings thou delud'st with thy
enchanting call.

VIII

I wonder not unbridled fools run
on ;
  Since all their Heav'n's on earth
  alone ;
Which, though thou seem'st to give,
as soon as giv'n, 'tis gone.

IX

Kiss, and betray, then Nero's rage
outdare ;
  He, whom thou hugg'st, should
  most beware :
I shall unmask thy guiles, and thy
fond gulls unsnare.

X

Thy smile is but a trap, thy frown a
bubble,
  Thy praise a squib, thy beauty
  stubble ;
Who know thee best, have found a
theatre of trouble :   30

XI

Where men and devils meet ; and
sense, compact
  With fraud, gild every vicious
  fact:

---

[1] As has been noted in Introduction, and as carefull (or even careless) readers of *Theophila* will notice at once, this piece is a sort of cento of *Theophila* itself.   But the mosaic is a curious one, the constituent pieces are sometimes slightly altered, and, unless I mistake, there are new links and patches.   At any rate, as extremely rare and as a sort of authentic abridgement, it seemed worth giving.

Where we must evil hear, or suffer
it, or act.

XII

Thy friends are thieves of Time;
The chat they vent
(Light airs please toyish ears) is
spent
On trash, which minds seduce with
cheating blandishment.

XIII

Thy gifted scythemen have Religion
mown,
Which, in their meeting-barns,
is grown
From best to all (like Corinth's
schism) from all, to none.

XIV

Thy shop vents braided ware of
apish fashion;   40
Thy gauds (Wealth, Sport, Pride)
breed vexation;
Like hautboys, on Earth's stage, oft
ushering in—damnation.

XV

Ah, while, like larks, fools with vain
feathers play,
Pleas'd with Sin's glass, are
snatch'd away,
In midst of their excess, to Hell's
tormenting bay!

XVI

World, thou soul-wracking ocean!
Flatteries blow

Thee up, thou blue with spite
dost grow,
Brinish with lust, like the Red-Sea
with blood, dost flow.

XVII

And, like the Basilisk's prodigious
eyes,
Thy first sight kills, but thyself
dies   50
First seen: quick-sighted Faith thy
darts prevents, and spies.

XVIII

Hadst been less cruel, thou hadst
been less kind;
Thy gall, prov'd medicine, heals
my mind:
Thus Hell may help to Heav'n, the
Fiend a soul befriend.

XIX

The age-bow'd earth groans under
sinners' weight!
Justice, oppress'd, to Heav'n takes
flight,
Vengeance her place supplies, which
with keen edge will smite.

XX

False World! is Hell the legacy to
thy friend?
Crawl with thy trifles to the
Fiend:
We scorn thy pack,—this year may
burning close, thy end.   60

*For all that is in the world, the lust of the eyes, is not of the Father, but is of the
world, &c.*

XXI

Midas, to th' bar; thou void of
grace, yet stor'd
With gold, thy minted god, ador'd:
Thou, and thine idol, perish in thy
wretched hoard.

XXII

Thy heart is lock'd up in thy shrined
chink:
Oh, heavy gold, bred near Hell's
brink!

Misgotten elf, thou Heav'n-designed
souls dost sink!

XXIII

Whose gain is godliness,—the scrip-
ture he
Perverts: days him with interest see,
Who incest still commits with his
coins' progeny.

XXIV

Thou hast too much, yet still thou
whin'st for more;   70

39 like Corinth's schism] This may serve, once for all, as an instance of the altera-
tions noteworthy here and justifying the reprint. These words do not appear in the
line as given and annotated above at Canto xii. st. vii. l. 21 of *Theophila*.

Thou, wishing, want'st ; art, want-
ing, poor :
Thou wouldst ev'n plunder Hell for
cash to cram thy store.

XXV

While gripes of famine mutiny with-
in,
And tan, like hides, the shrivell'd
skin
Of those thou hast decoy'd into thy
tangling gin.

XXVI

Whose skin, sear as the bark of sap-
less wood,
Clings to their bones, for want of
food ;
Friendless, as are sea-monsters
thrown ashore by th' flood.

XXVII

Though fasts be all their physic,
their corpse all
Their earth, who for thy pity
call, 80
Yet art thou harder to them than
their bed, the stall.

XXVIII

' Penurious churl, when shall I '
(says thine heir)
' Ransack thy chests ? so ease thy
care :
Purchase, instead of ground, a
grave !—Die, wretch, to spare !

XXIX

' Hath treach'rous coin swell'd by
thy curse ?—Live still
Lay-Elder : soon thy crimes ful-
fil : '
The heaviest curse on this side
Hell 's to thrive in ill.

XXX

How cursed Love of Money doth
bewitch
The leprous Mind with pleasing
itch !
This slave to his own servant, ne'er
was poor, till rich ! 90

XXXI

Graves may be sooner cloy'd, than
craving eyes :

Bribes blanch Gehazi till he dies.
' Thou fool, Death shall this night
thy dunghill soul surprise.'

XXXII

Nor would this city-wolf lead men to
snares,
Nor vex his mind with carking
cares,
View'd he himself i' th' mirror which
Despair prepares.

XXXIII

So wasteful, usurer, as thyself,
there 's none ;
Who part'st with three true gems,
for one
Brittle as glass ;—thy fame, rest,
soul for ever gone !

XXXIV

Who nettles sow, shall prickles reap ;
the train 100
To Hell is idolizèd gain :
Unless thou fiends canst bribe, thou
go'st to endless pain !

XXXV

His hidebound conscience opens
now.—' I've run
On rocks ' (he howls) ' too late to
shun !
Grace left, Wrath seiz'd me ! Gold,
my god, hath me undone !

XXXVI

' Often to Hell in dreams I head-
long fall !
From devils then I seem to crawl,
While furies round about with
whips my soul appal !

XXXVII

' Atheism our root, for boughs were
Faction's store,
Hypocrisy our leaves gilt o'er, 110
Wrath, Treachery, and Extortion,
were the fruit we bore.

XXXVIII

' Like profane Esau have we sold
our bliss,
For shine of pelf, that nothing is !
This desperates our rage, we still
blaspheme at this ! '

The Summary of Wisdom

XXXIX

Thus cursed gripers restless tortures feel,
  Whose hearts seem'd rocks, whose bowels steel.
'I burn' (cries Dives) 'for one drop, denied, I kneel!

XL

'Fire each where broils me, fire as black as night!
  Goblins mine eyes, ears shrieks affright!'
Sin's debt still paying, ne'er discharg'd, is infinite!   120

For all that is in the world, the lust of the flesh, is not of the Father, but is of the world, &c.

XLI

Strow flowers for spendthrift; Antemasks he might
  Act before Apes, Spectators right:
Whose dops, shrugs, puppet-plays, show best by candlelight.

XLII

Hot shows the season by his dusty head;
  With fancied ribbons round bespread;
Modish, and maddish, all untruss'd, as going to bed.

XLIII

'Ho! First brisk wine, next let a sparkling dame
  Fire our high blood, then quench our flame!
Blest is the son, whose father's gone i' th' Devil's Name.

XLIV

'Each pottle breeds a ruby, drawer, score 'um: 130
  Cheeks dyed in claret, seem o' th' quorum,
When our Nose-Carbuncles, like linkboys, blaze before 'um.'

XLV

Complete thy funeral-pile; shouldst thou mark well
  How down the drunkard's throat to Hell
Death smoothly glides; to swim so sadly would thee quell!

XLVI

Spawns of Excess, dropsies and surfeits are;
  From tenants' sweat's thy bill of fare:
Each glutton digs with 's teeth his grave, whose maw's his care.

XLVII

He's sick, and staggers. Doctor, his case state us,
  'His Cachexy results from flatus
Hypochondruncicus, ex crapula creatus.'   141

XLVIII

Scarce well, he swills what should the needy store;
  And grinds between his teeth the poor,
Who beg dry crumbs, which they with tears would moisten o'er.

XLIX

He a sharp reck'ning shall, with Dives, pay;
  Whose feasts did hasten his audit-day;
Death brought the voider, and the Devil took away!

L

Enter his courtesan, who fans his fire;
  Her prattling eyes teach loose desire:
Fondlings to catch this art-fair fly, like trouts aspire.   150

LI

With paint, false hair, and naked breasts she jets

121 Strow flowers, &c.] Another change; see xi. vi. 16. But it is not necessary to note all.
141 Hypochondruncicus] Here, as noticed above, some timid person has crossed out the right word in the B. M. copy of the *Summary* and substituted *hypochondriacus*.

And patches (Lust's new lime-
twigs) sets ;
Like tickets on the door, herself (for
gold) she lets.

LII

Her basilisk-like glances taint the air
Of virgin-modesty, and snare
His tangling thoughts in trammels
of her ambush-hair.

LIII

With her profusely he misspends
his days
  In balls, and dances, treatments,
  plays ;
And in his bosom this close-biting
serpent lays.

LIV

Death, after sickness, seize this
Helen must ;   160
  Whose radiant eyes, now orbs of
  lust,
Shall sink, as falling stars, which,
jellied, turn to dust.

LV

How wildly shows corrupted Nature's
face,
  Till deck'd by Reason, Learning,
  Grace !
Without which politure the noblest
stem is base !

LVI

Fools rifle out Time's lottery : who
misspend

The soul's rich joys, alive de-
scend,
And antedate with stings their never-
ending end !

LVII

Thy acts outsin the Devil ; who 's
ne'er soil'd
  With gluttony or lust, ne'er
  foil'd   170
By drink ; nor in the net of sloth-
fulness entoil'd.

LVIII

Therefore in time beware ; let not
sin-charms
  Bewitch thee, till Wrath cries to
  arms.
Sin's first face smiles, her second
frowns, her third alarms.

LIX

How blind mad sinners are when
they transgress !
  All woes are, than such blindness,
  less !
That wretch most wretched is who
slights his wretchedness !

LX

When Death shall quench thy flames,
and fiends thee seize,
  In brimstone-torrents, without
  ease,
Thou'lt broil midst blackest fires, and
roar midst burning seas !   180

*For all that is in the world, the pride of life, is not of the Father, but is of the world ;
and the world passeth away, and the lusts thereof, &c.*

LXI

Usher Aspiro in with 's looms of state,
  To weave Fraud's web, and his
  own fate ;
Who, mounted up, throws down the
steps him rais'd of late.

LXII

His posture is ambiguous, his pace
  Is stately high, who thinks it Grace,
If he casts forth a word, and deigns
but half a face :

LXIII

Nor minds he what he speaks ; for
by false light,

Like to his faith, he thrives ; whose
sight,
Clouded with jealousy, can never
judge aright.

LXIV

By dubious answers he is wont to
guess   190
  At men's dislikes ; and fears no less
Feign'd quips, than just reproofs :
fear haunts him in each dress.

LXV

Ambition prompts to precipices steep,
  Which Envy gets, and Hate doth
  keep ;

His daily thoughts of climbing break
his nightly sleep.

LXVI

Could he with 's foot spurn empires
into air,
And sit i' th' universal chair
Of state ; were pageants made for
him, as the World's Mayor ;

LXVII

Those fond disguisements could not
long him fence,
But crosses still would vex his
sense,   200
And leave him blest but in the
preterperfect tense.

LXVIII

Ev'n that at which Pride's tow'ring
project flies,
If gain'd obliquely, sinks, and
dies :
Earth's potentates ! great aims, plots,
fears makes tragedies.

LXIX

Achitophel and Absalon prove this,
(Who of their plots, not plagues
did miss)
To Macchiavels : 'That ill worst to
the plotter is.'

LXX

Pompey and Caesar so ambitious
grow,
A battle must be fought to show
Which of those cocks o' th' game
o'er Rome at last should crow.

LXXI

The world, as great—Cham, Turk,
Mogul upcries,   211
Tuscan's Great Duke (all, no
great prize),
Great Alexander :—the Nine Worthy
ironies.

LXXII

Ev'n sceptres reel like reeds : who
had no bound,
Is bounded in six foot of ground ;
'Here lies the Great'—thou li'st,
here but his dust is found.

LXXIII

Who lately swell'd to be his lord-
ship's slave,
May trample now upon his grave,
That levels all.   Best lectures dust-
seal'd pulpits have.

LXXIV

Where 's now   the Assyrian lion ?
Persian bear ?   220
Greek leopard ? Rome's spread-
eagle where ?
Where now fam'd Troy, that did in
old time domineer ?

LXXV

Troy 's gone, yet Simois stays. See
Fate's strange play !
That which was fix'd, is fled away ;
And what was ever sliding, that doth
only stay !

LXXVI

Therefore, why gap'st thou thus for
shadows ? who
Neglected lets the substance go,
Led by false hope, he makes sad
end in endless woe !

LXXVII

The Mighty mighty torments shall
endure,
If impious : Hell admits no cure :
Ambition 's never safe, though often
too secure.   231

LXXVIII

If Pride on wing could reach the
stars ; yet shall,
Like Lucifer, its carcass fall :
Pride mounted Babel's tower, and
arched Satan's hall.

LXXIX

In centre of the terrible abyss,
Remotest from supernal bliss,
That hapless, hopeless, easeless,
endless dungeon is !

LXXX

Where nought is heard, but yelling !
'Oh, that I
Might once more live ! or once
more die !'
Cursing his woes, he wooes GOD's
curse eternally !   240

But he that doeth the will of God, abideth for ever.
Lord, teach us so to number our days, that we may apply our hearts unto wisdom.

LXXXI

Lust brings forth Sin; Sin shame;
    Shame cries, ' Repent ; '
Repentance weeps ; tears Prayer
    do vent ;
Prayer brings down Grace ; Grace
    Faith ; Faith Love ; Love Zeal
    upsent.

LXXXII

Who fears GOD, is, without despon-
    dence, sad ;
    Timorous, without despair ; and
    glad,
Without wild freaks : whereas the
    World's knave, fool, or mad.

LXXXIII

Part should the world what are in
    man combin'd ;
    The body melts to be refin'd ;
Grace cheers the suffering, Glory
    crowns the conquering mind.

LXXXIV

Nor chance, change, fraud, nor
    force, the just man fright,   250
    In greatest pressures he stands
    right ;
Ever the same (while Sloth feels
    want, Ambition spite).

LXXXV

From costly bills of greedy empirics
    free ;
    From plea of Ambidexter's fee ;
From hypocritic schism of kirkish
    tyranny.

LXXXVI

He with observance honours Virtue's
    friends ;
    And to their faithful counsel
    bends ;
But not on empty forms of worldly
    gauds depends.

LXXXVII

In praising GOD, above the stars he
    climbs ;
    And pitying courts, with all their
    crimes,   260

And fawns, and frowns, dares to be
    good in worst of times.

LXXXVIII

Joy, little world, spite of the greater,
    blest ;
    Scanted abroad, within dost feast,
Hast CHRIST Himself for cates.
    The Holy GHOST for guest.

LXXXIX

Thou walk'st in groves of myrrh,
    with CHRIST thy guide
    (The best of friends that e'er was
    tried),
·By thee in vale of tears spiritual
    joy's descried.

XC

Knew but the World what glorious
    joys still move
    In Faith's bright orb, 'twould
    soar above
All sense, and centre in the point of
    heav'nly love !   270

XCI

Oh, Love's high'st height ! Thou
    art the wise man's bliss !
    T' enjoy thee's Heav'n, Hell thee
    too miss !
The Earth, yea, Heav'n hath its
    beatitude from this!

XCII

No Christian kings win by each
    other's loss ;
    What one gets by retail, in gross
All lose ; while still the Crescent
    gains upon the Cross.

XCIII

As children fight for toys ; so kings
    for clods :
    Heav'n's heir's more great, and
    rich by odds :
For All is his, and he is CHRIST's,
    and CHRIST is GOD's.

XCIV

No bank on earth such sums of
    wealth can lend,   280

As saints, who on Heav'n's grace
   depend;
God's Word their law, His SPIRIT
   their guide, the LAMB their
   friend.

XCV

But, what's vain man? what his
   earth-crawling race?
That GOD should such a shadow
   grace,
And him eternally in GLORY's region
   place?

XCVI

No surfeits' maw-worm's there, no
   itch of Lust,
No tympany of Pride, no rust
Of Envy, no Wrath's spleen, nor
   Obduration's crust.

XCVII

But, there, though Bliss exceeds, it
   never cloys;
   For, sweet Fruition's feast em-
   ploys   290

Still new desire; where none can
   count his least of joys!

XCVIII

The soul there (throwing off her
   rags of clay,
   Laid in Earth's wardrobe, till last
   day)
Ever triumphs in every beatific ray.

XCIX

There, each saint doth an endless
   kingdom own!
   There each king hath a starry
   crown!
Each sceptre there o'erpowers the
   world, and Devil's frown!

C

None blest, but he who finds the
   JUDGE his friend,
   When the last trump shall sum-
   mons send!   299
The End doth crown, the Work, may
   JESUS crown   THE END.

Edward Benlowes

A POETIC DESCANT
UPON A PRIVATE MUSIC-MEETING[1]

I

Muse! Rise, and plume thy feet,
and let's converse
This morn together: let's re-
hearse
Last evening's sweets; and run one
heat in full-speed verse.

II

Prank not thyself in metaphors;
but pound
Thy ranging tropes, that they
may sound
Nothing but what our Paradise did
then surround.

III

Thron'd first Parthenian heav'n-bred
beauties were
Near crystal casements' Eastern
sphere;
Who like to Venus sparkled, yet
more chaste than fair.

IV

'Mongst which, one radiant star so
largely shone,   10
She seem'd a constellation;
Her front 'bove lily-white, cheek
'bove rose-red, full blown.

V

Yet be not planet-struck, like some
that gaze
Too eagerly on Beauty's blaze;
There's none like thine, dear Muse!
theirs are but meteor-rays.

VI

Suitors to idols offer idle suits,
Which hold their presence more
recruits
Their broken hopes, than viols,
pedals, organs, lutes.

VII

But, whist! The masculine sweet
planets met,
Their instruments in tune have
set,   20
And now begin to ransack Music's
cabinet.

VIII

Sol! Thou pure fountain of this
streaming Noise!
Patron of Sweetness! Soul of
Joys!
How were we ravish'd with thy viol's
warbling voice!

IX

Thy nectar-dropping joints so
played their part,
They forced the fibres of our
heart
To dance: thy bow's swift light-
ning made the tears [to?] start.

X

Thou didst ev'n saw the grumbling
catlines still,
And tortured'st the base, until
His roaring diapasons did the whole
room fill.   30

XI

Luna the pedal richly did adorn;
If 'twixt the cedar and the
thorn
There's ought harmonious, 'twas
from this sweet fir-tree born.

XII

As Philomel, Night's minstrel, jugs
her tides
Of rolling melody; she rides
On surges down to th' deep; and,
when she lifts, up glides.

[1] This is taken from the B. M. copy (669 f. 15. 2), a single sheet not noted in Hazlitt's *Hand-book*. It is extremely characteristic, and perhaps as good an *average* example of Benlowes as could be given. If never at his very best in it, he is nowhere near his worst.

XIII

Jove cataracts of liquid gold did pour,
  More precious than his Danaë's show'r ;
From pedal-drops to organ-deluge swell'd the stour.

XIV

Mars twang'd a violin (his fierce drums for fight   40
  Turn'd to brisk Almans) with what sprite
His treble shrill'd forth marches, which he strain'd to the height!

XV

His active bow, arm'd with a war-like tone,
  Rallied his troops of strings, as one,
Which volleys gave i' th' chase of swift division.

XVI

So the Pelean youth was vanquish'd still
  By his renown'd musician's skill,
Which could disarm, and arm the conqueror at will.

XVII

Last Mercury with ravishing strains fell on,
  Whose violin seem'd the chymic-stone,   50
For every melting touch was pure projection.

XVIII

Chair'd midst ' the spheres of Music's Heav'n, I hear,
  I gaze ; charm'd all to eye and ear ;
Both which, with objects too intense, even martyr'd were.

XIX

Th' excess of fairs, distill'd through sweets, did woo

My wav'ring soul, maz'd what to do,
  Or to quit eyes for ears, or ears for eyes forgo.

XX

Giddy i' th' change which sex to crown with praise ;
  Time swore he never was with lays
More sweetly spent ; nor Beauty ever beam'd such rays.   60

XXI

'Twixt these extremes mine eyes and ears did stray,
  And sure it was no time to pray ;
The Deities themselves then being all at play.

XXII

The full-throng'd room its ruin quite defies :
  Nor fairs, nor airs are pond'rous ; skies
Do scorn to shrink, though pil'd with stars and harmonies.

XXIII

Form, Beauty, Sweetness, all did here conspire,
  Combin'd in one Celestial Quire,
To charm the enthusiastic soul with enthean fire :

XXIV

These buoy up care-sunk thoughts ; their power endues   70
  A castril brain with eagle-muse :
When Saints would highest soar they Music['s] pinions use.

XXV

Music ! thy med'cines can our griefs allay,
  And re-inspire our lumpish clay :
Muse ! Thou transcend'st ; Thou without instruments canst play.

BLANDULIS LONGUM VALE CANTILENIS.

---

39 stour] 'Assault,' 'din.' A favourite word of Spenser's.
41 Almans] German marches.   'Sprite' = 'sprightliness.'
71 castril] 'Kestrel,' &c., an ill-bred hawk.

POEMS

By the most deservedly Admired

Mrs Katherine Philips,

The Matchless
1724.

ORINDA.

To which is added

MONSIEUR CORNEILLES

POMPEY
&
HORACE,
TRAGEDIES.

With several other Translations out of

FRENCH

LONDON,

Printed by *T. N.* for *Henry Herringman* at the Sign of
the *Blew Anchor* in the *Lower Walk* of the
New Exchange. 1 6 7 8.

INTRODUCTION
TO KATHERINE PHILIPS

THE Poems of 'the matchless Orinda[1]' are better suited to stand the test on which Joe Gargery apologized for his indulgence at the public house than that on which William Taylor of Norwich judged poetry and was laughed at by Carlyle for judging it. They 'do not over-stimilate': on the division of 'Quotidian and Stimulant' they approach nearer to the former than to the latter. But this is no reason for excluding them from such a collection as this, where some at least of the constituents are rather too much than too little heady. And even if it deserved consideration there are many things on the other side to overrule it. Mrs. Philips as a poetess has been much more talked of than read, a state of things which it is one of the primary duties of editors to combat or cure; the references to her, from Dryden downwards, are more than sufficient vouchers for her reintroduction; and her intrinsic interest, though mild, is by no means insignificant. It is an obvious fancy, but neither too obvious nor too fanciful, to compare the attraction of her verse to that of the large portrait-bust which serves as frontispiece to the

[1] She was born on New Year's Day, 1631, the daughter of John Fowler, a merchant of Bucklersbury in the City of London; and educated at one of the famous Hackney boarding-schools, which, however, she must have left full twenty years before the unhallowed eyes of Samuel Pepys gloated over 'the young ladies of the schools, whereof there is great store, very pretty' on Sunday, April 21st, 1667. John Fowler dying, his widow married a Welshman, Hector Philips of Porth Eynon, whose son, by his first wife, Katherine herself married in 1647. The *Dictionary of National Biography* assigns to her a son (named after his grandfather Hector, and living but forty days) in the year of her marriage. But she expressly says in his epitaph

> *Twice forty months of wedlock did I stay,*
> Then had my vows crowned by a lovely boy.

She had, however, another child, a daughter christened after herself, who was born in 1656, and lived to be married. 'Orinda' began her appearance as a poetess with verses on Vaughan's poems in 1651: and soon attained a considerable (coterie and other) reputation. In 1662 she went to Dublin and had her version of Corneille's *Pompey* performed there. She died of small-pox in Fleet Street, London, on June 22, 1664, having been vexed a little earlier by an unauthorized issue of her *Poems*. (This irritation though excusable, was a little unreasonable, for the delinquent book is a prettier volume than the authorized version, and the variants are neither many nor important.) A further unfinished version of *Horace* was completed by Denham, but neither of these falls within our scope. The *Poems* were collected and published in 1667, and more than once reprinted, without any substantive changes as far as I have noticed. The principal modern treatment of her is in Mr. Gosse's *Seventeenth-century Studies*, and there is a selection, with Introduction by Miss Guiney, in *The Orinda Booklets*. J. R. Tutin, 1904.

Introduction

folio edition of her poems, and which is delicately apologized for as 'a poor paper shadow of a statue made after a portrait not very like her.' In this portrait the features are too much accentuated and the expression hardened and vulgarized a little by adherence to fashion, and supposed proportion, and the like : but there is still an *aura* of possible charm about it[1]. The *Poems* of Orinda are studiously adjusted to Romantic-Platonic ideas of friendship, studiously artificial, studiously 'proper.' But there is more than a suggestion that not merely must 'Rosania' and 'Lucasia' and the rest have possessed and lost a friend worth having, but that 'my Antenor' (less romantically Mr. Philips,) was by more than convention a fortunate man in his marriage, and an unlucky one in his widower-hood.

Part of the interest and value of Orinda's poems for us lie in the way in which they exhibit the settling down of poetry to its more prosaic kinds and expressions about the period of the Restoration : and it is very curious that another poetess, born just after Orinda's death, shows us in like manner the rise from this. Katherine Philips and Lady Winchelsea cover in their lives ten years short of a century, for the elder was still young and the younger not yet old when she died. But between them they give us the curve almost complete. Orinda in such a poem as 'The Soul' shows us the insolent and passionate Elizabethan poetry still trying to soar, but with flagging wings and in a too rare atmosphere ; Ardelia's 'Nocturnal Reverie' shows us the recovery of the way to the empyrean by a diligent and loving attention to the things of terrestrial nature.

The greatest danger for a modern reader of Katherine Philips is of course the associations of the *Précieuse* School, with Rosania and Lucasia and their little harmless plays at being each a Sappho *non doctior sed pudica* (to vary the epigrammatist). But one fashion is very much like another ; seldom much more absurd, almost always as well worth understanding. In England, as in France, there was undoubtedly a good deal of roughness and coarseness to be worn off and cleansed away, and Mrs. Philips and her friends, though Addison was to give their successors a little of his milder satire, were practically doing Addison's work before he himself was born. And the whole thing is a sort of 'side-show' to the Heroic entertainment which is one of the main things that our time has to provide. It does not appear that 'Antenor' objected, or that he had any reason to object; indeed he seems to have played his part with all the mixture of gravity and zeal that could have been required in the Hôtel de Rambouillet itself, and no doubt regarded his gifted spouse as more ingenious if less in quality than even 'Julie.'

To come to details, her couplet verses are rarely very good, and she

---

[1] This is, perhaps not quite fancifully, brought out in a mezzotint by Beckett, inserted by some one in the B. M. copy of the 1678 ed., a really attractive face, and with character in it. Beckett's work is mostly dated about twenty years after Orinda's death. Another later portrait in the same copy is prettified, but mawkish.

Katherine Philips

seldom anticipates, as Chamberlayne and others do after Fairfax, the clench and grip of her contemporary Dryden. But she has retained something of the mysterious charm of earlier Caroline poetry in the shorter and intertwisted measures. For instance, quite early in

Come, my Lucasia, since we see

the quintet, though it has no extraordinary poetical ideas or images to carry, carries its actual burden with something of the strange throb and pulse of pace which we find in the greatest things of Marvell. The next poem is far less effectual, but why? because the couplet added to the quatrain in its six-line arrangement is infinitely less effective than the single line. She is again at home in the simpler octosyllabic quatrain

Come, my Ardelia, to this bower

and hardly less (though she cannot approach the best things of the time) in that unique form of the 'common measure' which that time invented, and which makes one wonder how it can possibly be the same in mere mathematical respects with the jogtrot of Delony or Sternhold.

I did not love until this time
Crowned my felicity,
When I could say without a crime
I am not thine but thee.

How did Donne or Jonson (for it was apparently one or the other) discover this ineffable cadence? How did they manage to teach it to (all but) all and sundry, for half a century? How did it get utterly lost? and how has it been only occasionally and uncertainly recovered? But these are questions, themselves 'begotten of Despair upon Impossibility' yet delightfully suggested by such matter as that which we here collect for study.

Of less strange piquancy, but too good to be left inaccessible, are the 'Lines to Regina Collier on her cruelty to Philaster.' 'Regina,' it may be observed, appears to have been a real name and not of the Orinda kind. Those to Rosania herself

As men that are with visions graced

apply the spell once more. 'A Prayer' is fine; but somehow Orinda is always more at home with her Sapphic-Platonics as in 'To Mrs. M. A. [Mary Aubrey] at Parting':

I have examined and do find
Of all that favour me,
There's none I grieve to leave behind
But only, only thee.

Once more the commonest of commonplaces in sentiment, the most ordinary—almost to the Wordsworthian paradox-level—of words: yet of cadence ineffable, and such that Keats *found* it, and knew it. 'The Enquiry,' 'To My Lucasia' and others, are hardly inferior. She was less happy at the ode ; but she could often manage song-measures featly enough ; as, for instance, in

How prodigious is my fate

which does not ill deserve a place in the too little known anthology of Second-Caroline songs. 'The Parting of Lucasia, Rosania and Orinda at a fountain' (which the sensible Platonics mitigated with Bacchus) is not contemptible : and the epitaph on her own infant son is not the worst of the school of Jonson.

Nor will the reader who really cares for poetry fail to find other things in the Matchless Orinda which will please him ; nor would she have been very sorry not to please the reader who does not so care.

THE PREFACE

WHEN the false Edition of these Poems stole into the light, a friend of that incomparable Lady's that made them, knowing how averse she was to be in Print, and therefore being sure that it was absolutely against her consent, as he believed it utterly without her knowledge, (she being then in Wales, above 150 miles from this town) went presently both to the Gentleman, who licens'd it upon the stationer's averment that he had her leave, and to the stationer himself for whom it was printed, and took the best course he could with both to get it suppress'd, as it presently was (though afterward many of the books were privately sold) and gave her an account, by the next post, of what he had done. A while after he received this answer, which you have here (taken from her own hand) under that disguised name she had given him, it being her custom to use such with most of her particular friends.

Worthy Poliarchus,

IT is very well that you chid me so much for endeavouring to express a part of the sense I have of your obligations ; for while you go on in conferring them beyond all possibility of acknowledgement, it is convenient for me to be forbidden to attempt it. Your last generous concern for me, in vindicating me from the unworthy usage I have received at London from the press, doth as much transcend all your former favours[1], as the injury done me by that Publisher and Printer exceeds all the troubles that I remember I ever had. All I can say to you for it, is, that though you assist[2] an unhappy, it is yet a very innocent person, and that it is impossible for malice itself to have printed those Rimes[3] (you tell me are gotten abroad so impudently) with so much abuse to the things, as the very publication of them at all, though they had been never so correct, had been to me ; to me (Sir) who never writ any line in my life with an intention to have it printed, and who am of my Lord Falkland's mind, that said,

He danger fear'd than censure less,
Nor could he dread a breach like to a
    Press.

And who (I think you know) am sufficiently distrustful of all, that my own want of company and better employment, or others' commands have seduc'd me to write, to endeavour rather that they should never be seen at all, than that they should be expos'd to the world with such effronters[4] as now they most unhappily are. But is there no retreat from the malice of this World ? I thought a rock and a mountain might have hidden me, and that it had been free for all to spend their solitude in what Reveries[5] they please, and that our rivers (though they are babbling) would not have betray'd the follies of impertinent thoughts upon their banks ; but 'tis only I who am that unfortunate person that cannot so much as think in private, that must have my imaginations rifled and exposed to play the mountebanks, and dance upon the ropes to entertain all the rabble ; to undergo all the raillery of the Wits, and all the severity of the Wise ; and to be the sport of some that can, and some that cannot read a verse. This is a most cruel accident, and hath made so proportionate an impression upon me, that really it hath cost me a sharp fit of sickness since I heard it ; and I believe would be more fatal but that I know what a Champion I have in you, and that I am sure your credit in the World will gain me a belief from all that are knowing and civil, that I am so innocent of that wretched

---

[1] Orig. usually the 'or' form.   [2] I substitute 'assist' for 'assert.'
[3] I think it fair to keep this spelling, more especially because I think it the wrong one.
[4] effrontery ?   [5] Orig. Resveires.

artifice of a secret consent (of which I am, I fear, suspected) that whoever would have brought me those copies corrected and amended, and a thousand pounds to have bought my permission for their being printed, should not have obtained it. But though there are many things, I believe, in this wicked impression of those fancies, which the ignorance of what occasion'd them, and the falseness of the copies may represent very ridiculous and extravagant, yet I could give some account of them to the severest Cato, and I am sure they must be more abus'd than I think is possible (for I have not seen the Book, nor can imagine what's in 't) before they can be render'd otherwise than Sir Edward Dering says in his Epilogue to Pompey,

——No bolder thought can tax
Those Rimes of blemish to the blush-
    ing Sex,
As chaste the lines, as harmless is the
    sense,
As the first smiles of infant innocence.

So that I hope there will be no need of justifying them to Virtue and Honour; and I am so little concern'd for the reputation of writing sense, that, provided the World would believe me innocent of any manner of knowledge, much less connivance at this publication, I shall willingly compound never to trouble them with the true copies, as you advise me to do: which if you still should judge absolutely necessary to the reparation of this misfortune, and to general satisfaction; and that, as you tell me, all the rest of my friends will press me to it, I should yield to it with the same reluctancy as I would cut off a limb to save my life. However I hope you will satisfy all your acquaintance of my aversion to it, and did they know me as well as you do, that apology were very needless, for I am so far from expecting applause for any thing I scribble, that I can hardly expect pardon; and sometimes I think that employment so far above my reach, and unfit for my sex, that I am going to resolve against it for ever; and could I have recovered those fugitive papers that have escap'd my hands, I had long since made a sacrifice of

(491)

them all. The truth is, I have an incorrigible inclination to that folly of riming, and intending the effects of that humour, only for my own amusement in a retir'd life; I did not so much resist it as a wiser woman would have done; but some of my dearest friends having found my Ballads, (for they deserve no better name) they made me so much believe they did not dislike them, that I was betray'd to permit some copies for their divertisement; but this, with so little concern for them, that I have lost most of the originals, and that I suppose to be the cause of my present misfortune; for some infernal spirits or other have catch'd those rags of paper, and what the careless blotted writing kept them from understanding, they have supplied by conjecture, till they put them into the shape wherein you saw them, or else I know not which way it is possible for them to be collected, or so abominably transcrib'd as I hear they are. I believe also there are some among them that are not mine, but every way I have so much injury, and the worthy persons that had the ill luck of my converse, and so their names expos'd in this impression without their leave, that few things in the power of Fortune could have given me so great a torment as this most afflictive accident. I know you Sir, so much my friend, that I need not ask your pardon for making this tedious complaint; but methinks it is a great injustice to revenge myself upon you by this harangue for the wrongs I have received from others; therefore I will only tell you that the sole advantage I have by this cruel news, is that it has given me an experiment, That no adversity can shake the constancy of your friendship, and that in the worst humour that ever I was in, I am still,

Worthy Poliarchus,
Your most faithful, most obliged
Friend, and most humble Servant
ORINDA.

Cardigan, *Jan.* 29, 166¾.

She writ divers letters to many of her other friends, full of the like resentments; but this is enough to show

how little she desired the fame of being in print; and how much she was troubled to be so exposed. It may serve likewise to give a taste of her prose to those that have seen none of it, and of her way of writing familiar letters, which she did with strange readiness and facility, in a very fair hand, and perfect orthography; and if they were collected with those excellent discourses she writ on several subjects, they would make a volume much larger than this, and no less worth the reading.

About three months after this Letter she came to London, where her Friends did much solicit her to redeem herself by a correct impression; yet she continued still averse, though perhaps in time she might have been over-rul'd by their persuasions if she had lived.

But the small-pox, that malicious disease (as knowing how little she would have been concern'd for her handsomeness, when at the best) was not satisfied to be as injurious a printer of her face, as the other had been of her Poems, but treated her with a more fatal cruelty than the stationer had them: for though he, to her most sensible affliction, surreptitiously possess'd himself of a false copy, and sent those children of her fancy into the World, so martyred, that they were more unlike themselves than she could have been made, had she escaped; that murtherous tyrant, with greater barbarity, seiz'd unexpectedly upon her, the true original, and to the much juster affliction of all the world, violently tore her out of it, and hurried her untimely to her grave, upon the 22nd of June, 1664, she being then but 31 years of age.

But he could not bury her in oblivion, for this monument which she erected for herself, will, for ever, make her to be honoured as the honour of her sex, the emulation of ours, and the admiration of both. That unfortunate surprise had robb'd it of much of that perfection it might else have had, having broke off the Translation of *Horace* before it was finish'd, much less review'd, and

hindered the rest from being more exactly corrected, and put into the order they were written in, as she possibly herself would have done, had she consented to a second Edition. 'Tis probable she would also have left out some of those pieces that were written with less care and upon occasions less fit to be made public, and she might also have added more: but all industry has been us'd to make this Collection as full and as perfect as might be, by the addition of many that were not in the former impression, and by divers Translations, whereof the first has the Original in the opposite page; that they who have a mind to compare them, may, by that pattern, find how just she has been in all the rest to both the Languages, exactly rendering the full sense of the one, without tying herself strictly to the words, and clearly evincing the capaciousness of the other, by comprising it fully in the same number of lines, though in the Plays half the verses of the French are of thirteen syllables, and the rest of twelve, whereas the English have no more but ten [1]. In short, though some of her pieces may perhaps be lost, and others in hands that have not pro-duc'd them; yet none that upon good grounds could be known to be hers, are left out; for many of the less considerable ones were publish'd in the other; but those, or others that shall be judged so, may be excused by the politeness of the rest which have more of her true spirit, and of her diligence. Some of them would be no disgrace to the name of any Man that amongst us is most esteemed for his excellency in this kind, and there are none that may not pass with favour, when it is remembered that they fell hastily from the pen but of a Woman. We might well have call'd her the English Sappho, she of all the female poets of former Ages, being for her verses and her virtues both, the most highly to be valued; but she has call'd herself ORINDA, a name that deserves to be added to the number of the muses, and to live with honour as long as they. Were our language

---

[1] It has seemed sufficient to meet this by giving *one* stanza of the orig. in a note.

as generally known to the world as the Greek and Latin were anciently, or as the French is now, her verses could not be confin'd within the narrow limits of our islands, but would spread themselves as far as the continent has inhabitants, or as the seas have any shore. And for her virtues, they as much surpass'd those of Sappho as the Theological do the Moral, (wherein yet Orinda was not her inferior) or as the fading immortality of an earthly laurel, which the justice of men cannot deny to her excellent poetry, is transcended by that incorruptible and eternal Crown of Glory, wherewith the Mercy of God hath undoubtedly rewarded her more eminent piety. Her merit should have had a statue of porphyry wrought by some great artist, equal in skill to Michael Angelo, that might have transferr'd to posterity the lasting image of so rare a person: but here is only a poor paper-shadow of a statue made after a picture not very like her, to accompany that she has drawn of herself in these Poems, and which represents the beauties of her mind with a far truer resemblance, than that does the lineaments of her face.

They had sooner performed this right [1] to her memory, if that raging Pestilence which, not long after her, swept away so many thousands here and in other places of this Kingdom; that devouring Fire, which since destroy'd this famous City; and the harsh sounds of War, which with the thunderings of cannon, deafn'd all ears to the gentle and tender strains of Friendship, had not made the publication of them hitherto unseasonable. But they have outliv'd all these dismal things to see the blessing of Peace, a conjuncture more suitable to their Nature, all compos'd of kindness; so that I hope Time itself shall have as little power against them, as these other storms have had, and then [2] Ovid's conclusion of his *Metamorphosis* may, with little alteration, more truth, and less vanity than by him to himself, be applied to these once transformed, or rather deformed Poems, which are here in some measure restor'd to their native shape and beauty, and therefore certainly cannot fail of a welcome reception now, since they wanted it not before, when they appeared in that strange disguise.

The Earl of Orrery to Mrs. Philips

Madam,
WHEN I but knew you by report,
I fear'd the praises of th' admiring Court
Were but their compliments, but now I must
Confess, what I thought civil is scarce just:
For they imperfect trophies to you raise,
You deserve wonder, and they pay but praise;
A praise, which is as short of your great due,
As all which yet have writ come short of you.

You, to whom wonder's paid by double right,
Both for your verses, smoothness and their height.   10
In me it does not the least trouble breed,
That your fair sex does ours, in verse, exceed,
Since every Poet this great truth does prove,
Nothing so much inspires a Muse as Love;
Thence has your sex the best poetic fires,
For what's inspir'd must yield to what inspires.

[1] I am in two minds as to substituting ' rite ' for this.
[2] Nec Jovis ira, nec ignis, nec poteris (*sic in orig. side-note*) ferrum, nec edax abolere vetustas, &c.

And as our sex resigns to yours the
due,
So all of your bright sex must yield to
You.
Experience shows, that never fountain
fed
A stream which could ascend above
its head;   20
For those whose wit fam'd Helicon
does give,
To rise above its height durst never
strive,
Their double hill too, though 'tis often
clear,
Yet often on it clouds and storms
appear.
Let none admire then that the ancient
wit
Shar'd in those elements infused
[in ?] it;
Nor that your Muse than theirs ascends
much higher,
She sharing in no element but fire.
Past ages could not think those things
you do,
For their Hill was their basis and
height too: 30
So that 'tis truth, not compliment, to
tell,
Your lowest height their highest did
excel;
Your nobler thoughts warm'd by a
heav'nly fire,
To their bright centre constantly
aspire;
And by the place to which they take
    their flight,
Leave us no doubt from whence they
have their light.
    Your merit has attain'd this high
degree,
'Tis above praise as much as flattery,
And when in that we have drain'd all
our store,
All grant from this nought can be
distant more.   40
    Though you have sung of friend-
ship's power so well,
That you in that, as you in wit excel;
Yet my own interest obliges me
To praise your practice more than
theory;

For by that kindness you your friend
did show
The honour I obtain'd of knowing
You.
    In pictures none hereafter will
delight,
You draw more to the life in black
and white;
The pencil to your pen must yield the
place,
This draws the soul, where that draws,
but the face.   50
    Of blest retirement such great
Truths you write,
That 'tis my wish as much as your
delight;
Our gratitude to praise it does think
fit,
Since all you writ are but effects of it.
    You English Corneil[le]'s Pompey
with such flame,
That you both raise our wonder and
his fame;
If he could read it, he like us would
call
The copy greater than th' original;
You cannot mend what is already
done,
Unless you'll finish what you have
begun: 60
Who your Translation sees, cannot but
say,
That 'tis Orinda's work, and but his
play.
The French to learn our language
now will seek,
To hear their greatest Wit more nobly
speak;
Rome too would grant, were our tongue
to her known,
Caesar speaks better in 't than in his
own.
And all those wreaths once circl'd
Pompey's brow,
Exalt his fame, less than your verses
now.
    From these clear truths all must
acknowledge this,
If there be Helicon, in Wales it is.   70
Oh happy Country which to our Prince
gives
His Title, and in which Orinda lives!

The Earl of Roscommon to Orinda :
an imitation of Horace

Integer vitae, &c.
Carm. lib. i. od. 22.

I

VIRTUE (dear Friend) needs no defence,
No arms, but its own innocence ;
Quivers and bows, and poison'd darts,
Are only us'd by guilty hearts.

II

An honest mind, safely, alone
May travel through the burning *Zone*,
Or through the deepest *Scythian* snows,
Or where the fam'd *Hydaspes* flows.

III

While (rul'd by a resistless fire)
Our great ORINDA I admire.   10
The hungry wolves that see me stray
Unarm'd and single, run away.

IV

Set me in the remotest place
That ever *Neptune* did embrace,
When there her image fills my breast,
Helicon is not half so blest.

V

Leave me upon some *Lybian* plain,
So she my fancy entertain,
And when the thirsty monsters meet,
They'll all pay homage at my feet.   20

VI

The magic of ORINDA's name,
Not only can their fierceness tame,
But, if that mighty word I once rehearse,
They seem submissively to roar in verse.

Upon Mrs. Philips her Poems

I

WE allow'd you beauty, and we did submit
    To all the tyrannies of it.
Ah cruel Sex! will you dispose us too in Wit ?
Orinda does in that too reign,
Does man behind her in proud triumph draw,
And cancel great Apollo's Salic Law.
    We our old Title plead in vain :
Man may be head, but Woman 's now the brain.
    Verse was love's fire-arms heretofore :
In beauty's camp it was not known,
Too many arms beside that conqueror bore.   11
'Twas the great cannon we brought down,
    T' assault a stubborn town.
Orinda first did a bold sally make,
    Our strongest quarter take,
    And so successful prov'd that she
Turn'd upon Love himself his own artillery.

II

Women, as if the Body were the whole,
    Did that, and not the Soul,
    Transmit to their posterity ;   20
If in it sometimes they conceiv'd,
Th' abortive issue never liv'd.
'Twere shame and pity, Orinda, if in thee
A spirit so rich, so noble, and so high,
    Should unmanur'd or barren lie.
But thou industriously hast sow'd and till'd
    The fair and fruitful field :
And 'tis a strange increase that it doth yield.
    As when the happy Gods above
    Meet all together at a feast,   30
A secret joy unspeakably does move
In their great Mother Cybele's contented breast :
With no less pleasure thou, methinks, shouldst see
This thy no less immortal progeny,
And in their birth thou no one touch dost find,
    Of th' ancient curse to woman-kind ;

Thou bring'st not forth with pain,
It neither travel is, nor labour of thy
brain.
So easily they from thee come,
And there is so much room,　　40
In the unexhausted and unfathom'd
womb ;
That, like the Holland Countess, thou
might'st bear
A child for ev'ry day of all the fertile
year.

III

Thou dost my wonder, wouldst my
envy raise,
If to be prais'd I lov'd more than to
praise.
Where'er I see an excellence,
I must admire to see thy well-knit
sense,
Thy numbers gentle, and thy fancies high,
Those as thy forehead smooth, these
sparkling as thine eye.
'Tis solid, and 'tis manly all,　　50
Or rather, 'tis angelical :
For, as in Angels, we
Do in thy verses see
Both improv'd sexes eminently meet ;
They are than Man more strong, and
more than Woman sweet.

IV

They talk of nine, I know not who,
Female Chimaeras, that o'er Poets
reign ;
I ne'er could find that fancy true,
But have invok'd them oft I'm sure in
vain.
They talk of Sappho, but, alas the
shame !　　60
Ill manners soil the lustre of her fame.
Orinda's inward virtue is so bright,
That, like a lantern's fair enclosèd light,

It through the paper shines where she
doth write.
Honour and Friendship, and the gen'-
rous scorn
Of things for which we were not born,
(Things that can only, by a fond
disease,
Like that of girls, our vicious stomachs
please)
Are the instructive subjects of her pen.
And as the Roman victory　　70
Taught our rude land arts, and
civility,
At once she overcomes, enslaves, and
betters men.

V

But Rome with all her arts could ne'er
inspire
A female breast with such a fire.
The warlike Amazonian train,
Which, in Elysium, now do peaceful
reign,
And Wit's mild empire before Arms
prefer.
Hope 'twill be settled in their sex by
her.
Merlin the seer (and sure he would not
lie
In such a sacred Company)　　80
Does Prophecies of learn'd Orinda
show,
Which he had darkly spoke so long
ago.
Even Boadicia's[1] angry Ghost
Forgets her own misfortune and dis-
grace,
And to her injur'd Daughters now does
boast,
That Rome's o'ercome at last by a
Woman of her race.

ABRAHAM COWLEY.

To the excellent Orinda

LET the male Poets their male Phoebus
choose,
Thee I invoke, Orinda, for my
Muse ;
He could but force a branch, Daphne
her tree
Most freely offers to her sex and thee,
And says to verse, so unconstrain'd as
yours,

Her laurel freely comes, your fame
secures :
And men no longer shall with ravish'd
bays
Crown their forc'd Poems by as forc'd
a praise.
Thou glory of our sex, envy of men,
Who are both pleas'd and vex'd with
thy bright pen :　　10

[1] Boadicia in orig. and better kept for metre.

Its lustre doth entice their eyes to gaze,
But men's sore eyes cannot endure its rays;
It dazzles and surprises so with light,
To find a noon where they expected night:
A woman translate Pompey! which the fam'd
Corneille with such art and labour fram'd!
To whose close version the Wits club their sense,
And a new lay-poetic SMEC[1] springs thence!
Yes, that bold work a woman dares translate,
Not to provoke, nor yet to fear men's hate. 20
Nature doth find that she hath err'd too long,
And now resolves to recompense that wrong:
Phoebus to Cynthia must his beams resign,
The rule of Day, and Wit's now Feminine.
That sex, which heretofore was not allow'd
To understand more than a beast, or crowd;
Of which problems were made, whether or no
Women had souls; but to be damn'd, if so;
Whose highest contemplation could not pass,
In men's esteem, no higher that the class; 30
And all the painful labours of their brain,
Was only how to dress and entertain:
Or, if they ventur'd to speak sense, the wise
Made that, and speaking ox like prodigies.
From these the more than masculine pen hath rear'd
Our sex; first to be prais'd, next to be fear'd.
And by the same pen forc'd, men now confess,
To keep their greatness, was to make us less.
Men know of how refin'd and rich a mould

Our sex is fram'd, what sun is in our cold: 40
They know in lead no diamonds are set,
And jewels only fill the cabinet.
Our spirits purer far than theirs, they see;
By which even men from men distinguish'd be:
By which the soul is judg'd, and does appear
Fit or unfit for action, as they are.
When in an organ various sounds do stroke,
Or grate the ear, as birds sing, or toads croak;
The breath, that voices every pipe, 's the same,
But the bad metal doth the sound defame. 50
So, if our souls by sweeter organs speak,
And theirs with harsh, false notes the air do break;
The soul's the same, alike in both doth dwell,
'Tis from her instruments that we excel,
Ask me not then, why jealous men debar
Our sex from books in peace, from arms in war;
It is because our parts will soon demand
Tribunals for our persons, and command.
Shall it be our reproach, that we are weak,
And cannot fight, nor as the schoolmen speak? 60
Even men themselves are neither strong nor wise,
If limbs and parts they do not exercise,
Train'd up to arms, we Amazons have been,
And Spartan virgins strong as Spartan men:
Breed Women but as Men, and they are these:
Whilst Sybarit Men are Women by their ease.
Why should not brave Semiramis break a lance,
And why should not soft Ninyas curl and dance?

[1] *Smectymnuus.*

Ovid in vain bodies with change did vex,
Changing her form of life, Iphis
   chang'd sex. 70
Nature to females freely doth impart
That, which the males usurp, a stout,
   t.
   :male beasts fear to assail :
   wks more metalled than
   t then courage and wit
   x lives, the lion, or the
   ght men both to them-
   fine,
   n, such as you, Orinda,
   friendship brought thee
   ast,
   casia, and thy courage 80
   wave could not Orinda
fright,
Fearless she acts that friendship she
   did write :
Which manly Virtue to their sex confin'd,
Thou rescuest to confirm our softer
   mind ;
For there 's required (to do that virtue
   right)
Courage, as much in friendship as in
   fight.
The dangers we despise, doth this truth
   prove,
Though boldly we not fight, we boldly
   love.
   Engage us unto books, Sappho comes
   forth,
Though not of Hesiod's age, of Hesiod's
   worth. 90
If souls no sexes have, as 'tis confest,
'Tis not the He or She makes Poems
   best :
Nor can men call these verses feminine,
Be the sense vigorous and masculine.
'Tis true, Apollo sits as judge of Wit,
But the nine Female learnèd troop
   are it :
Those laws for which Numa did wise
   appear,
Wiser Egeria whisper'd in his ear.
The Gracchi's Mother taught them
   eloquence;
From her breasts courage flow'd, from
   her brain sense; 100
And the grave beards, who heard her
   speak in Rome,

Blush'd not to be instructed, but o'er-
   come.
Your speech, as hers, commands re-
   spect from all,
Your very looks, as hers, rhetorical:
Something of grandeur in your verse
   men see,
That they rise up to it as Majesty.
The wise and noble Orrery's regard,
Was much observ'd, when he your
   Poem heard :
All said, a fitter match was never seen,
Had Pompey's Widow been Arsamnes'
   Queen. 110
   Pompey, who greater than himself 's
   become,
Now in your Poem, than before in
   Rome ;
And much more lasting in the poet's pen,
Great Princes live, than the proud
   towers of men.
He thanks false Egypt for its treachery,
Since that his ruin is so sung by thee;
And so again would perish, if withal,
Orinda would but celebrate his fall.
Thus pleasingly the bee delights to die,
Foreseeing, he in amber tomb shall lie.
If that all Egypt, for to purge its crime,
Were built into one pyramid o'er him,
Pompey would lie less stately in that
   hearse, 123
Than he doth now, Orinda, in thy verse :
This makes Cornelia for her Pompey vow,
Her hand shall plant his laurel on thy
   brow :
So equal in their merits were both found,
That the same Wreath Poets and
   Princes Crown'd :
And what on that great captain's brow
   was dead,
She joys to see re-flourish'd on thy
   head. 130
In the French rock Cornelia first did
   shine,
But shin'd not like herself till she
   was thine :
Poems, like gems, translated from the
   place
Where they first grew, receive another
   grace.
Dress'd by thy hand, and polish'd by
   thy pen,
She glitters now a star, but jewel then :
No flaw remains, no cloud, all now is
   light,
Transparent as the day, bright parts
   more bright.

Cornelia, now made English, so doth
  thrive,
As trees transplanted do much lustier
  live.   140
Thus ore digg'd forth and by such
  hands as thine
Refin'd and stamp'd, is richer than the
  mine.
Liquors from vessel into vessel pour'd,
Must lose some spirits, which are
  scarce restor'd :
But the French wines, in their own
  vessel rare,
Pour'd into ours, by thy hand, spirits
  are ;
So high in taste, and so delicious,
Before his own Cornelia thine would
  choose.
He finds himself enlightened here,
  where shade
Of dark expression his own words had
  made :   150
There what he would have said, he
  sees so writ,
As generously, to just decorum fit.
When in more words than his you
  please to flow,
Like a spread flood, enriching all
  below,
To the advantage of his well-meant
  sense,
He gains by you another excellence.
To render word for word, at the old rate,
Is only but to construe, not translate :
In your own fancy free, to his sense true,
We read Cornelia, and Orinda too :   160
And yet ye both are so the very same,
As when two tapers join'd make one
  bright flame.
And sure the copier's honour is not
  small,
When artists doubt which is original.
But if your fetter'd Muse thus praisèd
  be,

What great things do you write when
  it is free ?
When it is free to choose both sense
  and words,
Or any subject the vast World affords ?
A gliding sea of crystal doth best
  show
How smooth, clear, full, and rich your
  verse doth flow :   170
Your words are chosen, cull'd, not by
  chance writ,
To make the sense, as anagrams do hit.
Your rich becoming words on the sense
  wait,
As Maids of Honour on a Queen of
  State.
'Tis not white satin[1] makes a verse
  more white,
Or soft ; Iron is both, write you on it.
Your Poems come forth cast, no file
  you need,
At one brave heat both shap'd and
  polished.
  But why all these encomiums of you,
Who either doubts, or will not take as
  due ?   180
Renown how little you regard, or need,
Who like the bee, on your own sweets
  do feed ?
  There are, who like weak fowl with
  shouts fall down,
Doz'd with an army's acclamation :
Not able to endure applause, they
  fall,
Giddy with praise, their praises' funeral.
But you, Orinda, are so unconcern'd,
As if when you, another we commend[2].
Thus, as the Sun, you, in your course,
  shine on,
Unmov'd with all our admiration. 190
Flying above the praise you shun,
  we see
Wit is still higher by humility.
                        PHILO-PHILIPPA.

To the memory of the excellent Orinda

I

FORGIVE, bright Saint, a vot'ry, who
  No missive Orders has to show,
Nor does a call to inspiration owe :
  Yet rudely dares intrude among

This sacred, and inspirèd throng ;
Where looking round me, ev'ry one
  I see,
Is a sworn Priest of Phoebus, or of
  thee,

---

[1] It was not unusual to print on white satin. Pepys mentions instances.
[2] In this rhyme 'Philo-Philippa' has out-Barretted Mrs. Browning 150 years before-
hand. Even a careful student of all ages of English poetry might be puzzled to find
a worse.

Forgive this forward zeal for things
   divine,
If I strange fire do offer at thy shrine :
  Since the pure incense, and the gum
  We send up to the Pow'rs above, 11
  (If with devotion giv'n, and love)
Smells sweet, and does alike accepted
   prove,
As if from golden censers it did come ;
  Though we the pious tribute pay
In some rude vessel made of common
  clay.

II

What by Pindarics can be done,
  Since the great Pindar's greater [1] Son
(By ev'ry Grace adorn'd, and ev'ry
  Muse inspir'd)
From th' ungrateful World, to kinder
  Heaven 's retir'd :   20
He, and Orinda from us gone,
What Name, like theirs, shall we now
  call upon ?
  Whether her Virtue, or her Wit
  We choose for our eternal theme,
  What hand can draw the perfect
   scheme ?
None but herself could such high
  subjects fit :
  We yield, with shame we yield
  To Death and Her the field :
For were not Nature partial to us men,
The World's great order had inverted
  been :   30
Had she such souls plac'd in all women-
  kind,
Giv'n 'em like wit, not with like good-
  ness join'd,

Our vassal sex to hers had homage
  paid :
Women had rul'd the World, and
  weaker Man obey'd.

III

To thee O Fame, we now commit
Her, and these last remains of gen'rous
  wit ;
  I charge thee, deeply to enroll
This glorious Name in thy immortal
  scroll ;
  Write ev'ry letter in large text,
  And then to make the lustre hold, 40
  Let it be done with purest gold,
To dazzle this age, and outshine the
  next :
  Since not a name more bright than
   Hers,
  In this, or thy large book appears.
And thou impartial, powerful Grave,
These Reliques (like her deathless
  Poems) save
  Ev'n from devouring Time secure,
May they still rest from other mixture
  pure :
Unless some dying Monarch shall to
  try
Whether Orinda, though herself could
  die,   50
Can still give others immortality ;
Think, if but laid in her miraculous
  Tomb,
As from the Prophet's touch, new life
  from hers may come.

            JAMES TYRRELL.

To the memory of the incomparable Orinda
A Pindaric Ode

I

A LONG Adieu to all that 's bright,
  Noble, or brave, in Womankind,
To all the wonders of their wit,
  And trophies of their mind ;
The glowing heat of th' holy fire is gone,
  To th' altar, whence 'twas kindled,
   flown ;
There 's nought on Earth, but ashes
  left behind ;
  E'er since th' amazing sound was
  spread
      ORINDA 's Dead,

Every soft and fragrant word, 10
All that language could afford,
  Every high and lofty thing
That 's wont to set the soul on wing,
No longer with this worthless
  World would stay :
Thus when the death of the great
  PAN was told,
Along the shore the dismal tidings
  roll'd,
  The lesser Gods their fanes for-
  sook;
Confounded with the mighty stroke,

[1] Mr. A. Cowley. (*Orig. note at side.*)

(500)

They could not over-live that fatal
     day,
But sigh'd, and groan'd their gasping
     Oracles away.   20

II

How rigid are the laws of Fate,
     And how severe that black de-
     cree?
No sublunary things is free,
     But all must enter th' adamantine
          gate:
Sooner, or later shall we come
     To Nature's dark retiring-room;
     And yet 'tis pity, is it not?
The learnèd as the fool should die,
     One full as low as t'other lie;
Together blended in the general lot; 30
Distinguish'd only from the common
          crowd,
By an hing'd coffn, or an Holland
          shroud,
Though Fame and Honour speak them
          ne'er so loud;
     Alas ORINDA, even thou!
Whose happy verse made others live,
     And certain immortality could give;
Blasted are all thy blooming glories
          now:
The Laurel withers o'er thy brow:
Methinks it should disturb thee to
          conceive
That when poor I this artless breath
          resign,   40
My dust should have as much of Poetry
     as thine.

III

Too soon we languish with desire
     Of what we never could enough
          admire;
On th' billows of this world some-
          times we rise
     So dangerously high,
We are to Heaven too nigh;
     When (all in rage
Grown hoary with one minute's age,)
     The very self-same fickle wave,
Which the entrancing prospect gave,
Swoll'n to a mountain, sinks into a
          grave.   51
Too happy mortals if the Pow'rs above
     As merciful would be,
And easy to preserve the thing we love,
     As in the giving they are free!
But they too oft delude our weary'd
          Eyes,
They fix a flaming sword 'twixt us and
          Paradise;

A weeping evening crowns a smiling
     day,
Yet why should heads of gold have
     feet of clay?
Why should the man that wav'd th'
     almighty wand,   60
That led the murmuring crowd,
     By pillar and by cloud,
Shivering atop of aëry Pisgah stand,
Only to see, but never, never tread the
     Promis'd Land?

IV

Throw your swords and gauntlets by,
     You daring sons of war,
     You cannot purchase e'er you die
One honourable scar,
Since that fair hand that gilded all
     your bays,
That in heroic numbers wrote your
     praise,   70
While you securely slept in honour's
     bed,
Itself, alas! is withered, cold, and
     dead;
     Cold and dead are all those
          charms,
     Which burnish'd your victorious
          arms:
Inglorious arms hereafter must
     Blush first in blood, and then in rust:
No oil, but that of Her smooth words
     will serve
Weapon, and warrior to preserve.
Expect no more from this dull age,
     But folly, or poetic rage,   80
Short-liv'd nothings of the stage,
Vented to-day, and cried to-morrow
     down,
With HER the soul of poesy is gone;
     Gone, while our expectations flew
As high a pitch as She has done,
     Exhal'd to Heaven like early dew,
Betimes the little shining drops are
     flown,
Ere th' drowsy World perceived that
     Manna was come down.

V

You of the sex that would be fair,
     Exceeding lovely, hither come 90
Would you be pure as Angels are,
     Come dress you by ORINDA's tomb,
And leave your flatt'ring glass at
     home;
     Within this marble mirror see
     How one day such as She
You must, and yet alas! can never be.

Think on the heights of that vast soul,
And then admire, and then con-
dole.
Think on the wonders of Her pen,
'Twas that made Pompey truly
Great,   100
Neither th' expense of blood nor
sweat

Nor yet Cornelia's kindness made him
live agen.
With envy think, when to the
grave you go,
How very little must be said of
you,
Since all that can be said of virtuous
Woman was her due.

THOMAS FLATMAN, M.A.

On the Death of Mrs. Katherine Philips

I

CRUEL Disease! Ah, could it not suffice
Thy old and constant spite to exercise
Against the gentlest and the fairest
sex,
Which still thy depredations most do
vex?
Where still thy malice most of all
(Thy malice or thy lust) does on the
fairest fall;
And in them most assault the fairest
place,
The throne of Empress Beauty, even
the face?
There was enough of that here to
assuage
(One would have thought) either thy
lust or rage: 10
Was 't not enough, when thou, profane
Disease,
Didst on this glorious temple seize?
Was 't not enough, like a wild zealot
there,
All the rich outward ornaments to tear;
Deface the innocent pride of beauteous
images?
Was 't not enough thus rudely to
defile,
But thou must quite destroy the goodly
pile?
And thy unbounded sacrilege commit
On th' inward Holiest Holy of her
Wit?
Cruel Disease! there thou mistook'st
thy power;   20
No mine of Death can that devour;
On her embalmèd name it will abide
An everlasting Pyramid,
As high as Heaven the top, as Earth
the basis wide.

II

All ages past, record; all countries
now

In various kinds such equal beauties
show,
That even Judge Paris would not
know
On whom the Golden Apple to bestow
Though Goddesses to his sentence did
submit,
Women and lovers would appeal from
it;   30
Nor durst he say, of all the female
race
This is the sovereign face.
And some (though these be of a kind
that's rare,
That's much, oh much less frequent
than the fair)
So equally renown'd for virtue are,
That it the Mother of the Gods might
pose,
When the best Woman for her guide
she chose:
But if Apollo should design
A Woman-Laureat to make,
Without dispute he would Orinda take,
Though Sappho and the famous
Nine   41
Stood by, and did repine.
To be a princess or a Queen
Is great, but 'tis a greatness always
seen;
The World did never but two women
know
Who, one by fraud, the other by wit
did rise
To the two tops of Spiritual dignities;
One female Pope of old, one female
Poet now.

III

Of female Poets who had names of
old,
Nothing is shown, but only told,   50
And all we hear of them, perhaps may be
Male flattery only, and male Poetry;

Few minutes did their beauties' light-
ning wast,
The thunder of their voice did longer
last,
  But that too soon was past.
The certain proofs of our Orinda's
Wit
In her own lasting characters are writ,
And they will long my praise of them
survive,
  Though long perhaps too that may
  live.
The trade of glory manag'd by the pen
Though great it be, and everywhere
is found,   61
Does bring in but small profit to us
men ;
'Tis by the number of the sharers
drown'd,
Orinda in the female coasts of fame
Engrosses all the goods of a poetic
name,
  She does no partner with her see ;
Does all the business there alone
which we
Are forc'd to carry on by a whole
company.

                IV

But Wit's like a luxuriant vine,
  Unless to Virtue's prop it join,   70
Firm and erect towards Heaven
bound,
Though it with beauteous leaves and
pleasant fruit be crown'd,
It lies deform'd, and rotting on the
ground.
  Now shame and blushes on us all
Who our own sex superior call ;
Orinda does our boasting sex out-do,
Not in wit only, but in virtue too :
She does above our best examples
rise,
In hate of vice and scorn of vanities.
Never did spirit of the manly make, 80

And dipp'd all o'er in learning's sacred
lake,
A temper more invulnerable take ;
No violent passion could an entrance
find
Into the tender goodness of her mind :
Through walls of stone those furious
bullets may
  Force their impetuous way ;
When her soft breast they hit, damped
and dead they lay.

                v

The fame of Friendship, which so
long had told
Of three or four illustrious Names of
old,
Till hoarse and weary of the tale she
grew,   90
  Rejoices now to have got a new,
  A new, and more surprising story
Of fair Lucasia and Orinda's glory.
As when a prudent man does once per-
ceive
That in some foreign country he must
live,
The language and the manners he
does strive
  To understand and practise here,
  That he may come no stranger there ;
So well Orinda did herself prepare,
In this much different clime for her
remove,   100
To the glad world of Poetry and Love ;
There all the bless'd do but one body
grow,
And are made one too with their
glorious Head,
  Whom there triumphantly they wed,
After the secret contract pass'd below ;
Their Love into Identity does go,
'Tis the first unity's Monarchic Throne,
  The Centre[1] that knits all, where the
  great Three's but One.

                      ABRAHAM COWLEY.

[1] In orig. This destroys the value of 'cen*ter*' found elsewhere. And so constantly.

The Table

[1] I keep this in order to show how little authority, even of its own, the earlier 'rimes' has.

The Table

[1] Orig. 'resvery.'

Katherine Philips

[1] This, which in text is 'Lloyd,' possibly indicates the double pronunciation.
[2] See note in text.

IMPRIMATUR

Aug. 20, 1667.   ROGER L'ESTRANGE.

POEMS

Upon the double Murther of King Charles I, in Answer to a Libellous Copy of Rimes by Vavasor Powell[1]

I THINK not on the State, nor am
    concern'd
Which way soever the great helm is
    turn'd :
But as that son whose Father's
    danger nigh
Did force his native dumbness,
    and untie
The fetter'd organs; so this is a cause
That will excuse the breach of
    Nature's laws,
Silence were now a sin, nay passion
    now
Wise men themselves for merit
    would allow.
What noble eye could see (and
    careless pass)
The dying Lion kick'd by every ass ?
Has Charles so broke God's Laws,
    he must not have   11
A quiet Crown, nor yet a quiet grave ?
Tombs have been sanctuaries;
    Thieves lie there
Secure from all their penalty and
    fear.
Great Charles his double misery was
    this,
Unfaithful friends, ignoble enemies.
Had any heathen been this Prince's
    foe,
He would have wept to see him
    injur'd so,
His title was his crime, they'd reason
    good
To quarrel at the right they had
    withstood.   20
He broke God's Laws, and therefore
    he must die ;

And what shall then become of thee
    and I ?
Slander must follow Treason ; but
    yet stay,
Take not our reason with our King
    away.
Though you have seiz'd upon all
    our defence,
Yet do not sequester our common
    sense.
Christ will be King, but I ne'er
    understood
His subjects built His Kingdom up
    with blood,
Except their own; or that He would
    dispense
With His commands, though for His
    own defence.   30
Oh ! to what height of horror are
    they come
Who dare pull down a crown, tear
    up a tomb ?

On the numerous Access of the English to wait upon the King in Flanders

HASTEN, Great Prince, unto thy
    British Isles,
Or all thy subjects will become
    exiles.
To thee they flock, thy Presence is
    their home,
As Pompey's camp, where e'er it
    mov'd, was Rome.
They that asserted thy Just Cause
    go hence
To testify their joy and reverence ;
And those that did not, now, by
    wonder taught,
Go to confess and expiate their
    fault.

---

[1] A bitter Welsh Nonconformist, and a great harrier of the Church before the Restoration, after which he had rather less than due reward (1617-70).

So that if thou dost stay, thy gasping land
Itself will empty on the Belgic sand : 10
Where the affrighted Dutchman does profess
He thinks it an invasion, not address.
As we unmonarch'd were for want of thee,
So till thou come we shall unpeopled be.
None but the close fanatic will remain,
Who by our loyalty his ends will gain ;
And he th' exhausted land will quickly find
As desolate a place as he design'd.
For England (though grown old with woes) will see
Her long deny'd and sovereign remedy. 20
So when old Jacob could but credit give
That his prodigious Joseph still did live,
(Joseph that was preservèd to restore
Their lives that would have taken his before)
It is enough (said he), to Egypt I
Will go, and see him once before I die.

Arion on a Dolphin, To his Majesty at his passage into England

WHOM does this stately navy bring ?
O ! 'tis Great Britain's glorious King.
Convey him then, ye Winds and Seas,
Swift as Desire and calm as Peace.
In your respect let him survey
What all his other subjects pay ;
And prophesy to them again
The splendid smoothness of his reign.
Charles and his mighty hopes you bear :
A greater now than Caesar's here ; 10

Whose veins a richer purple boast
Than ever hero's yet engrost ;
Sprung from a Father so august,
He triumphs in his very dust.
In him two miracles we view,
His virtue and his safety too :
For when compell'd by traitors' crimes
To breathe and bow in foreign climes,
Expos'd to all the rigid fate
That does on wither'd greatness wait.
Plots against life and conscience laid, 21
By foes pursu'd, by friends betray'd ;
Then Heaven, his secret potent friend,
Did him from drugs and stabs defend ;
And, what's more yet, kept him upright
'Midst flattering hope and bloody fight.
Cromwell his own Right never gain'd,
Defender of the Faith remain'd,
For which his predecessors fought
And writ, but none so dearly bought.
Never was Prince so much besieged,
At home provok'd, abroad obliged ;
Nor ever man resisted thus, 33
No not great Athanasius.
No help of friends could, or foes' spite,
To fierce invasion him invite.
Revenge to him no pleasure is,
He spar'd their blood who gap'd for his ;
Blush'd any hands the English Crown
Should fasten on him but their own.
As Peace and Freedom with him went, 41
With him they came from banishment,
That he might his dominions win,
He with himself did first begin ;
And, that best victory obtained,
His kingdom quickly he regain'd.
Th' illustrious suff'rings of this Prince
Did all reduce, and all convince.

He only liv'd with such success,
That the whole world would fight
　　with less.　　　　　　　　　50
Assistant Kings could but subdue
Those Foes which he can pardon
　　too.
He thinks no Slaughter-trophies
　　good,
Nor laurels dipt in subjects' blood ;
But with a sweet resistless art
Disarms the hand, and wins the
　　heart ;
And like a God doth rescue those
Who did themselves and him
　　oppose.
　　Go, wondrous Prince, adorn that
　　　Throne
Which birth and merit make your
　　own ;　　　　　　　　　　60
And in your mercy brighter shine
Than in the glories of your line ;
Find love at home, and abroad fear,
And veneration everywhere.
Th' united world will you allow
Their Chief, to whom the English
　　bow ;
And Monarchs shall to yours resort,
As Sheba's Queen to Judah's Court ;
Returning thence constrainèd more
To wonder, envy, and adore.　　70
Discovered Rome will hate your
　　crown,
But she shall tremble at your frown.
For England shall (rul'd and restor'd
　　by You)
The suppliant world protect, or else
　　subdue.

On the Fair Weather just at the Coronation, it having rained immediately before and after

So clear a season, and so snatch'd
　　from storms,
Shows Heav'n delights to see what
　　man performs.
Well knew the Sun, if such a day
　　were dim,

It would have been an injury to
　　him :
For then a cloud had from his eye
　　conceal'd
The noblest sight that ever he
　　beheld.
He therefore check'd th' invading
　　rains we fear'd,
And in a bright Parenthesis ap-
　　pear'd.
So that we knew not which look'd
　　most content,
The King, the people, or the firma-
　　ment.　　　　　　　　　　10
But the solemnity once fully past,
The storm return'd with an impetu-
　　ous haste
And Heav'n and Earth each other
　　to out-do,
Vied both in cannons and in fire-
　　works too.
So Israel past through the divided
　　flood,
While in obedient heaps the Ocean
　　stood :
But the same sea (the Hebrews once
　　on shore)
Return'd in torrents where it was
　　before.

To the Queen's Majesty on her Arrival at Portsmouth, May 14, 1662

Now that the Seas and Winds so
　　kind are grown,
For our advantage to resign their
　　own ;
Now you have quitted the triumphant
　　fleet,
And suffered English ground to kiss
　　your feet,
Whilst your glad subjects with
　　impatience throng
To see a blessing they have begg'd
　　so long ;
Whilst Nature (who in compliment
　　to you
Kept back till now her wealth and
　　beauty too)

Hath, to attend the lustre your eyes
  bring,
Sent forth her lov'd Ambassador the
  Spring;   10
Whilst in your praise Fame's echo
  doth conspire
With the soft touches of the sacred
  Lyre;
Let an obscurer Muse upon her
  knees
Present you with such offerings as
  these,
And you as a Divinity adore,
That so your mercy may appear the
  more;
Who, though of those you should
  the best receive,
Can such imperfect ones as these
  forgive.
  Hail, Royal Beauty, Virgin bright
  and great,
Who do our hopes secure, our joys
  complete.   20
We cannot reckon what to you we
  owe,
Who make him happy who makes
  us be so.
But Heav'n for us the desp'rate debt
  hath paid,
Who such a Monarch hath your
  Trophy made.
A Prince whose Virtue did alone
  ˙subdue
Armies of men, and of offences too.
So good, that from him all our
  blessings flow,
Yet is a greater than he can bestow.
So great, that he dispenses life and
  death,
And Europe's fate depends upon his
  breath.   30
(For Fortune in amends now courts
  him more
Than ever she affronted him before:
As lovers that of jealousy repent
Grow troublesome in kind acknow-
  ledgement.)

Who greater courage show'd in
  wooing you,
Than other Princes in their battles
  do.
Never was Spain so generously defied;
Where they design'd a prey, he
  courts a bride.
Hence they may guess what will his
  anger prove,
When he appear'd so brave in making
  love;   40
And be more wise than to provoke
  his arms,
Who can submit to nothing but your
  charms.
And till they give him leisure to
  subdue,
His enemies must owe their peace
  to you.
Whilst he and you mixing illustrious
  rays,
As much above our wishes as our
  praise,
Such heroes shall produce, as even
  they
Without regret or blushes shall obey.

To the Queen-Mother's Majesty, Jan. 1, 166$\frac{0}{1}$

You justly may forsake a land which
  you
Have found so guilty and so fatal too.
Fortune, injurious to your innocence,
Shot all her poison'd arrows here,
  or hence.
'Twas here bold rebels once your
  life pursu'd
(To whom 'twas Treason only to be
  rude,)
Till you were forc'd by their
  unwearied spite
(O glorious Criminal!) to take your
  flight.
Whence after you all that was
  humane[1] fled;

---

[1] The old confusion (or rather not yet division) of 'human' and 'humane' is not always to be got over by distributing the spelling. Something of both senses is wanted here.

For here, oh! here the Royal
  Martyr bled, 10
Whose cause and heart must be
  divine and high,
That having you could be content
  to die,
Here they purloin'd what we to you
  did owe,
And paid you in variety of woe.
Yet all those billows in your breast
  did meet
A heart so firm, so loyal, and so
  sweet,
That over them you greater conquest
  made
Than your immortal Father ever
  had.
For we may read in story of some
  few
That fought like him, none that
  endur'd like you : 20
Till Sorrow blush'd to act what
  Traitors meant,
And Providence itself did first
  repent.
But as our active, so our passive,
  ill
Hath made your share to be the
  sufferer's still.
As from our mischiefs all your
  troubles grew,
'Tis your sad right to suffer for them
  too.
Else our great Charles had not been
  hence so long,
Nor the illustrious Glou'ster died so
  young :
Nor had we lost a Princess all
  confest
To be the greatest, wisest, and the
  best ; 30
Who leaving colder parts, but less
  unkind,
(For it was here she set, and there
  she shin'd,)
Did to a most ungrateful climate
  come
To make a visit, and to find a tomb.
So that we should as much your
  smile despair,

(511)

As of your stay in this unpurgèd air ;
But that your mercy doth exceed
  our crimes
As much as your example former
  times,
And will forgive our off'rings, though
  the flame
Does tremble still betwixt regret
  and shame. 40
For we have justly suffered more
  than you
By the sad guilt of all your suff'rings
  too.
As you the great Idea have been seen
Of either fortune, and in both a
  Queen,
Live still triumphant by the noblest
  wars,
And justify your reconcilèd stars.
See your offenders for your mercy
  bow,
And your tried virtue all mankind
  allow ;
While you to such a race have given
  birth,
As are contended for by Heaven
  and Earth. 50

Upon the Princess Royal her Return into England

WELCOME, sure pledge of reconcilèd
  Powers ;
If Kingdoms have Good Angels, you
  are ours :
For th' Ill ones, check'd by your
  bright influence,
Could never strike till you were
  hurried hence.
But then, as streams withstood more
  rapid grow,
War and confusion soon did over-
  flow :
Such and so many sorrows did
  succeed,
As it would be a new one now to
  read.
But whilst your lustre was to us
  denied,

You scatter'd blessings everywhere
    beside.   10
Nature and Fortune have so curious
    been,
To give you worth, and scene to
    show it in.
But we do most admire that gen'rous
    care
Which did your glorious Brother's
    sufferings share ;
So that he thought them in your
    presence none,
And yet your suff'rings did increase
    his own.
O wond'rous prodigy ! O race divine !
Who owe more to your actions than
    your line.
Your lives exalt your father's death-
    less name,
The blush of England, and the
    boast of Fame.   20

    Pardon, Great Madam, this unfit
    address,
Which does profane the glory 'twould
    confess.
Our crimes have banish'd us from
    you, and we
Were more remov'd by them than
    by the Sea.
Nor is it known whether we wrong'd
    you more
When we rebell'd, or now we do
    adore.
But what Guilt found, Devotion
    cannot miss ;
And you who pardon'd that, will
    pardon this.
Your blest Return tells us our storms
    are ceas'd,
Our faults forgiven, and our stars
    appeas'd,   30
Your mercy, which no malice could
    destroy,
Shall first bestow, and then in-
    struct, our joy.
    For bounteous Heav'n hath, in
    your Highness sent
    Our great example, bliss and orna-
    ment.

On the Death of the Illustrious Duke of Gloucester

GREAT Glou'ster 's dead! and yet in
    this we must
Confess that angry Heaven is wise
    and just.
We have so long and yet so ill en-
    dur'd
The woes which our offences had
    procur'd,
That this new stroke would all our
    strength destroy,
Had we not known an interval of
    Joy.
And yet perhaps this stroke had
    been excus'd,
If we this interval had not abus'd.
But our ingratitude and discontent,
Deserv'd to know our mercies were
    but lent :   10
And those complaints Heaven in
    this rigid fate
Does first chastise, and then legiti-
    mate.
By this it our divisions does reprove,
And makes us join in grief, if not in
    love :
For (Glorious Youth !) all parties do
    agree,
As in admiring, so lamenting Thee ;
The Sovereign's, subject's, foreigner's
    delight ;
Thou wert the Universal Favourite.
Not Rome's Belov'd, and brave
    Marcellus, fell
So much a darling or a miracle.   20
Though built of richest blood and
    finest earth,
Thou hadst a heart more noble than
    thy birth ;
Which by th' afflictive Changes thou
    didst know,
Thou hadst but too much cause and
    time to show.
For when Fate did thy infancy
    expose
To the most barbarous and stupid
    Foes ;

Yet thou didst then so much express
the Prince,
As did even them amaze, if not con-
vince.
Nay, that loose tyrant whom no bound
confin'd,
Whom neither laws, nor oaths, nor
shame could bind,   30
Although his soul was than his look
more grim,
Yet thy brave innocence half soft'n'd
him ;
And he that worth wherein thy soul
was drest,
By his ill-favour'd clemency confest;
Lessening the ill which he could not
repent,
He call'd that travel which was
banishment.
Escap'd from him, thy trials were
increas'd ;
The scene was chang'd, but not the
danger ceas'd :
Thou from rough guardians to sedu-
cers gone,
Those made thy temper, these thy
judgement known ;   40
Whilst thou the noblest champion
wert for truth,
Whether we view thy courage or thy
youth.
If to foil Nature and Ambition claims
Greater reward than to encounter
flames,
All that shall know the story must
allow
A martyr's crown prepar'd for thy
brow.
But yet thou wert suspended from
thy throne,
Till thy Great Brother had regain'd
his own :
Who though the bravest suff'rer,
yet even He
Could not at once have mist his
crown and thee.   50
But as commission'd angels make no
stay,
But having done their errand go
their way :

So thy part done, not thy restorèd
state,
The future splendour which did for
thee wait,
Nor that thy Prince and country
must mourn for
Such a support, and such a counsellor,
Could longer keep thee from that
bliss, whence thou
Look'st down with pity on Earth's
Monarchs now ?
Where thy capacious soul may
quench her thirst,
And younger brothers may inherit
first.   60
While on our King Heav'n does
this care express,
To make his comforts safe he makes
them less.
For this successful heathens use[d?]
to say,
It is too much, (great Gods) send
some allay.

To Her Royal Highness the Duchess of York, on her commanding me to send her some things that I had written

To you whose dignity strikes us with
awe,
And whose far greater judgement
gives us law,
(Your mind b'ing more transcendent
than your state,
For while but knees to this, hearts
bow to that)
These humble papers never durst
come near,
Had not your pow'rful word bid
them appear ;
In which such majesty, such sweet-
ness dwells,
As in one act obliges, and compels.
None can dispute commands vouch-
saf'd by you :
What shall my fears then and con-
fusion do ?   10

They must resign, and by their just
    pretence
Some value set on my obedience.
For in religious duties, 'tis confest,
The most implicit are accepted best.
If on that score your Highness will
    excuse
This blushing tribute of an artless
    Muse,
She may (encourag'd by your least
    regard,
Which first can worth create, and
    then reward)
At modest distance with improvèd
    strains
That Mercy celebrate which now
    she gains.   20
But should you that severer justice
    use,
Which these too prompt approaches
    may produce,
As the swift hind which hath es-
    capèd long,
Believes a vulgar shot would be a
    wrong;
But wounded by a Prince falls with-
    out shame,
And what in life she loses, gains in
    fame:
So if a ray from you chance to be
    sent,
Which to consume, and not to warm,
    is meant;
My trembling Muse at least more
    nobly dies,
And falls by that a truer sacri-
    fice.   30

On the Death of the Queen of Bohemia

ALTHOUGH the most do with offi-
    cious heat
Only adore the living and the
    great;
Yet this Queen's merits Fame so far
    hath spread,
That she rules still, though dispossest
    and dead.

For losing one, two other Crowns
    remain'd;
Over all hearts and her own griefs
    she reign'd.
Two Thrones so splendid, as to
    none are less
But to that third which she does
    now possess.
Her heart and birth Fortune so well
    did know,
That seeking her own fame in such
    a foe,   10
She drest the spacious theatre for
    the fight:
And the admiring World call'd to
    the sight:
An army then of mighty sorrows
    brought,
Who all against this single virtue
    fought;
And sometimes stratagems, and
    sometimes blows
To her heroic soul they did oppose:
But at her feet their vain attempts
    did fall,
And she discovered and subdu'd
    them all.
Till Fortune weary of her malice
    grew,
Became her captive and her trophy
    too: 20
And by too late a tribute begg'd t'
    have been
Admitted subject to so brave a
    Queen.
But as some hero who a field hath
    won,
Viewing the things he had so greatly
    done,
When by his spirit's flight he finds
    that he
With his own life must buy his victory,
He makes the slaughter'd heap that
    next him lies
His funeral pile, and then in triumph
    dies:
So fell this Royal Dame, with con-
    quering spent,
And left in every breast her monu-
    ment;   30

Wherein so high an Epitaph is writ,
As I must never dare to copy it.
But that bright Angel which did on
　her wait,
In fifty years' contention with her
　fate,
And in that office did with wonder see
How great her troubles, how much
　greater she—
How she maintain'd her best prero-
　gative,
In keeping still the power to forgive :
How high she did in her devotion go,
And how her condescension stoop'd
　as low ;　　　　　　　　　40
With how much glory she had ever
　been
A Daughter, Sister, Mother, Wife,
　and Queen—
Will sure employ some deathless
　Muse to tell
Our children this instructive miracle,
Who may her sad illustrious life re-
　cite,
And after all her wrongs may do her
　right.

On the 3rd of September, 1651

As when the glorious magazine of
　light
Approaches to his canopy of night,
He with new splendour clothes his
　dying rays,
And double brightness to his beams
　conveys ;
And (as to brave and check his
　ending fate)
Puts on his highest looks in 's lowest
　state,
Drest in such terror as to make us all
Be Anti-Persians, and adore his fall;
Then quits the World depriving it
　of day,
While every herb and plant does
　droop away :　　　　　　　10
So when our gasping English Royalty
Perceiv'd her period was now drawing
　nigh,

She summons her whole strength to
　give one blow,
To raise herself, or pull down others
　too.
Big with revenge and hope she now
　spake more
Of terror than in many months be-
　fore ;
And musters her attendants, or to
　save
Her from, or else attend her to, the
　grave :
Yet but enjoy'd the miserable fate
Of setting Majesty, to die in state.
Unhappy Kings, who cannot keep a
　throne,　　　　　　　　21
Nor be so fortunate to fall alone !
Their weight sinks others : Pompey
　could not fly,
But half the World must bear him
　company ;
And captiv'd Samson could not life
　conclude,
Unless attended with a multitude.
Who'd trust to greatness now, whose
　food is air,
Whose ruin sudden, and whose end
　despair ?
Who would presume upon his
　Glorious Birth,
Or quarrel for a spacious share of
　Earth,　　　　　　　　　30
That sees such Diadems become so
　cheap,
And Heroes tumble in a common
　heap ?
Oh give me Virtue then, which sums
　up all,
And firmly stands when Crowns and
　Sceptres fall.

To the Noble Palaemon, on his incomparable Discourse of Friendship

We had been still undone, wrapt in
　disguise,
Secure, not happy ; cunning, and
　not wise ;

War had been our design, interest
our trade ;
We had not dwelt in safety, but in
shade,
Hadst thou not hung our light more
welcome far
Than wand'ring sea-men think the
Northern Star ;
To show, lest we our happiness
should miss,
'Tis plac'd in Friendship, men's and
angels' Bliss.
Friendship, which had a scorn or
mask been made,
And still had been derided or be-
tray'd;   10
At which the great physician still had
laugh'd,
The soldier storm**è**d[1], and the gallant
scoff'd ;
Or worn not as a passion, but a plot,
At first pretended, and at last forgot;
Hadst thou not been her great deli-
verer,
At first discover'd, and then rescu'd
her,
And raising what rude malice had
flung down,
Unveil'd her face, and then restor'd
her crown ;
By so august an action to con-
vince,
'Tis greater to support than be a
Prince.   20
Oh for a voice which loud as thunder
were,
That all mankind thy conqu'ring
truths might hear !
Sure the litigious as amaz'd would
stand,
As Fairy Knights touch'd with
Cambina's Wand,
Drawn by thy softer, and yet stronger
charms,
Nations and armies would lay down
their arms :
And what more Honour can on thee
be hurl'd,

Than to protect a virtue, save a
World ?
But while great friendship thou hast
copied out,
Thou'st drawn thyself so well, that
we may doubt   30
Which most appears, thy candour or
thy art,
Whether we owe more to thy brain
or heart.
But this we know without thy own
consent,
Thou'st rais'd thyself a glorious
monument :
Temples and statues Time will eat
away,
And tombs (like their Inhabitants)
decay ;
But there Palaemon lives, and so
he must,
When marbles crumble to forgot-
ten dust.

To the Right Honourable Alice Countess of Carbery, at her coming into Wales

I

As when the first day dawn'd, Man's
greedy eye
Was apt to dwell on the bright pro-
digy,
Till he might careless of his organ
grow,
And let his wonder prove his danger
too :
So when our country (which was
deem'd to be
Close-mourner in its own obscurity,
And in neglected Chaos so long lay)
Was rescu'd by your beams into a
day,
Like men into a sudden lustre
brought,
We justly fear'd to gaze more than
we ought.   10

[1] The print in full of 'storm**e**d' doubtless indicates its disyllabic value.

II

From hence it is you lose most of
    your right,
Since none can pay 't, nor durst do 't
    if they might.
Perfection's misery 'tis that Art and
    Wit,
While they would honour, do but
    injure it.
But as the Deity slights our expense,
And loves Devotion more than
    Eloquence :
So 'tis our confidence you are divine,
Makes us at distance thus approach
    your Shrine.
And thus secur'd, to you who need
    no art,
I that speak least my wit may speak
    my heart.   20

III

Then much above all zealous injury,
Receive this tribute of our shades
    from me,
While your great splendours, like
    eternal spring,
To these sad groves such a refresh-
    ment bring,
That the despisèd country may be
    grown,
And justly too, the envy of the town.
That so when all mankind at length
    have lost
The Virtuous Grandeur which they
    once did boast,
Of you like pilgrims they may here
    obtain
Worth to recruit the dying world
    again.   30

To Sir Edward Dering (the Noble Silvander) on his Dream and Navy, personating Orinda's preferring Rosania before Solomon's Traffic to Ophir

Then am I happier than is the King;
My merchandise does no such danger
    bring :

The fleet I traffic with fears no such
    harms,
Sails in my sight, and anchors in my
    arms.
Each new and unperceivèd grace
Discovered in that mind and face,
Each motion, smile and look from
    thee,
Brings pearls and Ophir-Gold to me.
        Thus far Sir Edw. Dering.

Sir, To be noble, when 'twas voted
    down,
To dare be good, though a whole
    age should frown ;
To live within, and from that even
    state
See all the under-world stoop to its
    fate ;
To give the Law of Honour, and
    dispense
All that is handsome, great and
    worthy thence ;
Are things at once your practice and
    your end,
And which I dare admire, but not
    commend.
But since t' oblige the world is your
    delight,
You must descend within our reach
    and sight :   10
For so Divinity must take dis-
    guise,
Lest mortals perish with the bright
    surprise,
And thus your Muse (which can
    enough reward
All actions she vouchsafes but to
    regard,
And Honours gives, than Kings more
    permanent,
Above the reach of Acts of Parlia-
    ment)
May suffer an acknowledgement
    from me,
For having thence receiv'd Eternity.
My thoughts with such advantage
    you express,
I hardly know them in this charming
    dress.   20

And had I more unkindness from my friend
Than my demerits e'er could apprehend,
Were the fleet courted with this gale of wind,
I might be sure a rich return to find.
So when the Shepherd of his Nymph complain'd,
Apollo in his shape his mistress gain'd:
She might have scorn'd the swain, and found excuse;
But could not his great Orator refuse.
But for Rosania's Interest I should fear
It would be hard t' obtain your pardon here.   30
But your first goodness will, I know, allow
That what was bounty then, is mercy now.
Forgiveness is the noblest charity,
And nothing can worthy your favour be.
For you (God-like) are so much your own fate,
That what you will accept you must create.

To Mr. Henry Lawes

NATURE, which is the vast creation's soul,
That steady curious agent in the whole,
The art of Heaven, the order of this frame,
Is only Number in another name.
For as some King conqu'ring what was his own,
Hath choice of several Titles to his Crown;
So harmony on this score now, that then,
Yet still is all that takes and governs Men.
Beauty is but composure, and we find
Content is but the concord of the mind,   10

Friendship the unison of well-tun'd hearts,
Honour the Chorus of the noblest parts,
And all the world on which we can reflect
Music to th' ear, or to the intellect.
If then each man a Little World must be,
How many Worlds are copied out in thee,
Who art so richly formèd, so complete,
T' epitomize all that is good and great;
Whose stars this brave advantage did impart,
Thy nature's as harmonious as thy art?   20
Thou dost above the Poets, praises live,
Who fetch from thee th' eternity they give.
And as true Reason triumphs over sense,
Yet is subjected to intelligence:
So Poets on the lower World look down,
But Lawes on them; his Height is all his own,
For, like Divinity itself, his lyre
Rewards the wit it did at first inspire
And thus by double right Poets allow
His and their laurel should adorn his brow.   30
Live then, Great Soul of Nature, to assuage
The savage dullness of this sullen Age.
Charm us to Sense; for though experience fail,
And Reason too, thy numbers may prevail
Then, like those ancients, strike, and so command
All Nature to obey thy gen'rous hand.
None will resist but such who needs will be
More stupid than a stone, a fish, a tree.

Be it thy care our age to new-create:
What built a World may sure repair
a state.   40

A Sea-Voyage from Tenby to Bristol, begun Sept. 5, 1652, sent from Bristol to Lucasia, Sept. 8, 1652

Hoise[1] up the sail, cry'd they who
understand
No word that carries kindness for
the land :
Such sons of clamour, that I wonder
not
They love the sea, whom sure some
storm begot.
Had he who doubted Motion these
men seen,
Or heard their tongues, he had con-
vincèd been.
For had our Barque mov'd half as
fast as they,
We had not need cast Anchor by the
way.
One of the rest pretending to more
wit,
Some small Italian spoke, but mur-
ther'd it ;   10
For I (thanks to Saburra's Letters)
knew
How to distinguish 'twixt the false
and true.
But t' oppose these as mad a thing
would be
As 'tis to contradict a Presbyt'ry.
'Tis Spanish though, (quoth I) e'en
what you please :
For him that spoke it 't might be
Bread and Cheese.
So softly moves the barque which
none controls,
As are the meetings of agreeing souls:
And the moon-beams did on the
water play,
As if at midnight 'twould create a
day.   20

The amorous wave that shar'd in
such dispense
Exprest at once delight and rever-
ence.
Such trepidation we in lovers spy
Under th' oppression of a mistress'
eye.
But then the wind so high did rise
and roar,
Some vow'd they'd never trust the
traitor more.
Behold the fate that all our glories
sweep,
Writ in the dangerous wonders of
the deep :
And yet behold man's easy folly more,
How soon we curse what erst we did
adore.   30
Sure he that first himself did thus
convey,
Had some strong passion that he
would obey.
The barque wrought hard, but found
it was in vain
To make its party good against the
main,
Toss'd and retreated, till at last we
see
She must be fast if e'er she should
be free.
We gravely anchor cast, and pa-
tiently
Lie prisoners to the weather's cruelty.
We had nor wind nor tide, nor aught
but grief,
Till a kind spring-tide was our first
relief.   40
Then we float merrily, forgetting quite
The sad confinement of the stormy
night.
Ere we had lost these thoughts, we
ran aground,
And then how vain to be secure we
found.
Now they were all surpris'd. Well, if
we must,
Yet none shall say that dust is gone
to dust.

---

[1] 'Hoist' as obligatory, is quite modern.

But we are off now, and the civil
  tide
Assisted us the tempests to out-ride.
But what most pleased my mind
  upon the way,
Was the ships' posture that in har-
  bour lay :   50
Which to a rocky grove so close were
  fix'd,
That the trees' branches with the
  tackling mix'd.
One would have thought it was, as
  then it stood,
A growing navy, or a floating wood.
But I have done at last, and do
  confess
My voyage taught me so much
  tediousness.
In short, the Heav'ns must needs
  propitious be,
Because Lucasia was concern'd in
  me.

Friendship's Mystery, To my dearest Lucasia

I

COME, my Lucasia, since we see
  That miracles men's faith do
    move,
By wonder and by prodigy
  To the dull angry world let's
    prove
  There's a religion in our Love.

II

For though we were design'd t' agree,
  That Fate no liberty destroys,
But our Election is as free
  As Angels', who with greedy
    choice
  Are yet determin'd to their
    joys.   10

III

Our hearts are doubled by the loss,
  Here mixture is addition grown ;
We both diffuse, and both ingross :
  And we whose minds are so much
    one,
  Never, yet ever are alone.

(520)

IV

We court our own captivity
  Than thrones more great and
    innocent :
'Twere banishment to be set free,
  Since we wear fetters whose intent
  Not bondage is but ornament. 20

V

Divided joys are tedious found,
  And griefs united easier grow :
We are ourselves but by rebound,
  And all our titles shuffled so,
  Both Princes, and both subjects
    too.

VI

Our hearts are mutual victims laid,
  While they (such power in Friend-
    ship lies)
Are Altars, Priests, and Off'rings
  made :
  And each heart which thus kindly
    dies,
  Grows deathless by the sacrifice. 30

Content, To my dearest Lucasia

I

CONTENT, the false World's best
  disguise,
  The search and faction of the wise,
  Is so abstruse and hid in night,
  That, like that Fairy Red-cross
    Knight,
Who treacherous Falsehood for clear
  Truth had got,
Men think they have it when they
  have it not.

II

For Courts Content would gladly
  own,
  But she ne'er dwelt about a
    throne :
  And to be flatter'd, rich, and great,
  Are things which do men's senses
    cheat.   10
But grave Experience long since this
  did see,
Ambition and Content would ne'er
  agree.

Content, To my dearest Lucasia

III

Some vainer would Content ex-
    pect
From what their bright outsides
    reflect :
But sure Content is more divine
Than to be digg'd from rock or
    mine :
And they that know her beauties will
    confess,
She needs no lustre from a glittering
    dress.

IV

In Mirth some place her, but she
    scorns
Th' assistance of such crackling
    thorns,   20
Nor owes herself to such thin
    sport,
That is so sharp and yet so
    short :
And painters tell us they the same
    strokes place,
To make a laughing and a weeping
    face.

V

Others there are that place Con-
    tent
In liberty from Government :
But whomsoe'er Passions deprave,
Though free from shackles, he 's
    a slave.
Content and Bondage differ only
    then,
When we are chain'd by vices, not
    by men.   30

VI

Some think the camp Content
    does know,
And that she sits o' th' victor's
    brow :
But in his laurel there is seen
Often a cypress-brow [1] between.
Nor will Content herself in that
    place give,
Where Noise and Tumult and
    Destruction live.

VII

But yet the most discreet believe,
The Schools this jewel do receive,
And thus far 's true without dispute,
Knowledge is still the sweetest
    fruit.   40
But whilst men seek for Truth they
    lose their peace ;
And who heaps knowledge, sorrow
    doth increase.

VIII

But now some sullen Hermit
    smiles,
And thinks he all the world be-
    guiles,
And that his cell and dish contain
What all mankind wish for in vain.
But yet his pleasure 's follow'd with
    a groan,
For man was never born to be alone.

IX

Content herself best comprehends
Betwixt two souls, and they two
    friends,   50
Whose either joys in both are fix'd,
And multiplied by being mix'd :
Whose minds and interests are so
    the same ;
Their griefs, when once imparted,
    lose that name.

X

These far remov'd from all bold
    noise,
And (what is worse) all hollow joys,
Who never had a mean design,
Whose flame is serious and divine,
And calm, and even, must contented
    be,   59
For they've both Union and Society.

XI

Then, my Lucasia, we who have
Whatever Love can give or crave ;
Who can with pitying scorn survey
The trifles which the most betray ;
With innocence and perfect friend-
    ship fir'd,
By Virtue join'd, and by our choice
    retir'd.

[1] bough ?

XII

Whose mirrors are the crystal
  brooks,
Or else each other's hearts and
  looks ;
Who cannot wish for other things
Than privacy and friendship
  brings :   70
Whose thoughts and persons chang'd
  and mixt are one,
Enjoy Content, or else the World
  hath none.

A Dialogue of Absence 'twixt Lucasia and Orinda. Set by Mr. Hen. Lawes

Luc. Say, my Orinda, why so sad ?
Orin. Absence from thee doth tear
  my heart ;
Which, since with thine it union had,
  Each parting splits. *Luc.* And
  can we part ?
Orin. Our bodies must. *Luc.* But
  never we :
  Our souls, without the help of
  Sense,
By ways more noble and more free
  Can meet, and hold intelligence.
Orin. And yet those Souls, when
  first they met,
  Lookt out at windows through
  the eyes.   10
Luc. But soon did such acquaint-
  ance get,
  Nor Fate nor Time can them
  surprise.
Orin. Absence will rob us of that
  bliss
  To which this friendship title
  brings :
Love's fruits and joys are made by this
  Useless as crowns to captiv'd
  Kings.
Luc. Friendship 's a Science, and we
  know
  There Contemplation 's most em-
  ploy'd.
Orin. Religion 's so, but practic too,
  And both by niceties destroy'd. 20

(522)

Luc. But who ne'er parts can never
  meet,
  And so that happiness were lost.
Orin. Thus Pain and Death are
  sadly sweet,
  Since Health and Heav'n such
  price must cost.

Chorus.

But we shall come where no rude
  hand shall sever,
And there we'll meet and part no
  more for ever.

To my dear Sister Mrs. C. P. on her Marriage

I

We will not like those men our
  offerings pay
Who crown the cup, then think
  they crown the day.
We make no garlands, nor an altar
  build,
Which help not Joy, but Ostentation
  yield.
Where mirth is justly grounded,
  these wild toys
Are but a troublesome, and empty
  noise.

II

But these shall be my great Solem-
  nities,
Orinda's wishes for Cassandra's
  bliss.
May her Content be as unmix'd
  and pure
As my Affection, and like that
  endure ;   10
And that strong happiness may she
  still find
Not owing to her fortune, but her
  mind.

III

May her Content and Duty be the
  same,
And may she know no grief but in
  the name.

May his and her pleasure and love be so
Involv'd and growing, that we may not know
Who most affection or most peace engrost;
Whose love is strongest, or whose bliss is most.

IV

May nothing accidental e'er appear,
But what shall with new bonds their souls endear; 20
And may they count the hours as they pass,
By their own joys, and not by sun or glass:
While every day like this may sacred prove
To Friendship, Gratitude, and strictest Love.

To Mr. Henry Vaughan, Silurist, on his Poems

HAD I ador'd the multitude, and thence
Got an antipathy to Wit and Sense,
And hugg'd that fate in hope the World would grant
'Twas good affection to be ignorant;
Yet the least ray of thy bright fancy seen,
I had converted, or excuseless been;
For each birth of thy Muse to after-times
Shall expiate for all this Age's crimes.
First shines thy Amoret, twice crown'd by thee,
Once by thy love, next by thy poetry: 10
Where thou the best of unions dost dispense,
Truth cloth'd in Wit, and Love in Innocence.
So that the muddiest lovers may learn here,
No Fountains can be sweet that are not clear.

There Juvenal reviv'd by thee declares
How flat Man's joys are, and how mean his cares;
And generously upbraids the World that they
Should such a value for their ruin pay.
But when thy sacred Muse diverts her quill,
The landskip to design of Leon's Hill; 20
As nothing else was worthy her or thee,
So we admire almost t' idolatry.
What savage breast would not be rap'd to find
Such jewels in such cabinets enshrin'd?
Thou (fill'd with joys too great to see or count)
Descend'st from thence like Moses from the Mount,
And with a candid, yet unquestion'd awe,
Restor'st the Golden Age when Verse was Law.
Instructing us thou so secur'st thy fame,
That nothing can disturb it but my name; 30
Nay, I have hopes that standing so near thine
'Twill lose its dross, and by degrees refine.
Live till the disabusèd World consent,
All truths of use, or strength, or ornament,
Are with such harmony by thee display'd,
As the whole World was first by Number made;
  And from the charming rigour thy Muse brings,
  Learn, there's no pleasure but in serious things.

(523)

A retir'd Friendship. To Ardelia

I

COME, my Ardelia, to this Bower,
  Where kindly mingling souls
    awhile,
Let's innocently spend an hour,
  And at all serious follies smile.

II

Here is no quarrelling for crowns,
  Nor fear of changes in our fate ;
No trembling at the Great One's
    frowns,
  Nor any slavery of state.

III

Here's no disguise nor treachery,
  Nor any deep conceal'd design ;
From blood and plots this place is
    free,   11
  And calm as are those looks of
    thine.

IV

Here let us sit and bless our stars,
  Who did such happy quiet give,
As that remov'd from noise of wars,
  In one another's hearts we live.

V

Why should we entertain a fear ?
  Love cares not how the World is
    turn'd :
If crowds of dangers should appear,
  Yet Friendship can be uncon-
    cern'd.   20

VI

We wear about us such a charm,
  No horror can be our offence ;
For mischief's self can do no harm
  To Friendship or to Innocence.

VII

Let's mark how soon Apollo's beams
  Command the flocks to quit their
    meat,
And not entreat the neighbouring
    streams
  To quench their thirst, but cool
    their heat.

VIII

In such a scorching age as this,
  Who would not ever seek a shade,
Deserve their happiness to miss, 31
  As having their own peace
    betray'd.

IX

But we (of one another's mind
  Assur'd) the boisterous World
    disdain ;
With quiet souls and unconfin'd
  Enjoy what Princes wish in vain.

To Mrs. Mary Carne, when Philaster courted her

As some great Conqueror who
    knows no bounds,
But hunting Honour in a thousand
    wounds,
Pursues his rage, and thinks that
    triumph cheap
That's but attended with the common
    heap,
Till his more happy fortune doth
    afford
Some Royal captive that deserv'd
    his sword,
And only now is of his laurel proud,
Thinking his dang'rous valour well
    bestow'd ;
But then retreats, and spending
    hate no more,
Thinks Mercy now what Courage
    was before :   10
As cowardice in fight, so equally
He doth abhor a bloody victory:
So, madam, though your Beauty
    were allow'd
To be severe unto the yielding
    crowd,
That were subdu'd ere you an Object
    knew
Worthy your conquest and your
    mercy too ;
Yet now 'tis gain'd, your victory's
    complete,
Only your clemency should be as
    great.

None will dispute the power of
your eyes,
That understands Philaster is their
prize.   20
Hope not your glory can have new
access,
For all your future trophies will
grow less :
And with that homage be you
satisfi'd
From him that conquers all the
world beside.
Nor let your rigour now the triumph
blot,
And lose the honour which your
beauty got.
Be just and kind unto your peace
and fame,
In being so to him, for they're the
same :
And live and die at once, if you
would be
Nobly transmitted to posterity.   30
Take heed lest in the story they
peruse
A murther which no language can
excuse :
But wisely spare the trouble of one
frown ;
Give him his happiness, and know
your own.
Thus shall you be as Honour's self
esteem'd,
Who have one sex oblig'd, your own
redeem'd.
Thus the religion due unto your
shrine
Shall be as universal, as divine :
And that Devotion shall this bless-
ing gain,
Which Law and Reason do attempt
in vain.   40
The world shall join, maintaining
but one strife,
Who shall most thank you for
Philaster's life.

To Mr. J. B. the noble Cratander, upon a Composition of his which he was not willing to own publicly

As when some injur'd Prince assumes
disguise,
And strives to make his carriage
sympathize,
Yet hath a great becoming mien and
air,
Which speaks him Royal spite of
all his care :
So th' issues of thy soul can ne'er
be hid,
And the Sun's force may be as soon
forbid
As thine obscur'd ; there is no
shade so great
Through which it will not dart forth
light and heat.
Thus we discover thee by thy own
day,
Against thy will snatching the cloud
away.   10
Now the piece shines, and though
we will not say,
Parents can souls, as taper [1] lights,
convey ;
Yet we must grant thy soul trans-
mitted here
In beams almost as lasting and as
clear.
And that's our highest praise, for
but thy mind,
Thy works could never a resem-
blance find.
That mind whose search can Nature's
secret hand
At one great stroke discover and
command,
Which cleareth times and things,
before whose eyes
Nor men nor notions dare put on
disguise.   20

---

[1] Tapers ?

And were all authors now as much forgot
As prosperous Ignorance herself would plot,
Had we the rich supplies of thy own breast,
The knowing World would never miss the rest.
Men did before from Ignorance take their fame,
But Learning's self is honour'd by thy name.
Thou studiest not belief to introduce
Of novelties, more fit for show than use ;
But think'st it nobler charity t' uphold
The credit and the beauty of the old:
And with one hand canst easily support 31
Learning and Law, a Temple and a Court.
And this secures me: for as we below
Valleys from hills, houses from churches know,
But to their fight who stand extremely high,
These forms will have one flat equality :
So from a lower soul I well might fear
A critic censure when survey'd too near ;
But not from him who plac'd above the best,
Lives in a height which levels all the rest. 40

To the Excellent Mrs. Anne Owen, upon her receiving the Name of Lucasia, and Adoption into our Society, December 28, 1651

WE are complete, and Fate hath now
No greater blessing to bestow :

Nay, the dull World must now confess,
We have all worth, all happiness.
Annals of State are trifles to our fame,
Now 'tis made sacred by Lucasia's name.

But as though through a burning-glass
The Sun more vigorous doth pass,
Yet still with general freedom shines ;
For that contracts, but not confines : 10
So though by this her beams are fixèd here,
Yet she diffuses Glory everywhere.

Her mind is so entirely bright,
The splendour would but wound our sight,
And must to some disguise submit,
Or we could never worship it.
And we by this relation are allow'd
Lustre enough to be Lucasia's cloud.

Nations will own us now to be
A Temple of Divinity ; 20
And pilgrims shall ten ages hence
Approach our tombs with reverence.
May then that time which did such bliss convey,
Be kept by us perpetual Holy-day.

To the truly Noble Mrs. Anne Owen, on my first Approaches

MADAM,
As in a triumph conquerors admit
Their meanest captives to attend on it,
Who, though unworthy, have the power confest,
And justifi'd the yielding of the rest :
So when the busy World (in hope t' excuse
Their own surprise) your Conquests do peruse,

And find my name, they will be apt
to say,
Your charms were blinded, or else
thrown away.
There is no honour got in gaining me,
Who am a prize not worth your
victory.   10
But this will clear you, that 'tis
general,
The worst applaud what is admir'd
by all.
But I have plots in 't : for the way
to be
Secure of fame to all posterity,
Is to obtain the honour I pursue,
To tell the World I was subdu'd by
you.
And since in you all wonders
common are,
Your votaries may in your virtues
share,
While you by noble magic worth
impart :
She that can conquer, can reclaim a
heart.   20
Of this creation I shall not despair,
Since for your own sake it concerns
your care.
For 'tis more honour that the world
should know
You made a noble Soul, than found
it so.

Lucasia

NOT to oblige Lucasia by my voice,
To boast my fate, or justify my
choice,
Is this design'd ; but pity does
engage
My pen to rescue the declining Age.
For since 'tis grown in fashion to be
bad,
And to be vain or angry, proud or mad,
(While in their vices only men agree)
Is thought the only modern gallantry;
How would some brave examples
check the crimes,
And both reproach, and yet reform,
the times ?   10

Nor can Morality itself reclaim
Th' apostate World like my Lucasia's
name :
Lucasia, whose rich soul had it been
known
In that time th' Ancients call'd the
Golden one,
When Innocence and Greatness were
the same,
And men no battles knew but in a
game,
Choosing what Nature, not what Art,
prefers ;
Poets were Judges, Kings Philo-
sophers ;
Even then from her the wise would
copies draw,
And she to th' infant world had
giv'n a law.   20
That souls were made of Number
could not be
An observation, but a prophecy.
It meant Lucasia, whose harmonious
state
The Spheres and Muses only imitate.
But as then Music is best under-
stood,
When every chord 's examin'd and
found good :
So what in others Judgement is and
Will,
In her is the same even Reason still.
And as some colour various seems,
but yet
'Tis but our diff'rence in considering
it :   30
So she now light, and then does
light dispense,
But is one shining orb of excellence :
And that so piercing when she
judgement takes,
She doth not search, but intuition
makes :
And her discoveries more easy are
Than Caesar's Conquest in his Pontic
War.
As bright and vigorous her beams
are pure,
And in their own rich candour so
secure,

That had she liv'd where legends
were devised,
Rome had been just, and she been
canonized.   40
Nay Innocence herself less clear
must be,
If Innocence be anything but she.
For virtue's so congenial to her
mind,
That liquid things, or friends, are
less combin'd.
So that in her that sage his wish had
seen,
And virtue's self had personated
been.
Now as distillèd simples do agree,
And in th' alembic lose variety:
So virtue, though in pieces scatter'd
'twas,
Is by her mind made one rich useful
mass.   50
Nor doth Discretion put Religion
down,
Nor hasty Zeal usurp the judgement's
crown.
Wisdom and Friendship have one
single throne,
And make another friendship of
their own.
Each sev'ral piece darts such fierce
pleasing rays,
Poetic Lovers would but wrong in
praise.
All hath proportion, all hath come-
liness,
And her Humility alone excess.
Her modesty doth wrong a worth
so great,
Which Calumny herself would
noblier treat: 60
While true to Friendship and to
Nature's trust,
To her own merits only she's un-
just.
But as Divinity we best declare
By sounds as broken as our notions
are;
So to acknowledge such vast
eminence,
Imperfect wonder is our eloquence.

(528)

No pen Lucasia's glories can re-
late,
But they admire best who dare
imitate.

Wiston Vault

AND why this vault and tomb?
Alike we must
Put off distinction, and put on our
dust.
Nor can the stateliest fabric help to
save
From the corruptions of a common
grave;
Nor for the Resurrection more
prepare,
Than if the dust were scatter'd into
air.
What then? Th' ambition's just,
say some, that we
May thus perpetuate our memory.
Ah false vain task of Art! ah poor
weak Man!
Whose monument does more than's
merit can: 10
Who by his friends' best care and
love's abus'd,
And in his very Epitaph accus'd:
For did they not suspect his Name
would fall,
There would not need an Epitaph
at all.
But after death too I would be
alive,
And shall, if my Lucasia do, sur-
vive.
I quit these pomps of death, and am
content,
Having her heart to be my monu-
ment:
Though ne'er stone to me, 'twill
stone for me prove,
By the peculiar miracles of Love. 20
There I'll inscription have which no
tomb gives,
Not, Here Orinda lies, but, Here
she lives.

Friendship in Emblem, or the Seal. To my dearest Lucasia

I

THE Hearts thus intermixèd speak
A love that no bold shock can
 break;
For join'd and growing both in one,
None can be disturb'd alone.

II

That means a mutual Knowledge
 too;
For what is 't either heart can do,
Which by its panting sentinel
It does not to the other tell?

III

That Friendship hearts so much
 refines,
It nothing but itself designs: 10
The hearts are free from lower
 ends,
For each point to the other tends.

IV

They flame, 'tis true, and several
 ways,
But still those Flames do so much
 raise,
That while to either they incline,
They yet are noble and divine.

V

From smoke or hurt those flames are
 free,
From grossness or mortality:
The heart (like Moses' Bush pre-
 sumed)
Warm'd and enlightened, not
 consumed.   20

VI

The Compasses that stand above,
Express this great immortal Love;
For friends, like them, can prove
 this true,
They are, and yet they are not, two.

VII

And in their posture is exprest
Friendship's exalted interest:
Each follows where the other leans,
And what each does, this other
 means.

(529)

VIII

And as when one foot does stand fast,
And t' other circles seeks to cast,   30
The steady part does regulate
And make the wand'rer's motion
 straight:

IX

So friends are only two in this,
T' reclaim each other when they miss:
For whosoe'er will grossly fall,
Can never be a friend at all.

X

And as that useful instrument
For even lines was ever meant;
So Friendship from good Angels
 springs,
To teach the world heroic things. 40

XI

As these are found out in design
To rule and measure every line;
So Friendship governs actions best,
Prescribing unto all the rest.

XII

And as in Nature nothing 's set
So just as lines in number met;
So Compasses for these b'ing made,
Do friendship's harmony persuade.

XIII

And like to them, so friends may own
Extension, not division: 50
Their points, like bodies, separate;
But head, like souls, knows no such
 fate.

XIV

And as each part so well is knit,
That their embraces ever fit:
So friends are such by destiny,
And no third can the place supply.

XV

There needs no Motto to the Seal:
But that we may the mind reveal
To the dull eye, it was thought fit
That Friendship only should be
 writ.   60

XVI

But as there are degrees of bliss,
So there's no Friendship meant by
 this,
But such as will transmit to Fame
Lucasia and Orinda's Name.

In Memory of F. P. who died at Acton on the 24 of May, 1660, at Twelve and an Half of Age

IF I could ever write a lasting verse,
It should be laid, dear Saint, upon
    thy hearse.
But Sorrow is no Muse, and does
    confess,
That it least can, what it would most
    express.
Yet that I may some bounds to
    Grief allow,
I'll try if I can weep in numbers
    now.
Ah, beauteous blossom, too untimely
    dead !
Whither, ah, whither is thy sweet-
    ness fled ?
Where are the charms that always
    did arise
From the prevailing language of thy
    eyes ?   10
Where is thy beauteous and lovely
    mien,
And all the wonders that in thee
    were seen ?
Alas ! in vain, in vain on thee I rave ;
There is no pity in the stupid grave.
But so the bankrupt sitting on the
    brim
Of those fierce billows which had
    ruin'd him,
Begs for his lost estate, and does
    complain
To the inexorable floods in vain.
As well we may enquire when roses
    die,
To what retirement their sweet odours
    fly ;   20
Whither their virtues and their
    blushes haste,
When the short triumph of their life
    is past ;
Or call their perishing beauties back
    with tears,
As add one moment to thy finish'd
    years.

No, thou art gone, and thy presaging
    mind
So thriftily thy early hours de-
    sign'd,
That hasty Death was baffled in his
    pride,
Since nothing of thee but thy body
    di'd.
Thy soul was up betimes, and so
    concern'd
To grasp all excellence that could
    be learn'd,   30
That finding nothing fill her thirsting
    here,
To the spring-head she went to
    quench it there ;
And so prepar'd, that being freed
    from sin
She quickly might become a
    Cherubin.
Thou wert all Soul, and through
    thy eyes it shin'd :
Asham'd and angry to be so con-
    fin'd,
It long'd to be uncag'd, and thither
    flown
Where it might know as clearly as
    'twas known.
In these vast hopes we might thy
    change have found,
But that Heav'n blinds whom it
    decrees to wound.   40
For parts so soon at so sublime a
    pitch,
A judgement so mature, fancy so
    rich,
Never appear unto unthankful Men,
But as a vision to be hid again.
So glorious scenes in masques,
    spectators view
With the short pleasure of an hour
    or two ;
But that once past, the ornaments
    are gone,
The lights extinguish'd, and the
    curtains drawn.
Yet all these gifts were thy less
    noble part,
Not was thy head so worthy as thy
    heart ;   50

Where the Divine Impression shin'd
  so clear,
As snatch'd thee hence, and yet
  endear'd thee here :
For what in thee did most command
  our love,
Was both the cause and sign of thy
  remove.
Such fools are we, so fatally we
  choose,
That what we most would keep, we
  soonest lose.
The humble greatness of thy pious
  thought,
Sweetness unforc'd, and bashfulness
  untaught,
The native candour of thine open
  breast,
And all the beams wherein thy
  worth was drest,   60
Thy wit so bright, so piercing and
  immense,
Adorn'd with wise and lovely inno-
  cence,
Might have foretold thou wert not
  so complete,
But that our joy might be as short
  as great.
So the poor swain beholds his
  ripen'd corn
By some rough wind without a sickle
  torn.
Never, ah ! never let sad parents
  guess
At one remove of future happiness :
But reckon children 'mong those
  passing joys,
Which one hour gives, and the
  next hour destroys.   70
Alas ! we were secure of our con-
  tent ;
But find too late that it was only
  lent,
To be a mirror wherein we may see
How frail we are, how spotless we
  should be.
But if to thy blest soul my grief
  appears,
Forgive and pity these injurious
  tears :

(531)

Impute them to Affection's sad
  excess,
Which will not yield to Nature's
  tenderness,
Since 'twas through dearest ties and
  highest trust
Continued from thy cradle to thy
  dust ;   80
And so rewarded and confirm'd by
  thine,
That (woe is me !) I thought thee
  too much mine.
But I'll resign, and follow thee as
  fast
As my unhappy minutes will make
  haste.
Till when the fresh remembrances
  of thee
Shall be my Emblems of Mortality.
For such a loss as this (bright Soul !)
  is not
Ever to be repaired, or forgot.

In Memory of that excellent Person Mrs. Mary Lloyd of Bodidrist in Denbigh-shire, who died Nov. 13, 1656, after she came thither from Pembroke-shire.

I CANNOT hold, for though to write
  were rude,
Yet to be silent were ingratitude,
And folly too ; for if posterity
Should never hear of such an one as
  thee,
And only know this age's brutish
  fame,
They would think Virtue nothing
  but a name.
And though far abler pens must her
  define,
Yet her adoption hath engagèd
  mine :
And I must own where merit shines
  so clear,
'Tis hard to write, but harder to
  forbear.   10

Sprung from an ancient and an honour'd stem,
Who lent her lustre, and she paid it them ;
Who still in great and noble things appear'd,
Whom all their country lov'd, and yet they fear'd.
Match'd to another good and great as they,
Who did their country both oblige and sway.
Behold herself, who had without dispute,
More than both families could contribute.
What early beauty Grief and Age had broke,
Her lovely reliques and her offspring spoke. 20
She was by Nature and her parents' care,
A woman long before most others are.
But yet that antedated season she
Improv'd to Virtue, not to Liberty.
For she was still in either state of life,
Meek as a virgin, prudent as a wife.
And she well knew, although so young and fair,
Justly to mix Obedience, Love, and Care ;
Whil'st to her children she did still appear
So wisely kind, so tenderly severe,
That they from her rule and example brought 31
A native Honour, which she stampt and taught.
Nor can a single pen enough commend
So kind a sister and so clear a friend.
A wisdom from above did her secure,
Which as 'twas peaceable, was ever pure.
And if well-order'd Commonwealths must be
Patterns for every private family,

Her house, rul'd by her hand and by her eye,
Might be a pattern for a Monarchy.
Solomon's wisest woman less could do ; 41
She built her house, but this preserv'd hers too.
She was so pious that when she did die,
She scarce chang'd place, I'm sure not company.
Her Zeal was primitive and practice too ;
She did believe, and pray, and read, and do.
A firm and equal soul she had engrost,
Just ev'n to those that disoblig'd her most.
She grew to love those wrongs she did receive
For giving her the power to forgive.
Her alms I may admire, but not relate, 51
But her own works shall praise her in the gate.
Her life was chequer'd with afflictive years,
And even her comfort season'd in her tears.
Scarce for a husband's loss her eyes were dried [1],
And that loss by her children half supplied,
When Heav'n was pleas'd not these dear props t' afford,
But tore most off by sickness or by sword.
She, who in them could still their father boast,
Was a fresh widow every son she lost.
Litigious hands did her of right deprive, 61
That after all 'twas penance to survive.
She still these griefs had nobly undergone,
Which few support at all, but better none.

---

[1] Orig. 'dri'd' and 'suppli'd' which is not quite negligible.

Such a submissive greatness who can
    find ?
A tender heart with so resolv'd
    a mind !
But she, though sensible, was still
    the same,
Of a resignèd soul, untainted fame ;
Nor were her virtues coarsely set,
    for she
Out-did example in civility.   70
To bestow blessings, to oblige,
    relieve,
Was all for which she could endure
    to live.
She had a joy higher in doing good,
Than they to whom the benefit
    accru'd.
Though none of Honour had a
    quicker sense,
Never had woman more of compla-
    cence[1] ;
Yet lost it not in empty forms, but
    still
Her Nature noble was, her soul
    gentile[2].
And as in youth she did attract (for
    she
The verdure had without the vanity),
So she in age was mild and grave
    to all,   81
Was not morose, but was majestical.
Thus from all other women she
    had skill
To draw their good, but nothing of
    their ill.
And since she knew the mad
    tumultuous World
Saw crowns revers'd, temples to
    ruin hurl'd ;
She in retirement chose to shine and
    burn,
As a bright lamp shut in some Roman
    urn.
At last, when spent with sickness,
    grief and age,
Her Guardian Angel did her death
    presage   90

(So that by strong impulse she
    cheerfully
Dispensèd blessings, and went home
    to die ;
That so she might, when to that
    place remov'd,
Marry his ashes whom she ever
    lov'd) :
She died, gain'd a reward, and paid
    a debt.
The Sun himself did never brighter
    set.
Happy were they that knew her and
    her end,
More happy they that did from her
    descend :
A double blessing they may hope to
    have,
One she convey'd to them, and one
    she gave.   100
All that are hers are therefore sure
    to be
Blest by inheritance and legacy.
    A Royal Birth had less advantage
    been.
    'Tis more to die a Saint than
    live a Queen.

To the truly competent Judge of Honour, Lucasia, upon a scandalous Libel made by J. J.

HONOUR, which differs man from
    man much more
Than Reason differ'd him from
    beasts before,
Suffers this common fate of all things
    good,
By the blind World to be misunder-
    stood.
For as some heathens did their Gods
    confine,
While in a bird or beast they made
    their shrine ;

[1] Note the French accent.
[2] This seems worth keeping, both as a document of form and because of the horrible degradation of ' gen*teel* ' in meaning.

Depos'd their Deities to earth, and then
Offer'd them rites that were too low for Men :
So those who most to Honour sacrifice,
Prescribe to her a mean and weak disguise ;   10
Imprison her to others' false applause,
And from Opinion do receive their laws.
While that inconstant Idol they implore,
Which in one breath can murther and adore.
From hence it is that those who Honour court,
(And place her in a popular report)
Do prostitute themselves to sordid Fate,
And from their being oft degenerate.
And thus their Tenents[1] too are low and bad,
As if 'twere honourable to be mad :
Or that their Honour had concernèd been   21
But to conceal, not to forbear, a sin.
But Honour is more great and more sublime,
Above the battery of Fate or Time.
We see in Beauty certain airs are found,
Which not one grace can make, but all compound.
Honour 's to th' mind as Beauty to the sense,
The fair result of mixèd excellence.
As many diamonds together lie,
And dart one lustre to amaze the eye :   30
So Honour is that bright aetherial ray
Which many stars doth in one light display.
But as that Beauty were as truly sweet,
Were there no tongue to praise, no eye to see 't ;

And 'tis the privilege of a native Spark,
To shed a constant splendour in the dark :
So Honour is its own reward and end,
And satisfied within, cannot descend
To beg the suffrage of a vulgar tongue,
Which by commending Virtue doth it wrong.   40
It is the charter of a noble action,
That the performance giveth satisfaction.
Other things are below 't ; for from a clown
Would any Conqueror receive his crown ?
'Tis restless cowardice to be a drudge
To an uncertain and unworthy judge.
So the Cameleon, who lives on air,
Is of all creatures most inclin'd to fear.
But peaceable reflections on the mind,
Will in a silent shade Contentment find.   50
Honour keeps court at home, and doth not fear
To be condemn'd abroad, if quitted there.
While I have this retreat, 'tis not the noise
Of slander, though believ'd, can wrong my joys.
There is advantage in 't : for gold uncoin'd
Had been unuseful, not with glory shin'd :
This stamp'd my innocency in the ore,
Which was as much, but not so bright, before.
Till an Alembic wakes and outward draws,
The strength of sweets lies sleeping in their cause :   60

---

[1] 'Tenant' or 'tenet'? The latter better.

So this gave me an opportunity
To feed upon my own Integrity.
And though their judgement I must
still disclaim,
Who can nor give nor take away
a fame :
Yet I'll appeal unto the knowing
few,
Who dare be just, and rip my heart
to you.

To Antenor, on a Paper of mine which J. J. threatens to publish to prejudice him

MUST then my crimes become thy
scandal too ?
Why, sure the Devil hath not much
to do.
The weakness of the other charge
is clear,
When such a trifle must bring up
the rear.
But this is mad design, for who
before
Lost his repute upon another's score ?
My love and life I must confess are
thine,
But not my errors, they are only
mine.
And if my faults must be for thine
allow'd,
It will be hard to dissipate the cloud :
For Eve's rebellion did not Adam
blast,   11
Until himself forbidden fruit did
taste.
'Tis possible this magazine of Hell
(Whose name would turn a verse
into a spell,
Whose mischief is congenial to his
life)
May yet enjoy an honourable wife.
Nor let his ill be reckoned as her
blame,
Nor yet my follies blast Antenor's
name.

(535)

But if those lines a punishment
could call
Lasting and great as this dark
lanthorn's gall ;   20
Alone I'd court the torments with
content,
To testify that thou art innocent.
So if my ink through malice prov'd
a stain,
My blood should justly wash it off
again.
But since that mint of slander could
invent
To make so dull a rhyme his instru-
ment,
Let verse revenge the quarrel.   But
he 's worse
Than wishes, and below a Poet's
curse ;
And more than this Wit knows not
how to give,
Let him be still himself, and let him
live.   30

Rosania shadowed whilst Mrs. Mary Awbrey

IF any could my dear Rosania hate,
They only should her Character
relate.
Truth shines so bright there, that an
enemy
Would be a better orator than I.
Love stifles language, and I must
confess,
I had said more, if I had lovèd
less.
Yet the most critical who that face
see,
Will ne'er suspect a partiality.
Others by time and by degrees
persuade,
But her first look doth every heart
invade.   10
She hath a face so eminently bright,
Would make a Lover of an Anchorite :
A face where conquest mixt with
modesty,
Are both completed in Divinity.

Not her least glance but sets a heart
on fire,
And checks it if it should too much
aspire.
Such is the magic of her looks, the
same
Beam doth both kindle and refine
our flame.
If she doth smile, no painter e'er
would take
Another rule when he would Mercy
make.   20
And Heav'n to her such splendour
hath allow'd,
That no one posture can her beauty
cloud :
For if she frown, none but would
fancy then
Justice descended here to punish
men.
Her common looks I know not how
to call
Any one Grace, they are compos'd
of all.
And if we mortals could the doctrine
reach,
Her eyes have language, and her
looks do teach.
And as in palaces the outmost,
worst
Rooms entertain our wonder at the
, first ;   30
But once within the Presence-
Chamber door,
We do despise whate'er we saw
before :
So when you with her mind acquaint-
ance get,
You'll hardly think upon the
cabinet.
Her soul, that ray shot from the
Deity,
Doth still preserve its native purity ;
Which earth can neither threaten
nor allure,
Nor by false joys defile it, or ob-
scure.
The innocence which in her heart
doth dwell,
Angels themselves can only parallel.

More gently soft than is an evening
shower :   41
And in that sweetness there is
coucht a power,
Which scorning Pride, doth think it
very hard
That modesty should need so mean
a guard.
Her Honour is protected by her eyes,
As the old Flaming Sword kept
Paradise.
Such constancy of Temper, Truth
and Law,
Guides all her actions, that the
World may draw
From her one soul the noblest
precedent
Of the most safe, wise, virtuous
government.   50
And as the highest element is clear
From all the tempests which disturb
the air :
So she above the World and its rude
noise,
Above our storms a quiet calm
enjoys.
Transcendent things her noble
thoughts sublime,
Above the faults and trifles of the
time.
Unlike those gallants which take far
less care
To have their souls, than make their
bodies fair ;
Who (sick with too much leisure)
time do pass
With these two books, Pride, and a
looking-glass :   60
Plot to surprise men's hearts, their
pow'r to try,
And call that Love, which is mere
Vanity.
But she, although the greatest
Murtherer,
(For ev'ry glance commits a
Massacre)
Yet glories not that slaves her power
confess,
But wishes that her monarchy were
less.

And if she love, it is not thrown
   away,
As many do, only to spend the day;
But hers is serious, and enough alone
To make all Love become Religion.
And to her friendship she so faith-
   ful is,   71
That 'tis her only blot and pre-
   judice:
For Envy's self could never error
   see
Within that soul, 'bating her love to
   me.
Now as I must confess the name of
   friend
To her that all the World doth
   comprehend,
Is a most wild ambition; so for me
To draw her picture is flat lunacy.
Oh! I must think the rest; for
   who can write,
Or into words confine what's
   infinite?   80

To the Queen of Inconstancy, Regina Collier, in Antwerp

I

UNWORTHY, since thou hast decreed
Thy Love and honour both shall
   bleed,
My Friendship could not choose to
   die
In better time or company.

II

What thou hast got by this exchange
Thou wilt perceive, when the re-
   venge
Shall by those treacheries be made,
For which our Faith thou hast
   betray'd.

III

When thy idolaters shall be
True to themselves, and false to
   thee,   10
Thou'lt see that in heart-merchandise,
Value, not number, makes the
   price.

IV

Live to that day, my Innocence
Shall be my Friendship's just
   defence:
For this is all the World can find,
While thou wert noble, I was kind.

V

The desp'rate game that thou dost
   play
At private ruins cannot stay;
The horrid treachery of that face
Will sure undo its native place.   20

VI

Then let the Frenchmen never fear
The victory while thou art there:
For if sins will call judgements down,
Thou hast enough to stock the Town.

To my Excellent Lucasia, on our Friendship

I DID not live until this time
   Crown'd my felicity,
When I could say without a crime,
   I am not thine, but Thee.

This carcase breath'd, and walkt,
   and slept,
   So that the World believ'd
There was a soul the motions kept;
   But they were all deceiv'd.

For as a watch by art is wound
   To motion, such was mine: 10
But never had Orinda found
   A soul till she found thine;

Which now inspires, cures and
   supplies,
   And guides my darkened breast:
For thou art all that I can prize,
   My Joy, my Life, my Rest.

No bridegroom's nor crown-
   conqueror's mirth
   To mine compar'd can be:
They have but pieces of this Earth,
   I've all the World in thee.   20

Then let our flames still light and
   shine,
   And no false fear control,
As innocent as our design,
   Immortal as our soul.

Rosania's private Marriage

IT was a wise and kind design of
    Fate,
That none should this day's glory
    celebrate :
For 'twere in vain to keep a time
    which is
Above the reach of all solemnities.
The greatest actions pass without a
    noise,
And tumults but profane diviner
    joys.
Silence with things transcendent
    nearest suits,
The greatest Emperors are serv'd by
    mutes.
And as in ancient time the Deities
To their own priests reveal'd no
    mysteries   10
Until they were from all the World
    retir'd,
And in some cave made fit to be
    inspir'd.
So when Rosania (who hath them
    out-vied,
And with more justice might be
    deified ;
Who if she had their rites and
    altars, we
Should hardly think it were
    idolatry)
Had found a breast that did deserve
    to be
Receptacle of her Divinity ;
It was not fit the gazing World
    should know
When she convey'd herself to him,
    or how.   20
An eagle safely may behold the
    Sun,
When weak eyes are with too much
    light undone.
Now as in oracles were understood,
Not the priest's only, but the
    common good :
So her great soul would not imparted
    be,
But in design of general Charity.

She now is more diffusive than
    before ;
And what men then admir'd, they
    now adore.
For this exchange makes not her
    power less,
But only fitter for the World's
    address.   30
May then that Mind (which, if we
    will admit
The Universe one Soul, must sure
    be it)
Inform this All (which, till she
    shin'd out, lay
As drowsy men do in a cloudy day),
And Honour, Virtue, Reason so
    dispense,
That all may owe them to her
    influence :
And while this age is thus employ'd,
    may she
Scatter new blessings for posterity.
I dare not any other wish prefer, 39
For only her bestowing adds to her.
And to a soul so in herself complete
As would be wrong'd by any
    epithet,
Whose splendour's fix'd unto her
    chosen sphere,
And fill'd with love and satisfaction
    there,
What can increase the triumph, but
    to see
The World her Convert and her
    History ?

Injuria Amicitiae

LOVELY Apostate ! what was my
    offence ?
Or am I punish'd for obedience ?
Must thy strange rigour find as
    strange a time ?
The act and season are an equal
    crime.
Of what thy most ingenious scorns
    could do,
Must I be subject and spectator
    too ?

Injuria Amicitiae

Or were the sufferings and sins too few
To be sustain'd by me, perform'd
    by you?
Unless (with Nero) your uncurb'd
    desire
Be to survey the Rome you set on
    fire.   10
While wounded for and by your
    power, I
At once your Martyr and your
    Prospect die.
This is my doom, and such a
    riddling fate
As all impossibles doth complicate.
For Obligation here is Injury,
Constancy Crime, Friendship a
    Heresy.
And you appear so much on ruin
    bent,
Your own destruction gives you
    now Content:
For our twin-spirits did so long
    agree,
You must undo yourself to ruin me.
And, like some frantic Goddess,
    you're inclin'd,   21
To raze the temple where you are
    enshrin'd.
And, what's the miracle of cruelty,
Kill that which gave you immortality.
While glorious friendship, whence
    your honour springs,
Lies gasping in the Crowd of common
    things;
And I'm so odious, that for being
    kind
Doubled and studied murthers are
    design'd.
Thy sin's all paradox, for shouldst
    thou be
Thyself again, th' wouldst be severe
    to me.   30
For thy repentance coming now so
    late,
Would only change, and not relieve
    my fate.
So dangerous is the consequence
    of ill,
Thy least of crimes is to be cruel
    still.

(539)

For of thy smiles I should yet more
    complain,
If I should live to be betray'd again.
Live then (fair Tyrant) in security,
From both my kindness and revenge
    be free;
While I, who to the swains had
    sung thy fame,
And taught each echo to repeat thy
    name,   40
Will now my private sorrow enter-
    tain,
To rocks and rivers, not to thee,
    complain.
And though before our union
    cherish'd me,
'Tis now my pleasure that we
    disagree.
For from my passion your last rigour
    grew,
And you kill'd me because I
    worshipp'd you.
But my worst vows shall be your
    happiness,
And not to be disturb'd by my
    distress.
And though it would my sacred
    flames pollute,
To make my heart a scornèd pros-
    titute;   50
Yet I'll adore the author of my death,
And kiss the hand that robs me of
    my breath.

To Regina Collier, on her cruelty to Philaster

TRIUMPHANT Queen of scorn! how
    ill doth sit
In all that sweetness, such injurious
    Wit!
Unjust and Cruel? what can be
    your prize,
To make one heart a double
    Sacrifice?
Where such ingenious rigour you do
    show,
To break his heart, you break his
    image too;

And by a tyranny that's strange and new,
You murther him because he worships you.
No pride can raise you, or can make him start,
Since Love and Honour do enrich his heart.   10
Be wise and good, lest when fate will be just,
She should o'erthrow those glories in the dust,
Rifle your beauties, and you thus forlorn
Make a cheap victim to another's scorn ;
And in those fetters which you do upbraid,
Yourself a wretched captive may be made.
Redeem the poison'd Age, let it be seen
There's no such freedom as to serve a Queen.
But you I see are lately Round-head grown,
And whom you vanquish you insult upon.   20

To Philaster, on his Melancholy for Regina

GIVE over now thy tears, thou vain
  And double Murtherer;
For every minute of thy pain
  Wounds both thyself and her.
Then leave this dullness ; for 'tis our belief,
Thy Queen must cure, or not deserve, thy grief.

Philoclea's parting

KINDER than a condemnèd man's reprieve,
Was your dear company that bad me live.

When by Rosania's silence I had been
The wretched'st martyr any age hath seen.
But as when traitors faint upon the rack,
Tormenters strive to call their spirits back ;
Not out of kindness to preserve their breath,
But to increase the torments of their Death :
So was I raisèd to this glorious state,
To make my fall the more unfortunate.   10
But this I know, none ever died before
Upon a sadder or a nobler score.

To Rosania, now Mrs. Montague, being with her

I
As men that are with visions grac'd,
Must have all other thoughts displac'd,
And buy those short descents of Light
With loss of sense ; or spirit's flight :
II
So since thou wert my happiness,
I could not hope the rate was less ;
And thus the Vision which I gain
Is short t' enjoy, and hard t' attain.
III
Ah then ! what a poor trifle's all
That thing which here we Pleasure call,   10
Since what our very souls hath cost
Is hardly got and quickly lost !
IV
Yet is there justice in the fate ;
For should we dwell in blest estate,
Our joys thereby would so inflame,
We should forget from whence we came.
V
If this so sad a doom can quit
Me for the follies I commit ;

Let no estrangement on thy part
Add a new ruin to my heart.   20

VI

When on myself I do reflect,
I can no smile from thee expect :
But if thy kindness hath no plea,
Some freedom grant for charity.

VII

Else the just World must needs deny
Our Friendship an eternity :
This love will ne'er that title hold :
For mine's too hot, and thine too
    cold.

VIII

Divided rivers lose their name ;
And so our too unequal flame   30
Parted, will Passion be in me,
And an indifference in thee.

IX

Thy absence I could easier find,
Provided thou wert well and kind,
Than such a presence as is this,
Made up of snatches of my bliss.

X

So when the Earth long gasps for
    rain,
If she at last some few drops gain,
She is more parchèd than at first ;
That small recruit increas'd the
    thirst.   40

To my Lucasia

LET dull philosophers enquire no
    more
In Nature's womb, or causes strive
    t' explore,
By what strange harmony and course
    of things
Each body to the whole a tribute
    brings;
What secret unions secret neigh-
    bourings make,
And of each other how they do par-
    take.
These are but low experiments :
    but he
That Nature's harmony entire would
    see,

Must search agreeing souls, sit down
    and view
How sweet the mixture is, how full,
    how true ;   10
By what soft touches spirits greet
    and kiss,
And in each other can complete their
    bliss.
A wonder so sublime, it will admit
No rude spectator to contemplate it.
The object will refine, and he that can
Friendship revere, must be a noble
    man.
How much above the common rate
    of things
Must they then be, from whom this
    union springs !
But what's all this to me, who live
    to be
Disprover of my own mortality ?   20
And he that knew my unimprovèd
    soul,
Would say I meant all friendship to
    control.
But bodies move in time, and so
    must minds ;
And though th' attempt no easy
    progress finds,
Yet quit me not, lest I should des-
    p'rate grow,
And to such friendship add some
    patience now.
O may good Heav'n but so much
    virtue lend,
To make me fit to be Lucasia's
    Friend !
But I'll forsake myself, and seek a
    new
Self in her breast that's far more
    rich and true.   30
Thus the poor Bee unmark'd doth
    hum and fly,
And dron'd with age would unre-
    garded die,
Unless some lucky drop of precious
    gum,
Do bless the insect with an Amber-
    tomb.
Then glorious in its funeral the Bee
Gets Eminence, and gets Eternity.

On Controversies in Religion

RELIGION, which true policy be-
friends,
Design'd by God to serve Man's
noblest ends,
Is by that old Deceiver's subtle play
Made the chief party in its own
decay,
And meets that eagle's destiny,
whose breast
Felt the same shaft which his own
feathers drest.
For that great Enemy of souls per-
ceiv'd,
The notion of a Deity was weav'd
So closely in Man's soul; to ruin
that,
He must at once the World depopu-
late.   10
But as those tyrants who their wills
pursue,
If they expound old laws, need make
no new :
So he advantage takes of Nature's
light,
And raises that to a bare useless
height;
Or while we seek for Truth, he in the
quest
Mixes a Passion, or an Interest,
To make us lose it; that I know
not how,
'Tis not our practice, but our quarrel
now.
As in the Moon's eclipse some Pagans
thought
Their barbarous clamours her deliver-
ance wrought :   20
So we suppose that truth oppressèd
lies,
And needs a rescue by our enmities.
But 'tis injustice, and the mind's
disease,
To think of gaining Truth by losing
Peace.
Knowledge and Love, if true, do
still unite ;
God's Love and Knowledge are both
infinite.

And though indeed Truth does
delight to lie
At some remoteness from a com-
mon eye ;
Yet 'tis not in a thunder or a noise,
But in soft whispers and the stiller
Voice.   30
Why should we then Knowledge so
rudely treat,
Making our weapon what was meant
our meat ?
'Tis Ignorance that makes us quarrel
so ;
The soul that's dark will be contracted
too.
Chimaeras make a noise, swelling
and vain,
And soon resolve to their own smoke
again.
But a true light the spirit doth
dilate,
And robs it of its proud and sullen
state ;
Makes Love admir'd because 'tis
understood,
And makes us wise because it makes
us good.   40
'Tis to a right prospect of things
that we
Owe our Uprightness and our
Charity.
For who resists a beam when shin-
ing bright,
Is not a sinner of a common height.
That state's a forfeiture, and helps
are spent,
Not more a Sin, than 'tis a punish-
ment.
The soul which sees things in their
native frame,
Without Opinion's mask or Custom's
name,
Cannot be clogg'd to Sense, or
count that high
Which hath its estimation from a
lie.   50
(Mean, sordid things, which by mis-
take we prize,
And absent covet, but enjoy'd
despise.)

(542)

But scorning these hath robb'd them
of their art,
Either to swell or to subdue the
Heart;
And learn'd that generous frame to
be above
The World in hopes, below it all in
love:
Touch'd with divine and inward
life doth run,
Not resting till it hath its centre won;
Moves steadily until it safe doth lie
I' th' root of all its immortality; 60
And resting here hath yet activity
To grow more like unto the Deity;
Good, Universal, Wise, and Just
as he,
(The same in kind, though diff'ring
in degree)
Till at the last 'tis swallowed up and
grown
With God and with the whole Crea-
tion one;
Itself, so small a part, i' th' Whole
is lost,
And generals have particulars en-
grost.
That dark contracted personality,
Like mists before the Sun, will from
it fly. 70
And then the soul, one shining
sphere, at length
With true Love's wisdom fill'd and
purgèd strength,
Beholds her highest good with open
face,
And like him all the World she can
embrace.

To the Honoured Lady E.C.

MADAM,

I do not write to you that men may
know
How much I'm honour'd that I may
do so:
Nor hope (though I your rich ex-
ample give)
To write with more success than
I can live,

(543)

To cure the age; nor think I can be
just,
Who only dare to write, because
I must.
I'm full of you, and something must
express,
To vent my wonder and your pow'r
confess.
Had I ne'er heard of your illustrious
name,
Nor known the Scotch or English
ancient fame; 10
Yet if your glorious frame did but
appear,
I could have soon read all your
grandeur there.
I could have seen in each majestic ray,
What greatness ancestors could e'er
convey;
And in the lustre of your eyes alone,
How near you were allièd to the
Throne:
Which yet doth lessen you, who
cannot need
Those bright advantages which you
exceed.
For you are such, that your descent
from Kings
Receives more honour from you
than it brings: 20
As much above their glories as our
toil.
A Court to you were but a hand-
some soil.
And if we name the stock on which
you grew,
'Tis rather to do right to it than
you:
For those that would your greatest
splendour see,
Must read your soul more than your
pedigree.
For as the sacred Temple had with-
out
Beauty to feed those eyes that gaz'd
about,
And yet had riches, state, and wonder
more,
For those that stood within the shin-
ing door; 30

But in the Holy Place the admitted few,
Lustre receiv'd and inspiration too :
So though your glories in your face be seen,
And so much bright instruction in your mien ;
You are not known but where you will impart
The treasures of your more illustrious heart.
Religion all her odours sheds on you,
Who by obeying vindicate her too :
For that rich beam of Heaven was almost
In nice disputes and false pretences lost ; 40
So doubly injur'd, she could scarce subsist
Betwixt the hypocrite and casuist ;
Till you by great example did convince
Us of her nature and her residence.
And chose to show her face, and ease her grief,
Less by your arguments than by your life ;
Which if it should be copied out, would be
A solid body of divinity.
Your principle and practice light would give
What we should do, and what we should believe : 50
For the extensive knowledge you profess,
You do acquire with more ease than confess,
And as by you knowledge has thus obtain'd
To be refin'd, and then to be explain'd :
So in return she useful is to you,
In practice and in contemplation too.
For by the various succours she hath lent,
You act with judgement, and think with content.

Yet those vast parts with such a temper meet,
That you can lay them at Religion's feet. 60
Nor is it half so bold as it is true,
That Virtue is herself oblig'd to you :
For being drest in your subduing charms,
She conquers more than did the Roman arms.
We see in you how much that Malice lied
That stuck on goodness any sullen pride ;
And that the harshness some professors wear
Falls to their own, and not Religion's share.
But your bright sweetness if it but appear,
Reclaims the bad, and softens the austere. 70
Men talk'd of Honour too, but could not tell
What was the secret of that active spell.
That beauteous mantle they to divers lent,
Yet wonder'd what the mighty nothing meant.
Some did confine her to a worthy fame,
And some to Royal parents gave her name.
You having claim unto her either way,
By what a King could give, a world could pay,
Have a more living honour in your breast,
Which justifies, and yet obscures the rest ; 80
A principle from fame and pomp untied,
So truly high that it despises Pride ;
Buying good actions at the dearest rate,
Looks down on ill with as much scorn as hate ;

(544)

Acts things so generous and bravely hard,
And in obliging finds so much reward ;
So self-denying great, so firmly just,
Apt to confer, strict to preserve a trust ;
That all whose honour would be justified,
Must by your standards have it stamp'd and tried.   90
But your perfection heightens others' crimes,
And you reproach while you inform the times.
Which sad advantage you will scarce believe ;
Or if you must, you do conceal and grieve.
You scorn so poor a foil as others' ill,
And are protector to th' unhappy still ;
Yet are so tender when you see a spot,
You blush for those who for themselves could not.
You are so much above your sex, that we
Believe your Life your greatest courtesy :   100
For women boast, they have you while you live
A pattern and a representative,
And future mothers who in child-birth groan,
Shall wish for daughters, knowing you are one.
The world hath Kings whose crowns are cemented,
Or by the blood they boast, or that they shed :
Yet these great idols of the stooping crew
Have neither pleasure sound, nor honour true.
They either fight, or play ; and power court,
In trivial anger, or in cruel sport. 110

You, who a nobler privilege enjoy,
(For you can save whom they can but destroy)
An Empire have where different mixtures kiss ;
You're grave, not sour, and kind, but not remiss.
Such sweetened Majesty, such humble State,
Do love and reverence at once create.
Pardon (dear Madam) these untaught essays,
I can admire more fitly than I praise.
Things so sublime are dimly understood,
And you are born so great, and are so good,   120
So much above the honour of your name,
And by neglect do so secure your fame ;
Whose beauty's such as captivates the wise,
Yet only you of all the World despise ;
That have so vast a knowledge so subdued,
Religion so adorn'd, and so pursued ;
A wit so strong, that who would it define,
Will need one ten times more acute than mine ;
Yet rul'd so that its vigour manag'd thus
Becomes at once graceful and generous ;   130
Whose honour has so delicate a sense,
Who always pardon, never give offence ;
Who needing nothing, yet to all are kind,
Who have so large a heart, so rich a mind ;
Whose Friendship still's of the obliging side,
And yet so free from Tyranny and Pride ;

Who do in love like Jonathan descend,
And strip yourself to clothe your happy friend ;
Whose kindness and whose modesty is such,
T' expect so little and deserve so much;   140
Who have such candid worth, such dear concern,
Where we so much may love, and so much learn ;
Whose every wonder though it fills and shines,
It never to an ill excess declines ;
But all are found so sweetly opposite,   ·
As are in Titian's pieces shade and light :
That he that would your great description try,
Though he write well, would be as lost as I,
Who of injurious Zeal convicted stand,
To draw you with so bold and bad a hand ;   150
   But that, like other glories, I presume
   You will enlighten, where you might consume.

Parting with Lucasia, A Song

I
WELL, we will do that rigid thing
   Which makes spectators think we part;
Though Absence hath for none a sting
   But those who keep each other's heart.

II
And when our sense is dispossest,
   Our labouring souls will heave and pant,
And gasp for one another's breast,
   Since their conveyances they want.

III
Nay, we have felt the tedious smart
   Of absent Friendship, and do know
That when we die we can but part ;
   And who knows what we shall do now ?   12

IV
Yet I must go : we will submit,
   And so our own disposers be ;
For while we nobly suffer it,
   We triumph o'er Necessity.

V
By this we shall be truly great,
   If having other things o'ercome,
To make our victory complete   19
   We can be conquerors at home.

VI
Nay then to meet we may conclude,
   And all obstructions overthrow,
Since we our passion have subdu'd,
   Which is the strongest thing I know.

Against Pleasure. Set by Dr. Coleman

I
THERE'S no such thing as Pleasure here,
   'Tis all a perfect cheat,
Which does but shine and disappear,
   Whose charm is but deceit :
The empty bribe of yielding souls,
Which first betrays, and then controls.

II
'Tis true, it looks at distance fair ;
   But if we do approach,
The fruit of Sodom will impair,
   And perish at a touch :   10
In being than in fancy less,
And we expect more than possess.

III
For by our pleasures we are cloy'd,
   And so Desire is done ;
Or else, like rivers, they make wide
   The channel where they run :
And either way true bliss destroys,
Making Us narrow, or our Joys.

IV

We covet pleasure easily,
   But it not so possess;   20
For many things must make it be,
   But one may make it less.
Nay, were our state as we could
   choose it,
'Twould be consum'd by fear to
   lose it.

V

What art thou then, thou wingèd air,
   More weak and swift than Fame?
Whose next successor is Despair,
   And its attendant Shame.
Th' experienc'd Prince then reason
   had,
Who said of pleasure, It is mad.   30

A Prayer

ETERNAL Reason, Glorious Majesty,
Compar'd to whom what can be said
   to be?
Whose attributes are Thee, who art
   alone
Cause of all various things, and yet
   but One;
Whose Essence can no more be
   search'd by man,
Than Heav'n, Thy Throne, be graspèd
   with a span.
Yet if this great Creation was de-
   sign'd
To several ends fitted for every
   kind;
Sure Man (the World's epitome)
   must be
Form'd to the best, that is to study
   Thee.   10
And as our dignity, 'tis duty too,
Which is summ'd up in this, to
   know and do.
These comely rows of creatures spell
   Thy Name,
Whereby we grope to find from
   whence they came,
By Thy own chain of causes brought
   to think
There must be one, then find that
   highest link.

Thus all created Excellence we see
Is a resembla nce faint and dark of
   Thee.
Such shadows are produc'd by the
   moon-beams
Of trees or houses in the running
   streams.   20
Yet by impressions born with us we
   find
How good, great, just Thou art, how
   unconfin'd.
Here we are swallowed up and gladly
   dwell,
Safely adoring what we cannot tell.
All we know is, Thou art supremely
   good,
And dost delight to be so under-
   stood.
A spicy mountain on the universe,
On which Thy richest odours do
   disperse.
But as the sea to fill a vessel heaves,
More greedily than any cask re-
   ceives,   30
Besieging round to find some gap
   in it,
Which will a new infusion admit:
So dost Thou covet that Thou mayst
   dispense
Upon the empty World Thy influence;
Lov'st to disburse Thyself in kindness:
   Thus
The King of Kings waits to be
   gracious.
On this account, O God, enlarge my
   heart
To entertain what Thou wouldst fain
   impart.
Nor let that soul, by several titles
   Thine,
And most capacious form'd for
   things Divine,   40
(So nobly meant, that when it most
   doth miss,
'Tis in mistaken pantings after
   bliss)
Degrade itself in sordid things' de-
   light,
Or by profaner mixtures lose its
   right.

Oh! that with fixt unbroken thoughts
    it may
Admire the light which does obscure
    the day.
And since 'tis Angels' work it hath
    to do,
May its composure be like Angels
    too.
When shall these clogs of Sense and
    Fancy break,
That I may hear the God within
    me speak?   50
When with a silent and retirèd art
Shall I with all this empty hurry
    part?
To the Still Voice above, my soul
    advance;
My light and joy plac'd in his
    countenance?
By whose dispense my soul to such
    frame brought,
May tame each treach'rous, fix each
    scatt'ring thought;
With such distinctions all things
    here behold,
And so to separate each dross from
    gold,
That nothing my free Soul may
    satisfy,   59
But t' imitate, enjoy, and study thee.

To Mrs. M. A. upon Absence

I

'Tis now since I began to die
    Four months, yet still I gasping
      live;
Wrapp'd up in sorrow do I lie,
    Hoping, yet doubting a reprieve.
Adam from Paradise expell'd
Just such a wretched being held.

II

'Tis not thy love I fear to lose,
    That will in spite of absence hold;
But 'tis the benefit and use
    Is lost, as in imprison'd gold: 10
Which though the sum be ne'er so
    great,
Enriches nothing but conceit.

III

What angry star then governs me
    That I must feel a double smart,
Prisoner to fate as well as thee;
    Kept from thy face, link'd to thy
      heart?
Because my love all love excels,
Must my grief have no parallels?

IV

Sapless and dead as Winter here
    I now remain, and all I see   20
Copies of my wild state appear,
    But I am their epitome.
Love me no more, for I am grown
Too dead and dull for thee to
    own.

To Mrs. Mary Awbrey

Soul of my soul, my Joy, my Crown,
    my Friend,
A name which all the rest doth
    comprehend;
How happy are we now, whose souls
    are grown,
By an incomparable mixture, one:
Whose well-acquainted minds are
    now as near
As Love, or Vows, or Friendship can
    endear?
I have no thought but what's to thee
    reveal'd,
Nor thou desire that is from me
    conceal'd.
Thy heart locks up my secrets richly
    set,
And my breast is thy private cabinet.
Thou shed'st no tear but what my
    moisture lent,   11
And if I sigh, it is thy breath is
    spent.
United thus, what horror can appear
Worthy our sorrow, anger, or our
    fear?
Let the dull World alone to talk and
    fight,
And with their vast ambitions Nature
    fright;

To Mrs. Mary Awbrey

Let them despise so innocent a
flame,
While Envy, Pride, and Faction
play their game :
But we by Love sublim'd so high
shall rise,
To pity Kings, and Conquerors
despise,   20
Since we that sacred union have
engrost,
Which they and all the factious
World have lost.

In Memory of Mr. Cartwright

STAY, Prince of Fancy, stay, we are
not fit
To welcome or admire thy raptures
yet :
Such horrid Ignorance benights the
times,
That Wit and Honour are become
our crimes.
But when those happy Pow'rs which
guard thy dust
To us, and to thy Mem'ry shall be
just,
And by a flame from thy blest Genius
lent,
Rescue us from our dull imprison-
ment,
Unsequester our Fancies, and create
A worth that may upon thy glories
wait :   10
We then shall understand thee, and
descry
The splendour of restorèd Poetry.
Till when let no bold hand profane
thy shrine ;
'Tis high Wit-Treason to debase thy
coin.

Mr. Francis Finch, the Excellent Palaemon

THIS is confest presumption, for
had I
All that rich stock of ingenuity

Which I could wish for this, yet
would it be
Palaemon's blot, a pious injury.
But as no votaries are scorn'd when
they
The meanest victim in Religion
pay ;
Not that the Pow'r they worship needs
a gum,
But that they speak their thanks for
all with some :
So though the most contemptible
of all
That do themselves Palaemon's ser-
vants call,   10
I know that Zeal is more than
sacrifice,
(For God did not the widow's mite
despise)
And that Palaemon hath Divinity,
And Mercy is his highest property :
He that doth such transcendent
merit own,
Must have imperfect off'rings or none.
He 's one rich lustre which doth rays
dispense,
As Knowledge will when set in
Innocence.
For Learning did select his noble
breast,
Where (in her native majesty) to
rest ;   20
Free from the tyranny and pride of
Schools,
Who have confin'd her to pedantic
rules ;
And that gentiler[1] error which does
take
Offence at Learning for her habit's
sake,
Palaemon hath redeem'd her, who
may be
Esteem'd himself an University ;
And yet so much a gentleman, that he
Needs not (though he enjoys) a
pedigree.
Sure he was built and sent to let us
know

---

[1] Spelling of 'gentiler' retained for reasons elsewhere given.

What man completed could both be
  and do.   30
Freedom from vice is in him Nature's
  part,
Without the help of discipline or
  art.
He's his own happiness and his own
  law,
Whereby he keeps Passion and Fate
  in awe.
Nor was this wrought in him by
  Time and growth,
His Genius had anticipated both.
Had all men been Palaemons, Pride
  had ne'er
Taught one man Tyranny, the other
  Fear;
Ambition had been full as monstrous
  then
As this ill World doth render
  worthy men.   40
Had men his spirit, they would
  soon forbear
Grovelling for dirt, and quarrelling
  for air.
Were his harmonious soul diffus'd
  in all,
We should believe that men did
  never fall.
It is Palaemon's soul that hath
  engrost
Th' ingenuous candour that the
  World hath lost;
Whose own mind seats him quiet,
  safe and high,
Above the reach of Time or
  Destiny.
'Twas he that rescu'd gasping
  Friendship when
The bell toll'd for her funeral with
  men: 50
'Twas he that made Friends more
  than Lovers burn,
And then made Love to sacred
  Friendship turn:
'Twas he turn'd Honour inward, set
  her free
From titles and from popularity.
Now fix'd to Virtue, she begs praise
  of none,

But 's witness'd and rewarded both
  at home.
And in his breast this Honour's so
  enshrin'd,
As the old Law was in the Ark
  confin'd:
To which posterity shall all consent,
And less dispute than Acts of
  Parliament.   60
He's our original, by whom we see
How much we fail, and what we
  ought to be.
But why do I to copy him pretend?
My rhymes but libel whom they
  would commend.
'Tis true; but none can reach what's
  set so high;
And though I miss, I've noble
  company:
For the most happy language must
  confess,
It doth obscure Palaemon, not
  express.

To Mrs. M. A. at parting

I

I HAVE examin'd and do find,
  Of all that favour me,
There's none I grieve to leave behind
  But only, only thee.
To part with thee I needs must die,
Could parting sep'rate thee and I.

II

But neither Chance nor Compliment
  Did element our Love;
'Twas sacred Sympathy was lent
  Us from the quire above.   10
That Friendship Fortune did create,
Still fears a wound from Time or
  Fate.

III

Our chang'd and mingled souls are
  grown
  To such acquaintance now,
That if each would resume their
  own,
  Alas! we know not how.
We have each other so engrost,
That each is in the union lost.

To Mrs. M. A. at parting

IV

And thus we can no Absence know,
  Nor shall we be confin'd ;   20
Our active souls will daily go
  To learn each other's mind.
Nay, should we never meet to Sense,
Our souls would hold Intelligence.

V

Inspired with a flame divine,
  I scorn to court a stay ;
For from that noble soul of thine
  I ne'er can be away.
But I shall weep when thou dost
    grieve ;
Nor can I die whilst thou dost
    live.   30

VI

By my own temper I shall guess
  At thy felicity,
And only like my happiness
  Because it pleaseth thee.
Our hearts at any time will tell,
If thou, or I, be sick, or well.

VII

All Honour sure I must pretend,
  All that is good or Great ;
She that would be Rosania's Friend,
  Must be at least complete. 40
If I have any bravery,
'Tis cause I have so much of thee.

VIII

Thy leiger [1] soul in me shall lie,
  And all thy thoughts reveal ;
Then back again with mine shall fly,
  And thence to me shall steal.
Thus still to one another tend ;
Such is the sacred Name of Friend.

IX

Thus our twin-souls in one shall
    grow,
  And teach the World new love, 50
Redeem the age and sex, and show
  A flame Fate dares not move :
And courting Death to be our friend,
Our lives together too shall end.

X

A dew shall dwell upon our Tomb
  Of such a quality,
That fighting armies, thither come,
  Shall reconcilèd be.
We'll ask no Epitaph, but say
  ORINDA and ROSANIA. 60

To my dearest Antenor, on his Parting

THOUGH it be just to grieve when
    I must part
With him that is the Guardian of
    my Heart ;
Yet by a happy change the loss
    of mine
Is with advantage paid in having
    thine.
And I (by that dear guest instructed)
    find
Absence can do no hurt to souls
    combin'd.
As we were born to love, brought
    to agree
By the impressions of Divine decree :
So when united nearer we became,
It did not weaken, but increase, our
    flame. 10
Unlike to those who distant joys
    admire,
But slight them when possest of
    their desire.
Each of our souls did its own
    temper fit,
And in the other's mould so fashion'd
    it,
That now our inclinations both are
    grown,
Like to our interests and persons,
    one ;
And souls whom such an union
    fortifies,
Passion can ne'er destroy, nor Fate
    surprise.

[1] The spelling 'leiger' may be worth keeping, though 'leaguer' (cf. leaguer-lass) is best known in this meaning. Some, however, dispute the identity of these two : and identify 'leiger' in the sense of 'resident,' 'stationary,' with 'ledger.' These words, in the passages in which they occur, admit of a good deal of argument, and were probably not seldom confused originally.

Now as in watches, though we do
    not know
When the hand moves, we find it
    still doth go :   20
So I, by secret sympathy inclin'd,
Will absent meet, and understand
    thy mind ;
And thou at thy return shalt find
    thy heart
Still safe, with all the love thou
    didst impart.
For though that treasure I have
    ne'er deserv'd,
It shall with strong religion be
    preserv'd.
And besides this thou shalt in me
    survey
Thyself reflected while thou art
    away.
For what some forward arts do
    undertake,
The images of absent friends to
    make,   30
And represent their actions in a
    glass,
Friendship itself can only bring to
    pass,
That magic which both Fate and
    Time beguiles,
And in a moment runs a thousand
    miles.
So in my breast thy picture drawn
    shall be,
My Guide, Life, Object, Friend,
    and Destiny :
And none shall know, though they
    employ their wit,
Which is the right Antenor, thou,
    or it.

Engraven on Mr. John Collier's Tomb-stone at Bedlington

HERE what remains of him doth lie,
Who was the World's epitome,
Religion's darling, merchants' glory,
Men's true delight, and Virtue's
    story ;

Who, though a prisoner to the
    grave,
A glorious freedom once shall have :
Till when no monument is fit,
But what 's beyond our love and wit.

On the little Regina Collier, on the same Tomb-stone

VIRTUE's blossom, Beauty's bud,
The pride of all that 's fair and good,
By Death's fierce hand was snatchèd
    hence
In her state of Innocence :
Who by it this advantage gains,
Her wages got without her pains.

Friendship

LET the dull brutish World that
    know not Love,
Continue heretics, and disapprove
That noble flame ; but the refinèd
    know,
'Tis all the Heaven we have here
    below.
Nature subsists by Love, and they
    do tie
Things to their causes but by
    sympathy.
Love chains the different Elements
    in one
Great harmony, link'd to the
    Heav'nly Throne.
And as on earth, so the blest quire
    above
Of Saints and Angels are maintain'd
    by Love ;   10
That is their business and felicity,
And will be so to all Eternity.
That is the ocean, our affections
    here
Are but streams borrow'd from the
    fountain there.
And 'tis the noblest argument to
    prove
A beauteous mind, that it knows
    how to Love.

Those kind impressions which Fate
    can't control,
Are Heaven's mintage on a worthy
    soul.
For Love is all the Arts' epitome,
And is the sum of all Divinity.   20
He 's worse than beast that cannot
    love, and yet
It is not bought for money, pains or
    wit ;
For no chance or design can spirits
    move,
But the eternal destiny of Love :
And when two souls are chang'd
    and mixèd so,
It is what they and none but they
    can do.
This, this is Friendship, that
    abstracted flame
Which grovelling mortals know not
    how to name.
All Love is sacred, and the marriage-
    tie
Hath much of honour and divinity.
But Lust, Design, or some unworthy
    ends   31
May mingle there, which are despis'd
    by Friends.
Passion hath violent extremes, and
    thus
All oppositions are contiguous.
So when the end is serv'd their Love
    will bate,
If Friendship make it not more
    fortunate :
Friendship, that Love's elixir, that
    pure fire
Which burns the clearer 'cause it
    burns the higher.
For Love, like earthly fires (which
    will decay
If the material fuel be away)   40
Is with offensive smoke accompanied,
And by resistance only is supplied :
But Friendship, like the fiery element,
With its own heat and nourishment
    content,
Where neither hurt, nor smoke, nor
    noise is made,
Scorns the assistance of a foreign aid.

Friendship (like Heraldry) is hereby
    known,
Richest when plainest, bravest when
    alone ;
Calm as a virgin, and more innocent
Than sleeping doves are, and as
    much content   50
As Saints in visions ; quiet as the
    night,
But clear and open as the summer's
    light ;
United more than spirits' faculties,
Higher in thoughts than are the
    eagle's eyes ;
What shall I say ? when we true
    friends are grown,
W' are like—Alas, w' are like our-
    selves alone.

The Enquiry

I

IF we no old historian's name
    Authentic will admit,
But think all said of Friendship's
    fame
    But Poetry or Wit :
Yet what 's rever'd by minds so pure,
Must be a bright Idea sure.

II

But as our immortality
    By inward sense we find,
Judging that if it could not be,
    It would not be design'd :   10
So here how could such copies fall,
If there were no original ?

III

But if truth be in ancient song,
    Or story we believe,
If the inspir'd and graver throng
    Have scornèd to deceive ;
There have been hearts whose
    friendship gave
Them thoughts at once both soft
    and brave.

IV

Among that consecrated few,
    Some more seraphic shade   20
Lend me a favourable clew
    Now mists my eyes invade.

Why, having fill'd the World with
fame,
Left you so little of your flame ?

V

Why is 't so difficult to see
Two bodies and one mind ?
And why are those who else agree
So differently kind ?
Hath Nature such fantastic art,
That she can vary every heart ;   30

VI

Why are the bands of Friendship
tied
With so remiss a knot,
That by the most it is defied,
And by the rest forgot ?
Why do we step with so light sense
From friendship to Indifference ?

VII

If Friendship sympathy impart,
Why this ill-shuffled game,
That heart can never mcct with
heart,
Or flame encounter flame ?   40
What does this cruelty create ?
Is 't the intrigue of Love or Fate ?

VIII

Had Friendship ne'er been known
to men,
(The Ghost at last confest)
The World had been a stranger then
To all that Heaven possest.
But could it all be here acquir'd,
Not Heaven itself would be desir'd.

To my Lucasia, in defence of declared Friendship

I

O MY Lucasia, let us speak our
Love,
And think not that impertinent can
be,
Which to us both doth such
assurance prove,
And whence we find how justly
we agree.

(554)

II

Before we knew the treasures of our
Love,
Our noble aims our joys did
entertain ;
And shall enjoyment nothing then
improve ?
'Twere best for us then to begin
again.

III

Now we have gain'd, we must not
stop, and sleep
Out all the rest of our mysterious
reign :   10
It is as hard and glorious to keep
A victory, as it is to obtain.

IV

Nay, to what end did we once barter
minds,
Only to know and to neglect the
claim ?
Or (like some wantons) our pride
pleasure finds,
To throw away the thing at which
we aim.

V

If this be all our Friendship does
design,
We covet not enjoyment then,
but Power :
To our opinion we our bliss confine,
And love to have, but not to
smell, the flower.   20

VI

Ah ! then let misers bury thus their
gold,
Who though they starve, no
farthing will produce :
But we lov'd to enjoy and to behold,
And sure we cannot spend our
stock by use.

VII

Think not 'tis needless to repeat
desires ;
The fervent turtles always court
and bill,
And yet their spotless passion never
tires,
But does increase by repetition
still.

VIII

Although we know we love, yet while
 our soul
 Is thus imprison'd by the flesh we
  wear,   30
There's no way left that bondage to
 control,
 But to convey transactions through
  the ear.

IX

Nay though we read our passions in
 the eye,
 It will oblige and please to tell
  them too :
Such joys as these by motion
 multiply,
 Were 't but to find that our souls
  told us true.

X

Believe not then, that being now
 secure
 Of either's heart, we have no more
  to do :
The spheres themselves by motion
 do endure,
 And they move on by circulation
  too.   40

XI

And as a river, when it once hath
 paid
 The tribute which it to the ocean
  owes,
Stops not, but turns, and having
 curl'd and play'd
 On its own waves, the shore it
  overflows.

XII

So the soul's motion does not end
 in bliss,
 But on herself she scatters and
  dilates,
And on the object doubles till by
 this
 She finds new joys which that
  reflux creates.

XIII

But then because it cannot all
 contain,
 It seeks a vent by telling the glad
  news,   50

First to the heart which did its joys
 obtain,
 Then to the heart which did
  those joys produce.

XIV

When my soul then doth such
 excursions make,
 Unless thy soul delight to meet it
  too,
What satisfaction can it give or
 take,
 Thou being absent at the inter-
  view ?

XV

'Tis not distrust ; for were that plea
 allow'd,
 Letters and visits all would useless
  grow :
Love's whole expression then would
 be its cloud,
 And it would be refin'd to nothing
  so.   60

XVI

If I distrust, 'tis my own worth for
 thee,
 'Tis my own fitness for a love like
  thine ;
And therefore still new evidence
 would see,
 T' assure my wonder that thou
  canst be mine.

XVII

But as the morning Sun to drooping
 flowers,
 As weary travellers a shade do
  find,
As to the parched violet evening
 showers ;
 Such is from thee to me a look
  that's kind.

XVIII

But when that look is drest in words,
 'tis like
 The mystic pow'r of music's
  unison ;   70
Which when the finger doth one
 viol strike,
 The other's string heaves to
  reflection.

XIX

Be kind to me, and just then to our love,
　To which we owe our free and dear converse;
And let not tract of Time wear or remove
　It from the privilege of that commerce.

XX

Tyrants do banish what they can't requite:
　But let us never know such mean desires;
But to be grateful to that love delight
　Which all our joys and noble thoughts inspires.　80

A Reverie [1]

A CHOSEN privacy, a cheap content,
And all the peace a friendship ever lent,
A rock which civil Nature made a seat,
A willow that repulses all the heat,
The beauteous quiet of a summer's day,
A brook which sobb'd aloud and ran away,
Invited my repose, and then conspir'd
To entertain my Fancy thus retir'd.
As Lucian's ferry-man aloft did view
The angry World, and then laugh'd at it too:　10
So all its sullen follies seem to me
But as a too-well acted tragedy.
One dangerous Ambition doth befool,
Another envies to see that man rule:
One makes his love the parent of his rage,
For private friendship publicly t' engage:
And some for Conscience, some for Honour die;
And some are meanly kill'd they know not why.
More different than men's faces are their ends,
Whom yet one common ruin can make friends.　20
Death, dust and darkness they have only won,
And hastily unto their periods run.
Death is a Leveller; Beauty, and Kings,
And Conquerors, and all those glorious things,
Are tumbled to their graves in one rude heap,
Like common dust as quiet and as cheap.
At greater changes who would wonder then,
Since Kingdoms have their Fates as well as men?
They must fall sick and die; nothing can be
In this World certain, but uncertainty.　30
Since Pow'r and Greatness are such slippery things,
Who'd pity cottages, or envy Kings?
Now least of all, when, weary of deceit,
The World no longer flatters with the great.
Though such confusions here below we find,
As Providence were wanton with mankind:
Yet in this chaos some things do send forth,
(Like jewels in the dark) a native worth.
He that derives his high Nobility,
Not from the mention of a pedigree;
Who thinks it not his praise that others know　41
His ancestors were gallant long ago;

---

[1] Spelt in orig. as usual 'resvery.'

A Reverie

Who scorns to boast the glories of
his blood,
And thinks he can't be great that is
not good ;
Who knows the World, and what
we Pleasure call,
Yet cannot sell one conscience for
them all ;
Who hates to hoard that gold with
an excuse,
For which he can find out a nobler
use ;
Who dares not keep that life that he
can spend,
To serve his God, his Country, and
his Friend ;   50
Who flattery and falsehood doth so
hate,
He would not buy ten lives at such
a rate ;
Whose soul, than diamonds more
rich and clear,
Naked and open as his face doth
wear ;
Who dares be good alone in such a
time,
When Virtue's held and punish'd as
a crime ;
Who thinks dark crooked plots a
mean defence,
And is both safe and wise in Inno-
cence ;
Who dares both fight and die, but
dares not fear ;
Whose only doubt is, if his cause be
clear ;   60
Whose Courage and his Justice
equal worn,
Can dangers grapple, overcome and
scorn,
Yet not insult upon a conquer'd foe,
But can forgive him and oblige him
too ;
Whose Friendship is congenial with
his soul,
Who where he gives a heart, bestows
it whole ;
Whose other ties and titles here do
end,
Or buried or completed in the Friend ;

Who ne'er resumes the soul he once
did give,
While his Friend's honesty and hon-
our live ;   70
And if his Friend's content could
cost the price,
Would count himself a happy sacri-
fice ;
Whose happy days no pride infects,
nor can
His other titles make him slight the
man ;
No dark ambitious thoughts do
cloud his brow,
Nor restless cares when to be great,
and how ;
Who scorns to envy wealth where'er
it be,
But pities such a golden slavery ;
With no mean fawnings can the
people court,
Nor wholly slight a popular report ;
Whose house no orphan groans do
shake or blast,   81
Nor any riot help to serve his
taste :
Who from the top of his pros-
perities
Can take a fall, and yet without
surprise ;
Who with the same august and even
state
Can entertain the best and worst of
fate ;
Whose suffering's sweet, if Honour
once adorn it ;
Who slights Revenge, yet does not
fear, but scorn it ;
Whose happiness in ev'ry fortune
lives,
For that no fortune either takes or
gives ;   90
Who no unhandsome ways can bribe
his Fate,
Nay, out of prison marches through
the gate ;
Who losing all his titles and his
pelf,
Nay, all the World, can never lose
himself ;

This Person shines indeed, and he
  that can
Be Virtuous is the great Immortal
  Man.

A Country-life

How sacred and how innocent
  A country-life appears,
How free from tumult, discontent,
  From flattery or fears !
This was the first and happiest life,
  When man enjoy'd himself ;
Till Pride exchangèd peace for
  strife,
  And happiness for pelf.
'Twas here the Poets were inspir'd,
  Here taught the multitude ; 10
The brave they here with Honour
  fir'd,
  And civiliz'd the rude,
That Golden Age did entertain
  No passion but of Love ;
The thoughts of ruling and of gain
  Did ne'er their fancies move.
None then did envy neighbour's
  wealth,
  Nor plot to wrong his bed :
Happy in friendship and in health,
  On roots, not beasts, they fed. 20
They knew no Law nor Physic then,
  Nature was all their Wit.
And if there yet remain to men
  Content, sure this is it.
What blessings doth this World
  afford
  To tempt or bribe desire ?
Her courtship is all fire and sword,
  Who would not then retire ?
Then welcome, dearest Solitude,
  My great felicity ; 30
Though some are pleas'd to call
  thee rude,
  Thou art not so, but we.
Them that do covet only rest,
  A cottage will suffice :
It is not brave to be possest
  Of Earth, but to despise.
Opinion is the rate of things,
  From hence our peace doth flow ;

I have a better Fate than Kings,
  Because I think it so. 40
When all the stormy World doth roar
  How unconcern'd am I !
I cannot fear to tumble lower
  Who never could be high.
Secure in these unenvied walls
  I think not on the State,
And pity no man's case that falls
  From his Ambition's height.
Silence and Innocence are safe ;
  A heart that's nobly true 50
At all these little arts can laugh
  That do the World subdue.
While others revel it in State,
  Here I'll contented sit,
And think I have as good a Fate
  As wealth and pomp admit.
Let some in courtship take delight,
  And to th' Exchange resort ;
Then revel out a winter's night,
  Not making love, but sport. 60
These never know a noble flame,
  'Tis lust, scorn, or Design :
While Vanity plays all their game,
  Let Peace and Honour mine.
When the inviting Spring appears,
  To Hyde-Park let them go,
And hasting thence be full of fears
  To lose Spring-Garden show.
Let others (nobler) seek to gain
  In knowledge happy fate, 70
And others busy them in vain
  To study ways of State.
But I, resolvèd from within,
  Confirmèd from without,
In privacy intend to spin
  My future minutes out.
And from this hermitage of mine
  I banish all wild toys,
And nothing that is not Divine
  Shall dare to tempt my joys. 80
There are below but two things good,
  Friendship and Honesty,
And only those of all I would
  Ask for felicity.
In this retir'd and humble seat
  Free from both war and strife,
I am not forc'd to make retreat,
  But choose to spend my life.

To Mrs. Wogan, my Honoured Friend, on the Death of her Husband

Dry up your tears, there's enough
    shed by you,
And we must pay our share of sorrows
    too.
It is no private loss when such men
    fall,
The World's concern'd, and grief is
    general.
But though of our misfortune we
    complain,
To him it is injurious and vain.
For since we know his rich integ-
    rity,
His real sweetness, and full har
    mony ;
How free his heart and house were
    to his friends,
Whom he oblig'd without design or
    ends ;   10
How universal was his courtesy,
How clear a soul, how even, and how
    high ;
How much he scorn'd disguise or
    meaner arts,
But with a native honour conquer'd
    hearts ;
We must conclude he was a treasure
    lent,
Soon weary of this sordid tenement.
The Age and World deserv'd him not,
    and he
Was kindly snatch'd from future
    misery.
We can scarce say he's dead, but
    gone to rest,
And left a monument in ev'ry breast.
For you to grieve then in this sad
    excess,   21
Is not to speak of love, but make it
    less.
A noble soul no friendship will
    admit,
But what's Eternal and Divine as it.
The soul is hid in mortal flesh we
    know,
And all its weaknesses must undergo,
Till by degrees it does shine forth at
    length,
And gathers Beauty, Purity, and
    Strength :
But never yet doth this immortal
    ray
Put on full splendour till it put off
    clay :   30
So infant Love is, in the worthiest
    breast,
By Sense and Passion fetter'd and
    opprest ;
But by degrees it grows still more
    refin'd,
And scorning clogs, only concerns
    the mind.
Now as the soul you lov'd is here
    set free
From its material gross capacity ;
Your love should follow him now he
    is gone,
And quitting Passion, put Perfection
    on.
Such Love as this will its own good
    deny,
If its dear object have felicity.   40
And since we cannot his great loss
    reprieve,
Let's not lose you in whom he still
    doth live.
For while you are by grief secluded
    thus,
It doth appear your funeral to us.

In memory of the most justly Honoured, Mrs. Owen of Orielton

As when the ancient World by
    Reason liv'd,
The Asian Monarchs' deaths were
    never griev'd ;
Their glorious lives made all their
    Subjects call
Their rites a triumph, not a funeral :
So still the Good are Princes, and
    their fate
Invites us not to weep but imitate.

Nature intends a progress of each
    stage
Whereby weak man creeps to succeed-
    ing Age,
Ripens him for that change for which
    he's made,
Where th' active soul is in her
    centre staid.   10
And since none stript of infancy
    complain,
'Cause 'tis both their necessity and
    gain :
So Age and Death by slow approaches
    come,
And by that just inevitable doom
By which the soul (her cloggy dross
    once gone)
Puts on perfection, and resumes her
    own.
Since then we mourn a happy soul,
    O why
Disturb we her with erring piety ?
Who's so enamour'd on the beau-
    teous ground,
When with rich autumn's livery hung
    round,   20
As to deny a sickle to his
    grain,
And not undress the teeming Earth
    again ?
Fruits grow for use, mankind is born
    to die ;
And both fates have the same neces-
    sity.
Then grieve no more, sad relatives,
    but learn ;
Sigh not, but profit by your just
    concern.
Read over her life's volume : wise
    and good,
Not 'cause she must be so, but
    'cause she wou'd.
To chosen Virtue still a constant
    friend,
She saw the times which chang'd,
    but did not mend.   30
And as some are so civil to the
    Sun,
They'd fix his beams, and make the
    Earth to run :

So she unmov'd beheld the angry
    Fate
Which tore a Church, and overthrew
    a State :
Still durst be good, and own the
    noble truth,
To crown her Age which had adorn'd
    her Youth.
Great without pride, a soul which
    still could be
Humble and high, full of calm
    majesty.
She kept true state within, and could
    not buy
Her satisfaction with her Charity.   40
Fortune or birth ne'er rais'd her
    mind, which stood,
Not on her being rich, but doing
    good.
Oblig'd the World, but yet would
    scorn to be
Paid with requitals, thanks or
    vanity.
How oft did she what all the World
    adore,
Make the poor happy with her use-
    ful store ?
So general was her bounty, that she
    gave
Equality to all before the grave.
By several means she different per-
    sons tied,
Who by her goodness only were
    allied.   50
Her Virtue was her temper, not her
    fit ;
Fear'd nothing but the crimes which
    some commit ;
Scorn'd those dark arts which pass
    for wisdom now,
Nor to a mean ignoble thing could
    bow.
And her vast prudence had no other
    end,
But to forgive a foe, endear a
    friend :
To use, but slight, the World ; and
    fixt above,
Shine down in beams of Piety and
    Love.

Why should we then by poor un-
just complaint
Prove envious sinners 'cause she is
a Saint ?   60
Close then the monument ; let not a
tear
That may profane her ashes now
appear :
For her best obsequies are that we be
Prudent and Good, Noble and Sweet,
as she.

A Friend

I

Love, Nature's plot, this great crea-
tion's soul,
    The being and the harmony of
    things,
Doth still preserve and propagate the
whole,
    From whence man's happiness and
    safety springs :
The earliest, whitest, blessed'st
times did draw
From her alone their universal Law.

II

Friendship's an abstract of this nobler
flame,
    'Tis Love refin'd and purg'd from
    all its dross,
The next to Angels' love, if not the
same,
    As strong as Passion is, though
    not so gross :   10
It antedates a glad eternity,
And is an Heaven in epitome.

III

Nobler than kindred or than mar-
riage-band,
    Because more free ; wedlock-feli-
    city
Itself doth only by this union stand,
    And turns to friendship or to
    misery.
Force or Design matches to pass
may bring,
But Friendship doth from Love and
Honour spring.

IV

If souls no sexes have, for men
t' exclude
    Woman from Friendship's vast
    capacity,   20
Is a design injurious or rude,
    Only maintain'd by partial tyranny.
Love is allow'd to us and Innocence,
And noblest friendships do proceed
from thence.

V

The chiefest thing in friends is
Sympathy :
    There is a secret that doth friend-
    ship guide,
Which makes two souls before they
know agree,
    Who by a thousand mixtures are
    allied,
And chang'd and lost, so that it is not
known
Within which breast doth now reside
their own.   30

VI

Essential Honour must be in a
friend,
    Not such as every breath fans to
    and fro ;
But born within, is its own judge
and end,
    And dares not sin though sure
    that none should know.
Where Friendship's spoke, Honesty's
understood ;
For none can be a friend that is not
good.

VII

Friendship doth carry more than
common trust,
    And Treachery is here the greatest
    sin.
Secrets deposèd then none ever
must
    Presume to open, but who put
    them in.   40
They that in one chest lay up all
their stock,
    Had need be sure that none can pick
    the lock.

VIII

A breast too open Friendship does
    not love,
    For that the other's trust will not
      conceal ;
Nor one too much reserv'd can it
    approve,
    Its own condition this will not
      reveal.
We empty passions for a double
    end,
To be refresh'd and guarded by a
    friend.

IX

Wisdom and Knowledge Friendship
    does require,
    The first for counsel, this for
      company ;   50
And though not mainly, yet we may
    desire
    Both Complaisance and Ingenuity.
Though everything may love, yet
    'tis a rule,
He cannot be a friend that is a
    fool.

X

Discretion uses parts, and best knows
    how ;
    And Patience will all qualities
      commend :
That serves a need best, but this
    doth allow
    The weaknesses and passions of
      a friend.
We are not yet come to the quire
    above :
Who cannot pardon here, can never
    love.   60

XI

Thick waters show no images of
    things :
    Friends are each other's mirrors,
      and should be
Clearer than crystal or the mountain
    springs,
    And free from clouds, design or
      flattery.

For vulgar souls no part of Friend-
    ship share :
Poets and friends are born to what
    they are.

XII

Friends should observe and chide
    each other's faults,
    To be severe then is most just
      and kind ;
Nothing can 'scape their search who
    knew the thoughts :
    This they should give and take
      with equal mind.   70
For Friendship, when this freedom
    is denied,
Is like a painter when his hands are
    tied.

XIII

A friend should find out each
    necessity,
    And then unask'd relieve 't at any
      rate :
It is not Friendship, but Formality,
    To be desir'd : for Kindness
      keeps no state.
Of friends he doth the benefactor
    prove,
That gives his friend the means t'
    express his love.

XIV

Absence doth not from Friendship's
    right excuse :
    Them who preserve each other's
      heart and fame,   80
Parting can ne'er divide, it may
    diffuse ;
    As a far stretch'd-out river's still
    the same.
Though presence help'd them at
    the first to greet,
Their souls know now without those
    aids to meet.

XV

Constant and solid, whom no storms
    can shake,
    Nor death unfix, a right friend
      ought to be ;
And if condemnèd to survive, doth
    make

No second choice, but Grief and
    Memory.
But Friendship's best fate is, when
    it can spend
A life, a fortune, all to serve
    a Friend.   90

L'Accord du Bien

I
ORDER, by which all things are
    made,
And this great World's foundation
    laid,
Is nothing else but Harmony,
Where different parts are brought t'
    agree.

II
As empires are still best maintain'd
Those ways which first their great-
    ness gain'd :
So in this universal frame
What made and keeps it, is the same.

III
Thus all things unto peace do tend,
Even discords have it for their end.
The cause why elements do fight, 11
Is but their instinct to unite.

IV
Music could never please the sense
But by united excellence :
The sweetest note which numbers
    know,
If struck alone, would tedious grow.

V
Man, the whole World's epitome,
Is by creation Harmony.
'Twas Sin first quarrell'd in his breast,
Then made him angry with the rest.

VI
But goodness keeps that unity, 21
And loves its own society
So well, that seldom we have known
One real worth to dwell alone.

VII
And hence it is we Friendship call
Not by one virtue's name, but all.
Nor is it when bad things agree
Thought union, but conspiracy.

VIII
Nature and Grace, such enemies,
That when one fell t' other did rise,
Are now by Mercy even set,   31
As stars in constellations met.

IX
If Nature were herself a sin,
Her Author (GOD) had guilty bin ;
But Man by sin contracting stain,
Shall, purg'd from that, be clear
    again.

X
To prove that Nature 's excellent,
Even Sin itself 's an argument :
Therefore we Nature's stain deplore,
Because itself was pure before.   40

XI
And Grace destroys not, but refines,
Unveils our Reason, then it shines ;
Restores what was depress'd by sin,
The fainting beam of God within.

XII
The mainspring (Judgement) recti-
    fied,
Will all the lesser motions guide,
To spend our Labour, Love and Care,
Not as things seem, but as they are.

XIII
'Tis Fancy lost, Wit thrown away,
In trifles to employ that ray,   50
Which then doth in full lustre shine
When both ingenious and divine.

XIV
To eyes by humour vitiated
All things seem falsely colourèd :
So 'tis our prejudicial thought
That makes clear objects seem in
    fault.

XV
They scarce believe united good,
By whom 'twas never understood :
They think one Grace enough for
    one,
And 'tis because their selves have
    none.   60

XVI
We hunt extremes, and run so fast,
We can no steady judgement cast :

He best surveys the circuit round,
Who stands i' th' middle of the ground.

XVII

That happy mean would let us see
Knowledge and Meekness may agree ;
And find, when each thing hath its name,
Passion and Zeal are not the same.

XVIII

Who studies God doth upwards fly,
And heighth still lessens to our eye ;
And he that knows God, soon will see   71
Vast cause for his humility.

XIX

For by that search it will be known
There's nothing but our Will our own :
And who doth so that stock employ,
But finds more cause for shame than joy ?

XX

We know so little and so dark,
And so extinguish our own spark,
That he who furthest here can go,
Knows nothing as he ought to know.

XXI

It will with the most learnèd suit, 81
More to inquire than dispute :
But vapours swell within a cloud ;
'Tis Ignorance that makes us proud.

XXII

So when their own vain heart belies,
Like inflammations quickly rise :
But that soul which is truly great,
Is lowest in its own conceit.

XXIII

Yet while we hug our own mistake,
We censures, but not judgements, make ;   90
And thence it is we cannot see
Obedience stand with liberty.

XXIV

Providence still keeps even state ;
But he can best command his fate,
Whose art by adding his own voice,
Makes his necessity his choice.

XXV

Rightly to rule one's self must be
The hardest, largest monarchy :
Whose passions are his masters grown,
Will be a captive in a throne.   100

XXVI

He most the inward freedom gains,
Who just submissions entertains :
For while in that his reason sways,
It is himself that he obeys.

XXVII

But only in Eternity
We can these beauteous unions see :
For Heaven itself and Glory is
But one harmonious constant bliss.

Invitation to the Country

BE kind, my dear Rosania, though 'tis true
Thy friendship will become thy penance too ;
Though there be nothing can reward the pain,
Nothing to satisfy or entertain ;
Though all be empty, wild, and like to me,
Who make new troubles in my company :
Yet is the action more obliging great ;
'Tis Hardship only makes Desert complete.
But yet to prove mixtures all things compound,
There may in this be some advantage found ;   10
For a retirement from the noise of towns,
Is that for which some kings have left their crowns :
And conquerors, whose laurel press'd the brow,
Have chang'd it for the quiet myrtle-bough.
For titles, honours, and the World's address,
Are things too cheap to make up happiness ;

The easy tribute of a giddy race,
And paid less to the person than
the place.
So false reflected and so short
content
Is that which Fortune and Opinion
lent,   20
That who most tried it have of
Fate complain'd,
With titles burthen'd and to great-
ness chain'd.
For they alone enjoy'd what they
possest,
Who relish'd most and understood it
best.
And yet that understanding made
them know
The empty swift dispatch of all
below.
So that what most can outward
things endear,
Is the best means to make them
disappear :
And even that Tyrant (Sense) doth
these destroy,
As more officious to our grief than
joy.   30
Thus all the glittering World is but
a cheat,
Obtruding on our sense things
gross for great.
But he that can inquire and undis-
guise,
Will soon perceive the sting that
hidden lies ;
And find no joys merit esteem but
those
Whose scene lies only at our own
dispose.
Man unconcern'd without himself
may be
His own both prospect and security.
Kings may be slaves by their own
passions hurl'd,
But who commands himself com-
mands the World.   40
A country-life assists this study
best,
Where no distractions do the soul
arrest :

There Heav'n and Earth lie open
to our view,
There we search Nature and its
Author too ;
Possess'd with freedom and a real state
Look down on Vice, and Vanity,
and Fate.
There (my Rosania) will we,
mingling souls,
Pity the folly which the World
controls ;
And all those grandeurs which the
World do prize   49
We either can enjoy, or will despise.

In Memory of Mrs. E. H.

As some choice plant cherish'd by
sun and air,
And ready to requite the gard'ner's
care,
Blossoms and flourishes, but then,
we find,
Is made the triumph of some ruder
wind :
So thy untimely grave did both
entomb
Thy sweetness now, and wonders
yet to come.
Hung full of hopes thou sell'st a
lovely prize,
Just as thou didst attract all hearts
and eyes.
Thus we might apprehend, for had
thy years
Been lengthen'd to have paid those
vast arrears   10
The World expected, we should then
conclude,
The Age of Miracles had been
renew'd.
For thou already hast with ease
found out
What others study with such pains
and doubt ;
That frame of soul which is content
alone,
And needs no entertainment but its
own.

Thy even mind, which made thee
    good and great,
Was to thee both a shelter and retreat.
Of all the tumults which this World
    do fill,
Thou wert an unconcern'd spectator
    still :   20
And, were thy duty punctually
    supplied,
Indifferent to all the World beside.
Thou wert made up within resolv'd
    and fix'd,
And wouldst not with a base allay be
    mix'd ;
Above the World, couldst equally
    despise
Both its temptations and its injuries;
Couldst sum up all, and find not
    worth desire
Those glittering trifles which the
    most admire ;
But with a nobler aim, and higher
    born,
Look down on greatness with con-
    tempt and scorn.   30
Thou hadst no arts that others this
    might see,
Nor lov'dst a trumpet to thy piety :
But silent and retir'd, calm and
    serene,
Stol'st to thy blessed Haven hardly
    seen.
It were vain to describe thee then,
    but now
Thy vast accession harder is to
    know ;
How full of light, and satisfied thou
    art,
So early from this treach'rous World
    to part ;
How pleas'd thou art reflections now
    to make,
And find thou didst not things below
    mistake ;   40
In how abstracted converse thou
    dost live,
How much thy knowledge is intui-
    tive ;

How great and bright a glory is en-
    joy'd
With Angels, and in mysteries,
    employ'd.
'Tis sin then to lament thy fate, but we
Should help thee to a new eternity ;
And by successive imitation strive,
Till time shall die, to keep thee still
    alive ;
And (by thy great example furnish'd)
    be
More apt to live than write thy
    Elogy [1].   50

On Rosania's Apostasy, and Lucasia's Friendship

GREAT Soul of Friendship, whither
    art thou fled ?
Where dost thou now choose to re-
    pose thy head ?
Or art thou nothing but voice, air
    and name,
Found out to put souls in pursuit of
    fame ?
Thy flames being thought immortal,
    we may doubt
Whether they e'er did burn that see
    them out.

Go, wearied Soul, find out thy
    wonted rest,
In the safe harbour of Orinda's
    Breast ;
There all unknown adventures thou
    hast found
In thy late transmigrations expound ;
That so Rosania's darkness may be
    known   11
To be her want of lustre, not thy own.

Then to the great Lucasia have
    recourse,
There gather up new excellence and
    force,
Till by a free unbiass'd clear com-
    merce,
Endearments which no tongue can
    e'er rehearse,

---

[1] This form once more.

Lucasia and Orinda shall thee give
Eternity, and make even Friendship
  live.

Hail, great Lucasia, thou shalt
  doubly shine,
What was Rosania's own is now
  twice thine ;   20
Thou saw'st Rosania's chariot and
  her flight,
And so the double portion is thy
  right :
Though 'twas Rosania's spirit be
  content,
Since 'twas at first from thy Orinda
  sent.

To my Lady Elizabeth Boyle, singing Now affairs [1], &c.

SUBDUING Fair ! what will you win
  To use a needless dart ?
Why then so many to take in
  One undefended heart ?

I came expos'd to all your charms,
  'Gainst which the first half-hour
I had no will to take up arms,
  And in the next no power.

How can you choose but win the
  day,
  Who can resist your siege,   10
Who in one action know the way
  To vanquish and oblige ?

Your voice which can in melting
  strains
  Teach Beauty to be blind,
Confines me yet in stronger chains,
  By being soft and kind.

Whilst you my trivial fancy sing,
  You it to wit refine,
As leather once stamp'd by a King
  Became a current coin.   20

By this my verse is sure to gain
  Eternity with men,
Which by your voice it will obtain,
  Though never by my pen.

I'd rather in your favour live
  Than in a lasting name,
And much a greater rate would give
  For Happiness than Fame.

Submission

'TIS so, and humbly I will resign,
Nor dare dispute with Providence
  Divine.
In vain, alas ! we struggle with our
  chains,
But more entangled by the fruitless
  pains.
For as i' th' great Creation of this All,
Nothing by chance could in such
  order fall ;
And what would single be deform'd
  confest,
Grows beauteous in its union with
  the rest :
So Providence like Wisdom we allow,
(For what created once does govern
  now)   10
And the same Fate that seems to
  one reverse,
Is necessary to the Universe.
All these particular and various
  things,
Link'd to their causes by such secret
  springs,
Are held so fast, and govern'd by
  such art,
That nothing can out of its order
  start.
The World's God's watch where
  nothing is so small,
But makes a part of what composes
  all :
Could the least pin be lost or else
  displac'd,
The World would be disorder'd and
  defac'd.   20
It beats no pulse in vain, but keeps
  its time,
And undiscern'd to its own height
  doth climb ;

---

[1] See Appendix, first Song from *Pompey*.

Strung first and daily wound up by
His hand
Who can its motions guide and
understand.
No secret cunning then nor multi-
tude
Can Providence divert, cross or
delude.
And her just full decrees are hidden
things,
Which harder are to find than births
of springs.
Yet all in various consorts[1] fitly
sound,
And by their discords Harmony
compound.　　　　30
Hence is that Order, Life and
Energy,
Whereby Forms are preserv'd though
Matters die ;
And, shifting dress, keep their own
living state :
So that what kills this, does that
propagate.
This made the ancient Sage in
rapture cry,
That sure the World had full eternity.
For though itself to Time and Fate
submit,
He 's above both who made and
governs it ;
And to each creature hath such por-
tion lent,
As Love and Wisdom sees con-
venient.　　　　40
For He 's no Tyrant, nor delights to
grieve
The beings which from him alone
can live.
He's most concern'd, and hath the
greatest share
In Man, and therefore takes the
greatest care
To make him happy, who alone can
be
So by submission and conformity.
For why should changes here below
surprise,

When the whole World its revolution
tries ?
Where were our springs, our harvests'
pleasant use,
Unless Vicissitude did them produce ?
Nay, what can be so wearisome a
pain,　　　　51
As when no alterations entertain ?
To lose, to suffer, to be sick and die,
Arrest us by the same necessity.
Nor could they trouble us, but that
our mind
Hath its own glory unto dross con-
fin'd.
For outward things remove not from
their place,
Till our souls run to beg their mean
embrace ;
Then doting on the choice make it
our own,
By placing trifles in th' Opinion's
throne.　　　　60
So when they are divorc'd by some
new cross,
Our souls seem widow'd by the fatal
loss :
But could we keep our grandeur and
our state,
Nothing below would seem un-
fortunate ;
But Grace and Reason, which best
succours bring,
Would with advantage manage every-
thing ;
And by right judgement would pre-
vent our moan,
For losing that which never was our
own.
For right opinion's like a marble grot,
In summer cool, and in the winter
hot ;　　　　70
A principle which in each fortune
lives,
Bestowing catholic preservatives.
'Tis this resolves, there are no losses
where
Virtue and Reason are continued
there.

---

[1] = 'concerts,' as commonly.

The meanest soul might such a for-
tune share,
But no mean soul could so that for-
tune bear.
Thus I compose my thoughts grown
insolent,
As th' Irish harper doth his instru-
ment ;
Which if once struck doth murmur
and complain,
But the next touch will silence all
again.   80

2 Cor. v. 19. God was in Christ reconciling the World to Himself

WHEN God, contracted to Humanity,
Could sigh and suffer, could be sick
and die ;
When all the heap of miracles com-
bin'd
To form the greatest, which was,
save Mankind :
Then God took stand in Christ,
studying a way
How to repair the ruin'd World's
decay.
His Love, Pow'r, Wisdom, must
some means procure
His Mercy to advance, Justice
secure :
And since Man in such misery was
hurl'd,
It cost him more to save, than make
the World.   10
Oh ! what a desp'rate load of sins
had we,
When God must plot for our felicity !
When God must beg us that He may
forgive,
And die Himself before Mankind
could live !
And what still are we, when our
King in vain
Begs His lost rebels to be friends
again !
What floods of Love proceed from
Heaven's smile,

At once to pardon and to reconcile !
What God Himself hath made He
cannot hate,
For 'tis one act to love and to
create :   20
And He's too perfect full of Majesty,
To need additions from our misery.
He hath a father's, not a tyrant's, joy ;
Shows more His pow'r to save, than
to destroy.
Did there ten thousand Worlds to
ruin fall,
One God could save, one Christ
redeem them all.
Be silent then, ye narrow souls, take
heed
Lest you restrain the Mercy you will
need.
But O my soul, from these be different,
Imitate thou a nobler precedent : 30
As God with open arms the World
does woo,
Learn thou like God to be enlargèd
too ;
As He begs thy consent to pardon
thee,
Learn to submit unto thy enemy ;
As He stands ready thee to entertain,
Be thou as forward to return again ;
As He was crucified for and by thee,
Crucify thou what caus'd His Agony :
And like to Him be mortified to sin,
Die to the World as He died for it
then.   40

The World

WE falsely think it due unto our
friends,
That we should grieve for their un-
timely ends.
He that surveys the world with
serious eyes,
And strips her from her gross and
weak disguise,
Shall find 'tis injury to mourn their
fate ;
He only dies untimely who dies
late.

For if 'twere told to children in the womb,
To what a stage of mischiefs they must come ;
Could they foresee with how much toil and sweat
Men count that gilded nothing, being great ; 10
What pains they take not to be what they seem,
Rating their bliss by others' false esteem,
And sacrificing their content, to be
Guilty of grave and serious vanity ;
How each condition hath its proper thorns,
And what one man admits, another scorns ;
How frequently their happiness they miss,
So far even from agreeing what it is,
That the same person we can hardly find,
Who is an hour together in one mind : 20
Sure they would beg a period of their breath,
And what we call their birth would count their death.
Mankind is mad ; for none can live alone,
Because their joys stand by comparison :
And yet they quarrel at society,
And strive to kill they know not whom, nor why.
We all live by mistake, delight in dreams,
Lost to ourselves, and dwelling in extremes ;
Rejecting what we have, though ne'er so good,
And prizing what we never understood. 30
Compar'd t' our boisterous inconstancy
Tempests are calm, and Discords harmony.
Hence we reverse the World, and yet do find

The God that made can hardly please our mind.
We live by chance and slip into events ;
Have all of beasts except their innocence.
The soul, which no man's pow'r can reach, a thing
That makes each woman man, each man a King,
Doth so much lose, and from its height so fall,
That some contend to have no soul at all. 40
'Tis either not observ'd, or at the best
By Passion fought withal, by Sin deprest.
Freedom of Will (God's image) is forgot ;
And if we know it, we improve it not.
Our thoughts, though nothing can be more our own,
Are still unguided, very seldom known.
Time 'scapes our hands as water in a sieve,
We come to die ere we begin to live.
Truth, the most suitable and noble prize,
Food of our spirits, yet neglected lies. 50
Error and shadows are our choice, and we
Owe our perdition to our own decree.
If we search Truth, we make it more obscure,
And when it shines, cannot the light endure,
For most men now, who plod, and eat, and drink,
Have nothing less their bus'ness than to think.
And those few that inquire, how small a share
Of Truth they find, how dark their notions are !

That serious evenness that calms
  the breast,
And in a tempest can bestow
  a rest,   60
We either not attempt, or else
  decline,
By ev'ry trifle snatch'd from our
  design.
(Others he must in his deceits
  involve,
Who is not true unto his own
  resolve.)
We govern not ourselves, but loose
  the reins,
Counting our bondage to a thousand
  chains ;
And with as many slaveries, content
As there are tyrants ready to tor-
  ment,
We live upon a rack extended still
To one extreme or both, but always
  ill.   70
For since our fortune is not under-
  stood,
We suffer less from bad than from
  the good.
The sting is better dress'd and longer
  lasts,
As surfeits are more dangerous than
  fasts.
And to complete the misery to us,
We see extremes are still contiguous.
And as we run so fast from what we
  hate,
Like squibs on ropes, to know no
  middle state ;
So, outward storms strengthen'd by
  us, we find
Our Fortune as disordered as our
  mind.   80
But that 's excus'd by this, it doth
  its part ;
A treach'rous World befits a treach-
  'rous heart.
All ill 's our own, the outward storms
  we loath

Receive from us their birth, their
  sting, or both.
And that our Vanity be past a
  doubt,
'Tis one new vanity to find it out.
Happy are they to whom God gives
  a grave,
And from themselves as from His
  wrath doth save.
'Tis good not to be born ; but if
  we must,
The next good is, soon to return
  to dust,   90
When th' uncag'd soul fled to
  Eternity
Shall rest, and live, and sing, and
  love, and see.
Here we but crawl and grovel, play
  and cry ;
Are first our own, then others'
  enemy :
But there shall be defac'd both
  stain and score,
For Time, and Death, and Sin shall
  be no more.

The Soul

I

How vain a thing is Man, whose
  noblest part,
  That soul which through the
    World doth roam [1],
Traverses Heav'n, finds out the
  depth of Art,
  Yet is so ignorant at home ?

II

In every brook or mirror we can
  find
  Reflections of our face to be ;
But a true optic to present our mind
  We hardly get, and darkly see.

III

Yet in the search after ourselves
  we run,
  Actions and causes we survey ; 10

---

[1] Orig. 'rome,' doubtless on the principle of which Spenser is the most distin-
guished exponent. It may be worth observing that this quatrain of 10, 8, 10, 8
is not very common, and for good reasons. The immense improvement in *The Palace
of Art* by the change to 10, 8, 10, 6 is an excellent subject for metrical study.

And when the weary chase is almost
    done,
  Then from our quest we slip away.

IV

'Tis strange and sad, that since we
    do believe
  We have a soul must never die,
There are so few that can a reason
    give
  How it obtains that life, or why.

V

I wonder not to find those that
    know most,
  Profess so much their ignorance ;
Since in their own souls greatest
    wits are lost,
  And of themselves have scarce
    a glance.   20

VI

But somewhat sure doth here ob-
    scurely lie,
  That above dross would fain
    advance,
And pants and catches at Eternity,
  As 'twere its own inheritance.

VII

A soul self-mov'd which can dilate,
    contract,
  Pierces and judges things unseen :
But this gross heap of Matter cannot
    act,
  Unless impulsèd from within.

VIII

Distance and Quantity, to bodies due,
  The state of souls cannot admit ;
And all the contraries which Nature
    knew   31
  Meet there, nor hurt themselves,
    nor it.

IX

God never body made so bright and
    clean,
  Which Good and Evil could dis-
    cern :
What these words Honesty and
    Honour mean,
  The soul alone knows how to learn.

X

And though 'tis true she is imprison'd
    here,
  Yet hath she notions of her own,
Which Sense doth only jog, awake,
    and clear,
  But cannot at the first make
    known.   40

XI

The soul her own felicity hath
    laid,
  And independent on[1] the sense,
Sees the weak terrors which the
    World invade
  With pity or with negligence.

XII

So unconcern'd she lives, so much
    above
  The rubbish of a sordid jail,
That nothing doth her energy im-
    prove
  So much as when those structures
    fail.

XIII

She's then a substance subtile, strong
    and pure,
  So immaterial and refin'd   50
As speaks her from the body's fate
    secure,
  And wholly of a diff'rent kind.

XIV

Religion for reward in vain would
    look,
  Virtue were doom'd to misery,
All actions were like bubbles in
    a brook,
  Were 't not for Immortality.

XV

But as that Conqueror who millions
    spent
  Thought it too mean to give
    a mite ;
So the World's Judge can never be
    content
  To bestow less than Infinite.   60

---

[1] It may be doubted whether we have done well to substitute 'independent *of*' (as is often done) while keeping 'dependent *on*.'

XVI

Treason against Eternal Majesty
    Must have eternal Justice too ;
And since unbounded Love did satisfy,
    He will unbounded Mercy show.

XVII

It is our narrow thoughts shorten these things,
    By their companion flesh inclin'd ;
Which feeling its own weakness gladly brings
    The same opinion to the mind.

XVIII

We stifle our own Sun, and live in shade ;
    But where its beams do once appear,   70
They make that person of himself afraid,
    And to his own acts most severe.

XIX

For ways, to sin close, and our breast disguise
    From outward search, we soon may find :
But who can his own soul bribe or surprise,
    Or sin without a sting behind ?

XX

He that commands himself is more a Prince
    Than he who nations keeps in awe ;
Who yield to all that does their soul convince,
    Shall never need another Law.   80

Happiness

Nature courts Happiness, although it be
Unknown as the Athenian Deity.
It dwells not in man's sense, yet he supplies
That want by growing fond of its disguise.
The false appearances of joy deceive,

And seeking her unto her like we cleave.
For sinking Man hath scarce sense left to know
Whether the plank he grasps will hold or no.
While all the business of the World is this,
To seek that good which by mistake they miss,   10
And all the several Passions men express
Are but for Pleasure in a diff'rent dress.
They hope for Happiness in being great,
Or rich, or lov'd, then hug their own conceit.
But the good man can find this treasure out,
For which in vain others do dig and doubt ;
And hath such secret full Content within,
Though all abroad be storms, yet he can sing.
His peace is made, all's quiet in that place,
Where Nature's cur'd and exercis'd by Grace.   20
This inward calm prevents his enemies,
For he can neither envy nor despise :
But in the beauty of his ordered mind
Doth still a new, rich satisfaction find.
Innocent epicure ! whose single breast
Can furnish him with a continual feast.
A Prince at home, and sceptres can refuse ;
Valuing only what he cannot lose.
He studies to do good ; (a man may be
Harmless for want of opportunity :)
But he's industrious kindness to dispense,   31
And therein only covets eminence.

Others do court applause and fame,
but he
Thinks all that giddy noise but
Vanity.
He takes no pains to be observ'd or
seen,
While all his acts are echoed from
within.
He 's still himself, when company are
gone,
Too well employ'd ever to be alone.
For studying God in all his volumes,
he
Begins the business of Eternity ; 40
And unconcern'd without, retains a
power
To suck (like bees) a sweet from
ev'ry flower.
And as the Manna of the Israelites
Had several tastes to please all
appetites :
So his Contentment is that catholic
food,
That makes all states seem fit as
well as good.
He dares not wish, nor his own fate
propound ;
But, if God sends, reads Love in
every wound :.
And would not lose for all the joys
of sense
The glorious pleasures of obedience.
His better part can neither change
nor lose, 51
And all God's will can bear, can do,
can choose.

Death

I

How weak a star doth rule mankind,
  Which owes its ruin to the same
Causes which Nature had design'd
  To cherish and preserve the
  frame !

II

As commonwealths may be secure,
  And no remote invasion dread ;

Yet may a sadder fall endure
  From traitors in their bosom bred :

III

So while we feel no violence, 9
  And on our active health do trust,
A secret hand doth snatch us hence,
  And tumbles us into the dust.

IV

Yet carelessly we run our race,
  As if we could Death's summons
  wave ;
And think not on the narrow space
  Between a table and a grave.

V

But since we cannot Death reprieve,
  Our souls and fame we ought to
  mind,
For they our bodies will survive ;
  That goes beyond, this stays
  behind. 20

VI

If I be sure my soul is safe,
  And that my actions will provide
My tomb a nobler epitaph,
  Than that I only liv'd and died.

VII

So that in various accidents
  I Conscience may, and Honour,
  keep ;
I with that ease and innocence
  Shall die, as infants go to sleep.

To the Queen's Majesty, on her late Sickness and Recovery

THE public gladness that 's to us
  restor'd,
For your escape from what we so
  deplor'd,
Will want as well resemblance as
  belief,
Unless our joy be measur'd by our
  grief.
When in your fever we with terror
  saw
At once our. hopes and happiness
  withdraw ;

And every crisis did with jealous
   fear
Inquire the news we scarce durst
   stay to hear.
Some dying Princes have their ser-
   vants slain,
That after death they might not
   want a train.   10
Such cruelty were here a needless
   sin;
For had our fatal fears prophetic
   been[1],
Sorrow alone that service would
   have done,
And you by Nations had been waited
   on.
Your danger was in ev'ry visage seen,
And only yours was quiet and serene.
But all our zealous grief had been in
   vain,
Had not great Charles's call'd you
   back again:
Who did your suff'rings with such
   pain discern,
He lost three Kingdoms once with
   less concern.   20
Lab'ring your safety he neglected
   his,
Nor fear'd he death in any shape
   but this.
His Genius did the bold distemper
   tame,
And his rich tears quench'd the
   rebellious flame.
As[2] once the Thracian Hero lov'd
   and griev'd,
Till he his lost felicity retriev'd;
And with the moving accents of
   his woe,
His spouse recover'd from the shades
   below.
So the King's grief your threaten'd
   loss withstood,
Who mourn'd with the same fortune
   that he woo'd,   30
And to his happy passion we have
   been

Now twice oblig'd for so ador'd a
   Queen.
But how severe a choice had you to
   make,
When you must Heav'n delay, or
   Him forsake?
Yet since those joys you made such
   haste to find
Had scarce been full if he were left
   behind,
How well did Fate decide your in-
   ward strife
By making him a present of your life?
Which rescu'd blessing he must
   long enjoy,
Since our offences could it not
   destroy.   40
For none but Death durst rival him
   in you;
And Death himself was baffled in it
   too.

Upon Mr. Abraham Cowley's Retirement

ODE

I

No, no, unfaithful World, thou hast
   Too long my easy heart betray'd,
And me too long thy foot-ball made:
   But I am wiser grown at last,
And will improve by all that I have
   past.
I know 'twas just I should be prac-
   tis'd on;
   For I was told before,
   And told in sober and instructive
   lore,
How little all that trusted thee have
   won:
And yet I would make haste to be
   undone.   10
Now by my suff'ring I am better
   taught,
And shall no more commit that
   stupid fault.

---

[1] So in orig., showing that 'bin' for this rhyme is more or less of an accident.
[2] Orig. 'at.'

Go, get some other fool,
　　Whom thou mayst next cajole :
On me thy frowns thou dost in vain
　　　bestow ;
　　For I know how
To be as coy and as reserved[1] as
　　　thou.

II

In my remote and humble seat
　　Now I'm again possest　　19
Of that late fugitive, my breast,
From all thy tumults and from all
　　　thy heat
I'll find a quiet and a cool retreat ;
　　And on the fetters I have worn
Look with experienc'd and revenge-
　　　ful scorn,
　　In this my sov'reign privacy.
　　'Tis true I cannot govern thee,
But yet myself I may subdue ;
And that's the nobler empire of the
　　　two.
　　If ev'ry Passion had got leave
　　Its satisfaction to receive,　　30
Yet I would it a higher pleasure call,
To conquer one, than to indulge
　　　them all.

III

For thy inconstant sea, no more
I'll leave that safe and solid shore :
No, though to prosper in the cheat,
Thou shouldst my Destiny defeat,
And make me be belov'd, or rich,
　　　or great :
　　Nor from myself shouldst me
　　　reclaim
With all the noise and all the pomp
　　　of Fame.
Judiciously I'll these despise ;　40
Too small the bargain, and too great
　　　the price,
　　For them to cozen twice.
　　At length this secret I have
　　　learn'd ;
Who will be happy, must be uncon-
　　　cern'd,

Must all their comfort in their bosom
　　　wear,
And seek their treasure and their
　　　power there.

IV

No other wealth will I aspire,
　　But that of Nature to admire ;
Nor envy on a laurel will bestow,
Whilst I have any in my garden grow.
　　And when I would be great, 51
　　'Tis but ascending to a seat
Which Nature in a lofty rock hath
　　　built ;
A throne as free from trouble as
　　　from guilt.
　　Where when my soul her wings
　　　does raise
　　Above what worldlings fear or
　　　praise,
With innocence and quiet pride
　　　I'll sit,
And see the humble waves pay tri-
　　　bute to my feet[2].
O life divine, when free from joys
　　　diseas'd,
Not always merry, but 'tis always
　　　pleas'd !　　60

V

A heart, which is too great a thing
To be a present for a Persian King,
Which God Himself would have to
　　　be His court,
Where Angels would officiously re-
　　　sort,
　　From its own height should much
　　　decline,
　　If this converse it should resign
(Ill-natur'd World !) for thine.
Thy unwise rigour hath thy empire
　　　lost ;
　　It hath not only set me free,
　　But it hath made me see,　70
They only can of thy possession
　　　boast,
Who do enjoy thee least, and under-
　　　stand thee most.

---

[1] Orig. 'reserv'e' (with suggestion of French ?).
[2] The rhyme here is worth comparison with that of 'been' (so spelt) with 'sin.'

For lo, the man whom all mankind
    admir'd,
(By ev'ry Grace adorn'd, and ev'ry
    Muse inspir'd)
Is now triumphantly retir'd.
The mighty Cowley this hath done,
And over thee a Parthian conquest
    won :
Which future ages shall adore,
And which in this subdues thee
    more
Than either Greek or Roman ever
    could before.   80

The Irish Greyhound

BEHOLD this creature's form and state,
Which Nature therefore did create,
That to the World might be exprest
What mien there can be in a beast ;
And that we in this shape may find
A lion of another kind.
For this heroic beast does seem
In majesty to rival him ;
And yet vouchsafes, to man, to show
Both service and submission too.   10
From whence we this distinction have,
That beast is fierce, but this is brave.
This dog hath so himself subdu'd,
That hunger cannot make him rude :
And his behaviour does confess
True courage dwells with gentleness.
With sternest wolves he dares engage,
And acts on them successful rage.
Yet too much courtesy may chance
To put him out of countenance.   20
When in his opposer's blood,
Fortune hath made his virtue good ;
This creature from an act so brave
Grows not more sullen, but more
    grave.
Man's guard he would be, not his
    sport,
Believing he hath ventur'd for 't ;

But yet no blood or shed or spent
Can ever make him insolent.
  Few men of him to do great things
    have learn'd,
And when th' are done, to be so
    unconcern'd.   30

Song

To the Tune of *Sommes nous pas
trop heureux*

I

How prodigious is my fate,
Since I can't determine clearly,
Whether you'll do more severely
Giving me your love or hate !
For if you with kindness bless me,
  Since from you I soon must part ;
Fortune will so dispossess me,
  That your Love will break my heart.

II

But since Death all sorrow cures,
Might I choose my way of dying,   10
I could wish the arrow flying
From Fortune's quiver, not from
    yours.
For in the sad unusual story
  How my wretched heart was torn,
It will more concern your glory,
  I by absence fell than scorn.

A Dialogue betwixt Lucasia and Rosania, imitating that of gentle Thyrsis [1]

Ros. My Lucasia, leave the moun-
    tain-tops,
    And like a nearer air.
Luc. How shall I then forsake my
    lovely flocks
    Bequeathèd to my care ?

---

[1] A coincidence with the lines in *The Princess*, Canto vii, 'Come down, O maid.'
The internal rhyme, *after* the first quatrain, is curious. It might be better to print the
lines separately—
        'Shepherdess,
    Thy flocks will not be less,' &c.

Ros. Shepherdess, thy flocks will
    not be less,
  Although thou shouldst come
    hither.
Luc. But I fear, the world will be
    severe,
  Should I leave them to go thither.
Ros. O! my friend, if you on that
    depend,
  You'll never know content.   10
Luc. Rather I near thee would live
    and die,
  Would fortune but consent.
Ros. But did you ask leave to love
    me too,
  That others should deprive me?
Luc. Not all mankind, a stratagem
    can find
  Which from that heart should drive
    me.
Ros. Better 't had been, I thee had
    never seen,
  Than that content to lose.
Luc. Such are thy charms, I'd dwell
    within thine arms
  Could I my station choose.   20
Ros. When life is done, the World
    to us is gone,
  And all our cares do end.
Luc. Nay, I know there's nothing
    sweet below,
  Unless it be a friend.
Ros. Then whilst we live, this joy
    let's take and give,
  Since death us soon will sever.
Luc. But I trust, when crumbled into
    dust,
  We shall meet and love for ever.

Song

To the Tune of Adieu, Phillis

'TIS true our life is but a long disease,
Made up of real pain and seeming
    ease.
You stars, who these entangled for-
    tunes give,

    O tell me why
    It is so hard to die,
      Yet such a task to live?

If with some pleasure we our griefs
    betray,
It costs us dearer than it can repay.
For Time or Fortune all things so
    devours;
    Our hopes are crost,   10
    Or else the object lost,
    Ere we can call it ours.

An Epitaph on my honoured Mother-in-Law, Mrs. Phil[l]ips of Portheynon in Cardiganshire, who died Jan. 1, anno 166⅔.

READER, stay, it is but just;
Thou dost not tread on common
    dust.
For underneath this stone does lie
One whose name can never die:
Who from an honour'd lineage
    sprung,
Was to another matchèd young;
Whose happiness she ever sought;
One blessing was, and many brought.
And to her spouse her faith did
    prove
By fifteen pledges of their love.   10
But when by Death of him depriv'd,
An honourable widow liv'd
Full four and twenty years, wherein
Though she had much afflicted been,
Saw many of her children fall,
And public ruin threaten all.
Yet from above assisted, she
Both did and suffer'd worthily.
She to the Crown and Church ad-
    her'd,
And in their sorrows them rever'd,   20
With piety which knew no strife,
But was as sober as her life.
A furnish'd table, open door,
That for her friends, this for the
    poor,

An Epitaph

She kept; yet did her fortune find,
Too narrow for her nobler mind ;
Which seeking objects to relieve,
Did food to many orphans give,
Who in her life no want did know,
But all the poor are orphans now. 30
Yet hold, her fame is much too safe,
To need a written epitaph.
Her fame was so confess'd, that she
Can never here forgotten be,
Till Cardigan itself become
To its own ruin'd heaps a tomb.

Lucasia, Rosania, and Orinda parting at a Fountain, July, 1663

I
HERE, here are our enjoyments done,
And since the love and grief we
wear
Forbids us either word or tear,
And Art wants here expression,
See Nature furnish us with one.

II
The kind and mournful nymph which
here
Inhabits in her humble cells,
No longer her own sorrow tells,
Nor for it now concern'd appears,
But for our parting sheds these
tears. 10

III
Unless she may afflicted be,
Lest we should doubt her inno-
cence ;
Since she hath lost her best pre-
tence
Unto a matchless purity ;
Our love being clearer far than she.

IV
Cold as the streams that from her
flow,
Or (if her privater recess
A greater coldness can express)
Then cold as those dark beds of
snow
Our hearts are at this parting blow. 20

V
But Time, that has both wings and
feet,
Our suffering minutes being spent,
Will visit us with new content.
And sure, if kindness be so sweet
'Tis harder to forget than meet.

VI
Then though the sad adieu we say,
Yet as the wine we hither bring,
Revives, and then exalts the spring ;
So let our hopes to meet allay
The fears and sorrows of this day. 30

A Farewell to Rosania

MY dear Rosania, sometimes be so
kind,
To think upon the friend thou leav'st
behind,
And wish thee here, to make thy joys
complete,
Or else me there, to share thy blest
retreat.
But to the heart which for thy loss
doth mourn,
The kindest thought is that of quick
return.

To my Lady Anne Boyle, saying I looked angrily upon her

ADOR'D Valeria, and can you con-
clude,
Orinda lost in such ingratitude ;
And so mis-spell the language of my
face,
When in my heart you have so great
a place ?
Ah ! be assur'd I could no look direct
To you, not full of passion and
respect.
Or if my looks have play'd that
treach'rous part,
And so much misinterpreted my heart,
I shall forgive them that one false-
hood, less
Than all their folly, and their ugli-
ness ; 10

(579)

And had much rather choose they
    should appear
Always unhandsome, than once un-
    sincere.
But I must thank your error, which
    procures
Me such obliging jealousy as yours.
For at that quarrel I can ne'er repine,
Which shows your kindness, though
    it questions mine.
To your concern I pardon your dis-
    trust,
And prize your love, ev'n when it is
    unjust.

On the Welsh Language

If Honour to an ancient name be
    due,
Or Riches challenge it for one that's
    new,
The British language claims in either
    sense,
Both for its age, and for its opulence.
But all great things must be from
    us remov'd,
To be with higher reverence belov'd.
So landscapes which in prospects
    distant lie,
With greater wonder draw the pleasèd
    eye.
Is not great Troy to one dark ruin
    hurl'd?
Once the fam'd scene of all the
    fighting world.   10
Where's Athens now, to whom Rome
    Learning owes,
And the safe laurels that adorn'd her
    brows?
A strange reverse of Fate she did
    endure,
Never once greater, than she's now
    obscure.
Ev'n Rome herself can but some
    footsteps show
Of Scipio's times, or those of Cicero.
And as the Roman and the Grecian
    State,

The British fell, the spoil of Time
    and Fate.
But though the Language hath the
    beauty lost,
Yet she has still some great Remains
    to boast.   20
For 'twas in that, the sacred Bards of
    old,
In deathless numbers did their
    thoughts unfold.
In groves, by rivers, and on fertile
    plains,
They civiliz'd and taught the list'n-
    ing swains;
Whilst with high raptures, and as
    great success,
Virtue they clothed in Music's charm-
    ing dress.
This Merlin spoke, who in his gloomy
    cave,
Ev'n Destiny herself seem'd to en-
    slave.
For to his sight the future time was
    known,
Much better than to others is their
    own: 30
And with such state, predictions from
    him fell,
As if he did decree, and not fore-
    tell.
This spoke King Arthur, who, if
    Fame be true,
Could have compell'd mankind to
    speak it too.
In this once Boadicca[1] valour taught,
And spoke more nobly than her
    soldiers fought:
Tell me what hero could be more
    than she,
Who fell at once for Fame and
    Liberty?
Nor could a greater sacrifice belong,
Or to her children's, or her country's
    wrong.   40
This spoke Caractacus, who was so
    brave,
That to the Roman Fortune check
    he gave:

---

[1] *Sic* in orig., and the form, which has some authority, is wanted for the verse.

And when their yoke he could decline
no more,
He it so decently and nobly wore,
That Rome herself with blushes did
believe
A Britain[1] would the Law of Honour
give ;
And hastily his chains away she
threw,
Lest her own captive else should her
subdue.

To the Countess of Thanet, upon her Marriage

SINCE you who credit to all wonders
bring,
That lovers can believe, or poets
sing ;
Whose only shape and fashion does
express,
Your virtue is your nature, not your
dress ;
In whom the most admir'd extremes
appear,
Humble and fair, prudent and yet
sincere[2] :
Whose matchless worth transmits
such splendid rays,
As those that envy it are forc'd to
praise.
Since you have found such an illus-
trious sphere,
And are resolv'd to fix your glories
there ;   10
A heart whose bravery to his sex
secures
As much renown as you have done
to yours ;
And whose perfections in obtaining
you,
Are both discover'd and rewarded
too ;
'Twere almost equal boldness to
invent

How to increase your merit, or
content.
Yet sure the Muses somewhat have
to say,
But they will send it you a better
way :
The Court, which so much to your
lustre owes,
Must also pay you its officious
vows.   20
But whilst this shows respect, and
those their art,
Let me too speak the language of my
heart ;
Whose ruder off'rings dare approach
your shrine,
For you, who merit theirs, can pardon
mine.
Fortune and Virtue with such heat
contend
(As once for Rome) now to make
you their friend :
As you so well can this prefer to
that,
As you can neither fear, nor mend
your fate :
Yet since the votes of joy from all
are due,
A love like mine must find some
wishes too.   30
May you in this bright constella-
tion set,
Still show how much the Good out-
shine the Great :
May you be courted with all joys of
sense,
Yet place the highest in your inno-
cence ;
Whose praise may you enjoy, but
not regard,
Finding within both motive and
reward.
May Fortune still to your commands
be just,
Yet still beneath your kindness or
your trust.

---

[1] This is not impossible, though 'a Briton' is more likely.
[2] This line in orig. illustrates the futility of retaining typographical peculiarities in-
discriminately. Besides 'Humble,' 'Fair' and 'Prudent' there have capitals, 'sincere'
not. Let him, who can, distinguish.

May you no trouble either feel or fear,
But from your pity for what others wear ;   40
And may the happy owner of your breast,
Still find his passion with his joys increas'd ;
Whilst every moment your concern makes known,
And gives him too, fresh reason for his own :
And from their Parents may your Offspring have
All that is wise and lovely, soft and brave :
Or if all wishes we in one would give,
For him, and for the world, Long may you live.

Epitaph [1] on her Son H. P. at St. Syth's Church, where her body also lies interred

WHAT on Earth deserves our trust ;
Youth and Beauty both are dust.
Long we gathering are with pain,
What one moment calls again.
Seven years childless marriage past,
A Son, a Son is born at last :
So exactly limb'd and fair,
Full of good spirits, mien, and air,
As a long life promisèd,
Yet, in less than six weeks dead.   10
Too promising, too great a mind
In so small room to be confin'd :
Therefore, as fit in Heav'n to dwell,
He quickly broke the prison shell.
So the subtle alchymist,
Can't with Hermes' Seal resist
The powerful spirit's subtler flight,
But 'twill bid him long good night :
And so the Sun, if it arise
Half so glorious as his eyes,   20
Like this Infant, takes a shroud,
Buried in a morning cloud.

On the Death of my Lord Rich, only son to the Earl of Warwick, who died of the small-pox, 1664

HAVE not so many lives of late
Suffic'd to quench the greedy thirst of Fate ?
Though to increase the mournful purple flood,
As well as noble, she drank Royal blood ;
That not content, against us to engage
Our own wild fury, and usurpers' rage ;
By sickness now, when all that storm is past,
She strives to hew our heroes down as fast ;
And by the prey she chooses, shows her aim
Is to extinguish all the English Fame.   10
Else had this generous Youth we now have lost,
Been still his friends' delight, and country's boast,
And higher rais'd the illustrious name he bore,
Than all our chronicles had done before.
Had Death consider'd ere he struck this blow,
How many noble hopes 'twould overthrow ;
The Genius of his House (who did complain
That all her worthies now died o'er again) ;
His flourishing, and yet untainted years ;
His father's anguish, and his mother's tears ;   20
Sure he had been persuaded to relent,
Nor had for so much early sweetness, sent

---

[1] See Introduction.

That fierce disease, which knows not
how to spare
The young, the great, the knowing,
or the fair.
But we as well might flatter every
wind,
And court the tempests to be less
unkind,
As hope from churlish Death to
snatch his prey,
Who is as furious and as deaf as they;
And who hath cruelly surpris'd in him,
His parents' joy, and all the World's
esteem.   30
  Say, treacherous Hopes that
whisper in our ear,
Still to expect some steady comfort
here,
And though we oft discover all your
arts,
Would still betray our disappointed
hearts;
What new delusion can you now
prepare,
Since this pale object shows how
false you are?
'Twill fully answer all you have to
plead,
If we reply, great Warwick's heir is
dead:
Blush, human Hopes and Joys, and
then be all   39
In solemn mourning [1] at this funeral.
  For since such expectations brittle
prove,
  What can we safely either hope or
love?

The Virgin

The things that make a Virgin please,
She that seeks, will find them these;
A Beauty, not to Art in debt,
Rather agreeable than great;

An eye, wherein at once do meet,
The beams of kindness, and of
wit;
An undissembled Innocence,
Apt not to give, nor take offence:
A conversation at once free
From Passion, and from Sub-
tlety;   10
A face that's modest, yet serene,
A sober, and yet lively mien;
The virtue which does her adorn,
By Honour guarded, not by Scorn;
With such wise lowliness endu'd,
As never can be mean, or rude;
That prudent negligence enrich,
And Time's her silence and her
speech [2];
Whose equal mind does always
move,
Neither a foe, nor slave to love; 20
And whose Religion's strong and
plain,
Not superstitious, nor profane.

Upon the Graving of her Name upon a Tree in Barn-Elms Walks

Alas, how barbarous are we,
Thus to reward the courteous;
Tree,
Who its broad shade affording us,
Deserves not to be wounded thus!
See how the yielding bark complies
With our ungrateful injuries!
And seeing this, say how much
then
Trees are more generous then
men,
Who by a nobleness so pure,
Can first oblige, and then endure. 10

---

[1] Orig. 'morning.'
[2] This very 'metaphysical' couplet seems to mean, 'If you add riches to her wise retiringness, Time will have nothing bad and everything good to say of her.' But I could add other interpretations, and am not sure of any.

Katherine Philips

To my dearest Friend Mrs. A. Owen, upon her greatest loss

As when two sister-rivulets who crept
From that dark bed of snow wherein
    they slept,
By private distant currents under
    ground,
Have by maeanders [1] either's bosom
    found,
They sob aloud, and break down
    what withstood,
Swoln by their own embraces to
    a flood :
So when my sympathy for thy dear
    grief
Had brought me near, in hope to
    give relief,
I found my sorrow heighten'd when
    so join'd,
And thine increas'd by being so
    combin'd,   10
Since to the bleeding hopes of many
    years,
I could contribute nothing but my
    tears ;
Fears which to thy sad fate were
    justly due,
And to his loss, by all who that
    loss knew ;
For thy Charistus was so much above
The eloquence of all our grief and
    love,
That it would be injurious to his
    hearse,
To think to crowd his worth into
    a verse :
Could I by miracle such praise
    indite,
Who with more ease and justice
    weep than write,   20
He was all that which History can
    boast,
Or bolder Poetry had e'er engross'd.

So pious, just, noble, discreet, and
    kind,
Their best ideas know not how to
    find.
His strong Religion not on trifles
    spent,
Was useful, firm, early, and eminent,
Never betray'd to indigested heat,
Nor yet entic'd from what was
    safely great.
And this so soon, as if he had
    foresight,
He must begin betimes whose noon
    is night.   30
His virtue was his choice, and not
    his chance,
Not mov'd by Age, nor born of
    Ignorance.
He well knew whom, and what he
    did believe,
And for his faith did not dispute,
    but live,
And liv'd just like his infant inno-
    cence,
But that was crown'd with free
    obedience.
How did he scorn design, and
    equally
How much abhorr'd this age's vanity !
He neither lik'd its tumults, nor its
    joys,
Slighted alike Earth's pleasures, and
    her noise.   40
But unconcern'd in both, in his own
    mind
Alone could power and satisfaction
    find.
A treasury of merit there lay hid,
Which though he ne'er confess'd,
    his actions did.
His modesty unto his virtue lent
At once a shadow and an ornament.
But what could hide those filial rites
    he paid ?
How much he lov'd, how prudently
    obey'd ?

---

[1] The orig. has the diphthong ; but as it also has capital initial and italic spelling, it is open to any one to contend that Orinda, or her printer, was uncertain whether the word had yet become a common noun. I wish it had kept the diphthong as such.

To Mrs. A. Owen, upon her greatest loss

How as a brother did he justly share
His kind concern betwixt respect and care?   50
And to a wife how fully did he prove
How wisely he could judge, how fondly love?
As husbands serious, but as lovers kind,
He valu'd all of her, but lov'd her mind;
And with a passion made this riddle true,
'Twas ever perfect, and yet still it grew.
Such handsome thoughts his breast did ever fill,
He durst do anything, but what was ill;
Unlike those gallants who so use their time,
As opportunity to act their crime, 60
And lost in wine or vanity when young,
They die too soon, because they liv'd too long:
But he has hallowed so his early death,
'Tis almost shame to draw a longer breath.
I can no more, they that can must have learn'd
To be more eloquent, and less concern'd.
But all that noble justice to his name,
His own good Angel will commit to Fame.
Could grief recall this happiness again,
Of thy dear sorrow I would ne'er complain,   70
But such an opportunity would take
To grieve an useless life out for thy sake.
But since it cannot, I must pray thee live,
That so much of Charistus may survive,

And that thou do not act so harsh to Love,
As that his glory should thy sorrow move:
Endure thy loss till Heav'n shall it repay,
Upon thy last and glorious wedding-day,
When thou shalt know him more, and quickly find
The love increas'd by being so refin'd,   80
And there possess him without parting fears,
As I my friendship free from future tears.

Orinda to Lucasia parting, October, 1661, at London

ADIEU, dear Object of my Love's excess,
And with thee all my hopes of happiness,
With the same fervent and unchangèd heart
Which did its whole self once to thee impart,
(And which, though fortune has so sorely bruis'd,
Would suffer more, to be from this excus'd)
I to resign thy dear converse submit,
Since I can neither keep, nor merit it.
Thou hast too long to me confinèd been,
Who ruin am without, passion within.   10
My mind is sunk below thy tenderness,
And my condition does deserve it less;
I'm so entangl'd and so lost a thing
By all the shocks my daily sorrow[s] bring,
That wouldst thou for thy old Orinda call,
Thou hardly couldst unravel her at all.

And should I thy clear fortunes interline
With the incessant miseries of mine?
No, no, I never lov'd at such a rate,
To tie thee to the rigours of my fate.   20
As from my obligations thou art free,
Sure thou shalt be so from my injury.
Though every other worthiness I miss,
Yet I'll at least be generous in this.
I'd rather perish without sigh or groan,
Than thou shouldst be condemn'd to give me one;
Nay, in my soul I rather could allow
Friendship should be a sufferer, than thou:
Go then, since my sad heart has set thee free,
Let all the loads and chains remain on me.   30
Though I be left the prey of sea and wind,
Thou, being happy, wilt in that be kind;
Nor shall I my undoing much deplore,
Since thou art safe, whom I must value more.
Oh! mayst thou ever be so, and as free
From all ills else, as from my company;
And may the torments thou hast had from it,
Be all that Heaven will to thy life permit.
And that they may thy virtue service do,
Mayst thou be able to forgive them too: 40
But though I must this sharp submission learn,
I cannot yet unwish thy dear concern.

Not one new comfort I expect to see,
I quit my Joy, Hope, Life, and all but thee;
Nor seek I thence aught that may discompose
That mind where so serene a goodness grows.
I ask no inconvenient kindness now,
To move thy passion, or to cloud thy brow;
And thou wilt satisfy my boldest plea
By some few soft remembrances of me,   50
Which may present thee with this candid thought,
I meant not all the troubles that I brought.
Own not what Passion rules, and Fate does crush,
But wish thou couldst have done 't without a blush;
And that I had been, ere it was too late,
Either more worthy, or more fortunate.
Ah, who can love the thing they cannot prize?
But thou mayst pity though thou dost despise.
Yet I should think that pity bought too dear,
If it should cost those precious eyes a tear.   60
Oh, may no minute's trouble thee possess,
But to endear the next hour's happiness;
And mayst thou when thou art from me remov'd,
Be better pleas'd, but never worse belov'd:
Oh, pardon me for pouring out my woes
In rhyme now, that I dare not do 't in prose.
For I must lose whatever is call'd dear,
And thy assistance all that loss to bear,

And have more cause than e'er
I had before,
To fear that I shall never see thee
more.   70

On the first of January, 1657

Th' Eternal Centre of my life and
me,
Who when I was not, gave me room
to be,
Hath since (my time preserving in
his hands)
By moments number'd out the
precious sands,
Till it is swell'd to six and twenty
years,
Chequer'd by Providence with smiles
and tears.
I have observ'd how vain all glories
are,
The change of Empire, and the
chance of War :
Seen Faction with its native venom
burst,
And Treason struck, by what itself
had nurs'd :   10
Seen useless crimes, whose owners
but made way
For future candidates to wear the
bay.

To my Lady M. Cavendish, choosing the name of Policrite

That Nature in your frame has
taken care,
As well your birth as beauty do
declare,
Since we at once discover in your
face,
The lustre of your eyes and of your
race :
And that your shape and fashion
does attest,
So bright a form has yet a brighter
Guest,

To future times authentic fame shall
bring,
Historians shall relate, and Poets
sing.
But since your boundless mind
upon my head,
Some rays of splendour is content
to shed ;   10
And lest I suffer by the great
surprise,
Since you submit to meet me in
disguise,
Can lay aside what dazzles vulgar
sight,
And to Orinda can be Policrite.
You must endure my vows, and
find the way
To entertain such rites as I can pay :
For so the Pow'r Divine new praise
acquires,
By scorning nothing that it once
inspires :
I have no merits that your smile
can win,
Nor offering to appease you when
I sin ;   20
Nor can my useless homage hope to
raise,
When what I cannot serve, I strive
to praise :
But I can love, and love at such a
pitch,
As I dare boast it will ev'n you
enrich ;
For kindness is a mine, when great
and true,
Of nobler ore than ever Indians
knew ;
'Tis all that mortals can on Heav'n
bestow,
And all that Heav'n can value here
below.

Against Love

Hence, Cupid ! with your cheating
toys,
Your real Griefs, and painted Joys,
Your Pleasure which itself destroys.

Lovers like men in fevers burn
  and rave,
And only what will injure them
  do crave.
Men's weakness makes Love so
  severe,
They give him power by their
  fear,
And make the shackles which they
  wear.
  Who to another does his heart
    submit,
  Makes his own Idol, and then
    worships it.   10
Him whose heart is all his own,
Peace and liberty does crown,
He apprehends no killing frown.
  He feels no raptures which are
    joys diseas'd,
  And is not much transported, but
    still pleas'd.

A Dialogue of Friendship
multiplied

Musidorus

WILL you unto one single sense
Confine a starry Influence ;
Or when you do the rays combine,
To themselves only make them
  shine ?
  Love that's engross'd by one
    alone,
  Is envy, not affection.

Orinda

No, Musidorus, this would be
But Friendship's prodigality ;
Union in rays does not confine,
But doubles lustre when they shine,
And souls united live above   11
Envy, as much as scatter'd Love.
  Friendship (like rivers) as it
    multiplies
  In many streams, grows weaker
    still and dies.

Musidorus

Rivers indeed may lose their force,
When they divide or break their
  course ;

For they may want some hidden
  Spring,
Which to their streams recruits may
  bring :
But Friendship's made of purest
  fire,
Which burns and keeps its stock
  entire.   20
  Love, like the Sun, may shed his
    beams on all,
  And grow more great by being
    general.

Orinda

The purity of Friendship's flame,
Proves that from sympathy it came,
And that the hearts so close do knit,
They no third partner can admit ;
Love like the Sun does all inspire,
But burns most by contracted fire.
  Then though I honour every
    worthy guest,
  Yet my Lucasia only rules my
    breast.   30

Rosania to Lucasia on her
Letters

AH ! strike outright, or else forbear ;
Be more kind, or more severe ;
For in this chequer'd mixture I
Cannot live, and would not die :
And must I neither ? Tell me why.

When thy pen thy kindness tells,
My heart transported leaps and
  swells.
But when my greedy eye does stray,
Thy threaten'd absence to survey,
That heart is struck, and faints
  away.   10

To give me title to rich land,
And the fruition to withstand,
Or solemnly to send the key
Of treasures I must never see,
Would it contempt, or bounty be ?

This is such refin'd distress,
That thy sad lovers sigh for less,

Though thou their hopes hast over-
thrown,
They lose but what they ne'er have
known,   19
But I am plunder'd from my own.

How canst thou thy Rosania prize,
And be so cruel and so wise?
For if such rigid policy
Must thy resolves dispute with me,
Where then is Friendship's victory?

Kindness is of so brave a make,
'Twill rather death than bondage
take;
So that if thine no power can have,
Give it and me one common grave,
But quickly either kill or save.   30

To my Antenor, March 16, 166½

My dear Antenor, now give o'er,
For my sake talk of graves no more;
Death is not in your power to gain,
And is both wish'd and fear'd in
vain.
Let's be as angry as we will,
Grief sooner may distract than kill,
And the unhappy often prove
Death is as coy a thing as Love.
Those whose own sword their death
did give,
Afraid were or asham'd to live;   10
And by an act so desperate,
Did poorly run away from Fate;
'Tis braver much t' outride the
storm,
Endure its rage, and shun his harm[1];
Affliction nobly undergone,
More greatness shows than having
none.
But yet the wheel in turning round,
At last may lift us from the ground,
And when our Fortune's most severe,
The less we have, the less we fear.   20

And why should we that grief permit,
Which can nor mend nor shorten it?
Let's wait for a succeeding good,
Woes have their ebb as well as flood:
And since the Parliament have rescu'd
you,
Believe that Providence will do so
too.

A Triton to Lucasia going to Sea, shortly after the Queen's arrival

I

My Master Neptune took such pains
of late
To quiet the commotions of his
state[2],
That he might give, through his
fierce winds and seas,
Safe passage to the Royal Portuguese,
That he e'er since at home has kept,
And in his crystal palace slept,
Till a swift wind told him to-day,
A stranger was to pass this way,
Whom he hath sent me out to view,
And I must tell him, Madam, it is
you.   10

II

He knows you by an honourable
fame:
Who hath not heard Lucasia's worthy
name?
But should he see you too, I doubt
he will
Grow amorous, and here detain you
still:
I know his humour very well,
So best can the event foretell,
But wishing you better success,
And that my Master's guilt be less,
I will say nothing of your form,
Till you are past the danger of a
storm.   20

---

[1] The concurrence of 'its' and 'his' is rather curious, especially in view of the rather recent establishment of the former. Of course both *may* not refer to 'storm'; but Orinda would hardly have made Fate masculine, and Death is some way behind.
[2] Quite a Drydenian line: cf. *MacFlecknoe*, l. 10.

III

Fear nothing else, for eyes so sweet as
    these,
No power that is sea-born can dis-
    please ;
You are much more than Nymph or
    Goddess bright ;
I saw 'm [1] all at supper t' other night :
They with far less attraction draw,
They give us Love, you give us Law.
Your charms the winds and seas
    will move,
But 'tis no wonder, not to Love.
Your only danger is, lest they
Stiff with amazement should becalm
    your way.   30

IV

But should they all want breath to
    make a gale,
What's sent in prayers for you will
    fill your sail ;
What brought you hither will your
    way secure,
Courage and Kindness can no slip
    endure ;
The winds will do as much for you.

V

Yet since our birth the English Ocean
    boasts,
We hope sometimes to see you on
    these coasts,
And we will order for you as you pass,
Winds soft as lovers' vows, waves
    smooth as glass.
Each Deity shall you befriend, 40
And all the Sea-Nymphs shall
    attend ;
But if because a ship 's too strait [2],
Or else unworthy such a freight,
A coach more useful would appear,
That and six Danish steeds you know
    are here.

Orinda upon little Hector Philips

I

[3] TWICE forty months of wedlock I did
    stay,
Then had my vows crown'd with a
    lovely boy.
And yet in forty days he dropt away ;
O swift vicissitude of human joy !

II

I did but see him, and he dis-
    appear'd,
I did but pluck the rosebud and
    it fell ;
A sorrow unforeseen and scarcely
    fear'd,
For ill can mortals their afflictions
    spell.

III

And now (sweet Babe !) what can my
    trembling heart
Suggest to right my doleful fate or
    thee ?   10
Tears are my Muse, and sorrow all
    my art,
So piercing groans must be thy
    Elogy [4].

IV

Thus whilst no eye is witness of my
    moan,
I grieve thy loss (Ah, Boy too dear
    to live !),
And let the unconcernèd World
    alone,
Who neither will nor can refreshment
    give.

V

An off'ring to [5] for thy sad tomb I
    have,
Too just a tribute to thy early herse,

---

[1] *Sic* in orig., and just worth noting for prosody's sake.
[2] Orig. 'straight'; but this confusion is incessant.
[3] Again see Introduction.
[4] *Sic* The reader may choose between 'eulogy' and 'elegy'—the latter being of course the more obvious.
[5] *Sic* in orig. It is of course wrong; but to substitute 'too' would make an awkward clash with the next line. I am inclined to read 'offering' in full and to suppose that she wrote 'to thy' first, and substituted 'for' without cancelling 'to'—when the thirst of the age for apostrophes would do the rest.

Receive these gasping numbers to
  thy grave,
The last of thy unhappy mother's
  verse.   20

To the Lady E. Boyle

Ah, lovely Celimena ! why
  Are you so full of charms,
That neither sex can from them fly,
  Nor take against them arms ?
Others in time may gain a part,
But you at once snatch all the heart.

Dear Tyrant, why will you subdue
  Orinda's trivial heart,
Which can no triumph add to you,
  Not mèriting your dart ?   10
And sure you will not grant it one,
If not for my sake, for your own.

For it has been by tenderness
  Already so much bruis'd,
That at your altars I may guess
  It will be but refus'd.
For never Deity did prize
A torn and maimèd sacrifice.

But oh ! what madness can or dare
  Dispute this noble chain,   20
Which 'tis a greater thing to wear,
  Than empires to obtain ?
To be your slave I more design,
Than to have all the World be
  mine.

Those glorious fetters will create
  A merit fit for them,
Repair the breaches made by Fate,
  And whom they own redeem.
What thus ennobles and thus cures,
Can be no influence but yours.   30

Pardon th' ambition of my aim,
  Who love you at that rate,
That story cannot boast a flame
  So lasting and so great.
I can be only kind and true,
But what else can be worthy you ?

To my Lord Duke of Ormond, upon the late Plot

Though you, great Sir, be Heav'n's
  immediate care,
Who show'd you danger, and then
  broke the snare :
And our first gratitude to that be
  due,
Yet there is much that must be paid
  to you :
For 'tis your prudence Ireland's
  peace secures,
Gives her her safety, and (what's
  dearer) yours,
Whilst your prevailing Genius does
  dispense,
At once its conduct and its influence.
Less honour from a battle won, is
  got,
Than to repel so dangerous a plot ;
Fortune with Courage may play booty
  there,   11
But single Virtue is triumphant here :
In vain the bold ungrateful rebels
  aim
To overturn when you support the
  same :
You who three potent Kingdoms late
  have seen
Tremble with fury, and yet steadfast
  been ;
Who an afflicted Majesty could
  wait,
When it was seemingly forsook by
  Fate ;
Whose settled loyalty no storms dis-
  mayed,
Nor the more flattering mischiefs
  could dissuade :   20
And having 'scap'd so dangerous a
  coast,
Could you now fall, expiring Treason's
  boast ?
Or was it hop'd by this contemnèd
  crew,
That you could Fortune and not
  them subdue ?

But whilst these wretches at this impious rate,
Will buy the knowledge of your
mighty fate;
You shall preserve your King's entrusted crown,
Assisted by his fortune and your
own.
And whilst his sword Kingdoms
abroad bestows,
You, with the next renown, shall this
dispose.   30

To the Countess of Roscommon, with a Copy of *Pompey*

GREAT Pompey's Fame from Egypt
made escape,
And flies to you for succour in this
shape:
A shape, which, I assur'd him, would
appear,
Nor fit for you to see, nor him to
wear.
Yet he says, Madam, he's resolv'd to
come,
And run a hazard of a second doom:
But still he hopes to bribe you, by
that trust
You may be kind, but cannot be unjust;
Each of whose favours will delight
him more
Than all the laurels that his temples
wore: 10
Yet if his name and his misfortunes
fail,
He thinks my intercession will prevail;
And whilst my numbers would relate
his end,
Not like a Judge you'll listen, but a
Friend;
For how can either of us fear your
frown,
Since he and I are both so much
your own.

But when you wonder at my bold
design,
Remember who did that high task
enjoin;
Th' illustrious Orrery, whose least
command
You would more wonder if I could
withstand: 20
Of him I cannot which is hardest
tell,
Or not to praise him, or to praise
him well;
Who on that height from whence
true glory came,
Does there possess and thence distribute fame;
Where all their lyres the willing
Muses bring,
To learn of him whatever they shall
sing;
Since all must yield, whilst there are
books or men,
The universal empire to his pen;
Oh! had that powerful Genius but
inspir'd
The feeble hand, whose service he
requir'd,   30
It had your Justice then, not Mercy
pray'd,
Had pleas'd you more, and better
him obey'd.

On the Death of the truly honourable Sir Walter Lloyd, Knight

AT obsequies where so much grief
is due,
The Muses are in solemn mourning
too,
And by their dead astonishment
confess,
They can lament this loss, though
not express:
Nay, if those ancient Bards had seen
this herse,
Who once in British shades spoke
living verse,

Their high concern for him had made
    them be
Apter to weep, than write his Elogy[1].
When on our land that flood of
    woes was sent,
Which swallow'd all things sacred as
    it went,   10
The injur'd Arts and Virtues made
    his breast
The ark wherein they did securely
    rest :
For as that old one was toss'd up
    and down,
And yet the angry billows could not
    drown ;
So Heav'n did him in this worse
    deluge save,
And made him triumph o'er th' un-
    quiet wave :
Who while he did with that wild
    storm contest,
Such real magnanimity exprest,
That he dar'd to be loyal, in a time
When 'twas a danger made, and
    thought a crime :   20
Duty, and not Ambition, was his
    aim,
Who studied Conscience ever more
    than Fame ;
And thought it so desirable a thing,
To be preferr'd to suffer for his King,
That he all Fortune's spite had
    pardon'd her,
Had she not made his Prince a
    sufferer ;
For whose lov'd cause he did both
    act and grieve,
And for it only did endure to live,
To teach the World what Man can
    be and do,
Arm'd by Allegiance and Religion
    too.   30
His head and heart mutual assist-
    ance gave,
That being still so wise, and this
    so brave,
That 'twas acknowledg'd all he said
    and did,

From Judgement, and from Honour
    did proceed :
Such was the useful mixture of his
    mind,
'Twas at once meek and knowing,
    stout and kind ;
For he was civil, bountiful, and
    learn'd,
And for his friends so generously
    concern'd,
That both his heart and house, his
    hand and tongue,
To them, more than himself, seem'd
    to belong ;   40
As if to his wrong'd party he would be
Both an example and apology :
For when both swords and pens
    ceas'd the dispute,
His life alone Rebellion did confute.
But when his vows propitious
    Heaven had heard,
And our unequall'd King at length
    appear'd,
As aged Simeon did his spirits yield,
When he had seen his dearest hopes
    fulfill'd ;
He gladly saw the morning of that day,
Which Charles his growing splendour
    did display ;   50
Then to eternal joys made greater
    haste,
Because his present ones flow'd in
    so fast ;
From which he fled, out of a pious fear,
Lest he by them should be rewarded
    here ;
While his sad country by his death
    have lost
Their noblest pattern, and their
    greatest boast.

Orinda to Lucasia

I

OBSERVE the weary birds ere night
    be done,
How they would fain call up the
    tardy Sun,

---

[1] This hybrid has been already noted.

With feathers hung with dew,
And trembling voices too,
They court their glorious planet to
appear,
That they may find recruits of
spirits there.
　The drooping flowers hang their
　heads,
　And languish down into their
　beds :
While brooks more bold and fierce
than they,
　Wanting those beams, from
　whence　　　　　　　　10
All things drink influence,
Openly murmur and demand the
day.

II

Thou, my Lucasia, art far more to
me,
Than he to all the under-world
can be ;
　From thee I've heat and light,
　Thy absence makes my night.
But ah ! my friend, it now grows
very long,
The sadness weighty, and the dark-
ness strong :
　My tears (its due [1]) dwell on my
　cheeks,
　And still my heart thy dawning
　seeks,　　　　　　　　20
And to thee mournfully it cries,
　That if too long I wait,
　Ev'n thou mayst come too late,
And not restore my life, but close
my eyes.

To Celimena

Forbear, fond heart (say I), torment
　no more
That Celimena whom thou dost
　adore ;
For since so many of her chains are
　proud,

How canst thou be distinguish'd in
　the crowd ?
But say, bold Trifler, what dost thou
　pretend ?
Wouldst thou depose thy Saint into
　thy Friend ?
Equality of friendship is requir'd,
Which here were criminal to be
　desir'd.

An Answer to another per-suading a Lady to Marriage

I

Forbear, bold Youth, all 's Heaven
　here,
　And what you do aver,
To others courtship may appear,
　'Tis sacrilege to her.

II

She is a public Deity,
　And were't not very odd
She should depose herself to be
　A petty household god ?

III

First make the Sun in private shine,
　And bid the World adieu,　　10
That so he may his beams confine
　In compliment to you.

IV

But if of that you do despair,
　Think how you did amiss,
To strive to fix her beams which are
　More bright and large than this.

Lucasia and Orinda parting with Pastora and Phillis at Ipswich

I

In your converse we best can read,
　How constant we should be ;
But, 'tis in losing that, we need
　All your philosophy.

---

[1] *Sic* in orig., and quite probable with 'absence.' But 'dew' with 'darkness' is possible, and a play on the two words perhaps most likely of all.

II

How perish'd is the joy that's past,
  The present how unsteady !
What comfort can be great, and last,
  When this is gone already ?

III

Yet that it subtly may torment,
  The memory does remain ;   10
For what was, when enjoy'd, Content,
  Is, in its absence, Pain.

IV

If you'll restore it, we'll not grieve
  That Fate does now us sever ;
'Tis better by your gift to live,
  Than by our own endeavour.

Epitaph on my truly honoured Publius Scipio

To the officious marble we commit
A name, above the art of time or wit ;
'Tis righteous, valiant Scipio, whose
  life we
Found the best sermon, and best
  history :
Whose courage was no aguish,
  brutish heat[1],
But such as spoke him good, as well
  as great ;
Which first engag'd his arms to prop
  the state
Of the almost undone Palatinate,
And help the Netherlands to stem
  the tide
Of Rome's Ambition, and the
  Austrian Pride ;   10
Which shall in every History be
  fam'd,
Wherein Breda or Frankendale are
  nam'd.
And when forc'd by his country's
  angry stars
To be a party in her Civil Wars,
He so much conduct by his valour
  taught,

So wisely govern'd, and so bravely
  fought,
That th' English Annals shall this
  record bear,
None better could direct or further
  dare.
Form'd both for war and peace, was
  brave in fight,
And in debate judicious and upright :
Religion was his first and highest
  care,   21
Which rul'd his heart in peace, his
  hand in war :
Which at the least sin made him
  tremble still,
And rather stand a breach, than act
  an ill ;
For his great heart did such a
  temper show,
Stout as a rock, yet soft as melting
  snow.
In him so prudent, and yet so
  sincere,
The serpent much, the dove did
  more appear :
He was above the little arts of
  State,
And scorn'd to sell his peace to
  mend his Fate ;   30
Anxious of nothing, but an inward
  spot,
His hand was open, but his con-
  science not ;
Just to his word, to all religions
  kind,
In duty strict, in bounty unconfin'd ;
And yet so modest, 'twas to him
  less pain
To do great things, than hear them
  told again.
Perform, sad Stone, thy honourable
  trust
Unto his memory, and thyself be
  just,
For his immortal name shall thee
  befriend,
And pay thee back more fame than
  thou canst lend.   40

---

[1] Orig. 'bru*t*ish,' which could be forced into a sense, but very idly.

To Mr. Sam. Cooper, having taken Lucasia's Picture given December 14, 1660

I

IF noble things can noble thoughts infuse,
Your art might ev'n in me create a Muse,
And what you did inspire, you would excuse.

II

But if it such a miracle could do,
That Muse would not return you half your due,
Since 'twould my thanks, but not the praise pursue.

III

To praise your art is then itself more hard,
Nor would it the endeavour much regard,
Since it and Virtue are their own reward.

IV

A pencil from an Angel newly caught,   10
And colours in the Morning's bosom sought,
Would make no picture, if by you not wrought.

V

But done by you it does no more admit
Of an encomium from the highest wit,
Than that another hand should equal it.

VI

Yet whilst you with creating power vie,
Command the very spirit of the eye,
And then reward it with eternity—

VII

Whilst your each touch does Life and Air convey,
Fetch the soul out, like overcoming day,   20
And I my friend repeated here survey—

VIII

I by a passive way may do you right,
Wearing in that, what none could e'er indite,
Your panegyric, and my own delight.

Parting with a Friend

I

WHOEVER thinks that joys below
  Can lasting be and great,
Let him behold this parting blow,
  And cure his own deceit.

II

Alas ! how soon are Pleasures done
  Where Fortune has a power !
How like to the declining Sun,
  Or to the wither'd flower !

III

A thousand unconcernèd eyes
  She'll suffer us to see,   10
But of those [1] we chiefly prize,
  We must deprivèd be.

IV

But we may conquer if we will,
  The wanton Tyrant teach,
That we have something left us still
  Which grows not in her reach.

V

That unseen string which fastens hearts,
  Nor time, nor chance e'er tied,
Nor can it be in either's arts
  Their unions to divide.   20

VI

Where sympathy does Love convey,
  It braves all other powers ;
Lucasia, and Rosania, say,
  Has it not formèd ours ?

VII

If forty weeks' converse has not
  Been able yet to tie

[1] One feels inclined to insert 'joys' or 'which' or something similar.

Your souls in that mysterious knot,
How wretched then am I !

VIII

But if I read in either's mind,
As sure I hope to do,   30
That each to other is combin'd,
Absence will make it true.

IX

No accident will e'er surprise,
Or make your kindness start ;
Although you lose each other's eyes,
You'll faster keep the heart.

X

Letters as kind as turtle-doves,
And undisguis'd as thought,
Will entertain those fervent Loves
Which have each other bought. 40

XI

Till Fortune vexèd with the sight
Of Faith so free from stain,
Shall then grow weary of her spite,
And let you meet again.

XII

Wherein may you that rapture find,
That sister Cherals [1] have,
When I am in my rocks confin'd,
Or seal'd up in my grave.

To my dearest Friend, upon her shunning Grandeur

SHINE out, Rich Soul ! to Greatness be,
What it can never be to thee,
An ornament. Thou canst restore
The lustre which it had before
These ruins ; own it, and 'twill live ;
Thy favour 's more than Kings can give.
Hast more above all titles then [2]
The bearers are 'bove common men ;
And so heroic art within,   9
Thou must descend to be a Queen.
Yet honour may convenient prove,
By giving thy soul room to move :

Affording scene unto that mind,
Which is too great to be confin'd.
Wert thou with single virtue stor'd,
To be approv'd but not ador'd ;
Thou might'st retire ; but who e'er meant
A palace for a tenement ?
Heaven has so built thee, that we find
Thee buried when thou art confin'd :
If thou in privacy wouldst live,   21
Yet lustre to thy virtues give ;
To stifle them for want of air,
Injurious is to Heaven's care.
If thou wilt be immured [3], where
Shall thy obliging soul appear ?
Where shall thy generous prudence be,
And where thy magnanimity ?
Nay, thy own darling thou dost hide,
Thy self-denial is denied ;   30
For he that never greatness tries,
Can never safely it despise.
That Antoninus writ well, when
He held a sceptre and a pen :
Less credit Solomon does bring
As a philosopher than king ;
So much advantage flows from hence,
To write by our experience.
Diogenes I must suspect
Of envy more than wise neglect, 40
When he his Prince so ill did treat,
And so much spurnèd at the great :
A censure is not clear from those
Whom Fate subjects, or does depose ;
Nor can we Greatness understand
From an oppress'd or fallen hand :
But 'tis some Prince must that define,
Or one that freely did resign.
A great Almanzor teaches thus,
Or else a Dionysius.   50
For to know Grandeur we must live
In that, and not in perspective ;
Vouchsafe the trial then, that thou
Mayst safely wield, yet disallow

---

[1] Chorals (?) connected with 'choir.' Orinda elsewhere uses 'Quire' as = 'the assembly of the blest.'
[2] Then = 'than' as so often.
[3] Orig. 'immur'd,' with the usual thirst for apostrophes.

The world's temptations, and be
still
Above whatever would thee fill.
Convince mankind, there 's some-
what more
Great than the titles they adore :
Stand near them, and 'twill soon be
known
Thou hast more splendour of thy
own ;   60
Yield to the wanting Age, and be
Channel of true nobility :
For from thy womb such heroes
need must rise,
Who honours will deserve, and can
despise.

To Pastora being with her Friend

I

WHILE you the double joy obtain
Of what you give, and what you
gain :
Friendship, who owes you so much
fame,
Commands my tribute to your
name.

II

Friendship that was almost forlorn,
Sunk under every critic's scorn ;
But that your Genius her protects,
Had fled the World, at least the
sex.

III

You have restorèd them and us,
Whence both are happy ; Caesar
thus   10
Ow'd Rome the glories of his reign,
And Rome ow'd him as much
again.

IV

You in your friend those joys have
found
Which all relations can propound ;

What Nature does 'mong them
disperse,
You multiply in her converse.

V

You her enjoyment have pursu'd
In company, and solitude ;
And wheresoever she'll retire,
There 's the diversion you desire. 20

VI

Your joys by this are more immense,
And heat contracted grows intense ;
And friendship to be such to you,
Will make these pleasures, honours
too.

VII

Be to each other that Content,
As to your sex y' are ornament ;
And may your hearts by mixture
lost,
Be still each other's bliss and boast.

VIII

Impossible your parting be
As that you e'er should disagree ; 30
And then even Death your friend
will prove,
And both at once (though late)
remove.

IX

But that you may severely [1] live,
You must th' offending World for-
give,
And to employ your charity,
You have an object now in me.

X

My pen so much for you unfit,
Presents my heart, though not my
wit ;
Which heart admires what you
express,
More than what Monarchs do
possess.   40

XI

Fear not infection from my Fate,
Though I must be unfortunate,
For having paid my vows due, I
Shall soon withdraw, wither and
die.

[1] Securely (?).

To my Lord and Lady Dunganon

To my Lord and Lady Dunganon, on their Marriage, May 11, 1662

To you, who, in yourselves, do comprehend
All you can wish, and all we can commend ;
Whom worth does guide, and destiny obey,
What offerings can the useless Muses pay ?
Each must at once suspend her charming lyre,
Till she hath learnt from you what to inspire :
Well may they wonder to observe a knot,
So curiously by Love and Fortune wrought,
To which propitious Heaven did decree,
All things on earth should tributary be ;   10
By gentle, sure, but unperceiv'd degrees,
As the Sun's motion, or the growth of trees,
Does Providence our wills to hers incline,
And makes all accidents serve her design :
Her pencil (Sir) within your breast did draw
The picture of a face you never saw.
With touches, which so sweet were and so true,
By them alone th' original you knew ;
And at that sight with satisfaction yield
Your freedom which till then maintain'd the field.   20
'Twas by the same mysterious power too,
That she has been so long reserv'd for you ;
Whose noble passion, with submissive art,
Disarm'd her scruples and subdu'd her heart.
And now that at the last your souls are tied,
Whom floods nor difficulties could divide,
Ev'n you that beauteous union may admire,
Which was at once Heaven's care, and your desire.
You are so happy in each other's love,
And in assur'd protection from above,   30
That we no wish can add unto your bliss
But that it should continue as it is.
O ! may it so, and may the Wheel of Fate,
In you no more change than she feels, create ;
And may you still your happinesses find,
Not on your fortune growing, but your mind,
Whereby the shafts of chance as vain will prove,
As all things else did that oppos'd your Love.
Be kind and happy to that great degree,
As may instruct latest posterity,   40
From so rever'd a precedent [1] to frame
Rules to their duty, to their wishes aim.
May the vast sea for your sake quit his pride,
And grow so smooth, while on his breast you ride,
As may not only bring you to your port,
But show how all things do your virtues court.
May every object give you new delight,
May Time forget his scythe, and Fate his spite ;

---

[1] Orig. 'President,' but the error is common, and 'president' could only be forced into sense.

(599)

And may you never other sorrow
know,
But what your pity feels for others'
woe : 50
May your compassion be like that
Divine,
Which relieves all on whom it does
but shine,
Whilst you produce a race that may
inherit
All your great stock of Beauty,
Fame, and Merit.

To his Grace Gilbert, Lord Archbishop of Canterbury, July 10, 1664

THAT private shade, wherein my
Muse was bred,
She always hop'd might hide her
humble head ;
Believing the retirement she had
chose
Might yield her, if not pardon, yet
repose ;
Nor other repetitions did expect,
Than what our Echoes from the
rocks reflect.
But hurried from her cave with wild
affright,
And dragg'd maliciously into the
light,
(Which makes her like [the] Hebrew
Virgin mourn
When from her face her veil was
rudely torn) 10
To you (my Lord) she now for
succour calls,
And at your feet, with just confusion
falls.
But she will thank the wrong deserv'd
her hate,
If it procure her that auspicious
fate,
That the same wing may over her
be cast,

Where the best Church of all the
World is plac'd,
And under which when she is once
retir'd,
She really may be come to be inspir'd ;
And by the wonders which she
there shall view,
May raise herself to such a theme
as you, 20
Who were preserv'd to govern and
restore
That Church whose Confessor you
were before ;
And show by your unwearied present
care,
Your suff'rings are not ended, though
hers are :
For whilst your crosier her defence
secures,
You purchase her rest with the loss
of yours,
And Heav'n who first refin'd your
worth, and then,
Gave it so large and eminent a
scene,
Hath paid you what was many ways
your due,
And done itself a greater right
than[1] you. 30
For after such a rough and tedious
storm
Had torn the Church, and done her
so much harm ;
And (though at length rebuk'd, yet)
left behind
Such angry relics, in the wave and
wind ;
No Pilot could, whose skill and
faith were less,
Manage the shatter'd vessel with
success.
The Piety of the Apostles' times
And Courage to resist this Age's
crimes ;
Majestic sweetness, temper'd and
refin'd,
In a polite, and comprehensive
mind, 40

[1] Orig., as before, 'then.'

Were all requir'd her ruins to repair,
And all united in her Primate are.
In your aspect so candid and serene,
The conscience of such virtue may be seen,
As makes the sullen schismatic consent,
A Churchman may be great and innocent.
This shall those men reproach, if not reduce,
And take away their fault, or their excuse,
Whilst in your life and government appear
All that the pious wish, and factious fear.   50
Since the prevailing Cross her ensigns spread,

And Pagan Gods from Christian Bishops fled,
Time's curious eye till now hath never spied
The Church's helm so happily supplied,
Merit and Providence so fitly met,
The worthiest Prelate in the highest seat.

If noble things can noble thoughts infuse,
Your life (my Lord) may, ev'n in me, produce
Such raptures, that of their rich fury proud,
I may, perhaps, dare to proclaim aloud ;   60
Assur'd, the World that ardour will excuse ;
Applaud the subject, and forgive the Muse.

TRANSLATIONS

La Solitude de St. Amant [1]

Englished.

I

O ! SOLITUDE, my sweetest choice,
Places devoted to the night,
Remote from tumult, and from noise,
How you my restless thoughts delight !
O Heavens ! what content is mine,
To see those trees which have appear'd
From the nativity of Time,
And which all ages have rever'd,

To look to-day as fresh and green,
As when their beauties first were seen !   10

II

A cheerful wind does court them so,
And with such amorous breath enfold,
That we by nothing else can know,
But by their height that they are old.
Hither the demi-gods did fly
To seek a sanctuary, when
Displeasèd Jove once pierc'd the sky,
To pour a deluge upon men,

[1] O ! Que j'aime la Solitude,
Que ces lieux sacrez à la nuict,
Eloignez du monde & de bruit,
Plaisent a mon inquietude !
Mon Dieu ! que mes yeux sont contens,

De voir ces Bois, qui se trouverent
A la nativité du Temps,
Et que tous les Siècles reverent,
Estre encore aussi beaux & vers,
Qu'aux premiers jours de l'Univers.

This (see Preface) will satisfy the reasonable demands of Orinda's first editor without giving the whole.

And on these boughs themselves
did save,
Whence they could hardly see a
wave.   20

III

Sad Philomel upon this thorn,
  So curiously by Flora dress'd,
In melting notes, her case forlorn,
  To entertain me, hath confess'd.
O ! how agreeable a sight
  These hanging mountains do ap-
pear,
Which the unhappy would invite
  To finish all their sorrows here,
When their hard fate makes them
endure   29
  Such woes, as only death can cure.

IV

What pretty desolations make
  These torrents vagabond and
fierce,
Who in vast leaps their springs for-
sake,
  This solitary Vale to pierce.
Then sliding just as serpents do
  Under the foot of every tree,
Themselves are changed to rivers too,
  Wherein some stately Nayade [1],
As in her native bed, is grown
  A Queen upon a crystal throne.   40

V

This fen beset with river plants,
  O ! how it does my senses charm !
Nor elders, reeds, nor willows want,
  Which the sharp steel did never
harm.
Here Nymphs which come to take
the air,
  May with such distaffs furnish'd be,
As flags and rushes can prepare,
  Where we the nimble frogs may
see,
Who frighted to retreat do fly,
  If an approaching man they spy. 50

VI

Here water-fowl repose enjoy,
  Without the interrupting care,
Lest Fortune should their bliss
destroy
  By the malicious fowler's snare.
Some ravish'd with so bright a day,
  Their feathers finely prune and
deck ;
Others their amorous heats allay,
  Which yet the waters could not
check :
All take their innocent content
  In this their lovely element.   60

VII

Summer's, nor Winter's bold ap-
proach,
  This stream did never entertain ;
Nor ever felt a boat or coach,
  Whilst either season did remain.
No thirsty traveller came near,
  And rudely made his hand his
cup ;
Nor any hunted hind hath here
  Her hopeless life resignèd up ;
Nor ever did the treacherous hook
  Intrude to empty any brook.   70

VIII

What beauty is there in the sight
  Of these old ruin'd castle-walls,
On which the utmost rage and spight
  Of Time's worst insurrection falls ?
The witches keep their Sabbath here,
  And wanton devils make retreat,
Who in malicious sport appear,
  Our sense both to afflict and cheat ;
And here within a thousand holes
  Are nests of adders and of owls. 80

IX

The raven with his dismal cries,
  That mortal augury of Fate,
Those ghastly goblins gratifies,
  Which in these gloomy places
wait.

---

[1] The retention of the trisyllabic value of the French *Naiade* and the accentuation of the *e* are interesting, though the latter is of course unjustifiable. Saint-Amant has the word in the middle of the line.

'Ou quelque Nayade superbe.'

But, after all, the classical teaching of Hackney may have been slightly defective, and Orinda may have thought that ' Naiad*es* ' authorized a singular ' Naiad*ee*.'

On a curs'd tree the wind does move
   A carcase which did once belong
To one that hang'd himself for love
   Of a fair Nymph that did him wrong,
Who though she saw his love and truth,
With one look would not save the youth. 90

X

But Heaven which judges equally,
   And its own laws will still maintain,
Rewarded soon her cruelty
   With a deserv'd and mighty pain :
About this squalid heap of bones,
   Her wand'ring and condemnèd shade,
Laments in long and piercing groans
   The destiny her rigour made,
And the more to augment her fright,
Her crime is ever in her sight. 100

XI

There upon antique marbles trac'd,
   Devices of past times we see,
Here age hath almost quite defac'd
   What lovers carv'd on every tree.
The cellar, here, the highest room
   Receives when its old rafters fail,
Soil'd with the venom and the foam
   Of the spider and the snail :
And th' ivy in the chimney we
Find shaded by a walnut tree. 110

XII

Below there does a cave extend,
   Wherein there is so dark a grot,
That should the Sun himself descend,
   I think he could not see a jot.
Here sleep within a heavy lid
   In quiet sadness locks up sense,
And every care he does forbid,
   Whilst in the arms of negligence,
Lazily on his back he 's spread,
And sheaves of poppy are his bed. 120

XIII

Within this cool and hollow cave,
   Where Love itself might turn to ice,
Poor Echo ceases not to rave
   On her Narcissus wild and nice :

Hither I softly steal a thought,
   And by the softer music made
With a sweet lute in charms well taught,
   Sometimes I flatter her sad shade,
Whilst of my chords I make such choice,
They serve as body to her voice. 130

XIV

When from these ruins I retire,
   This horrid rock I do invade,
Whose lofty brow seems to inquire
   Of what materials mists are made :
From thence descending leisurely
   Under the brow of this steep hill,
It with great pleasure I descry
   By waters undermin'd, until
They to Palaemon's seat did climb,
Compos'd of sponges and of slime. 140

XV

How highly is the fancy pleas'd
   To be upon the ocean's shore,
When she begins to be appeas'd,
   And her fierce billows cease to roar !
And when the hairy Tritons are
   Riding upon the shaken wave,
With what strange sounds they strike the air
   Of their trumpets hoarse and brave,
Whose shrill report does every wind
Unto his due submission bind ! 150

XVI

Sometimes the sea dispels the sand,
   Trembling and murmuring in the bay,
And rolls itself upon the shells
   Which it both brings and takes away.
Sometimes exposes on the strand,
   Th' effects of Neptune's rage and scorn,
Drown'd men, dead monsters cast on land,
   And ships that were in tempest torn, 158
With diamonds and ambergreece,
And many more such things as these.

XVII

Sometimes so sweetly she does
    smile,
  A floating mirror she might be,
And you would fancy all that while
    New Heavens in her face to see :
The Sun himself is drawn so well,
  When there he would his picture
    view,
That our eye can hardly tell
    Which is the false Sun, which the
    true ;
And lest we give our sense the lie,
We think he's fallen from the sky. 170

XVIII

Bernieres ! for whose belovèd sake
  My thoughts are at a noble strife,
This my fantastic landskip take,
    Which I have copied from the
    life.
I only seek the deserts rough,
  Where all alone I love to walk,
And with discourse refin'd enough,
    My Genius and the Muses talk ;
But the converse most truly mine,
Is the dear memory of thine.   180

XIX

Thou mayst in this Poem find,
  So full of liberty and heat,
What illustrious rays have shin'd
    To enlighten my conceit :
Sometimes pensive, sometimes gay,
  Just as that fury does control,
And as the object I survey,
    The notions grow up in my soul,
And are as unconcern'd and free 189
As the flame which transported me.

XX

O ! how I Solitude adore,
  That element of noblest wit,
Where I have learnt Apollo's lore,
    Without the pains to study it :
For thy sake I in love am grown
  With what thy fancy does pursue ;
But when I think upon my own,
    I hate it for that reason too,
Because it needs must hinder me 199
From seeing, and from serving
    thee.

Tendres desirs out of a French Prose

Go, soft desires, Love's gentle pro-
    geny,
  And on the heart of charming
    Sylvia seize,
Then quickly back again return to me,
  Since that 's the only cure for my
    disease ;
But if you miss her breast whom I
    adore,
Then take your flight, and visit mine
    no more.

Amanti ch' in pianti, &c.

LOVERS who in complaints yourselves
    consume,
And to be happy once perhaps pre-
    sume ;
  Your Love and hopes alike are
    vain,
  Nor will they ever cure your pain.
They that in Love would joy attain,
  Their passion to their power must
    frame ;
  Let them enjoy what they can gain,
    And never higher aim.

Complaints and Sorrows, from me
    now depart,
You think to soften an ungentle
    heart,   10
  When it not only wards such
    blows,
But from your sufferance prouder
    grows.
They that in Love would joy, &c.

A Pastoral of Mons. de Scudery's in the first volume of 'Almahide'

Englished.

SLOTHFUL deceiver, come away,
With me again the fields survey ;
And sleep no more, unless it be
My fortune thou shouldst dream
    of me.

A Pastoral of Mons. de Scudery's

The sky, from which the night is fled,
Is painted with a matchless red,
'Tis day; the morning greets my
   eyes :
Thou art my Sun, wilt thou not rise?

Now the black shadows of the night
From Heav'n and Earth are put to
   flight :   10
Come and dispel each ling'ring
   shade,
With that light which thy eyes have
   made.

That planet, which so like thee seems,
In his long and piercing beams,
At once illuminates and gilds
All these valleys, and these fields.

The winds do rather sigh than blow,
And rivers murmur as they go,
And all things seem to thee to say,
Rise, fair one, 'tis a lovely day.   20

Come, and the liquid pearls descry,
Which glittering 'mong the flowers
   lie ;
Day finds them wet, when it appears,
And 'tis too often with my tears.

Hearken, and thou wilt much ap-
   prove
The warbling consort[1] of this grove ;
Complete the pleasure of our ears,
Mixing thy harmony with theirs.

Feather'd musician step aside,
Thyself within these bushes hide,   30
While my Aminta's voice affords
Her charming notes to clothe my
   words.

Hasten to sing them, then, my fair,
And put this proud one to despair,
Whose voice, the bass and trebles
   part,
With so marvellous an art.

Come, Philomel, and now make use
Of all thy practice can produce,
All the harmonious secrets thou
Canst try will do no service now.   40

Thou must to her this glory give,
For nothing can thy fame relieve.
Then ere thou dost the conquest try,
Choose to be silent here or die.

Come, my Shepherdess, survey
(While a hundred pipes do play,)
From every fold, from every shed,
How the herds and flocks are fed.

Hear the pleasing, harmless voice,
Of thy lambs, now [2] they rejoice,   50
While with their bleating notes are
   mix'd,
Their pretty bounds, and leaps be-
   twixt.

See, see, how from the thatchèd
   rooms
Of these our artless cabins, comes
A rustic troop of jolly swains,
From every side, unto the plains.

Their sheep-hooks' steel, so bright
   and clear,
How it shines, both far and near ;
A bag-pipe here, and there a flute,
With merrier whistles do dispute.   60

Hear thy flocks, which for thee bleat
In language innocent, and sweet;
See here thy shepherd who attends
   'em,
And from the ravenous wolf defends
   'em.

Thy Melampus him endears,
And leaps, and sports, when he
   appears,
He complains that thy sloth is such ;
And my poor heart does that as
   much.

Among the rest here's a ram, we
So white, so blithe, so merry see,   70
In all our flocks, there is not one,
Deserves such praise, as he alone.

On the grass he butts and leaps,
Flatters, and then away he skips ;
So gentle, and yet proud is he,
That surely he hath learn'd of thee.

---

[1] = 'concert,' as often.
[2] 'Now' is possible, but one rather suspects 'how.'

The fairest garlands we can find,
Unworthy are, his horns to bind ;
But flowers that death can never know,
Are fittest to adorn his brow.   80

He is full of modest shame,
And as full of amorous flame ;
Astrologers in heaven see
A beast less beautiful than he.

I have for thee a sheep-hook brought,
On which thy shepherd hard hath
    wrought,
Here he thy character hath trac'd ;
Is it not neatly interlac'd ?

To that a scrip is tied for thee,
Which woven is so curiously,   90
That the art does the stuff excel,
And gold itself looks not so well.

Here 's in a cage that he did make,
All the birds that he could take,
How glorious is their slavery,
If they be not despis'd by thee !

A garland too for thee hath staid ;
And 'tis of fairest flowers made :
Aurora had this offering kept,
And for its loss hath newly wept. 100

A lovely fawn he brings along,
Nimble, as thyself, and young,
And greater presents he would bring,
But that a shepherd is no king.

Come away, my lovely bliss,
To such divertisement as this,
And bring none to these lovely places,
But only Venus, and the Graces.

Whatever company were nigh,   109
Would tedious be, when thou art by ;
Venus and Fortune would to me
Be troublesome, if I had thee.

She comes ! from far, the lovely maid
Is by her shining charms betray'd :
See how the flowers sprout up, to
    meet
A noble ruin from her feet.

How sprightly, and how fair is she !
How much undone then must I be ?
My torment is, I know, severe,
But who can think on't when she 's
    near ?   120

(606)

My heart leaps up within my breast,
And sinks again with joy opprest ;
But in her sight to yield my breath,
Would be an acceptable death.

Come then, and, in this shade, be
    sure,
That thy fair skin shall be secure ;
For else the Sun would wrong, I fear,
The colours which do flourish there.

His flaming steeds do climb so fast,
While they to our horizon haste, 130
That by this time his radiant coach,
Does to his highest house approach.

His fiercer rays in heat, and length,
Begin to rob us of our strength ;
Directly on the Earth they dart,
And all the shadows are grown short.

This valley hath a private seat,
Which is a cool and moist retreat,
Where th' angry Planet which we spy,
Can ne'er invade us with his eye. 140

Behold this fresh and florid grass,
Where never yet a foot did pass,
A carpet spreads for us to sit,
And to thy beauty offers it.

Th   delicate apartment is
Roof'd o'er with agèd stooping trees,
Whose verdant shadow does secure
This place a native furniture.

The courts of Naiades are such,   149
In shades like these, ador'd so much,
Where thousand fountains round
    about
Perpetually gush water out.

How finely this thick moss doth look,
Which limits this transparent brook ;
Whose sportful wave does swell and
    spread,
And is on flags and rushes shed !

Within this liquid crystal, see
The cause of all my misery,
And judge by that, (fair murtheress)
If I could love thy beauty less.   160

Thy either eye does rays dispense
Of modesty and innocence ;
And with thy seriousness, we find
The gladness of an infant join'd.

Thy frowns delight though they torment,
From thy looks life and death are sent;
And thy whole air does on us throw
Arrows, which cureless wounds bestow.

The stature of a mountain pine 169
Is crooked when compar'd to thine:
Which does thy sex to envy move,
As much as it does ours to love.

From thy dividing lips do fly
Those pointed shafts that make us die:
Nor have our gardens e'er a rose,
That to thy cheeks we dare oppose.

When by a happy liberty,
We may thy lovely bosom see,
The whitest curds, nor falling snow,
Can any such complexion show. 180

Thyme and Marjoram, whose scent,
Of all perfume's most innocent,
Less fragrancy than thy breath have,
Which all our senses does enslave.

Even when thou scornest, thou canst please,
And make us love our own disease.
The blushes that our cherries wear,
Do hardly to thy lips come near.

When upon the smoother plains,
Thou to dance wilt take the pains,
No hind, when she employs her feet,
Is half so graceful, or so fleet. 192

Of thy garments fair and white,
The neatness gives us most delight,
And I had rather them behold,
Than clothes embroider'd with gold.

I nothing in the world can see
So rare as unadornèd thee,
Who art (as it must be confess'd)
Not by thy clothes, but beauty dress'd. 200

Thy lovely hair thou up hast tied,
And in an unwrought veil dost hide;
In the meantime thy single face
All other beauties does disgrace.

Yes, yes, thy negligence alone,
Does more than all their care hath done:
The Nymphs, in all their pompous dress,
Do entertain my fancy less.

A nosegay all thy jewel is,
And all thy art consists in this; 210
And what from this pure spring does pass,
Is all thy paint, and all thy glass.

Adorèd beauty, here may we
Ourselves in lovely glasses see:
Come then, I pray thee, let us look,
I in thy eyes, thou in the brook.

Within this faithful mirror see
The object which hath conquer'd me,
Which though the stream does well impart, 219
'Tis better form'd here in my heart.

In th' entertainment of thy mind,
When 'tis to pensiveness inclin'd,
Count if thou canst these flowers, and thou
The sum of my desires wilt know.

Observe these turtles, kind and true,
Hearken how frequently they woo:
They faithful lovers are, and who
That sees thee, would not be so too?

Of them, my fair Aminta, learn 229
At length to grant me thy concern;
Follow what thou in them dost see,
And thou wilt soon be kind to me.

Those mighty bulls are worth thy sight,
Who on the plains so stoutly fight;
Fiercely each other's brow they hit,
Where beauty does with anger meet.

Love is the quarrel they maintain,
As 'twas the reason of their pain.
So would thy faithful shepherd do,
If he should meet his rival too. 240

Thy shepherd, fair and cruel one,
In all these villages is known:
Such is his father's herd and flock,
The plain is cover'd with the stock.

He the convenient'st pastures knows,
And where the wholesome water flows ;
Knows where the coolest shadows are,
And well hath learn'd a shepherd's care.

Astrology he studies too,   249
As much as shepherds ought to do ;
Nay, Magic nothing hath so dim,
That can be long conceal'd from him.

When any do these secrets dread,
He for himself hath this to plead ;
That he by them such herbs can pick,
As cure his sheep when they are sick.

He can foresee the coming storm,
Nor hail, nor clouds, can do him harm,   258
And from their injuries can keep,
Safely enough his lambs and sheep.

He knows the season of the year,
When shepherds think it fit to shear
Such inoffensive sheep as these,
And strip them of their silver fleece.

He knows the scorching time of day,
When he must lead his flock away
To valleys which are cool and near,
To chew the cud, and rest them there.

He dares the fiercest wolves engage,
When 'tis their hunger makes them rage ;   270
The frighted dogs, when they retire,
He with new courage can inspire.

He sings and dances passing well,
And does in wrestling too excel ;
Yes, fair maid, and few that know him,
But these advantages allow him.

At our feast, he gets the praise,
For his enchanting roundelays,
And on his head have oftenest been
The garlands and the prizes seen. 280

When the scrip and crook he quits,
And free from all disturbance sits,
He can make the bag-pipes swell,
And oaten reeds his passion tell.

When his flame does him excite,
In amorous songs to do the right,
He makes the verses which he uses,
And borrows none of other Muses.

He neglects his own affairs,
To serve thee with greater cares, 290
And many shepherdesses would
Deprive thee of him if they could.

Of Alceste he could tell,
And Silvia's eye, thou know'st it well :
But as his modesty is great,
He blushes if he them repeat.

When in the crystal stream he looks,
If there be any truth in brooks,
He finds, thy scorn can never be
Excus'd by his deformity.   300

His passion is so high for thee,
As 'twill admit no new degree.
Why wilt not thou his love requite,
Since kindness gives so much delight?

Aminta heark'ned all this while,
Then with a dext'rous, charming smile,
Against her will, she let him see,
That she would change his destiny.

I promise nothing, then said she,
With an obliging air, and free ;   310
But I think, if you will try,
The wolves are crueller than I.

When my sheep unhealthy are,
I have compassion, I have care ;
Nor pains, nor journeys then I grudge,
By which you may my nature judge.

When any of them goes astray,
All the hamlets near us may
Perceive me, all in grief and fear,
Run and search it everywhere.   320

And when I happen once to find
The object of my troubled mind,
As soon as ever it I spy,
O ! how overjoy'd am I !

I flatter her, and I caress,
And let her ruffle all my dress ;
The vagabond I kindly treat,
And mint and thyme I make her eat.

When my sparrow does me quit,
My throbbing heart makes after it ;
And nothing can relief afford,   331
For my fair inconstant bird [1].
When my dog hath me displeas'd,
I am presently appeas'd ;
And a tear is in my eye,
If I have but made him cry.
I never could a hatred keep,
But to the wolf that kills my sheep :
Gentle and kind, and soft I am,
And just as harmless as a lamb. 340
Dispel thy fear, cease thy complaint,
O Shepherd timorous and faint !
For I'm a mistress very good,
If you'll but serve me as you shou'd.
Words of a favourable strain,
(Cried out that now transported swain)
Which do in thy Leontius' fate,
So glad and swift a change create.

But look about, for now I mark
The fields already growing dark, 350
And with those shadows cover'd all,
Which from the neighbouring mountains fall.
The wingèd quire on every tree
By carolling melodiously,
Do the declining Sun pursue,
With their last homage, and adieu.
From the next cottages I hear
Voices well known unto my ear :
They are of our domestics who
Do pipe, and hollow for us too. 360
The flocks and herds do homewards go,
I hear them hither bleat and low,
Thy eyes, which mine so much admire,
Tell me 'tis time we should retire.

Go, then, destroying fair one, go,
Since I perceive it must be so,
Sleep sweetly all the night, but be,
At least, so kind to dream of me.

Translation of *Thomas à Kempis* into Verse, out of Mons. Corneille's lib. 3. cap. 2. Englished

SPEAK, Gracious Lord, Thy servant hears,
For I both am and will be so,
And in Thy pleasant paths will go
When the Sun shines, or disappears.

Give me Thy Spirit, that I may perceive [2],
What by my soul Thou wouldst have done :
Let me have no desire but one,
Thy will to practise and believe.

But yet Thy eloquence disarm,
And as a whisper to my heart, 10
Let it, like dew, plenty impart,
And like that let it freely charm.

The Jews fear'd thunderbolts would fall,
And that Thy words would Death procure,
Nor in the desert could endure
To hear their Maker speak at all.

They court Moses to declare Thy will [3],
And begg'd to hear no more thy voice,
They could not stand the dreadful noise, 19
Lest it should both surprise and kill.

---

[1] This rhyme is an instance of a law which has not, I think, been generally noticed as prevailing in late seventeenth-century poetry, that *for rhyme's sake a combination of letters may take a value which it actually possesses only in another word.* In 'word' itself *ord* does rhyme to *ird.*

[2] ' Spirit ' is of course constantly monosyllabic, and even if not lends itself easily to trisyllabic substitution. But the rest of the line makes it almost certain that Orinda, by oversight, put in a foot too much.

[3] This apparently hopeless verse is perhaps best mended into a *deca*syllable (*cf.* the first lines of stanzas 2 and 8) by reading ' court*ed*.'

Without those terrors, I implore,
  And other favours I entreat,
  With confident, though humble
    heart[1],
I beg what Samuel did of yore.

Though Thou art all that I can dread,
  Thy voice is music to my ears :
  Speak, Lord, then, for Thy servant
    hears,
And will obey what Thou hast said.

I ask no Moses that for Thee should
    speak,
  Nor Prophet to enlighten me ; 30
  They all are taught and sent by
    Thee,
And 'tis Thy voice I only seek.

Those beams proceed from Thee
    alone,
  Which through their words on us
    do flow ;
  Thou without them canst all be-
    stow,
But they without Thee can give none.

They may repeat the sound of words,
  But not confer their hidden force,
  And without Thee, their best dis-
    course,
Nothing but scorn to men affords. 40

Let them Thy miracles impart,
  And vigorously Thy will declare ;
  Their voice, perhaps, may strike
    the ear,
But it can never move the heart.

Th' obscure and naked Word they
    sow,
  But thou dost open our dim eye,
  And the dead letter to supply,
The Living Spirit dost bestow.

Mysterious truths to us they
    brought,
  But Thou expound'st the riddle
    too, 50
  And Thou alone canst make us
    do
All the great things that they have
    taught.

They may indeed the way direct,
  But Thou enablest us to walk ;
  I' th' ear alone sticks all they talk,
But thou dost even the heart dissect.

They wash the surface of the
    mind,
  But all her fruit Thy goodness
    claims,
  All that e'er enlightens, or enflames,
Must be to that alone assign'd. 60

APPENDIX

Songs from *Pompey*

SONG (*Pompey*, Act I)

SINCE affairs of the State are already
    decreed[2],
  Make room for affairs of the
    Court ;

Employment and Pleasure each
    other succeed,
  Because they each other support.
  Were Princes confin'd
    From slackening their mind,
  When by Care it is ruffled and
    curl'd,

[1] It is probably useless to try to mend this rhyme, though 'heat' in the earlier metaphysicals would not be impossible.
[2] It must be admitted that Orinda is not happy in these anapaests, and too much justifies in particular the generally unjust scorn of Bysshe for 'the disagreeableness of their measure.'

A crown would appear
Too heavy to wear,
And no man would govern the
world.   10
If the Gods themselves who have
power enough,
In diversions are various, and oft;
Since the business of Kings is
angry and rough,
Their intervals ought to be soft.
    Were Princes confin'd, &c.

To our Monarch we owe, whatsoe'er
we enjoy:
And no grateful subjects were
those,
Who would not the safety, he gives
them, employ
To contribute to his repose.
    Were Princes confin'd, &c. 20

SONG (*Pompey*, Act II)

1

SEE how victorious Caesar's pride
    Does Neptune's bosom sweep!
And with Thessalian fortune ride
    In triumph o'er the deep.

2

What rival of the Gods is this
    Who dares do more than they?
Whose feet the Fates themselves do
    kiss,
    And Sea and Land obey.

1

What can the fortunate withstand?
    For this resistless He,   10
Rivers of blood brings on the land,
    And bulwarks on the sea.

2

Since Gods as well as Men submit,
    And Caesar's favour woo,
Virtue herself may think it fit
    That Egypt court him too.

1

But Pompey's head 's a rate too dear,
    For by that impious price
The God less noble will appear
    Than does the Sacrifice.   20

2

If Justice be a thing divine,
    The Gods should it maintain,
For us t' attempt what they decline,
    Would be as rash as vain.

CHORUS

How desperate is our Prince's fate?
What hazard does he run?
He must be wicked to be great,
    Or to be just, undone.

SONG (*Pompey*, Act III)

FROM lasting and unclouded day
From joys refin'd above allay,
And from a spring without decay—

I come, by Cynthia's borrow'd beams,
To visit my Cornelia's dreams,
And give them yet sublimer themes.

Behold the man thou lov'dst before,
Pure streams have wash'd away his
    gore;
And Pompey now shall bleed no
    more.

By Death my Glory I resume;   10
For 'twould have been a harsher
    doom
T' outlive the liberty of Rome.

By me her doubtful fortune tried,
Falling, bequeaths my Fame this
    pride,
I for it liv'd, and with it died.

Nor shall my vengeance be with-
    stood
Or unattended with a flood
Of Roman and Egyptian blood.

Caesar himself it shall pursue,
His days shall troubled be and few,
And he shall fall by treason too. 21

He by severity divine
Shall be an offering at my shrine;
As I was his, he must be mine.

Thy stormy life regret no more,
For Fate shall waft thee soon
    ashore,
And to thy Pompey thee restore.

Where past the fears of sad removes
We'll entertain our spotless loves,
In beauteous and immortal groves. 30

There none a guilty crown shall wear,
Nor Caesar be Dictator there,
Nor shall Cornelia shed a tear.

SONG (*Pompey*, Act IV)

PROUD monuments of royal dust !
Do not your old foundations shake,
And labour to resign their trust ?
    For sure your mighty guests
      should wake,
    Now their own Memphis lies at
      stake.

Alas ! in vain our dangers call ;
  They care not for our destiny,
Nor will they be concern'd at all
    If Egypt now enslav'd, or free,
    A kingdom or a province be. 10

What is become of all they did ?
  And what of all they had design'd,
Now Death the busy scene hath hid ?
    Where but in story shall we find
    Those great disturbers of mankind ?

When men their quiet minutes spent
  Where myrtles grew and fountains
    purl'd,
As safe as they were innocent :
    What angry God among them
      hurl'd
    Ambition to undo the World ? 20

What is the charm of being great ?
  Which oft is gain'd and lost with sin,
Or if w' attain a royal seat,
    With guiltless steps what do we win,
    If Love and Honour fight within ?

Honour the brightness of the mind !
  And Love her noblest ecstasy :
That does ourselves, this others bind.
    When you, great pair, shall disagree
    What casuist can the umpire be ? 30

Though Love does all the heart
    subdue,
With gentle, but resistless sway ;

Yet Honour must that govern too :
  And when thus Honour wins the
    day,
Love overcomes the bravest way.

SONG (*Pompey*, Act V)

1

ASCEND a throne, great Queen ! to
    you
By Nature, and by Fortune due ;
  And let the World adore
One who Ambition could withstand,
Subdue Revenge, and Love com-
    mand,
  On Honour's single score.

2

Ye mighty Roman shades, permit
That Pompey should above you sit,
  He must be deified. 9
For who like him, e'er fought or fell ?
What hero ever liv'd so well,
  Or who so greatly died ?

1

What cannot glorious Caesar do ?
How nobly does he fight and woo !
  On crowns how does he tread !
What mercy to the weak he shows,
How fierce is he to living foes,
  How pious to the dead !

2

Cornelia yet would challenge tears,
But that the sorrow which she wears,
  So charming is, and brave. 21
That it exalts her honour more,
Than if she all the sceptres bore,
  Her generous husband gave.

CHORUS

Then after all the blood that 's shed,
Let 's right the living and the dead :
  Temples to Pompey raise ;
Set Cleopatra on the throne ;
Let [1] Caesar keep the World h' has
  won ;
And sing Cornelia's praise. 30

FINIS

[1] Orig. 'Let's.'

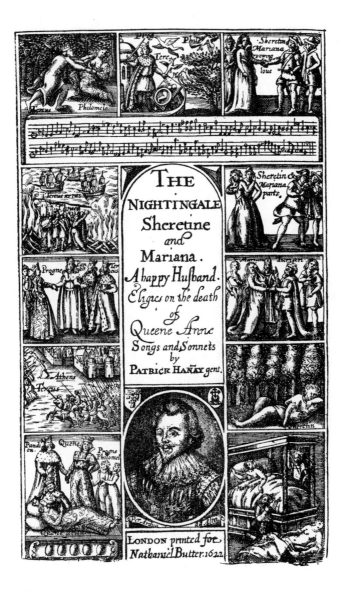

THE
NIGHTINGALE
Sheretine
and
Mariana.
A happy Husband.
Elegies on the death
of
Queene Anne
Songs and Sonnets
by
PATRICK HANAY gent.

LONDON printed foe
Nathaniel Butter. 1622.

INTRODUCTION TO
PATRICK HANNAY

THE interest of the poems of Patrick Hannay, though not wholly dependent upon, is no doubt to some increased by, that extreme rarity on which is based the calculation that there are not more than six known copies of the original, while Utterson reprinted but fifteen, and the only later edition (used in the present issue) is that of a private society—the Hunterian Club of Glasgow. He is not a great poet, and he comes in point of publication a very little before the strict 'Caroline' period, though he lived, according to some accounts, well into it, and into it according to all[1]. But he is quite of the type; and he contributes in *Sheretine and Mariana* one of those 'Heroic Poems' of which the collection and communication to the student is one of the main objects of this book. It has the peculiarity, unusual in a piece of such length, of being written in the first person, the story being told throughout by the heroine : nor is this the only thing which makes it a useful document as to the strange difficulty with which straightforward prose fiction got itself born. Hannay does not manage his six-line stanza very well. The more lyrical sixteen-line stave of the earlier *Philomela* is less well suited for a poem which also is of considerable length; but the poet is certainly less prosaic in it. In the original a musical setting is given for the first of these staves, and the author seems (from the note given below) to have thought it possible that some one might like to sing the whole poem—seventy pages, and nearly seventeen hundred lines ! The idea is a curious one. The 'Sonnets' (the name being applied quite *ad libitum*) and 'Songs' are not uninteresting; but here seems to be no need to take up precious space with much comment upon them. I am glad to have read Hannay, and to give others the opportunity of reading him.

[1] The personal history and even identity of our poet are things deeply wrapped in mystery. David Laing's rather elaborate genealogical introduction to the Hunterian reprint establishes practically nothing but that he was of the family of Hannay, or Ahannay, of Sorby in Galloway, now represented by the Hannays of Kingsmuir in Fife, and the Rainsford-Hannays of Kirkdale in Kirkcudbright. The Hannays seem to have christened themselves Patrick with the inveteracy of the Princes of Reuss in regard to another name, and not to have tempered this with the numerical niceness of that house. Laing does not seem to have accepted what the *Dictionary of National Biography* states with positiveness—that the poet was Master in Chancery in Ireland in the year 1627—or the rumour that he was drowned at sea two years later. That he was of the Sorby family, that he was Master of Arts, and that he was known to persons of distinction at the court of James I during the last years of his reign, may be said to be the only positively-known facts about him, except the dates of his works, which are, for *The Happy Husband* and the Elegies on Queen Anne (same year, but published separately) 1619, and for the Collected Poems 1622.

Patrick Hannay

To the most illustrious Princess FRANCIS [1] Duchess of Lenox, Countess of Hertford and Richmond

SWEET Philomela's long concealèd woe,
From dark oblivion now I bring to light;
That (though it help her not) the world may know,
The cause she sobbeth out her notes by night:
Which to you (greatest Lady) I present,
Fruit of some hours I with the Muses spent.

It is well known [2] honour hath been had
By patronizing of a work of worth,
Whilst skilful Art did cunningly o'ershade
The Patron's weakness, and his praise point forth: 10
Here it's not so, my work mean, your worth main,
Hereby I honour may, you none attain.

For such are you, whom Nature, Beauty, Grace,
So fair hath fram'd, adorn'd, so well endu'd:
As if those three contended had to place
In you perfection, which their store hath shew'd:

With whom virtue hath join'd and mak'st appear,
Deservedly you move first in this sphere.

So as thou canst not by a learn'der quill
Be honour'd, or receive an equal praise
Unto thy merits, they each press should fill,   21
Should go about with words thy worth to raise:
In it I'll rest: thy name which doth adorn
This frontispiece is my birds' April morn.

If that your Grace do but my labours grace,
Each lady's lodging shall a grove be thought:
The nightingale shall sing in every place;
Nay, thereby shall a miracle be wrought:
For if you but my Philomela cheer,
Her singing-spring-tide shall last all the year.   30

Ever most humbly devoted to your Grace's service,

PATRICK HANNAY.

To his-friend the Author

LET those that study how to praise a friend,
Or seek to flatter him beyond desert,
Shake hands with me, for I have no such end,
That befits him that hath a fawning heart:
I only care to let the Author know
I love him, and his book, for virtue's sake:
His work, his worth unto the world doth show,
Which for a pattern doth his practice take.

It needs no sycophant to set it forth,
(The wine is good, you well the bush may scorn:)   10
My praise defective should detract the worth,
Which with such lustre doth each leaf adorn.
All I will say is this, it's done so well,
Some may come nigh; some match; but none excel.

EDWARD LEVENTHORPE.

---

[1] It is well known that the distinction between Francis and Frances was so little observed that the usual abbreviation of the latter, as of the former, was 'Frank.'
[2] 'How' dropped before 'honour' (?).

Commendatory Poems

To my loving Kinsman the Author

Thy Philomela's sad (yet well-sung) note ;
Wrong'd Sheretine and Mariana's love :
Home's Husband : Anna's Elegies so wrote,

Thy Songs and Sonnets passion deep did move ;
Do well approve that thy ingenious wit,
For every measure, every subject's fit.

ROBERT HANNAY.

Authori

Qvis tibi Hannææ veteri pro stemmate certet?
Gente à Romulidum gens tua quando venit ;
Annæi micuere duo, vatesque sophusque,
His etiam Hannæus tertius esse potest.

IOHANNES DUNBAR [1].

To his much respected friend Master PATRICK HANNAY

HANNAY, thy worth bewrays well whence thou'rt sprung,
And that that honour'd Name thou dost not wrong :
As if from Sorby's stock no branch could sprout,
But should with rip'ning-time bear golden fruit :
Thy ancestors were ever worthy found,
Else Galdus' grave had grac'd no Hannay's ground :
Thy father's father Donald well was known
To th' English by his sword, but thou art shown
To them by pen (times changing). Hannays are
Active in acts of worth, be't peace or war.   10
    Go on in virtue, After-times will tell,
    None but A Hannay could have done so well.

                                    IO. MARSHALL.

King *Galdus* (that Worthy who so bravely fought with the Romans) lies buried in the lands of *Patrick Hannay* of *Kirkdale* in *Galloway*.

Of the Author

READER, I'm brief, this Poem's penn'd so well,
Of Muses Nine his is the Philomel.

                    IOHN HARMAR.

[1] The identification of the Senecas and the Hannays is ingenious, especially considering the form ' Ahannay.' But I wish Iohannes Dunbar had written a better first line.

Patrick Hannay

To his friend the Author

Laus tua, non tua res, cogit me scribere, vultus
Gratia sic dulcis : os facit, haud jubet ars.

M AEONIAN Chorus now incline to me,
A ssist my muse from your Parnassus high :
S ome influence infuse you in my brain,
T hat I this Author in a higher strain
E fforc'd may be to praise : a simple wit
R are ones to praise, nor able is nor fit.

P ierian virtues with Homerian wit,
A ffixèd are to thy ingenious brain :
T he penning of these Poems proveth it
R ais'd from oblivion in a lofty vein :   10
I n this our age (though many do affect
C unning in verse, and would be counted rare)
K now I none worthy of the like respect,
E ver green Laurel must fall to thy share.

H erein yet do I nothing flatter thee,
A lthough in part thy parts I do display :
N or none will doubt thereof that doth thee see,
N eedless were feigning where such virtues sway :
A rt shows itself by thy sweet flowing pen,
Y ielding the Wreath to thee from rarest men.   20

I. M. C.

To the Author [1]

HERE view the map of greatness, re-
gal states,
Kings thrown from thrones, crowns
thrown from royal mates :
Where treach'rous greed to reign,
ambitious ends
Main rights divide, intrude false foes
for friends :
Here try the course of wars, there see
that stem,
The awful Sceptre, glorious Diadem,
Which once Hungarian Kings majes-
tic sway'd,
(Born to command, though never well
obey'd)
How rear'd, subvers'd, replac'd, defac'd
again,
Their Kingdom (uncontinu'd) did re-
main.   10
But what in Thee (than rare) I most
admire,
Is this fierce flame, fraught with
Castalian fire ;

Thy pleasant strain, fram'd in this art
divine
And quick invention, th' essence of
engine ;
Wherein Apollo harps, the Muses
prance
The fount-drawn forkèd sharps, with
gleamings glance
This tragic tune to grace ; the Nymphs
adorn
Thee, with immortal fame, of lives for-
lorn :
So do thy Lyrics, set in tripping
measures,
Show skilful wit, sprung from Alcinoos
treasures,   20
Which swim on Demthen, sweet Per-
messen pleasures :
Thus may thy worth, thy curious
works Thee raise ;
Few have deserv'd (or can attain)
more praise.
WILLIAM LITHGOW.

---

[1] For Hannay's repayment of this *v. sub fin.* In l. 11, 'than rare' must be wrong.
'Thou rare,' as well as a dozen other things, occurs. In l. 21, 'Permessen' is of course
'Permessian' : 'Demthen' is what anybody likes. 'Engine,' l. 14 = *ingenium*, as later
in Scots.

Commendatory Poems

In Imaginem

T' EXPRESS the Author face, brass, ink
and Art
Have done their best, but for his better
part,
The Grecian Philomel in English
tongue,
Marian, a Husband, Elegies well sung,
Have given a touch, as in a cloudy
night
Obscurèd Phoebe shows her veilèd light;
And at some turns where clouds do
ill cohere,
With full beams shines out from her
silver sphere;
So are his shaded passages of wit,
(Where birds do speak, and women in
a fit :)   10
Who could so well have told fair
Marian's wrong,
Or taught the Athenian bird a London
song,
As he to whom the depth of love is
known,
And carving others can cut out his
own :
Which in some part is here so well
exprest,
None but himself can represent the
rest.

ROBERT ALANE.

Philomela, or the *Nightingale*, which here follows, is to be sung (by those
that please) to the tune set down before in the frontispiece [1].

[1] See Introd.   It has been thought best to reproduce the music *exactly*.

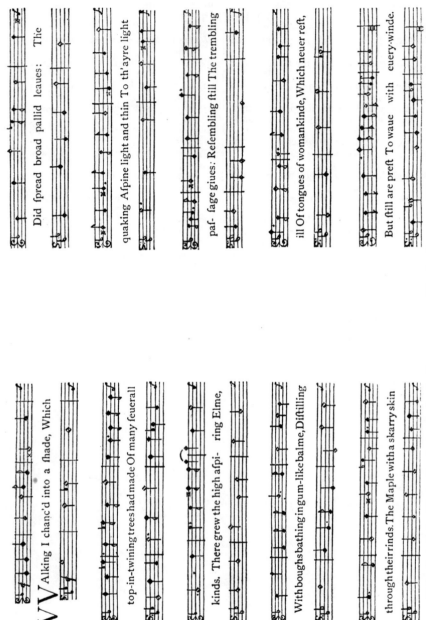

Alking I chanc'd into a shade, Which

top-in-twining trees had made Of many feuerall

kinds. There grew the high afpi-   ring Elme,

With boughs bathing in gum-like balme, Diftilling

through their rinds. The Maple with a skarry skin

Did fpread broad pallid leaues: The

quaking Afpine light and thin To th'ayre light

paf- fage giues: Refembling ftill The trembling

ill Of tongues of womankinde, Which neuer reft,

But ftill are preft To waue   with   euery winde.

All the Rests (being Minom Rests) must be Crochet Rests.

Therefore I pray mend them with your pen, or remember them.

PHILOMELA
THE NIGHTINGALE

THE ARGUMENT

PANDION, *King of* Athens, *takes
a wife,
He dearly loves her, she him with
like strife:
They issue have, two daughters (who
excel)*
Progne *the fair; and fairer* Philo-
mel.
*Fortune befriends not long, death her
surpriseth:*
Pandion *grieves, new cause of grief
ariseth.
Barbarians him invade, the Thracian
King
Them foils; and succours to the
sieg'd doth bring.
He's entertain'd;* Cupid *with loving
fires
Of* Progne *warms him; she hath
like desires.*   10
*He woos, she's won, her father's glad
he sped:
With Princely pomp they solemnly
do wed.*
Tereus *with* Progne *unto* Thrace
returns:
Thrace *joys therefore, therefore sad*
Athens *mourns.
Five years in* Thrace *they glad
together live,*
Progne *for* Philomela *'gins to grieve:
Longs for her sight, her husband
doth entreat,
To work a way they may together
meet.
He yields, takes sail, to* Athens *back
returns,
Unlawful love of* Philomel *him
burns.*   20

*Her native beauty, and her rich
attire,
Enrich'd by cunning Art he doth
admire.
With lust enrag'd he sore* Pandion
*prest
That she might with him go, at last
did wrest
Unwilling grant: he her commits
with tears
To* Tereus' *charge, his love suspecting
fears.
He takes his faith, moves her to
swift return;
They weeping part,* Pandion *left doth
mourn.
They sail, see shore, they land, no
more delay*
Tereus *can brook, nor doth he her her
assay*   30
*By words, knowing it bootless: to a
wood
He drew her, spoke his thought;
amaz'd she stood.
He forc'd, she faints; reviv'd, revenge
of wrong
She vow'd to take; he fearful lest her
tongue
Should blaze his crime, he cuts't out
with his blade,
That woful wood a prison for her
made.
Then home returns, feigneth her
funeral,*
Progne *her mourns, she unto work
doth fall;
Of party-coloured wool by skilful
art,
A web she made that did her woes
impart.*   40

(621)   S S   811846·1

Progne *a sharp revenge doth under-*
take ;
Time favours her designs with
Bacchus' wake,
She takes her out, comes home, her
flatt'ring child
She kills and dresses ; fury made
her wild :
To his sire for food she gives him, he
doth eat
His own flesh ; his fault Progne *lets*
him weet,
The sisters he pursues, with rage he
burn'd,
Both he and they on sudden birds are
turn'd.

I

WALKING I chanc'd into a shade,
Which top-in-twining trees had made
Of many several kinds.
There grew the high aspiring elm,
With boughs bathing in gum-like
balm,
Distilling through their rinds.
The maple with a scarry skin
Did spread broad pallid leaves :
The quaking Aspen light and thin
To th' air light passage gives :   10
Resembling still
The trembling ill
Of tongues of womankind,
Which never rest,
But still are prest
To wave with every wind.

II

The Myrtle made of nought but
sweets,
Love-loathing *Daphne's* offspring
greets,
Whose top no steel e'er lopp'd ;
Nor under-boughs with biting
beasts   20
Returning from their fodder-feasts,
For banquet ne'er had cropp'd.
The lowly banks did bathe in dew,
Which from the tops distill'd :
There Eglantine and Ivy grew,
Sweet Mint and Marjoram wild :

With many more,
Pomona's store
Was plentifully plac'd,
That nought did want,   30
Nor seem'd scant,
To please sight, scent, or taste.

III

The blooming borders fresh and
fair,
Were clad with clothes of colours
rare,
Which fairest *Flora* fram'd :
The Hyacinth, the self-lov'd lad,
Adonis, Amaranthus sad,
There pleasing places claim'd.
The Primrose, pride of pleasing
Prime,
With roses of each hue :   40
The Cowslip, Pink, and savoury
Thyme,
And Gilly-flower there grew.
The Marygold,
Which to behold
Her lover loaths the night,
Locking her leaves
She inward grieves,
When *Sol* is out of sight.

IV

Upon the boughs and tops of trees,
Blithe birds did sit as thick as bees
On blooming beans do bait :   51
And every bird some loving note
Did warble through the swelling throat
To woo the wanton mate.
There might be heard the throbbing
thrush,
The bull-finch blithe her by ;
The black-bird in another bush,
With thousands more her nigh.
The ditties all,
To great and small,   60
Sweet *Philomel* did set,
In all the grounds
Of Music sounds,
Those darlings did direct.

V

With pleasure which that place did
bring,
Which seem'd to me perpetual
spring,

Philomela

I was inforc'd to stay :
Leaning me lowly on the ground,
To hear the sweet celestial sound
These Sylvans did bewray.⠀⠀70
Ravish'd with liking of their songs,
I thought I understood
The several language to each 'longs,
That lodges in the wood.
Most *Philomel*
Did me compel
To listen to her song,
In sugar'd strains,
While she complains
Of tyrant *Tereus*' wrong.⠀⠀80

VI

Compos'd to sing her saddest dit,
She shrouded in a shade did sit,
Under a budding briar ;
Whose thickness so debarr'd the light,
It seem'd an artificial night,
Leaves link'd in love so near.
It seem'd she was asham'd to show
Herself in public place,
By sight, lest seers so might know
Her undeserv'd disgrace.⠀⠀90
Hid from the eye,
She thought none nigh
Was for to pen her plaints ;
She 'gins relate
Her adverse fate,
And thus her passion paints.

VII

'When Prince *Pandion* held that state
Which was the mirthful Muses' seat,
With learning beautified ;⠀⠀99
Governing there with peaceful rest,
Where no disturbing storms distrest
Those that did there reside :
In prime of youth he took a Dame,
By nature kind decor'd
With beauty virtue vow'd that frame
Should with her gifts be stor'd.
I know not which
Did seem most rich,
By lavishness in giving ;
Each gave so much,⠀⠀110
I think none such
Was left amongst the living.

VIII

With equal heat love so combin'd
Their hearts, as they were still inclin'd
To nill and will the same :
Their minds so mingled were together,
They had nought proper unto either,
Both fires one common flame.
Thus surfeiting on love's delight,
Where with a matching measure
The one the other doth requite⠀⠀121
In equal pitch of pleasure,
Their days they spent
In sweet content,
Deeming all others wretched,
Whose lesser joys,
Mixt with annoys,
To their full height not stretchèd.

IX

To add unto their happiness
And further to increase their bliss,⠀⠀130
The heavenly powers conspire,
Of which they (Joy-drown'd) did not dream,
So perfect did their pleasures seem,
They could no more desire.
Yet was their comfort so increas't,
With offsprings' happy store,
As now they think they were not blest
With benefits before.
Thus is it known
That none doth own⠀⠀140
So much of earthly pleasure,
But that the heart,
A little part,
May hold a greater measure.

X

We were by Muses Nine nurst up,
We drunk with Heliconian cup,
Their number did increase,
The goodly gifts, the Graces Three
Gave to us, we did multiply
To number numberless.⠀⠀150
No syllable could from us slide,
But in consenting sound
Our looks, and gestures, who espied
The graces in them found.

Each had such feature,
And good stature,
As just proportion grac'd,
With colours rare
To make us fair,
By Nature's pencil plac'd. 160
XI
Thus did both heaven and earth
conspire
To fill our father's dear desire,
With heapèd happiness.
But when things here are at the
height,
Unlook'd for lot doth often light,
And drives them to distress.
As when the Moon hath fill'd her
horn,
She straight begins to wane,
And when the flowing force is worn,
The tide then turns again : 170
For here no state
Is free from fate,
With Time all turns about :
Oft rise the small,
The great oft fall,
When they do nothing doubt.
XII
If pleasures here were permanent,
Free from disturbing discontent,
Not any ways annoy'd,
We should not relish our delights, 180
So dull should be our appetites,
With senseless surfeit cloy'd.
Therefore that we may better taste,
Each sweet hath many sours,
The brightest blink is quickly past,
And banishèd with showers :
Also to show
That we do owe
To changing Time, we're tost
When least we fear, 190
It is most near,
And our designs are crost.
XIII
So with my father did it fare,
Whom meagre death did unaware
Deprive of his belov'd,
My mother ; sickness so her seiz'd,
As pain itself did seem displeas'd,
And senses all remov'd :

(624)

She seiz'd with ceaseless sleep, gave
first
Pandion cause of cares ; 200
Which *Athens'* woe soon after nurst,
And bath'd in briny tears.
Thus ever still
Preceding ill
Is followed fast with more :
Ne'er comes alone
One cause of moan,
It's companied with store.
XIV
Before her death-bred grief was
'suag'd,
Barbarians were so enrag'd, 210
(Gaping for greedy gain,
Encourag'd by his carelessness,
Whom they deem'd drunken with
excess,
They doubt not to obtain.)
As they wall'd round rich *Athens'*
walls,
With warriors about,
So fainting fear our force appals,
It dares nowhere look out,
Fear forc'd some sound,
And did confound 220
In others resolution ;
All were dejected,
So unexpected,
Was Fortune's revolution.
XV
In midst of this our great distress,
Which did our former fears in-
crease,
Such troops we did behold,
As with their brav'ry brav'd the
skies,
And dazzled the beholders' eye
With beam-rebating gold, 230
In front with lofty plume in pride,
Mounted on stately steed,
The likeliest of all did ride,
Who seem'd the rest to lead,
Curveting oft,
Prancing aloft,
His courser proud disdains
To be control'd
By bit of gold,
Scorning commanding reins. 240

XVI

But when he did approach more near
He banishèd that former fear
Conceivèd by his sight :
He forc'd our foes soon to retire,
Who to resist had small desire,
They faintly fell in flight.
We musèd much what he should be,
Who with unaskèd aid,
So suddenly did set us free,
And all our foes dismay'd ;   250
All ran to see,
As he came nigh,
And fixt on him their sight,
And all those eyes
Which him espies,
Were taken with delight.

XVII

The streets as he did pass along,
With gold were garnishèd and hung,
All bravely beautified ;
The pavement pav'd with pleasing
flowers,   260
The spoils of *Flora's* fragrant bowers,
Where *Tereus* did ride :
Such was his name who us restor'd,
Of warlike *Thracia* King,
Whom in triumphant wise decor'd,
My father in did bring :
In manner meet
Each other greet,
And kindly entertain :
T'his Palace fair,   270
To solace there,
He brings him and his train.

XVIII

There banqueting with dainties best,
To please the too too curious taste,
Which sea or land doth yield,
With sweet discourses mixt among,
Where a delightful pleasing tongue
Did rove in Rhet'ric field.
When *Tereus* saw my sister fair,
Progne, he pric'd her such,   280
As he believ'd no beauties were
Beside, she had so much.

His heart desires,
His eye admires
Her pleasing form and feature :
He thinks all else
She far excels
In goodly gifts of Nature.

XIX

When that his fancy on her face
Doth feed, there grows no other
grace,   290
He thinks, in other parts :
It seems the curious cabinet,
Where Nature had that treasure set
That most bewitches hearts.
A rolling eye, whence thousand
flights
Of gold-dipt-darts do fly ;
Whereof the least with love-delights
Could wound a deity.
Th' alluring glances
Which by chances   300
From those two suns did dart,
Love borrow'd still,
When he had will
To fire a frosty heart.

XX

A forehead where inthronizit
Grave majesty in state did sit,
With humbleness attir'd ;
Where meekness made the meaner
hope,
And majesty cut short the scope
Of Pride, that high aspir'd.   310
Soft waving seas of sable hair—
That hue was judg'd by love
The best, and aptest to ensnare,
Mild *Zephyrus* did move.
In careless curls,
He oft it hurls,
He wantonness bewrays :
He oft it flung
Her back along,
And beauty best displays.   320

XXI

A cheek where purest white, with red
Of deepest dye, was overspread,

---

280 pric'd] A modern would probably have written 'prized' : but the distinction is not necessary.

305 inthronizit] The Scots participle, kept for rhyme's sake, is always worth noticing in these seventeenth-century writers.

And meeting so were mixt,
As neither red nor white they seem,
But both in one made beauties beam,
These colours two betwixt.
Her ruby lips, when they do kiss,
　Cover prime pearly rows ;
When they that kind conjunction miss,
　　Arabian sweet outflows :　330
　　One sure would think,
　　As she did drink,
That blood light *Bacchus* fills,
　　That it did pass,
　　As through a glass
Gray Claret wine distils.

XXII

What shame permits not to espy,
He with Imagination's eye
　Doth see, and values most :
He views it o'er, and o'er again, 340
Seeks for a fault, but all in vain,
　His labour there was lost ;
It 's seldom seen but some defect,
　By prudent Nature's plac'd,
To make the best be more respect,
　With glory more be grac'd ;
　　Yet nowhere here
　　There doth appear
Least foil, all was so fair,
　　As fir'd him so,　350
　　He did not know,
To hope, or to despair.

XXIII

Thus was he first enamourèd,
And still his loving fancy fed,
　While on her face he gaz'd,
His prying prest a beauty-blush,
In crimson coat, her face to flush,
　In *Cupid's* fire it blaz'd.
Thus forc'd with fainting fever's fit,
　His quaking heart did tremble, 360

Where love's deep grounded, there's no wit
Can his sure signs dissemble.
　He cools and burns,
　Heart inward mourns.
He hopes, he oft doth fear ;
　She may consent,
　May not relent,
May yield, may chance not hear.

XXIV

My father (as physician good)
By signs his sickness understood,
　(Having like passion prov'd)　371
He knew the salve could soonest slack
His sickness and his pain beat back,
　Was *Progne*, his belov'd.
By matching him and her, he thinks
　Such friendship to endear,
As bound by wedlock's holy links,
　He needs no foe to fear.
　　Thus policy,
　　Long time we see,　380
Hath ever had two ends,
　　One is a train,
　　But still the main
To private profit tends.

XXV

He gives these lovers leave together,
Tereus speaks not alone left with her,
　But in his heart doth pray
That she had boldness to begin,
In such a muse his mind was in,
　He knew not what to say :　390
Still rumbling is the little rill,
　Deep rivers silent move ;
That deepest passion is most still,
　Experience doth prove.
　He much doth fear
　She will not hear

336 'Gray' is very interesting as bearing on the much-vexed question of the history of the term 'Claret.' 'Claret' has never been used in France of a full red wine : but only of the wines betwixt red and white.

345 Respect = 'respeckit,' 'respected.'

361 I retain the italics in these passages, though there sometimes seems very little reason for them, because they appear to be intended as 'asides' of the author's, separate from Philomela's speech. In some cases, however, the printer has almost certainly gone wrong with them.

Philomela

If he good will should proffer;
 His often dread,
 Not to come speed,
Drives him he dares not offer.   400
XXVI
She muses thus to see him mute,
She fears he follow not his suit,
 (Which she deems her undoing.)
When he resolvèd had to speak,
What he should say, he had to seek,
 (He was not wise in wooing.)
When plainly we our passion tell,
It maketh much in moving,
A simple innocence so well
 Bewrays a heart much loving: 410
 For ever those
 Who (apt to glose)
Too speedy are in speech,
 Love do not show,
 But make maids know,
They kindly can beseech.
XXVII
His speeches had more pleasing
 sound,
With rhetoric did more abound,
 Unto my sister's sense,
Then theirs who by their skilful
 art,   420
With sophistry can truth pervert,
 To clear a foul offence.
She willingly doth hear him woo,
She 's pleas'd to hear him plead,
She could at first encounter, bow,
But doubts do make her dread
 Lest quickly won,
 He should have done,
His fancy should take flight:
 Oft soon obtain'd   430
 Are soon disdain'd:
Such love is counted light.
XXVIII
Thus on she draws him with delay,
She neither grants, nor gives a nay,
 (For fear he flee the field;)
Her yielding blush doth make him
 bold,

To reinforce, and to unfold
 All means to make her yield;
He vows, protests, and deeply
 swears,
His love to her shall never   440
Languish, with length of ling'ring
 years,
Nor faith fail he doth give her.
 'I grant' she said,
 No more he staid,
But at her word did take her;
 With purple red,
 All overspread,
Sweet virgin shame did make her.
XXIX
My father knowing th' had decreed
To wed, and were thereon agreed,
 He left his pausing pain: 451
For he had mused in his mind,
To make her heart thereto inclin'd,
 And beat his busy brain.
Now all do haste with like desire,
 To solemnize those rites,
Which holy *Hymen* doth require,
 'Fore lawful love-delights.
 They make such haste,
 The time they chas't,   460
Which little list makes long,
 The smallest stay
 That doth delay
Enjoying 's judg'd a wrong.
XXX
The longèd day is come should
 crown
Their wish'd desires, sweet Doric
 sound
 Doth deaf the itching ear,
Shrill echo in the rocks did ring,
Repeating what the sisters sing
 In Prince *Apollo's* quire;   470
Kind Nature's Quiristers increast,
 Mounting in crystal skies,
The gods invite unto this feast,
 Which angry Heaven denies.
 They did envy
 Felicity

398–400 This compressed phrase seems to mean 'his dread not to succeed [we must read 'sped'] has such force with him *that* he does not offer.' There are others like it.
419 'Then,' as constantly, = 'than.' It will not be again noted.
461 'List' seems here to mean 'inclination.'

Should such on earth be seen :
To Tragic end
These joys should tend,
The grievèd gods do mean.   480

XXXI

The Furies' brands aloft did bear
For *Hymenean* candles clear,
Which lent a dismal light :
The raven and the night-crow cry,
The ominous owl abroad doth fly
By day, and not by night.
Juno, that blesseth first the bed
Of happy wedded lovers,
Came not, in saffron colours clad,
Hymen affrighted, hovers,   490
Not daring there
Make his repair,
(With presage dire dismay'd.)
The Muses dread,
The Graces fled,
They were no less afraid.

XXXII

Yet did they dally in delights,
And revel at unhallowed rites,
Till Time, (which nought can stay)
Told *Tereus* his love delays,   500
His home-left-*Thracian* dismays,
Their comfort can decay.
They fear his safety, he farewell
Must bid, *Progne* doth plaine :
A pearly shower of liquid hail
Out o'er her cheeks did rain.
A tender heart,
Such bitter smart,
With sorrow doth suppress,
When bitter cup   510
Doth interrupt
New tasted happiness.

XXXIII

Yet boots it not, she must be gone,
Tereus her trains (though weeping) on,
And we alike lament :
Our sorrow so divided was,
Half with us staid, and half did
pass,
Whither that couple went.
They shipp'd, a lusty gale of wind
So prosp'rously did blow,   520
The sails suffice fill'd from behind,
There needeth none to row :

(628)

They soon came nigh,
Where they would be,
And do perceive the land ;
They see the shore
All peopled o'er
With those he did command.

XXXIV

For Fame, the air-wingèd post,
(By going greater) fills the coast   530
Of Thrace, with coming-cries ;
Her trumpet sounds his safe return,
The shores with blazing beacons burn,
Where cries confus'dly rise,
Which untir'd Echo in the hills
(With her redoubling voice)
So multiplies, the air it fills ;
The gods seem to rejoice :
The multitude
Confus'dly stood   540
Upon the shelvy shore,
He happiest seems
Next *Neptune's* streams,
Can draw, though drown therefore.

XXXV

The smaller (yet the sager) sort,
Do mind a more majestic sport,
Rough rudeness they disdain ;
Most stately triumphs they devise,
After the victor's gorgeous guise,
Tereus to entertain.   550
Altars with incense sweetly smoke,
Priests *Io Paean* sing :
The tottering steeples reel and rock,
(So rolling bells do ring.)
This day so glad,
To those they add
Which sacred they observ'd,
From yearly mirth
For *Itys'* birth,
His first-born they ne'er swerv'd.   560

XXXVI

WHAT time *Titan* our height had
scal'd,
Summer had sweat, winter had
hail'd,
Autumn had fill'd her lap,
Five times the Spring in fragrant
flowers
Was deck'd, warm sliding sunny
showers

The soaking earth did sap.
When pleasing *Progne's* longing love
For *Philomela's* sight
Grew wakerife, and such thoughts
 did move,
 As lessens largè delight,   570
 When we depart
 From what our heart
With liking once hath lov'd,
 Absence intires,
 And more endears,
The more it is remov'd.

XXXVII

This absence kindling longing love,
Makes *Progne* all her practiques
 prove,
 Defers not her desire.   579
Woman (who would) delay disdains,
Who doth deny, and who detains
 With hope, hath equal hire.
Fearing refusal, she puts on
 A look that most allures,
And draws the eye, nor that alone,
 Her of her suit assures.
 Such weighty words
 Her wit affords,
As for to move were meet,
 With loving charms   590
 Him in her arms
Kissing, doth thus entreat.

XXXVIII

" Dearer to me then sweet repose
To misers, seiz'd with ceaseless woes,
 Who ne'er of comfort tasted ;
More pleasing to me then is light
Unto the silly sleepless wight,
 Whom waking nights have wasted,
Who present put'st those fears to
 flight,
Which absent make me die :   600
As Titan *makes the ugly night,*
 With forcing flames to fly ;
 Methinks far more
 I now adore,
Love more, if such desire
 Could be increast,
 Which when at least,
Was such could soar no higher.

XXXIX

Great love in length doth often dull ;
Mine, (though so main) is not at
 full,   610
 It daily doth increase :
No intermission makes it stay,
No surfeit takes its edge away,
 It grows, but never less :
Which by effects may be perceiv'd,
 For since I first was fir'd,
No other happiness I crav'd,
 Than do as you desir'd :
 My chiefest grace,
 I there did place,   620
Held that my high'st content,
 Gladdest did pass
 The time that was
In loving service spent."

XL

" Dost think I doubt " (the Prince
 replies ;)
Meanwhile looks babies in her eyes,
 And dallies with delight ;
Kind kisses on her fairest face,
With soft impressions he doth place,
 Her lips have no respite ;   630
Her pretty parly so doth please,
 Her lips so sweetly taste :
He doubts, which rather he had leese,
 Both are to be embrac'd.
 He bids her say,
 Yet still doth stay
With kissing her discourse,
 Whilst from her lips
 He nectar sips,
As from celestial source.   640

XLI

" Speak, love " (he said) ; then she
 proceeds,
" If favour so affect my deeds,
 As deem them of desert,
I'll boldly beg, but such a suit,
As kindness cannot so confute,
 But I shall ease my heart,
Since fate from fairest *Philomel*
 (With that she deeply sigh'd)
And destinies have doom'd me dwell,
 To make the loss more light,   650

---

574 ' Intires ' = ' makes whole.' 633 ' leese ' = ' lose.'

Suffer
(If you
I may myse
Or els(
Some
That she m

XLII

The goodliest gift that thou canst
    give,
I for this grant with liking leave,
    It seems to me the best :
Promise *Pandion* swift return,   660
Whose aged eyes will overrun,
    At this unlook'd request."
Thus having said with kind embrace,
    Him in her arms she clings,
With soaking tears bedews his face,
    Forc'd from her sunny springs :
        She doth attend,
        How he will end,
    To do, or to deny :
        With speaking signs,   670
        She him entwines,
    Who makes her this reply :

XLIII

" What, is this all? sweet, sue for
    more,
Thou seem'st a niggard of my store,
    Out of my kingdom cull :
And eke unto thy late request
Seek more, so more I shall be
    blest,
    By being bountiful."
She only this : He more would add
    If he knew fit propine :   680
It seems so slender he is sad,
    None dearer can divine.
        Thus they do prove,
        Which most should love,
    That only was their strife,
        Which breeds no wars,
        Nor jealous jars,
    'Twixt happy man and wife.

XLIV

Then did he haste him to the sea,
That she might wit how willingly
    He granted her desire.   691
I leave the piteous plaints to tell,
That passion pour'd at this fare-
    well ;

(630)

e did nigh expire.
this forc'd affection, feign'd
ove a more belief
re love, the tears that rain'd
g from an inward grief :
Ariost
His foul-mouth'd host   700
Of *Iocund's* parting prate :
    Whose wife did swound,
    But of that wound
A groom the grief did bate.

XLV

This was not such, but as the
    show,
Such was the substance of the woe,
    Which thus their souls possess.
For she like lonely dove doth lan-
    guish ;
He goes with grief where bitter
    anguish
    Bides in his boiling breast.   710
At last *Pireus'* port he spies :
    The sailors raise a song,
The country, wakened with their
    cries,
    Unto the shore do throng :
        They feed their sight
        With sweet delight
    Of this unlook'd for guest ;
        They thrust him so,
        He scarce can go,
    Rude people so him prest.   720

XLVI

Pandion's state the street refrains,
Yet at the gate him entertains,
    And lovingly embrac'd.
The right hand friendship's firmest
    pledge,
They mutually for love engage,
    (Yet no good signs it grac'd :)
Without inquiry he doth tell
    The cause why he doth come,
Is for his sister *Philomel*,
    (Fresh beauty's budding bloom :)
        The presage bad,   731
        His speech then had,
    My future ill divin'd :
        It lowring brake,
        That day of wrack,
    Which dismal deadly shin'd.

Philomela

The glad congratulation past,
He goes on with his Heart's behest,
 Which had him thither brought.
He tells how pleasing *Progne* pines,
Her mirth with melancholy dwines,
 In solitary thought. 742
He tells how for her *Philomel*,
Progne did pensive long :
All her discourse on her doth dwell,
 She wholly hath her tongue :
 He doth request,
 With speeches best,
And aptest to persuade :
 As yet the end 750
 To nought did tend,
But his love's life to glad.

XLVIII
Straight he doth after me inquire,
Who him to see had like desire,
 I to his presence rush'd.
He at my sight amazèd grew,
He staid astonish'd at my view,
 (My face such fairness flush'd)
Our salutations had no touch
 Of complimenting strains : 760
Light love is lavish where it's much,
 From flattery it refrains :
 He kist, embrac't,
 About my waist
His winding arms he wrung :
 I did him meet
 With love as great,
And to his body clung.

XLIX
My goodly garment all of gold,
His griping made his eyes behold, 770
 And note more narrowly :
For though my robe itself were rich,
Musing *Minerva's* stately stitch
 It more did beautify.
She had made it the masterpiece
 Of all her studious store.
Art, Art itself to pass did press,
 Her cunning to decore.
 Reviewing still,
 Deeming all ill 780
(Though well) if skill could better,

So jealousy
 The slyest spy,
To needless work did set her.

L
There was *Apollo* in a chair
Of burnish'd gold, his flame-like hair
 Against that brightness beam'd,
An ivory harp with silver strings,
With trembling touch which lightly
 rings,
 Did sound or sounding seem'd. 790
With leafy laurel he was crown'd,
 And canopied o'erhead,
Wherein chaste *Daphne* lately wound,
 Did quiver yet for dread.
 The slender flim,
 Which hid each limb,
So offer'd to the eye ;
 And was so wrought,
 You would have thought
It to be maid and tree. 800

LI
Her leafy top (late hair) did shade
The welkin, part it twilight made,
 And part a mirthful morn,
For lower was an azur'd sky,
Where eastern beams did beautify
 Half, half the stars adorn.
Among the slender boughs some birds
 Their list'ning ears incline,
Others hover about in herds,
 To hear these dits divine : 810
 Some's swelling breast
 The joy exprest,
To hear how they did earn :
 Some's opening bill
 Bewray'd the will
These wantons had to learn.

LII
A little lower from this state,
Where Prince *Apollo* proudly sate,
 With brightness overblown :
The merry Muses rang'd in ranks, 820
Were seated on the sunny banks,
 With favour sweets o'ergrown :
While one doth tune her lute, or voice,
 One notes, one time doth measure.
A silent sound, an unheard noise

795 Note 'flim' for 'film.'   813 'earn'='yearn.'

(631)

Doth take the sight with pleasure.
Some garments grave
　Others did have,
Some light, some long, some short,
Some chaplets wore,　830
　And some forbore,
Some mus'd, and some made sport.

LIII

Nearer the border one might see
Orpheus and *Eurydice*,
　Returning from the dead :
He play'd, and with swift pace did
　haste,
Longing till she our air should taste,
　Whom he to light did lead :
But whether a desire of sight,
　Or fear she did not follow,　840
Made him look back, his dear de-
　light
　The opening earth did swallow :
　He quickly snatch'd,
　And would have catch'd,
But when it prov'd in vain,
　Her look did shriek,
　And in his cheek,
Pale grief was pictur'd plain.

LIV

A sea circled the lowest seam,
With welling waves, and of that
　stream　850
　The people pastime take :
Fearful on fish *Arion* sits,
He seeming seiz'd with quaking fits,
　Did mournful music make.
The *Dolphins* dance now up, now
　down,
　And as much pleasure have,
As he hath pain, for fear to drown,
　He sings his life to save,
　His hands scarce hold
　(With fear and cold　860
Benumb'd) his instrument :
　The swelling wave
　The motion gave,
The saving sound that lent.

LV

This gorgeous garment large and
　wide,

Before was with a button tied,
　And careless hung about :
My forepart was of purest lawn,
Whereon the fairest flowers were
　drawn,
　That Nature e'er brought out : 870
Their roots a seeming earth did
　hide,
　Clad in a grassy green ;
The stalk stood out, as if beside
　The ground a growing sien :
　Some thought a scent
　Out from them went ;
(So wrought they on conceit,)
　One maketh faith,
　He tasted hath
Some leaf that fell of late.　880

LVI

Thus was I cloth'd.　My breast was
　bare,
Never till then was white so fair,
　Which made the world profane,
And dare the mighty gods upbraid,
That they such pureness never
　made,
　Nor could to such attain.
Whereat the gods incensèd grew,
　And did together 'gree,
Even with a curse their skill to
　show,
　Blaming world's-blasphemy.　890
　No year doth fail
　But snow or hail,
Since candies o'er the earth,
　Whose joy doth vanish,
　For it doth banish
The beauty of its birth.

LVII

Yet he had not well view'd my
　face,
Which beauty-bringing years did
　grace
　With rays of most respect :
The buds he left so fair had
　flourish'd,　900
So kindly Nature had them nour-
　ish'd,
　As he did not expect.

874 sien] Is this = 'scion,' a word of many spellings ? Or should it be 'agrowing
seen'?

The infant lustre lightly laid,
Was curiously o'errun,
And careful Nature perfect made
Her beauty-board begun :
Each lineament
She did acquaint
With a proportion due,
And every limb,   910
Fashion'd so trim,
Was hid in heavenly hue.

LVIII

The favour of my face was such,
That beauty else, though ne'er so
        much,
(If that I came in place)
Was but a foil to make mine fairer,
That fairness made mine seem the
        rarer,
That glory gave mine grace.
As former eye-contenting flowers
Lose lustre by the Rose,   920
As *Phoebe's* glore eclips'd lowers,
When *Sol* his sight out-throws :
Even so did mine
Others outshine,
Though fair in their degree ;
The looks they lost,
Which more them boast,
If parallel'd with me.

LIX

Some would say *Venus*, when at
        rarest,
And fancied most for to be fairest,
(With *Adon* hot in love)   931
Look'd like me, but that I more
        chaste,
Look'd constant, she did care to
        cast
Such looks as lust could move.
Others would say such *Dian's* look
(But more to wrath inclin'd)
When hapless (bathing in a brook)
Acteon did her find.
Of goddesses
They did express   940
The goodly gifts by mine,

Not mine by theirs,
Their doom declares
They deem'd me more divine.

LX

These, these the tyrant so admir'd,
As with their sight his heart was fir'd
With more then lawful love :
He now thinks *Progne's* parts were
        poor :
He wonders how they could allure,
Or his affection move.   950
He wishes now he were unwed,
So I would hear him woo.
He sighs, he with my sister sped,
Or had with her to do :
As parchèd hay,
Whereto we lay
Quick fire, takes sudden flame,
So burn'd his heart
With every dart
That light-like from me came.   960

LXI

He's so enrag'd, he would not spare
To tempt my fellows' faithful care,
(If that could do the deed)
My Nurse's faith, nay e'en myself
He would seduce with precious pelf,
If so he could come speed ;
He cares not for the Kingdom's broil
To take me thence perforce,
And to maintain his ravish'd spoil
By slaughter'd souls' divorce : 970
His reinless love
So much doth move,
What is it but he dares ?
Nor can his breast
Those flames invest
Which provocate his cares.

LXII

Nor can he now delay endure,
He thinks with cunning to procure,
Doth *Progne's* suit renew ;
He makes it cloak his damn'd
        desire,   980
When more then right he did require,
So *Progne* did pursue,

905 Orig. 'perfit.' The odd phrase 'beauty-board' in the next line must be derived from the practice of painting portraits on panel, unless it means 'palette.'
921 The form 'glore,' with 'glory' just before, is interesting as showing the tyranny of strict syllabic scansion. It recurs below.

He would affirm his tongue did
glose,
(*Lovers are eloquent*)
E'en moving tears his cheeks
o'erflows,
(As if those *Progne* sent)
How human minds,
Oft error blinds,
He's thought to be sincere,
His wickedness   990
We kindness guess,
Which doth him more endear.

LXIII

Behold, I for the same do sue,
About my father's neck I threw
My arms, and him embrace,
I maiden kisses intermixed,
He notes them, for his eye is fixed
Still on my firing face :
Each kiss he (covetous) did crave,
He wished he were my sire,   1000
I to him sought, each gesture gave
Good to his fond desire.
My sire at last,
By our request,
Against his will is won :
Having obtain'd,
I good had gain'd
Did deem, but was undone.

LXIV

Now *Phoebus'* steeds so swift had run,
His daily course was almost done,
The height they passèd have ; 1011
And now the steepy sky they beat
With angry hoofs, to cool their heat,
Hasting in western wave.
On table kingly cates were plac'd
For to content the taste,
Blithe *Bacchus'* golden goblets grac'd.
After this rich repast,
To quiet rest
Each him addrest,   1020
But *Tereus'* tiring care
Lets silken sleep
On him to creep,
His woes so wakerife are.

LXV

The true Idea of each part
He saw, was seated in his heart :
What was hid from the sight,
He fains it such as he would have it,
And better then sight could con-
ceive it,
More delicate delight ;   1030
He thinks he sees face, feature,
gait,
And doth survey each limb,
So apprehensive quick conceit
Did represent to him.
The night was worn,
A weeping morn
Usher'd the doleful day,
When hast'ning Fate,
Full of deceit,
Permits no longer stay.   1040

LXVI

Pandion then with gushing eyes,
Where gorgèd grief a-bathing lies,
Me to him thus betakes :
" This jewel, (dearest son) this pearl,
My last, most lov'd, my dearest
girl,
(His hand then shivering shakes)
I give thee, and thy faith conjure
By all the gods above,
To guard, her safety to assure
With a paternal love :   1050
Let knowen bed
Which you have had,
In firmness keep your faith,
And bear in mind
What *Progne* kind
With me committed hath.

LXVII

And darling, now my sweetest stay,
My age's hope, that from decay
Detains these turning hairs,
Whose presence doth me primely
nourish,   1060
Whose sight yet makes this face to
flourish,
And curbs my coming cares :

1021 Orig. 'tiring-care,' but these unnecessary hyphens were then frequent. One
suspects 'tyrant.'
1022 'Lets' of course = 'prevents,' not 'allows.'
1056 'me' = 'thee.'

Philomela

Sweet *Philomel*, I thee beseech
Thou wouldst with speed return :
While thou art absent, I must teach
These moist'ned eyes to mourn.
  Though loath to want,
  Three months I grant,
(So long to stay you have)
  One day behind   1070
  That time assign'd,
Will bring me to my grave."

LXVIII

Thus speaks he with tear-dropping
    eyes,
Drownèd in his brain-breeding seas,
  Which doth his sorrow tell.
I seem to go and oft turn back,
And slender slips excuses make
  To take a fresh farewell.
Such was kind *Ovid's* ling'ring leave
  Departing from his wife,   1080
And so did *Cleopatra* grieve,
  Pity produc'd like strife,
  " *Caesario* go,
  O do not, no,
Fly from *Augustus'* snare ;
  Nay, stay a while,
  Fortune may smile,
Yet go, it 's best beware."

LXIX

So far'd it here, so we entreat,
Kiss'd, amongst kisses still we wet
  Our cheeks with mixèd tears : 1091
To firm our faith he takes our hands,
Joins them, and mute amazèd stands,
  Full fraught with future fears.
" At last, *Jove* witness this (he says)
  And punish those offend,
And, daughter, do not use delays,
  To *Progne* me commend " :
  Scarce speaks he more,
  He faints so sore,   1100
As if his spirits were past,
  Yet bids farewell,
  Which seems to tell,
(With staying) 'twas the last.

LXX

The night which did this day pre-
    cede,
Did wrap itself in mourning weed
  Of saddest sable hue,
Such pitchy clouds were interpos'd,
Phoebe was hid, small stars were los'd,
  Their splendour none did view.
At day *Aurora's* eyes so wept 1111
  As drunk each hill and dale,
As if for *Memnon* now she kept
  The sad fresh funeral.
  Her eyes did soak
  The parchèd cloak
Which *Tellus* then had on,
  The grass outsprung
  From clay was clung,
At fall of *Phaeton*.   1120

LXXI

Thus parted, we unto the sea,
Our canvas wings we do display
  Against the growing gale,
Which there resistance takes in
    scorn,
Whereby the bulk is forward borne
  By proudly swelling sail.
Though wat'ry hills were interpos'd,
  Yet followed he with sight,
Till his dim dazzled eyes were
    clos'd,
  'Fore their time bringing night :
  Returning then   1131
  He doth complain
His late receivèd loss,
  As mounting waves,
  And falling graves,
With stubborn billows toss.

LXXII

Now *Tereus* can no more contain
His (yet hid) joy, it is so main,
  Which vaunting voice doth vent.
" The day is ours, the prize is won,
  My love whose light obscures the
    Sun,   1141
Whose beams breed more content,

1066 moist'ned] It is perhaps worth noticing, once for all, that seventeenth-century
printers seem to have preferred the apostrophe for the first *e* in such forms as this
' threat'ned,' &c. Modern practice, not perhaps with much reason, seems to incline
the other way.

Goes with me: hath her sorrowing sire
(Who did her so much tender)
Twin'd with her? or drunk with
    desire,
  Do I dream he doth send her?
    Rouse, rouse you spirits,
    Conceited sweets
  Of a fantastic love
    No power have   1150
    So to bereave,
  Nor can such pleasure move."

LXXIII
Thus says he; nor doth turn aside
His eyes from me, which still do
    bide
  Beholding with delight:
As Adamant the Iron draws
By Nature's close compelling laws,
  So did I draw his sight:
Look as the Eagle sharp doth pry
  Upon his panting prey,   1160
Which in his cruel claws doth lie
  Hopeless to scape away:
    So he beheld,
    So I compell'd
  Was for to wait his will,
    Whom yet in mind
    I counted kind, ·
  Not conscious of ill.

LXXIV
Our fleeing sails had made such haste,
That now the tedious travel's past,
  The toiling sea brings forth: 1171
We touch upon the tyrant's coast,
Where hapless I, alas! was lost,
  And left of little worth.
To shore the tired troops do hie,
  Refreshment there to find:
The anchor'd bulk lies at a bay,
  With sail strook from the wind.
    All do rejoice,
    With cheerful voice,   1180
  Their gesture shows they're glad,
    They think them blest,
    That with such haste
  They happy voyage made.

LXXV
A winter-wasted aged wood
Near to the landing-place there stood,
  Spoilèd (with length of years)
Of beauty, no buds it had borne
For many springs, the wet had worn
  The trunk with tempest-tears: 1190
The barkless boughs spreading
    abroad,
  Unto the grassy ground
Yielded no shade, with leafy load
  The branches were not crown'd.
    Whereby the heat
    So sore did beat
  From *Phoebus'* fiery face:
    Flora for fear
    Durst not draw near
  To beautify that place.   1200

LXXVI
The winding ivy with soft moss
The bodies bound, and did emboss
  The rent and ragged rind,
They wrap with warmness to restore
Decayèd age, and to decore
  Time's ruins, 'bout them wind:
It seem'd sad Desolation's seat
  Far sever'd from resort,
Where nought did grow was good of
    late
  For profit or for sport.   1210
    No harmony
    From tree or sky
  The birds made, all was sad:
    The bad aspect,
    Show'd the neglect
  That nature thereof had.

LXXVII
Obscure bushes of fur and fern,
Confus'dly mixt, where robbers learn
  For to entrap the prey,   1219
Were rudely rangèd here and there,
Woven with brier and bramble bare,
  Which close together lay;
A place most fit for such a fact,
  For such a damn'd despite,
Where Mischief meant his part to act,

1145 'Twin'd' = 'twinned,' 'separated' or 'parted.'
1147 Note 'spirit,' not only = 'sprite,' but = 'spreet.'
1177 'Bulk' and 'hulk' are often interchanged at this time.
1217 'fur[ze]'?

And hide it from the sight.
The most obdur'd,
Would be obscur'd,
When they commit a crime:
Sin is so sham'd,   1230
Lest it be blam'd,
It seeks out place and time.

LXXVIII

Thither he hales me, I did quake,
My heart did faint, my limbs did
    shake,
I doubted and grew pale :
I for my sister ask'd with tears,
Not daring to confess my fears ;
Yet that did not avail :
He did confess his foul intent,
Me to the ground he flung,   1240
His late-lov'd hair he rudely rent,
And careless from me wrung.
  I call'd amain,
  But all in vain,
On sister and on sire,
  On gods above,
  But could not move
Them mitigate his ire.

LXXIX

He forc'd me, O how I did tremble !
Grief seem'd to kill, but did dis-
    semble,   1250
And would not prove so kind :
O had I then given up the ghost,
Before my virgin gem was lost,
As spotless as my mind ;
Then had my body without stain,
In sweet Elysian shade,
With the untainted virgin-train,
A merry mansion had,
  Where now, alas !
  It hath no place,   1260
Free from tormenting thought,
  Of that forc'd ill,
  Which 'gainst my will
On woful me was wrought.

LXXX

The harmless unsuspecting lamb,
Torn from the teats of fearful dam,
  By hungry wolves' surprise ;

Pursu'd by mast'ring mastiff fast,
The robber leaves his prey for haste,
  Which much amazèd lies,   1270
Still doubting if it be redeem'd
  From such a deep distress,
So fainting I confounded seem'd,
  My fear was nothing less :
  Fraught with despair,
  I did not care
What mischief might betide ;
  As in a trance,
  Forsook of sense,
I for a time did bide.   1280

LXXXI

When to myself I did return,
My heart did heave, my cheeks did
    burn,
My breast I boldly beat ;
Rap'd with revenge I did not spare,
As cause, (though guiltless) face and
    hair,
So lovely look'd of late,
From eye no tear, from tongue no
    words
My passion did permit.
The grief that such relief affords,
Is soon freed from his fit: 1290
  With sighs and sobs,
  And thrilling throbs,
My body did rebound.
  Mine eye him blam'd,
  Then straight asham'd,
It stares upon the ground.

LXXXII

But when as greater grief gave
    place,
Swift trickling tears did other trace,
  My glowing cheeks bedew'd :
Abortive words for birthright
    long'd,   1300
Each pressing first, his fellow
    throng'd,
  And hastily pursu'd.
As respite gave me further leave,
  I rat'd him in my rage,
Thinking I gain'd if he did grieve,
  My sorrow to assuage.

1233 Orig. ' hails.'
1284 ' Rap'd,' though not certainly, probably = ' rapt,' ' distraught.'
1300 Orig. ' Obortive.'

So raging spite
Doth take delight,
(Though thereby not reliev'd)
To vex the heart　　　　1310
Procur'd its smart,
And glores to see it griev'd.

LXXXIII

" O perjur'd, cursèd, cruel wretch,
To such a wickedness to stretch,
Respectless of the gods :
Thou blinded canst them not espy,
Yet doubtless they do draw thee
　　nigh,
With new revenging rods.
Could not *Pandion's* prayers move
Thee keep thy promise past,　1320
Nor *Progne's* charge? must mar-
　　riage prove
Thee base, which should make
　　blest?
A maid to stain,
A bed profane
With an incestuous lust,
Me to deflore,
My sister's whore,
What can be more unjust !

LXXXIV

If there be gods, they'll be reveng'd ;
If not, even I (as far estrang'd　1330
　　From shame, as thou from grace)
This heinous action shall proclaim,
Notorious shall be thy name,
　　Hateful in every place.
If here detain'd, with mirthless
　　moans
The mountains I'll acquaint :
My cries shall cause the trees and
　　stones
To pity my complaint :
To heaven I vow
I shall strive how　　　　1340
To taint him me betray'd ;
The world shall know
I was not slow
To wreck a wrongèd maid."

LXXXV

These words the monster so com-
　　mov'd,

He hates her now he lately lov'd,
For sin hath this farewell ;
It relish'd, straight a loathing breeds,
A minute's pleasure pain succeeds
That lastingly doth dwell.　1350
Though Conscience he cannot calm,
　　Which restless now is rent ;
Whose sore to salve he knows no
　　balm,
　　Yet seeks he to prevent,
Lest I to Fame
Should blaze his shame,
He minds with more mischief
　　Still to go on,
　　Regardless grown,
So name may find relief.　　1360

LXXXVI

Thus arm'd with hate my hands he
　　bound
Behind my back, my hair he wound
　　About a stubborn tree,
He drew his sword, I hopèd death,
Detesting a distainèd breath,
　　My soul I sought to free :
Yet he proves not so pitiful,
　　But to be out of doubt
That I should blab, his pinchers pull
　　My tongue with torment out :
　　Thus joy-bereft,　　　1371
　　No comfort left,
He loos'd and left alone
　　To tigers wild,
　　Then he more mild,
With worthless speech to moan.

LXXXVII

Then to my sister he returns,
She asks for me, therewith he mourns,
　　Sighs, sorrow suits his face.
He feigns my funeral, which drew
The tears, which made his tale seem
　　true,　　　　　　1381
　　None doubting my disgrace.
Progne her precious garments gay,
　　That daintily did deck
Her joyful, now she lays away,
And d'ons the mournful black :
　　A sable veil
　　To ground did trail,

1380 Orig. ' fains.'

(638)

A tomb for me did make,
    There incense burns,   1390
    And for me mourns,
That needed no such wake.
         LXXXVIII
His flaming chariot 'bout the world,
Posting through signs the Sun had
    hurl'd
And yearly course dispatch'd
While there I stay'd. No hope of
    flight,
My careful keeper day and night
    So warily me watch'd ;
I dumb could not the cause delate
    Of this my strict restraint ;   1400
But subtile wit on woe doth wait,
    Cunning's to caitifs lent :
        I cast about
        How to bring out
His lewdness to the light ;
    Which while I mind,
    Occasion kind
Doth offer to the sight.
         LXXXIX
The blissless briers the coat had torn
The fleecy flock had lately worn,
    And still retain'd that spoil : 1411
Of party-coloured wool there was
Store sticking on the stalks, on grass
    Some lay, some on the soil :
A web I wrought of colour white,
    Letters with blood distain'd
I interweav'd, which his despite,
    And my care's cause contain'd.
        Thus brought to end,
        By signs I send   1420
Unto my sister-Queen ;
    Nor did he know
    To her did go,
What these mixt marks did mean.
         XC
This petty present she o'erviews,
And narrowly doth note the hues,
    As she doth it unfold.
These careful characters express'd,
How doleful I was so distress'd,

She blush'd for to behold,   1430
O'er her proud cheek no tear
    distill'd,
    No bitter word brake out,
With vengeance and with hate she
    fill'd,
Like fury flies about :
    She meditates
    To move the Fates
To further her intent :
    To take revenge
    By means most strange,
Her mind is fully bent.   1440
         XCI
The hellish hags, hatchers of ill,
That can seduce a doubtful will,
    Finding her thus inclin'd,
Rejoic'd, and with the Furies join'd
To mould a mischief yet uncoin'd,
    So to content her mind.
The crime (admitting no excuse)
    These imps do aggravate,
They malice in the mind infuse
    That is at height of hate ;   1450
    Thus do these elves
    Busy themselves
To banish from the mind
    Pity that pleads
    For the misdeeds
Of a dear friend unkind.
         XCII
Thousand ideas in her brain
They stamp of distinct sorts of pain,
    To punish each doth press.
She's loath the least of them should
    perish,   1460
Pitiless passion doth them cherish,
    Till grown to excess
They long for birth, the time in-
    vites,
Swoll'n *Bacchus'* feast drew near,
Which *Thracian* dames with solemn
    rites
Should celebrate that year.
    Both old and young,
    In confus'd throng,

1419 One feels rather inclined to read 'This' : but Hannay is so fond of elliptic constructions that 'Thus,' with 'it' remembered after 'send,' is possible.
1462 Till] 'Until' or 'unto' probably written.

Do raving run about ;
   Like beldams mad   1470
    That day they gad,
No danger then they doubt.

XCIII

When *Phoebus'* fiery Car withdrew,
The Queen with a selected crew
   Her princely palace left :
The sounding brass so beat the walls,
Glib Echo answering the calls,
   The crystal covering cleft.
A hair-lace of a leafy vine,
   About her temples twin'd,   1480
A hart's hide was her habit fine,
   Which 'bout her she did bind,
    A small short spear
    Her shoulders bear :
Thus arm'd away she hies
    To search the wood,
    Rites of that god
She counterfeits with cries.

XCIV

She with disordered fury roves
Through coverts, dens, and shady
    groves,   1490
   With whoops and hollows loud.
"So ho!" she sounds : a scarce-pac'd-
   path
Her prying eye discovered hath,
   Which seem'd as stain'd with
    blood :
Her mind that mus'd on my mis-
   chance,
   Seeing the withered knops
Of parchèd grass, her sudden glance
Doth deem them bloody drops.
    What first the brain
    Doth entertain,   1500
There such impression takes,
That oft the sight
It changeth quite,
And false resemblance makes.

XCV

So was 't with her, which makes her
   more
Long for revenge then theretofore,
   She hastes, she thinks she hears
My woful plaint, she presseth on,

My prison door, a moss-grown stone,
   She breaks, and bushes tears ; 1510
She takes me out, she hides my face
   With blooming heather sweet :
She doth with *Bacchus'* livery grace
   Me, as the time was meet :
    She leads me home,
    Where when I come,
My panting breast bewray'd
    That my poor heart
    With bitter smart
And sorrow was assay'd.   1520

XCVI

She having found a fitting place
To vent her woe, unveils my face,
   Off *Bacchus'* tokens takes ;
She stares on me, I on the ground,
A guiltless shame did me confound,
   My face aflame it makes :
With scalding tears she strives to
   stench
   The fervour of my face,
Yet could not her eye-conduits
   quench
My fires, fed by disgrace.   1530
    If I had had
    A tongue to plead,
I had apologiz'd,
    And sworn, constrain'd
    I had been stain'd,
She 'gainst my will displeas'd.

XCVII

My eloquence did so prevail,
Which in sad silence told my tale,
   It deep impression took :
She reads the story in my face 1540
Of her wrong, and of my disgrace,
   Pointed with pity's look.
My tears that trickled down amain
   She blames, " That's not the way
(Says she in anger and disdain)
   My fury to allay :
    It's fire and sword
    Must means afford,
To take a sharp revenge ;
    Or if aught else   1550
    Their force excels
In torment ne'er so strange."

1478 'Crystal covering,' strictly the crystalline sphere of Ptolemaic astronomy : but of course here used loosely for 'welkin' or 'heaven' generally.

XCVIII

While thus she speaks, her pretty
child
Itys came, whom with looks unmild
She eyes : " How like his sire
He looks ! " (her heart could not
afford
Her woe-tied tongue another word,
Swelling with inward ire)
Yet comes he nigh, and 'bout her
neck
He winds his wanton arms,   1560
He toys, he kisses, wrath doth check
His childish snaring charms,
Against her will
Her eyes distil,
She (mov'd with pity) mourn'd,
But when on me
She set her eye,
Her tears to traitors turn'd.

XCIX

" See I my sister thus defil'd ?
And toy I with the traitor's child ?
Doth he with prating sport,   1571
And sits she silent ? calls he dame,
And cannot she her sister name,
Distressèd in such sort ?
First let him die ; I gave him breath,
And what hath he deserv'd ?
His sire gave what is worse than death,
Should his seed be preserv'd ?
What, shall she grieve ?
And shall he live   1580
Still to upbraid our shame ?
I'll not dispense
With such offence
For a kind mother's name."

C

Thus reason'd she, thus wrath pre-
vail'd,
A parent's part in pity fail'd,
Sister she prov'd too dear,
Rudely the tender boy she hales,
Who flatteringly, *kind mother* calls,
Her fury made him fear :   1590
Remorse and pity from her fled,

Fell fury took the place ;
She in his bosom bath'd a blade,
As he would her embrace ;
Nor so content,
She cut, and rent
Him piece-meal, part she boils,
Some part she roasts,
And thereof boasts,
Blithe of her proper spoils.   1600

CI

She hereof makes a dainty feast
For him that it suspected least ;
Her husband she invites,
Feigning the custom did permit
But one man at the most, to sit
At *Bacchus'* blessèd rites :
He set in state, that food before
Him plac'd, thereon he feeds,
Too dear a dish he doth devour,
Yet nothing thereof dreads :   1610
He says " Bring here
My darling dear,
Itys my lovèd lad : "
Progne could nought
More hide her thought,
Revenge made her so glad.

CII

" Thou seest him " (says she);
" Where ? " (he said).
I that no more could hide his head
Which quietly I kept,   1619
As it was stain'd with bark'ned blood,
Did hurl at him ; as he were wood,
He from the table leapt ;
He wails, he weeps, he mad doth
run,
Full fraught with fury's fits,
" My infant's herse, his tomb, un-
done
I am, bereft of wits, "
(He said).   O'erjoy'd
To see him 'noy'd
We were ; Revenge did smile,
With naked blade   1630
He doth invade
Us, authors of this guile.

1606 blessèd] Orig. ' blissed.'
1607 ' set ' is participial, as is ' plac'd.'   Hannay likes these absolute combinations.
1620 bark'ned] ' clotted ' : cf. Scott's *Guy Mannering*, where Dandie Dinmont uses it.
It is Northern English, and not merely Scots.

CIII

He eagerly doth us pursue
So swift, as feather'd we flew,
  Thereto enforc'd by fear,
Soft pens sprout out, our arms turn
    wings,
New shape we take, (who'll trust such
    things?)
  Soft plumes our bodies bear:
We become birds, *Progne* to town
  Doth take a sudden flight,   1640
I wand'ring to the woods did bowne
  To wail my woes by night:
    Some bloody stain
    We still retain,
The mark of that misdeed,
    Such crimson taint
    Our feathers paint,
As they seem still to bleed.

CIV

Nor he who us pursu'd doth 'scape
For his foul fault, he loseth shape,
  He to a Tewghet turns;   1651
His blade is turn'd into a bill
To exercise his angry will:
    His voice still sadly mourns,
'Cause once a King, a crown-like crest

He bravely yet doth bear;
His issue hatch'd, away do haste,
  Their father they do fear.
    Pandion heard
    These news and barr'd   1660
All comfort, fed on care,
    Before his day
    Grief made a way
To death, by dire despair.'

CV

So far sweet *Philomela* sung,
But here sad sorrow staid her tongue,
  Her throbbing breast did bound,
Whereby I well might guess her grief,
And 'cause I could not yield relief,
  Her woe my heart did wound.   1670
Pity with passion so me pierc'd,
  I press'd her how to please,
Her legend if it were rehears'd,
  I deem'd would do her ease:
    Not knowing well
    How she could tell
Her tale so well agen,
    Returning back
    I was not slack,
Thus her complaint to pen.   1680

FINIS

1651 Tewghet, teuchit, &c. = 'peewit.' This seems to be pure Scots.

(642)

SHERETINE AND MARIANA

To the truly Honourable and Noble Lady Lucy Countess of Bedford [1]

IT is a continued custom (Right honourable) that what passeth the Press, is Dedicated to some one of eminent quality : Worth of the personage to whom, or a private respect of the party by whom it is offered, being chief causes thereof, the one for protection and honour, the other for a thankful remembrance. Moved by both these, I present this small Poem (now exposed to public censure) to your Honour : first knowing the fore-placing of your Name (for true worth so deservedly well known to the world) will not only be a defence against malignant carpers, but also an addition of grace. Secondly, the obligation of gratitude (whereby I am bound to your Ladyship's service) which cannot be cancelled, shall be hereby humbly acknowledged. If it please (that being the end of these endeavours) I have my desire. Deign to accept thereof (Madam) with a favourable aspect, whereby I shall be encouraged, and more strictly tied to remain

Ever your Honour's, in
all humble duty,
PATRICK HANNAY.

A brief collection out of the Hungarian History for the better understanding of this ensuing poem

AFTER the loss of the battle of Mohacz, Lewis (the second of that name, King of Hungary and Bohemia) found dead in a rift of the earth half a mile above Mohacz ; the Turk invests John Zappoly (chosen at Alberegalis) King of Hungary. The Arch-Duke Ferdinand pretending to be heir of Ladislas, is elected King of Bohemia, and growing great thinks of the conquest of Hungary ; alleging it did appertain to him by right of Prince Albert, and Anne his wife, sister to King Lewis : He gathering together a strong army, enters therewith into Hungary. King John unprovided of forces, retires to Transilvania : Ferdinand pursues and overthrows him : he flees towards Polonia, and Ferdinand is crowned King of Hungary. Jerome Lasky (a man of great power) receives John, and practiseth with the Turk for his restitution. Solyman undertakes his defence, and brings him back. Many hostilities past twixt John and Ferdinand : Fortune now favouring the one, now the other ; at last (wearied, and their forces weakened) they agreed : The conditions were, that John should enjoy all he then possessed during his natural life ; and at his death it should descend to Ferdinand : John's children (if he left any) to be honourably maintained. Within short time after this agreement John dieth, leaving a son (named Stephen) of eleven days of age. Isabella (wife to John, and daughter to Sigismond King of Poland) together with a Friar named George (who had been a follower of John's fortunes) are left tutors to this young Prince. John dead, Ferdinand requires performance of the agreement ; which (by the Friar's means) is denied. The Queen with her son and George retire to Buda, which Ferdinand (by his Lieutenant

[1] Lucy Harington, wife of the third earl, d. 1627, one of the most famous and favourite patronesses of men of letters in the first half of the seventeenth century.

(643)

Raccandolph) straitly besieges. Ma-
humet Basha succours the Queen,
Solyman himself coming to Andrionop-
olis. Mustapha Basha is sent into Tran-
silvania against Malliat Ferdinand's
Lieutenant there. Raccandolph is quite
defeat at Buda by Mahumet, who takes
Pesth and divers other fortresses.
Malliat hearing of this overthrow
(and despairing of succours from Ferdi-
nand) retires to Fogare, a strong Castle,
which by a thousand assaults of the
Turks could not be taken. He comes
to a parly with Mustafa[1], who sends
into Fogare four principal Captaines
of the Cavalry[2] as hostages; Malliat on
this assurance coming forth is betrayed
in a banquet, seized on as a prisoner,
and sent to Constantinople, where he
remained prisoner till his death. Soly-
man (having thus driven Ferdinand's
forces out of Hungary) cometh to Buda,
from whence he sends Isabel and her son
with the Friar to govern Transilvania,
depriving her of Hungary against his
passed faith. The Friar (of an insolent
and haughty spirit) governeth all in
Transilvania as he listeth, little regard-
ing the Queen: She (disdaining to be
curbed by one risen from so mean a
quality) complaineth to Soliman. The
Friar (fearing the Turk's force)
sendeth privately to Ferdinand, entic-
ing him to a new attempt, promising
him the aid of the Transilvanians, with
divers fortresses. Ferdinand (glad of
this offer) sends to his brother Charles
the Fifth, then warring in Germany:
He (jealous of Frederick Duke of
Saxon, and Philip Landgrave of Hess,
whom yet he detained prisoners) sends
him only John Baptista Castalde to be
his Lieutenant, who comes to Vienna
for his instructions. With him came
divers Gentlemen, amongst whom was
John Sheretine, who there becomes
enamoured of Mariana, daughter to
Lazare Ardech, and is requited with
like affection: friends willingly con-
sent, and they are contracted. Cast-
alde (with instructions) leaves Vienna,
whom Sheretine (after a sad farewell
of Mariana) doth accompany. While
they are in journey to Hungary, Maxi-
milian son to Ferdinand returns from
Spain, having wedded Mary, daughter
to Charles the Fifth, in honour whereof
divers triumphs are done. Nicholas
Turian (a young Nobleman) coming
with Maximilian to Vienna, and seeing
Mariana, falls in love with her; by
means of her father's kinsman (his
entire friend) he comes acquainted
with Mariana's parents: he sues for
Mariana: Her parents better liking his
present and better means than Shere-
tine's, (which most depended on hope)
force her against her will and plighted
faith, to wed Turian.
Castalde (come into Hungary) causeth
Agria (a town of great importance,
yet neither strong by site nor Art) to be
strongly fortified, committing the charge
thereof to Erasmus Tewfle. Castalde
proceeds on his journey to Transilvania.
Arriving at Tiss or Tibiscus, (a large
and deep river, which taketh his be-
ginning in Poland, at the foot of the
hill Carpatus, and thwarteth Hungary
towards the South till it fall in Danu-
bius, between Belgrad and Cenedin,
where it loseth the name. It is in some
places eight miles broad, by reason of
quagmires) and having passed the river,
they marched in battle till they came
to Debrezen: there he met with two of
the greatest and richest Lords of Hun-
gary, Andrew Buttor, and Thomas
Nadasdy, who joined with him. By
the way Dalmas, holding for the Queen,
is besieged, and taken by John Baptista
of Arco. The Queen hearing of Cas-
talde his approach, calleth a Diet at
Egneth, which (by the Friar's cunning)
is dissolved without anything con-
cluded. She retires with her son to
Albeiula with such force as she had.
The Friar pursues her, and she fear-
ing the weakness of the town, retires
to Sassebess (a place by situation
far stronger than Albeiula:) George
besiegeth Albeiula. The Queen
hearing of the approach of ten thousand
Spaniards to his aid, seeks an accord,
which George easily grants, knowing
Castalde was not nigh. The Queen
yields the Town on condition to have
her movables saved. George consents
thereto, not suffering one of his soldiers
to enter, till her goods were brought

[1] The variation is orig.   [2] Orig. 'Cavallarie.'

out and carried to her. Castalde and George meet soon after at Egneth; they go to seek the Queen to Sassebess: there they sit in council: Castalde declares his charge: that the Queen should render, the kingdom according to the former agreement made with her Husband John. He adds also, that the Infanta Joan (youngest daughter to Ferdinand, with 100,000 Crowns for a Dowry) should be given to her son Stephen in marriage: with other offers, all seeming good to that assembly. They send her that message by George; whereupon she (knowing the impossibility to keep it by force, being destitute of all aid) yields herself to Ferdinand. The Friar (fearing lest this agreement might eclipse his greatness) seeks to dissolve it; but she (jealous of his inconstancy and cunning, and not able longer to suffer his insolencies) accuseth him to Castalde; seeketh to confirm the agreement, and at a Diet held at Egneth in presence of her son and Nobility, delivers up the kingly Ornaments, which were a Crown of plates of gold mounting on high in form of a high-crowned hat, enriched with Pearl and stones, with a small golden Cross on the top, a Sceptre of Ivory, a Mantle of cloth of gold set with stones: a Gown and a pair of shoes of gold: The Friar would have had the Crown in keeping, which she with disdain denied him, saying, 'She would never consent that a Friar should be King of that kingdom, whereof she dispossessed herself and son.' Then (with great effusion of tears) delivers Castalde the Crown; earnestly imploring Ferdinand's relief to her and her son (whose grief showed he disliked the surrender) considering they were sprung from a noble stock. The next day after she took her journey towards Cassovia with her sickly son, manifesting the great sorrow and discontent she felt to see herself deprived of her Kingdom; and by agreement to leave her own, which (in time) small help of friends could still have kept. At Cassovia she stays, with patience expecting a change of Fortune. At last is made Vayvod of Transalpinia, seeketh aid of the Turk. The Transilvanians (wearied with the Austrian oppression) practise her return. She coming, drives out Ferdinand's forces; is re-established, and rewardeth those who had still stuck to her. Castalde after receipt of the Crown diligently kept it. At last finding fit opportunity sends it to Ferdinand by John Alphonse Castalde Pescaire (his nephew) whom Sheretine (longing to see Mariana) accompanieth to Vienna; there seeing the inconstancy of Mariana (who had promised never to yield to any other) and the ill dealing of her parents, within short time he falleth sick with extreme sorrow, and dieth; whose death bringeth on their tragic ends, as in this Poem more at large doth appear.

Canto I

I

ONE evening 'twas when the declining Sun
 Wearied, gave place to the ensuing night:
And silver *Phoebe* had her course begun

To cheer the world with her more feeble light:
 To rest myself upon a bed I cast,
 Till gentle sleep seiz'd on me at the last.

II

As soon as sleep me wholly had possest,
 And bid sad cares a time for to depart,
I thought to me a lovely maid addrest,

Whose sight might pierce the most
obdurate heart : 10
Soft was her gate, and heavy was
her cheer,
Ghostly, yet mild, her visage did
appear.

III

Her golden tramels trailèd down
her back,
And in her hand a gory knife she bare :
Down from her breast streamèd a
bloody track ;
A sable sarsenet was all that she ware,
Thoro' which that blood appear'd,
as I on lawn
Have seen with crimson silk
a currant drawn.

IV

Then gently did she by the hand
me take,
Saying, ' Fear not, with me vouch-
safe to go, 20
Even for thine only Saint fair *Coelia's*
sake,
Where thou shalt all my forepast
fortunes know' :
Then to a flow'ry green she forth
me led,
Which was in *Flora's* finest livery
clad.

V

The Sun nor Moon there never
show their face,
Nor yet doth horrid darkness there
appear ;
Nor nights, nor days, nor seasons
there take place,
One night, one day, one season
serves the year.
Such light as when the early
lark doth sing,
Such season as 'twixt summer and
the spring. 30

VI

Down by this field there runs a
deep black lake,
O'er which a ferry-man doth steer
a boat
So smear'd with blood, that doubt-
ful it doth make,
Or black or red, with gory pitchèd coat,
With twisted long black hair, and
blue lips side,
Lamp-burning eyes, mare-brows
and nostrils wide.

VII

To him there flock'd of every sort
and fashion,
Over that river waftage for to have ;
But he devoid of all love and com-
passion,
Would none transport, but such as
passport gave : 40
Here would she fain have past,
but back he held
Her with his pole, and churlishly
repell'd.

VIII

Then back she brought me to that
flow'ry green,
And set me down, then pitifully said,
' Thou seest how fain I would trans-
ported been ;
But churlish *Charon* hath my pas-
sage staid :
Nor ere can I pass o'er this grisly
lake,
Unless thou deign pity on me to
take.

IX

For still I'm stay'd till one do write
my story,
Whose infant Muse is by a maid
inspir'd, 50
To write her worth, and to set forth
her glory,

---

13 ' tramels '='chains,' or rather 'network' of hair.
23 flow'ry] Orig. 'floorie,' which might possibly, though not probably = 'level,' if it
were not for stanza viii, where it is ' flowry.'
35 'side' in this engaging picture seems to have the old Scots sense of 'long,'
'trailing.'
36 ' mare-brows ' are penthouse-eyebrows.
49 I keep the variation of ' staid ' and ' stay'd ' in four lines only, for the moral.

Who for her parts deserves to be
    admir'd ;
Such is thy fairest *Coelia*, such
    the Muse
Which her rare beauty bred and
    did infuse.

X

By thy sweet *Coelia's* name I thee
    conjure,
My rueful legend that thou wouldst
    relate,
This may from her some pity thee
    procure,
For as hers now, such once was my
    estate :
    I bid her say, and I would do
    my best
    To please my mistress, and pro-
    cure her rest.   60

XI

Then thus. At *Vien* first I drew
    my breath,
And at my birth I *Marian* was nam'd,
I at *Vienna* gave myself my death,
For that alone not worthy to be
    blam'd ;
    My parents had not base, nor
    noble blood,
    But betwixt both in a mean
    order stood.

XII

At my wretch'd birth appear'd no
    ominous star,
Which might my future misery
    divine ;
None opposite, they all according
    were
To show my rise, but not my sad
    decline :   70
    All did agree to grace my infant
    years
    With happiness, but drown mine
    age in tears.

XIII

Kind *Nature* freely her best gifts
    bestow'd,
And all the *Graces* join'd to do me
    grace :
In giving what they gave, they
    nothing ow'd,

(647)

Which well to those appear'd, who
    saw my face ;
There was no maid who durst
    with me compare,
My beauty and my virtues were
    so rare.

XIV

My parents plac'd in me their whole
    content,
I was their joy, they had no children
    more,   80
Kin and acquaintance all of me
    did vaunt,
And bragg'd to see my youth produce
    such store
    Of budding blossoms, fairest
    fruit presaging,
    All which were nipp'd by adverse
    fortune's raging.

XV

My parents' care was chiefly how to
    train
Me up in virtue from my tender years,
They us'd all means, sparing nor
    cost nor pain,
Nor day nor night, me to instruct
    forbears,
    So in short time my virtue had
    such growth,
    As age whiles brings, but is not
    seen in youth.   90

XVI

Like as the rising Sun with weaker
    light,
Steals from the bed of bashful
    blushing *Morn*,
Permitting freely to the feeblest sight
Him to behold, but such beams him
    adorn
    Mounting our height, as who him
    then beholds,
    Is blinded, with the brightness
    him enfolds.

XVII

So I an Infant at the first appearance,
With hopèd beauty did but weakly
    shine ;
But as in years I further did ad-
    vance,
Perfection's pencil so did me refine,

As my accomplish'd beauty at
the height   101
Dazzled the bold beholder's dar-
ing sight.

XVIII

ABOUT this time th' Hungarian state
distrest,
(King *John* being dead) by civil
discord torn,
Some *Ferdinand* would in the state
invest,
The Friar for young *Stephen* others
doth suborn ;
He with Queen *Isabel* calls in
the Turk,
Who seems her friend, but for
himself doth work.

XIX

Buda by sieging *Ferdinand* is girt,
By *Solymon* his Army's there
defeat ;   110
Who taketh *Pesthe*, *Mustafa* doth
hurt,
On *Malliat* wars : The *Transilvanian*
state
Swears homage unto . *Stephen* ;
Malliat betray'd
To *Stambol's* sent, where till he
died he staid.

XX

Solyman having *Ferdinand* o'er-
thrown,
To *Buda* comes ; deprives the
woful Queen
Of *Hungary*, seizing it as his own :
Sends her distressèd with her Infant
Stephen
To *Transilvania* with the crafty
Friar
Her coadjutor, for to govern there.

XXI

You easily may guess her heart was
sorry,   121
Being depriv'd of what she held
most dear :

Robb'd of her state, degraded of her
glory
By th' injust Lord she call'd to free
her fear :
Buda bears witness of her sad
complaint,
Which mine own woe permits me
not to paint.

XXII

To *Transilvania* come, no sorrow
ceaseth,
Th' ambitious Bishop governs as
him listeth :
The Queen he curbs, command in
her decreaseth,
Whilst he grows greater and in
pride persisteth :   130
Till her abusèd patience cannot bear
More the demeanour of the saucy
Friar.

XXIII

Her Father *Sigismond* no comfort
sends her,
He was but careless, though she
thus was crost :
Not one of his confederates befriends
her,
Seeing him leave her should relieve
her most.
Ah, wretched Queen, what help
can moaning make thee,
When father, friends, kin, and
allies forsake thee ?

XXIV

Her sorrows now she can no more
support,
(Yet peremptory *George* was great-
est grief :)   140
Since who should love, had left her
in such sort,
Her discontented mind hopes small
relief :
To *Solyman* she sends ; O woful
wight,
To seek an injurer to do thee right.

---

111 *Pesthe*] The orig. spelling ' Pesthe ' is required here *met. grat.*
118 The evident scansion of this line is ' distressèd,' with ' Stephen ' pronounced
' Ste'en ' as in ' Steenie,' to rhyme to Queen. This pronunciation may also save l. 113 :
but of the versification of these historical parts perhaps the less said the better.
132 Friar] = ' Frere ' : but Frier in orig.

XXV

The *Turk* commiserates her sad
  estate ;
George knowing this, to *Sassebess*
  retires,
Scours ditches, heightens walls
  debas'd of late,
Lays in munition that a siege
  requires :
Then raiseth forces. *Isabel* pro-
  vides
Force 'gainst his force, which the
  whole land divides.   150

XXVI

The *Turk Chiauss* in *Is'bel's* favour
  sent
Threatens the Friar, and those to
  him adhere ;
Which did no good but ill, it from
  her rent
Most part of those that erst her
  fautors were :
Such inbred hatred to the *Turk*
  they bore,
They hate her cause, 'cause he
  would her restore.

XXVII

The Queen (misdoubting of the
  Turk's supply)
Seeks an agreement, which is lightly
  granted :
For the *Friar* knew that the *Turk's*
  force drew nigh,
Intelligence there to her hurt she
  wanted :   160
Agreed, the *Friar* forceth the
  Turk retire,
Still misregards her, still doth
  high aspire.

XXVIII

She once again the Nobles doth
  incite,
(Disdaining his neglect) and they
  once more
In a firm league to her do reunite.
The crafty *Friar* thinks to provide
  therefore :

XXIX

To *Ferdinand* he sends, his aid
  doth proffer,
Which *Ferdinand* accepts, glad of
  that offer.

XXIX

To *Charles* the Fifth his brother he
  doth send,
In such affair to have his present
  aid,   170
Yet knowing no great succour he
  could lend,
(In *Germany* his whole force being
  staid :)
Yet at the least an expert Captain
  brave
For his Lieutenant he doth press
  to have.

XXX

Charles weighing what this enter-
  prise importeth,
John Baptist Castald, Count of
  Piaden,
Doth single out, and to this charge
  exhorteth ;
He willingly accepts, but with few men
He takes his leave, and unto *Vien*
  comes,
Where he is welcom'd with the
  pressing-drums.   180

XXXI

One of his train, (and what concerns
  me most,
With that she sigh'd) was one in
  Vien born,
John Sheretine, his kin of him did
  boast,
As if his stock he chiefly did adorn.
And those who have no int'rest
  in his blood,
Honour him more, the more he's
  understood.

XXXII

From native home he long time had
  remain'd,
In *Padua* ten years at school he staid,
And in that time he so much learn-
  ing gain'd,

---

169 Fifth] Orig. here and elsewhere 'Fift,' *Scotice*. These survivals in the Angli-
cized Scots of this period are perhaps worth noting.

As virtue's firm foundations sure were
    laid :   190
His father hereof knowing, him
    commends
To *Castald*, who on bloody *Mars*
    attends.

XXXIII

He willingly his father's hest obeys,
And in short time made to the
    world appear
That learning ne'er the haughty
    spirit allays,
Which honour'd glory for his badge
    doth bear.
    And though that *Envy* still doth
        hate brave deeds,
    'Yet his worth even in *Envy*
        liking breeds.

XXXIV

He with *Castalde* to *Vien* comes
    back,
Where hungry expectation longs to
    see him,   200
Kin and acquaintance to the case-
    ments make,
They think him happiest that first
    can eye him:
    Yet when they see, they know not
        whom t' affect,
    All-changing *Time* had alter'd his
        aspect.

XXXV

To see these soldiers in the town
    received,
The confus'd multitude in clusters
    throng :
The better sort, (yet novelty that
    craved)
In spacious windows rangèd were
    along ;
    There was I plac'd, I clothèd was
        in green,
    Embroidered o'er with flowers
        like Summer's Queen.   210

XXXVI

As each did pass, he did our censure
    pass,

Whom one did like, another did
    disdain :
Sheretine came, and none knew
    what he was,
Yet each one's approbation he did
    gain,
    Each one him prais'd, and I
        amongst the rest,
    Of all that pass'd said he deservèd
        best.

XXXVII

Nor was this favour forcèd from
    affection,
It was desert that drew this verdict
    fra me,
Love had not then inflam'd me
    with infection,
No object had had hap from me to
    draw me ;   220
    Though love had found me fit to
        show his power,
    Yet did I live at liberty that hour.

XXXVIII

Though mine eyes were the arsenal
    where he hid
His choicest arms, from whence he
    might take fires,
(Which in continual lightning from
    them slid)
To kindle in cold hearts most hot
    desires ;
    Yet I not knowing what their
        power meant,
    My youth's sweet spring, free from
        disquiet spent.

XXXIX

Some noble thought possessing still
    my mind,
Whilst gold on canvas ground my
    fingers place,   230
Or nimbly on a lute light notes out find,
Which with sweet airs my charming
    voice did grace :
    These gave no leave to Love to let
        mine ease,
    Which disrespect did the Love-
        god displease.

---

199 *Castalde*] The addition of the *e* to get an extra syllable is interesting.
218 fra me] Note Hannay's utilizing of a Scots form for rhyme and the evidence
for 'draw' as 'dra'.' But he drops into it again *infra*, stanza xlix, where no rhyme calls.

XL

He languish'd that the flames which
in mine eyes
Were plac'd, had yet but darted
feeble rays :
Now did the bruit of *Sheretine* him
please,
Of him all speak, all listen to his
praise ;
   He thinks him only worthy of
those fires
   Which had not kindled others'
deep desires.   240

XLI

Whilst at *Vienna* they for dispatch
stay,
They're visit'd by their country
gallantry,
Which to express affection doth assay :
They with requital quit their curtesy ;
   For *Sheretine* the *Fates* do lay a
train,
   My father woos, he may him enter-
tain.

XLII

He willing to his suit doth con-
descend,
To be eye-witness (to his house
resorted)
Whether that *Fame* me falsely did
commend,
Or if I were such as I was
reported :   250
   For she had blaz'd my beauty
everywhere,
   Call'd others fair and fairer, me
most fair.

XLIII

The day did seem to break even at
the noon,
My coming so eclips'd the former
light,
Small stars are dimm'd so, by a
rounded moon
Which from a cloud comes suddenly
to sight :
   My beauty blaz'd so at the first
appearing,
   He thinks report my worth had
wrong'd by bearing.

XLIV

What learned Padua could not
effect,
Nor spacious Germany where he
had stayed,   260
That Vien doth, one beauty there
respect
Bred, which all theirs conjoin'd in
vain assayed :
   His heart from their attracting
baits left free,
   At Vien he doth offer up to me.

XLV

My father his affection to express,
Bids him kind welcome as his dear-
est friend,
Vows lasting love, meanwhile *Love*
doth address
His surest shaft, his golden bow
doth bend ;
   Mine eye the quiver whence he
took the dart
   With unavoiding stroke, that hit
his heart.   270

XLVI

One might have seen mid-day of his
desires,
Even from the East of their new-
taken birth :
He strove to hide the new flame of
his fires,
But grounded passion is not masqu'd
with mirth :
   His mirth to melancholy sighs
redoubled,
   Did well bewray, his musing mind
was troubled.

XLVII

Thus was he first enamoured, yet
he strove
To hide his passion ; but we did
perceive
Some unaccustom'd accident did
move
These sudden fits, yet we no cause
would crave :   280
   He takes his leave, unto his home
returns,
   Whilst in his heart, that new fire
hotly burns.

XLVIII

He careless casts himself upon his
    bed,
And 'gins to reason with his restless
    thought :
He curseth Chance that first him
    thither led,
He straight doth bless it 'cause it
    there him brought,
    He blames it for the breeding his
        unrest,
    Loves it for showing what could
        make him blest.

XLIX

" How did I live with unperturbèd
    mind,
Passing the day with joy, the night
    with sleep,   290
(Saith he) where wakerife cares I
    now do find,
And new disquiet for my late de-
    light :
    Are these th' effects of Beauty and
        of Love ?
    Heaven Love and Beauty fra me
        then remove.

L

Ah, hateful tongue, recant this foul
    amiss,
Love is the God that first gave life a
    being :
Beauty 's the breeder of this greater
    bliss,
How dar'st thou then profane their
    power weying ?
    Beauty breeds Love, Love beauty
        doth requite
    With the attractive lines of sweet
        delight.   300

LI

Then welcome Love, I now will
    entertain thee,
Beauty, I'll thee with reverence
    adore;
But what if beauteous love should
    now disdain me,
Since love and beauty I have brav'd
    before ?

Nay, they will not take that as a
    disgrace,
I saw nor knew not them, till first
    her face.

LII

Her face where wanton love keeps
    residence,
He takes no progress but when she
    removes :
Beauty projects from thence unto
    the sense
Such beaming glances, as their
    brightness proves   310
Young Eaglets, pardon Love, for I
    had been
Sooner your subject, if she sooner
    seen."

LIII

Thus passed he the night withouten
    slumber,
Longing for day, nor did I take such
    rest
As theretofore, new thoughts 'gan me
    to cumber,
Making me wakerife whilst my sleep
    decreast.
    Nor could I think what did pro-
        cure that change,
    'Cause unaccustom'd I did hold
        it strange.

LIV

Whilst sleep remov'd, on *Sheretine* I
    thought,
(The mind must still be busied) I
    his shape   320
Did think that Nature curiously had
    wrought,
On which the Graces did their
    blessings heap ;
    And Virtue that she part of him
        might claim,
    Had deck'd with rarest ornaments
        his frame.

LV

" Why should I think on him more
    than another ? "
(I say :) And straight begin my
    thought to blame,

298 weying = ' weighing ' ?

(672)

I would forget his shape, his virtues
smother,
Place where he sate, the time he
went and came :
Yet still the more I wish him out
of mind,
Him livelier represented there I
find.   330

LVI

I sleepless spend the night, I early
rise,
He restless longeth for to leave his bed,
Ev'n then our thoughts began to
sympathize ;
Abroad he walk'd as Morn the East-
heaven clad :
To put him out of mind I did repair
T' a Garden, yet in thought I
found him there.

LVII

Ere noon he came (acquaintance
loath to lose)
To visit and give thanks ; I joy'd to
see him,
As he to be with me of all did
choose ;
So I was well contented to be nigh
him :   340
Thus did the *Destinies* draw on our
fate,
I knew not *Love*, fear'd not his
hidden bait.

LVIII

After we often walk'd into the fields,
Passing the time with sport and harm-
less mirth,
Where nought did want, that fairest
Flora yields,
Or *Tellus* from her treasure bringeth
forth :
But discontented minds seld find
relief
By outward show for inward
hidden grief.

LIX

For in his countenance we might
behold

Some hidden grief, though gilded
o'er with gladness,   350
Sudden abortive sighs unto us told ;
His pensive mind was seiz'd with
inward sadness ;
Ignorant of the cause, I thought
to please him,
The more I cherish'd, more I did
disease him.

LX

Sheretine's love still more and more
increast,
The more he did my company
frequent :
His beating breast bewrayed his
heart's unrest,
Yet could not (though he strove) my
sight absent.
So doth *Farfalla* dally with the
flame,
Till, his wings sear'd, he sinks
down in the same.   360

LXI

Oft would he strive to look another
way,
And still endeavour'd me for to
neglect :
Yet did his eye more steadfast on me
stay,
Endeav'ring to dislike bred more
respect.
Now look'd he pale, now red, cold,
straight in fire,
Merry, soon sad ; *how changing
is desire !*

LXII

Yet his desire he strove to cover still,
And each way to conceal his passion
tried,
But love resisted, like a close-pent
kill
Most hotly burns, when least the
flame 's espied,   370
He thought it would have kill'd it
to conceal it,
The salve hurt most, which most
he thought should heal it.

340 nigh] 'nigh' and 'see' rhymed as above, st. xxxiv : 'see' and 'eye.'
359 *Farfalla*] 'butterfly,' 'moth.'
369 kill] = 'kiln.'

LXIII

Within short time his hid fire out
  doth blaze,
His strength no longer able to sup-
  press it :
He woos *Occasion*, then blames her
  she stays
To fit him *Time* when he might well
  express it :
  Time soon befriends, we to a
  garden walk,
  Unseen, unheard, where we might
  freely talk.

LXIV

" How comes it, Sir," taking him by
  the hand,
Then said I, "that grief taketh on you
  seizure :   380
(Without presumption if I might
  demand,)
Where nothing is intended but your
  pleasure ?
  For in your visage *Care's* idea 's
  plac'd,
  Which hath your late-joy sem-
  blance clean defac'd."

LXV

" Love-worthiest *Maiden*, blameless
  if I durst
(Saith he) lay ope my heart and
  thought reveal,
I would tell how my sobbing sighs
  were first
Conceiv'd, took birth, and why they
  still do dwell."
  Then finding me willing to hear
  inclined,
  He thus begins to tell his troubled
  mind.   390

LXVI

" Fair (if that fair be not too base a name
For thee, sweet deity of my affection,)
Before this boldness receive check,
  or blame,
(My tongue is free from flattery's
  infection :)
  Vouchsafe to hear, (and hear
  without offence)
  My rude, yet love-enforcèd
  eloquence.

LXVII

Love now the sole commander o'er
  my soul,
Elsewhere that could not by his
  craft or might
Captive my thought, or liberty
  control,
Hath brought me here (using that
  cunning slight)   400
  To see thy face, which in an hour
  hath gain'd
  Love conquest o'er him, who erst
  love disdain'd.

LXVIII

'Gainst his assaults, hitherto as
  defence,
A constant resolution I prepar'd :
His beauty-batteries poorly beat my
  sense,
Beauty's neglect 'bout me kept
  watch and ward.
  Ne'er could love gain till thy com-
  manding look
  Surpris'd my fort and guard, me
  captive took.

LXIX

I am thy prisoner, but no freedom
  seek,
In this captivity I joy to bide,   410
Only I crave my heart's keeper be
  meek ;
Dear, let not this desire be me
  denied :
  For it 's my joy, since *Love doth
  conquer all*,
  That I had hap to be thy beauty's
  thrall.

LXX

And thy sweet look (if I do right
  divine)
Doth promise, thou wilt not so cruel
  prove,
Nor pitiless to make thy captive
  pine
By base disdain, and so requite his
  love,
  Which is not touched with least
  part of folly,
  My aim is honest, my pretension 's
  holy.   420

LXXI

Then dear (but dearer far if thou
  wer't mine),
Let pity (the companion of sweet
  beauty)
Move thee to love him, whom *Love*
  hath made thine :
Love to requite with love is but love's
  duty.
  Grant love ; if not, say thou scorn'st
    my desires,
  That death may quickly quench
    my loving fires."

LXXII

As doth a prisoner at the bar expect
With pity-moving look the doubtful
  doom,
And by the judge's more severe
  aspect,
Doth rather fear than hope what is
  to come :   430
  So *Sheretine* torn betwixt hope and
    fear,
  His joy or sorrow so awaits to
    hear.

LXXIII

A purple blush with native tincture
  dyed
My cheek's late lily in a deepest red,
Whilst I (abashèd) to his speech
  replied,
Whose fainting eyes still on my face
  do feed :
  I was amaz'd, I musèd what to
    say,
  Love seeks consent, modesty bids
    deny.

LXXIV

At last " Brave Sir (said I), I am not
  train'd
So in love's school as make a quaint
  reply,   440
Nor think I lovers can be so much
  pain'd
As they make shew, but thereby
  only try
  Their wit on woman's weakness,
    to ensnare
  That harmless sex before it be
    aware.

(655)

LXXV

Or if they be, it's by some rarer
  beauty.
My poor perfection cannot passion
  move,
Your courage should propose else-
  where that duty ;
Vain-glory cannot so puff me with
  self-love
  As to believe mine such ; the
    looks I scatter
  Are feeble, ne'er inflame, nor such
    I'll flatter."   450

LXXVI

" My speech (saith he) of flattery
  cometh not,
Love brings it from the oracle of
  truth :
I cannot flatter, I, nor fain God wot,
Nor doth it need where beauty hath
  such growth :
  With cunning I would not com-
    passion move,
  Nor try my wit with an imagin'd
    love.

LXXVII

My protestations whence they do
  proceed,
Will soon be seen by sighing out
  my breath,
Unless my martyrdom thy mercy
  meed,
Thou'lt know thy beauty's force by
  timeless death :   460
  Then shall you see character'd on
    my heart
  True holy love, not flattery nor
    art."

LXXVIII

" I must not enter in intelligence
Of such love-passion, gentle Sir (I
  said),
If I have answer'd (prompt with
  innocence)
Seek not the rather to entrap a
  maid.
  Th' access which my simplicity
    doth give,
  Hence I will bar, unless such suit
    you leave."

LXXIX

My father's coming hindered his
reply,
With him the residue of the day he
spent, 470
Then to his chamber went, there
down did lie,
Bathing his bed with tears of
discontent;
Accompanied with every kind of
care
He tumbling lay, *Hope* yielding
to *Despair*.

LXXX

My mind no less than his was sore
perplex'd,
It griev'd me that I granted not his
suit:
It vex'd my heart to know that he
was vex'd,
I reason'd, and my reason did
confute.
Should I have yielded? no, who
soon are won,
Are soon disdain'd, then I had
been undone. 480

LXXXI

Yet who doth love, and can torment
her lover:
Yield then, unask'd? may be he'll
sue no more.
Alas, how shall I then my love
discover?
Oh! would to God I granted had be-
fore.
His love's extreme; if it kill, or
take flight,
Or turn to hate, then, all my joys,
good night.

LXXXII

May be it was not serious that he
said,
Oh! I am lost if that he only tried me;
Then my own self I seriously survey'd,
And saw that loving Nature nought
denied me: 490
Yet priz'd I not my parts, 'cause
they were rare,
But 'cause they could my *Sheretine*
ensnare.

(656)

LXXXIII

Yet being doubtful of his back
returning,
I call myself too cruel, too unkind:
And he that could not hinder inward
mourning,
Absents not long, returns to know
my mind.
He vows, protests, thereto adds
sighs and tears,
Which sweeter than sweet'st
music pierc'd mine ears.

LXXXIV

I was well pleasèd that he came
again,
(But better far his love was not
decay'd) 500
I thought it folly longer to detain
With doubtful *Hope*, lest *Love* should
die denay'd:
I (seeming loath) granted all that
he crav'd,
Mine honour and my reputation
sav'd.

LXXXV

Those who have felt the fits of
fervent Love,
Which hath the strength decay'd,
and vigour wasted
With strongest Passion, and in end
did move
Their Saint to pity, and some
comfort tasted:
Such and none else, can tell if he
were glad,
When of my love, this overture I
made. 510

LXXXVI

My hands he kisses, doth not speak
a word,
(Joy chaining fast the passage of his
speech)
His gesture did more eloquence
afford
By moving signs, than Rhetoric can
teach:
Therewith o'ercome, I open laid
my heart,
And all my loving-secrets did
impart.

LXXXVII

I told him that I did no less affect
His virtuous parts, than he admirèd
  mine,
How I delay'd not 'cause I did
  neglect,
Or joy'd to see him for my sake to
  pine :   520
  But only love's continuance did
    doubt,
  *The soonest kindled fire goes soonest
    out.*

LXXXVIII

No more we then on ceremony
  stand,
Each unto other firmly plighteth
  troth,
In sign whereof I took his, gave my
  hand,
Call'd *God* to witness with religious
  oath :
  He unto me vow'd a ne'er-bating
    love,
  I vow'd my fancy ne'er should
    other prove.

LXXXIX

Our next care was, to gain our
  friends' consent,
Who heard no sooner we did other
  like,   530
But they did yield, and are so well
  content,
They joy and thank the heavens,
  that so did strike
  Our hearts with equal heat, they
    hop'd to see
  Honour and joy of our wish'd-
    progeny.

XC

We sometimes after walk'd to take
  the air,
Sometimes to see them hunt the
  fearful roe :
Sometimes we to the Temple did
  repair :

Sometimes to the Theatre we would
  go.
  Thus did we banquet still with
    fresh variety,
  Yet ne'er did cloy or surfeit with
    satiety.   540

XCI

Methinks the sweet remembrance
  yet me glads,
How in my father's flore-perfumèd
  garth,
Where leafy tops chequer'd out
  motley shades,
And *Flora's* minions diaper'd the
  earth :
  How we have walk'd discoursing of
    our love,
  With kindest appellations *Dear*
    and *Dove.*

XCII

An arbour there, fenc'd from the
  southern Sun
With honeysuckle, thorn, and
  smelling brier,
Which intermix'd through others
  quaintly run,
Oft hath had hap our loving lays to
  hear :   550
  There hath he laid his head down
    in my lap
  To hear me sing, feigning to steal
    a nap.

XCIII

There sitting once, I told him how
  I dream'd,
And wish'd my dream were true!
  he long'd to know it :
And then most eager for to hear it,
  seem'd ;
Yet shamefastness would never let
  me show it
  Before our plighted-faith ; then I
    it read,
  It was how I was first enamourèd.

538 Theatre] Note the accent (of course in strictness justifiable, like so many vulgar-
isms) 'The*a*yter.'
542 flore-perfumèd] 'flore-perfumèd garth ' is good, methinks.
557 read] = 'expounded.'

XCIV

There have we talk'd, chaste kisses
 interrupping
Our kind discourse, which every
 word did point: 560
I from his lips, he from mine nectar
 supping.
Mix'd tears of *Pity* oft our cheeks
 anoint :
 There have we spent long time in
 such like sport,
 And that long time, we still
 thought very short.

XCV

Such happiness we had, we none
 envied,
We counted Keasars caitiffs match'd
 with us.
But permanent felicity's denied
To mortals here, none can enjoy that
 bliss :
 Our joy soon turns to sorrow, we
 must part,
 Which with grief's sharpest prickles
 pierc'd each heart.   570

XCVI

Now *Ferdinand* had everything
 prepar'd
Was necessary the war to maintain :
Castalde who for conduct thereof
 car'd,
Was ready, and gave warning to his
 train
 To be in readiness him to attend
 To *Hungary* to make their valour
 ken'd.

XCVII

Young *Sheretine* prepareth for to go,
Though all his friends persuade him
 stay behind,
Yet he will forward, though even I
 say no :
"Sweet," (saith he) "*Love* doth not
 debase the mind.   580
 What! shall I now obscure my
 former worth ?
 No, no, thy love doth no such fruit
 bring forth.

XCVIII

Weep not," (for then the tears stood
 in mine eye)
"Life of my Life, for so my sorrow's
 doubled,
Although thereby signs of thy love
 I see
Which it assureth, yet therewith I'm
 troubled :
 If thou wouldst have me to enjoy
 content,
 Leave, dearest Love, with sorrow
 to lament."

XCIX

The hapless day being come that
 must us sunder,
All such persuasions he pour'd out
 in vain,   590
That my heart broke not then it was
 a wonder,
Swift scalding tears out o'er my
 cheeks did rain,
 "What, wilt *thou* go ? and meanst
 thou thus to leave *me* ? "
 (Said I) "And wilt thou of all bliss
 bereave me ?

C

Thou saidst thou wouldst my prisoner
 abide,
Is this thy craft thy keeper to
 betray ?
What, wilt thou, cruel now, my soul
 divide ?
I know thou wouldst not kill me,
 Dear, then stay;
 Ah, wilt thou go ? and must I stay
 behind ?
 Oh ! Is this *Love* ? Is this it to be
 kind ? "   600

CI

No more could *Passion* suffer me
 produce,
To whom my grieving *Sheretine*
 replied,
Each eye a tear-evacuating sluice ;
 "My *Heart*, my *All*, my *Star* that
 doth me guide,

---

559 interrupping] This useful if not elegant form does not seem common.

Leave now to grieve, my chiefest
  care shall be
Soon to return, then still to stay
  with thee.

CII

Nor mean I now to leave thee
  altogether,
With its affection I leave thee my
  Heart,
Let Destiny or Fortune draw me
  whither
They will, yet from thee that shall
  never part :   610
In nought I'll joy deprivèd of thy
  sight,
Except the minding of thee breed
  delight.

CIII

Dear, let the hope of a soon joyful
  meeting,
Better to bear this separation move
  thee,
Think of the joys that will be at our
  meeting,
The *Fates* do force my absence but
  to prove thee :
Hence from my thoughts all else
  shall be debarr'd :"
(I said) *My constancy may chance
  be heard.*

CIV

Passion no more permits, we did
  embrace,

Each other wringing in our winding
  arms,   620
With mixèd tears bedewing other's
  face,
One's heart the other's rous'd with
  love-alarms :
  Oh ! none but such as have felt like
    distress,
  Can think how sorrowful this sever-
    ing was.

CV

I think *Ulysses* (feigning to be
  mad,
Loath to depart from lov'd *Penelope*)
No such distracting fits (through
  fancy) had,
As had my *Sheretine* going away ;
  Ulysses had reapèd the longèd
    crop,
  Sheretine in the blade had bloom-
    ing-hope.   630

CVI

Thus did we part, he with *Castalde*
  goes ;
Yet while in sight he still did look
  behind him,
I stay'd, steeping mine eyes in seas of
  woes :
Oft unawares I look'd about to find
  him :
  Imagination did delude my sense,
  I thought I saw him, who was far
    from thence.

Canto II

THE ARGUMENT

Turian Mariana loves,
  She 's forced by her friends
To marry him : This luckless match
  With blood and sorrow ends.

I

OF all the Passions which perturb
  the mind,
Love is the strongest, and molests it
  most ;
Love never leaves it as it doth it
  find ;

By it some goodness is or got, or lost :
  None yet ere lov'd, and liv'd in
    like estate,
  But did to Virtue add, or from it
    bate.

II

Sometimes it makes a wise man
  weakly dote,
And makes the wariest sometimes to
  be wild,
Sometimes it makes a wise man of a
  sot,

Sometimes it makes a savage to be
   mild :   10
It maketh Mirth to turn to sullen
   Sadness,
And settled brains it often cracks
   with Madness.

III

By cursed all-suspecting Jealousy,
Faint doubtful Hope, and ever-shak-
   ing Fear,
(Whom pale-fac'd Care still keepeth
   company)
It is attended : These companions are
   No minute's rest who let the lover
   find,
But with their several thoughts do
   rack his mind.

IV

So was't with me : I everything did
   fear   19
That might unto my *Sheretine* befall ;
Sometimes I thought I clatt'ring
   arms did hear,
Sometimes for help I thought I heard
   him call :
   Sometimes I fear'd new beauty him
   allur'd,
   Sometimes my hope his honesty
   assur'd.

V

Now (absent) I did love him more
   intearely,
It taught me deprivation was a hell,
The parting pangs did touch my
   heart but nearly ;
But now in centre of the same they
   dwell :
   I oftentimes lov'd to consult with
   Hope,
   And of his swift return propos'd the
   scope.   30

VI

But now the Fates with Fortune do
   conspire,
To cross the kind intendements of
   Love ;
And with salt tears to quench his
   kindled fire,

Not satisfied with my dear friend's re-
   move :
   My Joys are in the wane, daily
   grow less,
   My Sorrows waxing, daily do in-
   crease.

VII

To Vien back comes Maximilian,
(King of Bohemia) Ferdinand his son,
With Mary daughter unto Charles of
   Spain,
In honour whereof divers sports are
   done ;   40
   Tilting and Turnay, Feasts to
   entertain
   (With pomp) the coming stranger
   they ordain.

VIII

'Mongst others who to Vien then
   resorted,
Nicholas Turian (a brave youth) was
   one ;
Most of his friends him from the
   feast dehorted,
Yet he from it will be detain'd by
   none :
   Such warnings oft the unknown
   Fate forerun,
   Yet misconceiv'd, by those must
   be undone.

IX

His straying eyes which wander'd
   every way,
('Mongst the rare beauties that assem-
   bly bred)   50
Seeking fit subject their roving to
   stay,
At last unto my firing looks were led ;
   Which with one glance (that *Cupid*
   fra them prest)
   Dazzl'd his sight, and did his eyes
   arrest.

X

He thinks he ne'er such fairness saw
   beforn,
It did eclipse the beauty that was by,
As doth the fresh-forth-streaming
   ruddy Morn

25 intearely] I keep this form intact because of the rhyme. Hannay would
doubtless have justified himself from the Fr. *entier*.

Put out the lesser-lights of nighted sky.
  He thinks there is not any of such
    prize,
  If inward worth do outward
    equalize.   60

XI

He longs to know, and presseth to
  be near,
The nearer he his courage did
  abase :
Approach'd he speaks not, seems to
  quake for fear,
He shames so to be daunted in that
  place :
  Shame him encourag'd, prick'd
    him on to prove,
  The more my mind was known,
    it more did move.

XII

" I thought not, Lady " (said he) " if
  in one
The rarest beauties of the world had
  been
By Nature plac'd, that that one
  could have shown   69
So great perfection as in you is seen :
  Whose lustre doth exceed each
    beauty else,
  As lively diamond dull glass
    excels."

XIII

"The beauty which you speak of"
  (I reply)
"Is pale, but by reflex is fairer made :
If it receiv'd not light by those are by,
It should be veilèd with an obscure
  shade."
  Some time thus spent in talk he
    doth depart,
  Leaving his freedom with a fettered
    heart.

XIV

Then home he goes with new-bred
  thoughts turmoiling
The late-sweet quiet of his beating
  brains :   80
His heaving heart with bitter anguish
  boiling,

He Love with his effects now enter-
  tains :
He's pensive, musing, company
  absents,
With frequent sighs his smoulder'd
  fire forth vents.

XV

One of my father's kindred very near,
(In whom much trust my parents
  did repose.)
True friendship did to *Turian* en-
  dear,
Secrets were common, he by grieving
  shows
  Perceives his friend's distress,
    demands the cause :
  Turian tells all, compell'd by
    Friendship's laws.   90

XVI

My kinsman told him who, and how
  I was
To *Sheretine* by solemn oath con-
  tracted.
No sooner *Turian* heard but cries
  " Alas,"
(By loving frenzy well-nigh dis-
  tracted :)
  "Now see I" (said he) " that the
    Fates pretend
  To bring my wretched life to wo-
    ful end."

XVII

My cousin was astonish'd that to hear,
Knowing how hard the enterprise
  would be
To undo what was done, wills him
  forbear,
Instantly urges it, letting him see 100
  The stopping lets, which would
    his love disturb,
  Therefore whiles young, he wishes
    it to curb.

XVIII

But he (whom no dissuasive argument
From that resolve had force for to
  withdraw)
Unwilling hears, to go on still is
  bent,

88 shows] Orig. ' shoes.'

Though likelihood of no good end he
  saw :
  "In things difficult" (saith he)
   "worth is shown, '
  By light achievements courage is
   not known."

          XIX

His friend (whose oratory was in
  vain)
Doth condescend to aid him to his
  power :   110
He vows to lose his life, or to obtain
Help for the ill that did his friend
  devour :
  Hence my mishap, hence had my
   grief first breeding,
  Hence my successive sorrows still
   had feeding.

          XX

No more I afterward in public go,
(Loath to bewray my beauty to his
  eyes :)
I shun all that might trouble or
  o'erthrow
The order I propos'd to eternize
  My constant love, unto the Love
   that hath
  My Hand, my Heart, Affection,
   and my Faith.   120

          XXI

He cannot brook delay, spurs on
  his friend
To know the issue, *Danger's in*
  deferring :
Though it prove bad, yet best to
  know the end,
Protraction is the worst of all love-
  erring :
To know the worst of ill is some
  relief,
Faint hope and feverish fear are
  food for grief.

          XXII

The agent (that his cause had under-
  taken)
Doth first address himself unto my
  mother :

He thinks if that weak fortress were
  shaken,
He with assurance may assail an-
  other :   130
With doubtful speeches he doth
  try her mind,
Meaning to prosecute, as she's
  inclin'd.

          XXIII

He him commends, with best praise
  tongue affords,
(Yet in no commendation did belie
  him)
He had *Youth, beauty, virtue, winning-*
  words,
Behaviour from *detracting hate* to
  free him :
  So well he mov'd, my mother was
   content,
  Turian (if 't pleas'd him) should
   her house frequent.

          XXIV

He seeks no more, goes, tells his
  friend, who's glad,
So soon he lookèd not for free
  access :   140
No more he can forbear ; he came,
  did shade
His deep Desire, his Passion did
  suppress :
  Acquainted, he comes more than
   compliment
  Requir'd, but cunning Love did
   cause invent.

          XXV

He in my father's good opinion
  grows,
My mother 'gins him well for to
  affect :
As time permits his friend his worth
  out throws,
With poison'd words, he doth their
  ears infect :
  Himself to me imparteth still his
   love,
  And languisheth 'cause it did no-
   thing move.   .   150

122–6 I keep the italics in such passages as this because, as noted above in regard to
Philomela, they seem to represent a sort of proverbial *aside* rather than part of the text.

XXVI

In his pale cheek the lily loseth
    white,
The red, the rosy livery off did
    cast:
His favour lately that did so de-
    light,
With ardour of his hot desire did
    waste.
    In inapparent fire he now con-
        sumes,
    His beauty fades, as forward frost-
        nipp'd blooms.

XXVII

I grieve because I cannot help his
    grieving,
His pain relenting pity in me bred:
I do accompt him worthy of reliev-
    ing,
That he deserv'd to speed if none
    had sped.   160
    I blame my beauty 'cause it breeds
        his woe:
    I cherish it 'cause *Sheretine*
        would so.

XXVIII

His friend (perceiving what such
    signs portend)
Knows if he salve not suddenly his
    sore,
Protraction with a perfect cure must
    end
His woes in death: he doth provide
    therefore.
    My mother now he plainly doth
        assail,
    And by preferment thinks for to
        prevail.

XXIX

Women by Nature are ambitious,
With *Turian's* titles tickles first her
    ear: 170
She of her daughter's state solicit-
    ous,
That honour is her aim, doth gladly
    hear.
    He tells to her his riches and his
        land,
    And then for wealth she more
        than worth doth stand.

XXX

Ah, that base earth, and baser excre-
    ment
(Placed by Nature underfoot,) should
    move
The mind of greedy age with more
    content
Than Love, the life of things that's
    from above!
    Wealth for their Summum bonum
        oft is taken,
    Loving it most when it must be
        forsaken.   180

XXXI

My serpent-seduc'd mother, *Eva-*
    like,
Tempts and entraps my pelf-affect-
    ing sire:
Judge ye what pensive pangs my
    soul did strike,
Seeing parents, friends, and furious
    love conspire
    To work my ruin, and their power
        bend
    To prostitute my Faith, and wrong
        my friend.

XXXII

My Father with authority commands,
My Mother with enticing blandish-
    ment
Allures, for *Turian* my kinsman
    stands,
With kind persuasions, *Turian* doth
    vent   190
    With sobs and sighs his too
        apparent love,
    All join my faith and fancy to
        remove.

XXXIII

Yet I resist: my Father 'gins to
    rage:
" How now, you minion, must you
    have your will?
Becomes it you to cross us in our
    age?
It is thy due our pleasure to fulfil:
    Is this the way for to requite the
        pain
    Which for thy education we have
        ta'en?

(663)

XXXIV

Thou canst ne'er that repay, thou'lt
still be debtor,
Yet still we travail to have thee
preferr'd :   200
Wants *Turian* worth? deserves *He*
not thy better ?
Reform thyself, acknowledge thou
hast err'd.
  The law divine (which you so
much pretend,)
  *Commands thee to thy parents' will
to bend.*

XXXV

What though that *Sheretine* be
gentle, free ?
Yet he hath left thee languishing
alone :
Turian is no less courteous than
he,
He flies not from thee, gives no cause
of moan :
  Had *Sheretine* but half so dearly
lov'd,
  He had not from thy sight so far
remov'd.   210

XXXVI

Nor are their fortunes equal : near
our friends,
Is *Turian's* state, fair lands and
signories :
Sheretine's most on doubtful war
depends,
It is by others' ruins he must rise :
  Who would such Worth with
Certainty forgo,
  For Worth and Likelihood, with
fairest show ?

XXXVII

Then, foolish lass, leave off and con-
descend,
It is my will and I must have it so. "
My mother follows on, as he doth
end,
" Ah, daughter, I beseech thee by
that woe,   220
  By the sore throbs I did for thee
endure,
  Whilst (yet unborn) these sides
did thee immure ;

(664)

XXXVIII

By these lank breasts at which thou
oft hast hung,
And lookèd in mine eyes with child-
ish toys,
Oft fallen asleep whilst I have to
thee sung,
Do not now strive to stop our
coming joys :
  Who now can be more tender,
wish thee better,
  Than she, whom Love to such
kind work did set her ?

XXXIX

Shalt thou, the only pledge of ancient
Love,
The sweet-expected comfort of mine
age,   230
That hopèd happiness fra me remove,
Which thy ne'er-disobeying did
presage ?
  I know thou wilt not, dear
child ; then incline,
  Scorn to be his that left for to be
thine."

XL

My kinsman urges, adds to what
they said,
Turian extols, detracts my *Sheretine*,
Lessens his means, affirms he is
unstaid,
Hath wand'ring-thoughts : if his love
had not been
  Quench'd—with my beauty if he
still had burn'd,
  He had not gone, or sooner had
return'd.   240

XLI

Turian himself (with tears) doth tell
his woes,
He needeth not protest to move
belief.
Passion is soon perceiv'd, his out-
ward shows
Did well bewray great was his inward
grief,
  He doth not feignèd (for the
fashion) mourn,
  As widows oft, and rich heirs at the
urn.

XLII

" Children obedience to their parents
owe,
I grant," (said I) "but in a lawful thing;
This is not, you me freely did
bestow,
I did submit ; fra *Sheretine* to wring
Me now were wrong, in me a foul
offence :   251
To disobey here, is obedience.

XLIII

Parents give being, noble benefit,
If with 't content, if not, better un-
born :
Yet even the best doth oft-times
bring with it
A misery whereby the mind is torn,
For making children capable of
woe,
Must they *free Choice*, the best
of bests, forgo.

XLIV

Our Minds must like, none by
attorney loveth,
If Love decay, we cannot grieve by
friends :   260
From Marriage, Love Misery re-
moveth,
On Love all wedlock's happiness
depends.
*'Twixt those ne'er lik'd, what hope
is love will last,*
*When 'twixt those dearliest lov'd
oft falls distaste ?*

XLV

If *Turian* than he is more noble were,
More virtuous, more rich, of higher
degree :
Sheretine more mean, more poor, less
worthy far,
Yet he hath that, that more con-
tenteth me.
It's not in us to love or to despise,
*They love by Fate, whose souls do
sympathize.*   270

XLVI

I grant his worth is worthy of
respect,

Tears for his grief, my cheeks have
often stain'd :
Yet with that love I cannot him
affect,
Wherewith a husband should be
entertain'd.
*'Twixt those who wed, if wooing
love be cold,*
*The married friendship can no long
time hold.*

XLVII

Yet do suppose I could affect him
dearly,
How might I with my plighted faith
dispense ?
Oh, how my conscience is touchèd
nearly,
Even with the thought of such a
foul offence.   280
*How can that prosper, or have
happy end,*
*Which sin begins, and still must
God offend ?*

XLVIII

For I cannot be lawfully his wife,
*It's not the act that ties the marriage
knot,*
It is the Will; then must I all my
life
Be stainèd with *Unchastity's* foul
blot.
O grant me then my choice be
either free,
Or an unstainèd Virgin let me
die. "

XLIX

All would not do, my father so
austere
Commands, and must not, will not,
be denay'd.   290
My mother and my kinsman will not
hear ;
Turian still urgeth, they must be
obey'd:
"O Heaven, bear witness, since
you force me do it,"
(Say I) "my heart doth not con-
sent unto it."

L

Thus 'gainst my will I give myself
    away,
They (glad they gainèd) every thing
    do haste :
Fearing disturbance by the smallest
    stay,
They think them not secure till it be
    past.
    I to my chamber go, on bed me
      threw,
    Which my moist eyes do suddenly
      bedew.   300

LI

With these complaints I entertain
    the time :
"Ah, must I now my hopèd joys
    forgo ?
Must pleasure perish with me in the
    prime?
Must I be wedded to a lasting woe?
    Must I my settled fancy now
      remove,
    And leave a lawful for an unjust
      love ?

LII

Must I recall my promise freely
    given,
And falsify my faith unto my friend ?
Is not my oath now register'd in
    Heaven ?
Is not my Promise to its power
    ken'd ?   310
    Ah, ah, it is, and therefore they
      decree
    To tie my life to lasting misery.

LIII

Ah, *Sheretine*, if thou but now didst
    know
In what a case thy *Mariana* is :
How she's surpris'd and taken by thy
    foe,
Left comfortless, debarrèd of all
    bliss :
    Would not relenting pity make thy
      heart
    To melt with sorrow for thy sweet
      love's smart ?

LIV

Free from their forcing to thee shall
    remain,
Do what they can, my best, most
    noble part,   320
Which they shall want power and
    skill to gain,
Reserv'd for thee shall be my Love,
    my Heart,
    Farewell, dear love, and as much
      joy possess,
    As doth thy *Marian* unhappiness."

LV

The day is come, we solemnly are
    wed,
That part displeasing I do over-
    pass :
You easily may think my heart was
    sad,
When forcèd thus against my will I
    was.
    Vain were their wishes, who did
      bid us joy ;
    Sad grief my nuptial pleasure did
      destroy.   330

LVI

Castalde in *Hungaria* arriv'd ;
Agria in haste commands to fortify,
A town of great import, but yet
    depriv'd
Of natural strength, or artful industry.
    There was his *Rendez-vous*, his
      men there met,
    For *Transilvania* forth by *Tyss* they
      set.

LVII

They in battaillie march *Tibiscus*
    past,
Till they arrive at small, weak
    Debrezen,
While *Castald* with the Friar to
    meet doth haste,
A *Diet's* held at *Egneth* by the
    Queen.   340
    The *Friar* with craft hinders her
      enterprise,
    By fear or flattery makes the Lords
      to rise.

---

337 battaillie] The form 'battaillie' seems better kept.

LVIII

The *Diet* thus dissolv'd, the *Queen's*
        design
Is overthrown, vanisheth to smoke :
To *Albeiula* with her son, in fine,
She doth withdraw ; there fearing
        sieging shoake,
And weakness of the place, to
        Sassebess
Makes her retrait, which more
        strong sited was.

LIX

Albeiula George besiegeth strait,
To take it fairly, or to throw it
        down,   350
Is bent ; it kept the *Queen's* jewels
        and plate,
The Gown, the Mantle, Sceptre,
        Shoes and Crown.
The cannon vomiting forth fiery
        balls,
In divers places shakes the
        mould'ring walls.

LX

With braver courage than the *Priest*
        expected,
The valiant besiegèd did defend :
To *Castald* letters *George* in haste
        directed,
Post after post with diligence doth
        send,
Wills him to speed, yet 'cause he
        saw small haste,
T' accord with *Isabel* he thinks it
        best.   360

LXI

Ten thousand *Spaniards* thither to
        his aid
Were coming (and now nigh) *Fame*
        did report :
Whereby the *Queen* was troubled,
        sore afraid,
Accords with *George* to render in
        such sort,

As she might have her movables
        of worth
From *Albeiula* safely brought her
        forth.

LXII

The *Friar* at *Egneth* with *Castalde*
        meets,
Albeiula Dalmas being ta'en :
With joyful semblance one the
        other greets,
Yet craft and jealousies in heart
        retain.   370
Ferdinand's letters *George* chief
        guider made,
Whereof th' ambitious *Bishop's*
        very glad.

LXIII

To *Sassebess* they come to find the
        Queen,
And there arise at third hour of the
        night :
Within two days the Lords they do
        convene,
They sit in counsel, *Castald* to their
        sight
Shows his Commission, wills the
        Queen restore
That Province as it was agreed
        before.

LXIV

He many arg'ments to this end doth
        urge,
It was concluded by her late *Lord
        John :*   380
The *Turk* (the Christian's common
        foe and scourge)
Could not be daunted with so weak
        a one.
She held it but with trouble and
        unrest,
At the *Turk's* pleasure might be
        dispossest.

---

344 overthrown, vanisheth] Orig. 'overthrowne, vanisheth' may be 'overthrown, *e*vanisheth,' and so save the metre.

346-8] The poet, who, from his little doggrel mottoes downwards, shows various signs of acquaintance with Spenser, has taken an extreme Spenserian liberty with 'shock' to get the rhyme, though *Scotice* it is fairly phonetic. 'Retrait' is actually Spenser's, though he usually spells it 'ret*r*ate.'

372 Hannay does not often rise high : but he seldom sinks as low as this.

LXV

Not only *Hungary* thereon depends,
But the whole good of all the
    Christian state,
Her Power weak, she wanted help
    of Friends,
Unable his encroaching force to bate:
    A mighty *Prince* was meeter him
        to curb,
    If he the common peace durst to
        disturb.   390

LXVI

To the old offers, he now addeth more.
Th' Infanta *Joan* to her young son
    Stephen
With crowns a hundred thousand
    to her dower,
By *Ferdinand* should faithfully be
    given.
    All like this well, all willingly it
        hear,
    And send to her this message by
        the *Friar*.

LXVII

Whilst, unresolvèd, things thus doubt-
    ful hung,
She with *Castald* hath private con-
    ference:
Bitterly plaineth of the Prelate's
    wrong,
Wherewith her patience can no
    more dispense.   400
    Constrain'd by need, she yields
        to *Ferdinand*,
    George thereof knowing, seeks it
        to withstand.

LXVIII

He thinks if settled peace were surely
    plac'd,
And all the civil broils were fully
    ceas't :
His plumes were pluckèd, he should
    be disgrac'd,
Who now is most, should be regarded
    least.

Often a gold-affecting Prelate proud,
For private ends hinders a public
good.

LXIX

The *Queen* unto *Castalde* him
    accuseth,
(Inconstancy and cunning she did
    doubt :)   410
To ratify th' agreement rather chuseth,
Castalde labours how to bring't about:
    There is a *Diet* call'd at *Colosvar*,
    The States from all sides to it do
        repair.

LXX

The day come, and the regal orna-
    ments
Produc'd, the Priest desires the
    Crown in keeping :
With sobs and sighs her inward
    sorrow vents ;
Scorn and *Disdain* detain her eyes
    from weeping :
    " What, shall I to a base Friar give
        the Crown,
    Whereof I dispossessed myself and
        son ? "   420

LXXI

She said. Then in her hand the
    Crown she took,
In presence of *Castalde* and her *Son*,
And all the *Lords*, her eyes tears
    cannot brook ;
In pearly torrents o'er her cheeks
    they run.
    The tears which from her *Son's*
        eyes did distil,
    Show'd the surrender was against
        his will.

LXXII

" Since froward *Fortune* (that in
    change delights,
Wherewith her fickleness infects the
    world,
Hath us subverted loaded with
    despights,

392 *Joan*] ' Jo-an,' as in ' Joanna.'
429 despight] The influence of Spenser, which is often strong in the earlier seventeenth
century, appears again in this context with the present ' eye-rhyme-spelling,' the
rhyme of ' entreat ' and ' estate ' below, and ' Mutability ' lower still. Each separately
would prove nothing : but they are *all* Spenserian.

And all her mischiefs on our heads
   have hurl'd :)   430
Makes me this woful resignation
   make,
My Mates, thy father's Kingdoms
   to forsake ;

LXXIII

Yet shall She not amidst all these
   annoys
Let us but that in this we'll take
   content,   -
Since we must leave them, that he
   them enjoys
Who is a Christian ; Here I them
   present
   To thee, *Castald*, for *Ferdinand*,
      tell we
Not by constraint, but yield them
   to thee free.

LXXIV

Now we submit ourselves unto his
   Grace,
With all our fortunes, humbly him
   entreat   440
(Since sprung of princely blood and
   royal race)
To take some pity of our poor estate :
   Let not his bounty now deny
      relief,
   Nor breach of promise add unto
      our grief.

LXXV

And thou (sweet *John*) my dear and
   tender son,
Since now our fortune's not sufficient
That to repair, that malice hath
   o'erthrown
Without the aid of others : be con-
   tent ;
   Midst of such miseries, I thought
      it best
   With private loss to gain a public
      rest.   450

LXXVI

Like to a Prince (though not like to
   a King)
Yet thou mayst live with some good
   certainty,
When *Destiny's* disgrace on Kings
   do bring,

There they govern with Mutability :
   Dear Child, of friends, of aid, of
      hope forsaken,
   For thy repose this course is
      undertaken.

LXXVII

Yet 'mongst these troubles let us not
   despair,
Nor doubt but thou art kept for
   more command ;
Think it not strange, nor be dismay'd
   with care,
Where thou didst first take breath
   to leave that land,   460
   Love *Virtue*, *Virtue's dignity's so*
      great,
   Fortune cannot debar it long from
      state.

LXXVIII

I grant there's cause of grief, to
   give away
This Crown thy father's temples did
   adorn,
And if false *Fortune* had not put
   a stay,
Had now upon thy Kingly head
   been worn :
   But now with *Patience* we must be
      content,
   Each state doth change, no king-
      dom's permanent."

LXXIX

Thus spoke she with such penetra-
   ting words,
(And therewith did deliver up the
   Crown)   470
As they did pierce the hearts of all
   the Lords,
But chiefly *George*, in tears his eyes
   did drown.
   Castalde with kind words strives
      to appease
   Her sorrow, and to 'swage her
      swelling seas.

LXXX

Within few days she doth from
   thence depart,
With painful travel and in habit poor,
Dissembling not the anguish of her
   heart,

She manifests it to her utmost power;
Towards *Cassovia* she doth take
the way,
Where a steep hill enforceth her
to stay.   480
LXXXI
The roughness hinders her in coach
to ride,
She 's fain with labour on her foot to
go,
Her tender child and ladies by her
side,
The only now-copartners of her woe,
Whilst they 're on foot, a sudden
storm doth rise,
Black pitchy clouds enveloping
the skies.
LXXXII
The wind and rain them boister-
ously did beat,
She blameth *Fortune* that is not
content
To be her opposite in matters great,
But even in trifles, thus her spite to
vent.   490
She attributes it to her Destiny,
That she is subject to such misery.
LXXXIII
Therefore a little for to ease her
mind,
Under a tree for shelter she took
seat:
Sic fata volunt carvèd in its rind,
Regina Isabella under-wrait.
Ah, wretched Queen, no wonder
thou wast sorry
To fall so low, from such a height
of glory.
LXXXIV
She to *Cassovia* comes, and bears it
out
With patience, till *Fortune's* fury's
past: 500
With *Time*, her rolling wheel doth
come about,
And she is of her country repossest.
*God grant her soon her state, and
kingdom lost,*

*Who with more courage bears it,
though more crost.*
LXXXV
Castalde having what he would
obtain'd,
Lord John Alphonse Castald with
the Crown
He sends to *Ferdinand*: my Lover
pain'd,
With ling'ring-stay for *Vien's* ready
boun.
Castald (though unwilling) con-
descends,
Loath for to part at once with two
such friends.   510
LXXXVI
In journeying every hour he thinketh
two,
The nearer, he doth think the
leagues the longer:
His love increases, and he knows
not how,
The nearer to Me, his Desire is
stronger.
Long-look'd-for *Vien* he beholds
at last,
Spurr'd by *Desire*, he to it hasteth
fast.
LXXXVII
Thinks with himself, "O what a joy-
ful greeting
Will't be when *Marian* sees her
Sheretine!
How shall we bear ourselves at
this wish'd meeting?
Can the joy be express'd we shall be
in?"   520
Ah, *Sheretine*, how little didst thou
know,
How far from joy thou wast, how
near to woe.
LXXXVIII
No sooner he in *Vien's* come, but
hears
The sad news of the thing he least
suspected:
He thinks them mandrake-sounds,
he stops his ears,

496 under-wrait] A little *plusquam*-Spenserian.

He trows each tongue with poison
  is infected :
    He none believes, he thinks that
      each tongue lies,
    Longing to see me, to my home
      he hies.

        LXXXIX

He came, in *Turian's* arms me
  lockèd found,
He could not trust his eyes (though
  still he gazed) :   530
No doubt his heart receiv'd a deadly
  wound,
Long ere he spoke, he was so much
  amazed.
    At last, "Is this the constancy"
      (he said)
    "Should be heard of ?" that
      spoke, no longer staid.

        XC

My heart was no less cut with *Care*
  than his
Because he staid not to hear my
  excuse,
I know he deem'd I willing did amiss,
Which did more sorrow in my soul
  infuse :
    Taking no leave, he fair *Vienna*
      leaves,
    Accompanied with care-increasing
      griefs.   540

        XCI

All woe-begone, he wanders here
  and there,
Looks most for rest when furthest
  from resort,
Submits himself solely to sad *Despair*,
With cheering comfort he cannot
  comport :
    At last he came unto an obscure
      shade,
    Where mirthless *Melancholy* man-
      sion had.

        XCII

Low on the ground grew Hyssop,
  Wormwood, Rue,
The mourning mounting trees were
  Cypress green,

Whose twining tops so close together
  grew,
They all seem'd as they but one
  bough had been :   550
    Covering a spacious tomb where
      cursed *Care*
    Herself had sepulchriz'd with
      dire *Despair*.

        XCIII

No wanton bird there warbled loving
  lays,
There was no merry Merle, Gold-
  Finch, or Thrush ;
No other hopping bird in higher
  sprays,
No mourning Nightingale in lower
  bush :
    The carcass-craving Raven, Night-
      Crow, Owl,
    In this dark grove their hateful
      notes did howl.

        XCIV

This sullen seat doth suit well with
  his soul,
There throws himself down in the
  bitter weeds ;   560
His heart did thrust out sighs, his
  tongue condole,
His wat'ring eyes with bitter moisture
  feeds
    These hapless herbs, there 'gins he
      to lament,
    With interrupting sighs his woes
      to vent.

        XCV

"Ah, cursed *Time*," (and there a
  sigh him staid)
"That ere I saw" (that scarcely he
  had spoken
When that a groan his fainting speech
  allay'd,
With such abound as if his heart had
  broken ;
    When sighs and groans had got
      some little vent,
    He 'gins anew his sorrows to
      lament.)   570

---

550 bough] Orig. ' Bow,' perhaps for ' bower.'

XCVI

"Ah, cursed *Time*," (said he) "that
ere I saw
The light, and that my Nurse did
not o'erlie me ;
Ah, cursed *Time*, that first I breath
did draw,
Ah, cursed *Time*, that did not *Time*
deny me :
Ah, cursed *Time* ! Ah, cruel cursed
Time,
That let me pass the springtide of
my prime.

XCVII

Was it for this I was so sung and
dandled
Upon the knee, and watchèd when
I slept ?
Was it for this I tenderly was
handled ?
Was it for this I carefully was kept ?
Was it for this I was so neatly
nurst,   581
That I of all should be the most
accurst ?

XCVIII

Did *Fortune* smile in my young
tender years,
To make me better relish now my
pain ?
Then pour'd I out no bitter briny tears,
That I should now have store my
cheeks to stain ?
Did *Fortune* and the *Fates* strive
to content me,
That they might now with sorrow
more torment me ?

XCIX

Did cruel *Love* yield unto my *Desire*,
To know his pain by being dis-
possest ?   590
And did my *Marian* with *Love*
conspire,
Did all agree to rob me of my rest ?
Since it is *Marian's* will, welcome
Despair,
Farewell all *Joy*, welcome *Woe*,
Grief and *Care*.

C

Welcome, since it 's her will, now
wishèd *Death*,
Long may she live, and happy with
her choice :
I will wish that so long as I have breath,
Nay, even in death I will therein
rejoice.
Dear (though disloyal) Thou art
still to me,
So once (if thou not fain'dst) I
was to thee.   600

CI

If that one spark of thy old love
remain,
When thou shalt chance my timeless
death to hear ;
Let that so much favour for me obtain,
As offer at my hearse a sigh, and tear.
And if some chance be by when
them you spend,
And ask the cause, say *You have
lost a friend.* "

CII

Sorrow suffers no more, his tongue
there stays,
Heart-killing *Care* prepares to stop
his breath :
His strength and colour by degrees
decays,
Grief seems to grieve, and for his
help calls *Death*,   610
Who much displeasèd so to see
him languish,
Soon with his surest cure doth
help his anguish.

CIII

No sooner heard I how my dear
Friend died,
(Soon it was known, for his friends
had sought him :)
And that his destiny was so descried,
That to his timeless death my deeds
had brought him :
But that my ill-divining hapless
heart
Was suddenly assail'd with unseen
smart.

614 A syllable seems missing : perhaps another ' soon ' after ' for.'

(672)

CIV

Now *Turian* I will no more come
   nigh,
His flattering blandishments I now
   disdain :   620
He is despis'd, yet grieveth more to
   see
The mistress of his soul thus seiz'd
   with pain :
   He with my sadness such a con-
      sort bears,
   Sighs as I sigh, doth weep when I
      shed tears.

CV

Sad discontent so wholly me possest,
I seem'd not she that late I was be-
   fore :
My woe that was by fits, is an unrest
Which with a still increase grows
   ever more.
   From mirthful company I now
      absent,
   And melancholy walks alone
      frequent.   630

CVI

Thus many days only heart-killing
   Grief
Me still accompanied and did attend
With black *Despair*, which told me
   no relief
On earth could my least discontent-
   ment end :
   The days I spent in heavy plaints
      and moanings,
   In night I tire the answering
      walls with groanings.

CVII

Yet never could I sit, or walk, or lie,
But still I thought I saw my
   Sheretine,
With pale and meagre face standing
   me by,
With wrathful look upbraiding me of
   sin,   640
   Saying his soul could yet obtain
      no rest
   Amongst the souls in sweet
      Elysium blest.

CVIII

Twixt *Fear* and *Love* my heavy heart
   distract,
Knew neither what to follow, what to
   flee ;
Love bids me for my *Sheretine* to act
A part that might me ease and set
   him free ;
   Persuades me and affirms I shall
      remain
   With my *Love* after in *Elysian*
      Plain.

CIX

Fear 'fore my face makes horrid
   Death appear
In ugly shape seizèd with smarting
   pain,   650
Making to tremble as he draweth near ;
Yet I with scorn his terror do disdain :
   Love doth prevail, I am resolv'd
      to fly,
   By death to keep my Lover
      company.

CX

Thus mourning, on my bed myself
   I threw,
Saying, "Sweet *Sheretine*, behold and
   see,
For thy sweet sake I bid the world
   adieu ;
And now, dear Love, I come to live
   with Thee : "
   Then out I drew this blood-
      begorèd knife,
   Therewith to cut the fatal thread
      of life.   660

CXI

Thrice was my hand heav'd up to
   give the stroke,
Thrice down again my fearful hand
   did fall;
Still fear dissuades, and love doth
   still provoke,
Courage her forces to my heart did call ;
   Then gave this death's wound,
      whilst my latest cry
   Was, *Sheretine, behold thy Marian
      die.*

665 death's wound] Cf. ' deathsman,' &c.

CXII

My Mother (with my latest shriek
    affrighted,
Come in and finding me in such a
    guise)
With sudden fright is lastingly
    benighted ;
Fear-forcèd *Death* seals up her aged
    eyes :   670
  My Father rages, his gray hairs he
    tore,
  Turian (though still amazèd),
    grievèd more.

CXIII

Pull'd out the blade, pans'd the
    blood-weeping-wound,
Findeth it mortal, saw my soul de-
    part ;
A frantic fury did him clean
    confound,
He stroke himself on sudden to the
    heart ;
  Our blood doth mix in death, yet
    mine would run
  From his ; what life dislik'd e'en
    death would shun.

CXIV

My Father now doth find (though all
    too late,)
The misery forc'd marriage doth
    ensue :   680
Unto the poor he gives his whole
    estate,
The world (with his delights) he bids
    adieu.
  He as a pilgrim from *Vienna* goes ;
  Where, when, or how he died, yet
    no man knows.

CXV

Then to these fields my sad Soul did
    descend,
With my sweet *Sheretine*, abode to
    make :
But when I came, I found my
    faithful friend
With *Charon* passing o'er this grisly
    Lake:
  For my *Death* had his wrongèd
    Ghost appeas'd,
  So that He might pass over as he
    pleas'd.   690

CXVI

I followed fast, thinking with Him
    to go,
That I might still enjoy his company :
But I was stay'd as I before did show
Until thy *Muse* should pity taken on
    me :
  And now by thy sweet *Caelia's*
    name once more
  I thee conjure, keep promise past
    before.'

CXVII

Then back She brought me, and no
    longer stay'd,
But with more cheerful looks did
    thence depart,
With confidence she could not be
    denay'd
What she desir'd, for her sake, hath
    my heart :   700
  For *Caelia's* sake my sole-adorèd
    saint,
  The world with *Marian's* woes I
    thus acquaint.

FINIS

---

667 shriek] Orig. 'scrike.'

673 pans'd] Another Gallicism.

A Happy Husband:

OR

DIRECTIONS FOR
A MAID TO CHVSE HER
MATE.

Together with

A WIVES BEHAVIOVR
after Mariage.

The second Edition.

By Patrick Hannay Gent.

Proper.

Exemplo junctæ tibi sint in amore columbæ,
Masculus & totum fœmina coniugium.

LONDON,
Printed by *Iohn Haviland* for *Nathaniel Butter*,
and are to be sold at his shop at S. *Austins*
gate. 1622.

To the virtuous and noble lady, the Lady Margaret Home, eldest daughter to the Right Honourable Alexander Earl Home, Baron of Dunglas, &c.

THINKING with myself (Noble Lady) what I might present some way to express my love in remembrance of those not to be requited favours, which have wholly obliged me to your House: It came into my mind, that what is offered to Gods, or great ones, ought rather to be apt, than equal: and that it was held absurd in old time to offer an Hecatomb to the Muses, or an Ivy wreath to the God of War. I thought no offering could be more conformable to your virtues than this Husband, which of due doth challenge a maiden-Maecenas: and none so fit as yourself, who even in these years by your budding virtues, do well bewray what fruit your riper years will produce. Accept it then (Madam) as an acknowledgement of what is due by me to your deservings, which have bound me to abide ever yours

In all dutiful observance,
PATRICK HANNAY.

TO WOMEN IN GENERAL

IN things of weight and moment, care and circumspection are to be used, with a truly grounded judgement before resolution. Now in human actions none is of more consequence than marriage, where error can be but once, and that never after remedied. Therefore in it is great caution required before conclusion, the sequel of staid deliberation, or unadvised rashness, being a happy, or a wretched life. And therein is another's counsel most necessary (though through the whole course of man's life it be safer than the self-conceived): for affection, which in other affairs doth oft overrule reason (even in the wise) doth in this ever hide the faults of the affected under the blinding veil of love. This hath caused me for the weal of your Sex to produce this *Husband* to the light, not gain, or glory; knowing well the vulgar and critic censurers in this age do rather detract, than attribute: but I care not much for their opinion: who dislike, may freely abstain: if any give better, I shall willingly assent; take it as it is meant, for your good, to displease none, and to content all.

P. *Hannay.*

To Overbury's Widow, wife of this Husband

LEAVE, worthy Wife, to wear your
    mourning weed,
Or bootless stain your cheeks for
    him that's dead;
But rather joy, and thank this Author's
    pen,

Hath so well match'd thee with this
    matchless man:
For *Overbury's* Ghost is glad to see
His widow such one's happy wife
    to be.

R. S.

Overbury's Widow] Allusions to Overbury's poem of *A Wife*, complicated or not with others to his miserable fate, are abundant at the time.

To his Friend the Author

THY happy Husband shows thy high
    ingine,
Whose muse such method in her
    measures can,
The matter shows thy manners are
    divine;
Thy practis'd virtues shows thou art
    this Man :
I half envy that highly blessed Maid,
Whose happy lot shall be to link with
    thee,
And well-nigh wish that Nature had
    me made
A woman; so I such one's wife might
    be :
Detraction is distraught thy lines to
    see,
And swell'd with envy, can no words
    bring forth,   10
Her baseness cannot parallel thy
    worth,
Which still shall live unto eternity :
For after Ages reading of thy verse,
Shall deck with Laurel thy adorèd
    herse.

                                    P. S.

To his Friend Mr. Patrick Hannay

FRIEND, I am glad that you have
    brought to life
A Husband fit for *Overbury's* Wife ;
Whose chastity might else suspected
    be,
Wanting too long a Husband's com-
    pany :
But now being match'd so well by your
    endeavour,
She'll live a chaste *Penelope* for ever,
And you brave *Overbury* make to be
Your brother-in-law by act of
    ingeny.

                            W. Jewell.

To the Author

WHEN I behold the Author and his
    book,
With wonder and delight on both
    I look ;
Both are so like, and both deserve so
    well,
Were I not friend, I in their praise
    would dwell,
But since I should seem partial, I think
    fit
To leave their praises to a better wit :
Yet Husband like to this I wish God
    send
To those are chaste, and to me such a
    friend.
Live each in other, be each other's
    praise,
Time shall not end your glory with
    your days.   10

                    Edward Leventhorpe.

The Argument

MARRIAGE ordain'd ; the man made
    head,
That kind may be, like like doth
    breed :
God blest it ; youth it best befits :
The Author will not try his wits
To make one man of many parts,
Painters do so to show their Arts :
His birth and breeding first he shows,
Equal, and good ; the wants of those
What ills they breed, yet self-gain'd
    glore
He doth prefer both these before.   10
His shape must not deformèd be,
Nature makes house and guest agree.
His stature neither low, nor tall,
The mean in each is best of all :
Not curious to be counted fair,
It's womanish to take that care ;
Free from affecting gifts of others,
That self-weakness still discovers.
Such one found, then next is shown
What vice he s'd want, what virtue
    own :   20

20 he s'd] 's'd' for 'should' is, I think, one of the rarest of these contractions.
The absence of 'h' *Scotice.*

Wealth must be set aside to try,
(It is a beam in judgement's eye.)
What ill doth haunt her weds for gold,
Is told : with the content of old,
When virtue and simplicity
Did choose : then he doth let her see
The Worthies that the World brought
    forth,
Woo'd ne'er for wealth, but still for
    worth.
With virtue this man should be nurst,
If 't be deprav'd, he 's worse than
    first :   30
Drunkenness, gaming, he must want,
He shows what ills such unthrifts
    haunt ;
He must not haunt another's sheets,
With grace, foul whoredom never
    meets ;

He must have spent well his time
    past,
A wicked crime's bruit long doth
    last :
His humours must with hers agree,
Or else true friendship cannot be ;
He must fear God, for on that fear
Wisdom doth her building rear,   40
It 's that makes honest ; Honesty
In show, not deed, is policy.
He must propose a certain end,
Whereto his actions all must bend ;
He must have unfeign'd piety,
And serve in truth the Deity :
The four chief virtues, in some mea-
    sure,
Must hoard up in him their treasure,
Whereon the lesser do depend :
Age and behaviour do him end.   50

Another

To keep him good, his wife must be
Obedient, mild, her huswifery
Within doors she must tend ; her charge
Is that at home ; his that at large :
She must be careful ; idle wives
Vice works on, and to some ill drives :
Not toying, fond, nor yet unkind,
Not of a weak dejected mind,
Nor yet insensible of loss,

Which doth with care her Husband
    cross :   10
Not jealous, but deserving well,
Not gadding, news to know, or tell ;
Her conversation with the best,
In Husband's heart her thought must
    rest :
Thus if she choose, thus use her mate,
He promiseth her happy state.

A HAPPY HUSBAND:
OR,
Directions for a Maid to choose her Mate

In Paradise God Marriage first ordain'd,
That lawfully kind might be so maintain'd ;
By it the Man is made the Woman's head,
And kind immortalizèd in their seed :
For like produces like, it so should be,
God blest it with *Increase and multiply.*
Nature requires it, nothing is more just,
Who were begot, beget of duty must.
It Youth becomes, Age is unapt to breed,
Old stocks are barren, youthful plants have seed. 10
Then, virtuous Virgin, since such blessing springs
From wedlock (which earth's greatest comfort brings)
Compell'd by love, which to thy worth is due,
How to choose well thy mate, I will thee shew ;
Whose sympathizing virtues may combine
Your hearts in love, till death life's thread untwine.
It's not my mind the rarities to glean
Of blest perfections I have heard or seen ;
And take the best, where bounty doth abound,
And make a Husband, (nowhere to be found :) 20
The painter so from boys, and girls did take

Best of their beauties, Helen fair to make ;
No, I will paint thy mate in such a hew,
As *Care* may find : *Discretion* must allow.
To choose aright, know from what stock he's grown ;
The birth suits best, is nearest to thine own :
Dislike makes higher Birth deem lower base,
Lower will never by thy Birth take place :
In Man the fault is more to be excus'd,
Who of low birth (for beauty) hath one chus'd ; 30
His lightness therein ever love is deem'd,
Yet as his place, his Wife shall be esteem'd.
But when a Woman of a noble race
Doth match with Man of far inferior place,
She cannot him ennoble, he is still
In place as she first found him, good, or ill :
His breeding will his birth still to thee tell,
For as the Cask, the liquor still doth smell.
A crab, though digg'd and dung'd, cannot bring forth
A luscious fruit ; so hardly man of worth 40
Doth from base stock proceed : still like itself
Nature produces ; force of golden pelf

---

23 hew] In the general sense of 'character,' 'quality.' The rhyme of 'all*oo*' is of course Scots.

A Happy Husband

To alter that 's not able, yet we know
Oft Men of worth have come of
    Parents low :
For Parents' place is not the Children's
    merit,
Yet it adds grace, if they their worth
    inherit ;
If not, it adds to shame : for from
    high race
Virtue 's expected due to such a
    place :
For undegenerate heroic minds
They should possess, are come of noble
    kinds :   50
What man's own worth acquires with
    virtuous ends,
Is truly his, and not that which
    descends.
Cicero brags (and justly) that his
    line
He did in glorious virtue far out-
    shine,
Which was his honour : They no
    honour have,
Who (idle) add not to what they
    receive ;
It is his own worth every Man doth
    grace,
Less or more eminent, as is his place :
For Virtue (though aye clear) yet
    clearest shines
When she doth dart her lights from
    noble lines.   60
A glorious flame blazing in valley
    low,
Is soon barr'd sight, nor doth it far
    way show,
Obscur'd with neighbour objects :
    but on high
A little Beacon to both far and nigh
Shows like a bearded Comet in the
    air,
Admir'd of some, of most accounted
    rare.
Choose thou a Husband equal to thy
    race,
Who's grac'd by virtue, and doth
    virtue grace ;

Things different do never well agree,
True liking lodges in equality :   70
Better than birth his Parents' virtues
    know,
From poison'd springs no wholesome
    waters flow.
As for his shape, I would it should
    be free
From (Nature's note of spite) De-
    formity :
Deform'd shape is of so bad a nature,
That it 's dislik'd even in a noble
    creature ;
Where comely shape with love at-
    tracts the eyes,
By secret sympathy of all it sees.
England's third Richard, and the wife
    of Shore,
The one deform'd, the other grac'd
    with store   80
Of bounteous Nature's gifts, do show
    th' effects
Of Love and Hate, to good and bad
    aspects ;
She (when she bare-foot with a taper
    light,
Did open penance in the people's
    sight)
Went so demure, with such a lovely
    face,
That beauty seem'd apparell'd in dis-
    grace :
But most when shame summon'd the
    blood too high
With native stains, her comely cheeks
    to dye
In scarlet tincture. She did so
    exceed,
That e'en disgrace in her delight did
    breed ;   90
Firing beholders' hearts that came to
    scorn her,
So Beauty cloth'd in baseness did
    adorn her,
That e'en the good (who else the
    vice did blame)
Thought she deserv'd pity more than
    shame :

85, 86 A couplet not quite unworthy of Dryden, yet unborn.

Condemning cunning Richard's cruel
mind
Who caus'd her shame, the multitude
to blind,
Lest it his greater mischief should
behold,
Which his ambition-plotters had in
mould :
So in them was the force of feature
seen,
*Who, if less famous, had more happy
been.* 100
Thus Nature makes each body with
the mind
Some way to keep decorum : for we
find
Mark'd bodies, manners cross accom-
pany,
Which in well-shap'd we seld, or
never see :
For she doth, builder-like, a mansion
frame
Fit for the guest should harbour in
the same.
No stature choose too low, for so in
time
Thy offspring may prove dwarfs ;
yet do not climb
To one too tall : *for buildings mounted
high,*
*Their upper rooms seldom well
furnish'd be :* 110
Herein observe the mean, it 's best
of all,
Let him not be observ'd for low nor
tall.
Fresh, lively colours, which fair
woman grace,
Modest, effeminate, alluring face,
Is not so much in Man to be
respected,
As other graces are to be affected :
The bloom of beauty is a fading
flower,
Which *Age* and *Care* consumeth
every hour ;

It blasted once, is ever after lost,
Like to a rose nipt with untimely
frost. 120
A manly face in Man is more com-
mended
Than a fair face from sun and wind
defended.
A *Carpet Knight*, who makes it his
chief care
To trick him neatly up, and doth
not spare
(Though sparing) precious time for
to devour,
(Consulting with his glass) a tedious
hour
Soon flees (spent so) whiles each
irregular hair
His barber rectifies, and to seem
rare,
His heat-lost locks to thicken closely
curls,
And curiously doth set his misplac'd
pearls. 130
Powders, perfumes, are then profusely
spent,
To rectify his native nasty scent :
This forenoon's task perform'd, his
way he takes,
And chamber-practis'd craving curt-
sies makes
To each he meets ; with cringes, and
screw'd faces,
(Which his too partial glass approv'd
for graces :)
Then dines, and after courts some
courtly dame,
Or idle busy 'bout misspending
game ;
Then sups, then sleeps, then rises for
to spend
Next day as that before, as t'were
the end 140
For which he came : so womaniz'd,
turn'd Dame,
As place 'mongst *Ovid's* changelings
he might claim.

130 pearls] Orig. 'purles' = 'pearls' ? Or is it in the sense of 'purling' ? Cf.
'purling billow' in ' On the Queen ' *inf.*, and 'purling Zephyr ' in the second Elegy.
138] Orig. 'busy-bout.' But the subst. ' bout ' would make no sense, and my
alteration seems pretty certain.

What? Do not such discover their weak mind
(Unapt for active virtue) is inclined
To superficial things, and can embrace
But outward Habits for internal Grace?
The mind's gifts do the body's grace adorn,
Where that's defective, to affect is scorn.
For Action's hinder'd by too much observing
Of decency: but where a well-deserving   150
And settled reputation is; then there
Each thing becomes, and is accounted, rare:
Where that's defective, striving to affect
Another's worth, their weakness doth detect.
Let thy Mate be what such do strive to seem,
Thou must the substance, not the shade esteem:
When thou hast found this well-form'd cabinet,
Try what rich jewels are within it set:
Set wealth apart, thou shalt more clearly see
His Virtues *(Riches dazzle judgement's Eye.)*   160
Who weds for wealth, she only wealth doth wed,
Not Man which got, and in possession had,
Love languishes: yet till one's death she's forc'd
To live with him; though wealth fail, yet divorced
They cannot be; so is she all his life
His riches' Widow, though she be his Wife.
That golden Age when sullen Saturn reigned,
For Virtue's love, not gold's, the glory gained;

To be so styl'd, it was not then demanded
How rich in gold, or how that he was landed: 170
When they did woo, simplicity had wont
Be first, which now is last, in least account;
With *Virtue* leading *Love*, be Wedlock's aim,
And greatest wealth, a pure unspotted name:
They liv'd and lov'd, then joying each in other,
Not fearing that their *Mate* should love another,
Seduc'd by tempting Gold; their time they spent
Free from distrust, or open discontent.
But the next Age, when as our mother Earth
(Fertile before in voluntary birth)
Was sought into, and had her bowels torn   181
For hidden wealth: then when the keel was worn,
Ploughing the Ocean for his hidden store,
The sweet Content did vanish was before;
The silly Maid (then ignorant of ill)
Having no Wealth might live a Maiden still,
And die (except seduc'd) so; the poor swain
(Though virtuous) was straight held in disdain.
But yet the Worthies that the world brought forth
Since that blessed Age, postponèd wealth to worth.   190
Great Alexander did disdain the offer
Declining Darius with his Child did proffer,

---

192 Darius] Hannay is guilty either of 'Darïus' or of bad metre. 'Declining' is of course to be taken with D., not A., and equals 'falling.' In the next line 'Maced's' is textual and short for 'Macedon's,' but I do not know whether the genitive with 'full' as a noun or the plural with 'full' as an adjective is the more likely.

Nor Maced's full of Gold, nor Euphrates' brim,
To bound his Empire, could inveigle him :
But he for that rather contemn'd his foe,
For thinking he could have been conquer'd so.
True worth doth wealth as an addition take,
Defective virtue's wants of weight to make :
Virtue's best wealth wherewith he should be nurst,
That smell stays long, a vessel seasons first. 200
Yet build not there, for good natures depraved,
Are still the worst, so thou may'st be deceived.
See that he have so spent his fore-past time,
That he be free from censure of a crime.
Youth's apt to slip : but a notorious deed
From Nature, not from Age, doth still proceed ;
And though that Fortune herein oft hath part,
Yet th' actions still are judgèd from the heart.
Adrastus thinking to revenge the harms
Of his dead Love, his naked weapon warms 210
In his brother's bosom (too dear blood to spill)
Instead of his that did his Lady kill:
Fleeing to Croesus, he him entertain'd,
Where his behaviour so much credit gain'd,
As Lydia's hope, young Atis, Croesus' heir,
He got in charge ; whom, hunting, unaware
His hapless hand unfortunately slew,
Whiles at a boar his dismal dart he threw :

Yet was it thought intention, and not chance,
Till being freely pardon'd the offence,
Lest more disast'rous chances should fall out, 221
His own self-slaughter clear'd them of that doubt :
Thus when opinion hath possessed the mind,
It leaves a deep impression long behind ;
And they must do much good, that have done ill,
Ere they be trusted, wer't by fate or will.
See Drunkenness (from which all vices spring)
Do no way stain him ; for that still doth bring
Contempt, disgrace, and shame : *Circe* made swine
Of wise *Ulysses*' fellows, drunk with wine. 230
The Macedonian Monarch (lately nam'd)
Is not for worth so prais'd, as for that blam'd ;
He in his drink destroy'd his dearest friend,
That did 'fore him his Father's deeds commend :
Nor could his after-tears wash off that stain
Which doth to blot his actions still remain :
For if one would his glorious actions show,
How strong, chaste, valiant, mild to captiv'd foe ;
With such brave deeds though he the world hath fill'd,
Yet this still stays, He drunk, dear *Clytus* kill'd. 240
No Gamester let him be : for such a *Man*
Shall still be loser, do the best he can ;
His mind and money it frets, and destroys
And wastes the precious time he here enjoys :

Some in less time unto some Art attain,
Than others spend in play ; some's pleasing vein
Will seem so mild, in this dear double loss,
They outwardly not take it for a cross :
But when all's gone (for they but then give over)
Their smother'd anguish they at last discover ;　250
Whereof man's foe, the Fiend, advantage takes,
Whiles on self-slaughter'd rooks, he gathers wrakes.
Examples hereof we may daily see,
How some by halter, some by poison die ;
And who go not so far yet their last ends
Contemned need, and misery attends :
For this ill haunts them, who to play are bent,
They seldom leave till their estate be spent.
With other's sheets let him not be acquainted,
(They are still stain'd, whom once that sin hath tainted)　260
And never hope to have him true to thee,
Who hath oft prey'd on chang'd variety :
Be sure who hath had choice, will ne'er digest
To feed on one dish, (though of sweetest taste)
And whoso strays, loves not, but lusts ; in one
Doth *Love* delight, when that leaves, *Love* is gone ;
For *Grace* and *Lust* ne'er harbour in one Inn,

And where *Lust* lodges, ever lodgeth *Sin* :
Which *Sin* when it is to a habit grown,
Not fear of God (but Man, lest it be known)　270
Doth stay the execution : but be sure
Though the act be hinder'd, yet the heart's impure,
Whose lusts will predomine in time and place,
Not over-rul'd by God's preventing Grace.
Besides, he will be still suspecting thee,
Though thou beest pure as spotless *Chastity* :
For vice is ever conversant in ill,
And guilty as itself thinks others still.
Upon this Earth there is no greater Hell,
Than with suspecting Jealousy to dwell.　280
See that his humours (as near as may be)
Do with each humour of thy mind agree ;
Or else contention, and dissension still,
Will bar your sweet content ; while the one's will
The other's doth resist, Love cannot be,
'Twixt fire and water, they will ne'er agree.
True friendship must express 'twixt man and wife,
The comfort, stay, defence, and port of life,
Is perfect, when two souls are so confus'd,
And plung'd together (which free-will hath chus'd)　290

---

246 vein] Orig. ' vaine ' ; but this is a very usual spelling of ' vein,' and I do not think ' vain' makes sense.

252 rooks] ' pigeons ' rather ; but the birds often interchange parts. There is a complicated play on words in this line. ' Wrake ' is properly in Scots = ' wrack ' = ' sea-weed,' with which sense ' rook ' has to suggest ' rock.' But it may also mean ' anger,' ' revenge ' : cf. wr*eak*.'

As they can never sever'd be again,
But still one compound must of both
    remain :
From which confusèd mixture, ne're
    proceeds
Words of good turns, requitals, helps
    of needs ;
For it is ever after but one soul,
Which both their wills and actions
    doth control ;
And cannot thank itself for its
    own deeds,
*(What is done to itself, no self-love
    breeds :)*
But this holds not where humours
    disagree,
There's no concordance in disparity.
See he fear God, then will he fear
    to sin ;   301
Where Vice doth leave, there Virtue
    doth begin :
Sin is nipt in the bud, when we do
    mind
That God's all light, and can in
    darkness find
What we can hide from Man ; the
    reins and heart
He searches through, and knows
    each hidden part,
And each thought long before ; we
    cannot hide
Our faults from Him, nor from His
    censure slide.
The Wiseman saith, it's Wisdom's
    first degree,
To have a true fear of the Deity ;
For that makes Honest : Honesty's
    commended,   311
Whether sincere, or for a cloak
    pretended.
The vulgar *Honesty,* servant to
    Laws,
Customs, Religions, Hope and Fear
    it draws,
Be more or less according to the
    times,

It still is wavering, difference of climes
Makes it unequal, rather Policy
I may call such respect, than
    Honesty :
Which still aspiring, quickly oft
    mounts high,
And in short time unto that mark
    comes nigh   320
At which it aims : but builded on
    false grounds,
A sudden fall it unawares confounds.
But Honesty doth always go upright,
With settled pace ; not wavering for
    the might
Of winds, times, nor occasions : it
    goes slow,
But still attains the end, towards
    which doth go.
Now such an Honest man I wish
    thee find
As still is Honest, out of Honest
    mind :
That's Wisdom's first ground : next
    is to propose
A certain form of life ; for ever
    those   330
(Who divers in themselves) aim at
    no end,
But as occasion offers, each way tend,
Never attain the mark. *If Hawk
    assay*
*To truss two Birds, she doth on
    neither prey :*
These grounds being laid, an un-
    feign'd Piety
Must build thereon, and though
    that divers be
Religions, Laws ; yet ours amongst
    them all
Is truest, purest, most authentical.
Religion true, loves God, and quiets
    us,   339
And rests in a soul free and generous:
Where superstition is a frantic error,
A weak mind's sickness, and the own
    soul's terror :

293 ne're] Sic in orig. : but 'never,' which is the usual expansion of ' ne're,' does
not seem to suit. ' There ' is possible ; and no doubt there are other possibilities.
313-6 This passage is a mere *jam* of ellipses, &c.—expansible, but perhaps not
worth expanding.

A Happy Husband

Religious men do still fear God for love,
The superstitious, lest they torments prove.
Let thy Mate be a man, whose settled faith
In true Religion sure foundation hath:
For 'twixt those bodies love doth best reside,
Whose souls no self-opinions do divide :
The four chief Virtues next in order go,
From which the rest as from four fountains flow ; 350
Prudence the first place hath, to see and choose,
Which is so needful, and of so great use,
That with it weighty things do seem but light,
Without it nothing can be done of weight ;
By it things even 'gainst Nature are achieved,
A wise mind gains what many hands hath grieved.
Just he must be himself first to command,
For sensual things at *Reason's* Law must stand,
The *Spirit's* power keeps the *Passions* still in awe,
And strictly bounds them with an austere Law, 360
With *Moderation* it guides our desires
(We must not all condemn Nature requires)
To love things neat and needful, base things hate.
It's wantonness to live too delicate :
But it's mere madness to condemn the things
Which needful use, and common custom brings.
Next, to his Neighbour he that right must do

Which he expects, (freely, not forc'd thereto ;)
Whom Law constrains, they falsify all trust,
It's conscience, not constraint, that makes men just. 370
As just, so valiant would I have him be,
Not out of rashness or stupidity,
It is a constant patient resolution
Of bashless *Courage* 'gainst the revolution
Of times and fortunes : it regards not pains,
Where *Honour* is the Hire, *Glory* the gains :
It's sensible careful man's self to save,
Not daring offer wrong, more than receive.
As *Prudent, Just,* and *Valiant,* so he must
Be *Temperate,* this *virtue* hath foul lust, 380
And pleasure for its object : it commands,
Laps, and reforms our sensual thoughts ; it stands
'Twixt a desire, and dullness of our nature,
And is the spurrer on, or the abater
Of ill or good, shamefast in refusing
Things filthy, honest in things comely choosing.
Though with perfection these no one man fits,
Yet let him be free from their opposites :
He must be sober, not given to excess,
It cures, and keeps in health, *mind* it doth dress ; 390
Making it pure, and capable of good,
Mother, and good counsel is the Brood :
Excess doth dull the spirits, and breeds disease,
So after punish'd by what first did please.

362 I have shifted the bracket from ' condemn ' to ' requires.'
385 One might suggest ' is ' before ' shamefast.'

Learn'd let him be, his learning
general,
Profound in none, yet have some
skill in all ;
Who's deeply learn'd,' his Book is
most his Wife,
Conversing still with it, so of his Life
His Wife not half enjoys, for most
is spent
In study, so what should yield most
content,   400
Society's debarr'd ; I do wish then
Who are mere Scholars, may live
single men :
Learning besots the weak and feeble
mind ;
But polishes the strong, and well
inclin'd :
The one *Vain-glory* puffs with self-
conceit,
The other's brain is settled *Judge-
ment's* seat.
Then so learn'd let him be, as he
may choose
Flowers of best Books, whose sweet
scent he may use
To rectify his knowledge, and distil
From thence life-blessing precepts,
which so will   410
Temper his understanding, that the
frown
Of fickle *Fortune* never shall cast
down.
Not bold in speech, no man of many
words
Choose thou a Husband, leafy tree
affords
The smallest store of fruit : *Both
words and deeds
Seldom or never from one man
proceeds.*
Who guides his words, he in a word
is wise :
Yet let him not be sullenly precise,
But gentle, pleasing, not crabbèd, or
tart,
The wise man's tongue is ever in his
heart ;   420
The fool's heart's in his tongue : *it
is great gain*

For to be silent, and one's self contain ;
And see with whomsoever he
converse,
(Lest he be thought ill-nurtur'd, or
perverse)
That he be kind, obsequious,
affable ;
To fit himself unto their humours,
able
*To change condition with the time,
and place,
Is wisdom, and such levity doth grace :*
So Aristippus each face, each
behaviour
Did still become, and was a gracing
favour.   430
Choose thou a Husband older by
some years
Then thou thyself art, Man age
better bears
Then Women : for bearing of child-
ren makes
Their strength decay, soon beauty
them forsakes :
*Many crops make a field soon to be
bare,
Where that that bears not long con-
tinues fair.*
Now, Lady, such a man I wish you
find,
As here I have describ'd, with whom
to bind
Yourself, is to be blest, leading
a life
Full of content, free from conten-
tious strife.   440

A Wife's behaviour.

BUT to find good, is not enough to
show,
But having found him, how to keep
him so ;
Then since I have advis'd you how
to choose him,
I will give some advice how you
should use him.
Obedience first thy will to his must
fit,
(He is the pilot that must govern it)
It man condemns of inability,

A Happy Husband

When women rule, that are born to
  obey:
Nor is it honour to her, but a
  shame
To be match'd with one only man
  in name: 450
But if imperious he should more
  desire
Than due respect doth of a *Wife*
  require,
Think not harsh stubbornness will
  e'er procure him
To be more mild (it rather will
  obdure him);
The whip and lash the angry horse
  enrages,
Mild voice and gentle stroke his ire
  assuages:
From steel-struck flint we see the
  lightning flies,
But struck 'gainst wool, the flashing
  flame none spies;
Nor is the clangour heard: the one's
  soft nature
Is to the other's hardness an aba-
  ture.   460
Win thou thy mate with mildness:
  for each cross
Answer'd with anger, is to both
  a loss:
Like as the sea which 'gainst a
  churlish rock
Breaks braving billows with a bois-
  t'rous stroke,
Seeking by raging force to throw
  on sands
The stiff resisting rock, which
  unmov'd stands,
Repelling his bold billows with like
  scorn,
As th' others' bravery had bounced
  them beforne;
Thus both still strive, and striving
  are o'ercome,
The rock is worn, the billow's crush'd
  in foam: 470
Whereas the sea calmly the sand
  embraces,
And with smooth forehead lovingly
  it graces:

Being content that it should bound
  his shore,
Yielding to mildness where force
  fail'd before.
So let thy mildness win thy Husband
  to it,
If that do not, then nothing else will
  do it:
Beware you (willing) to no anger
  move him,
If he perceive't, he cannot think you
  love him:
If anger once begin twixt man and wife,
If soon not reconcil'd, it turns to
  strife: 480
Which still will stir on every light
  occasion,
What might have ceas'd in silence;
  then persuasion
Of friends will hardly end: *for every*
  jar
Is ominous presaging life-long war:
And where two join'd do jar, their
  state decays,
They go not forward, who draw
  divers ways,
Being yoked together: your first care
  must be,
That with your husband you in love
  agree.
As far from fondness be, as from
  neglect,
Mixing affection with a staid re-
  spect: 490
If toying fondness were man's only
  aim,
Not reason, but his lust should choose
  his dame;
Where whores lascivious, that can
  ways invent,
Should equalize thee, nay, give more
  content:
No, these are not the joys he hopes
  to find,
The body not so much he weds, as
  mind.
Be never fond, nor without cause
  unkind,
These are the fruits of an inconstant
  mind:

Thou must not if his fortunes do
   decline,
Be discontented, or seem to repine,
But bear a constant countenance,
   not dismayed,   501
As if you were of misery afraid :
His fortunes you must good or bad
   abide,
With chains of mutual love, together
   tied.
The loss of that which blindfold
   chance doth give,
Cannot a worthy generous mind
   aggrieve :
For it will never take it for a cross,
Which cannot make one wicked by its
   loss,
Nor by the gaining good. Both fool
   and knave
Are often rich : if such afflictions
   have,   510
They drive them to despair ; but
   draw the wise,
With elevated thoughts, such things
   despise.
Seneca saith, the gods did take
   delight
To see grave Cato with his fate to
   fight :
O ! what should we, whose hopes
   do higher rise,
If heathens thus could worldly things
   despise ?
Affliction oft doth mount the wiser
   high,
Joseph and Job rose by adversity :
It's sign of a weak mind to be
   dejected
For worldly loss (such never are
   respected).   520
If thou wouldst not be irksome
   to thy mate,
Be cheerful, not succumbing with
   his fate :
Yet if that anguish doth afflict his
   mind,
You must not seem so from the
   world refin'd
As to disdain what human cross
   brings forth,

Pride to be singular, that is not
   worth :
Nay, thou must be a mirror, to
   reflect
Thy husband's mind : for as is his
   aspect,
So should be thine. Pale Phoebe
   yields no light,
When th' interpos'd earth bars her
   Phoebus' sight :   530
But when no object intercepts his
   streams,
She decks herself with light-rebat-
   ing beams.
Even so as is thy husband's joy, or
   pain,
So must thy joy and sorrow wax
   or wane :
Be not too curious in his ways to
   pry,
Suspicion still makes the suspected
   try
Jealousy's fear : for why should she
   suspect
That knows herself guilty of no
   defect ?
If he perceive thee of thyself de-
   spair,
He will think sweeter joys are other-
   where,   540
Which thou dost want ; so thou
   thyself shalt give
The first occasion to what may
   thee grieve :
Thy own desert must him unto thee
   bind,
Desert doth make a savage to be
   kind :
It is an adamantine chain to
   knit
Two souls so fast, nought can them
   disunite ;
Where that most sweet communion
   of the minds
Save each in other, no contentment
   finds ;
And whatsoever the one touches
   near,
Jealous, the other ne'er conceals
   for fear.   550

Brutus his honour (dearer priz'd than life)
Concredited to Portia his wife;
What fear from dearest friends caus'd him conceal,
Worth and desert made him to her reveal.
Great Caesar's death, and who his consorts were,
With their designs, he did impart to her;
Nor is their birth, or beauty of such might,
To alienate their hearts, or give delight:
Who had more beauty than that captiv'd Queen,
The fair Statira, when in grief was seen   560
The pearly hail blasting her beauty-fields,
Which seemliness even cloth'd in sorrow yields?
Being grac'd with modesty, and unstain'd faith,
More force still fairness with such fellows hath:
Yet could not her fair beauty move the thought
Of Alexander (though less fair have brought
Oft captains to be captives), nor her state
(She being married) did affection bate:
For then her virgin daughter yet unstain'd,
(Whose beauty all comparison disdain'd,   570
Going her lovely mother so before,
As she did all the rest of Asia's store)
Should quickly have entangled his desire,
Whose heart all one, Roxane's love did fire:

For if proportion, colour, wealth, or birth,
Could have captiv'd the Monarch of the Earth;
These should have won: but he did her prefer,
Whose only merits pleaded *love* for her.
Deserve then not in show, but from the heart,
Love is perpetuated by desert.   580
As it befits not man for to embrace
Domestic charge, so it's not woman's place
For to be busied with affairs abroad:
For that weak sex it is too great a load,
And it's unseemly, and doth both disgrace,
When either doth usurp the other's place:
Leave his to him, and of thine own take charge,
Care thou at home, and let him care at large:
Thou hast enough thyself for to employ
Within doors, 'bout thy house and huswifery: 590
Remember that it's said of *Lucrece* chaste,
When some dames wantoniz'd, others took rest,
She with her maidens first her task would end,
E're she would sleep: she did not idle spend
Swift-running *Time*, nor gave alluring pleasure
The least advantage, to make any seizure
On her rare virtues. *A soul vacant still*
Is soon seduc'd to do good or ill:
For like perpetual motion is the mind,
In action still, while to this flesh confined;   600

552 Concredited] This rare English derivation from the not unclassical *concredo* might have been made common with advantage, for it expresses in one word what requires a long periphrasis without it.
590 huswifery] I keep this as well as ' housewifery.'

(From which soul-prison it takes
 often stains,
For absolutely good no man remains.)
Employ'd if not 'bout good, about
 some ill,
Producing fruits which do discover
 still
How it is labour'd like a fertile field,
Which fruit, or weeds abundantly
 doth yield,
As it is manur'd ; be not idle then,
Nor give vice time to work upon
 thy brain
Imagined ill : for what it there
 conceives,
It oft brings out, and in dishonour
 leaves :   610
*The purest things are easiest to be
 stain'd,
And it's soon lost which carefully
 was gain'd.*
Penelope did wheel and distaff
 handle,
And her day's work undid at night
 by candle ;
Nor labour-forcing need compell'd
 that task,
Which toiling days, and tedious
 nights did ask :
(For she was Queen of Ithacke)
 'twas her name,
Which virtuous care kept spotless,
 free from blame ;
One of so many suitors of each sort,
As for her love did to her Court
 resort,   620
Not speeding, would have spoke
 that might her stain,
*(The greatest hate, when love turns
 to disdain.)*
If colour could have made their
 knavery stronger,
But Envy could not find a way to
 wrong her.
Be thou as these, careful of house-
 wifery,
With *Providence* what's needful still
 supply ;
Look thy Maids be not idle, nor yet
 spend

Things wastingly : for they so oft
 offend,
When careless is the Mistress ; yet
 with need
Ne'er pinch them, nor yet let them
 e'er exceed :   630
The one doth force them seek thee
 to betray,
The other makes them wanton, and
 too gay ;
It is no shame to look to every
 thing,
The Mistress' eye doth ever profit
 bring.
Salomon saith, *the good Wife seeks
 for flax
And wool, wherewith her hands glad
 travail takes :
She's like a ship that bringeth bread
 from far,
She rises ere appear the morning
 Star ;
Victuals her household, gives her
 maidens food,
Surveys, and buys a field, plants
 vines, with good   640
Gain'd by her hands : what merchan-
 dise is best
She can discern, nor doth she go to
 rest
When Phoebus hides his head, and
 bars his sight,
But by her lamp, her hands do take
 delight'
To touch the wheel and spindle ; she
 doth stretch
Her hand to help the poor and needy
 wretch :
Her words are wisdom, she o'ersees
 her train
That idle none do eat their bread in
 vain ;
Her children rise and bless her, sweet
 delight
Her husband takes still in her happy
 sight.*   650
Be thou this careful goodwife, for to
 lend
Thy helping hand, thy husband's
 means to mend.

Last, let thy conversation be with such,
As foul-mouth'd malice can with no crime touch :
I cannot but condemn such as delight
Still to be sad and sullen in the sight
Of their own husbands, as they were in fear,
(*Sure guilty of some crime such women are*)
But when they gossip it with other wives
Of their own cut, then they have merry lives, 660
Spending, and plotting how they may deceive
Their husbands, rule themselves, and mastery have ;
O let such women (for they make-bates be
'Twixt man and wife) never consort with thee :
But shun them, as thou dost see one that's fair
Flee the small pox ; both like infectious are.
The grave, staid, blameless, and religious dames,
Whose carriage hath procur'd them honest names,
Are fit companions ; let such be thy mates,

When wearied with affairs, thou recreates 670
Thyself with harmless mirth : yet do not walk
Often abroad, that will occasion talk ;
Though thou hast store of friends, yet let none be
(Saving thy husband) counsellor to thee :
He 's nearest to thee, and it will endear him,
He is thyself, thou needest not to fear him :
Be free with him, and tell him all thy thought,
It's he must help, when thou hast need of ought ;
And constantly believe he'll love thee best,
When he sees thou preferr'st him 'fore the rest. 680
Thus, lady, have I show'd you how to chuse
A worthy mate, and how you should him use ;
So choose, so use, so shall you all your life
Be in a Husband blest, he in a Wife ;
And when death here shall end your happy days,
Your souls shall reign in heaven, on earth your praise.

FINIS

654 touch] Orig. 'tutch.'

ELEGIES

ON THE

DEATH OF OUR LATE SOVEREIGN

QUEEN ANNE

WITH

EPITAPHS

To the most Noble Prince Charles

*Disdain not, Sir, this offering which
    I make,
Although the incense smoke doth tower
    so black ;
Nor think my fires faint, 'cause they
    darkly shine,*
Tapers burn dim, are set before a
    shrine.
*Some better hap to have their first
    fruit glad,
This Common woe masques mine in
    mourning shade :
And 's strange, You (solely left for our
    relief)
For salve, do prove a cor'sive to our
    grief :
Weigh what is it to add to those
    opprest.*

*Then by Your woe, ours shall not be
    increast :* 10
*I grant, nor Son nor Subject good,
    can smother
Grief, for so great, and good, a Queen
    and Mother.
Yet moderate this sorrow ; as you're seen
To use in joy, so use in grief a mean,
O'ermatch thy matchless self, that all
    may see
Her courage, worth and love, do live
    in Thee :
Then may this pen, which with tears
    draws my plaint,
In gold Thy glorious actions after
    paint.*
Your Highness' most humble servant,
    Patrick Hannay.

The First Elegy [1]

As doth a Mother, who before her
    eyes,
Her age's hope, her only Son espies
Butcher'd, and bathing still in bloody
    strands,
Ravish'd with sudden grief amazèd
    stands ;
Nor weeps, nor sighs, nor lets one
    tear distil,
But (with fix'd eye) still gazeth on her
    ill :
But when with time her smothered
    grief forth vents,
She wastes her eyes in tears, her
    breath in plaints :
So we astonish'd could not tell our
    woe ;
*Who do grieve most, least signs of
    grief do show,* 10

Yet time to those, in time, a time
    affords,
To weep and wail, and show their woe
    in words.
Time grant us now in time, lest of
    her praise
Our offspring hearing, and when
    her swift days
Had run their course, they hear none
    of our plaints,
Do either think some Poet's pen her
    paints,
Or that they are of the same stones
    all sprung,
Which backward Pyrrha and Deuca-
    lion flung.
So that will seem no fable, but a story,
If we do leave no witness that we're
    sorry, 20

---

[1] This poem, in the original (as well as its companion) is a sort of debauch of italics, which the poet or his printer has showered on every line, for the most part with no discoverable excuse of emphasis or anything else. They have been most trouble-some to alter : but unaltered they would have been still more troublesome to read.

Each senseless thing shall us upbraid
  to them,
And as less sensible (than they)
  condemn :
Since in each object offer'd to the
  eye,
Signs of sad sorrow settled there we
  see :
The Heavens (tho' grac'd with her)
  for us are griev'd,
And weep in showers for that we
  are bereav'd
Of her : in, and for whom the World
  was blest,
In whom her kind's perfection did
  consist.
Aquarius seems to have a solemn
  feast,
And that each other sign's his house-
  hold guest.   30
Not one of them now influence down-
  pours,
But what distils in liquid weeping
  showers.
The Skies of Clouds now make
  them mourning weeds,
And general darkness all the world
  o'erspreads :
What? hath the Sun for a new
  Phaeton
Abandonèd the Heavens, and
  beamy throne?
Is the cause theirs? or doth it touch
  us nigh?
(Since with their sorrow we so
  sympathy :)
No, it's because our Cynthia left
  this sphere,
The world wears black, because she
  moves not here :   40
Her influence that made it freshly
  flourish,
Leaves it to fade, and will no more
  it nourish.
Leaves it? hath left. How can it
  then subsist?
Can that be said to be, which,
  dispossest

Of soul, wants vigour? this Queen
  was the soul,
Whose faculties world's frailties did
  control ;
Corrected the ill humours, and
  maintain'd
In it a wholesome concord, while
  she reign'd :
But now (she gone) the world seems
  out of frame,
Subord'nate passions now as Princes
  claim   50
Seignory o'er the soul, which do
  torment
The whole with anguish ; make the
  heart to faint,
Whose sad infection generally's so
  spread,
Grief's character on every brow is
  read.
Our eyes so drop (wer't not God
  frees those fears)
The world might dread a new deluge
  of tears.
Dread? (thus distress'd) we rather
  should desire
With the world's dissolution to
  expire
Our latest woes, 'twere better have
  no being,
Than live in woe, so as we are still
  dying.   60
Leave foolish passion, dares thou
  thus repine
'Gainst what's enacted by the powers
  divine?
Humbly submit, yet passion were a
  word,
Useless, a nothing's name, speech
  should afford
No place for it, if it should not now
  show
It's being by our grieving in this
  woe :
Yet the woe's short, which on each
  soul hath seiz'd,
It and the cause can ne'er be
  equaliz'd :

38] Note 'sympathy' as a verb.
the second person. Cf. *A Happy Husband*, l. 670.

61 dares] Hannay often uses this form for

I will not blaze her birth, descent or State,
Her princely progeny, her royal mate : 70
They are known best, and greatest, yet these are
But accidental honours : but this star
With proper beams was so resplendent here,
Others (though bright) yet when she did appear,
Did lose their lustre : she honour'd her place,
Her place not her : she Queen, was Queen's sole grace.
'Twas she the Antique Poets so admir'd,
When with prophetic fury they inspir'd,
Did feign the heavenly powers they did see,
(As in a dream) that such a one should be : 80
And for each several grace, she should contain,
One Deity they did for that ordain,
Not one for all, for that too much had been,
To feign her like, whose like was never seen.
Nor is their number equal to her merits,
For she afar off was show'd to those spirits ;
Now had they liv'd her virtues to have seen,
The Goddesses sure numberless had been,
But's well they did not, for then she should be
(Though guiltless) yet cause of Idolatry, 90
For they who honourèd her shade before,
Seeing her substance needs must it adore.
The Moralists did all of her divine,
When they made every virtue feminine ;

And but they knew that such a one should be,
Doubtless with them virtue should have been HE.
Peruse all stories are compil'd by Man,
Or Poets' fictions since the world began,
You shall not find (true or imaginary)
Like worth in one, whose all in nought doth vary. 100
Nay, take the abjects in these books revil'd
For basest parts, so vicious and defil'd,
As they seem Nature's monsters, made in scorn,
As foils, her other fair works to adorn,
(*Contrar's oppos'd do others best set forth*)
They serve not all, to parallel her worth.
They are deceiv'd, who say the world decays,
And still grows worse and worse, as old with days :
For then this Age could never that have shown
Which was long since to *Salomon* unknown, 110
A woman : but had he lived in our times,
He might have found one so devoid of crimes,
That her own merits (if merits could save)
Might justly (as of due) salvation crave.
I rather think the world's first infancy
Growing more perfect with antiquity,
(As younglings do) travail'd till now at height,
Big of perfection, brought this birth to light :
This second to that Maiden-Mother-Daughter,
She only was before, this only after : 120

For on this Grace and Nature spent
  such store,
As after her we need expect none
  more.
And those who read her praise
  when we are gone,
Would think we but describ'd a
  worthy one,
Not that there was one such, but
  that she here
Left part of her, which and its seed
  shall bear
Successive witness to all doubtful
  ages,
Of her rare virtues, which in those
  dear pledges
Still live : they'll say our praise came
  short, we dull,
With speech defective, could not to
  the full   130
Set forth her worth, which she at death
  did give :
Others may goods, not goodness' off-
  spring, leave.
But she bequeath'd her goodness,
  for her merit
Obtain'd her issue should that
  wealth inherit,
Which we possess in them, while
  they do prease
(As usurers) that stock still to
  increase :
Only ambitious to augment that store,
Robbing the world, which either is
  but poor,
Or seems so, set by them, beggars
  may boast,
But they alone have all that wealth
  ingrossed :   140
And though that God the world's
  gold hath refined,
And took the tried, He left this vein
  behind,
Pity'ng the dross the lustre should
  obscure,
Of her bright soul, while flesh did it
  immure.

Yet did He not with it of all bereave
  us,
But with her offspring, happiness
  did leave us.
For her preferment, why then should
  we toss
Our souls with torment ? or grieve
  that our loss
Hath Heaven enrich'd ? or 'cause
  we held her dear,
Wish we her punished, to be living
  here ?   150
We rather should rejoice she thus
  did leave us,
And nought but Heaven alone of
  her could reave us.
O ! since that Cedar fell so right at
  last,
Which way it standing lean'd, may
  well be guessed.
And since the End doth crown the
  actions still,
How lived she, who dying, died so
  well !
For asked, if she did willing hence
  depart,
Said (rapt with heavenly joy) WITH
  ALL MY HEART.
Though flesh be frail, yet hers so
  void of fear
(For Death did not in his own shape
  appear)   160
Did entertain so kindly its own foe,
(Who came to Court, but un'wares
  killed her so)
As she esteem'd it only one hard
  thrust
At that strait gate by which to life we
  must :
Faith, Hope, and *Love* possess'd her
  heart and mind,
Leaving no place for fearful thoughts
  to find :
Troops of white Angels did her bed
  impale,
To tend the soul's flight from the
  fleshly jail,

135 'prease' = ' press.'
167 impale] Orig. ' impaile,' in the sense apparently of ' surround like a paling.'
168 jail] Orig. ' gaile.'

It to conduct unto that heavenly
throne,
Which Christ prepared, with glore
to crown her on.   170
O ! how my flesh-clogg'd soul would
scale the sky,
And leave that dear companion here
to lie,
To see her entertain'd, with glory
crown'd,
While troops of Angels her arrival
sound
To that new kingdom : they all God
do praise
For her translation, and their voices
raise,
In sign of joy, but yet that joy
comes short
Of what they make for most to them
resort,
For, for the greater sinner, Christ
hath said,
That doth repent, the greater joy is
made :   180
Yet that's made up in glore, for she
so far
Doth those exceed, as one another
star :
What may we think unto her soul is
shown,
When from her baser part such
virtues flown
As a sad reverent fear their senses
pierce,
Who sighing see her sorrow-suited
hearse :
What would they do, if their veil'd
soul could spy
Her sitting crown'd above the starry
sky ?
Sure they would do (nay in their
hearts they do)
Even at the thought thereof with
reverence bow.   190
But leave to speak, nay, not so much
as think,
Least of those joys which ne'er in
heart could sink.
Let's not envy her, but inveigh 'gainst
our Fate,

That we behind her are staid here
so late :
And let 's not mourn for her, that
she 's gone hence,
But for ourselves, that we are kept
from thence
Whither she 's gone : yet let no tear
o'erflow,
(*Sorrow soon ceaseth that's disburd'ned
so*)
Let them strain inward, if they'll
needs distil,
And with their drops thy heart's sad
centre fill,   200
And when it's full, it can no more
contain,
Let the cask break, and drown thee
in that main.

On the Queen

The World's a Sea of errors, all must
pass,
Where shelves and sands the purling
billow blinds :
Men's bodies are frail barks of brittle
glass,
Which still are toss'd with adverse
tides and winds,
Reason's the Pilot that the course
directs,
Which makes the vessel (as it's hight)
hold out.
Passions are partners, a still-jarring
rout :
Succumbing thoughts are life-invading
leaks.
How built her body ! such a voyage
made ;
·How great her reason ! which so
rightly sway'd ;   10
How pliant passions ! which so well
obey'd ;
How dauntless thoughts, vain doubts
durst ne'er invade.
Her body, reason, passions, thoughts
did 'gree,
To make her life the Art to sail
this Sea.

The Second Elegy

EACH Country now contributes to the
  Thames,
Which a support of every current
  claims :
Why dost thou so, sweet *Thames* ?
  Is not thy sorrow
Sufficient for thyself, but thou must
  borrow ?
Or wants thy waters worth for such
  a charge,
As to conduct Great ANNE'S last
  body'd barge ?
Or is it 'cause so just and kind thou
  art,
Thou'lt not encroach that, wherein
  each hath part ?
Sure that's the cause ; the loss is
  general,
And that last Office must be help'd
  by all.   10
Yet wonder not they come not now
  so sweet,
As they do use, when they to solace
  meet :
They're not themselves, they are com-
  pounded things,
For every one his latest off'ring
  brings,
And sends it by these brooks, unto
  Her Shrine,
Whose waters with their tears are
  turnèd brine :
Each subject's cheek such falling
  drops distain,
As if to dew, sighs had dissolv'd
  the brain :
Which from their eyes still in abun-
  dance pour,
Like a moist hail, or liquid pearly
  shower :   20
Which in such haste, each one an-
  other chases,
Making swift torrents in late torrid
  places,
Disgorging in these brooks, making
  them rise,

So's sovereign *Thames* almost fear
  a surprise :
Fear not (fair Queen) it is not their
  ambition,
But swelling sorrow, that breeds thy
  suspicion :
Its sorrow feeds those currents and
  those rills,
Which thy vast channel with an
  ocean fills,
Which eye-bred humour so hath
  chang'd thy nature,
Thy fishes think they live not in thy
  water :   30
It or their taste is alter'd, for they
  think
For thy sweet streams they briny
  liquor drink :
How wearied is thy Sister, famous
  Forth,
Bringing sad Scotland's sorrows
  from the North ;
Who comes not out of duty, as the
  rest
Who unto *Thames* their careful
  course addrest ;
She comes, her equal will not yield
  in tears,
In subject's sorrows nor in country's
  cares.
Great *Neptune's* self doth fear
  invasive wrong,
Seeing her strange waves through his
  waters throng ;   40
And causeth *Triton* to found an
  alarm
To warn the Sea-Gods in all haste to
  arm ;
Who bringing billows in brave battle-
  'ray,
Do mean *Forth's* fury with their force
  to stay :
But when they see her thus all wrapt
  in woe,
And the sad cause of her just sorrow
  know ;
They lay not their defensive arms
  aside,
But as a guard, her through their
  gulfs do guide ;

The Second Elegy

Striving with all the pleasures of the Main,
This grieving stranger-*Queen* to entertain, 50
Out through their bowers of clear transparent waves,
Crystalline-wainscot pearl the bottom paves :
Her they conduct, and to abate her woe,
Their Sea-delights and riches all they show,
Which *Neptune* (now in love) would gladly give her
For love, yet dares not offer lest he grieve her ;
Who loves and would not have his love unkind,
Must woo a pleasant humour, vacant mind :
This makes him stay his suit, and strive to please
With all the love-allurements of the Seas. 60
Yet all do not so much as move one smile,
An anxious sorrow soon discover'th guile ;
Yet he will guide and guard her grieving streams,
Whom at her entry in the wishèd *Thames*
He leaves, and vows in discontent to mourn ;
Till fairest *Forth* back to the Sea return,
Her sister her receives with kind embrace,
Their liquid arms clasping, they interlace
In love so straight, they cannot be untwined,
They seem both one, in body and in mind. 70
O happy *union!* labour'd long in vain,
Reserv'd by God to James his joyful reign,
And *Anne's* ; O blessed couple, so esteem'd

By all fore-knowing Jove, that He them deem'd
Worthy each other, and to wear that Gem,
Blest *Britain's* now united-Diadem.
He esteem'd none worthy to wear't before them,
But kept it still in store, for to decore them.
How did He suffer those two Kingdoms try
All open power and private policy, 80
Yet still increasèd discord, other's force
Made separation greater, sued divorce.
How did one tear the other, spare no toil,
To bath[e] in blood the neighbour's fertile soil ;
Wrath, discord, malice, envy, rapine, strife,
Thefts, rapes, and murderous mischiefs were so rife,
None liv'd secure, while each King did protect
The other's fugitives, (for his respect)
Thus looking for no rest, or end of hate,
But with the ruin of the adverse State. 90
God, He effects it (that to Him alone
We might ascribe the honour ; and being one,
We might love better : '*Twixt united foes,*
And separated friends, love and hate grows
To greatest heights :) And for this end doth raise,
(Using the means) the honour of his days.
Great JAMES, the joy-presaging Northern Star,
Whose radiant light illuminates so far,
As it doth warm with its all-quick'ning beams
The frozen love betwixt the *Tay* and *Thames ;* 100

59, 60] A couplet nearly as early as Waller's earliest of the same style.

(703)

With wonder and delight, drawing
    all hearts
And eyes, to love and see his Princely
    parts.
And (what is strange) who hated
    most before,
With admiration, most his worth
    adore,
Wishing they were his subjects : He
    is King
Already of their hearts ; the poison'd
    sting
Of rancour is remov'd, for love they
    call him,
And with their Kingdom's ornaments
    instal him.
Great confidence his virtuous life
    must bring,
Whom, such old foes, love forces
    make their King.   110
Where was e'er heard, of emulating
    foes,
(Rooted in hate with others, over-
    throws
Such and so long) that did their
    wrath appease,
And yield (won but by love) to right,
    as these ?
Yet do they not repent, they find
    report
Sometime is wrong'd, and may in-
    deed come short
In commendations ; yet it's rare (as
    here)
For she's a woman, and (by kind)
    will bear
More than she should : but his last
    subjects find
Themselves with *Saba's Queen* of
    self-same mind,   120
That fame (though saying by belief)
    had wrong'd
Two Kings, not telling half to each
    that long'd.
For *England* heard not, nor could
    it have thought,
That *Scotland's king* such wonders
    could have wrought.
Long may he live, and die well, full
    of years,

And when his death shall draw us
    dry with tears,
On *Britain's* throne may his seed
    ever reign,
Till *Christ* do come (to judge the
    world) again.
Who would have thought from the
    Scot-hated Dane,
Whom vanquish'd England so much
    did disdain,   130
(Oppress'd with base subjection) they
    did turn,
(Being freed) *Lord-dane* to *lurdane*
    for a scorn ;
Who would have thought (I say) from
    Dane should spring
One, who from *Scots* and *English*
    eyes should wring
Such hearty tears ; must not her
    worth be much,
Since we do find its love-effects prove
    such,
How great that worth (in such, such
    love could breed) ?
O let it live for ever in her seed :
And let that love in our hearts never die,
But ever live to her Posterity :   140
And those sweet streams her mate
    and she combined
In love, O let their arms be ne'er
    untwined
From kind embraces, and though
    now their greetings
Be not so joyful as at other meetings ;
Yet is their love all one, they take
    one part,
The one joys not, the other sad at
    heart :
They surfeit now in sorrow, then in
    pleasure ;
Joy then exceeds, grief now is above
    measure.
To honour *Charles* (our hope) when
    they met last,
How did they rob each meadow as
    they past,   150
Of sweets, each bank a posy did be-
    stow,
Of fairest flowers, that on his brim
    did grow :

These and such like, they brought from every part,
And gratulations from each subject's heart :
They swell'd with pride, rising in lofty waves,
And all the neighbour bord'ring banks outbraves :
Their fishes frolick'd, showing joy by gesture,
The waters (wantonizing) woo'd their Master ;
So fast their billows 'bout his blest barge throng'd,
They hurt themselves oft, oft their fellows wrong'd :   160
Each would be first, on others' backs some ride,
Some under others' slipp'ry shoulders slide,
Though beat with oars, yet will they not turn back,
For they their humble prostrate homage make :
The Sun then gilt each glistring glassy coat
Those marine-masquers wore, danc'd 'bout his boat,
Who by the music measur'd not their paces ;
Deaf'd with a confus'd cry from divers places,
Of maidens, matrons, aged men and boys,
Which from each quarter made a confus'd noise   170
Of hearty *Aves,* welcoming their Prince,
Echo (with answering tir'd) was mute still since.
The City with the suburbs did appear
Like a large Theatre when he came near :
Each window, wall, each turret-top and steeple,
Was fill'd with every age, sex, sort of people :

So as some thought (who erst had never seen
Such numbers) that the buildings all had been
Of Imag'ry contriv'd, by cunning Art :
For on the ground, the brewer in his cart,   180
The sculler, carman, and the baser sort,
Seem'd strong and rudely carv'd clowns, to support
The stately frame : maids, prentices and grooms,
Made shop-door, window-stale, and lower rooms :
The battlements, house-coverings and the leads,
As tiles or slates, young boys and girls o'erspreads.
The middle rooms all round about the *Thames,*
Which ladies held, and choicer city dames,
Such took for spaces, which fair statues held,
Where carver and the painter both excell'd ;   190
So pure complexions these seem'd made by Art,
As *Nature* never did the like impart
To lovely youth ; the large, low, open breast,
Full, white, round, swelling, azure-vein'd, increast
The error, for they thought none living would
Lay out such parts, for all eyes to behold :
So curious were the colours which were shown,
As *Nature* hardly could from *Art* be known :
So that they could adjudge them due to neither,
But participles, taking part of either ;   200

184 stale] in the sense of 'sill.' It occurs dialectically as 'stool,' &c., and is of course a form of 'stall.'

Yet all by voice and gesture seemèd glad,
Wonder it was to see a thing look sad.
Now it's not so, the off'rings are but tears,
The sighs and groans of *Britain's* blest-reft sheres
Are now the acclamations; these two streams,
Compounded waters of mix'd sorrow seems;
Yet walk *they* hand in hand with equal pace,
T'wards that late pleasant, but now pensive place
Where sorrow suited in a sable weed,
Doth with a mourning veil each heart o'erspread,   210
And *Phoebus* for to make the world and mind
To wear one livery all his beams confin'ed,
Dimming each eye in darkness of the night,
Either asham'd to mourn in open sight,
Or loath to alter with his brighter streams,
Our late obscurèd *Cynthia's* lesser gleams;
For her fled soul which doth with glory shine,
Left with its lodging something that's divine,
Which with reflection smileth on these rays,
Which her bright soul now from the skies displays.   220
And these light orbs which with such swiftness roll
About the Heavens, acquainted with her soul

To light her corpse do set in every porch
Of the damantine *Heaven*, a starry torch,
Which dark'ned with the weeping Earth's moist vapours,
Are her last lamps and never-dying tapers.
Thames trembles, *Forth* doth feverize for fear,
Both roar to see their sovereign thus appear:
Their billows break their hearts against the shore.
Their fishes faint (yet cannot tell wherefore),   230
But when they float upon the water crop,
And see the tears from eyes and oars which drop,
They think them all too few, and add their own
And swim in proper *waters* (erst unknown);
The water-Nymphs now round about her boat,
Cloth'd in sad sable mourning habits float,
The Hamadryads, and the Silvans all
To bear a part in this complaint they call,
Who since her death had practis'd in their tears,
Streams deep enough: none now the water fears.   240
They brought with them sweet camomile and rue,
Mint, spikenard, marjoram, her way they strew,
With flowers of choicest colour and of scent,
Which from the slender weeping stalk was rent.

---

204 'blest-reft'='bl*iss*-reft'? Of 'shere' for 'shore' I do not know any other instance; but it is etymologically defensible, and the form 'shear' is actually used in senses very close. Of course it *may* be for 'shire,' not 'shore.'

224 'damantine' for 'adamantine,' if H. wrote it, is a particularly agreeable instance of the almost insane terror of hiatus or trisyllabic foot—for it happens to reverse the meaning.

231 'crop' for 'top' is quite conceivable.

The Second Elegy

Her Exequies these Nymphs together sing,
Till with this consort, Heaven and Earth doth ring :
Heaven's envying our waters, walks, and woods,
Hath 'reft our joy, and plac'd her 'mongst the Gods.
No more our wand'ring waves shall wantonize,
No more shall swelling billows brave the skies, 250
No more shall purling *Zephyr* curl our head,
No more we'll foamy powders thereon spread,
No more shall now Meandrian walks delight us,
No more Despair with Death shall now affright us,
Since Heaven envying our late happy floods,
Hath 'reft our joy, and plac'd her 'mongst the Gods.
We'll take no sport now to pursue the fawn,
We'll no more tread light measures on the lawn,
We'll deck our heads no more with *Flora's* flowers,
We'll woo no more our woody paramours, 260

We'll bear no part hereafter with the birds,
We'll weep for woe, and teach them wail in words ;
Since Heaven envying our late happy woods,
Hath 'reft our joy, and plac'd her 'mongst the Gods.
We'll hide our heads within our shores and shelves,
We'll dwell in darkest cypress groves with elves,
No more we'll solace in great *Neptune's* halls,
No more we'll dance at *Sylvan's* festivals,
Because she's gone, whose glory grac'd our floods,
Because she's gone, who honour'd walks and woods. 270
Thus sung they her along, but come to shore,
Where she must leave them, they ne'er see her more ;
They sink to bottom, either in a swoon,
Or else themselves (now loathing life) to drown ;
The *Forth* and *Thames* losing their so lov'd sight,
Vow, yearly to renew their woes, that night.

An Epitaph

Power to do ill, and practise only good,
Humblest in heart, highest in place and blood,
Fairest, and freest from loose desires in thought.
Pleasures to tempt, yet not disdain'd in aught :
With anxious care, in courage ne'er dejected ;
Though cause of joy with no vain joy affected,
Know Reader, whensoe'er these lines you scan,
Such (and none such but she) was our Queen Anne.

247, 248] The italics here and later are kept because they seem to indicate not merely the poet's usual asides, but a sort of stanza-burden to the unitalicized couplet-blocks behind them.

Patrick Hannay

An Epitaph

A Wife, a Daughter, Sister to a
    King,
Mother to those, whose hopes do
    higher spring,
Chaste, fair, wise, kind ; first, Crown-
    United wore,
We knew her such, and held her for
    no more.
That she was more, God's daughter
    and Heaven's heir,
We know, since parted hence He
    crown'd her there.

SONGS AND SONNETS

To the Right Honourable Sir Andrew Gray, Knight, Colonel of a foot regiment, and General of the Artillery to the high and mighty Prince Frederick, King of Bohemia

IF of these labours I did none direct,
Brave sir, to you for offering or for
  shield,
Since you so fatherly did me affect,
When first you did conduct me to the
  field :
  I justly might be taxèd as ingrate,
  Deservedly your love might turn to
    hate.

Let shriller Musket, Cannon, Culvering,
(Part of thy charge) with the sky-
  tearing balls,
Which treble, base, mean, tenor rudely
  sing
To bloody Mars, forcing the dancing
  walls,   10
  Give place a space, while I do enter-
  tain
  Your ears with Music of a milder
    strain.

Stern Mars himself hath ofttimes
  danc'd a measure,
(Arms laid aside) his Minions most dear
Have woo'd the Muses, and have
  taken pleasure
To tune their own, and others' notes
  to hear :
  Thou art a proof hereof thyself most
  plain,
  Who in their Art hast had so sweet
    a vein.

To none more aptly can I then direct
These lines than thee, who both hast
  skill to prove,   20
And worth (more than their errors) to
  protect,
To none I'm so indebted for such love.
  Accept them as they're sent with
  love sincere,
  With kind construction read them
    whilst you're here.

I know thy haughty spirit much disdains
This loath'd detention, for I have been by
When thy hot courage well-nigh crack'd
  the reins
Of strict command, (when the fierce
  foe drew nigh)

That to thy valour freedom was not
  given,
Those Popish hirelings might by
  thee be shriven.   30

Nor was it wage or want that spurr'd
  thee on,
No hope of spoil nor thirsting after
  blood :
But worth-bred love of that rare Para-
  gon,
Thy dear King's daughter, whose cause
  doubtful stood.
  Had doubted Mansfelt led, you had
  your will,
  Pylsen prevented had this hap'ned ill.

Yet shrinks He not, nor thou, you
  both earn more,
(That cross your courage rather doth
  inflame)
With sharp revenge the lost state to
  restore
To that most worthy, best deserving
  Dame,   40
  Whom even her enemies so much
  do honour,
  As women's rarest praises they
    throw on her.

There are nine Worthies hitherto of men,
But of all women, I not read of any :
I know not then, whether she makes
  them ten,
Or of her sex first number unto many :
  In spirit, courage, valour, to those nine
  She's equal ; Women none yet so
    divine.

Go in Her cause, success crown thy
  desires,
Soon may I change this softly tunèd
  song,   50
Inflam'd with new and unacquainted
  fires,
To sing the Enemies' revengèd wrong :
  Oh how I long in high heroic verse,
  Their ruin and Her rising to rehearse.
    Ever yours most affectionate in
    all humble duty,
      PATRICK HANNAY.

37 'earn' = 'yearn.'

Song I

SAD *Sheretine* was seiz'd,
  And wounded so with woe,
Fra he fair *Mariana's* faith
  Was falsified did know.
Fra time he knew that her
  Another did possess,
Whom in his heart he had propos'd
  His height of happiness :
His tongue was sorrow-tied,
  His passion inward pent,   10
His woes no passage could procure,
  Forth from his heart to vent.
He scarce believes it so,
  Although himself it sees :
To free her of so foul a fault,
  He blames his blameless eyes :
But when he found her false,
  Her vows and oaths untrue,
As after he could joy in nought,
  He bids the world adieu.   20
His woes to aggravate,
  He causes doth invent,
Though cause of care he had enough,
  How he might more lament,
A woful banishment
  He willing undertakes :
And comfort-causing company
  He utterly forsakes.
In a care-clothèd shade,
  From eye and ear removed,   30
He thus with woe begins to wail
  The loss of his beloved.
' Ah, *Mariana*, ah !
  Is thus my love repaid ?
Do my fires still so freshly burn :
  And are thy flames decayed !
How constant have I proved !
  Though many baits there were
Where I have been, yet none had force
  My fancy to ensnare.   40

Nor since thy favour first
  Kindled my quenchless fire,
Did I see beauty that could breed
  A dram of dear desire ;
Or if 'mongst fairest fairs
  I thought one did excel :
My love was jealous of that thought,
  And straight did it repel :
Wherein then did I fail ?
  My heart doth hold it strange,
That seeing I have lov'd so well, 51
  I should find such a change.
No doubt the gods were griev'd,
  That I did thee adore ;
'Cause therein I idolatriz'd,
  Have plaguèd me therefore.
Yet should not that in thee,
  Least alteration mov'd :
It rather should thy love endear
  To be so dearly lov'd :   60
Hadst thou with proud disdain
  My favour first refus'd,
I might have blam'd my hapless fate,
  But not thy crime accus'd.
My love with time had died :
  Or if it still had liv'd,
My care this comfort yet had had,
  That I for worth had griev'd.
But thou by granting love,
  Didst bring me to such height
Of hopèd joys, to such a low   71
  Hast cast me with despight,
That the sad souvenance
  Of such a love so lost,
Is now my greatest cause of grief,
  And doth molest me most.
For if I ne'er had gain'd,
  My grief had not been such,
The once-rich poor man grieveth more
  Than he that ne'er was rich. 80
Whom Nature with her gifts
  'Bove others did indue ;

3 ' Fra ' = ' from ' as usual : but, as shown by l. 5, in sense of ' from the time when.' It may be worth observing that in the *Songs and Sonnets* the pitiless rain of italics ceases. These are quite rare and generally justifiable. In the First Song the keeping of the old ' Poulter's Measure ' (Alexandrine and Fourteener, divided or not into a quatrain of 6, 6, 8, 6), which had given so much dreary work in the middle of the sixteenth century, may be worth noticing.

73 souvenance] Again a Gallicism.

79, 80 The, &c.] A somewhat vulgarized variant of *Nessun maggior*, but to be noted with others.

O ! that adds woe unto my woe,
　　That she should prove untrue.
If whilst on bloody *Mars*
　　I boldly did attend,
By some brave hand had I exhal'd,
　　Before thy crime was kend,
Then had my wrongèd Ghost
　　(Not conscious of this)　　90
With joy expected thy approach,
　　To thy *Elysian* bliss.
Or if it there had griev'd,
　　The sole cause of its moan
Had been lest that thou shouldst
　　have griev'd
　　To hear that I was gone.
But now methinks I hear
　　Thy *Turian* with scorn
Upbraid thy crime as my disgrace ;
　　Fond *Sheretin*'s forlorn.　　100
Methinks thou seconds him,
　　Not sensible thereof ;
And thy true loving *Sheretine*
　　Rememberest with a scoff.
Another being wrong'd
　　By such a deep disdain,
Enrag'd might count it greater good
　　To lose such than obtain.
But that the world may see,　　1c9
　　My first fires were not feign'd,
They shall not therefore be extinct,
　　'Cause I am thus disdain'd.
No, *Turian* whom I most
　　Do hate and least respect,
'Cause thou dost love and honour
　　him,
　　I'll honour and affect.
By that (still dear !) thou'lt know
　　By leaving me what's lost,
If love disdain'd can do so much,
　　What had it ne'er been crost ?
But now since it's thy will　　121
　　That I do suffer woe,
I do endeavour for thy sake
　　The greatest grief to know.
Bear witness with me, woods,
　　Weeds waterèd with tears,

How I do live devoid of joy,
　　But you there's none me hears :
Nor e'er shall more content
　　Seize on my heavy heart,　　130
Witness with me while from this clay
　　My sad soul do depart.
And *Mariana* fair,
　　My first and latest love,
My last words shall be that the
　　heavens
May bless thee from above :
That thou may'st still enjoy
　　The best of sweet content ;
And let my death (since love could
　　not)
Move thee this fault repent.　　140
That when from hence thou fleet'st,
　　Thy unafflicted spirit
May with of like fault guiltless souls
　　A joyful peace inherit.'
That said he and no more,
　　But on the bitter weeds
His flesh-forsaken feeble limbs
　　He languishingly spreads.
His weary soul removes,　　149
　　Death seiz'd him by degrees ;
So true Love's Martyr (not so wrong'd
　　As he deem'd) thus he dies.

Sonnet I

EYE, beauty, admiration, love, desire,
Did join in one to set my heart on
　　fire.
My eye did see that beauty did sur-
　　pass,
That boundless beauty made me
　　much admire :
With admiration love conceivèd was,
And love brought forth and nourish'd
　　my desire ;
　　Which now is grown unto so great
　　perfection,
　　It sees, admires, conceives, feeds
　　sans direction.

Sonnet I] That this is not strictly a sonnet at all is an almost unnecessary observation. It is less so that the printing illustrates the wholly *unprincipled* character of this typography. Italics, or at least initial capitals, would have been quite in place here : and there is not one in the original.

Patrick Hannay

Sonnet II

EXPERIENC'D nature in this latter age,
Willing her masterpiece should then
  be wrought,
Such my fair *Coelia* set on earth's
  large stage,
As all the Gods in emulation
  brought;
For they did think, if Nature only
  might
Brag of her worth, she should insult
  o'er them.
Wherefore they 'greed to have an
  equal right,
That they of her perfection part
  might claim.
Pallas gave wisdom, *Juno* stateliness,
And the mild Morning gave her
  modesty :   10
The *Graces* carriage, *Venus* loveli-
  ness,
And chaste *Diana* choicest chastity :
  Thus heaven and earth their
    powers did combine
  To make her perfect ; kind Love !
    make her mine.

Sonnet III

WHILST wand'ring thoughts unsettled
  in desire,
Did rove at random in the fields of
  love,
Where fancy found fair objects fit
  to fire
Frozen affection, choice did choice
  remove :
Cupid contemn'd taking it much at
  heart,
For spite his dame's loose darling
  made delight me ;
She, leaving *Venus*, taking *Juno's*
  part,
With new chaste thoughts and fires
  'gins to requite me.
Proud *Cytherea* angry with her wench,
Seeks in my heart a hate of her to
  breed,   10

So blaz'd her faults, which soon my
  fires did quench,
But Malice still lights on the owner's
  head :
  For this the ill that all her envy
    wrought ;
  It made her chaste, me author of
    that thought.

Sonnet IV

ONCE early as the ruddy bashful
  Morn
Did leave *Dan Phoebus'* purple-
  streaming bed,
And did with scarlet streams East-
  heav'n adorn,
I to my fairest *Coelia's* chamber sped :
She Goddess-like stood combing of
  her hair,
Which like a sable veil did clothe
  her round.
Her ivory comb was white, her hand
  more fair !
She straight and tall, her tresses
  trail'd to ground ;
Amaz'd I stood, thinking my dear
  had been
Turn'd Goddess, every sense to sight
  was gone.   10
With bashful blush my bliss fled, I
  once seen,
Left me transformed (as it were) in
  stone.
  Yet did I wish so ever t' have re-
    main'd,
  Had she but stay'd, and I my
    sight retain'd.

Sonnet V

WHILE I do hope my thoughts do
  high aspire,
In deep Despair these hopes are
  quickly drown'd ;
Sometimes I burn with an *Etnean*
  fire :
Sometimes I freeze : I swim, straight
  sink to ground.

O since such changes in my love
I find,
Death change my life; or Love my
Coelia's mind.

Sonnet VI

Alluding to Hope

Hope makes the Sea be plough'd in
furrows white,
That in the end sweet gain may
thence arise;
Hope makes the toiling tradesman
take delight
To labour ear' and late with watch-
ful eyes.
Hope makes the shepherd in the
Winter care
To tend his flock, and lodge them
from the cold.
Hope makes the Soldier fight, sense-
less of Fear
'Mongst hot alarms, both watch and
ward to hold.

The seaman's hope rich merchandise
repays:
The tradesman's hope is answer'd
with his hire,   10
Young lambs and wool, the shep-
herd's charge defrays,
The soldier's wage is that he doth
require.
  I do for *Hope* more than all these
  sustain,
  Yet *Hope* with no reward repays
  my pain.

Song II

*Amantium irae amoris redintegratio
est.*

I

Coelia jealous (lest I did
  In my heart affect another)
Me her company forbid,
  Women cannot passion smother.

II

The dearer love the more disdain,
  When truth is with distrust re-
  quited;
I vow'd (in anger) to abstain,
  She found her fault and me invited.

III

I came with intent to chide her
  ('Cause she had true love abus'd),
Resolv'd never to abide her,   11
  Yet her fault she so excus'd,

IV

As it did me more entangle,
  Telling, *True love must have fears;*
They ne'er lov'd that ne'er did
  wrangle,
  Lovers' jars but love endears.

Sonnet VII

When as I wake I dream oft of my
  dear,
And oft am serious with her in my
  sleep;
I am oft absent when I am most near,
And near whenas I greatest distance
  keep:
  These wonders love doth work,
  but yet I find
  That love wants power to make
  my Mistress kind.

Sonnet VIII

I lov'd, was lovèd, and joy'd in con-
  tent,
Our souls did surfeit on the sweets
  of love;
While equal heat our hearts affec-
  tions lent,
The one the other to content did
  prove.
Thus 'bove the pitch of other hap-
  less wights,
Whose sweets are sunk still in a sea
  of sours,

VI. 4 ear'] This abbreviation must be very rare: yet it is etymologically defensible,
without the apostrophe.
VIII. 4. This line in the original is another interesting example of the elision- and
apostrophe-mania of the time. It is printed 'Th'one th'other,' thereby quite falsifying
the metre.

Our hearts swam in the depth of
dear delights,
Pleasures seem pains, not equalizing
ours.

But love's not love, wherein are no
disasters,
Time tried my trust was by my love
betray'd,   10
And she (for state) had got for me
some tasters,
Which lovers like not, so our love
decay'd.

Though she lov'd others; hereof
I may boast,
I lov'd, was lovèd chastely first and
most.

Sonnet IX

Lover, Mistress

L. HENCE loose alluring looks, no
more of Love,
No more thy seeming virtues shall
deceive me.
M. Come, come my dearest, speak
not thus to prove
How well I love; thou think'st it
doth not grieve me.
L. Thy beauty was a bait to draw
mine eye.
M. And with thy blink my heart was
set on fire.
L. I thought to find a suiting soul
in thee.
M. Thy love's the limit that bounds
my desire.
L. Thy looseness makes my love's
date now expire.
M. Where then thy vows? *L.* Gone
with thy seeming worth.   10
M. And made to me? *L.* No, virtue
brought them forth.
Which failing now no fuel feeds my
fire.

M. My heart's the harbour where
thy hopes must stay.
L. Where ground's not good, an
anchor drags away.

Song III

I

I CAN love, and love entirely,
And can prove a constant friend:
But I must be lov'd as dearly,
And as truly to the end:
For her love no sooner slaketh,
But my fancy farewell taketh.

II

I cannot endure delaying,
I must have her quickly won:
Be she nice (though not denaying)
By her leave I then have done:
For I am not yet at leisure, 11
To dwine for a doubtful pleasure.

III

My eyes shall not still be wailing,
Where I'm answered with neglect;
My hurt is not at her hailing,
Who my pain doth not respect:
He's a fool that seeks relieving,
From her glories in his grieving.

IV

With beauty I will not be blinded,
Yet I will none foul affect: 20
With wealth I will not be winded,
If in behaviour be defect;
Beauty stained such love dieth,
Wealth decayed such love flieth.

V

Gifts do good, yet he is silly
That therein expendeth store,
If he win not, tell me, will he
Not be meetly mock'd therefore?
It is better to be keeping
Than to sow not sure of reaping.

VI

As I would not words be waring 31
Where there's no assurance had;

VIII. 10 Time tried] Orig. 'try'd.' The construction is ambiguous: 'time-tried'
with 'trust' would be, perhaps, most poetical; but I think 'Time tried my trust [and it]
was' more Hannayish.
Song III. 31 waring] = 'spending,' *Scotice.*

So I would not gifts be sparing,
Where I woo and know shall wed.
Giving so is no decreasing,
I have hers in her possessing.

VII

Be she rich, and fair, and gained ;
If I fickleness do find,
My desires are quickly waned,
I can steer with other wind.   40
For Virtue, I have vow'd to
chuse her,
When that fails I will refuse her.

Song IV [1]

I

Now do the Birds in their warbling
words
Welcome the year ;
While sugared notes they chirrup
thro' their throats,
To win a fere :
Sweetly they breathe the wanton love
That Nature in them warms :
And each to gain a mate doth prove,
With sweet enchanting charms.

II

He sweetly sings, and stays the
nimble wings
Of her in th' air,   10
She hovering stays, to hear his loving
lays
Which woo her there :
She becomes willing, hears him woo,
Gives ear unto his song :
And doth as *Nature* taught her do,
Yields, sued unto not long.

III

But *Coelia* stays, she feeds me with
delay,
Hears not my moan :
She knows the smart in time will kill
my heart
To live alone :   20
Learn of the birds to choose thee a fere,
But not like them to range :
They have their mate but for a year,
But sweet, let 's never change.

IV

The *Turtle-dove* let's imitate in love,
That still loves one :
Dear, do not stay, youth quickly flies
away,
Then desire 's gone.
Love is kindest, and hath most length,
The kisses are most sweet,   30
When it 's enjoy'd in heat of strength,
Where like affections meet.

Sonnet X

As doth *Solsequium*, lover of the light,
When *Sol* is absent lock her golden
leaves,
And seal'd mourns, till it regain his
sight,
Whose flaming rays soon counter-
vail its griefs—
Far more thy absence me of rest
bereaves.
The hop'd-morn the Marigold doth
cherish :
But when my Sun this blest horizon
leaves,
Hopeless of light my joys in darkness
perish.
Stay then, my Sun ! make this thy
Zodiac
And move, but make my arms to be
the sphere :   10
Make me thy West, with me thy
lodging take,
Move to my breast, and make thy
setting there.
So shall I be more glad of thy
decline,
Than *Phoebus*-flower when he be-
gins to shine.

Song V

I

SERVANT, farewell ; is this my hire,
Do my deserts no more require ?

---

[1] There is some music in this.

No, do not think to cheat me so,
I will have more yet ere you go.

II

Thy lov'd *Idea* I'll arrest,
And it imprison in my breast :
In sad conceit it there shall lie,
My jealous love shall keep the key.

III

The drops my wounded heart shall
  bleed,   9
Shall be food whereon it shall feed :
The tears are shed when I do think
On thee, shall be its only drink.

IV

My restless thoughts shall range
  about,
My cares shall care it come not out :
And when these fail their watch to
  keep,
I'll chain it fast in leaden sleep.

V

Nor think it ever shall part thence,
Or that I will with it dispense :
Thy love alone can me avail,
Thyself alone I'll take for bail.   20

Sonnet XI

SWEET is the Rose and fair, yet who
  the same
Would pluck, may wound his finger
  with the briar,
So sweet, so fair is my belovèd
  Dame :
Her darting eye wounds those that
  come her near.
  They both are fair, both sweet,
    they both make smart ;
  The rose the finger ; *Coelia* the
    heart.

Sonnet XII

MY love is such as I can ne'er obtain,
Nor can I think which way to ease
  my pain :
If I conceal 't, there 's no hope of
  relief,

If I bewray 't, scorn will increase my
  grief ;
Grief hid brings soonest death, there
  help remains,
Reveal'd life lingers, languishing in
  pains :
Since my love 's hopeless, and with-
  out relief,
I scorn her scorn should add unto
  my grief,
Therefore my thoughts I'll bury as
  they rise,
And smother in my soul my infant
  cries :   10
So hasten death : then if she chance
  to hear
I died for love of her I held too
  dear,
And say 'twas pity with her heavenly
  breath,
That shall requite me well even after
  death.

Sonnet XIII

WHEN I do love, let me a mistress
  find,
Whose hard repulse doth me small
  hope procure,
Not yielding *yielding-no :* the con-
  stant mind
Is long in gaining, but obtain'd is
  sure :
  The diamond is cut with care and
    pains,
  But being cut, it still one form
    retains.
That which is lightly got is valued
  least,
' The memory of care sweetens con-
  tent ' :
Most feelingly we do those pleasures
  taste,
That are procur'd with pain, made
  known by want :   10
  It 's better never any comfort taste,
  Than relish sorrows by the plea-
    sures past.

Song VI [1]

I

A MAID me lov'd, her love I not
  respected,
She mourn'd, she sigh'd, nay sued,
  yet I neglected :
Too late, too late, alas, I now repent,
For *Cupid* with her love hath me
  infected.

II

As erst *He* hers, so love my heart
  now burneth,
As I at her, she laughs at me that
  mourneth :
Too late, too late, alas, I now repent,
Since her disdainèd love to hatred
  turneth.

III

On her alone doth health and hope
  rely,
Yet still she scorns and doth me love
  deny :   10
Too late, too late, alas, I now repent,
Since she joys in my death, I for her
  die.

Sonnet XIV

THE loving *Lizard* takes so much
  delight
To look upon the face of living man,
As it seems for to feed even by the
  sight,
And lives by looks which it enjoyeth
  than.

But when that pleasing object leaves
  the place,
(As wanting that which only did it
  cherish)
It fainting dies, deprival of that face
The only cause is why it so doth
  perish.

Even so my *Coelia's* love hath lately
  proved,

It joy'd, it liv'd to me, while I was
  eyed   10
It vigorous was, but I from sight
  removed,
It fainted, soon grew weak, and
  quickly died.

My *Coelia's* love thus prov'd a
  lizard right,
I seen, it lived ; it died I out of
  sight.

A Paradox

I LOVE my *Love* the better she doth
  change,
(Which some may chance hold a
  position strange)
Women's extreme, if [2] love were still
  at height,
Like ever-shining sun 't could not
  delight.
A still-fruition dulls ; respite relieves :
An intermission still new relish
  gives.
A changing favour puffs not up
  with pride,
Because uncertain how long 't shall
  abide ;
It lets not languish with a long dis-
  dain,
No sooner ebb'd but it doth flow again.
Then in my turn I shall be well re-
  spected,   11
Late favourites as much shall be neg-
  lected.
I love her 'cause she 's woman (if her
  mind
Not wavering were, she were none
  of that kind) ;
The more she 's woman I the more
  do love her,
The more inconstant, I more woman
  prove her.
The more a woman 's of a woman's
  mind,
The better, (best degener least from
  kind :)

---

[1] Did **Hannay** know *Robene and Makyne ?*   [2] ' If women's extreme ' ?

The most inconstant they degener least,
The most inconstant therefore are the best.   20
  The best I vow'd to love, therefore none else
  I'll love but whose inconstancy excels.

Sonnet XV

WHILST Fortune's fondlings dandled in her lap,
Swim in the depth of undeserv'd desires,
Careless of cross, unmindful of mishap,
Still floating higher than their hope aspires:
Poor hapless I, whose hopes soar'd lately higher,
(With promise-pens plum'd which ne'er fail in flight)
Deferr'd, disdain'd, heartless dare(s) not draw nigh her,
My wearied wand'ring wing can nowhere light.
And Fortune, still the more to show her spite,
The nearer that my hope seems to obtain,   10
With unexpected crosses curbs them quite,
Which nigh gain'd good makes me but taste my pain.
  Yet, fickle Fortune, I disdain thy frown:
  'Base minds thou may'st, but never brave cast down.'

Sonnet XVI

THEY Fortune much do wrong that call her blind;
And that she knows not how to give her gifts;

That she's inconstant, wavering as the wind,
Which in a minute many corners shifts.
That she delights in nought but turning states,
The misers raising, mighty ones o'erthrowing;
She loves not long, and long she never hates,
At random (as it lights) her gifts bestowing.
If she were blind, some gift I might have got
By chance: if loving chance, I had rise higher,   10
If long to love or hate inclining not,
I once had found her friend; but I will free her.
  She sees, can give, is constant, long can hate,
  Too well I know 't, she still hath cross'd my state.

Sonnet XVII

WHEN I consider well how *Cupid* kind
First did inflame my heart with loving fires,
And did remove the quiet of my mind,
And for it plac'd wakerife (yet dear) desires:
And how the friend I truly did affect
With like sincerity repaid my love:
How we did strive each other to respect,
And no contention else did ever prove:
How that our souls so nearly sympathiz'd,
We oft did think and oft did dream the same,   10

XV. 7. If dare*s* is what H. wrote, he had either forgotten 'I' or, more probably, was thinking of 'hopes,' and gave them a singular verb—as he and his contemporaries so often do.
XVI. 1. 'Say' must be understood from 'call.'
10 rise] 'rose' for 'risen,' or 'ris'n' itself?

What one approv'd the other highly priz'd,
What one dislik'd the other's heart did blame.

O how thy envy, *Fortune*, makes me wonder,
Whom *Love* so join'd, thou shouldst have kept asunder.

Song VII

Horac. Car. lib. 3, Ode 9. ad Lydiam.

I

Ho. WHILST I was welcome, and thy chief delight,
And no youth else more wishèdly did bring
His arms about thy neck so lovely white,
I liv'd more happy than the *Persian* King.

II

Ly. Whilst thou didst not burn with the love of other,
And *Lydia* no less grace than *Cloe* found :
Lydia was famouser than any other ;
Liv'd more than Roman *Ilia* renown'd.

III

Ho. But *Thracian Cloe* now commandeth me,
Skilled in sweet Music, cunning on the Lute :   10
For whom I would not be afeard to die,
To save her life, so that my death could do 't.

IV

Ly. *Calais Ornith's* son with loving fire
Burns me, and I affect him with like strife :
For whom I willingly would twice expire,
If so the fates would spare my youngling's life.

(721)

V

Ho. What if our ancient love should come about,
And join us jarring with a lasting chain :
Were fair-hair'd *Cloe* fra my heart cast out,
And cast-off *Lydia* receiv'd again.

VI

Ly. Though *Calais* fairer than a blazing star,   21
Lighter than fleeting cork although you be :
And than the *Adrian* sea more testy far,
With thee I'd love to live and willing die.

Sonnet XVIII

WHY dost thou doubt (dear *Coelia*) that my love,
(Which beauty bred, and virtue still doth nourish)
That any other object can remove,
Or faint with time ? but still more freshly flourish.

No, know thy beauty is of such a force,
The fancy cannot flit that 's with it taken :
Thy virtue 's such my heart doth hate divorce
From thy sweet love, which ne'er shall be forsaken.

So settled is my soul in this resolve,
That first the stars from crystal sky shall fall :   10
The heavens shall lose their influence, dissolve,
To the old Chaos shall be turn'd this all,

Ere I from thee (dear *Coelia*) remove,
My true, my constant, and my sincere love.

Patrick Hannay

Song VIII

I

WHEN curious *Nature* did her cunning try,
In framing of this fair terrestrial round:
Her workmanship the more to beautify
With chang'd variety made it abound,
And oft did place a plot of fertile ground
  Fraught with delights, nigh to a barren soil,
  To make the best seem better by a foil.

II

Thus first were made by *Thames* the motley meads,
Wearing the livery of the Summer's Queen:
Whose flowery robe o'er them she freely spreads,   10
With colours more than are in *Iris* seen,
And all the ground and hem of grassy green,
  Whereon the silly sheep do fearless feed,
  While on a bank the shepherd tunes his reed.

III

Next shady groves where *Delia* hunteth oft,
And light-foot *Fairies* tripping still do haunt:
There mirthful *Muses* raise sweet notes aloft,
And wanton birds their chaste loves cheer'ly chant:
There no delightful pleasure e'er doth want;
  There *Sylvian* with his Satyrs doth remain,   20
  There Nymphs do love and are belov'd again.

IV

This place doth seem an earthly Paradise,
Where on fit object every sense may feed;
And fill'd with dainties that do thence arise,
Of superfluity help others' need;
Yet no satiety that store doth breed.
  For when the sense nigh surfeits on delight,
  New objects the dull'd appetite do whet.

V

This place, I say, doth border on a plain,
Which step-dame *Nature* seems t' have made in scorn,   30
Where hungry husbandmen have toil'd in vain,
And with the share the barren soil have torn;
Nor did they rest till rise of ruddy morn:
  Yet when was come the harvest of their hopes,
  They for their gain do gather grainless crops.

VI

It seems of starv'd *Sterility* the seat,
Where barren downs do it environ round:
Whose parchèd tops in Summer are not wet,
And only are with snow in winter crown'd,
Only with bareness they do still abound;   40
  Or if on some of them we roughness find,
  It 's tawny heath, badge of the barren rind.

VII

In midst of these stands *Croydon* cloth'd in black,
In a low bottom sink of all these hills:
And is receipt of all the dirty wrack
Which from their tops still in abundance trills.
The unpav'd lanes with muddy mire it fills.

20 *Sylvian*] Note the unnecessary *i*. It is probably a misprint, as the form is correct below.

(742)

If one shower fall, or if that bless-
 ing stay,
You may well smell, but never
 see your way.

VIII

For never doth the flower-perfumèd
 Air,   50
Which steals choice sweets from
 other blessed fields,
With panting breast take any resting
 there,
Nor of that prey a portion to it
 yields :
For those harsh hills his coming
 either shields,
 Or else his breath infected with
 their kisses,
 Cannot enrich it with his fragrant
 blisses.

IX

And those who there inhabit, suiting
 well
With such a place, do either negroes
 seem,
Or harbingers for *Pluto*, Prince of
 hell,
Or his fire-beaters one might rightly
 deem,   60
Their sight would make a soul of
 hell to dream,
 Besmear'd with soot, and breath-
 ing pitchy smoke,
 Which (save themselves) a living
 wight would choke.

X

These with the demi-gods still
 disagreeing,
(As vice with virtue ever is at jar)
With all who in the pleasant woods
 have being
Do undertake an everlasting war,
Cuts down their groves, and often
 do them scare,
 And in a close-pent fire their
 arbours burn,
 While as the *Muses* can do nought
 but mourn.   70

XI

The other *Sylvans* with their sight
 affrighted,
Do flee the place whereas these elves
 resort,
Shunning the pleasures which them
 erst delighted,
When they behold these grooms of
 Pluto's court,
While they do take their spoils and
 count it sport
 To spoil these dainties that them
 so delighted,
 And see them with their ugly
 shapes affrighted.

XII

To all proud dames I wish no
 greater hell,
Who do disdain of chastely proffered
 love,
Than to that place confin'd there
 ever dwell ;   80
That place their pride's dear price
 might justly prove :
For if (which God forbid) my dear
 should move
 Me not come nigh her for to pass
 my troth,
 Place her but there : and I shall
 keep mine oath [1].

Sonnet XIX

FOND doubtful *Hope*, *Reason* de-
 prav'd, false fires,
Deceiving thoughts and plaints prov-
 ing but wind :
Ill-grounded grief, springing from
 vain desires,
Have led me in a maze of error blind.

But *Thou* whose eye surveys this
 earthly ball,
And sees our actions ere they be
 begun :
High and Eternal Mover of this all,
Whose mercy doth man's misery
 fore-run :

58 negroes] Orig. ' Nigro's.'
[1] The *Collier* (charcoal-burner) *of Croydon* illustrates this song.

Now in the right way turn my
wand'ring heart,
Teach me to bid farewell to fond
desire.   10
Deceiving *Error* and *Vain-joy* de-
part,
With Thy all-quick'ning spirit my
soul inspire.
  Grant, Lord, I may redeem my
    mis-spent time,
  And (if I sing) to Thee I praise
    may chime.

Song IX

I

O HOW my sin-clogged soul would
soar aloft,
And scale the crystal sky to seek
remeed
But that foul Sin (wherewith I stain
it oft)
Makes it to sink through doubt of
my misdeed :
In scroll of guilty conscience I
read
The rueful legend of my passèd
life,
The thought whereof maketh my
heart to bleed,
Finding my foul offences are so rife.

II

Fear makes me faint to find such,
and so many
As there are ranked in that ragged
roll :   10
Despair doth say there was ne'er
such in any,
Weeping cannot them wash nor
heart condole.
God's Wrath and *Justice* showeth to
my soul,
For every sin that must be satis-
fied :
What will become of me with such
a scroll,
Since *Death* the wage of Sin is sure
decreed ?

III

Never to blooming virgin truest
mirror,
Did represent beauty with more
delight
Than subtil *Satan* with affrighting
terror,
My guiltiness doth show me with
despight.   20
What erst as trifles seemèd to my
sight
Now are death-worthy ; my late-
liking sin
Is now displeasing ; and would bar
me quite
All hope of help, since such I
wallowed in.

IV

Hope to my heart my *Saviour* doth
present,
With all His *Passions* prov'd for
sinners' sake,
Yet none but he that doth from
heart repent,
Can use of that great satisfaction
make :
I hold of Him by a firm faith must take,
And all His sufferings to myself
apply :   30
If penitence want not, nor *Faith* be
weak,
Of *Heaven* I know He cannot me
deny.

V

But where 's *Repentance* for so foul
a stain ?
Why stint you, eyes, continually to
shower ?
The humid liquor of your moist'ning-
rain
Doth make to sprout the fair *Repent-
ing-flower.*
Give tears no respite, nor no truce
an hour,
And since with wand'ring looks you
did offend :
With still-distilling drops your can-
ker scour,
With coming-care your passèd 'scapes
amend.   40

VI

Ah, hapless heart, why rend'st not
    with remorse?
For quick conceiving what the flesh
    hath wrought:
Hast thou (depravèd) bent to ill thy
    force?
And knows thy *Maker* thy most
    secret thought?
And wilt thou yet be negligent in
    aught
Thee may reclaim, or with contrition
    wound?
Bleed, bleed to think that who so
    dear thee bought,
Thou 'st crucifi'd *again*, with thorns
    hast crown'd.

VII

And thou, frail *Flesh*, shame not now
    to begin,
Thee to submit to the reforming
    spirit: 50
Think of the by-ways thou hast
    wander'd in,
Which lead to Hell, and Death-
    deserved merit.
Why art thou proud? Thou canst
    not heaven inherit;
Lie down in dust, do no works of
    thine own;
But what the soul commands, oh!
    willing hear it,
By thy obedience let its rule be
    known.

VIII

But, *Lord!* without Thy sweet assist-
    ing grace,
I can do nought, all my attempts
    are vain:
I cannot come without Thou call, alas!
Grant me this grace, and bring me
    home again;   60
Let Thy blest *Spirit, Faith, Hope*,
    and *Love* remain
Still in my soul: the *Flesh*, the *World*
    and *Devil*,
Deprive of power; let them no more
    reign,
Or if they tempt, deliver me from
    evil.

IX

Thou 'rt not desirous that a sinner
    die,
But that he may repent his sins and
    live:
Thou bidst the heavy laden come to
    Thee,
And Thou wilt ease the weight that
    doth him grieve.
Thou bidst him knock, and Thou
    wilt ope the leave
Of that strict gate that leadeth unto
    bliss;   70
Grant I repent, do come, do knock,
    receive
Life, lightning, entrance where no
    anguish is.

X

Lord! grant me grace my coming
    days to number,
To wisdom then I shall my heart
    apply:
Roll me out of this lethargy and
    slumber,
Of sin and sloth wherein I now do
    lie.
Sinners (that seeing) soon shall
    draw Thee nigh,
Shunning base thoughts, their *souls*
    to Thee shall raise,
And with a sweet consort shall
    pierce the skies,
Of Thy great mercy, and eternal
    praise.   80

Sonnet XX

O *Father-God*, who by Thy word
    didst make
The Azured-vault, and all the host
    of heaven,
The hills, vales, plains, fresh streams,
    and briny lake,
And unto each inhabitants hast
    given:
O *Word* which (for our sakes) didst
    flesh become,
With sinners to purge sin hadst
    habitation:

Patrick Hannay

Crimeless accus'd, condemn'd, the
  Cross Thy doom,
Suff'redst Death, Burial, rose for
  our salvation.

O *Holy Ghost*, which dost from Both
  proceed,
Sweet soul-inspiring Spirit, with
  peace and love,   10
Comfort to all, cast down for sinful
  deed,
Lessening their woes with hopes of
  Heaven above.

O *Trinal-one*, one *God* and *Persons*
  three,
Reform my ways, and draw me unto
  Thee.

FINIS

To his singular friend

Mr. William Lithgow [1]

The double travail (*Lithgow*) thou
  hast ta'en,
One of thy feet, the other of thy brain,
Thee, with thyself do make for to
  contend,
Whether the Earth thou'st better
  pac'd or penn'd:
Would *Malaga's* sweet liquor had
  thee crown'd,
And not its treachery; made thy
  joints unsound,
For Christ, King, Country, what
  thou there endur'd,
Not them alone, but therein all
  injur'd:

Their tort'ring rack, arresting of thy
  pace,
Hath barr'd our hope of the world's
  other face: 10
Who is it sees this side so well
  express'd,
That with desire, doth not long for
  the rest?
Thy travail'd countries so describèd
  be,
As readers think they do each
  region see:
Thy well-compacted matter, ornate
  style,
Doth them oft, in quick-sliding
  Time beguile,
Like as a maid, wand'ring in Flora's
  bowers,
Confin'd to small time, of few
  flitting hours,
Rapt with delight, of her eye-pleas-
  ing treasure,
Now culling this, now that flower,
  takes such pleasure,   20
That the strict time whereto she
  was confin'd
Is all expir'd: whiles she thought
  half behind,
Or more remain'd. So each attract-
  ing line
Makes them forget the time, they
  do not tine:
But since sweet future travail is cut
  short,
Yet lose no time, now with the
  Muses sport;
That reading of thee, aftertimes may
  tell,
In Travel, Prose, and Verse, thou
  didst excel.
                    Patrick Hannay.

[1] Printed by Laing, in his Introduction, from the third edition of Lithgow's *Travels*, 1623. The torture referred to in the poem is rather well known from the passage describing it in these *Travels*, which has found its way into books of 'Selections.' 'To his singular friend' seems not to occur till the fourth edition of 1632: but it would be unsafe to infer that the writer was still alive.